AN INTEGRATED THEORY OF LINGUISTIC ABILITY

The Language & Thought Series

AN INTEGRATED THEORY OF LINGUISTIC ABILITY

THOMAS G. BEVER
Columbia University

JERROLD J. KATZ
City University of New York

D. TERENCE LANGENDOEN
City University of New York

THOMAS Y. CROWELL COMPANY · NEW YORK · ESTABLISHED 1834

LIBRARY OF CONGRESS CATALOGING IN PUBLICATION DATA
Main entry under title:

An Integrated theory of linguistic ability.

  (The Language & thought series)
  Includes bibliographies and index.
  1. Generative grammar—Addresses, essays, lectures.
I. Bever, Thomas G. II. Katz, Jerrold J. III. Langendoen, D. Terence.
P158.I5 1976   415   75-43873
ISBN 0-690-00850-3

Thomas Y. Crowell Company, Inc.
666 Fifth Avenue
New York, New York 10019

Manufactured in the United States of America

For George Armitage Miller

We do not augment, but rather subvert the sciences, if we allow their boundaries to run together.

KANT

CONTENTS

LIST OF CONTRIBUTORS*

Thomas G. Bever (1, 11, 65, 115, 149, 239)
Columbia University

Manfred Bierwisch (271)
Deutsche Akademic der Wissenschaft zu Berlin

John M. Carroll, Jr. (149)
Columbia University

John Dore (195)
Baruch College, City University of New York

Robert M. Harnish (261, 313)
University of Arizona

Richard Hurtig (149)
Educational Testing Service, Princeton, New Jersey

Jerrold J. Katz (1, 11, 393, 415)
Graduate Center, City University of New York

Nancy Kalish-Landon (195)
California State University of Sacramento

D. Terence Langendoen (1, 89, 115, 183, 195, 225, 239, 393)
Graduate Center, City University of New York

*Numbers in parentheses indicate the pages on which the authors' contributions begin.

Introduction

THOMAS G. BEVER
JERROLD J. KATZ
D. TERENCE LANGENDOEN

In the late 1960s and early 1970s, generative grammar changed from a stable subject with a unified theory, called the "standard theory" and codified in Katz and Postal's *Integrated Theory of Linguistic Descriptions* (1964) and Chomsky's *Aspects of the Theory of Syntax* (1965), to a less than stable one with a number of different and conflicting theories. Not surprisingly, attitudes toward this change in the state of generative grammar vary depending on which of these theories one is committed to. Most generative grammarians have abandoned the the standard theory in favor of one or another of the theories that emerged in the late 1960s and early 1970s, and accordingly, they view the change as progress toward a more adequate model of grammar. Some have changed their theory many times and so have an even stronger sense of progress. Nonetheless, almost all generative grammarians view the overall condition of their field with some dismay. The proliferation of diverse theories, they can agree, is not a state of affairs in which the field can take pride. Moreover, the reaction of scholars and researchers in related disciplines such as psycholinguistics, anthropological linguistics, and philosophy of language has been unfortunate. These scholars and researchers, who often have to employ grammatical theory in their studies, have been confused about which theory to employ, and there is now a trend to try to avoid grammatical theory entirely by resorting to a purely data-oriented approach. In this situation, it seems reasonable to raise the question whether the change that took place when the standard theory was abandoned really represented progress toward a more adequate theory of grammar.

In the case of each of the new theories of grammar to which generative grammarians turned, the change from the standard theory was motivated by the desire to handle phenomena within grammar that did not seem to fit naturally into the available formulation of the standard theory. It was thought that the standard theory could not, in principle, accommodate the new phenomena and

1

THOMAS G. BEVER, JERROLD J. KATZ,
AND D. TERENCE LANGENDOEN

that therefore another theory, representing an extension of the standard theory, or a radical departure from it, would be required. A reconsideration of this revolutionary period in generative grammar must thus focus mainly on the question whether such phenomena should really be handled in grammar, and if so, whether the standard theory is really unable to handle them.

The aim of this book is to stimulate such a reconsideration. We think that the standard theory has been abandoned too hastily. Events moved too quickly for linguists to have had the time to carefully consider all the issues relevant to these major theoretical decisions, and linguists never carefully explored the important issue of whether the phenomena on which abandonment of the standard theory was based are genuinely grammatical phenomena. We think that the standard theory has many theoretical advantages over the theories proposed since, and that these advantages make it highly desirable to undertake such a reconsideration. In a sense, however, a reconsideration of this issue is already under way. This reconsideration has been taking place unnoticed in studies of questions that are seemingly unrelated to the issues surrounding the debate about the standard theory and its successors. These questions concern aspects of the theory of performance: speech perception, semantic aspects of speech production, stylistics, etc. This book pulls together a number of the more important and relevant of these studies, and focuses them on the question of whether linguists were right to abandon the standard theory. In this way, we hope to encourage a reconsideration of the status of the standard theory.

The standard theory contains the following principles: The structure of every sentence of a natural language must be stated in the form of an *underlying phrase marker* representing its deep structure, from which semantic rules construct its semantic interpretation; and a *superficial phrase marker* representing its surface syntactic structure, from which phonological rules construct its phonological interpretation. Syntactic transformational rules relate the underlying phrase marker of a sentence to its superficial phrase marker and thereby represent the sound/meaning correlation in the sentence. The underlying phrase markers of a sentence of a language are generated by a set of context-free phrase-structure rules and by local transformational rules that insert lexical items into the structures generated by the context-free phrase-structure rules. The superficial phrase markers are obtained by applying transformational rules, which are highly constrained operations that map phrase markers onto phrase markers. These transformations apply as a whole cyclically, from the most deeply embedded structures to the root of each structure, and within each cycle they apply in sequence, independently of each other.

The theory briefly sketched above represented the most natural formalization of Chomsky's original insights into linguistic structure, which had been responsible for overthrowing the earlier theory of taxonomic grammar. Chomsky's central insight into grammatical description was that taxonomic grammars were empirically inadequate because they provided only a description of the surface structure of sentences. Yet the most important grammatical relations in sentences cannot be represented adequately in their surface structures, but rather in their deep structures. This was the point of the now classic examples "John is easy to please" and "John is eager to please"; "Flying planes can be dangerous"; and so on. The crucial feature of the standard theory was its postulation of a level of deep syntactic structure with special properties that give it a unique place in the explanation of grammatical phenomena. These properties, that the entities at this level are the input both to the semantic component and to the syntactic transformations, established the deep structure as the unique level that determines the semantic interpretations of sentences (relative to the semantic rules) and their phonological interpretation (relative to the global transformations in the syntactic component and the phonological rules). On the standard theory, then, the all-important grammatical relations connecting sound and meaning are located far beneath the surface structure of sentences.

The standard theory was also the optimal embodiment of Chomsky's antiempiricist and antibehaviorist criticism of taxonomic grammar and structuralist linguistics generally. By making both the semantic and the phonological structures of sentences depend on their deep syntactic structure, which is both unobservable and too abstract to be inductively inferable from regularities in the surface structure of actual utterances, the standard theory takes the strongest antiempiricist and antibehaviorist position. No other plausible theory could state more clearly that the objective reality of a language consists not in corpora of utterances (actual or possible) or in stimulus-response relations between environmental features and verbal behavior, but rather in a speaker's internalization of its grammatical rules, that is, in internal psychological states. Similarly, no other plausible theory could state more clearly that the acquisition of grammar consists not in making inductive generalizations from observable distributional regularities but in developing innate schemata (which represent linguistic universals) into grammatical rules that embody hypotheses about the unobservable deep structure of the language.

Although much work early in the last decade fleshed out the standard theory and refined the formalization of theoretical insights (see for example Rosenbaum, 1967, and Chomsky, 1970) in the latter half of the sixties and the early seventies the emphasis shifted, and increasingly work in generative grammar has come to be concerned with developing alternatives to the standard theory. As codified in the early sixties, the standard theory was incomplete on several important points; the philosophical ideas and assumptions it embodied were not fully digested nor generally embraced; the philosophical and logical argumentation Chomsky introduced into linguistics was not well understood; the relations of grammar to the various disciplines that it now touched upon were unclear; and finally, describing natural languages using the apparatus of generative grammar was difficult.

The alternatives to the standard theory fall within either the *generative semantics* framework or Chomsky's *extended standard theory*. For generative semanticists the fundamental source of dissatisfaction was theoretical, while for

Chomsky it was almost entirely empirical. Ultimately, in both cases the issue came down to how well the various theories could handle the grammatical facts, to a blend of theoretical and empirical issues.

Generative semantics was the first alternative to appear. Its practitioners believed that the arguments supporting standard theory over taxonomic grammar had not been carried far enough and, if extended to their logical conclusion, would eliminate even the level of deep syntactic structure, leaving only a highly abstract and homogeneous mapping of semantic structures onto surface structures (see McCawley, 1968; Lakoff and Ross, 1967; Lakoff, 1971). Initially, the issue was between generative semantics and interpretive semantics, which was that part of the standard theory that embodied the particular thesis that grammars are *syntactically based* (derivations are initiated by the rules that generate underlying phrase markers), and that the meaning of a sentence is obtained as an *interpretation* of its syntactic structure, in particular, its underlying phrase markers. The question was whether the theory of *semantically based grammars* being proposed by generative semanticists was really new and simpler, or merely a notational variant of the standard theory itself, as both Katz (1971) and Chomsky (1972) argued. But before any clear conclusion was reached, a new set of issues arose with the development of Chomsky's extended standard theory. The generative semanticists then saw the extended standard theory, which of course was as interpretivist as the standard theory, as the "theory to beat." Their assumption was that if Chomsky extended his theory, abandoning the standard theory, it was pointless to argue directly against the latter, a position Chomsky no longer held.

Chomsky's prestige in the field at the time made this position almost irresistible; and indeed few linguists resisted it. But logically, of course, the assumption is only as strong as the reasons for the extension of the standard theory. If these reasons were insufficient, then perhaps the change in the theoretical scene, too, was misguided. We shall return to this question below.

The main stimulus for Chomsky's extended standard theory were linguistic phenomena that were difficult to account for within the framework of the standard theory. These phenomena included quantifier relations, the interaction of quantifiers and negation, topic-comment relations as in active/passive pairs, focus and presupposition, and certain apparent constraints on the operation of transformational rules. It was claimed that grammatical description should in principle be able to account for such phenomena, yet the standard theory seemed unable to do so. As Chomsky and a number of his students and colleagues saw it, the problem lay in the standard theory's restriction against semantic rules applying anywhere but at the level of deep structure. They argued that the recalcitrant linguistic facts could be described in grammars that allowed semantic interpretation rules to apply to both underlying and superficial phrase markers. Their contention that certain aspects of semantic interpretation occur at the level of surface syntactic structure was a denial of the Katz-Postal thesis that syntactic transformations make no contribution to the meaning of sentences (see Chomsky, 1971; and Jackendoff, 1972). They claimed that the theory of grammar should contain universals for *surface interpretive rules* in the semantic component. Such surface interpretation rules, as Katz points out in his contribution to this volume, constitute a major extension of the range of possible grammars, not simply of the range of objects that undergo semantic interpretation within a grammar. These rules are significantly more powerful, since in a derivation they can make use of the structure of noncontiguous phrase markers.

Generative semanticists, too, employ such more powerful rules in their semantically based grammars, in order to increase the homogeneity of grammatical rules. Generative semanticists oppose the extended standard theory, a relatively articulated theory involving several components and various types of rules from various categories, with a theory that appears to be far simpler conceptually. Postal (1972) proposes a homogeneous framework of relatively simple phrase structure rules, which define the notion "well-formed semantic structure," and derivational constraints, which define the permitted relations between semantic representations and surface structures. The issue has become: Which increase in the power of grammars, that advocated by the generative semanticists under the name "derivational constraint" or that advocated by extended standard theorists under the name "surface interpretive rule," is necessary to account for the phenomena that both take to be outside the scope of the standard theory?

More recently, this issue has been further complicated on both sides. There are some generative semanticists (Hankamer, 1973; and Lakoff, 1973) who advocate an even more powerful apparatus, "transderivational constraints," which operate beyond the context of a single derivation and block certain derivations on the basis of other derivations. This raises all the more sharply questions of the relation between increases in the homogeneity of rules and the size of the class of possible grammars: how much of an increase in the set of possible grammars can be tolerated as the price of increases in homogeneity? What considerations can legitimately enter into deciding this question? Most basically, is it clear that the facts that motivate such radical increases in generative power are not describable in terms of a less powerful apparatus of some kind?

Chomsky and his followers further complicate the issue. Chomsky (1975) and Fiengo (1974) now propose the *revised extended standard theory*, in which all semantic interpretation occurs at the level of surface structure. As Katz points out in his contribution to this volume, the advantage of the revised extended standard theory is that it makes "global" rules unnecessary by having all interpretation occur at the same level. For this, however, it is necessary to enrich the surface structure, so that it can represent all of the syntactic structure necessary to predict semantic properties and relations.

These more recent refinements in generative semantics and the extended standard theory do not alter the common assumption underlying them: that

THOMAS G. BEVER, JERROLD J. KATZ,
AND D. TERENCE LANGENDOEN

standard theory was abandoned for good reason; and that one or the other of these two theories is preferable to the standard theory. The present volume challenges this assumption. We think that it has been accepted too uncritically, and that it is based on a misconception about the linguistic phenomena motivating revisions of the standard theory. We think that the standard theory is *a priori* preferable to any of these extensions by virtue of its being the clearest expression of the original insights of transformational grammar and because it constitutes the narrowest constraints on the class of possible grammars. Thus, we think that linguistics stands to gain much if it can be shown that the best explanation of linguistic phenomena does not require extensions of the standard theory.

As we have already remarked, what fostered the development of the alternative theories was the belief that certain linguistic phenomena were (*a*) grammatical phenomena and (*b*) could not be handled in grammars in the framework of the standard theory. Although there has been much work in the latter area to demonstrate that linguistic phenomena cannot be handled in the standard theory, this means nothing unless it can be shown that the phenomena in question are indeed grammatical in nature. For example, it is meaningless to argue for a particular theory of intelligence on the grounds that that theory can, and other theories of intelligence cannot, handle a certain set of psychological facts if those psychological facts turn out to be about accident proneness rather than intelligence. Hence, what is necessary is a careful, systematic examination of the claim that the linguistic phenomena that motivate extensions of the standard theory are indeed grammatical, rather than extragrammatical facts of another sort. As we have indicated above, some investigations of this issue have been conducted, with, however, quite different aims and without any connection to each other. What we have done is bring some of the more important of these studies together in this volume as a first step toward a systematic examination of the issue of what are grammatical phenomena.

The picture revealed by integrating these independent studies is the following. For almost all linguistic phenomena that have provided empirical support for extensions of the standard theory, the assumption that they should be describable within a theory of grammatical competence is, at least, highly questionable. Recall that the early Chomskyan conception of grammars as theories of the internalization of a system of rules, and of linguistic theory as the initial competence of the language learner caused work in the description of languages to touch on a number of disciplines in a way that it had not earlier. Because the relation of grammar to these disciplines, in particular psychology, philosophy, sociology, and logic, was so new, it was as yet unclear. This meant that the boundaries of grammar and linguistic theory themselves were unclear, too. If, for example, we cannot say where the psychology of sentence perception begins, we are also unclear about where the grammar of sentence structure ends. At the same time, linguists working in grammar were successful in describing all sorts of grammatical phenomena that heretofore had not been describable in grammars. The new transformational model with its underlying levels of representation provided the possibility for description unavailable in previous theories; and grammarians were busy exploring the limits of this new descriptive apparatus. Therefore, when they came across linguistic phenomena that did not lend themselves to description directly, it was natural to think that one or another of the restrictions imposed on the use of this apparatus was at fault. On occasion, linguists did question whether the phenomena were really grammatical; consider Chomsky's argument that the loss of intelligibility in multiply center-embedded sentences is a matter of performance factors reflecting the limitation on immediate memory rather than a matter of ungrammaticality. But once these resistant phenomena became part of controversies about how to change the standard theory, little attention was paid to whether they were genuinely grammatical yet could not be incorporated properly into grammars modeled within the standard theory, or whether they were performance phenomena like loss in intelligibility of multiply center-embedded sentences.

When we pay attention to this question, it turns out that a good case can be made for the claim that such phenomena have been misclassified as grammatical in nature, and accordingly do not provide empirical support for "global" principles and other extensions of the theory of grammar. The studies collected in this volume offer various kinds of bases outside formal grammar—in psychology, philosophy, rhetoric, sociology—that account for very many of them in the same way that Chomsky accounted for loss of intelligibility in center-embedded sentences. They do not only show how such phenomena can be explained by theories belonging to areas outside grammar but how the obscurity of the boundaries between grammar and related disciplines can be clarified. They thus suggest various hypotheses about the scope and limits of grammar and also about its relations to neighboring disciplines. If these suggestions prove sound, much of the alleged evidence against the standard theory and in support of the various alternatives disappears.

The papers in this volume can be seen as attempts to develop theories of verbal ability that can in principle account for extragrammatical linguistic phenomena. Several papers in this volume develop Bever's initial effort (1970) to show that a theory of speech perception can account for many facts about acceptability and language universals. These are: "The Influence of Speech Performance on Linguistic Structure" by Bever; "A Dynamic Model of the Evolution of Language" by Bever and Langendoen; "Analogy" by Bever, Carroll, and Hurtig; "A Case of Apparent Ungrammaticality" by Langendoen; "Dative Questions" by Langendoen, Kalish-Landon, and Dore; and "Can a Not Unhappy Person Be Called a Not Sad One?" by Langendoen and Bever. Of these, the last three specifically address themselves to whether the standard theory jointly with a theory of speech perception and production can deal adequately with certain

THOMAS G. BEVER, JERROLD J. KATZ,
AND D. TERENCE LANGENDOEN

phenomena, where univocal treatment in the grammar would necessitate abandoning the standard theory.

Katz's "Global Rules and Surface Structure Interpretation," points out the magnitude of the extension embodied in the extended standard theory and suggests that a major segment of the evidence for this theory is irrelevant to the issue, because it is stylistic or rhetorical rather than grammatical in nature. "Pragmatics and Presupposition" by Katz and Langendoen, and Harnish's papers "The Argument from *Lurk*" and "Logical Form and Implicature" provide strong grounds for thinking that various extensions of the standard theory in generative semantics were mistakenly based on pragmatic rather than grammatical phenomena. "Social Differentiation of Language Structure" by Bierwisch is concerned with the proper treatment of sociolinguistic phenomena outside grammar. "Finite-State Parsing of Phrase-Structure Languages and the Status of Readjustment Rules in Grammar" by Langendoen further articulates the standard theory; it provides a formalism for the notion of a syntactic readjustment rule and settles a previously open question about the boundary between competence and performance.

Finally, two general papers address directly the inadequacy of generative semantics. "Acceptable Conclusions from Unacceptable Ambiguity" by Langendoen points out the problems inherent in a current version of the theory of transderivational constraints and shows that certain of the phenomena in question can be handled within the standard theory. "The Fall and Rise of Empiricism" by Katz and Bever traces the history of transformational grammar from the work of Zellig Harris to that of generative semantics, and demonstrates that one wing of generative semantics involves a return to the empiricism of taxonomic linguistics in the 1930s and 1940s.

REFERENCES

Bever, T. G. 1970. "The Cognitive Basis for Linguistic Structures." In *Cognition and the Development of Language*, ed. J. R. Hayes. Wiley.

Chomsky, N. 1965. *Aspects of the Theory of Syntax*. M.I.T. Press.

——1970. "Remarks on Nominalizations." In *Readings in English Transformational Grammar*, R. Jacobs and P. Rosenbaum, eds. Ginn-Blaisdell.

——1971. "Deep Structure, Surface Structure and Semantic Interpretation. In *Semantics*, D. Steinberg and L. Jakobovits, eds. Cambridge University Press.

——1972. "Some Empirical Issues in the Theory of Transformational Grammar." In *Studies on Semantics in a Generative Grammar*. Mouton.

——1975. "Questions of Form and Interpretation." *Linguistic Analysis* 1: 75–109.

Fiengo, R. 1974. *Semantic Conditions on Surface Structure*. Unpublished Ph.D. dissertatation. M.I.T.

Hankamer, J. 1973. "Unacceptable Ambiguity." *Linguistic Inquiry* 4: 17–68.

Jackendoff, R. 1972. *Semantic Interpretation in a Generative Grammar*. M.I.T. Press.

Katz, J. J. 1971. "Generative Semantics is Interpretive Semantics." *Linguistic Inquiry* 2: 315–331.

Katz, J. J., and P. Postal, 1964. *An Integrated Theory of Linguistic Descriptions*. M.I.T. Press.

Lakoff, G. 1971. "On Generative Semantics." In *Semantics*, D. Steinberg and L. Jakobovits, eds. Cambridge University Press.

———1973. "On Transderivational Constraints." In *Essays in Honor of Henry and Renée Kahane*, B. Kachru, ed. Linguistic Research.

Lakoff, G., and J. R. Ross. 1967. *Is Deep Structure Necessary?* Indiana University Linguistics Club.

McCawley, J. 1968. "The Role of Semantics in a Grammar." In *Universals in Linguistic Theory*, E. Bach and R. Harms, eds. Holt, Rinehart and Winston.

Postal, P. 1972. "The Best Theory." In *Goals of Linguistic Theory*, S. Peters, ed. Prentice-Hall.

Rosenbaum, P. S. 1967. *The Grammar of English Predicate Complement Constructions*. M.I.T. Press.

The Fall and Rise of Empiricism

JERROLD J. KATZ
THOMAS G. BEVER

The tradition of all the dead generations weighs like a nightmare on the brain of the living. And just when they seem engaged in revolutionizing themselves and things, in creating something that has never yet existed, precisely in such periods of revolutionary crisis they anxiously conjure up the spirits of the past to their service

MARX

SOME THINGS KUHN NEVER TOLD US

The transformationalist revolution in linguistics fits Thomas Kuhn's (1962) account of scientific revolutions. There was a prevailing structuralist paradigm —taxonomic grammar—in which grammatical analysis consisted of segmenting and classifying actual speech into a form resembling a library catalogue. This paradigm failed to provide an adequate framework for explaining such phenomena as syntactic ambiguity, grammatical relations, ellipsis, agreement, stress, constituent equivalences, and others. The revolution that overthrew structuralism replaced it with the new paradigm of generative grammar, which conceives of grammatical analysis as the constructing and testing of theories about the speaker's internalized linguistic competence. In this paradigm, the grammatical

The senior author wishes to acknowledge his gratitude to the John Simon Guggenheim Foundation for its support of this research. Both authors wish to thank Noam Chomsky for his comments on an earlier draft.

Source: This article appears for the first time in this volume.

JERROLD J. KATZ
THOMAS G. BEVER

analysis of a language is represented as a typical case in science of inference from behavior to a theory about the unobservable system responsible for it.

From the general intellectual viewpoint, the most significant aspect of the transformationalist revolution is that it is a decisive defeat of empiricism in an influential social science. The natural position for an empiricist to adopt on the question of the nature of grammars is the structuralist theory of taxonomic grammar, since on this theory every property essential to a language is characterizable on the basis of observable features of the surface form of its sentences. Hence, everything that must be acquired in gaining mastery of a language is "out in the open"; moreover, it can be learned on the basis of procedures for segmenting and classifying speech that presuppose only inductive generalizations from observable distributional regularities. On the structuralist theory of taxonomic grammar, the environmental input to language acquisition is rich enough, relative to the presumed richness of the grammatical structure of the language, for this acquisition process to take place without the help of innate principles about the universal structure of language. Rationalists, on the other hand, find the taxonomic theory uncongenial because, for them, the essential properties of language underlie the surface form of sentences and are thus unobservable in the sense in which atoms are unobservable.

Chomskyan transformational theory is rationalist because it allows for unobservable grammatical properties (which in the taxonomic model have no linguistic reality) to be stated as part of the rules of the linguist's theory about the speaker's internalized linguistic competence. Thus, the shift from a conception of grammar as cataloguing the data of a corpus to a conception of grammar as explicating the internalized rules underlying the speaker's ability to produce and understand sentences introduces "deep structure" levels of grammar, which provide the linguistic reality that unobservable features otherwise lack (Katz, 1971, Chaps. 1-5).

The transformational rules that relate these deeper levels to the surface forms also enable the new paradigm to surpass the old one in explanatory power. It is now possible to explain what had been inexplicable in the taxonomic framework: syntactic ambiguity, grammatical relations, ellipsis, agreement, stress, constituent equivalences, and so forth (Chomsky, 1957). But the language acquisition problem confronting linguists also changes. The input to the language acquisition process no longer seems rich enough and the output no longer simple enough for the child to obtain its knowledge of the latter by inductive inferences that generalize distributional regularities found in speech. For now the important properties of the language lie hidden beneath the surface form of sentences, and the grammatical structure to be acquired is seen as an extremely complex system of highly intricate rules relating the underlying levels of sentences to their surface phonetic form. The problem of language acquisition now is to discover sufficiently powerful principles about the universal form of language that compensate for the impoverished input to the child's language acquisition mechanism.

Linguistics today is in what may be called a "postrevolutionary period." To look at one aspect of this period from the viewpoint of the historian of science gives some needed perspective on the events now shaping the course of theoretical linguistics. From this perspective we shall discover a danger to the transformationalist revolution and to its restoration of rationalism. The picture we shall construct provides an interpretation of the present scene in linguistics that brings this danger clearly into focus.

One type of postrevolutionary situation occurs when a new paradigm does not succeed in restoring the field to the tranquil life of normal science. Instead, the introduction of the new paradigm is followed almost immediately by what seems to be another revolution that challenges one of its central features. Thus, rather than a return to the smooth routines of normal science, there is the increasing chaos characteristic of a new upheaval. Not only are there conflicts with the forces overthrown in the original revolution, but now there are also conflicts within the revolutionary camp itself between what may be called the "revolutionary old guard" and the "counterrevolutionaries."

There is little doubt that the current situation in theoretical linguistics fits this description. But there is no single satisfactory explanation of its underlying dynamics. An unregenerate member of the prerevolutionary "ruling class," that is, a linguist from the Bloomfieldian tradition of taxonomic theory, would see the current situation in transformational linguistics as the "revolution devouring itself." On the other hand, a counterrevolutionary, that is, a generative semanticist, would see the situation as a continuation of the transformationalist revolution, a necessary further step in the dialectic that moves linguistics upward toward scientific utopia. Last, a member of the revolutionary old guard, that is, an interpretive semanticist,[1] is likely to see it as an unfortunate fractionation of a once highly unified position, something like what happened when the younger generation of psychoanalysts broke from Freud and splintered into Jungians, Adlerians, and so on.

We find none of these explanations acceptable, although we admit that there is an element of truth in each. The prerevolutionary ruling class is right in seeing the possibility of the revolution destroying itself, at least in the danger to rationalism in linguistics. The revolutionary old guard is right that the paradigm offered by generative semantics provides no new insights into the structure of language. And the counterrevolutionaries are right that the present controversies signify a dialectical process out of which a more articulated theory of linguistic structure can emerge.

1. There is an unfortunate ambiguity in the use of "interpretive semantics" among linguists. On the one hand, the term contrasts with "generative semantics" and denotes the theory in which grammars are "syntactically based," that is, that have a level of deep syntactic structure and assign semantic representations interpretively to otherwise uninterpreted syntactic phrase markers (be they underlying or derived). This is the sense in which we use the term here. On the other hand, the term denotes what Chomsky now calls the "extended standard theory," the view that there are surface structure interpretive rules. This view contrasts with the theory in Katz and Postal (1964).

JERROLD J. KATZ
THOMAS G. BEVER

We do not, however, share the supposition of the counterrevolutionaries that the theory that will emerge as the next stage in the progress of linguistics will be generative semantics. We view as incorrect their claim that they offer a genuinely new paradigm embodying greater explanatory power and deeper insights into language while employing simpler descriptive machinery. We think their claim that their theory better achieves the original goals of the revolution against taxonomic theory is the very opposite of the truth. Rather, we think their theory, in its novel elements, constitutes the danger that threatens to replace the rationalism of the transformationalist movement by something very much akin to Bloomfieldian empiricism. We will present our view not simply as a vignette, but as a carefully detailed piece of "contemporary history of science," whose claim to truth is that it best describes the facts. We wish this picture to affect the course of events by making linguists aware of the broader intellectual implications of the present debates in the theory of grammar.

BEFORE THE REVOLUTION

The history of linguistics in this century displays at least one full cycle from rationalism to empiricism and back. At the beginning of the century, linguistics reflected the rationalism of the previous century. De Saussure (1916) emphasized the distinction between linguistic structure and speech, although for him sentential form was part of speech behavior rather than linguistic structure. Sapir (1921) argued that the speaker's linguistic knowledge is only abstractly related to observable phenomena in speech, and he sought a general definition of language.[2] Even Bloomfield's outlook was rationalist at this time. He published an enthusiastic exegesis and expansion of the views of Wundt, whose ideas on language were based on the linguistic rationalism of Humboldt, which in turn developed out of Kantian rationalism (Bloomfield, 1914).

The essential elements of Wundt's position, representing in the nineteenth century the culmination of the rationalist tradition that began with Descartes and the Port Royal grammarians (Chomsky, 1966b), are: (a) the sentence, intuitively defined, is a main unit of linguistic study, (b) there is a fundamental distinction between inner meaning and outer form in sentences, (c) language is a means for expressing propositions that are language invariant, and (d) this means is a distinctly human ability (see Blumenthal, 1970). But although this position at first strongly influenced Bloomfield, he ultimately rejected it as he came under the influence of the neopositivist school developing at the time. Bloomfield's attempt to outline the science of linguistics within the framework of Wundtian rationalism lacked an explicit methodology. Seeking to remedy this,

---

2. Sapir's speculations on the genetic basis for language are confused because he has a narrow notion of what counts as instinctive and fails to distinguish the universal from the particular in individual languages (1921, pp. 3–23).

he accordingly became interested in questions of methodology in science, which brought him into contact with the works of the neopositivists who were developing canons of methodology along more or less traditional empiricist lines. They stressed the Humean bias against speculative or metaphysical conceptions, the instrumentalistic view of theoretical concepts (on which such concepts express fictions), the reductionistic view of the relation of theories to observations, and an operationalistic, behavioristic, and physicalistic outlook on the domain of a science. Bloomfield brought these ideas into linguistics (1955, p. 251).

Each of the essential elements of the Wundtian position were casualties of these methodological canons. The notion of an intuitively defined sentence was removed as too subjective to be consistent with behaviorist principles. The notion of meaning could not be reduced to the observable properties of the acoustic signal, so it had to be given up as inconsistent with physicalism, to be replaced by a stimulus-response account of sentence use. The notion of language-invariant propositions was discarded along with the distinction between inner meaning and outer sentential form, because without this distinction the notion of invariance could not be specified. Finally, the idea of language as a distinctly human characteristic disappeared in favor of the empiricist idea of languages as culturally learned forms.

Linguistic descriptions could no longer be viewed as accounts of linguistic knowledge or explications of linguistic structure. Rather, to conform to these methodological canons, grammars came to be viewed as efficient data catalogues of linguistic corpora, and linguistic theory took the form of a mechanical discovery procedure for cataloguing linguistic data. This, then, was the origin of the taxonomic paradigm and Bloomfieldian structuralism, which dominated linguistic theorizing for thirty years.

The goal of linguistic investigation during this period was to determine explicit procedures for segmenting and classifying utterances that would automatically apply to a corpus to organize it in a form that meets conditions 1-4, and to apply these procedures in the study of particular languages:

(1) The grammar is a hierarchy of classes; the units at the lowest level in the hierarchy are temporal segments of speech events; at higher levels, the units are classes or sequences of classes.

(2) The elements of each level of the hierarchy are determined by their distributional features together with their representations at the immediately lower level.

(3) Information in the construction of a grammar flows only "upward" from level to level; i.e., no information at a higher level can be used to determine an analysis at a lower level.

(4) The main distributional principles for determining class memberships at level L_i are complementary distribution and free variation at level L_{i-1}.

JERROLD J. KATZ
THOMAS G. BEVER

As can be seen simply from inspection, these conditions are motivated by physicalist and operationalist considerations. For if these conditions are met, the grammatical analysis of a sentence will reflect observable physical events and consist only in classifying them so that no appeal is made to mental capacities or events anywhere from the beginning to the end of a grammatical analysis (Katz, 1964; Fodor *et al.*, 1974).

Such grammatical analysis was restricted to phonology, morphology, and the constituent structure of sentences until Harris found a way of extending it to the sentence level—that is, to relations among sentences in a language. Harris's particular achievement was to find a way of setting up substitution frames for sentences so that sentences could be grouped according to the environments they share, similar to the way that phonemes or morphemes were grouped by shared environments. Thus, distributional tests of the kind that taxonomic linguists employed below the sentence level could be used to determine cooccurrence relations of sentences. It was Harris's genius to see the need for such an extension of the taxonomic paradigm and to hit on the idea of using strings of sentences, comprising a discourse, to provide the substitution frames so that distributional features of sentences could be revealed by substitution of one sentence for another in such frames. Discourse analysis was thus the product of this attempt to extend the range of taxonomic analysis beyond the level of immediate constituents.

Syntactic transformations were developed by Harris as the formal means of stating the equivalence classes of sentences that emerged from the use of such substitution tests. The classes 'passive sentence', 'interrogative', and so on are thus the sentence-level counterparts of immediate constituent classes like 'noun', 'verb', and so on. For example, the passive transformation (5),

(5) $NP_1 \, V \, NP_2 \longleftrightarrow NP_2 \; is \; V + en \; by \; NP_1$

states the cooccurrence pattern that relates the subject and object in a sentence like (6),

(6) The cat bites the dog.

to the subject and object in a sentence like (7),

(7) The dog is bitten by the cat.

The regularity is that the same noun phrases that can occur as the subject and object of the verb in an active sentence can also occur as the subject and object (respectively) of the verb in the corresponding passive. Thus, just as two sounds can be said to be members of the same equivalence class of phonemes if one can substitute for the other without changing one word into another, two sentences can be said to be members of the same equivalence class of sentences (active/passive pairs, declarative/interrogative pairs, etc.) if the constituents of one sentence can appear at corresponding positions in the other without changing one discourse into another. Thus, transformational rules express cooccurrence regularities in essentially the same manner as the phrase structure rules of immediate constituent analysis.

Harris's conception of a grammar is an orthodox structuralist conception except for the addition of two new levels of grammatical structure beyond the structuralist levels of phones, phonemes, morphemes, words, and phrases. These are the level of *kernel sentence forms* and the level of *transformations*.[3] The kernel structures constitute a small, well-defined set of sentence forms, and they function as the base for the application of transformations. The application of transformations to kernels and to structures derived from kernels yields all the sentence constructions of a language (Harris, 1957, p. 444). These kernel structures represent the basic construction types out of which more complex sentences are built transformationally, and themselves comprise those constructions that are 'simple declaratives', including simple intransitives, transitives, predicate constructions, and so on. In addition, the level of kernel sentence structures serves as the point at which the cooccurrence restrictions on individual lexical items are stated. These restrictions, as Harris phrases it, "determine which member of a class occurs with which member of its neighbor class" (p. 446). Thus, Harris's distinction between the *level of kernel sentence forms* and *the transformational level* is the origin of the present, more sophisticated, distinction between the base and transformational components of a generative grammar.

Thus, contrary to common belief, transformations come into modern linguistics, not with Chomsky, but with Harris's rules relating sentence forms. These are genuine transformations, since they are structure-dependent mappings of phrase markers onto phrase markers. That this is so can be seen from the examples of transformations Harris gives. They perform the standard formal operations of permutation, deletion, and copying; and information about the bracketing of kernel strings and the category labels assigned to bracketed strings determine their application. Thus, they are more powerful than phrase structure rules because they use information beyond the left-right linear context of a symbol in a string.

Two points should be noted here. First, to be fully consistent with his empiricist approach Harris ought to have taken actual sentences as kernel forms rather than the constructions he uses—which use abstract categories and thus are only indirectly related to actual sentences. Had he done so, however, he would have sacrificed the possibility of stating transformations with any degree of

---

3. In discourse analysis, transformations serve as the means of normalizing texts, that is, of converting the sentences of the text into a standard form so that they can be compared and intersentence properties discovered. Harris sometimes regards transformational analysis as ancillary to structural linguistics, but he always relies on it to define a set of grammatical units and relations (on a par with those defined at other levels). This certainly qualifies transformational analysis as a grammatical level. In general, we rely heavily on Harris's descriptive practice to decide questions about his syntactic model.

JERROLD J. KATZ
THOMAS G. BEVER

generality. In practice, he used structures expressing the syntactic classification of sentential segments. This was similar to Bloomfield's practice of using ordering restrictions on phonological rules, even though in theory he refused to tolerate them as being inconsistent with physicalism (Bloomfield, 1933, p. 213).

Second, Harris's transformations are less sophisticated than present-day transformations, for his representations of syntactic structure in kernel forms are not as abstract as Chomskyan underlying phrase markers. This limitation does not imply that Harris's transformations are not true transformations, any more than the greater sophistication of contemporary transformations compared to those in *Syntactic Structures* shows that the latter are not true transformations. Chomsky's achievement was not to invent transformations, but to recognize the philosophical significance of Harris's transformational grammar, to clarify the role of transformations in grammar, and to provide a more general and complete formalization of transformations.

Harris's conception of transformational grammar had at least two further features of contemporary transformational theory. One is that he noted the existence of order restrictions on the sequences of transformational rules, excluding certain sequences of transformations from occurring. The other is that each sentence receives an analysis that decomposes it into a series of stages back to the kernel(s), and the intermediate stages describe both the sentence's relations to other sentences and its mode of construction out of them. In this connection, Harris had much to say about the particular characteristics of "parallel sentences," "overlapping sentences," and nominalizations (1957, pp. 442–443). However, these features had limited theoretical significance because Harris's approach contains no theory of the proper form for grammars, and hence no notion of how to decide what the correct derivation of a sentence is. Harris's conception of grammars as summaries of a corpus precludes a theory of the proper form for grammars, since the latter would pose questions of truth instead of questions of brevity.

From this brief review of Harris's early transformational theory, it is clear that his *formal model* of syntax was basically similar to Chomsky's in its first, *Syntactic Structure*, phase. The difference in Harris's and Chomsky's positions had to do with how this formal model was interpreted in the light of their different philosophical and methodological conceptions. On Harris's interpretation, transformational grammars are mathematical systematizations of the linguistic data of a corpus that express facts about the distribution of linguistic units from phones to sentences. On Chomsky's interpretation, such grammars are explications of the internalized rules that comprise the speaker's grammatical competence. Chomsky's revolution in linguistics therefore consisted in developing a rationalist and mentalist interpretation of the same formal, transformational model that Harris construed in empiricist and behaviorist terms. The primary differences between these two interpretations concern five major topics: *novelty*, *explanation, explication, absolute formulations*, and *transformational levels*. Let us look at each.

Novelty

Harris attached no special importance to the fact that speakers can produce and comprehend new sentences and other syntactic forms. He adopted a neo-Machian view on the question of whether the linguistic structures that must be presupposed to account for novelty are in any sense real. The essence of this view is that theoretical constructs do not represent a portion of reality but only computing machinery that enables the scientist to predict one set of observations from another (cf. Mach, 1911, p. 57). Harris acknowledges that such linguistic structures exist in language but denies that this linguistic structure represents anything in reality—in particular, anything in speakers. At best, distributional structure exists in speakers only in the Pickwickian sense of "reflecting their speaking habits." As Harris expresses his position:

> even when our structure can predict new utterances, we do not know that it always reflects a previously existing neural association in the speakers (different from the associations which do not, at a given time, produce new utterances). For example, before the word *analyticity* came to be used (in modern logic), our data on English may have contained *analytic, synthetic, periodic, periodicity, simplicity*, etc. On this basis, we would have made some statement about the distributional relation of *-ic* to *-ity*, and the new formation of *analyticity* may have conformed to this statement. But this means only that the pattern of habit existed in the speakers at the time of the new formation, not necessarily before: the 'habit'—the readiness to combine these elements productively—may have developed only when the need arose, by association of words that were partially similar as to composition and environment. . . . Aside from this, all we know about any particular language habit is the probability that new formations will be along certain lines rather than others, and this is no more than testing the success of our distributional structure in predicting new data or formations (1954, p. 150).

Contrast this with Chomsky's often repeated claim that the ability of speakers to produce and understand novel forms is a proof of the existence of a system of internalized grammatical rules. Even Chomsky's preferred term for novelty, "creativity of language," reflects the shift from data to speaker. Moreover, he even goes so far as to say that explanations of creativity that rely on habit have no force whatever (1966b, pp. 9–18).

Explanation

Harris took the prediction of distributional regularities in a corpus to be the primary concern of the linguist. What matters for him is the construction of formulas expressing observed distributional regularities, which permit us to anticipate further cooccurrence relations that will appear when the corpus is suitably enlarged. For Harris, transformations, like phrase structure rules, have

JERROLD J. KATZ
THOMAS G. BEVER

this function. Chomsky, on the other hand, takes explanation rather than prediction to be the linguist's primary concern. For Chomsky, the basic question is about the theory of language and theoretical psychology rather than about writing grammars of particular languages. Chomsky seeks to explain how a human being can acquire competence in a language on the basis of the information available in the formative period for language learning. Grammars of particular languages, although inherently interesting too, are of primary significance in that their common properties may tell us what universals may be regarded as innate principles functioning in the acquisition process. The properties of a grammar are significant in this sense insofar as they enable us to say how the child narrows down the class of systems of sound/meaning relations to a class of possible grammars from which a choice can be made, using sensory information available.

But besides the explanation of acquisition, Chomsky has stressed two other areas of explanation: the explanation, based on a hypothesis about universal grammar, of grammatical competence in a particular natural language; and the explanation, based on a hypothesis about the internalized grammar and the psychological mechanisms of production and perception, of both the speaker's ability to make judgments about grammatical properties and the speaker's other linguistic abilities. In all three areas, however, prediction of new forms plays the role of confirming or disconfirming hypotheses about the internalized grammar.

Explication

For Harris, there is no division of the strings of a language into two exclusive and jointly exhaustive sets, sentences and nonsentences, but only a sliding scale of acceptability on which strings can be ranked as more or less possible. As Harris puts this position:

> there is no well-defined set of sentences in a language. Rather, some word sequences are clearly sentences, some are odd or even undecidable as to sentencehood in one or another way, and some are entirely impossible (1965, p. 370).

Harris takes this position because he considers rules of a grammar to be nothing more than compact formulations of cooccurrence patterns in a corpus. Thus there is no way for him to explain away unclear cases of grammaticality. Doubtful intermediate cases must be so because that is their real status in the corpus. Chomsky, on the other hand, views each and every string of the language as belonging to one or the other of the two categories, 'grammatical' or 'ungrammatical'. For him, the middle range of 'undecidable cases' reflects not some inherent gradient in the phenomena that a descriptively adequate rule must represent, but simply incomplete knowledge on the part of the linguist.[4] As Chomsky writes:

> Notice that in order to set the aims of grammar significantly it is sufficient to assume a partial knowledge of sentences and non-sentences. That is, we may assume for this discussion that certain sequences of phonemes are definitely sentences, and that certain other sequences are definitely non-sentences. In many intermediate cases, we shall be prepared to let the grammar itself decide, when the grammar is set up in the simplest way so that it includes the clear sentences and excludes the clear non-sentences. This is a familiar feature of explication (1957, pp. 13-14).

Absolute Formulations

Viewing a grammar as an explication of the speaker's internalized rules makes it possible to frame them in absolute terms rather than as probability statements. Chomsky could take such rules as statements of what the ideal speaker-hearer knows about the language and thereby treat them as an idealization of the kind familiar from physics and other sciences. Harris, on the other hand, could treat grammatical rules only as compact mathematical expressions of the distributional regularities in a corpus. Statements of the likelihood of new forms occurring under certain conditions must express every feature of the situation that exerts an influence on likelihood of occurrence. This means that all sorts of grammatically extraneous features are reflected on a par with genuine grammatical constraints. For example, complexity of constituent structure, length of sentences, social mores, and so on, often exert a real influence on the probability that a certain n-tuple of morphemes will occur in the corpus. Thus, as long as the criterion of grammatical representation is what influences the distribution of linguistic forms in the corpus, such features will count equally with standard selectional relations in syntax. Chomsky's notion of absolute formulations as part of an idealization permits him to exclude from such formulations any factor that should be considered a matter of performance rather than competence by simply considering the former as something to be abstracted away from, the way the physicist excludes friction, air resistance, and so on from the formulation of mechanical laws.

Transformational Levels

Harris shared Bloomfield's positivistic views of the nature of language. He once put it as follows:

4. Note that Chomsky also proposed a theory of degrees of grammaticalness (Fodor and Katz, 1964, pp. 384–389) in which each ungrammatical string is assigned to some category representing the nature of its departure from grammaticality. Such a theory involves absolute categories, not a gradient in Harris's sense.

JERROLD J. KATZ
THOMAS G. BEVER

as part of nature . . . [language] can be objectively studied if one considers speech and writing not as an expression of the speaker which has particular, introspectively recognized, meanings to the hearer; but rather as a set of events—sound waves or ink marks (1958, p. 458).

Transformations, then, were thought of as just computing machinery for predicting cooccurrence relations, and therefore they constituted merely an extension of the scope of the devices for data-cataloguing in structuralist linguistics. But within the Chomskyan framework, transformations took on a new and revolutionary character. Because linguistic rules were interpreted as representations of a mental rather than a phonetic or orthographic reality, the postulation of transformations constituted the discovery of a new level of psychological structure. On Chomsky's interpretation, the existence of transformations constitutes for linguistics a discovery of roughly the same magnitude as the discovery in physics that matter has an atomic structure.

Thus, the significance of the Chomskyan revolution did not lie in the proposal of a new type of rule nor in its many improvements in the formalism of transformational theory. Indeed, the grammatical formalism found in Chomsky's earlier versions of transformational theory is fundamentally the same as what Harris constructed to extend the structuralist theory of taxonomic grammar, and even current models of the formal structure of transformational grammars are essentially a sophistication of Harris's original proposals. The profound contribution of the Chomskyan revolution was to reinterpret Harris's formal innovations, to see them from the opposite philosophical perspective, and to derive the important philosophical and psychological implications that follow from this change in the interpretation of the formal model.[5] Chomsky thus turned Harris's formalism against Harris's empiricist conception of linguistic structure. He saw that transformations, mentalistically viewed, implied the existence of unobservable levels of grammatical structure, that these had to be interpreted as constituting parts of the speaker's knowledge, and that their nature offered a basis for generalizing about the universal structure of language, which made the variations in surface form from language to language irrelevant to these generalizations. Finally, this analysis resembles in several interesting ways seventeenth-century universal philosophical grammar, the approach that had begun with Descartes and the Port Royal grammarians, flourished with Humboldt, and culminated in the nineteenth century with Wundt and ended in the early twentieth with Bloomfield's search for a sound, empirically oriented methodology.

5. In an interview Chomsky says: "From the very beginning of my work I have tried to explain the characteristics of a given stage of the language by trying . . . to attribute to [the speaker] certain mental characteristics from which one could derive the facts . . . I have tried to ask . . . how the speaker of the language organizes his knowledge so that the form is such and such or that the syntactic structure is such and such, and I think that this is the only innovation I've introduced into the field of linguistics" (Rosner and Abt, 1970, p. 76).

HOW EMPIRICISM COULD
MAKE A COMEBACK

Let us now examine aspects of both the formal structure of the theory of language and the sociological and historical structure of the postrevolutionary period in linguistics. We do this to illustrate how it would be possible for empiricism to make a comeback and what form it might take. In the next section, we present an important tendency in generative semantics as a case study of a movement that realizes this possibility in essentially the form sketched.

We begin with a few remarks about terminology. 'Empiricism' is the name of a metatheory. It is a theory about theories of how knowledge is acquired. It claims that the proper theory of how knowledge is acquired says that it comes from sensory experience by means of inductive principles. On empiricist theories, innate mental mechanisms are restricted to procedures for inductive generalization, and therefore contribute nothing to the content of our knowledge. 'Rationalism' is the name of the opposing metatheory. It claims that the general form of our knowledge comes not from experience but from innate schemata. On rationalist theories, much of the content of our knowledge is fixed as a biological disposition of our mind; the function of experience is simply to activate this disposition and thereby cause the innate schemata to be realized and differentiated.

'Behaviorism', 'operationalism', and 'physicalism' have to be distinguished from 'empiricism'.[6] Behaviorism contrasts with mentalism. Behaviorism is the doctrine that there are no internal, private mental states causally underlying behavior that are not themselves statable fully in terms of behavior. Operationalism is a methodological "safeguard" against mentalistic theories, requiring that each concept in a theory have a definition in terms of explicit operations that govern its application. Physicalism constitutes another such "safeguard." It holds that the concepts of any theory (in particular, psychological theories) must be in principle reducible, without loss of content, to concepts of physics, and that the laws of other theories must be expressible by laws of physics. Although these doctrines differ from empiricism, they often go together because they support each other and at bottom express the same conception of how to understand phenomena. Empiricism, behaviorism, and operationalism assume that such understanding requires us to consider only what is outside, what is public, what is observable to every experimenter.

We may extend the terms 'empiricism' and 'rationalism' to accounts of knowledge of one kind or another. That is, we may say about an account of a certain kind of knowledge that it is empiricistic or rationalistic, depending on

6. 'Empiricism' is also to be distinguished from 'empirical'. A theory is empirical if it is about the empirical world, and as such confirmable or disconfirmable on the basis of observation and experimentation. Chomsky's rationalism is every bit as empirical as Bloomfield's empiricism.

JERROLD J. KATZ
THOMAS G. BEVER

what properties the account ascribes to the knowledge. If it ascribes properties that make it difficult or impossible to explain that knowledge by an empiricist theory of acquisition, then the account is rationalistic. If it ascribes properties that make it easy to explain that knowledge by an empiricist theory, then it is empiricist. Since any account of how knowledge arises must begin with some notion of what that knowledge is like, it is clear that accounts of what the knowledge is like can be either more or less troublesome to philosophical theories about its acquisition. Traditionally, arguments for the existence of necessary truths (for example, "Bachelors are male," "If P, then P$\lor$Q," "All events have a cause," and so on) were taken as arguments for rationalism, because it was assumed that no inductive principles could account for the application of necessary connections (Katz, 1975, pp. 285–286).

Since grammars are accounts of linguistic knowledge, we can ask of a grammar (and a theory of grammars) whether it is rationalistic or empiricistic. Chomsky's account of grammar is clearly rationalistic, since, on it, linguistic knowledge is determined by unobservable mental structures that are invariant from language to language. For empiricism to make a comeback, this account would have to be changed so that the account of linguistic knowledge becomes empiricistic again.

What makes the comeback of empiricism possible is a deficiency in the theory of generative grammar that permits an empiricistic account of grammars. This deficiency is the incompleteness of the theory of the interpretation of formal grammars; nothing in the theory tells us how such formal systems are construed as empirical theories that make specific claims about linguistic behavior. Transformational linguistics has contributed to some extent to this theory, but its contributions are limited and fragmentary, never explicitly recognized as such, and in some cases less than coherent. The development of transformational linguistics has been lopsided in favor of contributions to the characterization of the formal model of a grammar. Indeed, what has come to be known as transformational theory is almost exclusively in account of the formal structure of sentence-generating grammars.

The distinction between the formal structure of a grammar, what we will call the 'formal model', and the principles that assign it empirical content, which we will call the 'interpretation', is a distinction between the abstract calculus that forms the skeletal structure of the theory and the statements about the parts of the calculus that give them empirical content. The formal model consists of a vocabulary of meaningless symbols, syntactic rules for forming strings in the calculus from the vocabulary, a set of such strings distinguished as the axioms, and, finally, principles that specify derivational relations between the axioms and other strings in the calculus. The interpretation consists of a set of what we shall call 'correspondence principles' that connect the symbols and strings of the calculus to states of affairs in the world. They supply empirical content by relating strings of symbols or sets of them to aspects of the behavior of the things in the domain of the theory. The formal model plus an interpretation is an empirical theory of the domain.[7]

Here and there in linguistics we find fragments of an interpretation, but they are not thought of as correspondence principles. Generally, they are seen as part of the apparatus for determining predictions about the intuitions of speakers, as providing a means of confirming or disconfirming rules. Three notable examples are Chomsky's (partial) explications of the notions 'grammatical sentence', 'ambiguous construction', and 'synonymous sentence' (1957, pp. 2-17, 88-91). The first explicates grammaticality in terms of the formal property of generation in an optimal grammar. This explication associates a derivation with the intuitive property of well-formedness and thereby enables the linguist to predict that a native speaker of English distinguishes between sentences like (8) and strings like (9):

(8) Colorless green ideas sleep furiously.
(9) Furiously sleep ideas green colorless.

The second explicates ambiguity in terms of the formal property of a sentence having two or more nonequivalent derivations. This explication associates the existence of multiple structural descriptions for the same sentence with a native speaker's intuitions of multiple senses. This enables the linguist to predict that the native speaker of English recognizes the ambiguity of sentences like (10):

(10) Flying planes can be dangerous.

The third explicates synonymy in terms of the formal property of the same underlying phrase marker initiating the derivations of different sentences. This explication associates derivations originating with the same underlying phrase marker with the native speaker's intuition of sameness of meaning and thereby enables the linguist to predict that the native speaker of English takes sentences like (11) and (12) or (13) and (14) to have the same sense:

(11) John hit Benny's sister.
(12) Benny's sister was hit by John.
(13) The woman who is old left.
(14) The old woman left.

These associations were originally thought of as *predictive*, as determining the specific empirical claims that grammars with certain formal properties are committed to (e.g., rules enabling us to derive such-and-such a sentence, or ones enabling us to derive it in different ways). They can also be thought of as *interpretive*, as specifying the empirical meaning of such formal properties in the grammar. That is, these associations function as correspondence principles that tell us the significance of some uninterpreted piece of formalism in the grammar.

7. This distinction is slightly different from some of those in the literature (cf. Nagel, 1961, pp. 90-105).

JERROLD J. KATZ
THOMAS G. BEVER

But not only have the correspondence principles offered so far been an exceedingly small and fragmentary piece of a full interpretation, they are each themselves less than adequate. The definition of grammaticality as generation in an optimal grammar is informative only to the degree that we have a complete notion of what an optimal grammar is. By itself, the failure of a system of rules to generate a string means *either* that the string is ungrammatical *or* that the system is not optimal. We must know that the system is optimal to know that the ungenerated string is ungrammatical. If we have a number of independent constraints that can be imposed on grammars that, apart from questions of grammaticality, permit us to argue that the grammar is optimal, then we have a basis for deciding questions of grammaticality. If we have no such constraints, there are no independent grounds for claiming the system is adequate and no basis for choosing between the alternatives of an ungrammatical string and an inadequate grammar. The situation is even worse if there are no other acceptable correspondence principles, for then the grammar is defined simply as a system that generates all and only the grammatical sentences; as a consequence, we face real circularity when we claim that a string is not grammatical because it is not generated.

In fact, the two other correspondence principles presently available (of ambiguity and synonymy) cannot bear the weight that is thus put on them. The explication of ambiguity fails completely if there are cases where different underlying phrase markers underlie synonymous sentences, since the explication takes multiple underlying phrase markers as a sufficient condition for ambiguity. Counterexamples are relatively easy to find, for example (15), (16), and (17):

(15)   It was done by an automated processing machine.
(16)   John wrote a letter about his experience.
(17)   Don't buy dark green paint.[8]

In each of these cases, there is alternative bracketing of the form (A (BC)) and ((AB) C), but no meaning difference corresponding to it. Any grammar that assigns such alternative bracketings as its explanation of the ambiguity of phrases like "ornamented lettering machine" will also assign such alternative bracketing to examples like (15).

An explication of synonymy in terms of sameness of underlying phrase marker is no better. Changes in transformational theory (such as the change in the conception of the passive transformation by which it became obligatory as the result of introducing a passive marker in the base) narrow the range of cases for which this explication has application. Such an explication has no relevance to the infinite set of cases in which sentences with vastly different underlying phrase markers are synonymous because the meanings of their

8. Example (16) is due to Barbara Hall Partee and (17) to D. Terence Langendoen.

lexical items combine compositionally to provide them with the same meaning, as in (18) and (19):

(18)   George is a bachelor.
(19)   George is a human who is male and an adult and an unmarried person to boot.

The area of application remaining for this explication is not only small, but trying to characterize it would be extremely complicated.

But it would be pointless even to try to characterize it. The reason is that these counterexamples show that there is a role for a semantic explication of ambiguity and synonymy, and any role for semantic explications makes syntactic explications of such notions irrelevant. Cases like (15)–(17) require us to explicate 'S is ambiguous in L' in terms of the condition that S receives more than one semantic representation in the grammar of L. But if we introduce such an explication for these cases, there is no point in keeping the syntactic explication for others, since every case of ambiguity that the syntactic explication covers is also covered by the new semantic explication. The same situation exists for synonymy. Cases like (18) and (19) require us to explicate 'S_1 is synonymous with S_2 in L' in terms of the condition that S_1 and S_2 receive the same semantic representation in the grammar of L. But if we introduce such an explication, there is, again, no point in retaining the syntactic explication, since every case of synonymy that the syntactic explication covers is also covered by the new semantic one.

We may obtain some further idea of the primitive state of the theory of interpretation if we look at what would be contained in a complete and systematic account of the interpretation of the formalism of grammars. Clearly, such a theory would list every grammatical property that a language could exhibit and provide a correspondence principle for each. These principles would associate a term denoting some grammatical property, such as intuitive *well-formedness*, with a description of some formalism in the uninterpreted calculus, such as a *complete derivation*. At the phonological level, we would find correspondence principles for the properties of *rhyme, alliteration, meter*, and so on. At the syntactic level, we would find correspondence principles for the properties of *grammaticality, ellipsis, sentence types, part-of-speech equivalences, pronominalization relations, agreement*, and so on. At the semantic level, we would find correspondence principles for the properties of *ambiguity, synonymy, analyticity, meaninglessness vs. meaningfulness, entailment, presupposition*, etc. Further, a theory of interpretation would have to state metaprinciples that guarantee that a system of correspondence principles provides a coherent interpretation of formal grammars. For example, there must be some metaprinciple to determine what part of the formal model is interpreted and what part can be left without direct connection to linguistic behavior.

JERROLD J. KATZ
THOMAS G. BEVER

One such metaprinciple might be based on the linguist's working assumption that similar formal structures must receive similar empirical interpretations. This assumption operated as one reason for eliminating generalized transformations from the grammar. On the one hand, if the assignment of different underlying phrase markers to the same surface structure is a condition for ambiguity, then, on this working assumption, assigning different T-markers to the same surface structure, in grammars with generalized transformations, should also be a condition for ambiguity. But, on the other hand, the existence of multiple T-markers underlying a sentence does not, empirically, correspond to any form of sentential ambiguity. Thus a reason for eliminating generalized transformations is that no situation arises where there is a distinction without a difference (Chomsky, 1965). The formulation of metaprinciples in a theory of interpretation would provide a place in the theory of grammars to state such assumptions explicitly.[9]

The present primitive state of the theory of interpretation is what provides the back door through which empiricism might return to linguistics. Since many different actual and possible empirical theories can have the same formal structure (a system of phrase structure rules can be a description of the genealogy of a family, a program for theorem-proving computers, a sentence-generating grammar), a given formal system can be made to mean different things, depending on what interpretation is imposed on its symbols and their formal relations in strings. Moreover, if this can be done for a whole system, nothing prevents a change in a central part of a system from changing the general character of the whole system in some specific direction. Thus, empiricism might return if it could capitalize on the near-vacuum in linguistic theory concerning a theory of interpretation, dislodging the rather weakly based rationalistic interpretation (based on Chomsky's proposals concerning novelty, explanation, explication, absolute formulations, and transformational levels) and replacing it with an empiricist interpretation.

The problem for the empiricist is how to find an interpretation that represents the internalized grammar that comprises the speaker's fluency in a way that makes an empiricist account of its acquisition seem natural. The focus of such an interpretation would clearly have to be the property of grammaticality. Grammaticality is the central notion in linguistic investigation, and it occupies

9. Also, there should be metaprinciples that determine the kinds of empirical events a formal structure in the grammar can be associated with. For example, it might be claimed that semantic correspondence principles can only connect grammatical formalisms to language universal cognitive structures, while phonological correspondence principles must often link grammatical formalisms to language-specific articulatory configurations. Further, there ought to be constraints that determine the conditions under which the same formal structure can be referred to by different kinds of correspondence principles. For instance, it would clearly be absurd if one principle connects ellipsis to the operation of erasure transformations as in most discussions, but another principle allowed mapping rules that correlate phonetic structures with physiological properties of the vocal tract to apply prior to such erasures.

a preeminent position in the Chomskyan theory as well. Chomsky's presentation of transformational theory emphasizes the property of grammaticality by its characterization of grammars as sentence-generating devices. Thus, to find an interpretation that is empiricist, perhaps the most important thing to do is to undermine fully Chomsky's notions of explication and absolute formulation, which provide the basis for his conception of grammaticality.

We should therefore expect the Chomskyan notion of grammaticality as generation in an optimal grammar to be the main target of an empiricist counterrevolution. This notion supports a rationalist conception of language acquisition by making a sharp, absolute distinction between the grammatical and the ungrammatical, and between the competence principles that determine the grammatical and anything else that combines with them to produce performance. Such cleavages are not found in linguistic experience, which better fits Harris's description of a sliding scale from the totally unacceptable to the clearly acceptable. Moreover, it is virtually inconceivable that inductive generalization applied to so heterogeneous a set of events as linguistic experience could give rise to so idealized a set of objects as Chomskyan grammars without the aid of strong *a priori* determinations of the form and content of their rules. Induction generalizes regularities in particular phenomena, but like photography it reflects only what is there. If sharp categorizations are not explicit in linguistic experience, then they have to be contributed by the principles the mind uses to organize its experience. However, if instead of Chomskyan grammars, theories of language acquisition had to explain the acquisition of something closer to a description of actual experience, empiricism would look far more plausible.

An important secondary target of an empiricist counterrevolution must be the absolute concepts of synonymy, analyticity, and entailment at the semantic level. Such absolute concepts lead directly to the existence of necessary truths, since these concepts force us to credit speakers with knowledge of meanings that by itself constitutes knowledge of necessary truth. Such knowledge poses a formidable stumbling block to empiricism, since no amount of repetition in experience can produce anything stronger than a highly confirmed association. It can never equal a necessary connection, and thus empiricist theories stand no chance of accounting for how speakers could have come to know sentences whose meaning involves necessary connection (Katz, 1975).

The absence of even a fairly well-developed theory of interpretation makes it easy for the empiricist to attack these notions, for without such a theory there is no rationalistic criterion for what is linguistic and what is not, what belongs in the grammar and what is extragrammatical. If there were such a theory, then relative to its correspondence principles we could set up the criterion that what belongs in the grammar is whatever formalism is necessary to explain the properties and relations (e.g., rhyme, meter, ellipsis, word order, sentence type, synonymy, ambiguity) appearing in these principles. Without such a theory, we tend not even to think of such a criterion, and in its absence the empiricist could re-

JERROLD J. KATZ
THOMAS G. BEVER

turn (without much notice being taken) to Harris's criterion that what belongs in the grammar is any aspect of the distribution of linguistic elements in actual speech. This criterion would easily do away with the Chomskyan conception of grammaticality as dealing with only a limited set of the factors that influence distribution. It would be replaced by a conception that relativizes grammaticality to all sorts of performance and contextual factors, thereby almost by itself reinterpreting the formal model empiricistically. Furthermore, the criterion would also obliterate the distinction between beliefs about the meanings of words and beliefs about what words refer to, since both sets of beliefs determine the distribution of words in speech. Consequently, absolute concepts of synonymy, analyticity, and entailment would be replaced by graded concepts[10], and because only contingent connections could be expressed with them, these would be no obstacle to empiricist theories of how speakers come to know what they do about their language.

A CASE STUDY: GENERATIVE
SEMANTICS, LAKOFF STYLE

Having seen how empiricism might come back into linguistics, we now will see how it *is* coming back. We do not claim that the linguists who are bringing it back are necessarily empiricists or are aware that their work has this thrust, but only that their work clears the way for return of empiricism in the manner we have described.

It may appear at first encounter that generative semanticists are developing a new and improved model of grammar, but there is clear reason to think that the model they are offering is either a notational variant of the model of grammar known as the "standard theory" or a modest extension of that model. We will not repeat the arguments for this claim (see Katz, 1972; 1973). What we wish to say here does not depend on them; rather, our claims here answer the question of how generative semantics can be a notational variant of interpretive semantics when it is perfectly clear that some new and controversial thesis is being put forth by generative semanticists. The answer is that the claim of equivalence is about the formal model, while the controversy is about the interpretation. The issue between generative and interpretive semantics is over different interpretation schemes for the transformational model, one of which is empiricist and the other rationalist.

Lakoff proposes to replace the absolute notions of grammaticality and of analyticity, synonymy, and entailment with graded ones. As we argued above, these aspects of the rationalist interpretation of the transformational model are the two key areas where an empiricist counterrevolution would have to concentrate its attack.

10. For the empiricist conception of graded concepts, cf. Quine, 1960, especially section 12.

Lakoff states his aims as follows:

> there are a great many cases where it makes no sense to speak of the well-formedness or 'grammaticality' of a sentence in isolation. Instead one must speak of relative well-formedness and/or relative grammaticality; that is, in such cases a sentence will be well-formed only with respect to certain pre-suppositions about the nature of the world . . . Given a sentence, S, and a set of presuppositions, PR, we will say, in such instances, that S is well-formed only relative to PR. That is, I will claim that the notion of relative well-formedness is needed to replace Chomsky's original notion of strict grammaticality . . . , which was applied to a sentence in isolation (1971a, p. 329).

Lakoff claims further that he is not "blurring the distinction between competence and performance," since he distinguishes between extralinguistic factors that enter into a speaker's judgments about well-formedness and "the linguistic competence underlying this," i.e., "the ability of a speaker to pair sentences with the presuppositions relative to which they are well-formed" (p. 330). Chomsky takes Lakoff at his word here and concludes that there is nothing more at stake than a question of terminology (1972, p. 121). As Chomsky argues, the relation between (20),

(20)   John called Mary a Republican and then *she* insulted *him*.

and its presupposition, say, that Mary believes that to be called a Republican is insulting, is agreed to hold independently of anyone's factual beliefs and to be a matter of competence, and therefore it doesn't matter whether we follow Lakoff and "define 'well-formed' as a relative concept, and . . . have the grammar generate (S, P) pairs such that S is well-formed relative to P," or we follow Chomsky and define 'well-formed' independently of Mary's, John's, or anyone else's beliefs and then "assign to the semantic component of the grammar the task of stipulating that (20) expresses the presupposition that for John to call Mary a Republican is for him to insult her." The substance of Chomsky's position is that: "For sentences with presuppositions in this sense, nothing hinges on this terminological decision . . . What may appear at first sight to be a profound issue dissolves into nothing on analysis" (p. 122).

But Chomsky is wrong here. There is a profound issue. Lakoff is allowing *a* competence-performance distinction, but not the one Chomsky has drawn, which characterizes the notion of well-formedness so that strings in a language can be divided into the well-formed and the ill-formed just on the basis of their syntactic structure, without reference to the way things are in the world, what speakers, hearers, or anyone else believe, etc. What makes the situation confusing is that Lakoff keeps the terminology 'competence', and 'linguistic knowledge', but changes what such terms mean. One has to read closely and put together things that he says in different places to see that 'competence' no longer refers exclusively to the system of grammatical rules that constitutes an idealized

JERROLD J. KATZ
THOMAS G. BEVER

(in Chomsky's sense) speaker-hearer's ability to associate sounds and meanings, but includes a host of nongrammatical facts about the way things are in the world, such as what speakers, hearers, people spoken about, and so on, believe. Lakoff says: "The study of the relationship between a sentence and those things that it presupposes about the nature of the world by way of systematic rules is part of the study of linguistic competence" (1971a, p. 329). Thus, for Lakoff, but *not* for Chomsky, the well-formedness of (20) turns in part on the empirical facts concerning what beliefs Mary, John, and the speaker, have about Republicans, whereas for both, at some level in the grammar, (20) is paired with the presupposition that for John to call Mary a Republican is for him to insult her.

Lakoff would of course argue about whether such facts about people's beliefs are nongrammatical facts, but such an argument would be beside the point, since here the conflict is between two conceptions of the distinction between the grammatical and the extragrammatical. Lakoff's criterion for what is grammatical is explicitly that of structuralist linguists like Harris—namely, that whatever determines the distribution of morphemes is *ipso facto* part of grammar.[11]   Thus, he argues that, since the beliefs of those involved in the speech situation determine the distribution of such features as the stress pattern of (20) as distinct from that of (21),

(21)   John called Mary a Republican and then she insulted him.

where the sentence expresses no more than that one event occurred and then another occurred (there is no sense of Mary insulting John back), information about the existence of beliefs about John's having insulted Mary must be an integral part of the study of competence. Lakoff's criterion leads to an almost indefinitely expandable competence domain: any factor in a linguistic situation that influences distribution becomes a matter of competence. As we shall see below, Lakoff capitalizes on this feature of his criterion to come up with a variety of "novel claims" about competence.

Chomsky's criterion is close to the Wundtian conception of the subject of grammar. The object of study is the sentence, intuitively understood, and the theory of competence is a theory about the principles that explain the intuitions we as speakers have about sentence structure (Chomsky, 1965, pp. 3-9). Thus, a rule is counted as grammatical if it plays a role in explaining the structure underlying intuitions about ambiguity in sentences like (10), about synonymy in sentence pairs like (11) and (12) or (13) and (14), and about well-formedness in sentences like (8). But linguistic competence is distinguished from performance, primarily in a negative way by the fact that the latter involves matters not relevant to the explanation of such intuitions—for example, limitations stemming from the nature of the organism's psychological mechanisms, which restrict immediate memory, computation time, and information access. On the positive side, it is readily conceded that this criterion is nowhere nearly as fully devel-

11. Lakoff uses this criterion in several places: 1971a, pp. 330, 331, 337, and so on.

oped as is desirable, principally because of the absence of a rich theory of the interpretation of formal grammars. The absence of this theory means that the range of intuitions required in a reasonably complete and convincing account of what a grammar must explain is drastically impoverished. Nonetheless, Chomsky made it quite clear that a factor that influences the distribution of linguistic forms cannot for that reason alone be taken to determine aspects of competence like grammaticality (rather than aspects of performance like acceptability), since, as he observed: "The more acceptable sentences are those that are more likely to be produced, more easily understood, less clumsy, and in some sense more natural. The unacceptable sentences one would tend to avoid and replace by more acceptable variants, wherever possible, in actual discourse. ... The unacceptable grammatical sentences often cannot be used, for reasons having to do, not with grammar, but rather with memory limitations, intonational and stylistic factors, 'iconic' elements of discourse ... and so on" (1965, p. 11).

Lakoff's criterion leads directly to a reintroduction of Harris's conception of acceptability, in which the sentences of the language form a gradient from clearly impossible strings on up to clearly well-formed ones, since well-formedness is made a function of parameters that may vary in any way from speaker to speaker and to any degree in the same speaker over time.[12] Thus, Lakoff's proposal of relative grammaticality, if accepted, would take what is perhaps the most important step toward preparing the way for a return of empiricism, since it would eliminate Chomsky's strict dichotomy between the grammatical and the ungrammatical. Given that actual speech is so messy, heterogeneous, irregular, fuzzy, and filled with one or another performance error, the empiricist's explanation of Chomskyan rules, as having been learned as a purely inductive generalization of a sample of actual speech is hard to take seriously to say the very least. On the other hand, something like Harris's or Lakoff's rules, which represent an acceptability gradient, stand a much better chance of being explained on the basis of inductive generalization because they reflect the character of actual speech.

Rationalism, however, is an empirical theory. It might be a true hypothesis about the acquisition of knowledge, or empiricism might be true. Hence, we

12. Lakoff allows for an absolute notion of grammaticality in an exceedingly narrow range of cases: "languages exhibit certain low-level or 'shallow' constraints on the form of sentences. ... Violation of such constraints does indeed make for ungrammaticality of an absolute sort: *'Hit Sam Irving' *'I went Boston to'" (1971a, p. 399). Two remarks should be made about this. First, it represents an acknowledgment of the existence of counterexamples to the thesis Lakoff wishes to put forth that there is no absolute notion of grammaticality. Second, it assumes, without argument, that such verb-subject constraints and preposition-noun constraints can be stated in isolation from everything else in the grammar, that is, they have no implications for "higher-level" or "deeper" aspects of sentence structure. Lakoff seems to be claiming that whatever rules are need to explicate these clear cases of ungrammaticality do not, as one might expect on Chomsky's notion of explication, imply decisions in unclear ones. Thus, whereas the unclearness of an unclear case for Chomsky is a matter of the state of our knowledge, for Lakoff, as for Harris, it is due to the inherent fuzziness of the phenomena themselves.

JERROLD J. KATZ
THOMAS G. BEVER

have to show more than that Lakoff's proposal is pro-empiricist; we have to show that the proposal provides no actual support for empiricism. We cannot hope here to restate the case against empiricism in linguistics (see, for example, Chomsky, 1968), and so we have to accept the fact that those linguists who still remain empiricists will reply to what we have said in this paper, "so much the better for generative semantics." But we can show that Lakoff's arguments in no way undermine or weaken the case Chomsky and others have erected for rationalism. Therefore, we now turn to the question of the adequacy of Lakoff's arguments for his proposal to relativize well-formedness to the beliefs of speakers, actors, and so on.

Typical of Lakoff's arguments is the one that claims that the grammaticality of sentences with verb phrases like "realizes that I'm a lousy cook," "believes I'm a fool," "enjoys tormenting me," etc., does not depend on whether their subject is marked 'Human' but instead on whether the speaker assumes that the thing(s) in the world that he or she refers to by the subject are sentient. Lakoff's argument for this conclusion is that people who believe that such things as cats, goldfish, amoebas, frying pans, sincerity, or births are sentient find sentences like (22) "perfectly alright" (Lakoff, 1971a, p. 332):

(22) My cat (goldfish, pet amoeba, frying pan, birth) enjoys tormenting me.

Thus, Lakoff concludes that well-formedness is not an absolute notion but a relative one that varies with belief.

The argument initially strikes one as a simple *nonsequitur*. Why should anyone conclude that a sentence like (23)

(23) My frying pan enjoys the fire because it's masochistic.

is well-formed in any sense from the mere fact that people who believe that frying pans have a mind find such a sentence "acceptable," "perfectly alright," or "perfectly normal"? What makes us take such judgments to be judgments about *well-formedness*, in the sense in which this term is used in the theory Lakoff is criticizing? Perhaps all that such people mean when they say these things is that the sentence expresses something they think is true. After all, deviant sentences can be used to make true statements.[13]

The argument is a *nonsequitur*, but the plot thickens if we look more closely. Lakoff himself finds the argument convincing, so one may assume that he has some principle in mind that enables him to conclude that the judgments are legitimately about well-formedness. One aspect of such a principle would have to be that ill-formedness is the only kind of sentential deviance to which the judgments of such people are relevant. This is, of course, dubious, but we may accept it for the sake of argument.[14] The other aspect of such a principle

13. This is what the interest in semi-sentences was all about (cf. Fodor and Katz, 1964, pp. 384–416).
14. Some argument is needed to show that there is no further type of deviance, such as semantic anomaly, exclusive of ill-formedness, to which the judgments are relevant.

is that there is no distinction between a speaker's knowledge of the grammatical or semantic properties of a word and his or her beliefs about the things in the world to which it refers. It is easy to show that this must be assumed to make the argument work. Assume it to be false. That is, assume that there is one criterion for determining the grammatical or semantic facts about a term like 'frying pan' and another for determining beliefs about frying pans. The former might be as follows: a hypothesis H_i representing a putative lexical sense of w is preferable to another hypothesis H_j just in case H_i predicts and explains the semantic properties and relations of sentences in which w occurs better than does H_j or they explain them equally well but H_i is simpler (Katz, 1972, pp. 284-286). The latter criterion might be as follows: a belief B_i about some class of things in the world is better than another B_j just in case it better explains the behavior of these objects or more simply if both explain such behavior equally well. Now, suppose that on the basis of the first criterion we learn that the meaning of 'frying pan' in English today is roughly, 'nonsentient, physical object, artifact, used for frying food'. Suppose, however, that you and your friends have been making a study of the behavior of frying pans when other people forget about them, and you find that this behavior is so strange that the only explanation for it is that frying pans are sentient and desire to enslave the human race. You rush to the TV station, seize the microphone, and begin to sound the warning. What do you say? There is no word in the language meaning 'sentient, physical object, artifact, used for frying food'. But this doesn't matter, for you can deliver the warning using the term 'frying pan'. There is nothing illegitimate about this; it is a perfectly straightforward case of reference under a false semantic description (cf. Donnellan, 1966, pp. 281-304; 1970, pp. 335-358).

But if beliefs about the referents of words are independent of the meaning of these words in the way suggested by the account above, Lakoff's conclusion does not follow. Hence, his argument must deny any possibility of such distinct criteria and any distinction between speakers' knowledge of the grammatical properties of words and their knowledge of the things in the world to which words refer. But since this is exactly what his argument against Chomsky's notion of absolute grammaticality is supposed to prove, the argument is circular. Lakoff is supposed to show that Chomsky's rationalist conception of a closed system of formal rules expressing the internal structure of sentence types and permitting us to make an absolute dichotomy between the ill-formed and the well-formed is untenable because it is incapable of handling the most interesting facts in the domain of syntax.[15] However, he begs the question because he simply assumes the empiricist principle that there is no distinction between grammatical information that includes dictionary information of both a syntactic and semantic nature, and extragrammatical information that includes information about what the speaker believes about others, encyclopedia information concerning what various referred to objects are, and so on.

15. Lakoff says: "It is not at all clear that very much that is interesting would be part of the study of presupposition-free syntax" (1971a, p. 337).

JERROLD J. KATZ
THOMAS G. BEVER

The actual grammatical status of sentences like (22) and (23) is, of course, another question. It might be that the hypothesis that Lakoff rejects out of hand is correct, that only 'uncle' is marked 'Human' so that only (24) is nondeviant.

(24)   My uncle enjoys tormenting me (realizes I'm a lousy cook, etc.).

Or, for all we know, (23) might be nondeviant. The problem is not the lack of a criterion to tell us how to decide matters of this kind; the criterion mentioned just above together with a suitable set of definitions of the semantic properties and relations that have to be predicted and explained serves well enough. What is absent is some clear enough set of examples of the semantic properties and relations that need to be predicted and explained. What is relevant here, however, is that, whatever the examples turn out to be, there is nothing in what Lakoff says to show that in principle such deviance phenomena will be outside the range of the standard theory.

This may not be as clear for some of Lakoff's cases as it is for the case of examples like (22)–(24). Thus, it is worthwhile to consider his examples (25) and (26):

(25)   We have just found a good name for our child, *who* we hope will be conceived tonight.

(26)   We have just found a good name for our child, *who* we hope will grow up to be a good citizen after he is born.

Lakoff's claim concerning the deviance of (25) is:

it seems clear that the distribution of the grammatical morpheme *who* cannot simply be determined by a syntactic feature like [+Human] ; rather, the relative *who* requires, at least, that the person referred to be presupposed to be alive at the time referred to in the relative clause (1971a, p. 331).

It is easy to show that an explanation of the deviance of (25) and the nondeviance of (26) can be given in the standard theory without reference to what the speaker believes. We can assume that the combination of a reading of an embedded sentence in the form of a relative clause with the reading of its head in the matrix structure is governed by the condition that the latter reading be identical to the reading of the pronominalized constituent. Taking the deviance of (25) to be semantic, this condition is a selectional restriction determining the existence of a derived reading for the whole sentence. In (25), the reading of the head noun phrase of the matrix structure contains the semantic marker '(Alive at Speech Point)'[16] while the reading of the pronominalized noun phrase in the embedded structure, i.e., the object of the verb 'conceive', contains the

16. The notion of the speech point is formulated in terms of the system of temporal specification in the semantic component; cf. Katz, 1972, pp. 306–362.

semantic marker '(A/(Alive at Speech Point))'.[17] Thus, the selectional restriction on the combination of readings is not satisfied, and the sentence as a whole is marked semantically anomalous.

Note that this explanation does not mention either presupposition or speakers' beliefs. Generative semanticists generally assume that selectional restrictions always determine presupposition, but this is mistaken, since the connection can fail in both directions (Katz, 1973, pp. 568-574). Actually, in the cases where a selection restriction predicts a presupposition, the latter is something like an epiphenomenon. Thus, the correspondence between the selectional restriction of verbs like 'enjoy', 'realize', 'believe', etc.—that the reading of their subject contain the semantic marker '(Sentient)'—and the presupposition that a sentence like (24) assumes the existence of some sentient creature (appropriately related to the speaker) is due simply to the fact that the reading of this subject determines such a presupposition just insofar as the reading of any noun phrase in referential position determines a presupposition to the effect that there exists something with the properties expressed by the semantic markers in its reading. The selection restriction merely excludes readings of sentences whose subject does not contain the marker '(Sentient)', thereby leaving only those with the presupposition that there exists some sentient creature. Although it appears that it is the selection restriction of the verb that determines the presupposition, the verb influences the presupposition of its subject only indirectly. Therefore our explanation makes no reference to presupposition, etc., but accounts for the semantically deviant and nondeviant cases in terms of whether or not a selection restriction on the semantic markers appearing in a reading is satisfied, that is, in terms of the internal semantic structure of a sentence.

Recently, Lakoff has extended his theory of relative well-formedness, making the notion of well-formedness depend on an even wider range of empirical facts about the beliefs of speakers. Lakoff says (we have renumbered the example):

"Take a typical example.

(27) Nixon was elected, but the blacks won't revolt.

(27) involves the assertion of [28], and is grammatical relative to a set of presuppositions like that given in [28].

(28) Assertion: Nixon was elected, and the blacks won't revolt.
$$S_1 \quad \text{and} \quad S_2$$

---

17. "A/" is the antonymy operator that converts a semantic marker into an n-tuple of incompatible ones (Katz, 1972, pp. 157-171). Note that the explanation here is highly simplified, and that this example is not intended to contrast with "the child *which* we hope. . . ," since these sentences with "which" are even less acceptable.

JERROLD J. KATZ
THOMAS G. BEVER

Presuppositions:

(29) (a) Nixon is a Republican.

 (b) If a Republican is elected, then social welfare programs will be cut.

 (c) If social welfare programs are cut, the poor will suffer.

 (d) Blacks are poor.

 (e) Blacks are discriminated against.

 (f) Blacks form a substantial part of the population.

 (g) One would expect that poor, suffering people who are discriminated against and who form a substantial proportion of the population would revolt.

I will not go through the deduction here, but it should be obvious that $\text{Exp}(S_1 \supset \sim S_2)$ can be deduced from these presuppositions. Thus, [27] will be grammatical relative to these presuppositions. Since these presuppositions do not conflict with our knowledge of the world, [27] is a perfectly normal sentence. Of course, there are innumerable other sets of presuppositions relative to which [27] would be grammatical—all of those from which $\text{Exp}(S_1 \supset \sim S_2)$ can be deduced" (1971b, p. 68).

Lakoff himself is in no doubt about the fact that in this theory the well-formedness of sentences depends on matters of empirical fact. He continues:

It should be clear that the general principles governing the occurrence of *too*, *but*, and reciprocal contrastive stress can be stated only in terms of presuppositions and deductions based on those presuppositions. This means that certain sentences will be grammatical only relative to certain presuppositions and deductions, that is, to certain thoughts and thought processes and the situations to which they correspond. This seems to me wholly natural (pp. 68–69).

Moreover, he happily embraces the consequence that the pairing of sentences with their presuppositions, and hence the determination of well-formedness generally, is no longer a matter of mechanical computation.[18]

From the viewpoint of those sympathetic to the old version of Lakoff's theory of relative well-formedness, this new version must be considered both a natural extension and an important improvement. It represents a generalization in that now no particular belief of a speaker's (say, about cats, goldfish, amoebas, frying pans, etc.) is necessary for a sentence about them (like those in (22)) to be grammatical. All that is required now is that the speaker's beliefs, taken together, bear the relation of logical implication to the presupposition of the sentence. This has the advantage of permitting the generative semanticist to

18. Mistaking his own theory for a fact about language, Lakoff even claims to have discovered that the well-formedness of sentences is undecidable (1971b, pp. 69–70).

determine the relative grammaticality of a sentence in certain of the cases where the speaker has no specific belief about the truth of the presupposition, namely, those in which the speaker's beliefs imply the presupposition. In the old version, these cases were treated on a par with cases in which the speaker has a belief that is inconsistent with the presupposition or in which the speaker's beliefs are independent of the presupposition.

From the viewpoint of those unsympathetic to the first version of Lakoff's theory because it is an attack on the rationalist distinction between the grammatical and the extragrammatical, the new version is, as already indicated, even more empiricistic. Fortunately, however, it has consequences so absurd as to pose no threat to rationalism. The new version says that a sentence S is grammatical relative to a set of beliefs, B, of a speaker in case B implies P, the presupposition of S. But this means that Lakoff's theory entails the absurd claim that every string is grammatical for anyone whose beliefs are at any point inconsistent. For suppose that someone has a set of beliefs containing one of the form B and another of the form $\sim B$.[19] Then, by a well known argument,[20] this set of beliefs implies any proposition whatever. Lakoff can, of course, try to avoid this conclusion by denying that anyone ever has inconsistent beliefs, but this would be a Pyrrhic victory since such a claim is only slightly less absurd than the claim that every string is grammatical.

Lakoff sometimes speaks as if he had in mind a weaker relation (between the presupposition of a sentence and the beliefs of a speaker) than that of logical implication, namely, independence—for example, "Since these presuppositions do not conflict with our knowledge of the world, [27] is a perfectly normal sentence" (1971b, p. 68). Thus it might be thought that he has a way out of the difficulty above: to require simply that the presupposition of a sentence be consistent with the speaker's knowledge (or beliefs). But the revision has equally absurd consequences. For example, for a radical skeptic who accepts no beliefs about anything every string in the language is grammatical, since every presupposition is consistent with a null set of beliefs. Thus, independently of their use of ancient Greek, we have to say that Pyrrho and Plato had entirely different competence in the language. Furthermore, every sentence about a subject that one knows nothing about (and modestly refrains from framing opinions on) is grammatical. Moreover, as we come to gain some knowledge about a subject and to have some beliefs about it, sentences about that subject start to become ungrammatical at a rate proportional to the increase in what we know and believe. Again, since most of us have different sets of beliefs, and

---

19. If a speaker's beliefs are treated as occurring essentially in contexts of the form 'X believes B' so that the inadmissibility of detaching B prevents the contradiction from being derived, then Lakoff's whole theory collapses, since now beliefs do not imply presuppositions.

20. $(B \,\&\, \sim B)$ imply B; B implies $(B \vee Q)$; $(B \,\&\, \sim B)$ also imply $\sim B$; but $(B \vee Q)$ and $\sim B$ together imply Q.

JERROLD J. KATZ
THOMAS G. BEVER

since languages are individuated (in part) by the set of sentences counted as grammatical, Lakoff's view entails the absurd consequence that almost all of us, except for the most "Tweedle-Dee, Tweedle-Dum" pairs, speak different languages.[21]

In our discussion of how empiricism might make a comeback, we said that a secondary target of an empiricist counterrevolution is the cluster of semantic notions 'synonymy', 'analyticity', and 'entailment', since such absolute notions lead directly to necessary truths. They permit us to determine the internal conceptual structure of linguistic constructions and distinguish their semantic properties from features of the things to which they refer. They enable us to use the purely internal conceptual structure to express connections that are independent of the features of the actual world and thus hold in any possible one. Accordingly, they lead to a rationalist account of the speaker's knowledge, insofar as they permit us to attribute knowledge of sentences expressing necessary truths to the speaker's competence. This, in turn, means that a theory of the acquisition of such a competence must contain more than the principles of inductive learning allowed by empiricism, since such principles provide only for probable connections. Hence, empiricism has to find some way of replacing these absolute semantic notions by graded ones that imply no sharp division between the inside and outside of a concept. Given concepts with vague boundaries that permit no precise division between internal conceptual structure and external features, the speaker's knowledge of the language can be characterized in a way that removes the obstacle of necessary truth that otherwise would block empiricist attempts to account for its acquisition on an inductive basis.

Now, turning to how generative semantics *is* clearing the way for a return of empiricism, we find Lakoff proposing just such an empiricist doctrine of concepts. He writes:

> natural language concepts have vague boundaries and fuzzy edges and . . . consequently, natural language sentences will very often be neither true, nor false, nor nonsensical, but rather true to a certain extent and false to a certain extent (1972, pp. 183).

In particular, he argues:

> Robins simply are more typical of birds than chickens and chickens are more typical of birds than penguins, though all are birds to some extent. Suppose now that instead of asking about category membership we ask instead about the truth of sentences that assert category membership. If an X is a member of a category Y only to a certain degree, then the sentence "An

21. Robin Lakoff (1973) seems willing to stick with the consequences of this theory to the bitter end. Similiar considerations lead her to claim that men and women (speakers of English) speak different languages (Valian, 1976).

X is a Y" should be true only to that degree, rather than being clearly true or false. My feeling is that this is correct, as (30) indicates.

(30) "Degree of truth (corresponding to degree of category membership)

    (a)   A robin is a bird. (true)
    (b)   A chicken is a bird. (less true than a)
    (c)   A penguin is a bird. (less true than b)
    (d)   A bat is a bird. (false, or at least very from from true)
    (e)   A cow is a bird. (absolutely false)" (1972, p. 185)

This doctrine of "fuzzy concepts" leads, of course, to a graded notion of entailment:

> . . . we will want to talk about such concepts as 'degree of validity' and 'degree of theoremhood', which are natural concomitants of the notion 'degree of necessary truth'. If one wants a natural example of entailment, consider [31] and [32]. We know that not all birds

(31) x is a bird
(32) x flies

> fly, but we might well want to say that once a bird has a certain degree of birdiness, say, 0.7, then it flies. We might then want to say that (31) entails (32) to degree 0.7 (1972, p. 186).

There is no point in belaboring the obvious. The absolute notion of analyticity on which examples like (30a–c) would be on a par as linguistic truths and on which examples like (30d) and (30e) would be on a par as linguistic falsehoods is replaced by a graded notion of degree of truth (or "degree of necessary truth," whatever this might mean). The absolute notion of entailment on which sentences of the form (33) entail ones of the form (34)

(33) x is a robin
(34) x is a bird

but sentences of the form (31) simply do not entail sentences of the form (32) is replaced by a graded notion of degree of entailment.

What needs to be clarified is how numerical values representing extent of inclusion are determined. Lakoff cites two ways of interpreting degree statements. On one, they reflect the results of testing subjects in experimental situations, (Rosch, 1973) where they are asked to rank birds as to their degree of birdiness, that is, how close the test item comes to their ideal of a bird. Here the statistical value obtained as the measure of degree of birdiness is taken by Lakoff to represent the degree of inclusion (the degree of truth, the degree of entailment, etc.). On the other way of interpreting degree statements, they are taken to represent a measure of the distribution of some physical property in nature rather than a statistical statement about judgments of people of a physical property. Lakoff says:

> It is common for logicians to give truth conditions for predicates in terms of classical set theory. "John is tall" (or "TALL(j)") is defined to be true just in case the individual denoted by "John" (or "j") is in the set of tall men. Putting aside the problem that tallness is really a relative concept (tallness for a pygmy and tallness for a basketball player are obviously different), suppose we fix a population relative to which we want to define tallness. In contemporary America, how tall do you have to be to be tall? 5′8″? 5′9″? 5′10″? 5′11″? 6′? 6′2″? Obviously, there is no single fixed answer. How old do you have to be to be middle-aged? 35? 37? 38? 39? 40? 42? 45? 50? Again, the concept is fuzzy. Clearly, any attempt to limit truth conditions for natural language sentences to true, false, and 'nonsense' will distort the natural language concepts by portraying them as having sharply defined rather than fuzzily defined boundaries (1972, p. 183).

The argument for the thesis that the meanings of words do not have sharply determined boundaries but grade off begs the question. In connection with the first way of interpreting inclusion, Lakoff argues as follows: "If category membership were simply a yes-or-no matter, one would have expected the subjects either to balk at the task (of ranking) or to produce random results" (1972, p. 183). But one has no right to have such expectations unless one can assume that the task Rosch's subjects were asked to perform, to rank different animals as to their degree of birdiness, is tapping their intuitions about the *meanings* of the words 'robin', 'chicken', 'penguin', 'bat', rather than, what is more plausible in this case, their stereotypes about such animals. The distinction can be put in terms of an example. The meaning of the expression 'airline hostess' is simply 'a woman who is employed by an airline in the capacity of a hostess'. Nothing in the meaning of the expression tells us (what is clearly true) that the American stereotype of an airline hostess includes such properties as attractiveness, a pleasant disposition, having a height of over three feet, and so on. If one may assume that Rosch's subjects are responding in terms of their stereotypes, then there is no reason to expect them to balk, since such stereotypes ought to vary in how close they come to the ideal of a bird. If there is no reason to expect the subjects to balk, then the fact that they do not is no argument against category membership in semantics being a "yes-or-no matter." Hence, Lakoff's argument has to assume that there is no distinction between the meanings of words and the stereotypes of theories people have about the things words refer to. On this assumption, and on this assumption alone, the responses obtained to the instruction "rank birds as to the degree of their birdiness" are evidence against meanings being sharp concepts, for these subjects were not instructed to rank the *meanings* of 'robin', 'chicken', and the others on a scale of degree of overlap with the category 'bird'. But this assumption is, of course, what has to be established to make an argument against category membership in semantics being a "yes-or-no matter" (Katz, 1972; Bever, 1973).

In connection with the second way of interpreting inclusion, Lakoff also begs the question by assuming there is no clear distinction between facts about the meaning of words and facts about the things words refer to in the world. Note in the first place that Lakoff's only argument is a "where do you draw the line?" argument, and such arguments are fallacious because they do not offer a reason to suppose that there is, in fact, no distinction. How do we know that the failure to find a fixed answer to questions like "In contemporary America, how tall do you have to be to be tall?" is due to the looseness of the boundaries of the concept that functions in the language as the meaning of 'tall,' or to some deficiency in our knowledge about the distribution of heights in contemporary America that makes it unclear how to apply the term 'tall' in certain "borderline" situations? Obviously, one can't decide that the latter difficulty is not responsible for this failure unless one assumes that the concept 'tall' reflects the knowledge and beliefs we have about how the heights of tall people merge, imperceptibly, into those of short people. But this assumption is exactly what needs to be established.

Thus, there is no argument against the rationalist view that the meaning of 'tall' and other such linguistic concepts have sharply defined boundaries. On this view, to say that something belonging to a certain class is tall is to say that it exceeds in height the average member of that class,[22] and the difficulty in applying 'tall' to someone derives from our imperfect knowledge concerning the average height for the class (or the amount of deviation permitted in determining the relation 'x exceeds y'). To see this, consider the following two questions (see also Katz, 1971, fn. 10). Which has the greatest height, a tall man (not a giant) or one short man (not a midget) standing on the shoulders of another? Which is bigger, one thick noodle or two thin ones stuck together? Almost everyone asked these questions replies easily to the first, saying that the two short men are higher, but almost everyone has difficulty in replying to the second question, most saying they don't know. The reason is clearly that in the case of the height of men we have a good idea of the average and of the distribution of heights, whereas in the case of the thickness of noodles we are much less well informed (and perhaps it is harder to be adequately informed here). Thus, it seems reasonable to conclude that the indecision experienced in the latter case is due not to any difference in the degree of vagueness of the words "tall" and "thick"

22. The class that serves as the standard varies with the comparison class. If the comparison class is dogs, then the standard is animals; if the comparison class is skyscrapers, then the standard is buildings. An alternative view is that the standard for any given case can be determined from the meaning of the word in question (cf. Katz, 1972, pp. 254–260).

JERROLD J. KATZ
THOMAS G. BEVER

(both are relative in the same manner) but to our failure to possess the critical facts about the world.[23]

Now, we wish to consider, first, how well Lakoff's doctrine of fuzzy concepts handles the meaning of sentences, and second, how good a theory of truth it offers. As we already noted, Lakoff provides two ways to interpret the meaning of a sentence in terms of fuzzy concepts. On both, however, the semantic characterization that sentences receive is fundamentally different from their meaning in the langugage. On the first scheme of interpretation, a sentence assigning some individuals to a class does so in terms of a coefficient expressing their degree of class membership, and the coefficient reflects an estimate of the judgments people make concerning how close these individuals come to the ideal represented by the class. Thus, on Lakoff's doctrine, sentence such as (30a–e) must be interpreted as asserting that people have a certain psychological propensity, that they tend to judge the animals in question as this close or that close to the ideal of birdiness. But these English sentences assert nothing of the sort. They simply assert that the animals in question *are* birds. The point can perhaps be brought home more forcefully if we consider what happens when two people disagree about such a sentence, say (30c). On Lakoff's doctrine, they are disagreeing about the outcome of typicality studies on how people judge penguins, when in fact they are disagreeing about whether penguins are birds. Moreover, if everyone wrongly believed that penguins are not birds, the party to such a dispute who claimed (falsely, from the point of view of the meaning of the sentence in English) that penguins are not birds would be right.

If Lakoff's interpretation were employed generally in science, confirmation would be replaced with public opinion polls and argument with propaganda.[24]

---

23. Indeed, there is nothing fuzzy or vague about the concept 'tall' as it appears in the meaning of sentences like "That pygmy is tall," "That basketball player is tall," and "Pygmies are as tall as basketball players," nor does this concept depend on the distribution of heights in the world. Suppose the world were to change so that pygmies grew to gigantic height and only midgets were allowed to play basketball. The meanings of these sentences would remain unchanged. The first would still denote some pygmy (using this term in its sense of a racial stock) and say of this designatum that it exceeds the average height of pygmies (whatever it is at the time). The second would still denote some basketball player and say of this designatum that it exceeds the average height of basketball players (whatever it is at the time). The third would neither change meaning nor be a contradiction (to some degree?) but would still be false (though with another change it could be true). This sentence expresses a proposition that clashes with our stereotype of pygmies and basketball players, nothing more.

24. There is also a problem about the selection of the subjects for such typicality experiments. If one selects them from the population at large, chances are that they can make no judgments at all. If one selects them from subpopulations that can be expected to have an opinion on these issues, then the value expressing the degree of truth that is empirically determined can be expected to vary, depending on whether the sample comes from the Cambridge or Berkeley area.

Using Lakoff's doctrine to interpret his own assertions of that doctrine (that natural language concepts are fuzzy), we obtain the paradoxical consequence that these assertions must be understood as claiming that most people tend to agree with him about these issues. Hence, since agreement between people bears no logical relation to what is the case, Lakoff's assertions become irrelevant to the issue of whether concepts are exact or fuzzy, since they are about how people will judge such questions when tested in typicality studies.

On the second scheme of interpretation, the coefficient expresses the actual degree to which the comparison class is close to the extreme of the property in terms of its empirical distribution. Thus, a sentence like (35)

(35)   Basketball players are tall.

would be understood as saying that basketball players are (on the average?) n units from the extreme of tallness in the empirical distribution of people's heights. But the English sentence (35) does not have a meaning that contains a fixed quantity expressing the percentile that basketball players are in in the distribution of heights. Thus, rather finding with Lakoff that restricting "truth conditions for natural language sentences to true, false, and nonsense will distort the natural language concepts,"[25] we have found that expanding truth conditions as Lakoff suggests distorts the meaning of sentences in natural language.

Finally, what is to be said about Lakoff's doctrine of degrees of truth, according to which assertions of truth assert a degree of truth? Either the degree of truth of such a metasentence is always the same as the coefficient associated with the class assignment in the object sentence, in which case it is wholly redundant and one might as well stick with an absolute notion of truth, or it is sometimes different, in which case the whole theory of truth becomes incoherent. Consider a sentence of the form (36) (the "S" is sentence (35)):

(36)   The sentence S is true to degree K.

Let us assume basketball players are tall to degree .9. Then, if K must be .9, we are saying no more than that basketball players are in the 90th percentile by saying that (35) is true. Thus, 'true' is not really a degree term. On the other hand, if K is different from .9, then we lose the Tarski equivalence, which is basic to any theory of truth, that asserting a sentence is equivalent to asserting that it is true.

In this section, we have considered Lakoff's attack on the absolute notion of grammaticality and on the absolute notion of meaning. These, we argued, would if successful remove the two major stumbling blocks to an empiricist effort to explain the acquisition of linguistic knowledge. Thus, we have claimed the generative-semantics interpretive-semantics controversy represents an at-

25. Note that the values true and false are not truth conditions but truth values, and that nonsense is not even a truth value. Nonsense says nothing, and so cannot even be a property of statement because nonsensical sentences express no proposition at all.

JERROLD J. KATZ
THOMAS G. BEVER

tempt at counterrevolution within linguistics and, is within philosophy, a further episode in the continuing struggle between rationalism and empiricism. We have concentrated on Lakoff because his work has spearheaded the generative semanticist's attack on grammaticality and meaning, but this should not lead the reader to think he is atypical of the leading generative semanticists in this. In connection with the absolute notion of grammaticality, Ross's recent work has the same thrust as Lakoff's in seeking to replace it with a graded notion of acceptability, but Ross goes even further than Lakoff by making the application of syntactic rules, membership of grammatical elements in classes like 'noun', 'verb', and so forth, all a matter of degree (1973). We note here that the heart of Ross's argument is his rejection of Chomsky's conception of explication in which the unclear cases are decided on the basis of the rules devised to deal with the clear ones. Ross rejects this conception because he wrongly thinks that it makes the empirical claim that hazy, incremental phenomena of the kind he analyzes do not exist. He fails to see that Chomsky' conception makes no such claim; it simply fails to treat these phenomena as purely syntactic (Bever, 1975).

In connection with absolute notions in semantics, McCawley's recent work seems to be heading toward an extreme contextualist theory of meaning, which cannot avoid conclusions about semantic properties and relations similar to Lakoff's. For example, McCawley writes:

> It will develop that I should be talking about sentence tokens rather than sentence types. A 'semantic structure' will thus specify not the 'meaning' of a sentence but the 'content' of a token of a sentence, e.g., *It's raining* will have different 'content' depending on when and where it is said (1972, fn. 7).

McCawley advocates a semantics in which the context of an utterance determines its semantic representation in the grammar, so that, for example, as two contexts are more alike (in the critical respects?) the sentence tokens occurring in them are more nearly synonymous. Such a notion of semantics precludes a formal theory of semantic structure (see Katz and Langendoen in this volume).

DISTINGUISHING BETWEEN GRAMMATICAL AND NONGRAMMATICAL REGULARITIES

At the beginning of the previous section, we argued that Lakoff's views on grammaticality and conceptual structure are based on an empiricist conception of the explanatory goals of a grammar. On this conception anything that influences the distribution, or cooccurrence patterns, of morphemes is *ipso facto* to be explained in the grammar. We also argued that Chomsky's position contains an alternative, rationalist conception, but because it had been so poorly developed this rationalist conception presented no real obstacle to Lakoff's reinstituting the traditional taxonomic conception and then applying it to erode the competence-performance distinction, thereby freeing grammars of properties disturbing to empiricist theories of acquisition. We tried to indicate that the development of a rationalist conception was retarded by the primitive state of the theory of the interpretation of the formal transformational model, because to extend this conception beyond Chomsky's first formulation of it, on which the goals of grammar are seen as accounting for speakers' intuitions about sentence structure, it is necessary to spell out what it meant by 'sentence structure' on the basis of a list of grammatical properties and relations and definitions of them—that is, on the basis of a theory of interpretation. In the present section, we try to explain in more detail what this conception looks like on a rich notion of interpretation and how it applies to distinguishing grammatical phenomena from extragrammatical ones.

On a rationalist conception, the pretheoretic intuition behind the study of grammar is that the central problem is to explain how features of the systematic relation between sound and meaning in a language account for the phonological, syntactic, and semantic properties of each of its sentences. The construction of grammars thus begins with pretheoretic intuitions about three classes of grammatical properties and relations; phonological, syntactic, and semantic. The first includes rhyme, alliteration, meter and so on; the second word order, agreement relations, ellipsis, part of speech equivalences, and so on; the third synonymy, ambiguity, meaninglessness, analyticity, and so on. Moreover, we also have pretheoretic intuitions that the phenomena judged to be phonological are related to each other by virtue of their having to do with speech sounds, that the phenomena judged to be syntactic are related to each other by virtue of their having to do with how sentences are built up out of their constituents, and that the phenomena judged to be semantic are related to each other by virtue of their having to do with the meaning of sentences and its compositional relations to the meanings of the sentences's constituents. Thus, in each of these cases, the properties and relations are grouped together (as phonological, syntactic, or semantic) on the basis of intuitions that they are about the same aspect of grammatical structure. Finally, speakers have pretheoretic intuitions that these three kinds of properties and relations are interrelated with each other in a grammar because they are each intuitively recognized as part of the sound/meaning correlation in the language.

In a rationalist approach to grammar that gives the theory of interpretation its proper place, this theory seeks to explicate these sets of intuitions in tandem with the construction of particular grammars. Such a theory defines these properties and relations in terms of universal features of the structural descriptions of sentences in grammars. It also seeks to explicate intuitions about the interconnectedness of phonological properties in terms of a theory of the phonological component, to explicate intuitions about the interconnectedness of syntactic properties in terms of a theory of the syntactic component, and to explicate intuitions about the interconnectedness of semantic properties in terms of a theory of the semantic component. The theory of grammar seeks finally to explicate intuitions of relatedness among properties of different kinds in terms of the systematic connections expressed in the model of a grammar that weld its components into a single integrated theory of the sound/meaning correlation in a language.

These remarks of course describe the theoretical ideal. But as the theory of grammar makes progress toward this ideal, it not only sets limits on the construction of grammars and provides a richer interpretation for grammatical structures, it also defines a wider and wider class of grammatical properties and relations. In so doing, it marks out the realm of the grammatical more clearly, distinctly, and securely than could have been done on the basis of the initial intuitions. As Foder has insightfully observed, such a theory literally defines its own subject matter in the course of its progress:

> There is then an important sense in which a science has to discover what it is about: it does so by discovering that the laws and concepts it produced in order to explain one set of phenomena can be fruitfully applied to phenomena of other sorts as well. It is thus only in retrospect that we can say of all the phenomena embraced by a single theoretical framework that *they* are what we meant, for example, by the presystematic term "physical event", "chemical interaction", or "behavior". To the extent that such terms, or their employments, are neologistic, the neologism is occasioned by the insights that successful theories provide into the deep similarities that underlie superficially heterogeneous events (1968, p. 10).

Therefore, on this rationalist view, our conception of the goals of the study of grammar is always a projection from the present state of linguistic theory to how it will define its subject matter in its optimal state. Nonetheless, this conception provides us with a sound criterion for properties and relations that are genuinely grammatical, for deciding whether a new phenomenon should be considered part of the subject of grammar or whether an old one, mistakenly assumed to be grammatical, should be excluded from grammar. This conception supplies the positive side of such a criterion to supplement Chomsky's proposal that the nongrammatical phenomenon is one whose explanation requires principles concerning memory, computation time, etc. This proposal clearly needs supplementation, since without a positive notion of the grammatical the "etc." can be specified only in the somewhat circular fashion of saying "and other extragrammatical matters." Thus we obtain a fully general criterion now that we can say that what makes a phenomenon grammatical is the fact that the principles that explain it are all required to explicate the properties and relations that have been systematically interrelated by the laws and concepts originally devised to account for speaker's intuitions about clear cases of grammatical properties and relations.

The empirical importance of such a criterion lies in the fact that linguistic behavior is an extremely complex integration of grammatical rules and other cognitive systems, so that grammatical rules often play an important role in phenomena which are not themselves grammatical, that is, matters of competence. Thus, if we fail to distinguish the role of grammatical rules in such hybrid phenomena from that of other cognitive mechanisms, we will mistakenly try to impose a homogeneous form of explanation on the phenomena. If we attempt to account for such hybrid phenomena within the grammar itself, we will obstruct the development of a simple and revealing theory of the grammatical structure of the language, since the demand to integrate principles unrelated to the explication of grammatical properties and relations will prevent the rules of the grammar from properly rendering genuine grammatical generalizations about the sound/meaning correlation in the language.

The classic example of the benefits that come from clearly separating the contributions of linguistic phenomena to different cognitive systems is Miller and Chomsky's treatment of the unintelligibility of multiply center-embedded sentences (1963). They make two points about such sentences that provide a basis for classifying them as grammatical but unacceptable. First, they show that to rule out such cases in the grammar requires that it contains a 're-cursion counter', that is, a device that is selectively sensitive only to those recursions that are center-embedded in their surface manifestation. But such a counter would involve formal mechanisms otherwise unknown in the grammar and for which no other use could be found. Second, Miller and Chomsky posit a treatment of the phenomena of unintelligible center-embedded sentences outside the grammar. They sketch a plausible perceptual theory that predicts the difficulty of understanding center-embedded sentences in terms of performance assumptions about computation and the limit on information stored in immediate memory. The phenomenon of loss of intelligibility in multiply center-embedded sentences is categorized as a extragrammatical, as a matter of acceptability rather than grammaticality (see Bever, 1974).

We shall now discuss three other kinds of systematic linguistic phenomena that are properly handled outside the grammar, on the basis of the interaction of grammatical principles with principles from some nongrammatical cognitive theory. In the first case, we try to show that the phenomenon can best be explained on the basis of perceptual theory; in the second, we try to show that it can best be explained on the basis of Grice's theory of conversational implicature;[26] and in the third, we try to show that it can be explained by the various

26. Grice has published a short version of his theory (1975).

JERROLD J. KATZ
THOMAS G. BEVER

disciplines in psychology that describe the conceptions of things that people have, their stereotypes, everyday theories, and so on, over and above the linguistic concepts that serve as the meanings of the words that name them. In each case, we pick our examples from those that generative semanticists have used to argue for some extension of the theory of grammar. We shall show that each of these cases is better handled on the model of the Miller-Chomsky treatment of the loss of intelligibility in multiply center-embedded sentences, and that the failure to treat them outside grammar has led generative semanticists to postulate devices that impute spurious power to the grammar.

Cases in which perceptual theory can account for phenomena that would otherwise require considerable expansion of the power of the grammar have been explored in the literature of generative semantics. They have been hailed as leading to the discovery of new grammatical principles, particularly, global derivational constraints,[27] and as providing strong evidence for one or another generative semantics model of the organization of a grammar.

The segmentation and labeling processes in speech perception group together one class of linguistic examples under the rubric of *perceptually suppressed sense*. Consider, for example, the sentence in (37), which is unacceptable on the reading in which "fiancé" is the subject:

(37) The friend of my brother's fiancée left town.

Yet, it is parallel in structure to the acceptable sentences in (38) and (39):

(38) The fiancée of my brother's friend was discovered to be a cat burglar so *the friend of my brother's fiancée* left town.
(39) It was the fiancée of my brother's idea to give him a surprise party.

Clearly, what is at issue is the salience of the sub-sequence ". . . brother's fiancée . . . ." Insofar as the general structure surrounding the sequence allows it to be interpreted as a *possessive noun + noun* sequence the sentence is blocked from having "fiancée" as its subject. *Any* aspect of the sentence that perceptually separates "brother's" from "fiancée" or emphasizes "fiancée" as the head noun has the effect of making the interpretation with "fiancée" as subject acceptable.

Suppose now we required of the grammar that it account for these facts. There is no straightforward restriction on the operation of grammatical rules themselves that can selectively restrict the interpretation of cases like (39). What is at issue is a restriction on the *surface string*, rather than a restriction on the rules that produce such strings (Chomsky, 1965; Bever, 1968; Perlmutter,

27. This is rather ironic since, in fact, Chomsky was the first to think of such mechanisms. In *Aspects of the Theory of Syntax*, he writes: "it is clear that we can characterize unacceptable sentences only in terms of some 'global' property of derivations and the structures they define—a property that is attributable, not to a particular rule, but rather to the way in which the rules interrelate," p. 12.

1971; Fodor, Bever, and Garrett, 1974). Perlmutter proposed that such cases be handled by an "output constraint," a rule that examines final trees in a derivation to make sure that they do not have specific properties. In this case, an output constraint would block any string having a complex noun phrase with a final possessive noun immediately preceding its head noun. Such well-formedness constraints, of course, would represent an increase in the power of the grammar, since they are constraints stated across tree configurations rather than constraints on the structural indices of transformational rules. Furthermore, it is not clear that such constraints would be sufficient to handle the continuum of acceptability facts exhibited by such cases. For example, *all* the cases in (37)–(39) would be marked as ungrammatical by such a restriction, yet (39) is acceptable.

To treat the phenomena correctly one could appeal to the perceptual attractiveness of the *N's N* sequence as an account of the relative acceptability of sequences that have this property to differing degrees. However, once such a device is formulated to handle the cases of varying acceptability, it obviates the necessity for introducing the same device within the grammar to account for certain perceptually extreme cases. That is, on the interpretation that all the cases in (37)–(39) are grammatically ambiguous, the acceptability facts can be accounted for and the grammar kept free of new theoretical devices. The perceptual strategy suppresses one of the interpretations, so it appears only when other conditions in the sentence, such as semantic constraints or structural parallelism, facilitate its interpretation with that structure.[28]

There are several other cases in the current literature of such perceptually suppressed interpretations. Consider, for example, the cases in (40)–(45):

(40) The man$_i$ likes the girl$_j$ who$_i$ lives in Chi.
(41) The idea$_i$ surprised the man which$_i$ Harry proposed.
(42) The man$_i$ left who$_i$ lives in Chi.
(43) The man$_i$ likes your idea who$_i$ lives in Chi.
(44) The man$_i$ left who$_i$ the girl likes.
(45) The man left the girl likes.

Clearly, they show that relative clauses can be extraposed so long as there is *some* property of the string that uniquely marks the extraposed relative as not

28. The existence of this behavioral strategy underlies cases of ungrammatical sentences that are nonetheless acceptable. For example, in English quantified possessive pronouns, as in (i)–(iii):

(i) The picture of the three of you;
(ii) The three of yours picture;
(iii) The three of yours'es picture

cannot be preposed. Even though (iii) is clearly recognized as ungrammatical, it is also more acceptable than (ii), presumably because the "-es" serves further to separate the possessive from its head noun and to make perspicuous the possessive morpheme. We owe this example to V. V. Valian (in conversation). See also Bever, Carroll, and Hurtig, and Bever, both in this volume, for a discussion of the perceptual theory.

JERROLD J. KATZ
THOMAS G. BEVER

modifying an immediately preceding noun phrase. Such cases could again be partially handled with "output constraints" that would block derivations without such unique marks. But this too would fail to account for the intermediate nature of many cases. Again, the perceptual principle of local-phrase salience could account for the tendency to misinterpret cases in which relatives are potentially attached to adjacent nouns, even though that is not their correct structure. Hence, if (40)–(45) are classified as grammatical, but (40) is classified as unacceptable by virtue of perceptual complexity, the grammar does not require added power.

A final case of this type is discussed by Postal and Ross (1970).

(46) Yesterday John said he will distill the liquor.
(47) Yesterday John said he distilled the liquor.
(48) Yesterday John will say he distilled the liquor.
(49) It was yesterday that John will say he distilled the liquor.

They point out that there appears to be a left-right constraint on the surface appearance of time adverbs such that an adverb cannot be displaced to the left across an intervening verb. Since adverbs are not morphologically indexed to English as to the verb they modify, such a constraint must refer both to the underlying tree in which the adverb is adjacent to its verb as well as to any of the surface structure trees that would destroy this property. That is, such a case would appear to motivate the use of a derivational constraint that states that certain relations between deep and surface trees cannot exist. Thus, a case like (48) can only be one in which the adverb-verb tense exhibits a mismatch and hence is semantically deviant.

Suppose we argued that there is a special case of the "phrase-gobbling" perceptual rule—an adverb within a *perceptual* clause modifies the first verb to appear after it. Then (46)–(48) could be generated freely in the grammar but would be perceptually interpreted only with difficulty as having the adverb modify the second verb. This formulation correctly predicts the acceptability of (49), in which the initial adverb is set off into its own surface clause, thus removing the applicability of the adverb-verb attachment principle, and leaving the adverb free to modify the second verb. Finally, we are now in a position to explain the acceptability of (50) as due to the perceptual closure around the first adverb; even though it is not in a *structurally* defined clause of its own, it is in a *perceptually* distinct clause (see Bever, 1975, for discussion of 'perceptual clause').

(50) Yesterday (pause) John will say he distilled the liquor.

These three cases share a number of characteristics. First, in each case a range of acceptability levels across closely related structures represents a challenge to grammatical theory that can be met within the grammar only by increasing its general descriptive power. At the same time, the basic principles of phrase and sentence segmentation postulated as part of the mechanism of speech perception account for the relative acceptability of the sentences. This interpretation allows the assumption that they are all grammatical but differentially acceptable as a function of the ease with which the structures are understood.

It is no doubt the case that the examples we have chosen are particularly revealing of the effects of the perceptual mechanism, since they all involve a structure that must be perceived despite the apparent presence of a perceptually more salient structure. We have emphasized these cases because the segmentation mechanisms that explain them have recently received experimental attention. Several behaviorally based proposals have also recently appeared to account for various aspects of pronominal reference and quantifier scope. These phenomena are important because they have been invoked by generative semanticists as motivating the need for more powerful grammatical mechanisms. If these proposals can be shown to be based on independently motivated perceptual principles, then the methodology we have outlined will succeed in showing that the grammar can be kept free of devices like derivational constraints, for the phenomena that would motivate such constraints are in fact due to the operation of the perceptual mechanism (Bever, 1970).

Now consider an example of the failure of generative semantics to make the distinction between grammatical phenomena and conversational phenomena. Gordon and Lakoff propose to make knowledge of conversational conventions an integral part of formal grammar. They write:

> Our purpose in this paper is twofold: first, to outline a way in which conversational principles can begin to be formalized and incorporated into the theory of generative semantics; and second, to show that there are rules of grammar, rules governing the distribution of morphemes in a sentence, that depend upon such principles. Our strategy for beginning to incorporate such observations in terms of them is based on the notions of natural logic and of transderivational rules (1971, p. 63).

Gordon and Lakoff propose that the grammar contain a set of "conversational postulates" formulated on the model of meaning postulates (conditional statements expressing a logical implication). Presumably, the conversational postulates define a class of implicatures relative to a characterization of a set of contexts. Thus, in Gordon and Lakoff's example, the sentence (51) uttered by the duke of Bordello to his butler in a cold room with an open window implies a command by the duke for the butler to shut the window.

(51) It is cold in here.

The idea is basically that the antecedent of a conversational postulate describes a class of contexts and the consequent expresses a conversational implication in

JERROLD J. KATZ
THOMAS G. BEVER

that class of contexts. The attempt to force conversational knowledge into grammar makes it necessary to include rules that are not required for any other purpose. To explain why a sentence like (52)

(52) Can you take out the garbage?

can conversationally imply a request to take the garbage out rather than a question about ability, Gordon and Lakoff introduce the following rule:[29]

[53] $\text{ASK}(a,b,\text{CAN}(b,Q)^* \rightarrow \text{REQUEST}(a,b,Q)$

Thus, the explanation of why the hearer interprets (52) to imply conversationally a request to take out the garbage is as follows: the speaker knows, as part of his/her grammatical competence, the rule [53] and also the appropriate context for its application.

Part of the trouble with conversational postulates stems from difficulties inherent in the rules they are modeled on, namely, Carnapian meaning postulates. These are brute-force statements of implicational relations arising from the meanings of words in the so-called extralogical vacabulary of a language. They provide no basis to account for other semantic properties and relations that are determined by the same aspects of meaning: such failures to capture semantic generalizations can be overcome only by revisions in systems of meaning postulates that convert them into a semantic component in the sense of a dictionary and projection rule (Katz and Nagel, 1974).

But the biggest trouble with conversational postulates is that, unlike meaning postulates, which at least represent semantic facts, which a grammar has to account for, they represent pragmatic facts that can be handled by an independently motivated system outside grammar. The theory of conversational implicature due to Grice offers an explanation of such phenomena. The relevant part of Grice's theory is this. Speakers attempt to cooperate as best as they can to achieve the aim of a conversation (e.g., to transmit information, convince someone) and listeners believe that the speaker is attempting to cooperate and that the speaker knows the listeners know this. There are certain principles, "conversational maxims," that spell out in detail what such cooperation means. On the basis of these suppositions Grice explains cases where someone's utterance conveys a certain proposition to the listeners even though it is not the case that the sentence uttered means that proposition in the language nor is it the

29. The asterisk marks such cases as special for the following reasons: "Strictly speaking, [53] [without asterisks] is inadequate in an important way. Sentences like "Can you take out the garbage?" are ambiguous in context: it can either be a real question, a request for information about your ability to take out the garbage, or it can convey a request to do so. However, it can only convey a request if it is assumed by the hearer that the speaker does not intend to convey the question. In this case, the conversationally implied meaning (the request) can be conveyed only if the literal meaning (the question) is not intended to be conveyed and if the hearer assumes that it isn't. We will indicate this notationally by putting an asterisk after the illocutionary content" (Gordon and Lakoff, 1971, p. 65).

case that the speaker literally said that proposition on that occasion. Consider how a Gricean theory would handle the fact that (52) can be used to make requests without assuming a rule in the grammar such as (53). Such an explanation would assume, contrary to Gordon and Lakoff, that the lexical reading of 'can' expresses a sense of ability or capacity to do something. The meaning that the grammar assigns to a sentence like (52) is that of a question asking for information as to whether the addressee has the ability or capacity to perform the task. The problem is to explain how an utterance of (52) can express a request for help when the semantic representation of the sentence that the utterance is a token of expresses only this question. Another way to put the fact to be explained is to ask why it is odd in an ordinary context to reply to the speaker of (52) by simply acknowledging that one is able to perform the task—that is, why it is odd to treat the utterance as a simple request for information.

The Gricean explanation is as follows. We may assume that the speaker who has uttered a token of (52) is observing the cooperative principle and that the listeners assume so too. Yet the speaker clearly seems to be violating the Gricean maxim to make one's contributions to a conversation relevant. This is because on the assumption that 'can' has only an ability sense, the utterance of (52) to an able-bodied person appears irrelevant because such a person seems capable of doing a simple task like taking the garbage out; and it must be obvious to the speaker that the addressee is able to do it. Thus, if the addressee and the other listeners are to maintain their assumption that the speaker is not violating the cooperative principle, they must suppose that the utterance is not being used with the meaning 'Tell me whether you are able to take out the garbage'. But since the addressee can reasonably assume that the speaker wants to have the garbage removed from the house, he or she can maintain the assumption that the speaker is not opting out by treating the utterance as a polite way of making a request to remove the garbage. It is polite because it indicates to the addressee that the speaker is offering him or her a basis of declining, namely, incapacity. (For further discussion of Grice's theory, see Harnish, "Logical Form and Implicature," in this volume.)

Note that we can place this case between two more extreme ones, (54) and (55):

(54) Can you tie your shoelace with one hand?
(55) Can you lift the log that is crushing my leg?

In connection with (54) in most contexts, there is no reason for the addressee to assume that the speaker has any desire to see the shoelace tied in so peculiar a manner, and accordingly (54) is not normally taken to carry the implicature of a request to do something. On the other hand, (55) is an extreme case in the other direction. Here, the addressee must conclude that the speaker's utterance is certainly no mere request for information because the addressee knows that the speaker, suffering as he is, is in no position to indulge in irrelevancies. The

JERROLD J. KATZ
THOMAS G. BEVER

speaker obviously desires to stop the pain by having someone lift the log from his leg and equally obviously the addressee knows this. Thus, in the general case, this implicature exists when there is reason in the situation for the addressee to think that the speaker wants the action in question done and doesn't want information about the addressee's ability to do it. This form of requesting has preference in situations where it is clearly desirable for the speaker to choose a form that is polite because a negative response need not reflect badly on the addressee. The existence of reasons to believe the speaker has such desires and his expression of them in this polite form permit the assumption of a request-implicature as the simplest way of preserving the supposition that the speaker is still abiding by the cooperative principle and its maxims.

These considerations show that the phenomenon can be handled in a natural way without introducing new rules into the grammar such as (53). To show this we have made use of the theory of conversational implicatures, which has general motivation as an independent component governing language use. In addition, it is clear that within such a theory there are independent grounds for a general system interpreting requests for information as requests for action that ranges well beyond sentences using 'can'. Consider the questions in (56)–(58), all of which have a request for information as their literal interpretation but are often answered by actions:

(56) Do you want to pass the salt?
(57) Do you know your *abc*'s?
(58) Will you shut up?

Indeed, a literal reply to these questions would often be a (bad) joke. Such instances are paralleled by cases in which a literal request for information *about* the listener's knowledge is correctly responded to by providing the knowledge itself. Thus (59) is generally interpreted as a request to be told the time, not an inquiry about the chronological competence of the listener:

(59) Do you know what time it is?

Similarly, the sentences in (60)–(62) can be responded to directly with the information asked about, rather than with statements to the effect that the listener indeed has the information in question:

(60) Did Harry say when he'd get here? (Tomorrow.) (*Yes.)
(61) Do you know where the book is? (On the table.) (*Yes.)
(62) Do you see any reason why I shouldn't stay? (It's late.) (*Yes.)

In each case, these questions have exactly the same implicature properties that we used to explain the conversational interpretation of (52). The form of question is polite in that the listener can decline the request by pleading incapacity or lack of knowledge rather than by direct refusal. Also, in each case the interpretation has the nonliteral meaning only if the listener has reason to believe that the speaker is not asking a question specifically about his or her capacity, but in fact wants to have the information asked about, if possible.

To treat the variety of implicature facts sketched above within the grammar would require a separate *ad hoc* rule for each of the different construction types that can have such an implicature. Clearly, rule (53) applies only to cases that include 'can' in their derivation, so that a separate rule is required for each of the other cases. Gordon and Lakoff recognize this by giving separate rules for cases involving *will, want*, and *can*. Thus, to treat these phenomena within the grammar misses the significant generalization covering them and at the same time forces an incorporation of factual assumptions about a speaker's desires into the grammar. In short, it not only would represent a vast increase in the domain of grammar, it also would misrepresent the facts.

The last of the three phenomena that we proposed to examine in the perspective of the rationalist criterion for the grammatical concerns the distinction between grammatical meaning and cultural stereotype. The phenomenon in question is that people make judgments about birds, dogs, and many other things in a way that indicates they have a conception of an ideal bird or dog and can rate members of these classes by how close they come to this ideal. The phenomenon has been studied by many psychologists, anthropologists, and sociologists, and recently interesting experimental work has been done by Rosch. As we have seen above, the latter work was construed by Lakoff as showing that the standard notion of lexicographical meaning is too narrow and should be replaced by a broader notion of meaning that reflects the features on which such ratings depend. We saw also that this proposal replaced absolute concepts with graded ones, and furthermore, required the introduction of an entirely new set of "grammatical principles," the machinery of 'fuzzy logic'. Thus, again, we find ourselves in a situation that fits perfectly the Miller-Chomsky paradigm. Lakoff's proposal complicates the grammar with *ad hoc* machinery and turns it into a compendium of information from such subjects as theories about stereotypes, without, as we have seen above, extending the semantic component's ability to explain a wider range of properties and relations.

Unlike the previous two kinds of cases, a full theoretical framework that would systematize such facts does not as yet exist. In the literature of anthropology, sociology, and social psychology, however, one finds the beginnings of a theory of how stereotypes arise and play a role in our conception of the reference of lexical items. At this point, such studies have concentrated on isolating the factors that influence the stereotype. For example, Sargeant (1939) has found that the political and economic policies of a newspaper are a direct influence on the character of the stereotype developed by its readers. The studies by Katz and Braly (1935) show that the stereotype of "foreign" is not a function of either actual contact with foreigners or direct knowledge of them. Lévi-Strauss (1964) points out that the stereotypical representation of notions like "well-cooked meat" are predictable functions of general properties of the

JERROLD J. KATZ
THOMAS G. BEVER

culture in question. Bettelheim and Janowitz (1949) argue that in cases of racial and religious prejudice the stereotype attached to racial labels functions as a justification of the aggression produced by feelings of anxiety, frustration, and deprivation.

A stereotype is thus a function of a complex set of factors and as yet there is no clear theory about how these factors combine to form the stereotype attached to a lexical item. But there is no doubt that social science is capable of finding the appropriate organizing principle to express the manner in which such factors combine. Thus, the grammar is not required to account for the acceptability differences in (30a–e) and is thereby free of the need to have new kinds of explanatory structures. Rather, we are suggesting that an independently motivated theory of cultural knowledge will account for such acceptability differences.

We are following in this case exactly the procedure used by Miller and Chomsky to remove the unacceptability of center-embedded sentences from the domain of grammar. While they had neither a full theory of speech perception nor a general theory of the relation between perception and language structure, they were able to make a plausible case that such theories would naturally predict the perceptual unacceptability of center-embedded sentences. Similarly, we are arguing that there is good reason to believe that a theory of stereotypes can be developed within social science that can explain such acceptability differences as in (30a–e).

THE EMPIRICIST AND THE RATIONALIST CRITERION FOR WHAT IS AND WHAT IS NOT GRAMMATICAL

The three cases just considered show how generative semantics has distorted grammar by including within its goals those of a complete theory of acceptability. This assimilation of the phenomena of performance into the domain of grammaticality has come about as a consequence of an empiricist criterion for determining what counts as grammatical. In almost every paper Lakoff makes explicit his assumption that the explanatory goal of a grammar is to state all the factors that influence the distribution of the morphemes in speech. On this view, any phenomenon systematically related to cooccurrence is *ipso facto* something to be explained in the grammar. Since in actual speech almost anything can influence cooccurrence relations, it is no wonder that Lakoff repeatedly discovers more and more new kinds of "grammatical phenomena." In fact, the generative semanticist program for linguistic theory represents, if anything, a more extreme approach than even Bloomfieldian structuralism, which recognized that a variety of phenomena concerning language are extragrammatical.

The point is simply that the generative semanticist's criterion of what calls for grammatical explanation is so broad that every performance factor counts as a legitimate part of grammar. Performance factors such as the psychobiological features of an organism that restrict the length of an utterance to those with fewer than a hundred billion words impose a restriction on the cooccurrence of very long strings of words and so must count as grammatical by the generative semanticist's criterion. Likewise, the attitudinal features of organisms that restrict the cooccurrence of obscenities in sentences with expressions character- istic of New England matrons also count. Everything from memory limitations, life span, and changes in technology to changes in morals has a systematic effect on the distribution of morphemes in that each of them is the basis of an unacceptability intuition.[30]

To tighten this criterion it would be necessary to specify antecedently the kind of oddity that does not count as grammatical. Yet to do this would reim- pose the distinction between a "grammatical source of acceptability orderings" and a nongrammatical source. Suppose an antecedent specification of the kind of oddity that counts as nongrammatical were to rule out those intuitions having to do with the expectations engendered by the rarity of the situation in which certain sentences can be used with their standard meaning. This would auto- matically exclude a string like (63) from the category of ungrammaticality:

(63) I just ate my toes and nose with hollandaise sauce.

But then this would assume a distinction between grammatical and nongram- matical determination of the distribution of morphemes. One such case would constitute the first domino. Once it fell, so would each other domino: conver- sational bizarreness; next cultural deviance, then, perceptual complexity, and so on. That is, the first distinction between the grammatical and the non- grammatical represents a departure from the pure criterion that whatever system- atically influences the distribution of a morpheme is grammatical. This departure would raise the question of why other cases that have just as much claim to extragrammatical status are not treated similarly.

A rationalist criterion of the grammatical rejects the conception of gram- maticality based on principles of distributional linguistics, as practiced by empiricist, taxonomic grammarians from Bloomfield and Harris to generative semanticists. Instead, it is based on the notion of explication, which as we have seen was a cornerstone of the Chomskyan revolution in linguistics. This criterion must take the form of the principle that what is grammatical is whatever has to be hypothesized as such in order to explicate the properties and relations of

30. For example, it would have been odd to ascribe "atomic power" to a detergent in 1900 but it is common today. Any factor of human experience, even the secular success of a scientific theory, can affect, 'linguistic distribution of words and morphemes'; hence any factor can assume 'grammatical' status.

JERROLD J. KATZ
THOMAS G. BEVER

sentences that are antecedently construed as grammatical. This criterion assumes that, pretheoretically, as the result of both our intuitions and the work of descriptive grammarians of the past, we can identify certain properties and relations as grammatical—for example, meter, rhyme, ellipsis, ambiguity, synonymy, word order, agreement—and that we can construct principles of grammar to explain them. These principles assume a simple and revealing form only by excluding a wide range of phenomena from the category of grammatical (that is, from explanation on the basis of these principles).

The pretheoretic intuition behind linguistic research holds that the central problem for grammars is to describe the way speech sounds are organized so that representations of meanings can be associated with them systematically to predict the phonological, syntactic, and semantic properties of each sentence. The construction of grammars for natural languages proceeds in tandem with the formulation of a linguistic theory. Linguistic theory seeks to formulate universal definitions of syntactic, semantic, and phonological properties in terms of features of the structural descriptions of sentences generated in grammars. For example, linguistic theory defines 'x is well-formed' in terms of the existence of a derivation of x in the grammar. It defines 'x is fully synonymous with y' in terms of x and y receiving the same semantic representation in every structural description. It defines 'x rhymes with y' in terms of an overlap of features in terminal segments of x and y in their phonological representations. Given general definitions of some grammatical properties and relations in linguistic theory, linguists construct rules that generate descriptions of sentences whose formal structure instantiates the defining features of these phonological, syntactic, and semantic definitions.

The rationalist conception of the aims of grammars is based on how definitions of grammatical properties function in an interpretation of the formal transformational model. On this conception, the development of linguistic theory sets limits on the construction of grammars and provides an interpretation of grammatical structures. Progress toward a fuller understanding of grammatical structure may then come in the development of further definition of grammatical properties in linguistic theory.

The issue between the rationalist and the empiricist conception of the domain of grammar is an empirical one. Our estimate of the evidence at present is that it heavily confirms the rationalist strict separation of grammatical phenomena in the traditional sense from extragrammatical phenomena. We choose the three cases discussed above because they have been the basis for the generative semanticists' attack on the rationalist distinction between grammaticality and acceptability. In each case, we have shown that the rationalist program can not only deal with the phenomena brought up but does so in a more satisfactory way. Moreover, as we have already indicated, the generative semanticists' criterion leads to a theory that rapidly becomes a study and compilation of everything. But a compilation of everything is a science of nothing: the advantage of the rationalist program, then, is that by distinguishing different contributions to linguistic behavior, explanation in terms of appropriate principles becomes possible in each case. Such an explanation would not be possible within a homogeneously grammatical account of everything, even if there were normally different rules for each kind of extragrammatical fact (one kind for conversational facts, one for perceptual facts, and so on).

Such a system might simply be a notational variant of the rationalist proposal, in which case the grammaticality/extragrammaticality distinction would be substantively maintained but expressed in different terminology. But if such a system were not simply a notational variant, it would make false claims about the extragrammatical phenomena that it deals with in terms of "grammatical" rules. For example, in the case of multiple center embeddings these rules would incorrectly categorize as syntactic the psychological apparatus that limits the load on immediate memory; in the case of conversational implicature they would incorrectly categorize as grammatical principles consequences of Grice's maxims; in the case of concept determination they would incorrectly categorize as semantic structures the stereotypes that people have about the things words refer to.

We have described how an empiricist interpretation is being imposed on the formal model of grammar. It is happening in three stages. The first stage was the transformational grammarians' neglect of a theory of the interpretation of the formal structure of grammar. This set up the conditions for a return to empiricism by making 'grammaticality' the critical formal property in a grammar with an empirical interpretation. This made it appear that the rationalist interpretation of grammar rested entirely on the grammatical/nongrammatical distinction.

The second stage in the return to empiricism is the direct attack on this distinction. This attack attempts to relativize grammaticality to presuppositions, which in turn are relative to the speaker's system of contingent beliefs. In this way, the grammatical/nongrammatical distinction is replaced by a graded notion of grammaticality, in which the beliefs of speakers determine the position of each sentence on the gradient.

The latest stage is the expansion of the domain of grammar to include all sentence acceptability phenomena. Thus, the connection of grammatical phenomena to contingent belief systems opened the way for the connection of grammar to any systematic psychological, pragmatic, and cultural factors that determine features of acceptability.

This attack on the grammaticality distinction was complemented by an attack on other categorical distinctions within a grammar. Thus, all the distinctions offered to linguistic description by the rationalist interpretation of grammar are being replaced by continua.

These three stages constitute a return to empiricism in the following sense. The internalized grammatical rules of a speaker are not differentiated from contingent beliefs. A theory that would explain the acquisition of such rules does not have to account for linguistic or logical connections. It can depend on the same principles of learning appropriate to the acquisition of contingent beliefs about the world. Since empiricists believe they can handle the acquisition of the latter, they must welcome the advent of generative semantics.

It might be thought that the fact that generative semantics eases the burden for empiricists is irrelevant, since their burdens are intractable in any case. However, the existence of categorical distinctions and necessary truths has always been the ultimate argument against empiricism. A proof that they do not exist would necessitate rethinking many aspects of such traditional arguments. Correspondingly, empiricists have always tried to establish their position by arguing against such concepts (Quine, 1953). Clearly, these concepts are the critical empirical issue in the controversy between rationalists and empiricists. Fortunately, generative semanticists have not proven that such distinctions do not exist, though we have shown that their viewpoint is moving toward this claim. *Caveat lector.*

REFERENCES

Bever, T. G. 1968. "A Survey of Some Recent Work in Psycholinguistics." In *Specification and Utilization of a Transformational Grammar*, Scientific Report No. 3, Air Force Cambridge Research Laboratories.

—— 1970. "The Cognitive Basis for Linguistic Structures." In *Cognition and the Development of Language*, J. R. Hayes, ed., Wiley.

—— 1973. "Perception, Thought, and Language." In *Language, Comprehension, and the Acquisition of Knowledge*, R. Freedle and J. Carroll, eds. Winston.

—— 1974. "The Ascent of the Specious, of There's a Lot We Don't Know about Mirrors." In *Explaining Linguistic Phenomena*, D. Cohen, ed. Hemisphere.

—— 1975. "Functionalist Explanations Presuppose Independently Motivated Theories of Speech Behavior." In *Papers from the Chicago Linguistic Society Parasession on Functionalism*.

Bettelheim, B., and M. Janowitz. 1949. "Ethnic Tolerance: A Function of Social and Personal Control." *American Journal of Society* SS: 137–145.

Bloomfield, L. 1914. *The Study of Language.* Holt.

—— 1933. *Language.* Holt.

—— 1955. "Linguistic Aspects of Science." In *International Encyclopedia of Unified Science*, Vol. I, University of Chicago Press.

Blumenthal, A. 1970. *Language and Society.* Wiley.

Chomsky, N. 1957. Syntactic Structures. Mouton.

—— 1965. *Aspects of the Theory of Syntax.* M.I.T. Press.

—— 1966a. *Cartesian Linguistics*. Harper and Row.

—— 1966b. *Topics in the Theory of Generative Grammar*. Mouton.

—— 1968. *Language and Mind*. Harcourt, Brace, and World.

—— 1972. *Studies on Semantics in Generative Grammar*. Mouton.

—— 1972. "Some Empirical Issues in the Theory of Transformational Grammar." *In Studies on Semantics in Generative Grammar*.

Donnellan, K. 1966. "Reference and Definite Descriptions." *Philosophical Review* 75: 281–304.

—— "Proper Names and Identifying Descriptions." 1970. *Synthese* 21; 335–358.

Fodor, J. A. 1968. *Psychological Explanation*. Random House.

Fodor, J. A., and J. J. Katz. 1964. *The Structure of Language*. Prentice-Hall.

Fodor, J. A., T. G. Bever, and M. Garrett. 1974. *The Psychology of Language*. McGraw-Hill.

Gordon, D., and G. Lakoff. 1971. "Conversational Postulates." *Papers from the Seventh Regional Meeting, Chicago Linguistic Society*. University of Chicago Press.

Grice, P. 1975. "Logic and Conversation". In *Syntax and Semantics*, Vol. 3, P. Cole and J. L. Morgan, eds., Academic Press.

Harris, Z. 1954. "Distributional Structure." *Word* 10: 146–162.

—— 1957. "Co-Occurrence and Transformation in Linguistic Structure." (LSA Presidential Address, 1955). *Language* 33: 283–340. Reprinted in Harris, 1970, p. 390–457.

—— 1958. "Linguistic Transformations for Information Retrieval." *Proceedings of the International Conference on Scientific Information*. 2, NAS-WRC. Washington. Reprinted in Harris, 1970, pp. 458–471.

—— 1965. "Transformational Theory." *Language* 41: 363–401.

—— *Papers in Structural and Transformational Linguistics*. 1970. Reidel.

Katz, D., and K. W. Braly. 1935. "Verbal Stereotypes and Racial Prejudice." *Journal of Abnormal and Social Psychology* 30: 175–179.

Katz, J. J. 1964. "Mentalism in Linguistics." *Language* 40: 124–137.

—— 1971. *The Underlying Reality of Language and Its Philosophical Import*. Harper and Row.

—— 1972. *Semantic Theory*. Harper and Row.

—— 1973. "Interpretive Semantics Meets the Zombies." *Foundations of Language* 9: 549–596.

—— 1975. "Where Things Now Stand with the Analytic-Synthetic Distinction." *Synthese* 28: 283–319.

Katz, J. J., and R. Nagel. 1974. "Meaning Postulates and Semantic Theory." *Foundations of Language* 11: 311–340.

Katz, J. J., and P. Postal. 1964. *An Integrated Theory of Linguistic Description*. M.I.T. Press.

JERROLD J. KATZ
THOMAS G. BEVER

Kuhn, T. S. 1962. *The Structure of Scientific Revolutions*. University of Chicago Press.

Lakoff, G. 1971a. "Presupposition and Relative Well-Formedness." In *Semantics*, D. Steinberg and L. Jakobovits, eds., Cambridge University Press.

—— 1971b. "The Role of Deduction in Grammar." In *Studies in Linguistic Semantics*, C. Fillmore and D. T. Langendoen, eds. Holt, Rinehart, and Winston.

—— 1972. "Hedges: A Study in Meaning Criteria and the Logic of Fuzzy Concepts." *Papers from the Eighth Regional Meeting, Chicago Linguistic Society*. University of Chicago Press.

Lakoff, R. 1973. "Language and Woman's Place." *Language in Society* 2: 45–79.

Lévi-Strauss, C. 1964. *The Raw and the Cooked*. Harper (1969).

Mach, E. 1911. *The History and Root of the Principle of the Conservation of Energy*. Chicago.

McCawley, J. D. 1972. "A Program for Logic." In *Semantics of Natural Language*, D. Davidson and G. Harman, eds. Reidel.

Miller, G. A., and N. Chomsky. 1963. "Finitary Models of Language Users." In *Handbook of Mathematical Psychology*, R. D. Luce, R. R. Bush, and E. Galanter, eds., Wiley.

Nagel, E. 1961. *The Structure of Science*. Harcourt, Brace, and Jovanovich.

Perlmutter, D. 1971. *Deep and Surface Structure Constraints in Syntax*. Holt, Rinehart, and Winston.

Postal, P., and J. R. Ross. 1970. *The Problem of Adverb Preposing*. *Linguistic Inquiry* 1: 145–146.

Quine, W. V. 1953. "Two Dogmas of Empiricism." In *From a Logical Point of View*. Harvard University Press.

—— 1960. *Word and Object*. M.I.T. Press.

Rosch, E. H. 1973. "On the Internal Structure of Perceptual and Semantic Categories." In *Cognitive Development and the Acquisition of Language*, T. E. Moore, ed., Academic Press, 111–144.

Rosner, S., and L. E. Abt. 1970. *The Creative Experience*. Dell.

Ross, J. R. 1973. "A Fake NP Squish." In *New Ways of Analyzing Variation in English*, C.-J. N. Bailey and R. Shuy, eds. Georgetown University Press.

Sapir, E. 1921. *Language*, Harcourt.

Saussure, Ferdinand de. 1916. *Cours de Linguistique Générale*. Payot, Paris.

Sargent, S. S. 1939. "Stereotypes and the Newspapers." *Sociometry* 2: 69–75.

Valian, V. 1976. "Linguistics and Feminism." In *Philosophy and Feminism*, F. Elliston, J. English, and M. Vetterling, eds. Prometheus Press.

The Influence of
Speech Performance
on Linguistic Structure

THOMAS G. BEVER

INTRODUCTION
AND SUMMARY

Recent theoretical developments in the study of language have depended on a strict distinction between linguistic "knowledge" and the implementation of that knowledge in speech performance. This distinction has been extremely useful, since it has allowed linguistic investigations of language structure to proceed without taking into consideration any behavioral properties of that structure as used in everyday speech. Linguists have reveled in the luxury of being able to ignore why we say what we say, how we say it and how others understand it. They have concentrated their efforts on the description of the 'formal' properties of language implied by the existence of particular well-formed sentences *in vitro*. The problem of understanding the behavior elicited by those sentences *in vivo* has been left to experimental psychologists.

Current study of the acquisition of language has depended upon the same distinction. It is generally assumed that language is learned in a series of "subgrammars." Each subgrammar the child develops as he grows older takes into account the structure of more and more sentences, until finally his grammar is that of an adult. The virtue of such a view of language acquisition is that it allows the investigator to ignore general changes in the child's cognitive system during this period: the investigator's task is merely to isolate and write a grammar for each linguistic stage. Such a structuralist approach underlies the current

I am indebted to R. Hurtig, S. Reder, J. Langer and J. Grinder for assistance with the manuscript. This research was supported by PHS PO 1 GM 16737.

Source: G. B. Flores d'Arcais and J. M. Levelt, eds., *Advances in Psycholinguistics* (Amsterdam: North-Holland Publishing Company, 1970). Reprinted by permission of the publisher.

fascination with how much of language development is determined by innate 'linguistic' structures, rather than by structures that characterize all of human cognition and of which linguistic structure is merely one instance.

In this paper I should like to explore some of the drawbacks in our pre-occupation with linguistic structure in the child and adult and its concomitant lack of attention to psychological mechanisms for the implementation of that structure. First, many intuitions about the grammaticality of potential sentences *in vitro* are influenced and sometimes determined by the properties those sentences would have in actual behavior: a sentence can sometimes be classified as ungrammatical even though closer inspection suggests that it is grammatically acceptable but behaviorally complex. Second, certain grammatical rules themselves may be shown to be structural accommodations to behavioral constraints. Thus certain universal structural properties of language may express general cognitive constraints rather than particular innate linguistic structures.

THE INFLUENCE OF
PERCEPTION ON
ACCEPTABILITY INTUITIONS

The linguist sets himself the task of finding a linguistic description of all and only those sentences that native speakers of a language feel are potentially grammatical, regardless of whether they have ever heard the sentences said or not. For example, speakers of English will agree that (1) is a possible grammatical sentence while (2) is not, even though (2) is perfectly comprehensible in many contexts:[1]

 (1) Phil discussed Sam in a sharp tone of voice.
 (2) *Phil spoke Sam about in a sharp tone of voice.

Thus, a sentence may be comprehensible without being grammatical, nor does incomprehensibility imply ungrammaticality.

Consider a now classic example of a type of sentence which is incomprehensible but alleged to be grammatical by linguists, doubly-embedded sentences (cf. Chomsky and Miller, 1963). For example, (3) has a clause embedded within the main clause and is grammatical and comprehensible, but what about (4), in which the clause within a clause has a clause embedded within it?

 (3) The boy the girl left then slept.
 (4) The boy the girl the man left watched then left.

There is no natural way to block such double-embeddings within a grammar which allows single embeddings such as (3). One *could*, of course, argue that a "subordinate-clause-counter" be included as part of the grammar and that the

1. An asterisk indicates an ungrammatical example sentence; I use a question mark to indicate an unacceptable sentence without specifying the basis for its unacceptability.

counter be set at "1" as an upper limit. However, this will not do, since the restriction is not on the number of embedded clauses, but on the number of *self*-embedded clauses. For example, both sentences (5a) with one subordinate clause and (5b) with two such clauses are comprehensible and acceptable:

(5a) The girl left the boy who then slept.
(5b) The man watched the girl who left the boy who then slept.

An enterprising linguist could argue that there is a specific linguistic restriction on center-embedded clauses. But this would merely catalogue the restriction, not explain it.[2] From the standpoint of the structural linguist such a taxonomic exercise is sufficient, since he is free to claim that such a restriction is merely an example of an innate structural constraint on linguistic forms. We should not be satisfied with the linguists' desire to place such restrictions *hors de combat*. If we can find a plausible behavioral account for the difficulty of double embedded sentences we can avoid this obscure and scientifically stultifying claim about what is innate to linguistic capacity.

In fact, several authors have attempted to formulate behavioral laws that would predict the difficulty of such sentences as (4). For example, Fodor and Garrett (1967) suggest that the difficulty of such sentences is due to their "density," i.e., to the number of underlying structure sentence units per word in the surface structure, which exceeds some critical threshold ("density" $= 3/10$ for (4); "density" $= 3/12$ for (5b)). This proposal is intriguing since it would suggest that at least one dimension of perceptual complexity is quantifiable in linguistic terms. However, that the proposal is incorrect is shown by the fact that the density of underlying sentences per word is even higher in (6) $(3/9)$, yet (6) is entirely comprehensible and acceptable:

(6) The man watched the girl leaving the sleeping boy.

The complexity of center-embedded sentences cannot be explained by appeal to this quantitative principle.

Chomsky and Miller (1963) have also attempted to define a perceptual principle that could account for the difficulty of center-embedded sentences. They argue that any perceptual rule may not interrupt its own operation more than once. In the case of a sentence like (3) (represented schematically in (7a)) the perceptual assignment of the 'actor'-'action' relation to the first noun and last

---

2. There is a current claim that all grammars include a set of "derivational constraints" which restrict the possible form of underlying/surface structure relations (cf. Postal, 1972; Lakoff, 1971). The restriction on doubly center-embedded sentences could be stated with such a device. Also it might be possible to account for the restriction on sentences like (4) in terms of a so-called "output restriction," which state constraints on the final form which surface phrase structures can have (cf. Perlmutter, 1971). However, the restriction appears to be on the underlying/surface relations rather than on the surface sequence itself, viz. examples (26)–(31) below.

verb is interrupted by the same assignment to the second noun and first verb. In (4) (represented in (7b)) the perceptual assignment of actor-action to the first noun and last verb is interrupted by the assignment of actor-action to the second noun and second verb, which is in turn interrupted by the assignment of the same function to the last noun and the first verb. (Upper lines in (7) represent subject-verb relations. Lower lines represent verb object relations.)

(7a)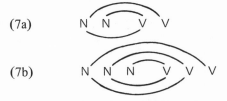

(7b)

It is intuitively clear that a self-interrupting operation is more complex than one which does not interrupt itself. However, there is no theoretical motivation for one interruption being acceptable (as in (3)) and two interruptions being entirely unacceptable (as in (4)). Chomsky and Miller's argument, as in the case of the hypothetical clause "counter" on double embeddings, also serves to describe the restriction but not to explain it.

The Operation of Mapping Rules in Speech Perception

The failure to explain the restriction on self-interruptions is partly due to the fact that this phenomenon is not viewed in the context of a general theory of sentence perception. An explanation of the existence of any particular case of perceptual complexity must follow from a theory which explains how the normal perceptual processes are strained by those complex constructions.

Some recent studies have illuminated normal perceptual processes by considering the way in which listeners extract basic grammatical relations (e.g., 'subject, predicate, object, modifier') from the actual appearance of sentences.[3] (See Fodor, Bever, and Garrett (1968) and Bever (1968) for experimental reviews.) The basic claim of these investigations is that there is a set of perceptual rules which map surface sequences onto the corresponding internal relations. According to this view, speech perception proceeds as outlined below.

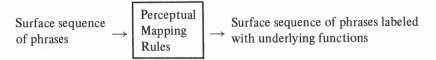

3. In this discussion I intentionally obfuscate the distinction between a semantic and a syntactic analysis of the underlying structure relations. That is, I shall not distinguish between a perceptual mechanism which extracts the syntactic 'logical subject, predicate, object' from one which extracts the semantic relations, 'actor, action, object,' or 'agent, action, patient.' This obfuscation does not vitiate the claims made about the general nature of speech perception. It is necessary in order not to make any claim about the form of underlying structure, which is a subject of current linguistic controversy.

For example, in English any sequence of several phrases of the same type (interrupted optionally with conjunctions), with a conjunction between the last two phrases, is a conjoint phrase of the same type as the compound phrases (e.g., 'noun phrase, verb phrase. . .'), (8).

(8) In ". . . x . . . y conjunction, z . . .", in which x, y . . . z are identical constituent types of type T then the entire sequence is a conjoint phrase of type T, each member of which has the same internal syntactic relation to other sentence constituents as the whole phrase.

(9a) The boy the girl and the man left.

(9b) The boy watched the girl, left the man and slept.

Thus the conjunct phrases in the sentences in (9) can be mapped directly onto their underlying syntactic relations. For example, after (8) has applied to (9a) it is labeled as in (10).

(10) The boy the girl and the man left.

(Conjoined noun phrase, each phrase being a separate subject of the verb.)

Such perceptual rules as (8) apply without reference to the full grammar. Rather than using the grammar in an analysis-by-synthesis recognition routine (cf. Halle and Stevens, 1964) or using an ordered series of "inverse transformations" each corresponding to a transformation to "detransform" the surface tree back to the underlying tree (Herzberger, 1966), many perceptual rules appear to provide *direct* mappings of the surface sequences onto the underlying syntactic relations.

The demonstration that this direct-mapping model is most appropriate for speech perception would be too time consuming for this discussion, particularly since much empirical work must still be done to test it adequately. However, if one accepts this view it is possible to subsume the unacceptability of double embedded sentences under a *general* conceptual restriction which simultaneously accounts for the perceptual difficulty of a number of other kinds of sentence constructions.

The Perceptual Basis for the Complexity of Double Embeddings

Given perceptual mapping rules such as (8), center-embedded sentences like (4) may be difficult because at first they may be misinterpreted as two compound phrases (e.g., (4) is misunderstood as "*the boy, the girl and the man left, watched and slept*"). Indeed Blumenthal (1967) found that subjects most often understand center-embedded sentences as though they were a compound noun followed by a compound verb. Furthermore, Fodor and Garrett found that sentences like (4) are a great deal easier to understand if the relative pronouns are included (e.g., "the boy *whom* the girl *whom* the man watched left slept").

Presumably this is partially due to the fact that the presence of the relative pronouns makes rule (8) inapplicable. Accordingly, part of the complexity of center-embedded constructions is that they present plausible sequences for inappropriate application of perceptual mapping rule (8). However, rule (8) does not explain why center-embedded sentences are difficult to process correctly; (8) applies to such sentences only after a correct interpretation cannot be found and explains only the attractiveness of the preferred inappropriate interpretation.

The action of another perceptual mapping rule does partially explain the initial complexity of double-embeddings. Consider the perceptual mapping rule that assigns the functions of underlying subject and object to noun phrases with relative clauses (11). This rule capitalizes on the fact that in clause initial (or postverbal) position two adjacent noun phrases followed by a verb other than *be* (with other noun phrases optionally intervening) are uniquely related such that the first noun phrase is the object (direct or indirect) of an underlying clause of which the second noun phrase is the subject. For example, the initial sequence of noun phrases in (3) and (4) would be assigned the appropriate relations by (11) as shown in (12) and (13):

(11) In a surface sequence '... NP_1 NP_2 ($\neq$ *who*) (NP*) V($\neq$ *be*)...', NP_1 is the object of a clause of which NP_2 is the subject.

(12) The boy   the girl   left   ...
     Object   Subject

(13) The boy   the girl   the man   left   ...
     Object   Subject/
              Object   Subject

Clearly (11) must apply twice to double-embeddings to mark the middle noun phrase as both a subject and an object. This double marking by the same perceptual rule lies at the heart of the difficulty of center-embedded sentences.

There is a general restriction on the utilization of any conceptual dimension, (14),

(14) A stimulus may not be perceived as simultaneously having two positions on the same classificatory relation.

which interacts with the double application of rules like (11) to double-embeddings. (14) articulates the tautology that a stimulus cannot be perceived in two incompatible ways at the same time. For example, a noun phrase in the surface sequence cannot simultaneously be subject and object of the same verb. This principle, when applied according to the view of speech perception as a direct mapping of external sequences onto internal structures, will predict the difficulty of any sequence in which a phrase has a 'double function' in such a mapping operation. However, before applying (14) to explain the difficulty of center-embedded sentences, let us consider its application to some well-known facts.

Miller and Selfridge (1950) found that sequences with low-order probability approximations to English are difficult to perceive, e.g., a sequence like (15) is more difficult than (16):

(15) he went to the newspaper is in deep   (2nd-order approximation)
(16) then go ahead and do it if possible   (7th-order approximation)

(a '2nd-order approximation' is generated by giving a subject a word (e.g., 'went') and asking him to produce the next word of a sentence ('to'); the next subject is given the last word of the sequence ('to') and produces the next word ('the') and so on. A '7th-order approximation' is generated by giving each subject the last six words of the sequence and asking for the next word.) The relative ease of perceiving sentences as they increase in order of approximation was taken by Miller and others as evidence for the organizing role of syntactic structure at levels higher than a single word. For example, in (16) the sequence forms a sentence, while in (15) it does not. However, reference to the 'organizing properties of syntax' does not explain why low orders of approximation are behaviorally difficult in the first place. In fact, if forming a sentence makes word strings easy to perceive, it might be predicted that sequence (15) should be psychologically simpler since it simultaneously forms *two* sentences (as shown in (17) and (18)):

(17) he went to *the newspaper*
(18)   *the newspaper* is in deep

The real basis of the psychological difficulty is clear: the italicized portion of the sequence is vital to both sentences, that is, it has a 'double function'. Psychological complexity results whenever such double functions appear, even in nonlinguistic stimuli. Consider, for example, the representation of the two adjacent squares in Figure 1. The line labeled 'y' is simultaneously shared by the right and left squares. As a result, Figure 1 is generally perceived as a divided rectangle rather than two adjacent squares. Often such double functions can produce 'impossible' figures from the combination of two 'possible' figures, e.g., Figure 2. The general psychological principle that governs these visual examples is a special case of (14): *in a closed system a component of a stimulus cannot serve two opposite functions at the same time.* For example, in Figure 1 line y cannot both end one square *and* begin another; or in Figure 2 the segment labeled

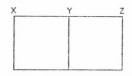

Figure 1. Figure most easily seen as a rectangle with one division at 'y', rather than two squares joined at 'y'.

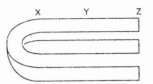

Figure 2. Figure that is 'impossible' because of combination of 2- and 3-dimensional projection at point 'y'.

'y' cannot both end one kind of figure (the 3-dimensional 'u' opening right in the segments labeled x—y) *and* begin the other (the three poles in the segments labeled y—z).

There is a related explanation for the psychological difficulty of 'center-embedded' sentences. Phillips and Miller (1966) noticed that in a sentence like (4) the second noun is the subject of one clause and the object of another (see 7) and suggested that this might be involved in the complexity of such sentences. According to our view, understanding a sentence involves labeling each phrase with its logical function in the underlying structure by means of perceptual mapping rules. The second noun in (4) could be interpreted as having a 'double function' with respect to perceptual rule (11) since the first noun is labeled by the same rule as the object of a verb of which the second noun is the subject. With respect to the preceding noun, the second noun is a subject, while it is an object with respect to the following noun (see 13).

The general double-function hypothesis for speech perception following from (14) is this:

(19) In a sequence of constituents x, y, z, if x has an internal relation R_i to y and y has the same internal relation to z, and x, y, and z are superficially identical in construction type, then the stimulus is relatively complex, due to y's double function in the perceptual mapping rule, r_i, in which y is both a p and q. (Note that $R_i \neq$ conjunction)

$$pq \xrightarrow{r_i} p\ R_i\ q$$

Thus doubly embedded sentences are complex because they involve the second noun phrase in a double function with respect to the perceptual mapping rule (11).

It should be emphasized that the difficulty implied by (19) does not refer to all cases in which a single phrase has more than one role in the deep structure. For example, in (3) "the boy" is both *object* of "left" and *subject* of "sleep," with no attendant perceptual complexity. Similarly in (20) "the boy" is simultaneously the underlying *subject* of "sleep," the *object* of "like," and the *indirect object* of "give." Yet the sentence is quite simple:

(20) The girl liked the sleeping boy Sam gave the sandwich to.

Principle (19) applies only to these cases in which exactly the same perceptual mapping rule is used to assign different functions to the same phrase. That is, it is not the 'double function' of the middle noun phrase in the underlying structure that makes such sentences complex. It is, rather, the double application to it of perceptual rule (11). In applying the rule the listener first categorizes the middle phrase as the right-hand member of a pair related by rule (11) and then must characterize it immediately as the left-hand member of the same kind of pair defined by the same rule. In the terms used in (19) the middle noun phrase of (4) is simultaneously a 'p' and 'q' of the same mapping rule.[4]

There are other examples of complex constructions explained by principle (19). Consider the relative complexity of sentences (21) and (22):

(21)? Maxine did not ask Harvey not to say he would not go.

(22) Maxine did not ask Harvey to say he would not go.

(21) is an example of "triple negation," which has often been recognized as extremely complex, if acceptable at all. Like single embedded sentences, sentences with two negation markers are perfectly comprehensible and acceptable (as in (22)). Principle (14) predicts the relative difficulty of sentences with three negations. The perceptual mapping operation corresponding to the negative marks the second 'not' in (21) as simultaneously the scope of the first negation and the operator on the third negation. The result of this mapping is outlined in (23):

(23)? Maxine did not ask Harvey not to say he would not go.

$$\text{Negator} \left(\begin{array}{l} \text{Negated} \\ \text{Negator} \left(\begin{array}{l} \text{Negated} \\ \text{Negator (Negated)} \end{array} \right) \end{array} \right)$$

Following principles (14) and (19), any sequence containing such a double perceptual function is perceptually complex.

Principle (19) also explains some examples of perceptually complex constructions which are intuitively of the same sort as the preceding examples. Consider the sentences in (24) and (25):

(24)? They were tired of discussing *considering* producing toys.

(25)? They were tired of the discussion of *the consideration* of the production of toys.

In each case the sentences are extremely difficult to understand, if they are acceptable at all. As in double-embedding and triple-negation sentences, the complexity of these sentences is a function of the presence of three superficially identical phrases in which the second phrase is modified by the first

---

4. Presumably there is an analogous strategy for relating the verbs to each other in sentences like (4), which also underlies the perceptual complexity of embedded sentences.

phrase in the same way that the second phrase modifies the third phrase (in the underlying structure). Consider the relative perceptual ease of these sentences if only two phases occur:

(26) They were tired of discussing producing toys.
(27) They were tired of the discussion of the production of toys.

The sentences in (24) and (25) also become much easier to understand if the internal relations among the three critical phrases are varied as in (28) and (29).

(28) They were tired of discussing *ceiling* producing toys.
(29) They were tired of the discussion of the *evolution* of the production of toys.

The explanation is that the middle phrase no longer has a double function since *different* perceptual mapping rules relate the first two and second two phrases. (Note that in (28) the middle phrase ("ceiling") is the underlying structure object of the following phrase ("producing") while the first ("discussing") and second phrase are not directly related. In (29) the middle phrase ("evolution") is the action carried out by the third phrase ("production") but the object of the first phrase ("discussion" . . .).

Finally, (26) and (27) become perceptually simpler if the superficial form of the critical phrases is varied, even while the internal relations are held constant; as in (30) and (31):

(30) They were tired of discussing the consideration of producing toys.
(31) They were tired of the discussion of considering the production of toys.

The explanation for the relative ease of (30) and (31) is that the middle phrase does not have a double function with respect to the same perceptual mapping rule. The superficial difference in the middle phrase allows the listener to use a different mapping rule for relating the first two phrases than for relating the second two phrases.[5]

In brief, I have tried to show that if speech perception is viewed (at least in part) as a direct mapping of external sequences onto internal structures, then the tautology in (14) predicts the principle in (19) which in turn, predicts the relative perceptual complexity of doubly embedded sentences, among others. In brief, in sequences of identical constructions, three's a crowd.

---

5. This suggests that a change in the superficial form of the noun phrases and verb phrase in double-embeddings should reduce their complexity. First, increasing the homogeneity does make the sentence harder, e.g. (a) is harder than (4). Furthermore (b) seems easier than (4), although it is still more complex than (6).

(a) The man the man the man left left left.
(b) The reporter everyone I met trusts says Thieu will resign in the Spring.

**Some Cases of Unacceptability of
Uncertain Etiology**

It is possible to argue that doubly embedded sentences are unacceptable due to their predictable perceptual difficulty, given our particular theory of sentence perception. If we had available a broad perceptual theory we could take any unacceptable sequence and analyze its complexity in order to determine whether its unacceptability is due to ungrammaticality or to perceptual difficulty. The problem for current research on language is that both our linguistic and perceptual theories are woefully inadequate. Consequently, much of the time, we may be trying to construct grammars in order to rule out constructions which could be discussed more appropriately by a perceptual theory, and vice versa.

Sometimes the decision about the basis for sequence acceptability is fairly straightforward. Consider (32) and (33):

(32) The boat floated on the creek and sank.
(33)? The boat floated on the creek sank.

Obviously (33) is not an acceptable version of (32) and at first appears to be completely ungrammatical. (Indeed when presented with these sentences out of context many linguists have assured me that (33) is completely ungrammatical.) But suppose (33) is considered in the context of (34) and (35).

(34) The boat that was floated on the creek sank.
(35) The boat put in the creek sank.

Suddenly one realizes that (33) is a version of (34) and that its construction is parallel to that of the entirely acceptable (35). The initial perceptual difficulty of (33) arises from the perceptual plausibility and dominance of the first six words as an independent sentence (e.g. "the boat floated on the creek ... "). The same problem accounts for the initial unacceptability of (36) in which the first nine words comprise a plausible but misleading sentence (e.g. "one editor authors all the newspapers and the magazine"). To understand (36) notice that it has a compound subject and one verb, "agree":

(36)? One editor authors all the newspapers and the magazine all agree.

Although the perceptual attractiveness of simple declarative sentences is clear on intuitive grounds, much of our research has been devoted to exploring the development and utilization in the adult of the perceptual strategy which maps any 'noun, verb, noun' sequence onto underlying subject-verb-object (Bever, 1970). Other studies have shown that perceptual segmentation occurs whenever there is a plausible underlying structure boundary reflected in the surface sequence (Bever, Lackner and Kirk, 1969). Thus the initial sequences in sentences like (33) and (36) appear to satisfy these perceptual schemata prematurely and make correct perception of the sentences more complex.

Not all cases of unacceptability due to perceptual difficulty are so easy to identify. Consider (37) which at first appears entirely ungrammatical. It would seem that the particle 'over' must be placed before the object noun phrase when that noun phrase is long, as in (38). Although it is clear that (38) is acceptable and (37) is not, it is entirely obscure to me whether (37) should be marked as ungrammatical, or as perceptually incomprehensible but grammatical.

(37)? I thought the request of the astronomer who was trying at the same time to count the constellations on his toes without taking his shoes off or looking at me over.

(38) I thought over the request of the astronomer who was trying at the same time to count the constellations on his toes without taking his shoes off or looking at me.

Consider the intermediate acceptability of (39):

(39)? I thought the request of the astronomer who was trying to count the constellations over.

(40) I thought over the request of the astronomer who was trying to count the constellations.

It is clearly not so acceptable as (40), but is (39) really ungrammatical? It is really grammatical?

There would appear to be a continuum of acceptability governed by the relative complexity of what intervenes between a verb and its particle. The general perceptual source for this restriction is a limit on immediate memory. In general, given two phrases following a verb, the less complex is ordered to come first (cf. Ross, 1967). I have argued elsewhere that placing the less complex phrase first allows less to be held in memory while the final phrase is being analysed (Bever, 1970). That is, in ordering phrases we save the hardest for the last.

However, the acceptability of such sentences is governed by other factors as well. Consider the unacceptability of (41) and (42) and the acceptability of (43) and (44):

(41)? I thought the request of the astronomer looking over the charts over.

(42)? I thought the request of the astronomer looking the charts over over.

(43) I thought over the request of the astronomer looking over the charts.

(44) I thought the request of the astronomer looking at the charts over.

Clearly it is not just complexity of the intervening sequence which determines whether a particle can be placed after the object noun phrase. Other restrictions have to do with apparent identity of adjacent phrases.

Another example of perceptual complexity arises in questions of superficial identity of phrases which appear to play a particularly baffling role in the assignment of pronominalization relations. For example in (45) there is no problem in understanding the way in which the pronouns 'her' and 'him' can cross-refer (i.e., there is one interpretation in which 'her' refers to 'the girl' and 'him' refers to 'the boy'):

(45) The boy kissed her only after the girl kissed him.

It is easy to see how (45) is composed by combining the two sentences reflected in (46) and (47):

(46) The boy kissed the girl only after the girl kissed him.
(47) The boy kissed her only after the girl kissed the boy.

However, within nominalized complement constructions such cross-referring does not occur. For example (48) and (49) cannot be combined to produce (50):

(48) The boy suggested the girl's prediction only after the girl predicted it.
(49) The boy suggested it only after the girl predicted the boy's suggestion.
(50)? The boy suggested it only after the girl predicted it.

That is, (50) cannot mean that the boy suggested that the girl would predict his suggesting her prediction only after the girl predicted that the boy would suggest her prediction of his suggestion). (I am indebted to G. Lakoff for calling examples like (50) to my attention.)

Is the cross-referring interpretation of (50) ungrammatical? At first it would appear that it is, and that there is a structural restriction against cross-referring complements. However, consider (51), which is syntactically parallel to (45), but unacceptable on the same cross-referring interpretation that was perfectly acceptable in (45) (i.e., the first "it" cannot refer to "the boulder" while the second "it" refers to "the rock"):

(51)? The rock bounced on it after the boulder struck it.

Apparently the difficulty lies in the confusion introduced by having the two identical pronouns, "it" cross-referring. Similarly (52) is easy to understand and (53) approaches total gibberish on the cross-referring interpretation (e.g. the interpretation that would mean "the rock bounced on the boulder after the boulder struck it"):

(52) The boy kissed the girl after she kissed him.
(53)? The rock bounced on the boulder after it struck it.

We might try to explain such a restriction as another extension of (14), applied in this case to nominal reference (54):

(54) Superficially identical definite noun phrases in the same discourse corefer.

Suppose we view the perceptual operation of nominal reference as a direct mapping of the surface form of the nominal onto the specific referent (whatever the psychological form of such referents may be). Then it follows that if the same superficial nominal has two different referents it will be in the position of having a double referential function. Thus (55)-(57) are unacceptable compared with (58)-(60) (notice, of course, that special contexts can be constructed for (55) (56) and (57) that make them more acceptable):

(55)? Bill and Bill left.
(56)? It and it fell.
(57)? Bill hit Bill.
(58) Bill and Mary left.
(59) He and she left.
(60) Bill hit Mary.

If the noun phrase is indefinite then these restrictions do not occur, presumably because such noun phrases do not map onto a unique specific referent; compare (61)-(63).

(61) Somebody hit somebody.
(62) A boy hit a boy.
(63) Boys hit boys.

Even a slight change in apparent form allows (54) not to apply. Thus while (56) and (57) are unacceptable, (64a, b) are acceptable, presumably due to the difference in surface form of 'he' and 'him':

(64a) He hit him.
(64b) He and him left.

Principle (54) explains the unacceptability of the cross-referring interpretation of (51) and (53) since it requires that "it" always refer to the same referent. This explains another fact about the interpretation of (51) that I have not mentioned: in (51) not only do the "it"s not cross their reference, they also cannot refer to *two* distinct objects not mentioned within the sentence. Rather, in each case, they must both refer to the same *single* object not mentioned in the sentence. We can now ask whether the unacceptability of (50) is due to the structural requirement that complement constructions cannot cross-refer, or whether it is due to the perceptual principle (54). Principle (54) explains the unacceptability of (51) and the acceptability of (45), both of which are superficially similar to (50). Principle (54) also predicts that (50) is unacceptable. How do we decide whether (50) is unacceptable for structural reasons or perceptual reasons, or both?

Such quandaries can be invented *ad nauseam*. Surely the crucial question for linguistic theory is not whether we can confuse ourselves about the basis for the unacceptability of particular sequences, but whether we can be sure of the cases in which we think we are *not* confused. I have presented some examples of unacceptability due to perceptual complexity which I partially understand and for which I can justify the claim that their unacceptability is not necessarily due to structural ungrammaticality. There are undoubtedly many other instances of unacceptable sequences which are taken today to be ungrammatical but which may have straightforward perceptual explanations when we come to understand more about perception.

The possibility that many judgments about grammaticality are judgments about perceptual difficulty does not mean that linguistic theory and formal description of intuitions about grammaticality are fruitless enterprises. It is simultaneously the greatest virtue and failing of linguistic theory that sequence acceptability judgments are used as the basic data. The fact that such judgments really are instances of behavior justifies the claim that linguistic theory is a serious psychological theory, not a mere intellectual artifact.

Although there are many properties of our intuitions about acceptability that we do not understand, certain intuitions appear to be stable enough to resist any obvious behavioral explanation. For example, the fact that for every transitive sentence with a direct object there is a corresponding passive sentence in English is not a fact which will someday be shown to be a by-product of our perceptual system. Nor are such facts as the unacceptability of sequences like (2) likely to be explained on trivial behavioral grounds. The purpose of this discussion is not to undercut one's confidence in linguistic theory, but to make one aware of its current empirical uncertainties and limitations.

THE INFLUENCE OF
PERCEPTUAL PROCESSES ON
LINGUISTIC RULES

In certain cases the perceptual system appears to influence the structure of linguistic rules themselves rather than merely influencing our acceptability judgments about particular sequences. I shall discuss an example in phonology and an example in syntax of how certain basic perceptual principles influence linguistic structure. The mechanism for this structural influence clearly is to be found in the young child. As he learns the linguistic rules of his language he will tend not to learn rules which produce speech forms that are behaviorally hard to understand or hard to say. Thus, whatever aspects of cognition are utilized directly in speech perception will be reflected in certain properties of linguistic grammars.

The Influence of Syllabic Structure
on Phonological Rules

One of the most basic characteristics of speech perception is the organization of the incoming speech signal into units at different levels. For example, the acoustic continuum can be divided up into syllables, which are themselves composed of individual speech sounds, 'phonemes'.[6] Accordingly, (65) can be analyzed as the syllable "dak" or as the sequence of three phonemes, 'd', 'a', and 'k':

(65) "dak"

Such a potential duality of description raises the behavioral question, which level of analysis is the "psychologically real" level and which is an artifact of linguistic theory or of the process of linguistic introspection? Most psychologists and many linguists have answered this question in favor of the syllable as the relevant psychological unit of speech production and perception.

The reasons for this are straightforward enough. The syllable can be defined in acoustic terms relatively easily, and it is the smallest unit that can be uttered in isolation (although vowel phonemes can be uttered in isolation, most consonants cannot). Furthermore, it has been shown by various techniques that the acoustic shape of many individual phonemes, both vowels and consonants, is influenced by the surrounding phonemes. That is, there is no acoustically definable invariant that corresponds uniquely to each phoneme. Not only does each phoneme represent a class of sounds acoustically, it is often the case that the acoustic representation of a phoneme in one context overlaps with the acoustic representation of a different phoneme in a different context. If the first step in speech perception were to identify the incoming speech signal, phoneme by phoneme, we would often not know what many of the phonemes were until we had analyzed the local context in which each phoneme occurs. Many researchers have argued that the natural and relevant definition of 'local context' in which to recognize particular phonemes is the syllable. The syllable is relatively invariant, and includes the information about consonant-vowel transitions that determines much of what we perceive.

Most of the studies that underlie the conclusion that the syllable is perceptually primary result from elegant experimental failures that attempted to account for speech perception in terms of sequential isolation of individual phonemes (Liberman et al., 1967). One can demonstrate that it is impossible to identify many individual phonemes out of syllabic context, while whole syllables are identified with relative ease. Similarly, one can demonstrate that there is no unique definition of the phoneme in terms of articulatory movements of the tongue and lips. Just as the perception of individual phonemes is influenced radically by their context, there are effects of equal magnitude on the articulatory movements involved in the production of a phoneme in a particular context.

Of course, the experimental and observational failure to find direct behavioral evidence for the phoneme as a valid perceptual entity does not explicate its obvious existence, its relation to syllables, nor the kind of role that it might

6. In this discussion I leave open the question of how abstract phonemes are for the same sort of reasons mentioned in footnote 2.

play in perception. To explore this kind of question, Harris Savin and I presented subjects with nonsense lists presented at the rate of one syllable/second, of varying length, like those in (66) (Savin and Bever, 1970):

(66)   skæm firt mowf kiyg gib nemp *bolf* dayts saymz

On some trials subjects were told to respond (on a telegraph key) as soon as they heard the first syllable beginning in a /b/ sound; on other trials the subjects were told to respond the first time they heard the particular syllable, which was presented in its entirety ahead of time.

We found that subjects respond about 70 msec faster when they are told the entire syllable than when they are looking for the first syllable beginning in /b/. This might be due to the fact that there are several acoustic versions of /b/, depending on the following context: subjects who were told the exact syllable knew exactly which acoustic variant of /b/ to listen for and so could respond faster. However, we found the same difference in responding to initial /s/-syllables (in sequences like (67)):

(67)   kæmf firt mowf kiyg gib nemp *solf* dayt baym

when subjects were told either the entire syllable or just that the target syllable would begin in /s/. This difference is critical, since the acoustic properties of the initial /s/ are only slightly affected by the following context, if at all. Furthermore, there is a recognizable acoustic invariant associated with every /s/ regardless of its context, a burst of high-frequency noise.

Another possible explanation for our results might be that subjects made very slow responses on just a few trials to initial phoneme targets but showed no difference the rest of the time. Therefore we analyzed the subjects fastest quartile of responses to syllable targets. These, too, were faster than the fastest quartile of responses to phoneme targets, so the difference was not due to only a few slow responses. Furthermore, while subjects' mean reaction time varied from 200 to 450 msec, there was no related difference in the relative delay in reacting to phoneme targets. Thus, consciously to discriminate and respond to the phoneme would appear to take a certain amount of time beyond the time it takes to respond to the syllable. In this sense we can argue that phonemes are perceptually subsidiary to the syllable.

Are phonemes then dispensable as psychological constructs internal to language, since neither the perceptual nor the articulatory facts require them? Not at all. It is quite impossible to do without phonemes in psychological theories of language, but for nonsensory and nonarticulatory reasons. To mention only a few aspects of the behavioral evidence for phonemes, there is the occurrence of alphabetic writing systems, of rhyme and alliteration in non-literate poetry, of segmental phonemic spoonerisms, and of the innumerable well-attested historical changes in language that are described very simply in terms of phonemes and only clumsily and arbitrarily without them.

In addition to evidence from such historical facts (which would hardly be facts but for some psychological facts about the people who make the history), there are numerous regularities in every modern language that can be stated satisfactorily only by referring to phonemic segments. Consider, for example, just part of the rule of plural-formation for modern English nouns (68):

(68) *If the (singular) noun ends in a voiced sound, add /z/ (boys) and if it ends in an unvoiced sound add /s/ (bits).*

To state such a rule in terms of unsegmented syllables would be a great deal more complex since all the syllables of each kind would have to be listed. Not only would it be inelegant, it would not represent the generalization that underlies the groupings of the three different kinds of syllables. Segmental phonemic features turn out to be just the appropriate concepts for such phenomena (cf. Chomsky and Halle, 1968), neither too specific nor too undifferentiated to describe regularities like this. Again, how could this be if those phonemic features were not part of a psychologically correct description of what people intuitively know about the sound structure of their language?

The conclusion that we draw from such considerations is that phonemes are neither perceptual nor articulatory entities. Rather, they are psychological entities of a nonsensory, nonmotor kind, related by complex rules to stimuli and to articulatory movements; but they are not a unique part of either system of directly observable speech processes. In short, phonemes are behaviorally *abstract*. Just by virtue of standing neutrally between the behavioral systems of sensory input and articulatory output, they can interrelate these perceptual and expressive speech processes.

Since it appears that the initial and primary step in speech perception is to isolate the syllables, we must account for the appearance of phonemes in language learning. One description can be based on work at Haskins' laboratory claiming that adults have a stored "library" of syllable templates. Each time speech stimulus is heard it is matched against the library to determine which syllable it is.[7] Presumably the young child acquires such a library as part of his initial language learning. If this is true, one of the first steps in acquiring the phonemic system which allows him to manipulate and subsequently represent the acoustic regularities in his language will be to acquire the acoustic regularities that characterize syllable structure. For example, in English, the child should acquire restrictions like (69) at an early age:

(69) Two sibilants do not occur in a row in one syllable.

Such a restriction would enable the child to recognize that (70) has three syllables, that (71) is not English, and so on:

(70) churchsteeple
(71)* churchs

---

7. Notice that it is not necessary to specify if the way in which the library is deployed is analysis-by-synthesis or direct analysis.

If acquisition of the acoustic regularities of syllables is one of the first steps in the child's acquisition of the phonemic system in his native language, we might expect that the syllabic properties of the language would influence the regularities that relate individual phonemic segments. For example, suppose the plural rule in (68) were applied to singular words that end in sibilants, like those in (72). The results would be incorrect forms like those in (73), which violate restriction (69):

(72)   church, ax, bush, fudge
(73)* churchs, axs, bushs, fudgz

Rule (68) must be modified so that it will not form syllables that violate the restriction against two sibilants in a row. The plural rule as stated in (74a, b) captures the regularities offered by the use of segmental phonemes with internal features and a system of ordered rules:

(74a) *If the singular noun ends in a sibilant add the neutral vowel, 'uh'.*
(74b) *Add /s/ to all forms, assimilating the voicing to the preceding sound* (giving 'z' following voiced consonants and vowels, including the vowel introduced by (a)).

But it does not reveal within the linguistic description any hint that (74a) is, in fact, an accommodation to the syllabic structure of English that would otherwise be violated by (74b).

Of course, one could argue that syllabic restrictions on the phonemic rules can be stated as part of the universal form of phonological grammar. On this view all phonological rules and systems of rules are evaluated against a paradigmatic statement of the syllable structure of that language. Those rule sequences that produce impossible syllable sequences are modified appropriately. In this way one could make it appear that syllabic constraints on phonological rules operate *within* linguistic structure, rather than being the result of the interaction of systems of speech perception and production with the system of linguistic structure. Such a move would formally save the descriptive linguist the embarassment of having to turn to nonstructural aspects of speech behavior. But the saving would be spurious. Including syllabic constraints within phonological theory is merely a way of stating that there is a descriptive problem of accounting for certain kinds of constraints on segmental sequences. The solution of the problem lies beyond the traditional domain of linguistic structure itself.

The Influence of Sentence Units on Syntactic Rules

At a higher level of analysis one must decide whether the sentence is the basic level of perceptual processing or whether we listen to and organize speech initially as a series of isolated words. At first it would appear obvious that sentences are composed of words and phrases perceptually—that is, as we hear the individual words and phrases we organize them into sentential units. Indeed some of the experiments reviewed above demonstrate the effects involved in the act of organizing a sequence of phrases into a sentence. But the question remains whether we hear sentences *before* the constituent words. For example, a classic experiment is baffling on this view of perception. If sentences are played in noise at certain levels, probable sentences (75) are perceivable but improbable sentences are not (76):

(75) The mother patted the dog.
(76) The dog patted the mother.

How can this be? Even more baffling is the fact that if the noise level behind a sentence like (75) is set so the words just cannot be perceived in isolation, they can be perceived when arranged in a sentence order. Somehow the bits and pieces of words that we hear can contribute mutual information when they are placed in a sentence. The striking aspect of this phenomenon is that as we hear sentences presented in noise we do not perceive that we hear bits and pieces. Rather, as the sentence organization brings the series of words into consciousness the perception of the individual sounds is simultaneous with it.

Of course, the technique of presenting sentences in noise or under other forms of distortion leaves a great deal to be desired and may introduce special properties of its own. To look at this in a different way, Savin, Hurtig and I are examining subjects' reaction times to target sentences beginning with the word "boys" in sequences like (77) (spoken at 1 sentence/second):

(77) Monks ring chimes, cows give milk, shoes help feet, plants have seeds, *boys like girls,* . . .

Before each trial, subjects are told the entire target sentence or told to respond to the first sentence beginning in "boys." Our results so far show that subjects respond consistently faster when they know the entire sentence target than the initial word target (the word 'boys' is always the initial word in the target). This difference is consistent even comparing the fastest quartile of responses to sentence and word targets for each subject (all these responses are *completed* before the end of the word "boys"). If these results hold up, and are not due to some artifact, they will demonstrate that conscious perception of a whole sentence is more direct than perception of the first word in the sentence (Bever, Savin and Hurtig, in preparation).

What then of the word? Is it a mere artifact of linguistic analysis? Obviously not. The kinds of evidence for the behavioral reality of the word are too numerous and obvious to list. But its reality may be analogous to that of the phoneme—words serve as the units with abstract properties that are intermediate between sentence production and perception. The word serves as the reflection of a point of intersection between acoustic, semantic, and syntactic structure.

Accordingly, many syntactic transformational rules are stated on constituents, ranging from clauses to individual words. For example, consider the sentences in (78), which exemplify the restrictions on the optional deletion of the complementizer markers "that" and "the fact":

(78a) John mentioned the fact that Sam is a fool.
(78b) John mentioned the fact Sam is a fool.
(78c) John mentioned that Sam is a fool.
(78d) John mentioned Sam is a fool.

It would appear that these words can be freely deleted, as represented by the syntactic rule (79):

(79) *Delete complementizers* that, the fact *freely*.

As the young child learns rules like these we can expect that he will bring to bear his perceptual strategies based on the sentence as the main unit of perception. We have found that at first (age 1½-2 years) young children repeat the first plausible sentence they hear; for example they repeat "the elephant jumped" in response to (80):

(80) The elephant that jumped kissed the cow.

That is, the young child takes the first noun-verb sequence as the main clause of a complex sentence, even in cases like (80) where that is inappropriate. Certain facts of adult English syntactic structure appear to accommodate this perceptual strategy: for example, R. Kirk (personal communication) has observed that a subordinate clause verb which precedes its main verb is generally marked as subordinate by the end of its verb phrase. The most obvious device is the subordinate clause conjunction, as in (81a, b):

(81a) *Although* the research was secret the liberated files revealed that it actually concerned the metabolization of sauce Bearnaise.
(81b) *Because* the demands were non-negotiable nobody wanted any.

In each case the first verb is marked by the subordinate conjunction as subordinate.

Subordinate conjunctions are specific lexical items which act as specific markers of those cases in which a subordinate clause occurs before its main clause. There are also certain syntactic rule systems that appear to have formed in response to the principle that initial subordinate clauses are marked in English: restrictions on the 'syntactically' allowed deletion of words which mark functional relations among clauses. The sentences in (82)-(84) exemplify a heterogeneous set of grammatical restrictions on the stylistic deletion of 'that' or 'the fact' in initial position.

(82) *Sam was a fool was mentioned by John.
(83) That Sam was a fool was feared by John.
(84) The fact Sam was a fool was feared by John.

Rule (79) is incorrect as shown by the incorrect sentence (82) in which both complementizers are deleted. However, one of the complementizers can be deleted in initial position, *so long as the other remains*. Thus rule (79) must be reformulated to (85):

(85) *Delete the complementizers, except in sentence initial position, in which case at least one complementizer must remain.*

Notice that (85) also applies to allow deletion of the complementizers so long as the complement clause is marked by some lexical item (e.g., "the discovery . . ." in (87)).[8]

(86) The discovery that Sam was a fool frightened John.

(87) The discovery Sam was a fool frightened John.

Thus as the child acquires the rules of syntax he applies global restrictions about sentences to the properties of sentences. One might argue that the fact that such restrictions are reflected in particular syntactic rules is sufficient evidence that the restrictions be included as a proper part of linguistic theory. For example, we might propose a universally available syntactic restriction that initial subordinate clauses always be uniquely marked as such. In a language which has such a restriction any set of syntactic rules that would produce constructions violating that constraint are modified appropriately. Of course, this would merely represent within the linguistic theory a structural property while leaving opaque the behavioral explanation for the existence of that property.

CONCLUSION

I have argued that there are two forms of interaction between speech behavior and linguistic description. First, certain intuitions about the unacceptability of possible sequences are due not to structural facts of the language, but to facts that make them hard to process behaviorally. Linguistic investigations sometimes may attempt to explain on structural grounds the unacceptability of sentences that have a more direct explanation on perceptual grounds. Second, some structures in adult language appear to be accommodations to behavioral strategies in the child's use of language. Consequently, certain structural properties of the grammar of a language can be attributed, not to the form of the child's (innate) *linguistic* structure, but to the interaction between the process of language

8. A similarly motivated restriction exists on the deletion of relative clause-introducing relative pronouns on initial nouns. Thus (b) is not a grammatical version of (a):
(a) The boy who is a fool frightened Sam.
(b) *The boy is a fool frightened Sam.
This, too, is presumably caused by the fact that in (b) the first sequence appears incorrectly as a main clause, cf. Bever and Langendoen (1971) for a discussion of this phenomenon in the history of English.

learning and behavioral strategies used by young children to process actual sentences.

Such facts must modify the dictum that a "correct" grammatical description of a language is at the "center" of all language behavior. A more accurate statement would be that language in its entirety is a function of an interaction between different systems of speech behavior. In the adult, different systems contribute to intuitions about particular utterances, and in the child different systems interact to determine the final form of the language in the adult. In this paper I have concentrated on the effects of the perceptual system on the structural system of language. Of course, both of these systems interact with systems of language learning, speech production, and so on. A fuller understanding of the complexities of language behavior will require study of the interactions among all the psychological systems that are recruited by our instinct to communicate.

REFERENCES

Bever, T. G. 1968. "A Survey of Some Recent Work in Psycholinguistics." *Specification and Utilization of a Transformational Grammar*, In W. J. Plath ed. Scientific Report No. 3, Air Force Cambridge Research Laboratories, Cambridge, Mass.

———. 1970. "The Cognitive Basis for Linguistic Structures." In *Cognition and the Development of Language*, J. R. Hayes ed. Wiley.

Bever, T. G., J. R. Lackner, and R. Kirk. 1969. "The Underlying Structures of Sentences Are the Primary Units of Immediate Speech Processing." *Perception and Psychophysics* 5: 225–234.

Bever, T. G., and D. T. Langendoen. 1971. "A Dynamic Model of the Evolution of Language." Reprinted in this volume.

Bever, T. G., H. Savin, and R. Hurtig. The Non-Perceptual Reality of the Word. In preparation.

Blumenthal, A. L. 1967. "Prompted Recall of Sentences." *Journal of Verbal Learning and Verbal Behavior* 6: 674–676.

Chomsky, N. and M. Halle. 1968. *The Sound Pattern of English*. Harper and Row.

Chomsky, N. and G. A. Miller. 1963. "Introduction to the Formal Analysis of Natural Languages." In R. D. Luce, R. R. Bush and E. Galanter eds. *Handbook of Mathematical Psychology*, Vol. 2, Wiley.

Fodor, J. A., T. G. Bever, and M. Garrett. 1968. "The Development of Psychological Models for Speech Recognition." Report on Contract No. AF 19 (628)-5705, M.I.T.

Fodor, J. A. and M. Garrett. 1967. "Some Syntactic Determinants of Sentential Complexity." *Perception and Psychophysics* 2: 289–296.

Halle, M. and K. N. Stevens. 1964. "Speech Recognition: A Model and a Program for Research." In *The Structure of Language*, J. A. Fodor and J. J. Katz, eds. Prentice-Hall.

Herzberger, H. 1966. "Perceptual Complexity in Language." Unpublished paper.

Lakoff, G. 1971. "On Generative Semantics." In *Semantics*, D. Steinberg and L. Jakobovits, eds. Cambridge University Press.

Liberman, A. M., F. S. Cooper, D. P. Shankweiler, and M. Studdert-Kennedy. 1967. "Perception of the Speech Code." *Psychological Review* 74: 431–461.

Miller, G. A. and J. A. Selfridge. 1950. "Verbal Context and the Recall of Meaningful Material. *American Journal of Psychology* 63: 176–185.

Perlmutter, D. 1971. *Deep and Surface Structure Constraints in Syntax*. Holt, Rinehart, and Winston.

Phillips, J. R., and G. A. Miller. 1966. "An Experimental Method to Investigate Sentence Comprehension." Unpublished paper.

Postal, P. 1972. "The Best Theory." In *Goals of Linguistic Theory*, S. Peters ed. Prentice-Hall.

Ross, J. R. 1967. *Constraints on Variables in Syntax*. Indiana University Linguistics Club.

Savin, H., and T. G. Bever. 1970. "The Non-Perceptual Reality of the Phoneme." *Journal of Verbal Learning and Verbal Behavior* 9: 295–302.

Finite-State Parsing of Phrase-Structure Languages and the Status of Readjustment Rules in Grammar

D. TERENCE LANGENDOEN

1. A THEOREM ABOUT FINITE-STATE PARSING OF PHRASE-STRUCTURE LANGUAGES

Chomsky (1959a,b) and independently Bar-Hillel, Perles, and Shamir (1961) proved that a context-free phrase-structure (CFPS) language L can be generated by a finite-state (FS) grammar if and only if there is a noncenter-embedding (NCE) CFPS grammar that generates L; we call this result the Chomsky–Bar-Hillel theorem.[1] This theorem asserts that, given a NCE–CFPS grammar G, there is a weakly equivalent FS grammar G', a grammar that can also be thought of as a finite acceptor (FA) for $L(G)$; that is, a device that accepts all and only all the sentences of $L(G)$. Chomsky (1959a), moreover, provides an algorithm for constructing FAs for sentences generated by arbitrary Chomsky-normal-form (CNF)[2] CFPS grammars with up to any fixed finite degree n of center embedding (CE).

Now let $L_B(G)$ be the language consisting of the set of structural descriptions (P-markers) that a CFPS grammar G associates with the sentences it generates. It is easy to see that $L_B(G)$ is a CFPS language; a CFPS grammar G_B that generates $L_B(G)$ can be constructed from G by replacing each production $A \to \omega$ in G by

---

1. For terminology and notation, see these papers or Chomsky (1963). I thank C. Kaniklidis and N. Chomsky for helpful discussions, and two reviewers whose painstaking critical efforts have resulted in numerous improvements.

2. The productions of a Chomsky-normal-form CFPS grammar are all of the form $A \to BC$, or $A \to a$ where A, B, and C are nonterminal elements and a is a terminal element.

Source: *Linguistic Inquiry* 5 (1975). Reprinted by permission of the publisher.

the production $A \rightarrow [_A \omega]_A$.[3] Can we find a FA for $L_B(G)$? The answer is negative just in case $L_B(G)$ is an infinite language; it does not matter if G is NCE or even FS, or if G generates only a finite language. If G associates infinitely many P-markers with the sentences it generates, $L_G(B)$ is not a FS language and hence cannot be accepted by a FA. Given that there is no FA for $L_B(G)$, there can also be no finite transducer (FT) that takes sentences of $L(G)$ as input and gives as output their P-markers with respect to G (such a FT may be called a finite parser (FP) for G). In other words, if we try to extend the Chomsky–Bar-Hillel theorem to strong equivalence in the direct sense that we determine the subclass of CFPS grammars for which there are FPs, we find that that subclass contains just those CFPS grammars that associate only a finite number of P-markers with the set of sentences they generate. The theorem and an outline of its proof are now given.

THEOREM 1

If G is a CFPS grammar that generates a language $L(G)$ and associates with the sentences of $L(G)$ a set $L_B(G)$ of P-markers, then there is a FS grammar G' that generates $L_B(G)$ if and only if $L_B(G)$ is finite.

Proof (outline). Clearly, if $L_B(G)$ is finite, there is a FS grammar G' that generates it, since there is a FS grammar for any finite language.

Suppose $L_B(G)$ is infinite. Then, by the method of the "*uvwxy*" theorem (Hopcroft and Ullman, 1969, pp. 57–59), for every nonnegative integer i, there are strings u, v, w, x, y (all except w possibly null) and terminal elements $[_A$ and $]_A$ such that $u([_Av)^i[_Aw]_A(x]_A)^iy$ is a sentence of $L_B(G)$, and such that u, v, x, y do not contain unmatched occurrences of $[_A$ and $]_A$. Suppose that the grammar G' that generates $L_B(G)$ is FS. Then, by the Nerode-Myhill theorem (Rabin and Scott, 1959, Theorem 2), there are distinct m and n such that $([_Av)^m$ and $([_Av)^n$ are equivalent, and hence such that $u([_Av)^m[_Aw]_A(x]_A)^my$ is in $L_B(G)$ if and only if $u([_Av)^n[_Aw]_A(x])^my$ is in $L_B(G)$. Since the former must be in $L_B(G)$, then so must the latter. But the latter cannot be in $L_B(G)$, since it contains an unequal number of occurrences of $[_A$ and $]_A$. Therefore no grammar G' that generates $L_B(G)$ can be a FS grammar. This completes the outline of the proof of the theorem.[4]

3. We assume that $[_A$ and$]_A$ are added to the terminal vocabulary of G_B for each nonterminal element A in G. The labels on either the left or right parentheses may be omitted without ambiguity. Either left or right parentheses may be omitted entirely under certain conditions; see footnote 4 for details.

4. As Chomsky (1963, p. 367) observes, however, it may not be necessary to construct a full P-marker in order to represent unambiguously the structural descriptions of sentences generated by a CFPS grammar. Under certain conditions, either the left or right parentheses may be omitted, yielding structures from which full P-markers can be unambiguously and effectively determined. Let us call a P-marker with left (respectively right) parentheses sup-

(Footnote *Continued*)

pressed a right- (respectively, left-) semi-P-marker (RSP-marker; respectively, LSP-marker). Let $L_R(G)$ be the set of RSP-markers that a CFPS grammar G associates with the sentences it generates, and let $L_L(G)$ be the set of LSP-markers that G associates with the sentences it generates.

I. Suppose G is FS; that is, suppose it is either left linear (LL) or right linear (RL). If G is LL, then $L_R(G)$ is a FS language that unambiguously represents $L_B(G)$, and if G is RL, then $L_L(G)$ is a FS language that unambiguously represents $L_B(G)$. This is so, because if G is LL, then all the left parentheses in sentences of $L_B(G)$ occur at the beginning of the corresponding sentences of $L(G)$, and any structural ambiguity in sentences of $L(G)$ will be represented in the positions of or labels on the right parentheses in $L_B(G)$. Therefore, $L_R(G)$ unambiguously represents $L_B(G)$. To form a FS grammar G' that generates $L_R(G)$, replace each production $A \longrightarrow (B)x$ in G by the corresponding production $A \longrightarrow (B)x]_A$. By the same argument, if G is RL, $L_L(G)$ is a FS language that unambiguously represents $L_B(G)$.

II. Suppose G is an unambiguous CFPS grammar. Then, both $L_L(G)$ and $L_R(G)$ unambiguously represent $L_B(G)$. Otherwise, there is some sentence s in $L_L(G)$ or in $L_R(G)$ that ambiguously represents sentences s' and s'' in $L_B(G)$. But then, there is a single sentence s''' in $L(G)$ that has two P-markers with respect to G, namely s' and s'', contrary to assumption.

III. Suppose G is a NCE–CFPS grammar. Then, either it generates a finite language, or it permits subderivations of the type $A \overset{*}{\longrightarrow} xA$ or $B \overset{*}{\longrightarrow} By$, or both (but not such that there are subderivations of the type $C \overset{*}{\longrightarrow} wCz$, where both w and z are nonnull). If subderivations of the first type are permitted, we say that G is (or permits) right embedding (RE); similarly, if subderivations of the second type are permitted, we say that G is (or permits) left embedding (LE).

Suppose G is unambiguous. From II, it follows that if G is RE, then $L_L(G)$ unambiguously represents $L_B(G)$, and that if G is LE, then $L_R(G)$ unambiguously represents $L_B(G)$. Moreover, if G is RE and not LE, then there is a RE–CFPS grammar G_L that generates $L_L(G)$, and if G is LE and not RE, then there is a LE–CFPS grammar G_R that generates $L_R(G)$. From the Chomsky–Bar-Hillel theorem, then, it follows that if G is an unambiguous strictly RE–CFPS grammar, then there is a FS grammar G' that generates $L_L(G)$, which unambiguously represents $L_B(G)$; and if G is an unambiguous strictly LE–CFPS grammar, then there is a FS grammar G' that generates $L_R(G)$, which unambiguously represents $L_B(G)$.

This result cannot be strengthened to unambiguous NCE–CFPS grammars in general, since such grammars may be both RE and LE, and if so, then any grammar that generates either $L_L(G)$ or $L_R(G)$ will not be FS.

IV. Even if G is ambiguous, it may be the case that either $L_L(G)$ or $L_R(G)$ unambiguously represents $L_B(G)$. Suppose, for example, that there is a variant of English that can be generated by a CFPS grammar G_1, and that the only parsing ambiguity occurs in sentences of the type illustrated in (i).

(i) (a) Ann said that Bill entered quietly.
    (b) [$_S$Ann said [$_S$that Bill entered quietly]$_S$]$_S$
    (c) [$_S$Ann said [$_S$that Bill entered]$_S$ quietly]$_S$

Clearly, $L_R(G_1)$ unambiguously represents $L_B(G_1)$. On the other hand, suppose that there is another variant of English that can be generated by a CFPS grammar G_2, and that the only parsing ambiguity occurs in sentences of the type (ii). (The symbol N may be read "noun phrase"–throughout this article, we use a simplified version of Chomsky's bar notation (Chomsky, 1970) for representing phrase categories.)

2. ON STRONG EQUIVALENCE
BETWEEN FINITE
TRANSDUCERS AND
PHRASE-STRUCTURE
GRAMMARS

As we previously noted, the first of Chomsky's proofs of the Chomsky–Bar-Hillel theorem is based on an algorithm for constructing a FA that accepts $L(G)$, given a NCE–CNF–CFPS grammar G (with certain additional limitations on its form). Moreover, there is an effective, one-one mapping Φ from the P-markers of each sentence generated by G onto the sequence of states that this FA goes through in accepting that sentence. Suppose, then, we equip this FA with an output tape on which it prints the sequences of states that it goes through when accepting each sentence x in $L(G)$. Such a device is a FT T that accepts x and assigns it elements $y_1, \ldots, y_n$ that the mapping Φ effectively and uniquely associates with the P-markers $z_1, \ldots, z_n$ that x has with respect to G. Briefly, we say that T generates $(x, \Phi(z_1, \ldots, z_n))$. We may now say, following Chomsky (1963, p. 396), that T and G are strongly equivalent if and only if T generates $(x, \Phi(z_1, \ldots, z_n))$ just in case G generates x with the P-markers $z_1, \ldots, z_n$ and no others. Let us call the FT, obtainable by Chomsky's algorithm from a NCE–CNF–CFPS grammar G, $\Psi(G)$. We have, then, the following theorem (Chomsky, 1963, Theorem 34).

THEOREM 2

There is an effective procedure Ψ such that, given a NCE–CNF–CFPS grammar G, $\Psi(G)$ is a FT that is strongly equivalent to G.

However, we see that the effective, one-one mapping Ψ cannot in general be a mapping that itself can be carried out by a FT, for if it could be so carried out, one could construct a FP for G from $\Psi(G)$ and Φ, since FTs are closed under composition. From Theorem 1, we know that such a FP exists only if the set of

---

(Footnote *Continued*)

    (ii) (a) The happy young children's teacher arrived.

       (b) $[_{\overline{N}}[_{\overline{N}}$the happy young children$]_{\overline{N}}$'s teacher$]_{\overline{N}}$ arrived

       (c) $[_{\overline{N}}$the happy $[_{\overline{N}}$young children$]_{\overline{N}}$'s teacher$]_{\overline{N}}$ arrived

Clearly, $L_L(G_2)$ unambiguously represents $L_B(G_2)$. Ambiguity of the type represented in (i) arises from the joint possibility of both RE and CE on the same recursive category, while ambiguity of the type illustrated in (ii) arises from the joint possibility of both LE and CE on the same recursive category. Thus, it would appear that if a CFPS grammar G does not permit both RE and LE, then either LSP-markers or RSP-markers are sufficient to represent unambiguously the structural descriptions of sentences with respect to G. It is the joint possibility of both LE and RE in CFPS English-like languages that contain sentences of both types (i) and (ii) that obligates the use of full P-markers to represent unambiguously the structural descriptions of the sentences of those languages with respect to the grammars that generate them.

P-markers associated with the sentences of $L(G)$ is finite. Thus, even though a general-purpose FS device (such as the human mind may be assumed to be) could internalize the procedure Ψ, it would not always be able to carry out Ψ in the course of associating P-markers with the sentences it accepts.

Now, the procedure Ψ of Theorem 2 can be thought of either as a model of how a CFPS grammar is represented in the mind (that is, as a model of competence),[5] or as a model of an aspect of linguistic performance that incorporates a CFPS grammar as a component. If Ψ is thought of as a model of competence, then from Theorem 2 we conclude that it is fully adequate for purposes of representing linguistic competence that a linguist would normally represent in the form of a CFPS grammar. However, there are at least three reasons for rejecting the view that Ψ is a model of competence, and correspondingly for accepting the view that it is a model of performance. First, if Ψ is a model of competence, then the theory of grammar must be formalized in terms of augmented FS grammars (the augmentation being required to deal with CE), rather than in terms of the conceptually more elegant theory of CFPS grammars. Second, given a linguistically adequate theory of competence with a CFPS base constructed in terms of Ψ, with transformations defined on the structures generated by that base, transformations would have to be defined as operations on sets of state sequences that Ψ goes through in generating a base string. While this could be done in principle, the characterization of the relations "factor of," "analyzable as," and "identical to," which are required by that theory of transformations, would be exceedingly complex and unnatural. Third, if Ψ is a model of competence, it is not at all clear how one would construct a reasonable model of performance that incorporated it; it would appear that the theory of performance would be totally independent of the theory of competence.

On the other hand, if Ψ is a model of performance, the base component (in the model of competence) could be given directly in the form of a CFPS grammar, and the basic relations of the transformational component could be directly defined as relations on strings (assuming, following the formalization of transformational grammar given in Peters and Ritchie (1973), that the base component directly generates strings with labeled brackets in them in the manner of G_B above). Further, the theory of performance is given directly by Ψ, which incorporates the grammar in the sense that the grammar is used in the construction of the states and instructions of Ψ (a matter we take up in detail below).

However, if Ψ is thought of as a model of linguistic performance, then one is interested not in Chomsky's indirect notion of strong equivalence, which requires the carrying out of a mapping that in general exceeds the capacity of any FS device, but rather in the direct notion of strong equivalence introduced in

---

5. We know that this hypothesis about competence is false, but only because the generative capacity (both weak and strong) of CFPS grammars is too small to be of linguistic interest. The class of CFPS grammars can still usefully serve, however, as a first approximation to the class of linguistically significant grammars.

section 1 above. We say that direct strong equivalence holds between a FT T and a CFPS grammar G if and only if T generates $(x; z_1, \ldots, z_n)$ just in case G generates x with the structural descriptions $z_1, \ldots, z_n$ and no others. From Theorem 1, it follows that there is no FT that is directly strongly equivalent to a CFPS grammar that associates an infinite number of P-markers with the set of sentences it generates.

From the conception of Ψ as a model of performance, moreover, we see how extremely limited the ability of FS devices is for parsing sentences generated by CFPS grammars. Since infinite numbers of phrase-markers can arise from CFPS grammars only by recursion (i.e., only by subderivations of the type $A \xrightarrow{*} \phi A \psi$), we conclude that it is recursiveness in general (not just CE) that gives rise to the inability of FPs to parse sentences generated by CFPS grammars. This observation, that it is recursiveness in general that limits the ability of a FP to associate P-markers with the sentences it accepts, leads us to conclude that if we wish to minimally augment the FP with a push-down store (PDS) so as to increase its direct strong generative capacity (in the manner in which Chomsky proposed minimally, or in his words, optimally, to augment the FA that accepts sentences generated by a NCE-CFPS grammar, to enable it to deal with up to some fixed finite degree n of CE), we would have to (ultimately) keep track of each recursion on the PDS. An algorithm for constructing a minimally augmented finite parser (MAFP) for any normal-form (NF)[6] CFPS grammar is presented in the next section.

3. CONSTRUCTION OF A MAFP
FOR A NF–CFPS GRAMMAR

Let G be a NF–CFPS grammar that has the single axiom $\#S\#$, the nonterminal vocabulary U, and the terminal vocabulary V, and that generates $L(G)$ and associates with the sentences of $L(G)$ the set of P-markers $L_B(G)$. We must also either impose the restriction that a nonterminal symbol cannot appear more than once on the right-hand side of production of G, or allow that possibility but construct M in terms of productions in a new grammar G', in which symbols that recur on the right-hand side in productions of G are replaced by distinct symbols. One obvious way to do this is to form G' by replacing each production $A \to X_1 B \cdots B X_{n+1}$ in G by the production $A \to X_1 B^1 \cdots B^n X_{n+1}$, and for each rule $B \to \omega$ in G, to add to G' the productions $B^i \to \omega$ for each i, $1 \leqslant i \leqslant n$, and to use G' in the construction of the MAFP for G.[7] For ease in formulating

6. The productions of a NF–CFPS grammar are all of the form $A \to X$, or $A \to a$, where A is a nonterminal element, X is a nonnull string of nonterminal elements, and a is a terminal element.

7. We are using the standard definition of CFPS grammar, which excludes the possibility of there being infinitely many production rules. However, the definition can readily be extended to include that possibility, as long as those productions can be indirectly repre-

the algorithm for constructing a MAFP for G, however, we accept the restriction on G that no nonterminal symbol may appear more than once on the right-hand side of each production of G, and note simply that this restriction is imposed for expository reasons only and that in principle it may be dispensed with.

We construct the MAFP M for G as follows. First we give a procedure for enumerating the set of states Σ of M. Let the set K consist of all rooted subsequences of labels on brackets of sentences of $L_B(G)$, such that no label occurs more than once. That is, $K = \{A_1 \cdots A_m \mid m \geq 1, A_1 = S$, and for all i,j such that $1 \leq i < j \leq m, A_i \neq A_j$, and there are strings X, Y such that $A_i \rightarrow X A_{i+1} Y$ is a production of $G\}$. Σ consists of the initial state S, the final state F, and all members of K subscripted by L or R (for "left" and "right" respectively). Thus, if $B_1 \cdots B_n$ is in K, then $(B_1 \cdots B_n)_L$ and $(B_1 \cdots B_n)_R$ are both in Σ. M has a reading head that scans from left to right an input tape, on which are written strings of the form $\#\sigma\#$, where σ is a string of elements of V together with left and right brackets labeled with elements of U (i.e., a string over the terminal alphabet of $L_B(G)$). The device M is also equipped with a PDS on which it may

---

sented by a finite number of finite rule schemata, and as long as from the schemata, the infinite set of rules they abbreviate can be enumerated by a procedure that is itself no more powerful than that of the theory of CFPS grammar (with a finite number of rules). The reason that the enumeration procedure must not be more powerful than the theory of CFPS grammar is to ensure that the weak generative capacity of CFPS grammars with possibly infinitely many productions is no greater than that of CFPS grammars with only a finite number of productions. For example, without this restriction, the well-known non-CFPS language $L = \{a^n b^n c^n : n > 0\}$ could be generated by the infinite CFPS grammar $S \rightarrow a^n b^n c^n, n > 0$ (the procedure that enumerates the rules abbreviated by this schema requires the power of a context-sensitive phrase-structure grammar).

The extension of the theory of CFPS grammars to include systems with infinitely many productions is linguistically motivated by considering the constituent structure of coordinate constructions in natural languages. However, the schemata that are so motivated are all of the general form $A \rightarrow \chi \psi^n \omega, n > 0$, for which the procedures that enumerate the productions, given these schemata, can all be carried out by FS devices (Chomsky and Schützenberger, 1963, p. 133; Chomsky, 1965, p. 224). Given such schemata, however, the procedure for constructing a grammar G' that does not contain repetitions of the same nonterminal symbol on the right-hand side of productions would not succeed, since it would require that G' have infinitely many nonterminal symbols. Fortunately, it turns out that for purposes of constructing the MAFP for a grammar G of that type, it is only necessary to index (or distinguish) the first occurrence of each repeating symbol. Thus, if G has the infinite set of rules abbreviated by the schema $A \rightarrow BC(BC)^n, n > 0$, then G' has the schema $A \rightarrow B^1 C^1 (BC)^n, n > 0$.

Note, finally that if the theory of CFPS grammar is extended to include grammars with infinitely many production rules (which, however, can be enumerated from finite schemata by a FS grammar), Theorem 1 is false, since clearly there is a FP for the grammar G consisting of the infinitely many productions abbreviated by the schema $S \rightarrow a^n, n > 0$, even though $L_B(G)$ is an infinite language. Indeed, Theorem 1 can be modified to state that for each CFPS grammar G that generates an infinite language solely by virtue of infinite sets of rules that can be enumerated by a finite automaton from finite schemata, there is a FT T that is directly strongly equivalent to G.

print or erase a string of elements of U, followed by the designated boundary symbol *, and an auxiliary reading head that scans the most recently printed string on the PDS. We say that M is in its initial configuration if it is in the state S, reading the first # on the input tape, and the PDS is blank. We say that M is in its final configuration if it is in the state F, reading the second # on the input tape, and the PDS is blank. Instructions in M are all in the form $Q \to I; x R$, where Q and R are members of Σ, x is a (possibly null) string of symbols on the input tape that the device must read to carry out that instruction, and I is a (possibly null) subinstruction to write and/or erase some string y^* (y a string of elements of U) on the PDS. The subinstruction $W(y^*)$ means to write y^* on the PDS and to push down whatever else appears on the PDS; the subinstruction $E(y^*)$ means to erase the string y^* on the PDS and to push up whatever else appears on the PDS. An erase subinstruction cannot be carried out if the auxiliary reading head is not scanning y^*. If both a write and an erase subinstruction appear in I, they are to be performed in the order indicated.

M accepts a string $\#\sigma\#$ on its input tape if and only if it can progress from its initial configuration to its final configuration exactly once while reading σ, using instructions constructed in accordance with the procedure now given.

I. If $B_n \to a$ is a production of G, then for all $B_1 \cdots B_n$ in K, the following is an instruction of M.

$$(B_1 \cdots B_n)_L \quad \to \qquad\qquad\qquad [_{B_n}a]_{B_n} \ (B_1 \cdots B_n)_R$$

II. If $B_n \to C_1 \cdots C_p$ is a production of G, then for all $B_1 \cdots B_n$ in K, the following are instructions of M.

A1. If $C_1 \neq B_k (1 \leq k \leq n)$:

$$(B_1 \cdots B_n)_L \quad \to \qquad\qquad [_{B_n} \qquad (B_1 \cdots B_n C_1)_L$$

B1. If $C_i, C_{i+1} \neq B_k (1 \leq i \leq p-1; 1 \leq k \leq n)$:

$$(B_1 \cdots B_n C_i)_R \ \to \qquad\qquad\qquad (B_1 \cdots B_n C_{i+1})_L$$

C1. If $C_p \neq B_k (1 \leq k \leq n)$:

$$(B_1 \cdots B_n C_p)_R \ \to \qquad\qquad]_{B_n} \qquad (B_1 \cdots B_n)_R$$

A2. If $C_1 = B_k (1 \leq k \leq n)$:

$$(B_1 \cdots B_n)_L \quad \to W(B_k \cdots B_n^*); \qquad [_{B_n} \qquad (B_1 \cdots B_k)_L$$

B2a. If $C_i \neq B_j, C_{i+1} = B_k (1 \leq i \leq p-1; 1 \leq j, k \leq n)$:

$$(B_1 \cdots B_n C_i)_R \ \to W(B_k \cdots B_n^*); \qquad\qquad (B_1 \cdots B_k)_L$$

B2b. If $C_i = B_j, C_{i+1} \neq B_k (1 \leq i \leq p-1; 1 \leq j, k \leq n)$:

$$(B_1 \cdots B_j)_R \qquad \to E(B_j \cdots B_n^*) \qquad\qquad (B_1 \cdots B_n C_{i+1})_L$$

B2c. If $C_i = B_j$, $C_{i+1} = B_k (1 \leqq i \leqq p-1; 1 \leqq j, k \leqq n)$:

$$(B_1 \cdots B_j)_R \quad \rightarrow E(B_j \cdots B_n^*), W(B_k \cdots B_n^*) \quad (B_1 \cdots B_k)_L$$

C2. If $C_p = B_k (1 \leqq k \leqq n)$:

$$(B_1 \cdots B_k)_R \quad \rightarrow E(B_k \cdots B_n^*) \qquad]_{B_n} \qquad (B_1 \cdots B_n)_R$$

III. The following are also instructions of M.

A. $\quad S \qquad\qquad \rightarrow \qquad\qquad\qquad\qquad \# \qquad (S)_L$

B. $\quad (S)_R \qquad\quad \rightarrow \qquad\qquad\qquad\qquad \# \qquad F$

The states Σ of M are designed to indicate what symbol on the input tape M is scanning when it is in that state. Thus, if M is in fact in the course of a computation that accepts a sentence of $L_B(G)$ written on its input tape, and it is in the state $(B_1 \cdots B_n)_L$, M is scanning the symbol $[_{B_n}$ on the input tape; similarly, if it is in the state $(B_1 \cdots B_n)_R$, M is scanning the symbol $]_{B_n}$. Moreover, the sequence of elements of U in the name of each state represents the labels on the unmatched left brackets that M has already read, in the order in which they were encountered, provided that no unmatched left bracket has been encountered more than once. When a given unmatched labeled left bracket is reencountered on the input tape, M enters the state that is appropriate for the first encounter of that bracket, in accordance with step IIA2, IIB2a, or IIB2c of the construction, and the labels of the unmatched left brackets that were encountered between the previous occurrence of the recurring bracket and the one being scanned are recorded on the PDS. When the labeled right bracket corresponding to the most recently scanned occurrence of the recursive labeled left bracket is encountered on the input tape, the PDS is erased back to the second occurrence of the boundary symbol* (if there is only one occurrence of * on the PDS, it becomes blank), and the erased symbols (except for *) are read back into the state name of the next configuration of M in accordance with step IIB2b, IIB2c, or IIC2 of the construction.[8] In this way M is able to keep a complete record of the unmatched left brackets it has previously read on the input tape, so as to be able to read labeled right brackets in the inverse order, as must be the case with sentences in $L_B(G)$.

The proof of the theorem that M accepts a string $\#\sigma\#$ just in case σ is a sentence of $L_B(G)$ would be too lengthy to give here. Instead, an illustration of the construction of a MAFP for a linguistically interesting grammar is given.

---

8. Step IIB2c of the construction is designed to deal with the situation in which M scans successively the right bracket of some recursive symbol followed by the left bracket of another recursive symbol. In this case, one can think of the string $B_j \ldots B_n$ as being read into the state name temporarily, so as to permit the string $B_k \ldots B_n$ to be transferred from the state name to the PDS.

4. ILLUSTRATION OF THE CONSTRUCTION

We illustrate the construction of a MAFP by considering the NF–CFPS grammar G, whose productions are given in the first section. The symbols $\overline{C}$, $\overline{V}$, and P may be read "complement phrase," "verb phrase," and "possessive," respectively.

(1)   (a) $S \to \overline{C}\,\overline{V}$
      (b) $S \to \overline{N}\,\overline{V}$
      (c) $\overline{V} \to V\,\overline{C}$
      (d) $\overline{V} \to V\,\overline{N}$
      (e) $\overline{C} \to C\,S$
      (f) $\overline{N} \to D\,N$
      (g) $D \to \overline{N}\,P$
      (h) $C \to$ that
      (j) $D \to$ the
      (k) $P \to$'s
      (l) $N \to$ {adult, boy, child, friend, girl, man, woman}
      (m) $V \to$ {amazes, believes, bothers, knows}

G is designed to illustrate certain recursions that are typical of English: subject complementation object complementation, and possessive modification. The MAFP M that parses sentences as generated by G has the instructions given in (2).[9]

(2)   (a)   i. $(S)_L$ $\to$ $(S\overline{C})_L$ IIA1.
          ii. $(S\overline{C})_R$ $\to$ [$_S$ $(S\overline{V})_L$ IIB1.
          iii. $(S\overline{V})_R$ $\to$ $(S)_R$ IIC1.
      (b)   i. $(S)_L$ $\to$]$_S$ $(S\overline{N})_L$ IIA1.
          ii. $(S\overline{N})_R$ $\to$ $(S\overline{V})_L$ IIB1.
      (c)   i. $(S\overline{V})_L$ $\to$ [$_{\overline{V}}$ $(S\overline{V}V)_L$ IIA1.
          ii. $(S\overline{V}V)_R$ $\to$ $(S\overline{V}\overline{C})_L$ IIB1.
          iii. $(S\overline{V}\overline{C})_R$ $\to$]$_{\overline{V}}$ $(S\overline{V})_R$ IIC1.
      (d)   i. $(S\overline{V}V)_R$ $\to$ $(S\overline{V}\overline{N})_L$ IIB1.
          ii. $(S\overline{V}\overline{N})_R$ $\to$]$_{\overline{V}}$ $(S\overline{V})_R$ IIC1.
      (e)   i. $(S\overline{C})_L$ $\to$ [$_{\overline{C}}$ $(S\overline{C}C)_L$ IIA1.
          ii. $(S\overline{C}C)_R$ $\to W(S\overline{C}^*)$ $(S)_L$ IIB2a.
          iii. $(S)_R$ $\to E(S\overline{C}^*)$]$_{\overline{C}}$ $(S\overline{C})_R$ IIC2.
          iv. $(S\overline{V}\overline{C})_L$ $\to$ [$_{\overline{C}}$ $(S\overline{V}\overline{C}C)_L$ IIA1.

9. The right-hand column in (2) gives the step of the construction that permits the establishment of each instruction of M. The numbering of the instructions reflects the numbering of the productions of the grammar G given in (1).

	v.	$(S\overline{V}CC)_R$	$\rightarrow W(S\overline{VC}^*)$		$(S)_L$	IIB2a.
	vi.	$(S)_R$	$\rightarrow E(S\overline{VC}^*)$;	$]_{\overline{C}}$	$(S\overline{VC})_R$	IIC2.
(f)	i.	$(S\overline{N})_L$	$\rightarrow$	$[_{\overline{N}}$	$(S\overline{ND})_L$	IIA1.
	ii.	$(S\overline{VN})_L$	$\rightarrow$	$[_{\overline{N}}$	$(S\overline{VND})_L$	IIA1.
	iii.	$(S\overline{ND})_R$	$\rightarrow$		$(S\overline{NN})_L$	IIB1.
	iv.	$(S\overline{VND})_R$	$\rightarrow$		$(S\overline{VNN})_L$	IIB1.
	v.	$(S\overline{NN})_R$	$\rightarrow$	$]_{\overline{N}}$	$(S\overline{N})_R$	IIC1.
	vi.	$(S\overline{VNN})_R$	$\rightarrow$	$]_{\overline{N}}$	$(S\overline{VN})_R$	IIC1.
(g)	i.	$(S\overline{ND})_L$	$\rightarrow W(\overline{ND}^*)$;	$[_D$	$(S\overline{N})_L$	IIA2.
	ii.	$(S\overline{VND})_L$	$\rightarrow W(\overline{ND}^*)$;	$[_D$	$(S\overline{VN})_L$	IIA2.
	iii.	$(S\overline{N})_R$	$\rightarrow E(\overline{ND}^*)$		$(S\overline{NDP})_L$	IIB2b.
	iv.	$(S\overline{VN})_R$	$\rightarrow E(\overline{ND}^*)$		$(S\overline{VNDP})_L$	IIB2b.
	v.	$(S\overline{NDP})_R$	$\rightarrow$	$]_D$	$(S\overline{ND})_R$	IIC1.
	vi.	$(S\overline{VNDP})_R$	$\rightarrow$	$]_D$	$(S\overline{VND})_R$	IIC1.
(h)	i.	$(S\overline{C}C)_L$	$\rightarrow [_C\text{that}]_C$		$(S\overline{C}C)_R$	I.
	ii.	$(S\overline{VC}C)_L$	$\rightarrow [_C\text{that}]_C$		$(S\overline{VC}C)_R$	I.
(j)	i.	$(S\overline{ND})_L$	$\rightarrow [_D\text{the}]_D$		$(S\overline{ND})_R$	I.
	ii.	$(S\overline{VND})_L$	$\rightarrow [_D\text{the}]_D$		$(S\overline{VND})_R$	I.
(k)	i.	$(S\overline{NDP})_L$	$\rightarrow [_P\text{'s}]_P$		$(S\overline{NDP})_R$	I.
	ii.	$(S\overline{VNDP})_L$	$\rightarrow [_P\text{'s}]_P$		$(S\overline{VNDP})_R$	I.
(l)	i.	$(S\overline{NN})_L$	$\rightarrow [_N\{\text{adult},\dots\}]_N$		$(S\overline{NN})_R$	I.
	ii.	$(S\overline{VNN})_L$	$\rightarrow [_N\{\text{adult},\dots\}]_N$		$(S\overline{N}VN)_R$	I.
(m)		$(S\overline{V}V)_L$	$\rightarrow [_V\{\text{amazes},\dots\}]_V$		$(S\overline{V}V)_R$	I.
(n)	i.	S	$\rightarrow \#$		$(S)_L$	IIIA.
	ii.	$(S)_R$	$\rightarrow \#$		F	IIIB.

M is capable of accepting any sentence of $L_B(G)$; in other words, of parsing any sentence of $L(G)$ in accordance with G. For example, M accepts the structures of (4) which are the P-markers of the sentences of (3) with respect to G.

(3)   a.   That the boy amazes the girl bothers the man.
      b.   The woman believes that the adult knows the child's friend.

(4)   a.   # $[_S[_{\overline{C}}[_C\text{that}]_C$ $[_S[_{\overline{N}}[_D\text{the}]_D$ $[_N\text{boy}]_N]_{\overline{N}}$ $[_{\overline{V}}[_V\text{amazes}]_V$
        $[_{\overline{N}}[_D\text{the}]_D$ $[_N\text{girl}]_N]_{\overline{N}}]_{\overline{V}}]_S]_{\overline{C}}$ $[_{\overline{V}}[_V\text{bothers}]_V$ $[_{\overline{N}}[_D\text{the}]_D$
        $[_N\text{man}]_N]_{\overline{N}}]_{\overline{V}}]_S$ #

      b.   # $[_S[_{\overline{N}}[_D\text{the}]_D$ $[_N\text{woman}]_N]_{\overline{N}}$ $[_{\overline{V}}[_V\text{believes}]_V$ $[_{\overline{C}}[_C\text{that}]_C$
        $[_S[_{\overline{N}}[_D\text{the}]_D$ $[_N\text{adult}]_N]_{\overline{N}}$ $[_{\overline{V}}[_V\text{knows}]_V$ $[_{\overline{N}}[_D[_{\overline{N}}[_D\text{the}]_D$
        $[_N\text{child}]_N]_{\overline{N}}$ $[_P\text{'s}]_P]_D$ $[_N\text{friend}]_N]_{\overline{N}}]_{\overline{V}}]_S]_{\overline{C}}]_{\overline{V}}]_S$ #

The sequence of transitions that M goes through in accepting (4a), the P-marker of (3a) with respect to G, is given in Table 1.[10]

---

10. In fact, Table 1 gives a complete analysis of the internal configurations of M at each point in the process of accepting (4a).

TABLE 1.
Transitions of M While Accepting Sentence (4A)

STEP	INSTRUCTION		IN STATE	SCANNING
1.	n.	i.	S	$\#$
2.	a.	i.	$(S)_L$	$[_S$
3.	e.	i.	$(S\bar{C})_L$	$[_{\bar{C}}$
4.	h.	i.	$(S\bar{C}C)_L$	$[_C$
5.	e.	ii.	$(S\bar{C}C)_R$	$[_S$
6.	b.	i.	$(S)_L$	$[_S$
7.	f.	i.	$(S\bar{N})_L$	$[_{\bar{N}}$
8.	j.	i.	$(S\bar{N}D)_L$	$[_D$
9.	f.	iii.	$(S\bar{N}D)_R$	$[_N$
10.	l.	i.	$(S\bar{N}N)_L$	$[_N$
11.	f.	v.	$(S\bar{N}N)_R$	$]_{\bar{N}}$
12.	b.	ii.	$(S\bar{N})_R$	$[_{\bar{V}}$
13.	c.	i.	$(S\bar{V})_L$	$[_{\bar{V}}$
14.	m.		$(S\bar{V}V)_L$	$[_V$
15.	d.	i.	$(S\bar{V}V)_R$	$[_{\bar{N}}$
16.	f.	ii.	$(S\bar{V}\bar{N})_L$	$[_{\bar{N}}$
17.	j.	ii.	$(S\bar{V}\bar{N}D)_L$	$[_D$
18.	f.	iv.	$(S\bar{V}\bar{N}D)_R$	$[_N$
19.	l.	ii.	$(S\bar{V}\bar{N}N)_L$	$[_N$
20.	f.	vi.	$(S\bar{V}\bar{N}N)_R$	$]_{\bar{N}}$
21.	d.	ii.	$(S\bar{V}\bar{N})_R$	$]_{\bar{V}}$
22.	a.	iii.	$(S\bar{V})_R$	$]_S$
23.	e.	iii.	$(S)_R$	$]_{\bar{C}}$
24.	a.	ii.	$(S\bar{C})_R$	$[_{\bar{V}}$
25.	c.	i.	$(S\bar{V})_L$	$[_{\bar{V}}$
26.	m.		$(S\bar{V}V)_L$	$[_V$
27.	d.	i.	$(S\bar{V}\bar{V})_R$	$[_{\bar{N}}$
28.	f.	ii.	$(S\bar{V}\bar{N})_L$	$[_{\bar{N}}$
29.	j.	ii.	$(S\bar{V}\bar{N}D)_L$	$[_D$
30.	f.	iv.	$(S\bar{V}\bar{N}D)_R$	$[_N$
31.	l.	ii.	$(S\bar{V}\bar{N}N)_L$	$[_N$
32.	f.	vi.	$(S\bar{V}\bar{N}N)_R$	$]_{\bar{N}}$
33.	d.	ii.	$(S\bar{V}\bar{N})_R$	$]_{\bar{V}}$
34.	a.	ii.	$(S\bar{V})_R$	$]_S$
35.	n.	ii.	$(S)_R$	$\#$

5. SOME PROPERTIES OF MAFPs

Since MAFPs are minimally augmented, their use of the extra power of a PDS is limited to just those situations in which that power is necessary for effective parsing. Consequently, they do not need to use their PDS to parse all noun phrases within sentences, unlike augmented transition networks (see Woods, 1969, 1970; Wanner and Maratsos, 1971), which use the PDS for parsing major

TO STATE	READING	PDS CONTENT
$(S)_L$	#	—
$(S\bar{C})_L$	$[_S$	—
$(S\bar{C}C)_L$	$[_{\bar{C}}$	—
$(S\bar{C}C)_R$	$[_C that]_C$	—
$(S)_L$	—	$S\bar{C}^*$
$(S\bar{N})_L$	$[_S$	$S\bar{C}^*$
$(S\bar{N}D)_L$	$[_{\bar{N}}$	$S\bar{C}^*$
$(S\bar{N}D)_R$	$[_D the]_D$	$S\bar{C}^*$
$(S\bar{N}N)_L$	—	$S\bar{C}^*$
$(S\bar{N}N)_R$	$[_N boy]_N$	$S\bar{C}^*$
$(S\bar{N})_R$	$]_{\bar{N}}$	$S\bar{C}^*$
$(S\bar{V})_L$	—	$S\bar{C}^*$
$(S\bar{V}V)_L$	$[_{\bar{V}}$	$S\bar{C}^*$
$(S\bar{V}V)_R$	$[_V amazes]_V$	$S\bar{C}^*$
$(S\bar{V}\bar{N})_L$	—	$S\bar{C}^*$
$(S\bar{V}\bar{N}D)_L$	$[_{\bar{N}}$	$S\bar{C}^*$
$(S\bar{V}\bar{N}D)_R$	$[_D the]_D$	$S\bar{C}^*$
$(S\bar{V}\bar{N}N)_L$	—	$S\bar{C}^*$
$(S\bar{V}\bar{N}N)_R$	$[_N girl]_N$	$S\bar{C}^*$
$(S\bar{V}\bar{N})_R$	$]_{\bar{N}}$	$S\bar{C}^*$
$(S\bar{V})_R$	$]_{\bar{V}}$	$S\bar{C}^*$
$(S)_R$	$]_S$	$S\bar{C}^*$
$(S\bar{C})_R$	$]_{\bar{C}}$	—
$(S\bar{V})_L$	—	—
$(S\bar{V}V)_L$	$[_{\bar{V}}$	—
$(S\bar{V}V)_R$	$[_V bothers]_V$	—
$(S\bar{V}\bar{N})_L$	—	—
$(S\bar{V}\bar{N}D)_L$	$[_{\bar{N}}$	—
$(S\bar{V}\bar{N}D)_R$	$[_D the]_D$	—
$(S\bar{V}\bar{N}N)_L$	—	—
$(S\bar{V}\bar{N}N)_R$	$[_N man]_N$	—
$(S\bar{V}\bar{N})_R$	$]_{\bar{N}}$	—
$(S\bar{V})_R$	$]_{\bar{V}}$	—
$(S)_R$	$]_S$	—
F	#	—

subconstituents regardless of recursion. The state names of MAFPs also directly reflect the grammatical relation (if any) of the constituent undergoing parsing (see Chomsky, 1965, p. 71), so that the device M of the section above requires no special routine to determine whether it is parsing, for example, a subject noun phrase or an object noun phrase. M is parsing a subject noun phrase with respect to G if and only if it is in states beginning $(S\bar{N}\ldots$, and a direct object noun phrase if and only if it is in states beginning $(S\bar{V}\bar{N}\ldots$.

D. TERENCE LANGENDOEN

The fact that access to a PDS is required for parsing not only CE structures, but also right-embedding (RE) and left-embedding (LE)[11] ones as well, follows from the fact that derivations of RE and LE structures with respect to any grammar that generates an infinite bracketing language are CE. In the case of RE structures, the labeled right brackets of the recursive symbol provide the necessary right-hand context for CE; for LE structures, the labeled left brackets provide the necessary left-hand context for CE. Thus, if $A \xrightarrow{*} \phi A$ is a subderivation with respect to a RE-CFPS G, where ϕ is nonnull, then $A \xrightarrow{*} \phi' A \psi$ is a subderivation with respect to G_B, where ϕ' is nonnull and where ψ consists of a nonnull string of right brackets; similarly, if $A \xrightarrow{*} A \psi$ is a subderivation with respect to G, where ψ is nonnull, then $A \xrightarrow{*} \phi A \psi'$ is a subderivation of G_B, where ψ' is nonnull and where ϕ consists of a nonnull string of left brackets. Since human beings do not have access to an unlimited PDS for parsing sentences, it follows that beyond some finite degree m of embedding, they must be unable to keep track of the number of recursions in LE and RE structures, and hence of the syntactic and semantic relations among their parts (the same, of course, is also true of CE structures).[12]

6. AN EXPLANATION FOR THE UNACCEPTABILITY OF EMBEDDING CONSTRUCTIONS IN NATURAL LANGUAGES

It has been known for some time that the human sentence recognition device is incapable of processing sentences of natural languages with greater than degree 3 or 4 of CE. From the foregoing discussion, it should also be the case that that device is unable to assign structural descriptions (say in the form of labeled

11. The terms "right embedding" and "left embedding," rather than the more customary designations "right branching" and "left branching," are used to emphasize the fact that we are dealing here with recursive structures, and also to highlight the parallelism with center embedding.

12. We can think of a perceptual or production model that incorporates a MAFP as imposing a fixed, finite limit m on the degree of embedding in the sentences of the bracketing language it accepts. Thus, sentences of $L_B(G)$ can be accepted by such a model if and only if those sentences have degree m or less of embedding. If the perceptual model also incorporates a minimally augmented FA for sentences of $L(G)$, in the manner suggested by Miller and Chomsky (1963), then it also imposes a (possibly different) fixed, finite limit n on the degree of CE in the sentences it accepts. Such a model predicts that, for a given CFPS grammar G, there may be sentences of $L(G)$ that are acceptable, whose corresponding structures in $L_B(G)$ are not acceptable; namely, all those sentences with less than degree n of CE, but with greater than degree m of embedding. In the next section we point out that this prediction is borne out in natural languages, thus suggesting strongly that a model for human sentence recognition and production should incorporate devices for both recognition and production of sentences and their corresponding structural descriptions, perhaps in the form of a minimally augmented FT that pairs sentences with their structures with respect to the internalized grammar.

bracketings for surface strings) to sentences with greater than some fixed finite amount of embedding, whether left, right, or center. Now, it may be observed that sentences of natural languages, like English, with degree of LE or RE greater than 3 or 4, are almost invariably produced with intonation breaks that do not correspond to the constituent structure assigned by the syntactic component of the grammar.[13] This readjustment of surface constituent structure effectively reduces multiple RE and LE structures to a kind of coordinate structure, in which the degree of embedding is reduced to degree 1. We take the fact that such readjustment is almost invariably performed in case the degree of embedding is greater than 3 or 4 to mean that the corresponding RE and LE structures are unacceptable, and the reason such structures are unacceptable to be that they cannot be recognized by the human sentence recognition device, since the latter incorporates a MAFP with a severe limit on the amount of PDS available to it for keeping track of embedding. In English, this readjustment of constituent structure has been specifically noted for RE structure of the type illustrated in (5).

(5) (a) the book that was on the table that was near the door that was newly painted (Chomsky, 1961, p. 127)

(b) This is the cat that caught the rat that stole the cheese. (Chomsky, 1965, p. 13; Chomsky and Halle, 1968, p. 372)

The structure assigned by the syntactic component of English grammar to the sentence (5b) is that given in (6a) (with irrelevant details omitted); however, such sentences are usually phrased as if they had the coordinate-like structure indicated in (6b).[14]

(6) (a) [$_S$this is [$_{\bar{N}}$the cat [$_S$that caught [$_{\bar{N}}$the rat [$_S$that stole the cheese]$_S$]$_{\bar{N}}$]$_S$]$_{\bar{N}}$]$_S$

(b) [$_S$ [$_S$this is [$_{\bar{N}}$the cat]$_{\bar{N}}$]$_S$ [$_S$that caught [$_{\bar{N}}$the rat]$_{\bar{N}}$]$_S$ [$_S$that stole the cheese]$_S$]$_S$

Since the relation between structures like (6a) and (6b) is systematic, we may assume that there is a linguistic rule that relates them. Following Chomsky and

13. As Chomsky (1965, pp. 13–14) puts it: "there are no clear examples of unacceptability involving only left-branching or only right-branching, although these constructions are unnatural in other ways—thus, for example, in reading the right-branching construction [(5b)], the intonation breaks are ordinarily inserted in the wrong places (that is after 'cat' and 'rat', instead of where the main brackets appear)...But it is unclear why left- and right-branching structures should become unnatural after a certain point, if they actually do." The hedge at the end of this passage presumably reflects the fact that Chomsky was not aware at the time of any "unnatural" LE constructions. As we observe below, the unnaturalness in question does extend to LE constructions.

14. That is, the embedded clauses become sisters of the matrix clause. This occurs whenever the embedded clauses are the rightmost constituents of the matrix. When the embedded clauses are internal to the matrix clause, then the embedded clauses become daughters of the matrix clause. Since the nature of the adjunction can be determined from the configuration of the input, we shall say nothing further about it here.

Halle (1968), we may call such a rule a readjustment rule (RR), about which class they have this to say:

> It seems clear that the grammar must contain readjustment rules that reduce surface structures, but it is very difficult to separate the study of these processes from the study of the theory of performance in any principled way (p. 371).

7. THE STATUS OF READJUSTMENT RULES IN GRAMMAR

One way that the study of the processes represented by RRs might be separated in a principled way from the study of the theory of performance is by an examination of the formal properties of RRs. If they should have formal properties in common with the formal properties of grammar, and not have properties in common with the properties of the theory of performance, then we would have clear evidence of their grammatical character. Moreover, we should be able to decide whether those rules belong in the syntactic component of the grammar, or in a separate component of their own.[15] Let us therefore state formally the RR that relates (6a) and (6b); such a statement is given in (7).[16]

(7) *Embedded-Sentence Readjustment (ESR)*

$$X - S - Y$$
$$1 \quad 2 \quad 3 \quad \xrightarrow{\text{opt}}$$
$$1 \quad \phi \quad 2+3$$

Conditions: a. The A-over-A condition is inapplicable.
b. 2 is on a right branch; i.e. $1 = X'A_1 \cdots A_n$, where $A_1 \cdots A_n S$ is a B.

From an examination of the properties of ESR, we see immediately that if such a rule is in the grammar, it is not in the syntactic component, since it is not a phrase-structure rule, and since it violates at least two well-motivated principles governing the structure of syntactic transformations. First, since it must be applicable to occurrences of the category S embedded within S, the A-over-A condition (Chomsky, 1964, 1973), which governs the mode of application of every syntactic transformation, must be suspended for ESR (see condition (a)).[17] Second, the structural description of ESR requires making explicit

---

15. Obviously, the other components of the grammar—base, semantic, and phonological—may be ruled out a priori.

16. The adjunction sign "+" is to be interpreted in the manner described in note 14.

17. Note that this suspension of the A-over-A condition cannot be gotten around by having the rule apply either cyclically or anticyclically, since in either case wrong derived constituent structures would be obtained. If the rule can apply more than once to a given P-marker, it applies simultaneously.

references to the internal constituent structure of its factors, contrary to other-wise well-motivated conditions on proper factorization (Chomsky, 1961; Peters and Ritchie, 1973). Even if such reference were to be allowed for syntactic transformations, however, condition (b) would still be in violation of the princi-ple of minimal factors, according to which a nonvariable factor must either be directly affected by the transformation (deleted or adjoined to something else) or provide the immediate context for such an operation.[18] Thus RRs, or at least those like ESR, cannot be part of the syntactic component of a grammar.

From the formal properties of ESR, however, there are several excellent reasons for considering the rule to be part of grammar, rather than part of per-formance. First, like syntactic rules, ESR makes no reference to the particular relations that the constituents it applies to bear to one another: it does not matter whether the embedded sentences to which it applies are complement clauses or relative clauses; whether those clauses have complementizers or rela-tive pronouns or not; or whether all of the clauses to which it applies in a given sentence are all of the same type, are similar in internal surface structure, or are dissimilar. If the rule were one of performance, one would expect that these particular properties of embedded clauses would play a role in the statement of the rule. Also, like syntactic transformations, ESR is capable of introducing structural ambiguity, hardly a property one would expect of rules of perfor-mance. To see this, consider again (6b). Not only can that structure be derived from (6a) by ESR, it can also be derived from (8) by ESR, in which the relative clauses are "stacked" modifiers of the head noun *cat*.[19]

(8) $[_S$this is $[_{\bar{N}}[_{\bar{N}}$the cat $[_S$that caught $[_{\bar{N}}$the rat$]_{\bar{N}}]_S]_{\bar{N}}$ $[_S$that stole the cheese$]_S]_{\bar{N}}]_S$

Second, the fact that the results of applying ESR to structures in which complementizers or relative pronouns are omitted (so that the clauses are no longer morphologically marked as being subordinate), or to structures in which the embedded clauses are of very different internal form are, to varying degrees, unnatural, is to be explained on the basis of the theory of performance as applied to those results, and that fact is not to be taken as limiting the applicability of the rule. On the other hand, the fact that ESR and other RRs like it appear to be "motivated" and perhaps even "explained" on the basis of the fact that human users of natural languages have very limited capacities for parsing multi-ply embedded structures, is no different in principle from the fact that many stylistic syntactic transformations also appear to be motivated on the basis of their ability to reduce CE structures to LE and RE ones (Yngve, 1960; Chomsky, 1961, p. 126; Miller and Chomsky, 1963, p. 471). In each case, we are clearly

---

18. To my knowledge, the principle of minimal factors has yet to be discussed in detail in the literature, but it has been presented and motivated by Chomsky and others in public lectures.

19. Despite the fact that the structure of (8) appears to be LE on $\bar{N}$, the recursive category is really S, which appears always on right branches in the stacked-relative-clause construction.

dealing with rules of grammar whose general properties are ultimately constrained by the systems of language use (on this point, see also Bever and Langendoen, 1971).[20]

Third, a striking reason for considering ESR to be a rule of grammar is the fact that the rule must be modified to express the idiosyncratic fact that certain phrases containing the verb *be* may be "pied piped" (Ross, 1967) along with an immediately following embedded clause. Thus, consider the sentences in (9).

(9) (a) I believe that his objection is that the election procedures are too complicated.

   (b) I believe that his objection cannot be that the election procedures are too complicated.

In both of these examples, an intonation break may appear after the noun *objection*, indicating that *is* in (9a), and *cannot be* in (9b), may be pied piped together with the embedded clause *that the election procedures are too complicated.*[21] That the pied piping of the verb along with the clause is limited to phrases with

---

20. In other words, rules of grammar are never specific responses to usage needs. Although it may be obvious that application of a specific rule, such as Extraposition or ESR, has desirable properties from the point of view of language users in a wide variety of cases, it also happens that these rules can have effects that are quite undesirable (with the result that certain sentences in which those rules apply are felt to be unacceptable). In the case of Extraposition, although it is true that its application in the derivation of a sentence like (i) results in a more comprehensible sentence than if it had not applied (as in (ii)), its application in (iii) results in a less comprehensible sentence than if it had not applied (as in (iv)).

   (i)   It's a pity that they don't want children.
   (ii) That they don't want children is a pity.
   (iii) It suggests that they consider parenthood a drag that they don't want children.
   (iv) That they don't want children suggests that they consider parenthood a drag.

Concerning ESR, it may also be observed that when it is applied to embedded clauses, it converts them into coordinate-like adjuncts of the main clause; when applied to coordinate structures, it destroys the coordinate relationship! Thus, consider a sentence like (v).

   (v) I believe that the cat chased the rat and that the rat stole the cheese.

This has the syntactic structure as indicated in (via); since the second complement clause is on a right branch, and since the A-over-A condition is suspended, ESR can extract the second conjunct and adjoin it as a sister to the main clause, resulting in (vib), assuming pied piping of *and*.

   (vi) (a) [$_S$I believe [$_S$[$_S$that the cat chased the rat]$_S$ and [$_S$that the rat stole the cheese]$_S$]$_S$]$_S$
       (b) [$_S$[$_S$I believe [$_S$that the cat chased the rat]$_S$]$_S$ and [$_S$that the rat stole the cheese]$_S$]$_S$

21. When the *be*-phrase is pied piped, the resulting derived structure looks a bit strange, since a verb phrase is adjoined as a sister to a sentence. The node that is introduced by the adjunction operation is, of course, S, and not $\overline{V}$. If *is* is not pied piped in (9a), it still cannot be contracted with *objection*, exactly as predicted by ESR and the well-known restriction that the copula in English cannot be contracted with a preceding element in case the constituent that follows it is removed (King, 1970; Baker, 1971; Zwicky, 1971). This observation provides independent evidence for the effect of ESR.

the head *be* can be seen from an example like (10), in which case an intonation break cannot appear between the noun *objection* and the following verb.

(10) I believe that his objection remains that the election procedures are too complicated.

While it is not out of the question, it is hard to imagine why a performance theory should contain the possibility of moving elements under the conventions governing pied piping (though such a theory independently must contain rules for interpreting structures in which pied piping has taken place). For these two groups of reasons, then, we take it to have established that ESR is a rule of English grammar, and that it belongs in a distinct readjustment-rule component of the grammar. We shall discuss its position in the grammar further below.

Before taking up the question of the existence of other RRs besides ESR in the RR-component of the grammar of English, let us examine more closely the applicability of ESR to a variety of structures other than the strictly RE type exemplified in (5). We have already considered one such variety, namely that illustrated in (8). Now consider (11), which has one degree of CE, although all of the embedded clauses are introduced on right branches. Its syntactically motivated constituent structure is that given in (12a); the result of applying ESR to that structure is given in (12b).

(11) The cat that caught the rat that stole the cheese was sick.
(12) (a) $[_S[_{\bar{N}}$the cat $[_S$that caught $[_{\bar{N}}$the rat $[_S$that stole the cheese$]_S]_{\bar{N}}]_S]_{\bar{N}}$ $[_{\bar{V}}$was sick$]_{\bar{V}}]_S$
      (b) $[_S[_{\bar{N}}$the cat$]_{\bar{N}}$ $[_S$that caught $[_{\bar{N}}$the rat$]_{\bar{N}}]_S$ $[_S$that stole the cheese$]_S$ $[_{\bar{V}}$ was sick$]_{\bar{V}}]_S$

The intonation breaks predicted by (12b) seem entirely natural, so that we may conclude that ESR has properly applied in this case.

Now consider the application of ESR to the doubly CE sentence (13), in which, nevertheless, all of the embedded clauses are introduced on right branches. Its syntactically motivated constituent structure is (14a); the result of applying ESR to (14a) is (14b).

(13) The cat that the rat that stole the cheese was afraid of was sick.
(14) (a) $[_S[_{\bar{N}}$the cat $[_S$that $[_{\bar{N}}$the rat $[_S$that stole the cheese$]_S]_{\bar{N}}$ $[_{\bar{V}}$was afraid of$]_{\bar{V}}]_S]_{\bar{N}}$ $[_{\bar{V}}$was sick$]_{\bar{V}}]_S$
      (b) $[_S[_{\bar{N}}$the cat$]_{\bar{N}}$ $[_S$that $[_{\bar{N}}$the rat$]_{\bar{N}}$ $[_S$that stole the cheese$]_S$ $[_{\bar{V}}$was afraid of$]_{\bar{V}}]_S$ $[_{\bar{V}}$was sick$]_{\bar{V}}]_S$

All that ESR did in this case was to flatten the structure somewhat; obviously, since the rule cannot affect the linearization of the string of formatives in any way, it cannot reduce the degree of CE. But, the intonation breaks that the application of the rule predicts (particularly those following *cat* and *rat*) accord perfectly with the phrasing of someone who has mastered the uttering of doubly

CE structures. In other words, ESR predicts the intonation pattern of an ideal speaker, exactly as we would expect from the hypothesis that ESR is a rule of grammar.

From the discussion in section 6, we might expect that for every recursive category that appears on a right or left branch, there is a RR that raises that category to be coordinate with or immediately subordinate to the highest available occurrence of that category. This expectation is borne out. English does not happen to embed sentences on left branches; however, it does embed noun phrases on both right and left branches, and there is a RR for each of these types of embeddings. Consider first the multiple occurrence of noun phrases on right branches, as illustrated in (15). The syntactically motivated constituent structure for (15) is given in (16a); its readjusted structure, as indicated by its possible rephrasing, is given in (16b).[22]

(15) This is the friend of the daughter of the ambassador to West Germany.

(16) (a) [$_S$this is [$_{\bar{N}}$the friend [$_{\bar{P}}$of [$_{\bar{N}}$the daughter [$_{\bar{P}}$of [$_{\bar{N}}$the ambassador [$_{\bar{P}}$to West Germany]$_{\bar{P}}$]$_{\bar{N}}$]$_{\bar{P}}$]$_{\bar{N}}$]$_{\bar{P}}$]$_S$

      (b) [$_S$this is [$_{\bar{N}}$ [$_{\bar{N}}$the friend]$_{\bar{N}}$ [$_{\bar{P}}$of [$_{\bar{N}}$the daughter]$_{\bar{N}}$]$_{\bar{P}}$ [$_{\bar{P}}$of [$_{\bar{N}}$the ambassador]$_{\bar{N}}$]$_{\bar{P}}$ [$_{\bar{P}}$to [$_{\bar{N}}$West Germany]$_{\bar{N}}$]$_{\bar{P}}$]$_{\bar{N}}$]$_S$

The RR that relates (16a) and (16b), together with conditions that will be motivated below, is given in (17).[23]

(17) *Embedded-Noun Phrase Readjustment* $(\bar{EN}R)$

$$W - X - \bar{N} - Y - Z$$
$$1 \quad 2 \quad 3 \quad 4 \quad 5 \xrightarrow{\text{opt}}$$
$$1 \quad 2 \quad \phi \quad 3+4 \quad 5$$

Conditions: a. 234 is a $\bar{N}$.

   b. 3 is on a right branch.

   c. If $2 = X'$ [$_{\bar{P}}$Pr, then [$_{\bar{P}}$Pr is pied piped, and if $4 =]_{\bar{P}}Y$, then]$_{\bar{P}}$ is pied piped.

   d. There do not exist X_1, X_2, Y_1, Y_2 such that $2 = X_1 [_S X_2$ and $4 = Y_1]_S Y_2$.

Condition (a) on $\bar{EN}R$ is required to ensure that only embedded occurrences of $\bar{N}$ are readjusted. Obviously, in a sentence like (18), the noun phrase *the movie* is not adjoined as a sister to the rest of the sentence, *I saw*.

(18) I saw the movie.

The need for conditions (b) and (c) is apparent. What condition (d) ensures is that no noun phrase will be readjusted out of a sentence that is itself part of a

22. $\bar{P}$ may be read "preposition phrase." Since P has already been used as a category symbol for the possessive element *'s*, we use the symbol Pr for the category "preposition."

23. From condition (a) it follows that A-over-A is not operative; hence violation of A-over-A is not mentioned specifically in the set of conditions in (17).

noun phrase. Without such a condition, the phrase *of the ambassador* in (19) would, incorrectly, be adjoined as a sister of the full noun phrase *the man who met the friend*, but with the condition, it can be adjoined to the smaller noun phrase *the friend*, in accordance with the facts.

(19) I know the man who met the friend of the ambassador.

Finally, consider the case of noun phrases embedded on left branches, as illustrated in (20). The syntactically motivated constituent structure of (20) is given in (21a). That structure may, however, be readjusted to yield (21b).

(20) My friend's oldest nephew's favorite teacher's strangest idea is that linguistics is profitable.

(21) (a) $[_S [_{\bar{N}} [_D [_{\bar{N}} [_D [_{\bar{N}} [_D [_{\bar{N}}$my friend$]_{\bar{N}}$'s$]_D$ oldest nephew$]_{\bar{N}}$'s$]_D$ favorite teacher$]_{\bar{N}}$'s$]_D$ strangest idea$]_{\bar{N}}$ $[_{\bar{V}}$is that linguistics is profitable$]$ $_{\bar{V}}]_S$

      (b) $[_S [_{\bar{N}} [_D [_{\bar{N}}$my friend$]_{\bar{N}}$'s$]_D$ $[_D [_{\bar{N}}$oldest nephew$]_{\bar{N}}$'s$]_D$ $[_D [_{\bar{N}}$favorite teacher$]_{\bar{N}}$'s$]_D$ $[_{\bar{N}}$strangest idea$]_{\bar{N}}]_{\bar{N}}$ $[_{\bar{V}}$is that linguistics is profitable$]_{\bar{V}}]_S$

The RR that relates (21a) and (21b) is given in (22).

(22) *Left-Embedded-Noun-Phrase Readjustment (LEN̄R)*

$$W - X - \bar{N} - Y - Z$$
$$1 \quad 2 \quad 3 \quad 4 \quad 5 \xRightarrow{\text{opt}}$$
$$1 \quad 2+3 \quad \phi \quad 4 \quad 5$$

Conditions: a. 234 is a $\bar{N}$.
  b. 3 is on a left branch.
  c. If $2 = X'$ $[_D$ and if $4 = $'s$]_D$ Y', then $[_D$ and 's$]_D$ are pied piped.
  d. There are no X_1, X_2, Y_1, Y_2 such that $2 = X_1 [_S X_2$ and $4 = Y_1]_S Y_2$.

The conditions on LEN̄R are motivated on the same grounds as the conditions on EN̄R.[24]

It is possible to construct an elaborate noun phrase containing both LE and RE noun phrases, resulting in CE of noun phrases within noun phrases. A case illustrating degree 2 of CE of noun phrase is illustrated in (23). The syntactically motivated constituent structure for (23) is given in (24a), and the result of applying EN̄R and LEN̄R to that structure is given in (24b), a derived structure that provides the basis for an ideal speaker's intonation pattern for (23).

---

24. Since pied piping of the determiner and possessive nodes is obligatory (one might be able to argue that the pied piping of the preposition and preposition phrase in EN̄R is optional), one might ask why it is not done directly in the structural change of the rule itself. The reason is that ultimately we shall be replacing these specific rules by a general rule schema (see (25)), in which the pied-piping conditions are listed separately.

(23) I borrowed the friend of the ambassador to West Germany's neighbor's sailboat.

(24) (a) $[_S$I borrowed $[_{\overline{N}}$ $[_D$ $[_{\overline{N}}$the friend $[_{\overline{P}}$of $[_{\overline{N}}$ $[_D$ $[_{\overline{N}}$the ambassador $[_{\overline{P}}$to $[_{\overline{N}}$West Germany$]_{\overline{N}}]_{\overline{P}}]_{\overline{N}}$'s$]_D$ neighbor$]_{\overline{N}}]_{\overline{P}}]_{\overline{N}}$'s$]_D$ sailboat$]_{\overline{N}}]_S$

(b) $[_S$I borrowed $[_{\overline{N}}$ $[_D$ $[_{\overline{N}}$ $[_{\overline{N}}$the friend$]_{\overline{N}}$ $[_{\overline{P}}$of $[_{\overline{N}}$ $[_D$ $[_{\overline{N}}$ $[_{\overline{N}}$the ambassador$]_{\overline{N}}$ $[_{\overline{P}}$to$[_{\overline{N}}$West Germany$]_{\overline{N}}]_{\overline{P}}]_{\overline{N}}$'s$]_D$ $[_{\overline{N}}$neighbor$]_{\overline{N}}]_{\overline{N}}]_{\overline{P}}]_{\overline{N}}$'s$]_D$ $[_{\overline{N}}$sailboat$]_{\overline{N}}]_{\overline{N}}]_S$

If we now compare the statements of the three RRs that we have proposed for English: ESR in (7), $\overline{EN}R$ in (17), and $LE\overline{N}R$ in (22), we see that they have much in common, suggesting that they can be collapsed into a single RR schema. To reconcile the differences among them, we note first that the various pied-piping conditions could be specified as separate conditions on the RR schema; second, that an analogue to condition (a) on $\overline{EN}R$ and $LE\overline{N}R$ can be imposed on ESR without altering the effect of that rule, so that the structural description of ESR can be written with the same five factors at $\overline{EN}R$ and $LE\overline{N}R$; third, that whether adjunction is to the left or to the right depends only on whether the recursive category is on a left branch or on a right branch; and fourth, that condition (d) on $\overline{EN}R$ and $LE\overline{N}R$, while not appropriate to ESR, can be specified in the schema so as not to affect the operation of ESR. Without specifying again the various pied-piping conditions, the RR schema for English may be stated as in (25).[25]

(25) *Readjustment-Rule Schema for English*

$$W - X - A - Y - Z$$
$$1 \quad 2 \quad 3 \quad 4 \quad 5 \xrightarrow{\text{opt}}$$

$$1 \left. \begin{cases} 2+3 \\ \\ 2 \end{cases} \right\} \phi \left\{ \begin{matrix} 4 \\ \\ 3+4 \end{matrix} \right. \left. \begin{matrix} \\ \\ \end{matrix} \right\} 5 \qquad \begin{matrix} \text{(i)} \\ \\ \text{(ii)} \end{matrix}$$

Conditions: (a) A is a recursive category.[26]

(b) 234 is an A.

(c) (i) results if 3 is on a left branch;

(ii) results if 3 is on a right branch.

(d) If $3 \neq S$, then there are no X_1, X_2, Y_1, Y_2 such that $2 = X_1 \; [_S X_2$ and $4 = Y_1]_S \; Y_2$.

(e) Various pied-piping conditions, such as condition (c) of (17) and (22).

25. The RR schema (25) does not abbreviate all of the RRs in English, but only those involving the reduction of degree of embedding. The formation of words from syntactically separate items, such as a rule that attaches 's to the noun it immediately follows no matter what its scope is in syntactic surface structure, or even in the output of the RR schema, are also RRs that belong in the RR component.

26. It may be correct to identify the categories that satisfy condition (a) as the cyclic categories S and $\overline{N}$. Categories that appear to be recursive in surface structure, but that are not in deep structure, such as $\overline{V}$, do not appear to undergo constituent readjustment.

Note that the only English-specific aspect of the schema (25) is contained in condition (e). The structural description and change, as well as conditions (a–d), are formulated so as to suitably represent the nature of constituent readjustment in any language, and hence constitute a hypothesis about universal grammar. The notion that a schema like (25) should be universal follows from four assumptions: (i) that recursive embedding is a property of languages generated by transformational grammars; (ii) that all acceptable strings (strings whose surface P-markers have less than some small degree of CE and that are otherwise acceptable) receive phonological interpretation in performance; (iii) that the input to the phonological component consists of well-formed P-markers; and (iv) that strings whose surface P-markers have some small degree of embedding cannot be parsed, and hence cannot receive phonological interpretation in performance. Assumptions (i)–(iii) are uncontroversial, and assumption (iv) follows from Theorem 1. Hence a readjustment-rule schema like (25) must be universal.

Moreover, the structural description and change, in addition to conditions (a–c) of (25), reasonably follow from these four assumptions, in that they minimally accomplish the desired effect of reducing the degree of embedding of acceptable strings to 1 (that of coordinate structures), and hence make them capable of being parsed. Condition (d) has the further desired effect of preventing nonsentential constituents from being removed from the sentences containing them, hence limiting the disruptive effect on intelligibility that application of RRs inevitably has. Thus the schema (25), less condition (e), is a very reasonable hypothesis about universal grammar.

As we have already argued, the formal properties of RRs are quite distinct from those of syntactic transformations. Thus, we are in a position to affirm not only that schema (25) without condition (e) is universal, but also that it belongs in a separate component of the grammar, one that relates syntax and phonology, thus confirming the conjecture by Chomsky (1973, p. 254) that rules that "never change the terminal string of phrase marker but only its structure . . . can be restricted to the readjustment rule component of the grammar, which relates syntax and phonology."[27,28]

27. Downing (1973, pp. 119–120) argues that a rule he calls Complement Detachment is a readjustment rule that must precede at least one movement transformation, namely a rule he calls Matrix Embedding. He concludes that "there is [thus] no reason to suppose that such purely restructuring rules belong in a special 'readjustment' component between syntax and phonology." However, his argument for the existence of the rule of Matrix Embedding depends on his analysis of the derivation of parenthetical expressions, an analysis which is easily challenged. In particular, he gives no arguments against the analysis in which parenthetical expressions are base generated as such, and for which no rule of Matrix Embedding is required.

28. The application of readjustment rules effectively destroys the stress contrasts that motivate Bresnan's (1971, 1972) analysis of stress assignment in the syntactic cycle. Apparently, stress must be reassigned from scratch (or nearly so) in the phonological cycle if readjustment rules have operated. More study of the interaction between pre- and post-readjustment stress assignment is obviously called for.

REFERENCES

Anderson, S., and P. Kiparsky, eds. 1973. *A Festschrift for Morris Halle*. Holt, Rinehart, and Winston.

Baker, C. L. 1971. "Stress Level and Auxiliary Reduction in English." *Linguistic Inquiry* 2: 167–182.

Bar-Hillel, Y., M. Perles, and E. Shamir. 1961. "On Formal Properties of Simple Phrase Structure Grammars." Reprinted in Luce, Bush, and Galanter, eds., 1965.

Bever, T. G., and D. T. Langendoen. 1971. "A Dynamic Model of the Evolution of Language." *Linguistic Inquiry* 2: 433–463. Reprinted in this volume.

Braffort, P., and D. Hirschberg, eds. 1963. *Computer Programming and Formal Systems*. North-Holland.

Bresnan, J. 1971. "Sentence Stress and Syntactic Transformations." *Language* 47: 257–281.

——. 1972. "Stress and Syntax." *Language* 48: 326–342.

Chomsky, N. 1959a. "On Certain Formal Properties of Grammars." Reprinted in Luce, Bush, and Galanter, eds., 1965.

——. 1959b. "A Note on Phrase Structure Grammars." *Information and Control* 2: 393–395.

——. 1961. "On the Notion 'Rule of Grammar'." Reprinted in Fodor and Katz, eds., 1964.

——. 1963. "Formal Properties of Grammars." In Luce, Bush, and Galanter, eds., 1963.

——. 1964. *Current Issues in Linguistic Theory*. Mouton.

——. 1965. *Aspects of the Theory of Syntax*. M.I.T. Press.

——. 1970. "Remarks on Nominalizations." In Jacobs and Rosenbaum, eds., 1970.

——. 1973. "Conditions on Transformations." In Anderson and Kiparsky, eds., 1973.

Chomsky, N., and M. Halle. 1968. *The Sound Pattern of English*. Harper and Row.

Chomsky, N., and M. P. Schützenberger. 1963. "The Algebraic Theory of Context-Free Languages." In Braffort and Hirschberg, eds.

Downing, B. T. 1973. "Parenthesization Rules and Obligatory Phrasing." *Papers in Linguistics* 6: 108–128.

Fodor, J. A., and J. Katz, eds. 1964. *The Structure of Language*. Prentice-Hall.

Hopcroft, J. E., and J. D. Ullman. 1969. *Formal Languages and their Relation to Automata*. Addison-Wesley.

Jacobs, R. A., and P. S. Rosenbaum, eds. 1970. *Readings in English Transformational Grammar*. Ginn-Blaisdell.

King, H. V. 1970. "On Blocking the Rules for Contraction in English." *Linguistic Inquiry* 1: 134–136.

Luce, R. D., R. R. Bush, and E. Galanter, eds. 1963. *Handbook of Mathematical Psychology*, Volume II. Wiley.

———. 1965. *Readings in Mathematical Psychology*, Volume II. Wiley.

Miller, G. A., and N. Chomsky. 1963. "Finitary Models of Language Users." In Luce, Bush, and Galanter, eds., 1963.

Peters, P. S., and R. W. Ritchie. 1973. "On the Generative Power of Transformational Grammars." *Information Sciences* 6: 49–83.

Rabin, M. O., and D. Scott. 1959. "Finite Automata and their Decision Problems." *IBM Journal of Research and Development* 3: 115–125.

Ross, J. R. 1967. *Constraints on Variables in Syntax*. Indiana University Linguistics Club.

Wanner, E., and M. Maratsos. 1971. "On Understanding Relative Clauses." Unpublished paper.

Woods, W. A. 1969. *Augmented Transition Networks for Natural Language Analysis*. Report CS-1, Computational Laboratory of Harvard University.

———. 1970. "Transition Network Grammars for Natural Language Analysis." *Communications of the ACM* 13: 591–602.

Yngve, V. H. 1960. "A Model and an Hypothesis for Language Structure." *Proceedings of the American Philosophical Society* 104: 444–466.

Zwicky, A. M. 1971. "Auxiliary Reduction in English." *Linguistic Inquiry* 2: 323–336.

A Dynamic Model of the Evolution of Language*

T. G. BEVER
D. T. LANGENDOEN

For use almost can change the form of nature.

HAMLET, III, iv

1. INTRODUCTION AND SUMMARY: THE THREE LINGUISTIC CAPACITIES

A person knows how to carry out three kinds of activities with his language: he can produce sentences, he can understand sentences, and he can make judgments about potential sentences. Recent linguistic investigations have concentrated on describing the facts brought out in speakers' predictions about sequence acceptability and structural relations within and among sentences. Such predictions have been assumed to reflect directly each speaker's knowledge of his language ("competence") while the capacities to speak and understand sentences have been viewed as revealing a person's linguistic knowledge only indirectly, due to the interposition of behavioral factors ("performance").

It clearly is the case that the activities of talking and listening can obscure much of a person's linguistic knowledge; but judgments about potential sentences are also behavioral manifestations of linguistic knowledge, and as such

*This research was supported in part by the Advanced Research Projects Agency Grant No. DAHC15 and by the National Institutes of Health Grant No. 1 POL GM 16735, to The Rockefeller University. This paper is based on a presentation at the UCLA conference on Historical Linguistics in the Perspective of Transformational Theory, January, 1969. A somewhat different version of this paper appears in the proceedings of that conference (Bever and Langendoen, 1972).

Source: *Linguistic Inquiry* 2 (1971): 433–463. Reprinted by permission of the publisher.

115

are not different in principle from the more ordinary uses of linguistic structure. Even though predictions about sentences may be the most direct evidence we have concerning linguistic structures, such judgments are not entirely free from behavioral effects. Thus, linguists and psychologists can utilize three kinds of manifest speech behaviors as data relevant to the study of linguistic knowledge: speech production, speech perception, and the prediction of new structures. In this paper, we shall discuss the evidence for the interaction of the systems of speech perception and sentence prediction in the history of the English language. We shall demonstrate that the history of a language, and therefore its synchronic state as well, are the products of a dynamic interaction between the rules required for the prediction of new sentences, and the behavioral mechanisms used to process actual sentences.

This demonstration implies that certain universal features of such grammars are due to laws governing their actual use by children and adults. This is distinct from the view that all of the universal properties are internal to the predictive grammatical mechanism (e.g., the principle that transformational rules are ordered). Since language learning includes the simultaneous acquisition of behavioral and predictive structures, the ultimate structure of the predictive system is partially a function of two kinds of simplicity: simplicity of the predictive mechanism itself, and simplicity of the processes of speech perception and production.

2. THE PERCEPTION OF SENTENCES BY ADULTS AND CHILDREN

Recent psychological studies have shown that the form in which sentences are understood corresponds closely to their internal grammatical structure (Miller, 1962; Mehler, 1963). Thus, any model for speech perception includes a mechanism which isolates the internal structure corresponding to each external form (1):

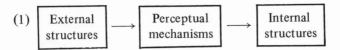

(1) External structures → Perceptual mechanisms → Internal structures

When transformational grammars were proposed, it was thought that the grammatical mechanisms were directly embedded within the operation of the perceptual mechanisms (Miller, 1962). A preliminary series of studies appeared to support this view; they showed that certain sentences which involve more transformations in the *grammatical* description of the relation between their internal and external structures are relatively hard to understand. For example, passive sentences (2b) involve one more rule than corresponding active ones (2a), and are indeed harder to understand. This was shown in many different kinds of studies; for example, McMahon (1963) demonstrated that generically true actives (2a) are verified more quickly than generically true passives (2b):

(2) (a) Five precedes thirteen.
     Thirteen follows five.

 (b) Thirteen is preceded by five.
     Five is followed by thirteen.

The basic principle at issue in these studies was that every grammatically defined rule corresponds to a psychological operation, and that therefore sentences with more rules mapping the internal onto the external structure should be relatively more complex psychologically.

However, this simple view of the relation between formal grammar and perceptual processes is incorrect. There are many examples of sentences that have relatively more transformations in their derivation and that are clearly *less* complex psychologically. Thus, in ((3)–(5)), the grammatical derivation of the second sentence (b) is more complex than the first (a), but is clearly easier to understand:

(3) (a) Harry ate the baklava that was green.
 (b) Harry ate the green baklava. (Relative Clause Reduction, Modifier Preposing)
(4) (a) That Harry liked the green baklava amazed Bill.
 (b) It amazed Bill that Harry liked the green baklava. (Subject-clause Extraposition)
(5) (a) The boy the girl the man liked hit cried.
 (b) The boy hit by the girl liked by the man cried. (Passive)

There are also various experimental demonstrations of an inverse relation between transformational and psychological complexity. Finally, recent reviews (Fodor and Garret, 1967; Bever, 1970a) have argued that the previous evidence in support of the hypothesis that grammatical transformations are part of perceptual operations is inconclusive on methodological grounds. The conclusion from all these considerations is that the perceptual mechanism which carries out the mapping operation outlined in (1) is at least partially independent of the predictive grammatical rules that relate internal and external structures. It is not the case that the perceptual mechanism is a direct behavioral exploitation of grammatical rules.

This conclusion leaves open the question of what the nature of the perceptual mechanism really is. Current research has suggested that listeners make primary use of an ordered set of perceptual strategies that directly map external strings onto their internal structures. For example, a series of experiments has given initial support to the claim that a set of perceptual strategies isolates lexical strings corresponding directly to internal structure clauses early in the perceptual process (Fodor and Bever, 1965; Garrett, Bever, and Fodor, 1966; Bever, Fodor, and Garrett, 1966; Bever, Kirk, and Lackner, 1969). These investigations have studied the perception of nonspeech interruptions in sentences with two clauses. The basic finding is that subjects report the location of a single click in a sentence as having occurred toward the point between the underlying structure clauses from its objective location. Accordingly more clicks in sentence (6b) are mislocated immediately following the main verb than in (6a). This is in accord with arguments that *the troops* is a direct object of the verb *defy* in (6a) while the entire complement sentence is the direct object of *desire* in (6b) (Rosenbaum, 1967):

(6) (a) The general defied the troops   to fight.
    (b) The general desired   the troops to fight.

Bever et al. interpret the experimental result as a demonstration of the claim that listeners know that the sequence following a verb like *desire* can begin a new internal structure sentence (as indicated by the spacing in (6b)). In contrast to this, a verb like *defy* is known to permit only a direct object immediately following it (as indicated by the spacing in (6a)); accordingly, listeners have a greater immediate tendency to establish internal structure segmentation following verbs like *desire* than they do for verbs like *defy*.

It is clear that the application of such specific lexical knowledge in perceptual segmentation is not the application of a particular grammatical rule. Rather it is the knowledge of the possible derivations associated with each word that is reflected in the perceptual operation. Similar nongrammatical perceptual strategies are sensitive to the external patterning of major syntactic categories. In particular, there is the following perceptual strategy, which is independent of grammar: (a) that a string consisting of a nominal phrase is the beginning of an internal structure sequence (i.e., sentoid); (b) that the verb phrase (optionally including a nominal) is the end of such a sequence. This perceptual rule may be stated formally as in (7):

(7) (a) X_1 Nominal $V_f X_2 \rightarrow X_1$ [$_S$ Nominal $V_f X_2$
    (b) X_1 [$_S$ Nominal V_f (Nominal) $X_2 \rightarrow X_1$ [$_S$ Nominal V_f (Nominal)]$_S X_2$

The application of strategy (7a) must precede that of (7b), in their application to certain verbs.[1]   The reason is that people have no difficulty understanding sentences like (8). However, if the right bracket were assigned before

---

1. We should emphasize that such strategies as (7) are explicitly probabilistic, and should not be confused with syntactic rules. At the moment we are uncertain as to the most appropriate formalization of the perceptual rules, and our presentation of them should be taken only as suggestive. For example, the rules in (7) assume a prior assignment of major phrase boundaries, although the experimental literature is extremely unclear on the question of whether the complete surface phrase structure is assigned initially during perception. (Cf. Bever et al., 1969) If one were to formalize the prior assignment of *Nominal* (including complements) and *Verbal* phrases within the rules, then the constraints on ordering the assignment of sentence boundaries would differ, at least for the examples under consideration. It seems intuitively likely that (7a) and (7b) apply simultaneously, moving from left to right in a sequence. However, specific verbs (e.g. noun phrase complement verbs like *believe*) appear to suspend (7b) before the second application of (7a). Bever et al.'s (1969) results suggested that such specific knowledge is indeed utilized actively during perception.

or simultaneous with the left bracket, then the incorrect initial bracketing in (9) would result, and the sentence would be incomprehensible.

(8)   John believed Bill was a fool.

(9)   [$_S$John believed Bill]$_S$ was a fool.

Thus, strategy (7a) applies first to an entire string, and then strategy (7b) applies. After application of (7a), example (8) would be analyzed, as in (10):

(10)   [$_S$John believed [$_S$Bill was a fool.

Strategy (7b) would then apply to produce (11):

(11)   [$_S$John believed]$_S$ [$_S$Bill was a fool]$_S$

Notice that (7b) is prevented from assigning a right bracket after *Bill* in (11) because (11) does not meet the structural index of (7b).

The presence of the perceptual strategies in (7) is demonstrated by the existence of many sentences in English in which they produce temporarily misleading analyses, thereby making them hard to understand. In each of the examples ((12)–(14)) below, (a) is hard to understand relative to (b) because there is a nominal-verb sequence present in its structure which does not, in fact, correspond to any internal structure cluster ((12), (14)), or which results in there being lexical material left over which cannot be assigned to such a cluster (13):

(12)   (a)   The umbrella the man sold despite *his wife is in the room.*

(b)   The umbrella the man sold despite his relatives is in the room.

(13)   (a)   *The horse raced past the barn* fell.

(b)   The horse that was raced past the barn fell.

(14)   (a)   The lecturer was believed by *John finished.*

(b)   The lecturer was believed by John not finished.

While such examples demonstrate the activity of the rules in (7), there are also experimental studies which give further direct evidence for it.[2]

2. For example, Blumenthal (1968) examined the kinds of errors that subjects make when attempting to paraphrase center-embedded sentences like (i). He found that the largest class of errors is to take the three nouns as a compound subject, and the verbs as a compound predicate. For example, (i) would be paraphrased as though it were (ii):

(i)   The boy the man the girl liked hated laughed.

(ii)   The boy, the man, and the girl liked, hated, and laughed.

That is, a simple "Nominal-Verb" schema is imposed on what is actually a complex sentence. In a related experiment, Bever (1969) found that center-embedded sentences which have plausible, but misleading noun-verb sequences (iii) in them are relatively hard to paraphrase compared with sentences not having such sequences (iv):

(iii)   *The editor authors the newspaper* hired liked laughed.

(iv)   The editor the authors the newspaper hired liked laughed.

A striking aspect of these results is that sentences like (iii) were difficult even with repeated practice.

The presence of such perceptual strategies in young children cannot be taken for granted just because they appear in adult intuitions and behavior. The main result of our investigations into the ways in which young children acquire perceptual strategies (see Bever, 1970a, for a review) is that the child from age two to five years is heavily dependent on perceptual strategies in speech perception, even to the point of overgeneralizing them to sentences to which they should not be applied. For example, within a clause, children of four years tend *more* than younger children to take the first noun as the actor, even in passive (15b) or cleft (15c) sentences in which that strategy leads to misperception:

(15) (a) *The cow* kisses the horse.
    (b) *The horse* is kissed by the cow.
    (c) It's *the horse* that the cow kisses.

Thus, while the adult has intuitive control over the application of such perceptual strategies in most cases, the child is more often at their mercy. Some of our recent experiments have also explored the basic dependence in the child on a strategy like (7). For example, we have found that children at one age tend to recall (and act out with toys) the first "nominal-verb" string that they hear, even if it is in a dependent clause (e.g., *dog jumped* in (16a), *dog fell* in (16b)). Children at another age tend to recall the main clause "nominal . . . verb" and to drop the dependent clause (they recall the *dog fell* in (16a and b)).

(16) (a) The dog that jumped fell.
    (b) The dog fell that jumped.

That is, at one stage, children assign priority on the basis of superordinate structure, while at another age children take the first nominal-verb string that they encounter. Just as the adult perceptual strategies are in a system distinct from the rules of predictive grammar, their development is partially independent of grammatical acquisition. This ontogenetic independence of the perceptual and predictive systems implies that the perceptual system could itself influence the form of the predictive system as it is learned. In the remainder of this paper we explore an example of this in the history of English: the way in which the perceptual strategy in (7) has influenced the evolution of grammatical restrictions on the presence of the relative pronoun in relative clauses.

3. THE SYNTAX OF RELATIVE CLAUSES IN CONTEMPORARY ENGLISH

The relative clause rules of English derive the external forms of (17a, b) from the underlying structure given in (17c).[3]

---

3. Well-formed relative clauses in underlying structures must contain a pronominal element that is understood to be the "same" as the noun phrase being modified. We call the modified noun phrase the "head nominal" and the pronominal element the "shared nominal."

(17) (a) Miss Hood met a ravenously hungry wolf.
    (b) Miss Hood met a wolf that was ravenously hungry.
    (c) [$_S$ Miss Hood met [$_{NP}$ *a wolf* # [$_S$ *he* Past be ravenously hungry]$_S$ #]$_{NP}$]$_S$

We assume that the transformational rules informally stated in (18) are applicable to structures like (17c) in the order given.

(18) (a) *Relative Clause Reduction.* Delete the shared nominal (see footnote 3) and tensed occurrence of *be* in initial position in relative clauses.
    (b) *Relative Pronoun Formation.* Copy the nominal in the relative clause containing the shared nominal at the beginning of the relative clause, and replace the shared nominal in this copy by the appropriate relative pronoun.[4]
    (c) *Shared Nominal Deletion.* Delete the original shared nominal in a relative clause.
    (d) *Modifier Preposing.* Move any reduced relative clause consisting of an adjective phrase ending with its head adjective to a position preceding the noun it modifies.

One can easily verify that rules (18b, c) have applied in the derivation of (17b) and that rules (18a, d) have applied in the derivation of (17a).

The formulation of the rules of Relative Clause Reduction and Relative Pronoun Formation in (18) differs from standard transformational accounts (e.g., Smith, 1964). In those accounts, Relative Pronoun Formation is obligatory, there being also a rule for deleting a relative pronoun under certain circumstances. Furthermore, the Pronoun Formation rule is standardly assumed to precede the Clause Reduction rule, so that the latter not only deletes the shared nominal and tensed *be*, but also the relative pronoun. Since there is no advantage in formulating the rules in this more cumbersome way either from a synchronic or diachronic perspective, we have chosen the form and order for these rules as given in (18). Rule (18a) is optional. Rule (18b) is generally optional,

---

The head nominal and shared nominal in (17c) are italicized. We do not consider here the difficult theoretical problem of how to state this well-formedness condition on relative clauses.

4. If the nominal containing the shared nominal is in fact just the shared nominal, then the relative pronoun is either the word *that*, or one of the interrogative pronouns *who*, *whom*, or *which* (the choice of the *who/whom* vs. *which* having to do with whether or not the shared nominal is assumed to designate a sentient being, and the choice of *who* vs. *whom* having to do with the syntactic functioning of the shared nominal in the relative clause).

If the shared nominal is wholly contained within a larger nominal expression, then the relative pronoun *whose* is chosen, and sentences like (i) are obtained.

(i) A man whose reputation I admire is looking for a job.

T. G. BEVER
AND D. T. LANGENDOEN

but is obligatory in most contexts in which the shared noun is subject of the relative clause and the finite verb of the relative clause has not been deleted. Thus, for most speakers of English the sentences of (20) are not grammatically acceptable as counterparts of those of (19):

(19) (a)　The man that wants to see the boss is waiting downstairs.
　　 (b)　The secretary discouraged the man that wanted to see the boss.
　　 (c)　There is a man that wants to see the boss downstairs.
　　 (d)　It was low wages and poor working conditions that caused the workers to strike.
(20) (a)　*The man wants to see the boss is waiting downstairs.
　　 (b)　*The secretary discouraged the man wanted to see the boss.
　　 (c)　*There is a man wants to see the boss downstairs.
　　 (d)　*It was low wages and poor working conditions caused the workers to strike.

Rules (18c, d) are, on the other hand, obligatory. Rule (18c) in particular is obligatory, since sentences which retain shared nominals within relative clauses (21) are ungrammatical (the shared nominal in the relative clause is italicized).[5]

(21) (a)　*Harry ate a baklava that *it* was slowly disintegrating.
　　 (b)　*The man that I saw *him* was wearing a polka-dot shirt.

---

5. In case the shared nominal occurs in a relative or noun complement clause within the relative clause, the sentence is ungrammatical both if the shared nominal is deleted or if it is retained:

(i)　*The choir limped through the anthem (that) the organist could not make up his mind at what tempo *it* should be played.
(ii)　*The choir limped through the anthem (that) the organist could not make up his mind at what tempo should be played.

Omission of the shared nominal in sentences such as (ii) leads to an even greater degree of ungrammaticality than its retention (as in (i)). This is due to the operation of the "Complex Noun Phrase Constraint" discussed in Ross (1967), according to which a constituent cannot be deleted under identity within a clause wholly contained within a nominal expression if the identical element is outside that expression. If the shared nominal is retained, then the Complex Noun Phrase Constraint is not violated; rather the violation is that of the obligatory Shared Nominal Deletion transformation. Obviously, the retention of the shared nominal in sentences like (i) serves to remind the speaker and hearer of the grammatical source of the relative pronoun in a situation where the syntactic complexity is so great that it is easy to forget what that source is. Ross' Complex Noun Phrase Constraint and similar "derivational constraints" in grammar (Lakoff, 1969) all seem to be reflections of perceptual strategies of one sort or another. To show this, however, would require extended discussion which would go far beyond the scope of this paper (but see also fn. 12, and Bever 1970a, b).

4. THE HISTORY OF RELATIVE CLAUSE FORMATION AND REDUCTION IN ENGLISH

It is convenient to distinguish six stages in the history of English relative clauses. Stage 1, Old English, dates from the time of the earliest manuscripts to about 1100 A.D.; Stage 2, Early Middle English, runs from 1100 to 1400; Stage 3, Late Middle English, from 1400 to about 1550; Stage 4, Early Modern English, from 1550 to 1700; Stage 5, Late Modern English, from 1700 to the beginning of this century; and Stage 6, Contemporary English.

A major general development during the first three stages was the loss of most nominal inflections by Stage 2 and verbal inflections by Stage 3. Simultaneously with these changes the structure of relative clauses was also evolving. In Stage I the element that could function as relative pronoun was the demonstrative *se* 'that', which was declinable, and which had a masculine, a feminine, and a neuter form. In Stage 2 the demonstrative as relative (which now existed only in a single indeclinable form *þæt*, a continuation of the neuter form in Stage 1), was joined by various interrogative pronouns (the modern forms of which are *who, whom, which, whose*, etc.), a situation which has continued to the present day (the demonstrative is now, of course, spelled *that*). In addition, in Stage 1, a relative clause could be introduced simply by the indeclinable relative particle (n.b. *not* pronoun) *þe*, or by the demonstrative plus *þe*. The latter was also a possibility in Stage 2; but by Stage 3 the use of the relative particle had been discontinued.[6]

In Stage 1 the shared nominal could be retained in all syntactic positions in the relative clause except in clauses introduced by neither a particle nor a pronoun; indeed in relative clauses introduced solely by the relative particle *þe*, the shared nominal could be deleted only if it was the subject of the relative clause. The situation was the same in Stage 2, except that since relative clauses could not be introduced just by the particle, the shared nominal was deletable everywhere. By Stage 3, however, the shared nominal had to be deleted if it occurred next to the relative pronoun, and was optionally deletable elsewhere. Still later (Stage 4), the shared nominal could only be retained in a subordinate clause within the relative clause; currently, the shared nominal can be nowhere retained.

We come now to a formal description of the historical development of the rule which introduces relative pronouns. As far as we can determine from the evidence cited by various grammarians,[7] at no stage in the history of English

---

6. In Stages 2 and 3 there were also relative clauses introduced by a string consisting of an interrogative followed by the demonstrative (*which that*, etc.); quite possibly, this use of *that* in second position was a continuation of *þe* in second position.

7. The grammarian who was the source for the various citations is indicated by the first letter of his surname; the number is the page on which the citation may be found in the work which is listed in the bibliography. The grammarians are Abbott (A), Curme (C), Jespersen (J), Mustanoja (M), Poutsma (P), Roberts (R), Sweet (S), Visser (V), and Wilson (W).

was a relative clause which modifies a nominal preceding the verb in its own clause allowed to begin with a finite verb.[8] That is, derivation of the sort given in (22) were never allowed:

(22) (a) the girl [$_S$she ate the baklava]$_S$ was fat.
          (Shared Nominal Deletion)
          $\longrightarrow$

    (b) *the girl [$_S$ate the baklava]$_S$ was fat.

On the other hand, it was possible up to the end of Stage 4 for a relative clause modifying a noun which followed the verb in its own clause to begin with a finite verb, so that derivations like (23) could be obtained, although such constructions were not frequent.[9]

(23) (a) Harry ate the baklava [$_S$it was disintegrating]$_S$
          Shared Nominal Deletion
          $\longrightarrow$

    (b) Harry ate the baklava [$_S$was disintegrating]$_S$

8. Two sentences from the works of Shakespeare may be cited as counterexamples to this claim:

   (i) Yet I'll move him to walk this way: I never do him wrong But he does buy my injuries to be friends, Pays dear for my offences. (A 166; Shakespeare, *Cymbeline* i, 1, 105) "... but he [who] does buy ..."

   (ii) Those men blush not in actions blacker than the night will shun no course to keep them from the light. (C 16; Shakespeare, *Pericles* i, 1, 135) "Those men [who] blush not ..."

But as Curme suggested, we may assume that the omission of the subject relative pronoun in these cases was done deliberately and consciously by Shakespeare, and that they do not reflect the rules of English syntax which he normally followed. Besides these, we have encountered very few other examples of this sort in all of English literature; one occurs in the writings of the Irish playwright John Synge:

   (iii) A lad would kill his father, I'm thinking, would face a foxy devil with a pitchpike. (V 14; Synge, *Playboy of the Western World* (1907)) "A lad [who] would kill ..."

Another (called to our attention by F. Householder) is from a recent detective novel:

   (iv) Anybody knows Harry'd say the same. (i.e. Anybody *who* knows Harry'd ...) (E. Livington, *Policeman's Lot* (1968)).

9. In Stages 1 and 2, omission of the subject relative pronoun in nonreduced relative clauses was largely limited to constructions involving the verbs *hatan* or *clepan* 'be named', and even here because of the possibility of having the object before the verb, the result was not always that the verb came first in the relative clause. For Middle English, Mustanoja (1960, 205) refers to a dissertation by G. Winkler, in which it is observed that "the relative subject-pronoun is more frequently left unexpressed in Chaucer than the object-pronoun but the ratio is reversed in Caxton." He also cites figures from a dissertation by J. Steinki on the ratio of nonexpressed to expressed object relative pronouns in the works of various late Middle and early Modern English writers. The figures he gives are Pecock 1: 950; Capgrave 53: 1250; Cely Papers 4: 172; Caxton 8: 2800; Fortescue 1: 245; Latimer 19: 3100; Bacon 15: 490; Sidney 331: 2180. From these figures, we may conclude that both subject and object relative pronoun omission were quite rare for Chaucer, Caxton, and the late ME period.

From Stage 4 to Stage 5 it became obligatory to introduce a relative pronoun into clauses modifying an object noun. In Stage 5, the subject relative could only be omitted in existential sentences like (20c) and (24a), cleft sentences like (20d) and (24b), including question word interrogative cleft sentences, either direct, as in (24c) or indirect, as in (24d).[10]

(24) (a) There are lots of vulgar people live in Grosvenor Square. (J 145; Wilde)
(b) It was haste killed the yellow snake. (J 145; Kipling)
(c) Who is this opens the door? (P 1001; Thackeray)
(d) I wonder who it was defined man as a rational animal. (J 146; Wilde)

Finally, in Stage 6, it seems that subject relative omission has become archaic or ungrammatical in existential and cleft sentences of the type (24a, b), and for some people also in interrogative cleft sentences of the type (24c, d).

Omission of the object relative pronoun, which necessarily leaves a nominal or some constituent other than the finite verb as the first element of the relative clause, has always been possible in English, although instances are very rare in Stages 1–3 (examples being even less frequent than those of subject relative pronoun omission in Stages 1–2, although in Stage 2, the formula represented in *by the faith I have to you* is fairly often instantiated). But, by Stage 4, the phenomenon had become quite common (see figures cited in footnote 9), and it is, of course, firmly established in idiomatic English today.[11]

10. Some examples which exhibit subject relative omission in relative clauses modifying direct objects can be found in the writings of certain nineteenth century novelists and poets such as Keats, Mrs. Browning, Thackeray, and Meredith, but these are deliberate archaisms. The construction has also been preserved dialectally, if we are to believe the testimony of Wright (1905, p. 280): "The relatives are; however, often omitted in the dialects, not only in the objective case in the literary language, but also in the nominative, as *I know a man will do for you*."

11. According to Visser (1963, p. 538), in about 98% of the cases of object relative omission found in early Modern English texts, the relative clause begins with a pronoun, rather than with a full nominal expression. That is, sentences like (i) are about fifty times more common than sentences like (ii):

(i) John saw the man she admires.
(ii) John saw the man the woman admires.

Visser assumes this is so for metrical reasons; the omission of the object relative (*whom* or *that*) before a pronoun insures that two weakly stressed elements do not occur together. This explanation cannot be true, however, since nominal expressions also generally begin with a weakly stressed element (*a* or *the*). The explanation probably has to do with a perceptual strategy which leads one to expect that when two independent nominal expressions of the same type (i.e., both full noun phrases or both pronouns) occur next to one another, they are part of a larger coordinate structure. The omission of an object relative before a full nominal expression modifying a full nominal expression leads to a violation of that strategy; e.g. when one hears

(iii) John saw the man the woman ——

one expects that it will be completed by another nominal, e.g., "and the child" rather than by a verb, e.g., "admires."

In brief, the historical developments in the structure of relative clause formation were the following:

(25) (a) relative pronoun not preceding the finite verb of the relative clause has always been omissible, whether the modified noun is initial within its own clause or not;

    (b) relative pronoun preceding the finite verb of the relative clause has never been omissible when the clause modifies a noun that is initial within its own clause;

    (c) relative pronoun preceding the finite verb of the relative clause is omissible through Stage 4 when the modified noun is not initial within its own clause;

    (d) after Stage 4, relative pronoun preceding the finite verb of the relative clause is not omissible, except:

        (i) through Stage 5, such relative pronoun is omissible if the modified noun is subject of existential or cleft sentence.

        (ii) for some speakers in Stage 6, such relative pronoun is omissible in interrogative cleft sentences; for other speakers such relative pronoun is never omissible (see the discussion at the end of Section 5).

(Appendix 1 outlines a synopsis of the historical developments relating to the form of the relative pronoun, the retention of shared nominals in relative clauses, the omission of the relative pronoun, and the loss of noun and verb inflections in English. In Appendix 2, examples that illustrate these developments are given, and in Appendix 3 a formal account of the rules relating to relative clause formation and reduction are given for each stage.)

5. THE ROLE OF PERCEPTUAL CONSTRAINTS IN THE EVOLUTION OF THE RELATIVE CLAUSE RULES

Recent investigations of the history of linguistic structures have sought explanations within the formal rules themselves (Halle, 1962; Kiparsky, 1968; Traugott, 1969). The goal of such investigations is to determine the way in which a linguistic change represents an "improved" grammar in formal terms. The primary attempts have been to argue that structural changes produce formally "simpler" grammars, or grammars with more general application of particular rules.

However, there is no general trend towards formal rule simplification or elaboration to be found in the developments we have discussed. Examination of the formal rules alone leaves us without any understanding of the processes which might be involved. For example, the shift from Stage 5 to Stage 6 represents a generalization of the restriction on the absence of relative pronoun in relative clauses. This generalization is represented formally as a simplification of the rule which inserts relative pronouns (cf. Appendix 3, Rule b). However, the shift from Stage 4 to Stage 5 represents a reduction in the generality of the restrictions on relative pronoun insertion since the relative pronoun is still optional before a verb in the relative clause if the head noun is preceded by an expletive construction. This loss of generalization is represented formally as an addition to the rule which inserts relative pronouns. (We emphasize that the oscillation of the formal complexity underlying the description of the relative pronoun system in English is not a consequence of our decision to treat the presence of relative pronouns as due to the operation of a single rule of relative pronoun formation, as opposed to an early rule of formation and then optional deletion proposed in previous accounts (Smith, 1964). If one adopted the previous solution, then one would find that the formal complexity of relative pronoun restrictions decreased from Stage 4 to Stage 5 but increased from Stage 5 to Stage 6.)

Of course, we do not want to exclude the possibility that some formal aspect of the rules might be found which represents a generally observed historical shift; nor can we claim that our formalization of the developments is not potentially subject to reformulation in the light of data that we have not considered. Such a reformulation might reveal a structural characteristic which would allow a satisfactory generalization about the historical developments. However, whatever formal account is found in terms of transformational rules, it will fail to represent that the two main historical changes (26a, b) we have discussed are related:

(26) (a) Disappearance of inflections, first in nouns then in verbs.
     (b) Appearance of restrictions on the absence of relative clause markers in clauses modifying noninitial nouns.

Yet it is the presence of such a relation which can explain the historical changes in the relative clause rules. We shall assume for the moment that the loss of inflections occurred spontaneously (but see discussion below), and argue that this development was a precondition for the changes in relative clause formation; the loss of inflections created certain perceptually ambiguous constructions which were then ruled out of the language by the changes in relative clause formation.

Consider first the operation of strategy (7) in the history of English. In Old English the nominal inflections allowed relative freedom of word order, which would have reduced the usefulness of an order-bound strategy like (7). However, by Stage 2 word order had become constrained, justifying (7). The loss of inflections had strong effects on the marking of subordinate and superordinate clause relations in general and the relation of a relative clause to its head noun in particular. First, it was apparently the case in Old English as well as in Modern English that the first "Nominal Verbal" sequence in a sentence was almost always part of the main clause unless specifically marked otherwise. Thus, if

T. G. BEVER
AND D. T. LANGENDOEN

the first verb introduced a relative clause, there had to be some marker present in the surface structure.[12]   Such a constraint must exist if the perceptual principles in (7) are to be maintained. If there were no marker on a relative clause modifying an initial noun, then it would be confused with the main clause of the sentence, as in (20a).

Sentences in which the verb initial relative clause modified a nonsubject noun would have created little ambiguity in Stage 1, first because the reliance on strategy (7) was less justified than in later stages, and secondly because the noninitial nominals were marked by their case endings as nonsubject.[13]   However, as inflections dropped and ordering constraints and strategy (7) became more important, relative clause constructions with no subject pronoun modifying initial nouns became perceptually complex. For example, by Stage 2 a construction like (23a) would be treated by strategy (7) as though it were a construction like (8) and would be assigned the same perceptual bracketing as shown in (11). That is, in (23b) *the baklava was disintegrating* would be segmented together as the sentential object of *Harry ate*. Or, in example (3a), Appendix 2, Stage 2-3, *a cherl was in the town* would have segmented together as the sentential object of *he sente after*. Such incorrect initial perceptual segmentations would make such constructions complex to understand. However, a certain amount of such perceptual complexity was tolerated, since as examples like (12)-(14) show, one cannot require of a language that it never generate a sentence which violates a perceptual generalization, only that the internal organization of actually uttered sentences be perceptually recoverable *in general*.[14]   The behavioral importance of the segmentation ambiguity in-

12. This sort of restriction on the surface structure expression in internal relations could be interpreted, following Perlmutter (1971), Lakoff (1969), Ross (1967), and Langendoen (1970), as an example of an "output constraint" which restricts the kind of derivation which is possible from an internal relative clause to an external form. We see nothing wrong with such a formulation except that it merely restates the facts at issue. Our quest is to explain such features of sentences rather than enumerate them. For example, Bever (1970b) has suggested that it is characteristic of such "output constraints" that they reflect general perceptual processes which are true of the perception of stimuli other than language. The observation that an initial subordinate "nominal-verbal" is always marked as such by the end of the verb phrase was suggested to us by R. Kirk.

13. It has been claimed that order dependent sentence syntax can appear early in the language of all children, even those learning a highly inflected order free language (cf. Slobin, 1970, for a review). Thus, a strategy like (7) may be used to some extent in all languages, even those where its use is limited by relative freedom of word order.

14. It is interesting to note that in all the cases of unmarked relative clauses in OE that we have found in the texts in which the object noun is object of a finite verb and confusable with a nominative, the relative clause verb is either a form of *be* or a modal. That is, the allowed ambiguity may have been restricted even further than we claim either by actual grammatical rule or simply by conventions of usage. This interpretation of the constraint would be further supported if it is true that sentences which began in initial nouns in the objective case could have a relative clause following with verb initial but without any relative clause marker, e.g. (i):

(i) Him likes me nobody likes.

creased as the number of alternative ways of marking a relative clause diminished to the interrogative relative pronoun and the indeclinable demonstrative *that* by the end of Stage 3. During Stages 2 and 3 the low frequency of subject pronoun omissions in actual usage implies that their perceptual complexity was only occasionally an issue for speakers. Consequently, these perceptually complex constructions died out gradually, rather than disappearing abruptly.

In sum, we interpret the appearance of an obligatory relative clause marker on non-initial nouns that are subject of the relative clause as a gradual response to the increase in perceptual ambiguity occasioned by the loss of declensions. In our view the two historical trends in (26a) and (26b) are directly related since the first is a sufficient motive for the second. As the number of false $NV =$ *Subject Verb* segmentations determined by perceptual strategy (7) became too great the independent marking of the relative clause became obligatory. This development stands as an example of the effect of behavioral mechanisms on the formal rules, in which the rules changed so as to accommodate the perceptual strategies.

However, rule simplification is also a motivating force in linguistic change. For example, the restriction on the obligatory presence of the relative pronoun is becoming increasingly general, such that it includes cases where the perceptual mechanisms would not lead to semantically inappropriate segmentation. Consider the sentences in (27):

(27) (a) ?? $\left\{ \begin{array}{l} \text{It's} \\ \text{There's} \end{array} \right\}$ a boy wants to see you.

   (b) ? Who is $\left\{ \begin{array}{l} \text{there} \\ \text{it} \end{array} \right\}$ wants to see me?

According to the data we have collected, sentences like (27a) are grammatically unacceptable for most speakers and sentences like (27b) are unacceptable for a subset of those speakers.[15] Consider the operation of perceptual strategies (7) on the last part of a sentence like (27a):

Cases like this would not have run afoul of the segmentation strategies like those in (7) since the fact that the first noun is not in the nominative case marks that it cannot be subject of any following verb. So far we have not found any data that would decide this question.

15. All of the intuitions in this section of our discussion are relatively evanescent. We suggest to the reader that he always compare each sentence in its versions with and without the relative clause marker in order to convince himself that our statements are correct, at least about the relative acceptability of the sentences. For example, in our dialects the difference in acceptability between (27a) and (a') is greater than the difference between (27b) and (b'). Indeed, while it is clear that (a') is more acceptable than (27a), it is not at all clear to us that (b') is more acceptable than (27b).

(a') $\left\{ \begin{array}{l} \text{It's} \\ \text{There's} \end{array} \right\}$ a boy $\left\{ \begin{array}{l} \text{who} \\ \text{that} \end{array} \right\}$ wants to see you.

(b') Who is $\left\{ \begin{array}{l} \text{it} \\ \text{there} \end{array} \right\}$ $\left\{ \begin{array}{l} \text{who} \\ \text{that} \end{array} \right\}$ wants to see me?

Note that the acceptability of (27a) is increased if *boy* is given contrastive stress.

(28) There is [$_S$a boy wants to see you]$_S$

It is important to note that this segmentation is appropriate to the meaning of the sentence, unlike the inappropriate segmentations which the strategy would yield with cases like ((12)-(14)). (27a) is synonymous with (29):

(29) A boy wants to see you.

That is, in cases like this operation of strategy (7) interferes little with the recovery of the appropriate internal grammatical relations. What is lost by such a preliminary segmentation of (27a) is the information that the sentence is an existential statement about *a boy*. This information however, is uniquely recoverable from the expletive use of the initial word *there*.[16]

Given that cases like (27a) and (27b) do not involve perceptual difficulty, we must ask why they appear to be in the course of becoming ungrammatical. We interpret this active development as due to the pressure for simplification of a rule of predictive grammar—that is, if both cases like (27a) and (27b) required a relative pronoun in all cases, then the relative pronoun formation rule (18c) would be as stated in Appendix 3 for Stage 6 but without any qualifications. Thus, this generalization can be taken as an instance in which the pressure to simplify the predictive rules is currently forcing a grammatical restructuring.

THE MUTATIONAL BASIS OF LINGUISTIC EVOLUTION AND LINGUISTIC UNIVERSALS

We have argued that the constraints which a child and adult have on the utilization of language in speech behavior limit the kind of sentences that are understood and therefore restrict the kind of grammatical structures which are learned. The historical relation between the loss of inflections and restrictions on relative clause formation exemplifies the historical competition between what makes a language easy to learn and what makes it easy to use. Between the 11th and 15th centuries the disappearance of most inflections simplified the learn-

---

16. If the locative use of *there* is intended then the absence of the relative marker involves a much less acceptable sequence, because the operation of strategy (7) on (i)

(i) (Over) there is the boy wants to see you.

leads to a nonsynonymous sentence (ii).

(ii) The boy wants to see you.

Notice that the cases with expletive *there* and *it* ought to have caused trouble in OE as well, since the initial noun is in the nominative case and therefore should have been segmented as the subject of the following verb. However, as we are arguing for modern English, this segmentation would not have involved a semantically inappropriate segmentation of the first clause.

ability of the language by reducing the number of lexical classes and suffix systems. Similarly the universality of the absence of the shared nominal in relative clauses also made the predictive rules easier to master. However, both developments increased the perceptual complexity of individual sentences. First, inflectional systems and lexical class markers carry a great deal of information as to the internal relations in any given sentence. Second, the combined loss of the oblique inflections on noninitial object nouns and the loss of all shared nominals created a perceptually confusing construction—a relative clause on a noninitial object noun. The possibility of such constructions had a gradual effect during Stages 2 and 3, when their actual frequency was low. Finally the perceptual difficulty was resolved in the 15th century by the restrictions on the presence of the relative pronoun in such constructions. This development constituted an increase in the grammatical complexity (and a decrease in the corresponding "syntactic regularity"). Finally, the modern generalization of the restrictions represent a grammatical resimplification.

These developments in the past millennium are not susceptible to any generalization about the evolution of formal grammars as such. No tendency appears *always* to simplify rules or to maximize a formal property of the rules, such as the extent to which the output of one rule is part of the input to a subsequent rule (cf. Kiparsky, 1968, for a discussion of this principle as a formalized motivating force underlying certain linguistic developments). Thus, while a plausible account can be found in the consideration of the interaction of the ease of learning and of understanding the language, the structure inherent to the formal account of what is learned and perceived does not itself reveal any plausible formal account of the historical changes.

Recent linguistic theorists have drawn a rigid distinction between linguistic structure ("competence") and speech behavior ("performance"). The corresponding theories of linguistic evolution have concentrated on the changes that take place within linguistic structure. The main proposal has been that suggested by Halle (1962) that children *restructure* their predictive grammar to provide simpler accounts of the language they hear than in the grammar of their parents. This presupposes that new forms appear in languages spontaneously (at least from the standpoint of the predictive grammar) which then motivate a grammatical restructuring. This picture of linguistic change is outlined in (30):

(30) *Stage*   *Sentence Types*   *Grammatical Structures*
     (a)   a . . . . . z   A . . . . Z
     (b)   a . . . . . z $+ \phi$ A . . . . Z $+ \emptyset$
     (c)   a . . . . . z $+ \phi$ A' . . . . Z'

On this view there is a period when adults may have one grammar (e.g., (30b)) while children in the same community have advanced to a restructured grammar (e.g., (30c)).

The application of this model to the facts we have discussed would be the following (in part). There was a period of time in which sentences like (24b, c, d) were all grammatical; i.e., the subject relative pronoun did not have to be expressed when the clause modified an object nominal or a nominal following *be* in an existential or cleft sentence. Relative Pronoun Formation was therefore obligatory only under the conditions listed in (31):

(31) Add the appropriate relative pronoun obligatorily to a relative clause which begins with the shared nominal and finite verb and which modifies a noun which precedes the verb in its own clause.

Somewhat later, however, sentences like (24b) became very infrequent (and presumably were viewed for a time as stylistic anachronisms). According to the theory of linguistic change we outlined above, there was a period when people learned the system described in (31) as children, but then added a rule to the end of their grammar, so that sentences like (24b) would be marked as ungrammatical. Such a rule is described in (32):

(32) Add the appropriate relative pronoun obligatorily to a relative clause which begins with a finite verb and which modifies a noun which is an object of the verb in its own clause.

The complexity of a grammar which contains rule (18c) with the stipulation given in (31) and rule (32) is quite great, since rule (32) redoes obligatorily what rule (18c) does optionally. Thus, the children who heard adult speakers of the system described in ((31)-(32)) would restructure it to the simpler grammar containing the provision described in (33) as a condition under which rule (18c) is obligatory:

(33) Add the appropriate relative pronoun obligatorily to a relative clause which begins with the shared nominal and a finite verb and which modifies a noun which either precedes the verb in its own clause or which is an object of the verb in its own clause.

This general model of linguistic evolution-by-simplification involves three claims:

(34) (a) children can replace learned grammatical structures while adults can only add rules to already learned structures;
    (b) grammars learned by children are maximally simple representations of the linguistic forms the children experience;
    (c) new linguistic forms appear spontaneously.

The first claim (34a) is related to the psychological hypothesis that there is a "critical period" for "creative" language learning which cuts off at about age 12. After that point new language learning is viewed as a relatively artificial process in which it is easier to learn new forms as a function of old structures rather than restructuring the already learned grammar de novo. This hypothesis has both clinical and anecdotal evidence in its favor (cf. Lenneberg, 1968). However, it is a moot point whether or not children from two through twelve years of age are themselves willing to restructure their own grammars totally when presented with new linguistic forms. Recent investigations of the development of grammatical structure (at least as revealed by speech production (cf. Brown, 1965; Bellugi, 1967; Bloom, 1970) have demonstrated that the child's linguistic ability itself developes at each point by minimal changes in highly articulated grammatical rules. Thus, the fact that the adult appears not to be able to change his grammar in a major way may also be true of the child at every point in his language development: it may simply be the case that during the ten years that the child is acquiring language he has the ability to perform many more slight grammatical restructurings than an adult. That is, principle (35) governs the restructuring that a child will carry out at each point.

(35) The child's grammar at one stage is a minimal change from the grammar at the preceding stage.

(35) raises an old theoretical problem: what constitutes a "minimal" change in grammatical structure? Detailed examination of the ontogenetic restructurings in the course of language acquisition may provide some empirical data which will clarify this theoretical question.

Proposal (34b), that children always learn the maximally "simple" grammar, would provide a natural basis for constraining the extent of restructuring that a child applies to his own grammar when he hears linguistic forms that are novel to him. The problem left open by (34b) is this: how does a child decide which of the sentences he hears are relevant data for a grammatical restructuring and which are not? Clearly if a child is presented with a foreign language at age four he does not learn it as a function of his already mastered linguistic structures: he recognizes intuitively that the difference between the foreign language and what he knows already is so great that it must be considered as entirely distinct (even if the same people in his environment speak both the first and second language). Presumably at each point in his speech development, there are certain possible additions to his first language that he will also be unable to learn as part of his language because their grammatical description represents too far a departure from the grammar he has already mastered. Thus, the possible novel forms that a child will try to take account of within his grammar are limited in part by the following sort of principle (36):

(36) Neologisms that are recognized by children as motivating a restructuring, must (a) be comprehensible and (b) imply grammatical structures that are "close" to the already learned structure.

Of course, like (35) this leaves open the definition of structural "closeness."

The third proposal, (34c), that neologisms occur, is not intended as an explanation of their occurrence nor of their form. No doubt new forms may be introduced into a language by cross cultural contacts, as well as by creative individuals within the culture. Whatever the source of a particular neologism the problem remains to characterize the general constraints on what kind of neologisms are likely to occur. Part of the argument in the present paper is that nonstructural behavioral constraints modify linguistic evolution by their presence in the language learning child. An additional way in which these behavioral systems influence language change is by limiting the neologisms that adult speakers themselves will produce and accept as "semisentences". Clearly semisentences (potential neologisms) which are incomprehensible or which violate some general behavioral laws will tend not to be uttered or picked up as part of a new argot (37):

(37) Possible neologisms are limited by the systems of speech behavior ("performance").

The main burden of this paper has been to point out that language learning and linguistic evolution are not merely the learning and evolution of grammatical structure, but also of the perceptual and productive systems for speech behavior. The novel structures that the child recognizes as relevant motivation for restructuring his grammar must be sentences he can (at least partially) understand, desire to say, and learn from. Thus, we can see that there are at least two sorts of requirements that the child applies to a novel sentence before attempting to modify his grammar to predict it: (1) it must be comprehensible in some way; (2) its grammatical description must not be radically different from the grammar he has already mastered.

On this view linguistic evolution is interpreted as an interaction between systematically constrained neologisms and an ontogenetically shifting filter in the child: those neologisms that are appropriate to the particular stage in the child "survive"; they are picked up by the child and incorporated within the predictive grammar of his language. In this sense the effect of linguistic neologisms is analogous to the role of biological mutations in species evolution: their form is somewhat constrained by existing synchronic structures and if they create a structure which is too much at variance with existing structures they "die out" and do not become part of the structural evolution. In brief, the linguistic future is highly constrained by the structural and behavioral systems implicit in the linguistic present.[17] One consequence of this is that certain

17. Such a view allows us to interpret the occurrence of particular developments in one language and their nonoccurrence in a closely related language. For example, German is highly inflected, such that singular nouns are uniquely marked as being in the objective case if they are not the internal structure subject of their verb. Yet relative pronouns may not be dropped in German sentences analogous to those in (24) above. This would seem to be at variance with our explanation of the deletability of relative pronouns in those positions in Old English as allowable because of the presence of noun inflections at the time. That is, while Old English had a rule for deletions of relative pronouns in certain positions German has no such rule. Thus to delete a relative pronoun in German even in positions which would not create perceptual confusions would be to change an exceptionless rule into a variable one. (Notice that the argument has the same form if one takes the view that relative pronouns are transformationally introduced in German since there is no rule that

universals of language which appear to be aspects of synchronic "linguistic structure" have sources in the ways in which language is learned and used. There is other evidence that this theoretical entailment of our empirical investigation of the history of English is correct (see Bever, 1970a, 1970b; Langendoen and Bever, 1973 for empirical investigations of the ways in which linguistic structures can be interpreted as linguistic reflections of cognitive structures).

Our investigations also bear on several issues which have been of traditional interest for all students of linguistic change: (1) the notion of "functional load" as an explanation for linguistic developments, (2) the claim that languages tend to change from dependence on inflections to express internal relations to dependence on superficial word order, and (3) the relative importance of factors external and internal to a culture in triggering linguistic change.

1. Various scholars have appealed to the notion of "functional load" as an explanation for the appearance of particular changes in the evolution of a language (cf. Martinet, 1962). Basically, the proposals depend on a notion of optimum distribution of information-bearing features in a language: if a particular sound or distinctive feature becomes too important in distinguishing words or sentences, then the disproportion of the "functional load" on that sound or feature can be taken as "forcing" a restructuring of the language so that other units or sentences can take over some of the information load. The interest of such arguments depends entirely on the postulated nature of the manner in which functional load is optimally distributed. Clearly, maximum equality of distribution across sound types or syntactic constructions is not a linguistic optimum: many languages reveal large disproportions between the most and least frequent structures. Our arguments in this paper suggest that optimum frequency of a construction or informational load must be measured vis-à-vis the particular mechanisms for language perception and production. With this proviso, we agree with those who argue that the motivation for linguistic change can be found partially in the ways in which the structure of language is used. However, our position is that it would be circular to define language structure in terms of its function (cf. Martinet, 1962) or function in terms of structure (cf. Kiparsky, 1972). Rather, the two systems of linguistic organization must be defined and studied independently in order to understand how they interact within the speaking child and adult. Our advantage today over

---

deletes them.) That is, if an adult or child makes a slip of the tongue in German and produces a relative clause without a relative pronoun it tends not to be picked up as a productive neologism since it is too much at variance with the existing linguistic structure. It would be tempting to argue for a principle like (a) as a specific subpart of (36), but the evidence is far too scanty to do any more than suggest it as a hypothesis for further investigation.

    (a) Changing an ungoverned (universal) rule into a governed rule (optional or restricted to certain environments), is not a minimal grammatical change.

Also, we have no explanation at present for why relative pronouns could be omitted in the older Germanic languages generally, e.g., Old High German, Old Saxon, etc., but not in modern German (cf. Williams, 1970; Bever and Langendoen, 1972, for further discussion).

T. G. BEVER
AND D. T. LANGENDOEN

earlier scholars concerned with this interaction is that we have available independently motivated theories of linguistic structure and speech performance.

2. The more explicit and unique the markers of the internal relations are in
the external sequence, the easier the sentence is to perceive. For example, a
language in which the first noun is always the internal subject would be perceptually simple, as would a language in which the subject is invariably marked
by one sort of case marking while the object is marked by another, regardless
of their order. While there may be no language which is entirely dependent on
the use of case markings or entirely dependent on surface order, Old English
was a relatively extreme case marking language with a variety of inflectional
paradigms.

From the standpoint of language learning it is clear that a rich inflectional
system is a mixed blessing. On the one hand, if the inflectional system is extremely general and without exception then the child need learn only one
inflectional system for nouns and for verbs and then can apply it ubiquitously.
However, it has been claimed (Jespersen, 1940, p. 59) that even if inflections
are small in number at one stage, they tend to multiply and become differentiated into many different systems of inflection which vary according to the
syntactic, semantic, or phonological property of each lexical item. Once learned,
such a varied inflectional system may increase the perceptual simplicity of the
language as a whole, since the inflectional endings would then carry partial
lexical class information. However, the learning problem itself is considerably
complicated. Many authors have noted that even in an inflectionally simple
language like modern English, children go through a period of great difficulty
with exceptional forms for which they overgeneralize the inflectional regularities
(e.g. they say "wented" instead of "went" or "childrens" instead of "children").
A language in which there is greater variety of inflectional classes than modern
English must be more difficult to learn, at least in that respect.

Old and Early Middle English had a large variety of distinct paradigms of
noun declension. Thus the child was faced with a formidable learning task.
When the opportunity for some restructuring of his language arose it is not
surprising that noun inflections were levelled. Of course, we have not explained
what the basis of the opportunity to change the language was, only why it was
utilized in this particular way.[18] Since many languages persist in maintaining

18. Subsidiary evidence for this interpretation of the loss of inflectional endings in English
is found in the fact that noun inflections disappeared before verb inflections. Indeed, a
system of verb inflection is residual in modern English. Our argument is that the basic
pressure to change the noun system came from the fact that there were so many different
paradigms. But the verb system was far more regular: there were two main classes, each
with its own system of inflectional endings. Thus, the learning problem for the verb system
was far less complex than for the noun systems, and the verb inflections dropped out of the
language at a later time. The traditional analysis of the verbal inflections would appear to
show that there were many different idiosyncratic kinds of verb inflections both among
the strong and weak verbs. These complexities have been shown to be more apparent than
real (Bever, 1963).

complex irregular declension systems we cannot claim that the proliferation of declension systems was the sole cause of the loss of all inflections. One might be tempted to argue that the real "cause" of the loss of inflections was the Germanic tendency for word initial stress. This "caused" a reduction of stress on other syllables which "caused" the ultimate loss of phonetic differentiation of the inflectional endings which "caused" their ultimate deletion. Such an "explanation" would merely beg the question as to why the inflectional endings were dropped entirely: there are many examples of neutralized vowels which remain in English and have not dropped. Thus vowel reduction may be a prerequisite for the loss of inflectional distinctions, but to take it as a direct cause would be as naive, as to take the complexity of the declension system as the single direct cause.

The evolutionary pattern of inflectional systems described by Jespersen may be interpreted as resulting from the conflict between the perceptual and predictive system of language. We assume that there is a continual evolutionary pressure for a language to maximize the recoverability of deep structure relations in individual sentences. Thus, languages tend to develop both surface order constraints (using function words) *and* inflectional markings. Consider a (hypothetical) language in an initially stable state, having both inflections and ordering restrictions. If this language has one regular declension class, it is easy to learn— but the homogeneity of a single class inflectional system contributes information only about the logical relations within a sentence and this information is also generally recoverable (by hypothesis) from surface order (and special morphemes). However, the perceptual simplicity of each individual sentence would be increased if the inflectional endings contributed differential information about each phrase and attributive relations between words separated from each other (e.g., as between adjectives and their head nouns). (Note that this would be relatively difficult to attain through proliferation of ordering restrictions— there is an upper limit to the number of possible lexical-class orders within an average size clause, but there is no theoretical limit to the possible number of inflectional classes in the lexicon.) Accordingly, the second phase of the hypothetical language is one in which the ordering restrictions are somewhat tightened and there is a large number of inflectional classes. This in turn strains the learning process, which provides the conditions for leveling all the inflections.

This description of a pattern of linguistic evolution in terms of competition between language learning and perception leaves open too many questions to count as an explanation. Rather, its value lies in articulating the explanation of the evolution into specific questions concerning the interaction of the learning and perception of language—questions which may be answered through further research.

(3) The question as to what triggers any particular linguistic change seems to us to be wildly premature. It is clear that major effects often result from such obvious observable events as the incursion of a foreign vocabulary, or a shift in stress reducing the phonetic differences in inflectional endings. Usually the

causes for such developments are attributed to extracultural factors such as being conquered by or conquering a group of speakers of a different language. However, our claim that linguistic evolution is in part a function of the balance between learnability and perceptibility raises the possibility that certain internal cultural developments can themselves motivate a linguistic shift, by changing what the language is used for. Suppose that there were a cultural change in the relative importance of the learnability of a language and its perceptibility. This would in itself place a new set of constraints on the evolution of the language since it would upset the previous balance in the culture between the language's learnability and perceptibility. For example, an increase in the relative importance of "educated forms" of sentences (e.g. sentences with many embeddings) might place a greater relative emphasis on perceptibility constraints, and motivate those linguistic shifts which increase the perceptibility of individual sentences, even though such shifts would increase the complexity of the predictive grammar which must be learned.[19]

Such questions await further empirical and theoretical investigation. The focus of this paper is to emphasize that linguistic structure and evolution are a joint function of the various systems for the use of language. Attempts to explain language universals as a formal function of just one of these systems are doomed to incompleteness whether the system considered is that of speech perception, production, or the grammatical prediction of new sentences. We cannot explain a linguistic restructuring as a function only of an out-of-balance perceptual load, or of a learning difficulty, or of the formal complexity of the predictive grammar. All of the systems of speech behavior interact in the child and naturally constrain each other as the language evolves.

19. The reader may have noticed that we do not discuss the putative effects of the interaction of structure learning and perception with the system of speech production. This is not because we think that such effects do not exist, but because the system of speech production has been largely unstudied.

APPENDIX I

Synopsis of Developments in Relative Clause Formation in the History of English, along with Some Other Developments.

PHENOMENON	STAGE					
	1 (OE) (to 1100)	2 (EME) (1100–1400)	3 (LME) (1400–1550)	4 (EMnE) (1550–1700)	5 (MnE) (1700–1900)	6 (CE) (1900–)
Relative clause introduced by:						
Particle þe	yes	no	no	no	no	no
Demons. pronoun + þe (*that* in 2)	yes	yes	no˙	no	no	no
Demons. pronoun (declinable)	yes	—	—	—	—	—
Demons. pronoun (indeclinable)	—	yes	yes	yes	yes	yes
Interrogative pronoun	no	coming	yes	yes	yes	yes
Shared nominal retainable						
Obligatorily if not subject & no rel. pronoun	yes	going	no	no	no	no
Next to rel. pron.	yes	yes	going	no	no	no
Elsewhere	yes	yes	yes	no	no	no
Subject rel. pron. form obligatory:						
On clause initial preverbal nouns	yes	yes	yes	yes	yes	yes
On obj. nouns	no	no	no	coming	yes	yes
On subjects of existential & cleft sentences	no	no	no	no	coming	yes
In interr. cleft sentences	no	no	no	no	no	coming
Nom./Acc. distinction	yes	going	no	no	no	no
Verb inflection	yes	yes	going	residual	residual	residual

APPENDIX 2. EXAMPLES BY STAGES.

Stage 1

(1) Relative clauses containing shared nominals
    a. Nænig forþum wæs, *þæt he* æwiscmod eft siþade. (V 59)
    'No one previously was there, that afterwards departed ashamed.'
    b. þonne fisc þe . . . mine geferen mid anum slege *he* mæg besencean. (V 59)
    'than a fish that . . . can sink my companions with one blow'
    c. Se god . . . þe þis *his* beacen wæs. (V 58)
    'the god whose beacon this was'
    d. We, þe *us* befæst is seo gyming Godes folces. (V 523)
    'we to whom is entrusted the care of God's people'

(2) Relative clauses introduced by se, þe and se þe
    a. Geseoh þu, cyning, hwelc þeos lar sie, *þe* us nu bodad is. (Bede's Ecclesiastical History)
    'Consider, king, what doctrine this is, which now is preached to us.'
    b. He þæt beacen geseah *þæt* him geiwed wearþ. (S118)
    'He saw the beacon that was shown to him.'
    c. Ond gif þu forþ his willan hearsom beon wilt, *þone* he þurh me bodaþ ond læreþ, . . . (Bede's Ecclesiastical History)
    'And if you henceforth are willing to be obedient to his desire, which he claims and teaches through me, . . .'
    d. Ure ieldran, *þa þe* þas stowa ær hioldan, hie lubodon wisdom. (Pastoral Care, Preface)
    'Our forebears, who previously possessed these places, they loved wisdom.'

(3) Relative clauses introduced by zero
    a. Hwa is þæt þe slog? (C16)
    'Who is that [who] smote thee?'
    b. Sum welig man wæs hæfde sumne gerefan. (C25)
    'There was a rich man [that] had a steward.'
    c. Alle mæhtiga þæm gelefes. (C 180)
    'All things are possible to him [who] believes.'
    d. Se fæder hire sealde ane þeowene Bala hatte. (J 133–4)
    'Her father gave her a maid [who] was called Bala.'
    e. Her on þys geare gefor Ælfred wæs æt Baþum gerefa. (J 133)
    'In this year died Alfred [who] was reeve at Bath.'[1]
    f. se þæt wicg byrþ (V 537)
    'He [whom] that steed bears'
    g. Wiste forworhte þam he ær wlite sealde (V 537)
    'He knew to be guilty those [to whom] he previously had given beauty.'

1. Notice that in these examples, the relative clause without an introducer modifies a subject nominal that has been inverted with its verb.

h. Bed him þet he scolde him giuen ealle þa minstre þa hæþen men hæfden ær tobroncon. (V 536)
'He asked him to give him entirely the monasteries [that] the pagans had earlier destroyed.'

Stages 2–3

(1) Shared nominal immediately following relative pronoun

a. Ther no wight is *that he* no dooth, or sei that is amys (V 59; Chaucer, *Canterbury Tales*)
'There is no person who does not do or say what is wrong.'

b. He knew sir Blamour de Ganys *that he* was a noble knyght. (V 59; Malory, *Morte d' Arthur*)
'He knew Sir Blamour de Ganys, who was a noble knight.'

(2) Shared nominal separated from relative pronoun

a. Our Lord *that* jn hevene ne Erthe *he* hath non pere. (V 59; Merlin)
'Our Lord that has no equal in heaven and earth.'

b. a jantyllwoman *that* semeth *she* hath grete nede of you. (V 59; Malory, *M. d' A.*)
'a gentlewoman who seems to have great need of you'

c. It was þat ilk cok þat peter herd *him* crau. (V 59; Cursor Mundi)
'It was the same cock that Peter heard crow.'

d. seynt lucie . . . , þat þe holy gost made *hire* so hevy þat sche myght not be draw . . . to þe bordelhous. (V 522; ab. 1400)
'Saint Lucia . . . whom the Holy Ghost made so heavy that she might not be drawn to the brothel.'

e. And this man began to do tristely in the synagoge, *whom* whanne Priscilla and Aquila herden, they token *hym*. (V 522; Wyclif)
'And this man began to behave sadly in the synagogue, who when Priscilla and Aquila heard, they took.'

(3) Subject relative pronoun omitted

a. He sente after a cherl was in the toun. (V 12; Chaucer, *C.T.*)
'He sent after a fellow [who] was in the town.'

b. Ye ryde as coy and stille as dooth a mayde, Was newe spoused. (W 41; Chaucer, *C.T.*)[2]
'You ride as coy and quiet as a maid does [who] was newly married.'

c. Ther was noon auditour coude on him winne. (J 146; Chaucer, *C.T.*)
'There was no listener [who] could beat him.'

d. This is the loue bes neuer gan. (C 184; Cotton MS)
'This is the love [that] never perishes.'

e. Whar es now Dame Dido was qwene of Cartage? (R 109; Parlement of the Thre Ages)
'Where is now Dame Dido [who] was Queen of Carthage?'

2. See fn. 1, p. 140.

    f. Where is the lady shold mete vs here? (J 147; Malory)
       'Where is the lady [who] should meet us here?'
    g. Lete fetche the best hors maye be founde. (J 143; Malory)
       'Go fetch the best horse [that] may be found.'
    h. With a knyght full sone she mette hyght Syr lucan de bottelere. (V 12; Malory)
       'She soon met a knight [who] called himself Sir Lucan de Bottelere.'

(4) Object relative pronoun omitted
    a. Sir be þe feith I haue to yow ... (V 538; Cursor Mundi)
       'Sir, by the faith [that] I have to you ...'
    b. The tresor they hadden, he it him reft. (V 538; Brunne Chronicle)
       'The treasure [that] they had, he took it from them.'
    c. He had a sone men cald Ector. (V 538; Brunne Chronicle)
       'He had a son [that] men called Ector.'

Stage 4

(1) Subject relative pronoun omitted on object noun
    a. My father had a daughter lov'd a man. (J 143; Shakespeare, *Two Gentlemen* ii, 4, 110).
    b. I see a man here needs not live by shifts. (J 143; Shakespeare, *Comedy of Errors* iii, 2, 186).
    c. I've done a deed will make my story quoted. (J 143; Otway)
    d. I bring him news will raise his dropping spirits. (J 143; Dryden)

(2) Subject relative omitted on nouns introduced by expletive constructions
    a. Some men there are loue not a gaping pigge. (J 134; Shakespeare, *Merchant of Venice* iv, 1, 47)
    b. There's one did laugh in's sleepe. (J 146; Shakespeare, *Macbeth* ii, 2, 24)
    c. 'Tis the God Hercules, whom Antony loued, Now leaves him. (J 145; Shakespeare, *Antony and Cleopatra* iv, 3, 16)

Stage 5

(1) Same as Stage 4 (1), but alleged "archaisms" (J 144)
    a. I had several men died in my ship. (J 147; Swift)
    b. I will advance a terrible right arm Shall scare that infant thunderer, rebel Jove. (J 144; Keats)
    c. You beat that great Maryland man was twice your size. (P 1001; Thackeray)
    d. I knew an Irish lady was married at fourteen. (P 1002; Meredith)[3]

(2) Same as Stage 4 (2)
    d. 'Tis thy design brought all this ruin on us. (J 144; Dryden)
    e. See who it is lives in the most magnificent buildings. (J 145; Fielding)

3. This example is not to be interpreted as containing a complement, according to Poutsma.

f. 'Tis I have sent them. (J 145; Hardy)[4]

g. Grandpa, what is it makes your eyes so bright and blue like the sky? (V 13; G. Cannan (1913))

APPENDIX 3. FORMAL ACCOUNT OF EACH STAGE.[5]

Stage 1

a. Relative Clause Reduction:

X_1 #, Pro, Tense + *be*, X_2

1	2	3	4
1	ϕ	ϕ	4

b. Relative Pronoun Formation:

X_1 #, ϕ, (þe) X_2, Pro, X_3 # X_4

$$1 \quad 2 \quad 3 \quad 4 \quad 5 \quad \Longrightarrow$$

$$1 \begin{bmatrix} 4 \\ \text{Demons} \end{bmatrix} 3 \quad 4 \quad 5$$

Condition: (i) Obligatory in case X_4 begins with V and $3 = \phi$

c. Shared Nominal Deletion:

X_1 #, (Demons), (þe), X_2, Pro, X_3

$$1 \quad 2 \quad 3 \quad 4 \quad 5 \quad 6 \quad \Longrightarrow$$

$$1 \quad 2 \quad 3 \quad 4 \quad \phi \quad 6$$

Conditions: (i) Not applicable in case $2 = \phi$; $3 \neq \phi$; $4 \neq \phi$.

(ii) Obligatory in case $2 = \phi$; $3 = \phi$.

Stage 2

a. Same as Stage 1.

b. Add Condition:

(ii) Obligatory in case þe is present.

Change Demons to $\left\{ \begin{matrix} \text{Demons} \\ \text{Interr} \end{matrix} \right\}$.

4. Jespersen (1927, 145) points out that a number of authors who use the accusative of the predicate nominal pronoun in simple sentences like:

(i) 'Tis me.

use the nominative (as in (2f)) when the pronoun is followed by a relative clause with the subject relative pronoun omitted. This observation provides additional independent evidence for the interaction of strategy (22) on grammar.

5. Note that nothing special about the history of the Relative Clause Reduction rule (18a) need be mentioned, given our decision to order that transformation before the rule of Relative Pronoun Formation (18b). The rule has remained optional in all environments throughout the entire history of English. If we were to remain with our earlier decision to have the rule follow Relative Pronoun Formation, we would find that the rule would have to be stated differently for each of the last two stages. We shall not discuss developments concerning the rule of Modifier Preposing.

c. Omit Condition (i).

Change Demons to $\left\{ \begin{matrix} \text{Demons} \\ \text{Interr} \end{matrix} \right\}$

Stage 3

a. Same as Stage 1.

b. Omit (þe) from structure index. Omit Condition (ii).

c. $X_1 \ \#, \ \left(\left\{ \begin{matrix} \text{Demons} \\ \text{Interr} \end{matrix} \right\} \right), \ X_2, \ \text{Pro}, \ X_3$

$$\begin{array}{cccccc} 1 & 2 & 4 & 5 & 6 & \Longrightarrow \\ 1 & 2 & 4 & \phi & 6 & \end{array}$$

Conditions: (i) Obligatory in case $4 = \phi$.

(ii) Obligatory in case $2 = \phi$.

Stage 4

a. Same as Stage 1.

b. Same as Stage 3.

c. Replace Conditions (i) and (ii) by:

(i) Obligatory.

Stage 5

a. Same as Stage 1.

b. $X_1 \ \#, \quad \phi \ , \quad X_2, \ \text{Pro}, \ X_3 \ \# \ X_4$

$$\begin{array}{ccccc} 1 & 2 & 3 & 4 & 5 \quad \Longrightarrow \end{array}$$

$$\begin{array}{ccccc} 1 & \begin{bmatrix} 4 \\ \left\{ \begin{matrix} \text{Demons} \\ \text{Interr} \end{matrix} \right\} \end{bmatrix} & 3 & 4 & 5 \end{array}$$

Conditions: (i) Obligatory in case X_4 begins with V and $X_2 = \phi$.

(ii) Obligatory in case $X_2 = \phi$ and X_1 ends in V (NP), unless V is in turn preceded by an expletive NP, such as *there* or *it*.

c. Same as Stage 4.

Stage 6

a. Same as Stage 1.

b. $X_1 \ \#, \quad \phi \ , \quad X_2, \ \text{Pro}, \ X_3 \ \# \ X_4$

$$\begin{array}{ccccc} 1 & 2 & 3 & 4 & 5 \quad \Longrightarrow \end{array}$$

$$\begin{array}{ccccc} 1 & \begin{bmatrix} 4 \\ \left\{ \begin{matrix} \text{Demons} \\ \text{Interr} \end{matrix} \right\} \end{bmatrix} & 3 & 4 & 5 \end{array}$$

Condition: (i) Obligatory when $X_2 = \phi$, except when $X_1 = $ Interr *it* Tense + *be*[6]

c. Same as Stage 4.

6. For those speakers of Contemporary English who, unlike us, find (24b, c) also ungrammatical, Condition (i) lacks the *except*-clause.

REFERENCES

Abbott, E. A. 1870. *A Shakesperian Grammar*. Macmillan.

Abrams, K., and T. G. Bever. 1969. "Syntactic Structure Modifies Attention During Speech Perception and Recognition." *Quarterly Journal of Experimental Psychology* 21: 280–290.

Bellugi, U. 1967. *The Acquisition of Interrogative and Negative Constructions*. Unpublished Ph.D. dissertation, Harvard University.

Bever, T. G. 1963. "The E/O Ablaut in Old English." *Quarterly Progress Report* M.I.T. 69: 203–207.

——. 1970a. "The Cognitive Basis for Linguistic Structures." In *Cognition and the Development of Language*, J. R. Hayes, ed. Wiley.

——. 1970b. "The Influence of Speech Performance on Linguistic Structure." In F. G. D'Arcais and W. Levelt, eds., *Advances in Psycholinguistics*, North-Holland. Reprinted in this volume.

Bever, T. G., R. Kirk, and J. Lackner. 1968. "An Autonomic Reflection of Syntactic Structure." *Neuropsychologia* 7: 23–28.

Bever, T. G., J. Lackner, and R. Kirk. 1969. "The Underlying Structure of Sentences is the Primary Unit of Speech Perception." *Perception and Psychophysics* 5: 225–234.

Bever, T. G., and D. T. Langendoen. 1972. "The Interaction of Speech Perception and Grammatical Structure in the Evolution of Language." In *Linguistic Change and Generative Theory*, R. Stockwell and R. Macaulay, eds. Indiana University Press.

Bloom, L. 1970. *Language and Development*. M.I.T. Press.

Blumenthal, A. L., and R. Boakes. 1967. "Prompted Recall of Sentences." *Journal of Verbal Learning and Verbal Behavior* 6: 674–676.

Brown, R. 1965. *Social Psychology*. Free Press.

Curme, G. O. 1912. "A History of the English Relative Constructions." *Journal of English and Germanic Philology* 11: 10–29; 180–204.

Fodor, J. A., and T. G. Bever. 1965. "The Psychological Reality of Linguistic Segments." *Journal of Verbal Learning and Verbal Behavior* 4: 414–420.

Fodor, J. A., and M. Garrett. 1967. "Some Syntactic Determinants of Sentenial Complexity." *Perception and Psychophysics* 2: 289–296.

Garrett, M., T. G. Bever, and J. A. Fodor. 1966. "The Active Use of Grammar in Speech Perception." *Perception and Psychophysics* 1: 30–32.

Halle, M. 1962. "Phonology in Generative Grammar." *Word* 18: 54–72.

Jespersen, O. 1927, 1940. *A Modern English Grammar on Historical Principles*, Vols. III, VII. Carl Winters Universitätsbuchhandlung.

Kiparsky, P. 1968. "Linguistic Universals and Linguistic Change." In *Universals in Linguistic Theory*, E. Bach and R. Harms, eds. Holt, Rinehart and Winston.

——. 1972. "Explanation in Phonology." In *Goals of Linguistic Theory*, S. Peters, ed. Prentice-Hall.

Lakoff, G. 1969. "On Derivational Constraints." In *Papers From the Fifth Regional Meeting, Chicago Linguistics Society*, University of Chicago.

Langendoen, D. T. 1970. "The 'Can't Seem To' Construction." *Linguistic Inquiry* 1: 25–36.

Langendoen, D. T., and T. G. Bever. 1973. "Can a Not Unhappy Person Be Called a Not Sad One?" In *A Festschrift for Morris Halle*, S. R. Anderson and P. Kiparsky, eds. Holt, Rinehart and Winston. Reprinted in this volume.

Lenneberg, E. 1967. *Biological Foundations of Language*. Wiley.

Martinet, A. 1962. *A Functional View of Language*. Oxford University Press.

McMahon, L. 1963. *Grammatical Analysis as Part of Understanding a Sentence*. Unpublished Ph.D. dissertation, Harvard University.

Mehler, J. 1963. "Some Effects of Grammatical Transformations in the Recall of English Sentences." *Journal of Verbal Learning and Verbal Behavior* 2: 346–351.

Meritt, H. D. 1938. *The Construction Apo Koinou in the Germanic Languages*. Stanford University Press.

Miller, G. A. 1962. "Some Psychological Studies of Grammar." *American Psychologist* 17: 748–762.

Mustanoja, T. F. 1960. *A Middle English Syntax*, Part 1. Société Néophilologique, Helsinki.

Perlmutter, D. 1971. *Deep and Surface Structure Constraints in Syntax*. Holt, Rinehart and Winston.

Postal, P. 1970. "On the Surface Verb 'Remind'." *Linguistic Inquiry* 1: 37–120.

Poutsma, H. 1916. *A Grammar of Late Modern English*. Noordhoff.

Roberts, W. J. F. 1937. "Ellipsis of the Subject-Pronoun in Middle English." *London Mediaeval Studies* 1: 107–115.

Rosenbaum, P. S. 1967. *The Grammar of English Predicate Complement Constructions*. M.I.T. Press.

Ross, J. R. 1967. *Constraints on Variables in Syntax*. Indiana University Linguistics Club.

Slobin, D. 1970. "Universals of Grammatical Development." In *Advances in Psycholinguistics*, F. D'Arcais and W. Levelt, eds. North-Holland.

Smith, C. S. 1964. "Determiners and Relative Clauses in a Generative Grammar of English." *Language* 40: 37–52.

Sweet, H. 1924. *A Short Historical English Grammar*, Clarendon Press, Oxford.

Traugott, E. C. 1969. "Toward a Grammar of Syntactic Change." *Lingua* 23: 1–27.

Visser, F. T. 1963. *An Historical Syntax of the English Language*, Vol. I, Brill.

Williams, G. 1970. "Restrictions on Relative Clause Reduction in German." Unpublished paper.

Wilson, L. R. 1906. *Chaucer's Relative Constructions*. North Carolina University Press.

Wright, J. 1905. *The English Dialect Grammar*. Clarendon Press.

Analogy
or
Ungrammatical Sequences That are Utterable and Comprehensible are the Origins of New Grammars in Language Acquisition and Linguistic Evolution

T. G. BEVER
J. M. CARROLL
R. HURTIG

That's the first time anybody ever sang to me like that before.
GLORIA STUART TO DICK POWELL IN *GOLD DIGGERS OF 1935*

1. INTRODUCTION AND SUMMARY

Recent linguistic discussion has focused on the power[1] of grammars needed to account for systematic variations in the acceptability of sequences. Constraints on derivations, as a formal means of describing variations in sequence acceptability,[2] have been considered. It has been proposed that 'acceptability' and 'grammaticality' are coextensive and therefore that formal derivational constraints belong within the arsenal of universal grammar. On this view, all systematic variations in acceptability judgments reflect properties of a single 'grammar.'

In contrast, it has often been argued that such constraints are due to interaction with linguistic knowledge outside the grammatical system.[3] On this view,

1. By 'power' we shall intend throughout 'descriptive power' rather than 'generative power.' See note 5, Langendoen and Bever, Chap. 9; and Bever, 1975a, Section 5.

2. "Output filters" (Perlmutter, 1972), "derivational constraints" (Lakoff, 1969; Lakoff and Ross, 1972), and "transderivational constraints" (Lakoff, 1974; McCawley, 1974).

3. The system of "ethnic style" (Labov, 1968, 1970; Ervin-Tripp, 1973); the system of speech production (Yngve, 1960); the system of memory (Miller and Chomsky, 1963; Bever, 1970); the system of speech perception (Bever, 1970; Grosu, 1971, 1972; Kimball, 1974; Tannenhaus and Carroll, 1975; Bever, 1975); the system of conversational implicatures (Grice, 1975) or nonspecific 'knowledge of the world' (Katz, 1972).

Source: This article appears for the first time in this volume.

T. G. BEVER, J. M. CARROLL,
AND R. HURTIG

sequence acceptability is a function of the interaction of grammar and other systems of linguistic knowledge and skill (see Chomsky, 1965, 1975; Bever, 1970, 1971, 1975a and 1975b for discussions). The proponents of the former, 'inclusive', view hold that any separation of grammatical facts from linguistic but nongrammatical facts is arbitrary and intuitively unmotivated. The proponents of the latter, 'interactionist', view contend that if a constraint may be adequately treated by independently motivated systems outside the grammar, its inclusion in the grammar is unwarranted and obscures the descriptive and explanatory power of the grammar. If grammars include unnecessary formal power, grammatical universals will be less constrained and make claims about the child's mind that are less precise and less testable. (See discussions of this in other papers in this volume, especially the introduction, Bever, Katz and Bever, and Langendoen and Bever.)

In this paper we explore the implications of the interactionist view for the concept of 'creative analogy' in linguistics. Creative analogy is the term that describes the emergence of new sequences in actual speech that are intuitively acceptable but marked as 'ungrammatical' by the synchronic grammar. These cases usually appear to be closely related to a fully grammatical sequence, and hence are traditionally referred to as cases that are 'analogous' to existing grammatical forms. Recently this concept has been brought into discussions of generative grammar (Chomsky, 1970) and attacked because it appears to be an *ad hoc* concept (Hankamer, 1972). The basic problem is that nobody has set constraints on *possible* analogical neologisms that can extend existing structures. Bever and Langendoen (1971, and this volume), Bever (1974, 1975b), and Carroll (1974) proposed that new sentence forms can occur if they are analyzable by the systems of speech perception and production. Since these systems are partially independent from grammatical knowledge, they allow for the creation of new, non-grammatical forms. However, the strategies in these behavioral systems are themselves based on grammatical sequences, so they naturally constrain the neologisms to be 'similar' or 'analogous' to fully grammatical forms. This view merely articulates the common-sense intuition that sometimes speakers utter and understand nongrammatical forms because of the communicative value of those forms and because they are "close enough" to fully grammatical forms.

The considerations in the present paper motivate and clarify a distinction between ungrammatical neologisms that are *usable* (i.e., utterable and comprehensible but recognized as "errors") and those that are *usable and acceptable* (i.e., intuitively accepted as an idiomatic part of the language). To quote two ungrammatical examples we shall explore in detail, (1) was an actually uttered sequence, but is clearly unacceptable upon reflection; (2) was also uttered but remains an intuitively acceptable idiom even after reflection:

(1) ? I really liked flying in an airplane that I understand how it works.

(2) Harry will try and do it.

Sentence (2) is marked as ungrammatical because it would require special formal power to generate *and* only where it is acceptable as a complementizer. 'Acceptable' and 'usable' grammatical errors have the property that they are uttered and understood through systematic failures of the mechanisms of speech production and comprehension. On the basis of the cases we analyze in this paper, we suggest the following principle of creative analogy:

> *An ungrammatical speech error that remains unacceptable is one for which there is a usable and grammatical alternative. An ungrammatical speech error that becomes 'acceptable' is one for which there is no comprehensible and utterable alternative of equal (or lower) behavioral complexity that shares the same deep structure.*

The intuitive basis for this distinction is clear: communicatively usable speech errors remain unacceptable so long as there are grammatical alternatives. If there are no equally usable alternatives, then the errors may become 'acceptable' even though they remain ungrammatical. The notion that a sequence can be ungrammatical but acceptable may appear jarring, if not wholly bizarre. However, it is clear that such cases are commonplace in the experience of the language-learning child—often the child appears to have mastered a new form as an idiom (i.e., *not* generated by its grammar) and only subsequently is the grammar extended to generate that form. On this model the child first incorporates a new form into his/her behavioral repertoire; then the grammar is restructured to generate it. Without such cases the child's grammar-learning process would depend entirely on negative feedback in response to its ungrammatical utterances. Acceptable sequences can motivate a change in the child's grammar only if the child can retain a category of cases that are 'acceptable' but not (yet) generated by its grammar (see Bever, 1975b).

The same principle holds for the interaction of adult grammar and language evolution. First, the notion of an acceptable but nongrammatically generated sequence is what is commonly referred to as an "idiom," and thus should not be a surprising concept for linguistic science. Second, if such cases did not exist then *there would be only one kind of extrinsic linguistic source for language change.* That is, if every 'acceptable' utterance were 'grammatical,' then the only possible kind of grammatical restructuring would be a reduction in the number of sentences that are 'grammatical' but 'unacceptable,' perhaps because of their behavioral complexity. Such cases are, by definition, usually not encountered, so it is unlikely that they are the only stimulus for grammatical change.

This discussion clarifies the source of extragrammatical neologisms that can force a restructuring of a grammar as the language evolves. Usable ungrammatical sequences that have usable grammatical alternatives drop in and out of usage without permanent consequence. Usable errors that lack easily usable alternatives can become encoded as extragrammatical "idiomatic" forms—it is these forms that children attempt to integrate within their own grammar. Such integration is one source for diachronic changes in grammatical structure.

This paper is addressed primarily to the principles that govern the occurrence of ungrammatical but acceptable sequences in the language of adults. It is clear, however, that the same principle could apply to the ontogenesis of grammar in children. This principle may answer a major question about the claim that language learning proceeds by way of a series of temporary "grammars" (e.g., Chomsky, 1965; McNeill, 1969): what are the restrictions on a new "hypothetical" grammar a child generates at each stage in the course of language learning? On our view, the child generates a new grammar when a number of new constructions have accumulated that he can understand or utter, even though they may not yet be treated by the child as 'grammatical'. The systems of speech perception and production in the child constrain which sequences are "acceptable" at each stage. In this way, these systems constrain and guide the evolution of each temporary grammar in the course of language acquisition (see Bever, 1975b).

Thus, the explanation of analogy figures crucially in both the evolution and ontogenesis of grammatical structures. This is reflected in our proposal that the emergence of new analogical forms is not only constrained by systems of language use, it is also constrained by a principle true for language acquisition: namely, in analogy a primary constraint is to *maintain the structure of a form while extending its use to a new meaning*. That is, adult analogical neologisms are constrained in the same way as the young child's acquisition of language— "old forms take on new functions" (Slobin, 1971).

The main nongrammatical system studied to date has been speech perception. We shall review that research to illustrate the study of the interactions of grammar and other systems of linguistic skill. We then turn to a brief account of speech production and explore its interactions with grammar. We propose a formalization of the traditional notion of 'analogy' as a set of production constraints on possible neologisms and ungrammatical utterances that arise during the course of speaking freely. Finally, we discuss the implications of analogy for language acquisition and linguistic evolution.

2. GRAMMAR AND SPEECH PERCEPTION

2.1 Prima Facie Cases of Behavioral Complexity

Traditionally, investigators have appealed to perceptual complexity as an intuitive account for the unacceptability of sequences that are difficult to mark distinctively as ungrammatical (Miller and Chomsky, 1963). For example, sentences like (3) and (4) are judged unacceptable by most speakers although they are clearly grammatical forms, as exemplified by the acceptability of (5) and (6), which have essentially the corresponding grammatical structures:

(3) *The oyster the oyster the oyster split split split.
(4) *The colonies' workers' forelegs' pincers' grip's duration hurt.
(5) The reporter everyone I met trusted said Nixon would resign.
(6) The big round splintering old wooden wheel rumbled on.

Such cases show that one can refer to behavioral complexity as the basis for sequence unacceptability: this relieves the grammar of the kind of descriptive power required to differentiate cases like (3) and (4) from (5) and (6), respectively. In these cases the unacceptability of fully grammatical sequences (3) and (4) is interpreted as due to their *perceptual* complexity.

There are many other behavioral sources of unacceptability. For example, observe in (7) the awkwardness of a compound verb phrase that does not maintain the logical or temporal ordering of the conjuncts in its surface form:

(7) (a) ?John landed on his head and attempted to pole vault the Great Divide.
     (b) ?John will make breakfast and get up.

Even though identical sentoids are conjoined, sentence (7a) does not paraphrase (8a) but rather describes a different "John" who had an accident and *then* tried to perform a great feat:

(8) (a) John attempted to pole vault the Great Divide and landed on his head.
     (b) John will get up and make breakfast.

To state the restriction on the surface order of conjuncts in the grammar would require sensitivity to a variety of wordly facts. That is, the formal grammar would have to include a specification of which activities can contingently or temporally precede others. On the other hand, the logical/temporal ordering restriction on coordinate structures seems a rather plausible principle of language behavior. Since the speaker utters and the listener hears conjoined forms in a linear sequence, it is reasonable to argue that these restrictions arise naturally out of what we do when we talk and listen. The independent motivation for such behavioral systems is not at issue: it is clearly plausible to claim that it is easier to build up contingent ideas in their temporal and causal order even if the sentences used are themselves simple conjuncts. The issue here is that to include such knowledge as part of the grammar would introduce considerable uncertainty as to the boundaries and content of grammar itself: almost any aspect of human knowledge can contribute to what is perceived as a temporal or causal relation. Thus, "grammar" would now include almost any aspect of human knowledge. Not only is this impossible to define, it places within "grammar" an aspect of the use of language which reflects general properties of cognition, and which would require independent description outside of language (e.g., to account for our perceptions of visual cause and effect). Thus, it is reasonable to argue that the sequencing of ideas is an extragrammatical property.

Surface order can interact with worldly knowledge to determine the scope of determiners. Consider for example, sentence (9) and (10):

(9) All cookies are not frosted.
(10) All bachelors are not married.

Even though the sentences are structurally identical, many speakers paraphrase them with different arrangements of the quantifiers as in (11) and (12) (see Labov, 1972a and b):

(11) Not all cookies are frosted. (i.e., some are and some aren't)
(12) No bachelors are married.

The ambiguity of such constructions is exemplified by sentence (13) which may be interpreted as either (14) or (15):

(13) All professors are not mean bastards.
(14) Professors are all (not mean bastards). (i.e., no professor is a mean bastard)
(15) Not (all professors are mean bastards). (i.e., some professors are not mean bastards)

The ambiguity of sentences like (13) can be interpreted as an ambiguity of quantifier scope. The problem then arises as to why (9) and (10) are behaviorally *un*ambiguous, and why their interpretations have opposite scope relations between the quantifiers *not* and *all*. The solution to this problem rests on the interaction of such sentences with ordinary conventions of discourse, as systematized by Grice (1975). Notice first that (13) is ordinarily interpreted as (16) while (17) is its literal interpretation:

(16) Some professors are not mean bastards while some are.
(17) Some professors are not mean bastards.

To explain this we refer to Grice's conversational maxim, "be relevant." Clearly, sentence (17) is of interest only if it is agreed that some professors *are* bastards.

A separate conversational maxim, "make sense," can now account for the structurally divergent interpretations of (9) and (10). Since (14) and (15) cannot be reliably distinguished by intonational stress contours or some other phonological property, the structurally opposite interpretation of cases (9) and (10) cannot be described with ordinary grammatical mechanisms. That is, the grammar would become considerably more complex if these phenomena are treated within it (see Jackendoff, 1972, and Lakoff, 1971, for discussions of the formal complexities that arise if such phenomena are treated within the grammar). However, reference to the Gricean conversational principles can account for these cases, thus allowing the grammar to mark all of them as structurally ambiguous. Suppose (9) and (10) were ambiguous, their structurally possible interpretations are given (18)–(21):

(18) No cookies are frosted.
(19) Some cookies aren't frosted while some are.
(20) No bachelors are married.
(21) Some bachelors aren't married and some are.

The reading in (18) is pragmatically ill-formed, since most speakers at least can conceive of a frosted cookie. The alternative in (21) is semantically ill-formed since bachelors are unmarried by definition. Accordingly, the unacceptable readings for (9) and (10) are effectively blocked by the conversational implicature "make sense." Thus, (9) and (10) are grammatically ambiguous like (13), although they are interpreted in structurally opposite ways because of conversational conventions. In this way we relieve the grammar of the descriptive burden of differentiating (9), (10), and (13), all of which are structurally identical. As above, we do so by referring to a system of knowledge that is independently motivated—in this case the system governing conversational interchanges.

2.2 Perceptual Strategies and Acceptability

The preceding cases exemplify some general ways that nongrammatical knowledge can restrict the acceptability and interpretations of grammatical sequences. To explain these cases we referred to general properties of extragrammatical systems of knowledge. The existence of a theory of speech perception makes explanation possible for more subtle phenomena. In recent years a good deal of research has been devoted to the development of a theory of speech perception (see Fodor, Bever, and Garrett, 1974; Bever (this vol.); Carroll and Bever (in press) for reviews). This research has isolated a set of perceptual segmentation strategies, operations that utilize information in surface constituents to assign directly their deep structure relations. Experimental evidence indicates that the words in a surface sequence are first assigned their possible lexical classification. Other experimental evidence supports the view that perceptual strategies are schemata that take the lexically labeled strings as input and mark them directly for deep structure relations without processing intermediate levels of representation.

A range of phenomena can be explained by reference to the perceptual strategies that assign modifier relations within phrases. For example, the perceptual strategy in (22) applies to English noun phrases as shown in (23):

(22) (det) N_1's $N_2 \rightarrow$ ($_{NP}$(det) N_1 + possessive, N_2 (=head))$_{NP}$
(23) (a) The newspaper's printing . . .
       (b) The horse's gait . . .
       (c) The bank's combination vault . . .

T. G. BEVER, J. M. CARROLL,
AND R. HURTIG

Such perceptual segmentation strategies can yield problematic parsings of constituent structure and therefore interact with judgments of acceptability. The
strategy in (22) can lead to incorrect parsing in certain cases. Consider the
operation of a Possessive Preposing rule of grammar (24):

(24) NP_1 of $NP_2 \Rightarrow NP_2 + poss\ NP_1$

This rule applies regularly, as in (25):

(25) (a) The printing of the vendor $\Rightarrow$ the vendor's printing.
      (b) The gait of the owner $\Rightarrow$ the owner's gait.
      (c) The combination lock of the president $\Rightarrow$ the president's com-
           bination lock.

However, if (24) applies to cases like (26), in which the possessive noun phrase
itself has an embedded possessive,

(26) (a) The printing of the vendor of the newspaper is unreadable.
      (b) The gait of the owner of the horse is rapid.
      (c) The combination lock of the president of the bank.

unacceptable sequences result as in (27) (cf. Wells, 1947; Carroll, 1975, and
Langendoen, this volume, p. 183 ff.):

(27) (a) *The vendor of the *newspaper's printing* is unreadable.
      (b) *The owner of the *horse's steps* are too rapid.
      (c) *The president of the *bank's combination lock* is efficient.

It would be possible to mark cases like (27) as ungrammatical by placing a
restriction on the transformational rule (24), so that it would not apply to
complex noun phrases of the form in (26). However, this restriction could not
operate uniformly, as shown by the acceptability of the cases in (28):

(28) (a) The vendor of the *newspaper's handwriting* was unreadable.
      (b) The owner of the *horse's speech* is too rapid.
      (c) The president of the *bank's daughter* is efficient.

which derive from the operation of rule (24) to sequences like those in (29):

(29) (a) The handwriting of the vendor of the newspaper is unreadable.
      (b) The speech of the owner of the horse is rapid.
      (c) The daughter of the president of the bank is
           efficient.

Since the sequences in (29) are structurally (and almost lexically) identical to
those in (26), there is no way of distinguishing them by reference to structural
grammatical properties alone. What appears to be at issue is the perceptual
plausibility of the *N's N* sequence created by rule (24), as italicized in (27) and
(28). In (28), such a sequence is not a plausible possessive noun phrase, while in
(27) it is. Accordingly, rule (24) must be restricted to apply only when the

sequence it creates would not be a semantically plausible possessive noun phrase. This would account for the facts we have outlined thus far, but at the cost of an added constraint on potential derivations, an example of a so-called transderivational constraint. To restrict the operation of rule (24) to a sequence like N_1 of N_2 of N_3, the possible plausibility of the potential sequence N_3 *possesses* N_1 must be checked; if the sequence is plausible then the derivation is blocked. The restriction is "transderivational" in that it must refer to a separate sentence derivation involving N_3 and N_1. However, the complexity of the restrictions goes beyond this. Consider the fact that the sentences in (30) are acceptable, even though the created *N's N* sequences are possible possessive noun phrases:

(30) (a) The vendor of the newspaper's printing revealed him to be fastidious.

(b) The owner of the horse's steps revealed his confidence as a former soldier.

(c) The president of the bank's combination lock frustrated his own attempts to steal the money.

The acceptability is apparently due to the implausibility of the *entire* sequence, *N's N VP*, as a separate sentence. To accommodate this fact, the "transderivational" constraint on (24) would not be restricted to a single extraderivational sentence frame (such as N_3 *possesses* N_1) but must range over *whatever material follows* the ultimate surface structure noun phrase being treated by (24). It is not clear that such a formalism can be constructed within any grammar. Even if it can, it would merely catalogue the facts rather than explain their nature.

The theory of speech perception offers a different account of the cases we have been discussing and also a possible explanation for their relative acceptability. The acceptability of cases like those in (31), which combine the effects of (28) and (30), suggest strongly that it is possible to have the possessive ending -'s attached to a complex noun phrase by rule (24):

(31) (a) The vendor of the newspaper's handwriting revealed him to be fastidious.

(b) The owner of the horse's speech was that of a former soldier.

(c) The president of the bank's daughter frustrated his attempts to steal the money.

However, the intuitively less complex versions of the same deep structure in (32) highlight the behavioral difficulty of such complex possessive noun phrases:

(32) (a) The newspaper's vendor's handwriting . . .

(b) The horse's owner's speech . . .

(c) The bank's president's daughter . . .

What appears to be difficult in (31) is not the complexity of a possessive with a possessive embedding (as in (32)), but the competition between the tendency to attach the bound possessive morpheme to the immediately preceding noun and

T. G. BEVER, J. M. CARROLL,
AND R. HURTIG

the tendency to attach it to the more distantly preceding noun. That this is so is demonstrated by the cases in (27), in which the immediately adjacent lexical material supports this misparsing. Thus, the theoretical claim that perceptual strategies apply to local sequences predicts that the strategy represented in (22) will tend to misapply to (27), thus rendering cases like (27) relatively difficult to understand and therefore relatively unacceptable. We can now explain why the cases in (28) and (30) are relatively acceptable—they include properties that are incompatible with the *N's N* misparsing, thus reducing its force and increasing the overall acceptability of the sentences.

We conclude that the relative acceptability phenomena in (27), (28), (30), and (32) are due to the operation of the system of speech perception; on this view, all these constructions are structurally grammatical. This solution relieves the grammar of otherwise unneeded formal power and utilizes an independently motivated theory to do so. There are several advantages to this analysis. If transderivational constraints are excluded, then universal grammar makes more constrained claims about the child's mind. Of course, this might seem to be a trivial advantage, since we do agree that the kinds of facts represented in the transderivational solution exist, but we claim that they are part of the perceptual system, not the grammar. However, their inclusion in the perceptual system allows the possibility of explaining *why* the facts are the way they are. The transderivational solution can *describe* the facts, but it does not offer any hypothesis as to their dynamic nature.

The critical advantage of the perceptual explanation is that it predicts new kinds of cases that would not be predicted by the transderivational restriction on rule (24). Consider the cases in (33):

(33) (a) ?*The owner of the horse's steps* were rapid.
     (b) Because he was in a hurry to place a bet, *the owner of the horse's steps* were rapid.

The critical sequence italicized in (33b) is more acceptable than in (33a) because the context increases the plausibility that the speaker is referring to *the owner's . . . steps* not the *horse's steps*. Accordingly, many speakers attempt to improve the acceptability of sentences like (33a) by unstressing the next-to-the-last noun of the complex noun of the complex noun phrase (*horse*), placing a pause before the -*s* and adding extra stress to the initial and the final noun, as schematized in (34):

(34) The ówner of the hòrse(pause)-es stéps
      were rapid.

The perceptual explanation predicts that such modifications would reduce the likelihood of misparsing due to gobbling and increase the perceived relation between the first and third nouns, thus increasing acceptability. The transderivational account of restrictions on (24) can make no such prediction (although it could describe such facts *post hoc*). The perceptual explanation not only offers a potential explanation for the original phenomena, but it also makes a wider variety of correct predictions.

We have gone through possessive noun phrase parsing in some detail, since it clarifies how the interactionist model of linguistic description deals with complex acceptability phenomena. The general principle is that if an acceptability phenomenon can be accounted for by reference to an independently motivated extragrammatical system and if the phenomenon would require adding formal mechanisms to universal grammar, then the property is classified as extragrammatical. Such cases highlight the theoretical position that grammaticality is a formal property that is variably mapped onto sequence acceptability. The cases reviewed above are ones in which this approach leads a number of sentences to be classified as grammatical but unacceptable. The interactionist form of explanation can also help us discover and explain an initially troublesome category of cases; namely, *sequences that are ungrammatical but acceptable—* that is, cases the grammar marks as ill-formed, but which are acceptable by virtue of their behavioral simplicity. Langendoen and Bever (in this volume) isolated such a case, as in (35) (for discussion of other such cases, see Bever, 1970; Carroll, 1974; and Carroll and Hennessey, 1975):

(35) A not unhappy man entered the room.

They note the cases in (36) are not acceptable although they have the same formal properties as (35):

(36) (a) *A not unearthly scream was heard by all.
      (b) *Some not unusual clothes lay on the bed.
      (c) *A not intrepid sailor stood at the bar.
      (d) *The not impious regent favored the bishop.

In formal grammatical terms the acceptability of the sequence *det not un-adj N* is assessed by comparing it with *det adj N*; if the latter is acceptable with the same meaning for the adjective, so is the former. The cases in (36) do not meet this test as shown in (37):

(37) (a) *An earthly scream was heard by all.
      (b) *Some usual clothes lay on the bed.
      (c) *A trepid sailor stood at the bar.
      (d) *The pious regent favored the bishop.
           (with "pious" pronounced 'píəs')

However, as shown in (38), (35) does meet this test.

(38) A happy man entered the room.

Example (36d) is particularly significant since the only difference between the adjective stem *-pious* and the lexical adjective *pious* is in the phonetic form, but even this difference is apparently sufficient to render (36d) unacceptable. To treat the difference between (35) and (36) as a grammatical phenomenon would

T. G. BEVER, J. M. CARROLL,
AND R. HURTIG

require sensitivity to the *phonetic* output of a separate derivation; surely one of the most farreaching transderivational constraints possible.

Langendoen and Bever point out that the same facts could be accounted for by the motivated misapplication of a strategy that is needed independently for the analysis of phrases and lexical compounds like those in (39), in which an adjective is preceded by an intensive adverb.

> (39) (a) A not very happy person walked in.
> (b) A not all-powerful diety is believed in by the islanders.

If this strategy were to apply to sequences like that in (35), then they would be analyzed by that strategy and treated in the same way semantically, which in fact is how they are understood. However, the misapplication of the perceptual strategy can occur only insofar as the adjective stem is recognizable as a separate lexical item, leaving the initial *un-* to be temporarily treated as an intensifying adverb. Thus, the phenomena in (36) can be accounted for without reference to transderivational constraints and in a way that offers an explanation of the facts rather than merely enumerating them. Thus, there are several advantages to classifying the sequences in (35) as ungrammatical but acceptable.

We mentioned above that if we are to understand the life and evolution of grammar we must pay close attention to the constraints that govern the creation of new ungrammatical idioms. Unfortunately, Langendoen and Bever's account leaves open what the general constraints are on possible ungrammatical forms. They suggest that the traditional notion of 'analogy' can be given theoretical and empirical content if we restrict it to cases in which a particular extragrammatical system of speech behavior accounts for the acceptability of an ungrammatical sequence. In the case of perception such cases would characteristically be ones in which a particular strategy is misapplied (successfully) to a sequence. The study of such cases in perception, however, is difficult, since the very acceptability of the critical sequences makes it likely that they will at first be classified as 'grammatical' and then discovered to be 'ungrammatical' only after attempts to describe their 'grammaticality' within a grammar have failed. Accordingly, we now turn to cases from speech production, for in speaking, we characteristically produce a class of utterances we recognize to be ungrammatical. It may be that the different kind of data will allow for further insight into what the constraints are on ungrammatical but acceptable sequences.

3. SPEECH PRODUCTION

An experimentally motivated theory of speech production is hard to develop for one obvious reason—it is hard to do controlled experiments on speech production. Ideally, we should do studies that are the converse of those used to verify perceptual models. We should control what a speaker intends to say, and then see how it is said. We could then sketch out the behavioral properties of the problem of how speakers map ideas onto surface sequences as they talk. Unfortunately (from the standpoint of this experimental line of research) one cannot control what subjects think as easily as one can control what they hear; in particular, one has almost no control over *when* subjects think a particular thought. Consequently, the study of speech production is based primarily on theoretical, observational, and anecdotal considerations.

Even such limited data constrain what the theory of speech production must be like (see Boomer, 1970; Valian, 1971; Fodor, Bever, and Garrett, 1974). Clearly, the problem for the speaker is to find a way of mapping ideas onto comprehensible utterances. At the same time, the speaker listens to his or her own utterances as they emerge and can modify ideas based on the utterances as they appear. That is, to some extent we think before we speak, but we also find out at a conscious level what we think by listening to what we say.

These two features of talking are reflected in two properties of speech production that have been studied relatively carefully. First, several observational and experimental studies suggest that the primary unit of speech planning is defined over the surface structure and probably is the surface structure 'clause' (Boomer, 1965, 1970; Valian, 1971). That is, in mapping ideas onto utterable sequences, the main goal is to formulate surface structure clauses that in themselves are coherent units. The second property is that as we talk we listen ahead to see if what we are going to say represents what we mean. Evidence for this comes primarily from the study of points at which false starts in free speech occur (Maclay and Osgood, 1959) and studies of spoonerisms (Fromkin, 1971; MacKay, 1970; Garrett and Shattuck, 1974). The existence of false starts suggests that we can listen ahead to how a particular construction is going to work out and decide that it is inadequate to our idea or to the conversational context, so we stop and start afresh. The existence of spoonerisms reveals that when we talk we have in mind parts of an utterance that are delayed by several words, although generally within the same surface structure clause.

A final property of the speech production system has been asserted, but there is still little direct evidence that proves it (Valian, 1971; Fodor, Bever, and Garrett, 1974; Schlesinger, 1969; and Bever, 1975b). That is the proposal that talking involves a set of speech production rules that map ideas onto standard phrases. It is unclear to what extent these production rules are literally the rules of grammar. They must differ in certain respects simply because they apply surface clause by surface clause, whereas many grammatical transformations apply to several clauses simultaneously. Furthermore, production rules are concerned only with creating linear order, while transformations can carry out other functions. Finally, all production rules apply during a single temporal scan of the surface structure and thus are not ordered; this insures that many transformations cannot be production rules.

Thus, just as in the case of the perceptual strategies, the speech production rules are not isomorphic to rules of grammar. What is of crucial importance for

T. G. BEVER, J. M. CARROLL,
AND R. HURTIG

the present paper is that the speech production system differs at least in part from the grammar. This allows for the possibility that speakers can utter sentences that in fact are ungrammatical but that are systematically predicted by the speech production system. Indeed, it is the partial mismatch between the speech production system and the grammar that is a dynamic source for potential neologisms.

3.1 Lexical Errors

This model of speech production can explain the occurrence of a variety of ungrammatical-but-utterable sequences. Characteristically, ungrammatical utterances are used as the solution to a bind that the speaker has created by what has been uttered up to that point. For example, in (40) the speaker presumably starts out with *both* because of the expectation that only two noun phrases will be conjoined, and during the later sequence utters a third noun phrase:

> (40) ?Both the senators, the congressmen and their assistants refused to appear.

The resulting utterance is clearly 'ungrammatical' in the sense that, if asked, speakers agree that it ought to be unacceptable by virtue of the fact that *both* requires exactly two conjoined noun phrases. Furthermore, there is a version of (40) which means the same and is grammatical, namely (41):

> (41) The senators, the congressmen and their assistants all refused to appear.

Sentence (42) has properties similar to (40) in that it is directly recognized as unacceptable, but is often uttered in preference to the grammatical (43a–c) because it avoids committing the speaker to the assumption that *everyone* is of one sex only, as in (43a and 43b); (42) also avoids the relative cumbersomeness of (43c):[4]

> (42) ?Everyone forgot their coat.
> (43) (a) Everyone forgot his coat.
> (b) Everyone forgot her coat.
> (c) Everyone forgot his or her coat.

4. In many similar cases the speaker is forced to select one of several ungrammatical forms. In such cases the third person singular seems to be the most favored, perhaps because it is the most unmarked. Consider (i–vi) (pointed out by G. K. Pullum).

(i) Either you or I am crazy.
(ii) Either you or I are crazy.
(iii) Either you or I is crazy.
(iv) Either you are going crazy or I am going crazy.
(v) It is I who am crazy.
(vi) It is I who is crazy.

Examples (i–iii) are all ungrammatical reductions of (iv). However (iii) seems to be the form most preferable. Similarly, (vi) is preferred over (v).

3.2 Syntactic Errors, Clause Relations

Sentences (40) and (42) are examples of intuitively ungrammatical utterances in which the structural difficulty occurs within one clause from the misuse of a single word. The view that speech production is planned clause-by-clause suggests that errors involving entire constructions occur across clauses but not within clauses. This follows from the fact that the misapplication of a syntactic process within a clause would be noticed by the speaker, and blocked; while across clauses the speaker might lose track of the exact syntactic form from one clause to the next. Consider (44) as an example of the misapplication of the pronominalization rule to the presumed underlying form in (45):

(44) ?Iroquoianists are strange because they want it to be a world language.
(45) Iroquoianists are strange because they want Iroquois to be a world language.

It is a misapplication because noun phrase identity does not occur in (45) (i.e., "Iroquoianists" ≠ "Iroquois"). Lakoff and Ross (1972) suggest that examples like (44) are acceptable because of a 'grammatical' principle that pronominalization can occur simply on the basis of semantically and phonologically *similar* commanding phrases. However, this description is difficult to state within the grammar since the notion of what counts as 'similar' differs from context to context (and from pronunciation to pronunciation). That is, the concept of 'similarity' is in part a function of language use, and thus would ordinarily be viewed as part of linguistic performance. On this view the appearance of "Iroquois" in (45) is interpreted by the speaker as a repetition of the phonologically and semantically similar element in "*Iroquoi*anists" that has just been uttered (or planned); the separation of it into a preceding clause makes it difficult to check. Hence, the pronominalization misapplies acceptably as in (44). It cannot misapply in a case like (46) from (47) because the second occurrence of the phonological sequence "Iroquois" is within the same clause (i.e., within the same unit of speech production planning); thus the speaker is not confused by the apparent similarity because the words are syntactically differentiated within the clause:

(46) *Because Iroquoianists want it to be a world language they're strange.
(47) Because Iroquoianists want Iroquois to be a world language they're strange.

The behavioral notion of 'similarity' can also explain the acceptability facts in (48a–c) (see McCawley, 1970):

(48) (a) ?I think I'd like the Mediterranean climate even though I've never been there.

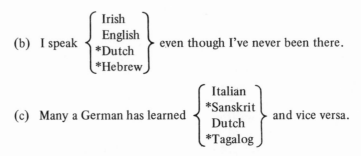

(b) I speak $\left\{\begin{array}{l}\text{Irish}\\ \text{English}\\ \text{*Dutch}\\ \text{*Hebrew}\end{array}\right\}$ even though I've never been there.

(c) Many a German has learned $\left\{\begin{array}{l}\text{Italian}\\ \text{*Sanskrit}\\ \text{Dutch}\\ \text{*Tagalog}\end{array}\right\}$ and vice versa.

Thus the view proposed by Lakoff and Ross (1972) is not only grammatically cumbersome, but it also fails to predict and explain already related facts.

The speech production model offers straightforward accounts of other frequent utterances that are intuitively ungrammatical. For example (49a) is presumably a rendition of (49b), which occurs because the speaker failed to insert *each* into the main clause (see Dougherty, 1970, 1971):

(49) (a) *Harry and Bill didn't realize that each other was at the meeting.
     (b) Harry and Bill each didn't realize that the other was at the meeting.

On the interactionist model of speech production *each other* is generated in the deep structure corresponding to the second surface clause; presumably the failure to move *each* into its proper position in the first clause results in part from the fact that the first clause is superficially well-formed without *each*; further, the speaker has uttered the first clause by the time he or she realizes that the second clause is ungrammatical. It is ungrammatical due to the fact that *each other* and *one another* can appear as a surface object (as in 50a, b) but not as surface subject (as in 50c):

(50) (a) Harry and Bill hit $\left\{\begin{array}{l}\text{one another}\\ \text{each other}\end{array}\right\}$.

     (b) Harry and Bill were hit by $\left\{\begin{array}{l}\text{one another}\\ \text{each other}\end{array}\right\}$.

     (c) $\left\{\begin{array}{l}\text{*One another}\\ \text{*Each other}\end{array}\right\}$ was hit by Harry and Bill.

A similar case that exemplifies the independence of surface clauses in speech production is given in (51) and (52):

(51) ?I really enjoyed flying in an airplane that I understand how it works.
(52) ?So we won't have keys lying around that we don't know where they are . . .

Sentence (51) arises from the utterance in (53); in (53) the speaker felt it was awkward to stop at that point since the dimension on which the airplane was 'understood' was not clear; (51) arises because there is no correct way of expanding (53) to represent the intended idea, as in (55). Similarly, having reached the point in (54) the speaker could find no natural way to expand it to contain the content of (56), and therefore utters (52).

(53) I really enjoyed flying in an airplane that I understand . . .

(54) So we won't have keys lying around that we don't know . . .

(55) I really enjoyed flying in an airplane the workings of which I understand.

(56) So we won't have keys lying around the whereabouts of which we don't know . . .

On this view the second clauses in (51) and (52) are utterable because of their full acceptability as independent clauses. The principle that speech production proceeds clause-by-clause explains why the speakers were willing to utter the sequences, in each case, the only difficulty arose from the incorrect syntax governing the relation *between* the two clauses, but leaving the intended meaning intact. (See Langendoen, 1970, for some discussion of such cases.)

3.3 Syntactic Errors, Repeated Items

In each of the preceding examples the utterance is clearly unacceptable upon reflection, although obviously utterable. We have argued that each critical ungrammatical utterance can be interpreted as due to a predicted potential failure of the speech production system. To treat each utterance as 'grammatical' (but 'unacceptable' due to processes outside the grammar) would weaken the power and interest of grammars unnecessarily, since there is an independently motivated system that explains the occurrence. Furthermore, it is characteristic of these examples that there are closely related alternatives that are fully grammatical.

In other ungrammatical but acceptable examples there seem to be no ready alternatives. It is characteristic of these cases that the ungrammatical forms are more readily accepted than those that have alternatives. Such cases are more subtle in that they are not clearly unacceptable even upon reflection; nevertheless, accounting for their acceptability within the grammar would still involve increasing its formal power. Consider example (57a), which represents (57b):

(57) (a) That Herbie was chewing his tongue amused them is normal.

      (b) ?That that Herbie was chewing his tongue amused them is normal.

Since (57a) is not obviously unacceptable, it is prudent first to examine the consequences of generating it as the grammatical version of (57b). A solution to the description of (57a) within the grammar would be to state a rule that obligatorily deletes the second *that* in any sequence of two. This, however, would be incorrect since (58) is entirely acceptable but it would be blocked by such a rule:

(58)   That that person is here surprised Harry.

In (58) deletion does not apply to the phonologically repeated form since the two *thats* have different grammatical functions in the sequence. An alternate solution within the grammar would be to state a rule that requires both phonological equivalence and identity of syntactic function in order for deletion to apply. However, this rule also will incorrectly derive many cases, as the unacceptable (60) from (59) and (62) from (61) show:

(59)   ?Who who I like will be at the party tonight?
(60)   *Who I like will be at the party tonight?
(61)   ?If if Sally is back interests you then we can find out.
(62)   ??If Sally is back interests you then we can find out.

The acceptable versions of (59) and (61) are (63) and (64):

(63)   Who $\begin{Bmatrix} \text{whom} \\ \text{that} \end{Bmatrix}$ I like will be at the party tonight?

(64)   If whether Sally is back interests you then we can find out.

These cases demonstrate a principle that a word cannot be immediately repeated if it has the same grammatical function in each instance, but *must* be replaced *if there is an available substitute*, as in (63) and (64).

The repetition of a phonological form with identical structural function involving different parts of the underlying structure can cause difficulties both for speech perception and production. The reason is that free speech involves a certain amount of spurious repetition as speakers search for the right words, especially of clause-initial function words like *that*, *who*, *if* as in (65) (see Fodor, Bever, and Garrett (1974) and Maclay and Osgood, 1959):

(65)   (a)   If . . . if . . . if Sally is back I'll call her.
        (b)   I didn't know that . . . that Marty likes hot dogs so much.
        (c)   I wonder who . . . who will be the one that has to tell him.

This makes it heuristically valuable to have a "repetition-collapser" that treats a sequence of words with the same phonological and structural role as a spurious repetition of the same word. Such a behavioral heuristic accounts for a number of variations in acceptability—for example, the unacceptability of (66a). The relative acceptability of (66b) is accounted for by the fact that the two instances of *over* have different grammatical properties:

(66)   (a)   ?I rolled the film clip of Lassie's rolling over over
        (b)   I looked the film clip of Lassie's rolling over over

In this regard, contrast (67a) (from Chomsky, 1953) with (67b) and (67c).

(67)   (a)   Whom will they name him after after his first birthday?

(b) *After after Oscar leaves Suzie kisses me then I'll really know for sure.

(c) *John said he would come after after the picnic clean-up work is finished.

The unacceptability of repetitions may involve units internal to words as well. Bever (1970) discusses the unacceptability of forms like (68) (also see Ross, 1972):

(68) They were considering discussing producing toys.

A similar restriction on repeated forms occurs in Spanish clitics. Perlmutter (1972) noted that forms like (69a) are realized as (69c):

(69) (a) *pero a los conscriptos se les los da
       (b) *pero a los conscriptos se se los da
       (c) pero a los conscriptos se los da ("but to the draftees one gives them")

Perlmutter argues that such facts can only be described by a set of "output constraints," which mark sequences like (69a) as ungrammatical. It is possible to recast Perlmutter's formally complex solution in the terms of the behavioral restriction on repeated forms. The ungrammatical *les los* of (69a) becomes *se los* as in (69b), since *se los* is a possible sequence. But now there is the sequence *se se* which is unacceptable: that is replaced by ϕ *se* since no other alternative is available. This results in the surface form (69c).

We can now understand the case in (57a) in which a repeated *that* is deleted. Alternative substitution items do not exist in this case as they do for (59) and (61). For this reason the null string is substituted. There are alternative similar strings, such as (70):

(70) That the fact that Herbie was chewing his tongue amused them is natural.

A substitution like this, however, does not even maintain the basic grammatical relations of the original form. In (70) *the fact* is the grammatical subject (modified by the complement clause *that Herbie was chewing his tongue*) of the verb phrase *amused them*, while in (57a) and (56b) *that Herbie was chewing his tongue* is the subject (cf Kiparsky and Kiparsky, 1970). Furthermore, even if *the fact that* in (70) were analyzed as having the same structure as *that* in (70), it repeats the initial *that* and can reasonably be interpreted as a spurious repetition, as in (71):

(71) That . . . the fact that Harry left upset many.

On these grounds, then, (70) does not constitute an alternative to (57b) in the sense that (60) and (62) may replace (59) and (61), respectively. Zwicky (1969) deals with related analogical simplifications that modify such sequences as (72a) to (72b):

(72) (a) *The The Hague airport is very modern.
     (b) The Hague airport is very modern.

Sequences of two possessive morphemes are often collapsed to one. Consider the form in (73a), which may be realized as in (73b):

(73) (a) My mother's dog's foot slipped but your mother's dog's foot didn't.
     (b) ?My mother's dog's foot slipped but your mother's's didn't.

Forms like (73b) are often actually rendered as in (74a) even though such replacement forms do not really mean the same thing. In particular, the *grammatical* source for (74a) would have to be a form like (74b):

(74) (a) My mother's dog's foot slipped but your mother's didn't.
     (b) My mother's dog's foot slipped but your mother's foot didn't.

Similarly, consider the embedding of (75b) in a form like (75a) as in (75c) (pointed out by Kuno). Forms like (75c) are usually realized as in (75d) with the extra *'s* 'analogically' deleted:

(75) (a) a friend of Mary's
     (b) this friend of Mary's
     (c) a friend of (this friend of Mary's)'s
     (d) a friend of this friend of Mary's

4. INTERACTION OF PERCEPTION AND PRODUCTION

A "minimax" principle governs the interactions between speech production and perception. The problem for the speaker is to map ideas onto a surface structure. The speaker attempts to minimize the surface structural complexity of the utterance while maximizing the information communicated to the listener. It is obviously in the speaker's interest to communicate effectively while not unnecessarily burdening himself in the process. Consider, as an example, self-embedded sentences like (3), (5), and (76a).

(76) (a) The bear the mole the grasshopper jumped bit growled.
     (b) The bear that the mole that the grasshopper jumped bit growled.

As Fodor and Garrett (1967) and others have observed, such difficult sequences are easier to perceive if the relative pronoun markers are not deleted (as in 76b).

This increases the complexity for the speaker since each *that* potentially signals the beginning of a new surface structure clause. However, it is just that property that facilitates comprehension. In this regard, Valian and Wales (1975) found that when speakers are asked to make a sentence "clearer" for the listener, they do so by altering the sentences so that the deep structure relations are more clearly marked in distinct surface structure clauses. For example, a sentence like (77a) might be clarified for the listener by a sentence like (77b):

(77) (a) The destruction of the building upset everybody.
(b) The building was destroyed and that upset everybody.

Of course, the goal of the speaker is to take potential utterances like (77b) and utter them in a form like (77a), which has fewer surface structure clauses. Indeed, forms like (78a) are quite typically changed into forms like (78b):

(78) (a) John runs faster than Bill runs.
(b) John runs faster than Bill.

Although (78a) is closer to its "deep structure" form, some of its structure is redundant (cf Fodor and Garrett, 1966, p. 150).

The main goal for the speaker is to maximize the information within each surface structure clause. For example, the convention that conjunctions must appear in the surface sequence in their logical order allows for the grammatical simplification of a variety of *originally* complex sentences (e.g., 79a to 79b; 79c to 79d):

(79) (a) Harvey left and then Harvey ate a sandwich.
(b) Harvey left and ate a sandwich.
(c) Marge inherited a million and then supported the ASPCA with it.
(d) Marge inherited a million and supported the ASPCA.

This pressure can even lead to the utterance of unacceptable sequences, as exemplified by (80) (after Schmerling, 1973):

(80) *(It) seems like (it is) a good idea (Do you) want Harvey to cut that out?

Although usable, cases like (80) are clearly unacceptable upon reflection.

4.1 Using *And* as a Complementizer

We turn now to a case of a usable sequence that is also fully acceptable. We shall argue that it is ungrammatical but acceptable because it simplifies surface structure complexity for the speaker, while remaining completely comprehensible for the listener.

Consider the sentences in (81b). They are a frequent version of the corresponding sentences in (81a).[5]

(81) (a) John will try to jump over the fence.
　　(b) John will try and jump over the fence.

　　(a) The foreman will leave to accept the better job.
　　(b) The foreman will leave and accept the better job.

　　(a) Harry wants to go to see the King.
　　(b) Harry wants to go and see the King.

　　(a) They asked us both to come to eat with them.
　　(b) They asked us both to come and eat with them.

　　(a) Malcomb hopes to stop to rest at Inverness.
　　(b) Malcomb hopes to stop and rest at Inverness.

　　(a) I need Calvin to testify to save me from jail.
　　(b) I need Calvin to testify and save me from jail.

It would appear that the sequences in (81a) could be treated as grammatical versions of those in (81b): *to* could be rewritten as *and*, as stated in the hypothetical transformation (82):

(82) $(V_1 (to V_2)) \Rightarrow V_1$ and V_2

However, there are a number of restrictions on (82). First, V_1 must be an infinitive in the surface structure, as shown by the unacceptability of (83a, b, c), in contrast with the acceptability of (83d, e):

(83) (a) *John tried and jumped over the fence.
　　(b) *John has tried and jumped over the fence.
　　(c) *John is trying and jumping over the fence.

5. Notice that for the verbs *come* and *go* the forms in (i) and (ii) also obtain.

　　(i) They asked us both to come eat with them.
　　(ii) Harry wants to go see the King.

This is consistent with the minimax principle. *Come* and *go* are very frequently used in 'V_1 (to V_2)' constructions, hence not only is the 'V_1 and V_2' analogy available (see below in text), but also '$V_1 V_2$'. The latter sequence further simplifies the verb structure by rendering conjoined verbs as a compound verb. See Ross (1967) and Zwicky (1969) for further discussion of related examples. Ross pointed out that V_1 need not be adjacent to V_2 in surface structure in order for (79) to apply as in (iii):

　　(iii) John wants to go to the store $\begin{Bmatrix} and \\ to \end{Bmatrix}$ buy some whiskey.

Ross also pointed out cases (iv) and (v), which appear to be related to the cases under discussion but are not examples of (81) since they are peculiar to *go* as V_1:

　　(iv) She went and solved a problem.
　　(v) She went and stained her dress.

(d) John didn't try and jump over the fence.
(e) John did try and jump over the fence.

In (83d) the negative element requires Do-Support, which leaves the main verb in the infinitival form, thus allowing (82) to apply (unlike 83a). Accordingly, rule (82) would have to be a late rule, applying after such rules as Do-Support, which leave the main verb form as an infinitive. At first, this appears to be an elegant solution, since the statement of (82) is itself simple and can easily be treated as a late optional rule.

The problem is, however, that many verbs are structurally and semantically indistinguishable late in a derivation from those above, but do not allow (82) to apply when they are V_1 —as demonstrated in (84b), which cannot be derived from (84a):

(84) (a) John will attempt to do it.
(b) *John will attempt and do it.

Other examples like (84b) are given in (85):

(85) (a) *Everyone will expect and greet you tonight.
(b) *Harry didn't want and read that book.
(c) *The queen will desire and meet the jester.
(d) *He did seem and get more money.

The complement verbs which can act as V_1 in (82) share one characteristic— they can stand alone, without an object phrase, in other constructions like (86a) and in the imperative (87a):

(86) (a) Harry really will try.
(b) *Harry really will attempt.

(87) (a) Try!
(b) *Attempt!

(Note that the contrast between *attempt* and *try* is crucial since they have identical meaning.)

It is important that the reason a verb can occur in constructions like (86a) and (87a) without an object can differ. For example, *go, come, . . .* never take objects, while *try, leave* may do so. A further restriction is that "V_1 and V_2" must be roughly paraphrasable as a "V_1 causes or facilitates V_2." For example, (88a) cannot appear as (88b), presumably because the activity of "waiting" does not cause or facilitate the "eating" (in fact, it does the opposite):

(88) (a) The devout Moslem will wait to eat until sunset.
(b) The devout Moslem will wait and eat until sunset.

However, there are instances in which "waiting" does facilitate or cause a predicate as in (89a):

(89) (a) To own your own car you're just going to have to wait to grow up.
(b) To own your own car you're just going to have to wait and grow up.

In this case, rule (82) *can* apply, producing (89b) as an acceptable version. These facts could be treated within some form of grammar, but would require sensitivity to a heterogeneous set of structural properties and would offer no explanation of the nature of the phenomenon. The grammar would simply list the properties governing the application of (82), as in (90):

(90) (a) The last formative of V_1 must be infinitival.
(b) V_1 must be: (i) intransitive.
                     (ii) subject to object deletion.
(c) V_1 must cause or facilitate V_2.

The condition in (90b) is 'global' in the sense that it makes reference to an earlier stage of derivation (i.e., lexical insertion). The condition in (90b, ii) is 'transderivational,' since it makes reference to the application of a rule of V-Object Deletion, which does not occur in the derivation of sentences like those in (81b). Condition (90c) requires sensitivity to the real-world contingencies governing which activities can cause or facilitate other predicates.

It remains for us to consider if there is an explanation for why the verbs and verb sequences that do undergo a change represented in (82) do so. The minimax principle seeks to minimize the (surface) structural complexity of utterances while maintaining comprehensibility. We have given examples showing that such a principle assigns a preferred status for the speaker to forms with reduced clause embeddedness. The sequences in (81b) compared with those in (81a) have this property. They represent an infinitival verb embedding a second infinitive with a pair of conjoined verbs. The behavioral preference for conjoined structures over embedded ones is supported by some research (e.g., Blumenthal, 1966). Accordingly, speakers would prefer to avoid uttering embedded constructions like those in (81a) if a grammatical alternative exists with conjoined rather than embedded verbs. In fact, such a construction does exist, as in (81b); that is, speakers have available a speech production rule which takes a linear sequence of superficially identical verb forms and conjoins them with *and*. Hence the conjoined verb sequence is a possible and utterable syntactic structure in the language. However, the grammatical derivation of conjoined structures as in (81b) involves a different meaning from (81a).

Nevertheless, the operation of the perceptual system guarantees that the intended meaning rendered in (81a) will be understood in (81b). This will occur because of the independently motivated perceptual strategies that normally apply to a sequence like "V_1 and V_2." As we observed above (see examples (7),

(8), and discussion), conjoined verbs are interpreted as coinciding with their temporal or logical order. This principle operates in sentences like (7) and (8) and exemplifies a natural constraint on speech behavior. The process in (82) also depends on this constraint. Thus, the listener in understanding sequences like those in (81) assumes that V_1 *necessarily* precedes V_2 logically or temporally. The grammatical relational information that V_1 takes V_2 as its complement can usually be recovered with this perceptual assumption. However, when this assumption is false, as in (88b), then the misapplication of the conjoined verb speech production schema is blocked. In this way, surface structural complexity is minimized by the speaker at no cost in comprehensibility for the listener.

At first this solution may appear merely to be a notational variant of the grammatical statements in (82) and (90). However, viewing the sequences in (81b) as produced by the misapplication of a speech production rule and the regular application of a perceptual strategy allows us to explain why the restrictions in (90) are the way they are. V_1 must end in an infinitive since V_2 is always infinitival in the source sequence "V_1 to V_2." If the *conjoined verb speech production rule* is to (mis)apply at all, V_1 must be superficially identical with V_2; i.e., V_1 must be an infinitival.

The restriction that V_1 must optionally be able to delete its object is also explicable if we interpret the sequence in (81b) as acceptable because of behavioral processes. If (82) were allowed to apply to the verbs in (84) and (85), which require an object phrase, the output would be homonymous with reduced compound structures like (91a), derived from (91b):

(91) (a) John will attempt and do it.
       (b) John will attempt it and John will do it.

In ordinary language usage, the compound interpretation of sentences like (91a) would be unavoidable since the verbs in (84) and (85) must have objects. Hence (82) is blocked in such cases, because the output would be *necessarily* homonymous with a fully grammatical sentence having a different meaning. This would leave no opportunity for the extended analogical meaning to obtain. In cases where V_1 does not require an object, the listener is not forced to interpret the sequence as a compound verb: so long as V_1 does cause or facilitate V_2, then the general perceptual strategy will lead the listener to hear such sentences as potentially having the complement meaning. In this way, our account explains why V_1 must at least optionally have no object and why V_1 must facilitate V_2.

In brief, the assumption that the sequences in (81b) are produced by behavioral processes relies on independently motivated structures, simplifies the grammar, and allows for a direct explanation of the restrictions on the phenomenon. It should be noted that we have demonstrated that the sequences in (81b) have the interpretation in (81a) only due to extragrammatical systems. That is, the sequences in (81b) are ungrammatical but acceptable on their complement interpretation.

4.2 The Interaction of Productive
Analogy and Perceptual Gobbling

We have argued that ungrammatical utterances become acceptable if they have no grammatical alternative that is behaviorally usable. The interaction of usability constraints and grammaticality can become quite intricate. Consider example (92) (actually uttered in a conversation), which is interpretable as (93):

(92)   The three of your's book will make you rich.

(93)   The book which $\begin{Bmatrix} \text{is by} \\ \text{belongs to} \end{Bmatrix}$ the three of you will make you rich.

On our analysis (92) is an ungrammatical but acceptable version of the grammatical but perceptually confusing sentence in (94):

(94)   The three of you's book will make you rich.

Example (94) is generated from (93) by the regular adjective phrase preposing transformation that forms standard prenominal possessive phrases. The perceptual difficulty of (94) is that the pronoun *you* gobbles the adjacent possessive morpheme. Since that morpheme is ordinarily a lexically absorbed suffix, it is particularly vulnerable to gobbling (see examples (22)-(34)). Now we must account for why the particular ungrammatical utterance in (92) is the one that replaces the perceptually complex grammatical sentence in (94). The production of (92) from (94) involves an interaction of productive analogy and further instances of perceptual gobbling. The first logical step is that *you's* in (94) becomes *your* as in (95):

(95)   The three of your book will make you rich.

This morphemic process is the same that applies to any possessive pronoun (changing *he's* to *his*, *they's* to *their*, etc.). Sentence (95) is itself unacceptable because the possessive pronoun *your* is gobbled by the apparent head noun *book* of the derived noun phrase, leading to an incomprehensible perceptual analysis as sketched in (96):

(96)   (The three of ((your book) (will make you rich))

To block this further gobbling and the resulting unacceptability, an alternate constituent is substituted. The principle of analogy requires that it be a constituent with similar syntactic and semantic properties. The constituent whose semantic content and morphological form are closest to that of the possessive pronoun *your*, and whose substitution would block gobbling, is the possessive pronoun *yours*. This analogical replacement yields sentence (97):

(97)   The three of yours book will make you rich.

In fact, some speakers find that (97) is the acceptable way to express (94). For those speakers our account stops here. However, this form is unacceptable for many speakers who prefer (92). This may be because a mandatory transformation reduces the possessive pronoun in the preposed position, as illustrated in (98):

(98) The book is yours $\Rightarrow$ yours book $\Rightarrow$ your book

The effect of this transformation precludes the occurrence of the possessive form *yours* in the prenominal position in sentence (97). Therefore, the alternative in (97) reduces to the unacceptable form in (95).

The unacceptability of (97) compels the speaker to resort to further analogical substitution. The next most likely alternative constituent that will block gobbling and whose occurrence in the prenominal position is not blocked by some mandatory transformation is the possessive pronoun *your's*. This form occurs in grammatical and acceptable sentences; e.g., (99b) (see also 73b above):

(99) (a) My guitar's strings are rusted but your guitar's strings are not.
     (b) My guitar's strings are rusted but yours's are not.

This establishes the form *yours's* within the system of speech production and makes it available for substitution of the perceptually complex forms in (94) and (95). This example illustrates the dynamic relationship in sentential acceptability among the productive analogy, perceptual constraints, and the grammar.

5. "DERIVATIVE GENERATION" AND ANALOGY

All the examples above involve misusing a constituent syntactically while maintaining the meaning of the misused constituent. For example, in (40) *both* maintains its lexical meaning; similarly *their* in (42) and *and* in (81b) have meanings that are independently motivated in other uses.

We can now apply the principle of analogy to explain a case of "derivative generation" raised by Chomsky (1970) and questioned by Hankamer (1972) and McCawley (1973). Chomsky points out that there are three kinds of deverbal noun phrases: the derived nominal (100a), the gerundive (100b), and the "mixed" forms (100c):

(100) (a) Harry's criticism of the book . . .
      (b) Harry's criticizing the book . . .
      (c) Harry's criticizing of the book . . .

Chomsky argues for the "lexicalist" position, that only the gerundive (100c) is derived from a deep-structure sentoid (e.g., "Harry criticized the book"). This would explain the fact that gerundive nominals can include verbal modifiers such as adverbials (101a), while derived nominals cannot (101b):

(101) (a) Harry's criticizing the book all evening long upset Bill.
      (b) *Harry's criticism of the book all evening long upset Bill.

Further support for this analysis is given by the fact that gerundive nominals have a "factive" interpretation while derived nominals are treated as simple nouns. For example, (102) is unacceptable because (*was . . . quoted*) is a predicate that cannot take a factive subject:

(102) *That Harry criticized the book was widely quoted.

This is consistent with the unacceptability of (103b) on the view that (103b) is derived from a sentence like (102) (see Jackendoff, 1974, for numerous arguments supporting this analysis):

(103) (a) Harry's criticism of the book was widely quoted.
       (b) *Harry's criticizing of the book was widely quoted.

Chomsky notes that for some speakers the derived nominal can include a verbal modifier. For example (104) is acceptable even though it is consistent with the lexicalist position since the nominal has a subordinate modifier:

(104) Harry's criticism of the book before he read it was widely quoted.

Chomsky proposes that (104) be accounted for by "derivative generation" from (105):

(105) Harry's criticizing the book before he read it . . .

That is, Chomsky argues that (104) is acceptable by "analogy," but remains ungrammatical, thus saving the lexicalist analysis. Hankamer (1972) and McCawley (1973) have attacked this proposal on the grounds that it is unmotivated by any general theory of "derivative generation." We can give force to Chomsky's claim and meet the objections to it by application of the analogy principle we have been illustrating. Suppose that a speaker wished to express the two propositions in (106) in one surface clause:

(106) (a) Harry criticized the book before he read it.
       (b) Harry's criticism was widely quoted.

There is no grammatical utterance that will represent this combination; rather there are two ungrammatical choices, (107) and (108):

(107) *Harry's criticizing the book before he read it was widely quoted.
(108) Harry's criticism of the book before he read it was widely quoted.

In (107), the regular meaning of the gerundive would have to be changed from a factive to a nonfactive. However, in (108) the normal meaning of the derived nominal is exactly the one intended. Thus the speaker uses (108) following the constraint that in analogy the meaning of individual phrases is preserved wherever possible.

    This analysis motivates the particular form used to express (106) and thereby explains (104) as an analogical formation. In this way, "derivative generation" may be given explanatory force.

6. EPILOGUE–IMPLICATIONS FOR A DYNAMIC MODEL OF LANGUAGE CHANGE AND ACQUISITION

Bever and Langendoen (1971, this vol.) articulated a problem in the model of linguistic evolution proposed by Halle (1962). According to this model, languages evolve according to specific constraints on the rules, for example, simplifying rules (Halle) or increasing the functional coherence of sets of rules (Kiparsky, 1968). As new cases come into linguistic usage, the child restructures its grammar to handle the new cases more efficiently than the grammar of its parents. The problem posed by such a model concerns the generation of "new" cases that motivate grammatical restructuring. Bever and Langendoen interpreted this problem as a question of constraints on possible neologisms and proposed that "possible neologisms are limited by the systems of speech behavior."

On this view, linguistic evolution is interpreted as an interaction between systematically constrained neologisms and an ontogenetically shifting filter in the child: those neologisms that are appropriate to a particular state in the child "survived"; they are picked up by the child and incorporated within the predicted grammar of the language. In this sense the effect of linguistic neologisms is analogous to the role of biological mutations in species evolution: their form is somewhat constrained by existing synchronic structures and if they create a structure which is too much at variance with existing structures they "die out" and do not become part of the structural evolution.

The present paper has fleshed out part of the view that was left unexplored: the source of acceptable neologisms. In their formulation Bever and Langendoen simply stated that neologisms are *constrained* to be "usable." They left the *source* of neologisms unexplained, relying on the possibility that they occur randomly and spontaneously. In the present paper, we have argued that behavioral limitations of the mechanism of speech production actually limit possible neologisms. Furthermore, they can *force* certain neologisms to become idiomatically "acceptable," though ungrammatical. That is, linguistic evolution is not merely a passive process in which randomly occurring neologisms are filtered out by behavioral and grammatical constraints. Rather, the process is partially an *active* one in which the needs of the system of speech production give rise to new constructions the grammar must accommodate to. Accordingly, linguistic evolution occurs in part as the by-product of mutual adjustments and interactions among different linguistic systems.

The notion that neologisms arise in an active process resolves a parallel problem in the standard models of language acquisition (see Chomsky, 1965; McNeil,

1969; Braine, 1964; Bloom, 1970). According to these models, language is acquired by way of a series of grammatical stages. At each stage the child attempts to incorporate within its grammar new sentences that it has come in contact with and to exclude sentences generated by its previous grammar that turned out to be unacceptable. Previous considerations of this model have left open the question of how the child brings new sentences into its behavioral repertoire before changing its grammar to generate them. That is, the previous discussions have characterized the language acquisition process as a passive one in which the child continually attempts to "weed out" unacceptable sentences that are generated by its grammar at each stage.

This view implies that the child's earliest grammars are the least constrained and become successively more restrictive. However, there is no evidence that this is the case. Also, grammar acquisition would be completely haphazard, depending entirely on *which* sentences the child happened to try out and which sentences the linguistic community happened to respond to appropriately.

The considerations in this paper allow for a more constrained and dynamic view of language acquisition (cf Bever, 1975b). On this view, the child is acquiring a behavioral system of speech perception and production partially independent from each other. "Grammar" develops primarily because of its functional role in easing the double burden on the child's memory imposed by the fact that there are a number of different systems for language use, each of which overlaps with the others. The main focus of the overlap are the shared lexical and syntactic sequences. For example, if the systems of speech production and perception are independent, then the set of words and sentences the child can understand will be represented in a distinct way from those words and sentences that he can utter. As this multiplication of information increases, so will the burden of the child's memory. On this view, the development of the "grammar" represents an organization of linguistic knowledge in which lexical items are listed only once each, and no sentences are listed. The syntactic and semantic components of the grammar specify how the lexical items can be combined to produce actual sentences.

An example may clarify this model of language acquisition. Consider simple adjectival sentences ("Harry was tall") and "truncated passives" ("Harry was hurt"). Children utter and understand both kinds of sentences at a very young age (about three years). This is puzzling if one were to assume that the child has developed a full grammatical analyses of truncated passives, since truncated passives are linguistically complex (i.e., they are derived from full passives such as "Harry was hurt by someone"). However, if the child uses only a minimal grammatical analysis to classify lexical items into types, then truncated passive past participles can be treated as "adjectives" and simply understood with the same perceptual schemata that are used to understand adjectives. By age six the child starts to understand and use full passives. By this hypothesis, this now creates a duplication of linguistic information in the child's repertoire—namely, the information that whatever can be the subject of the "adjectives" in truncated passives can also be the subject of full passives. Since truncated passive "adjectives" are homonymous with the past participle of the verbs they are related to, the grammatical solution to this replication of information is to derive truncated passives from full passives. This in turn would reclassify the "adjective" of truncated passives as a past participle. One would expect that the reorganization of truncated passives would make them more difficult for children to use at around age seven then they were at a younger age. In fact, there is evidence showing that this is the case. In a study of sentence retention, Slobin (1966) found that children at age eight have a relatively more difficult time with truncated passives than children at age six. This follows from the assumption that at age eight the child has ascribed a new grammatical analysis to truncated passives as derived from full passives.

This model of language acquisition is dynamic in that it depends on the interaction of different systems of linguistic knowledge and skill. At each stage, each of the systems attempts to represent the same set of sentences. However, one system (e.g., of speech production) may predict new cases that another system (e.g., of speech perception) does not allow. If the child tries these new cases out and finds them usable in the linguistic community, then this provides both internal and external pressure for all the systems of linguistic representation to accommodate to these cases. Thus, on this view, language acquisition not only depends on information from the linguistic community but on internal dynamics as well.

REFERENCES

Bever, T. G. 1970. "The Cognitive Basis for Linguistic Structures." In *Cognition and the Development of Language*, J. R. Hayes, ed. Wiley.

—— 1971. "The Integrated Study of Language." In *Biological and Social Factors in Psycholinguistics*, J. Morton, ed. Logos Press.

—— 1974. "The Ascent of the Specious, or There's a Lot we Don't Know about Mirrors." In *Explaining Linguistic Phenomena*, D. Cohen, ed. Hemisphere.

—— 1975a. "Functionalist Models of Linguistic Structures Presuppose Independent Models of Language Behavior." In *Papers from the Parasession on Functionalism*, *Chicago Linguistic Society*. University of Chicago Press.

—— 1975b. "Psychologically Real Grammar Emerges because of Its Role in Language Acquisition." In *Proceedings of the Georgetown Linguistics Roundtable*.

Bever, T. G., and D. T. Langendoen. 1971. "A Dynamic Model of the Evolution of Language." *Linguistic Inquiry* 2: 433–463. Reprinted in this volume.

Bloom, L. 1970. *Language Development: Form and function in emerging grammars*. M.I.T. Press.

Blumenthal, A. L. 1966. "Observations with Self-embedded Sentences." *Psychonomic Science* 6: 453–454.

Boomer, D. S. 1965. "Hesitation and Grammatical Encoding." *Language and Speech* 8: 148–158.

—— 1970. Review of F. Goldman-Eisler, *Psycholinguistics: Experiments in spontaneous speech. Lingua* 25: 152–164.

Braine, M. 1963. "On Learning the Grammatical Order of Words." *Psychological Review* 70: 323–348.

Carroll, J. M. 1974. "On the Historical and Synchronic Interaction of Verbal Systems: Diachronic Analogy." *Columbia University Working Papers in Linguistics*, pp. 29–66.

Carroll, J. M. 1975. "The Perceptual Principle of 'Gobbling': A Study in Functional Linguistic Explanation." *Northeast Linguistic Society*, University of Montreal.

Carroll, J. M., and T. G. Bever. In press. "Sentence Comprehension: A Case Study in the Relation of Knowledge and Perception." In *The Handbook of Perception*, Vol. 7, E. Carterette and J. Friedman, eds., Academic Press.

Carroll, J. M., and J. S. Hennessey. 1975. "Coordination Reduction and the English Comparative/Superlative: A Psycholinguistic Perspective." *Proceedings of the Berkeley Linguistic Society* 1: 25–36.

Chomsky, N. 1953. *The Logical Basis of Linguistic Theory*. Unpublished Ph.D. dissertation. M.I.T.

—— 1965. *Aspects of the Theory of Syntax*. M.I.T. Press.

—— 1970. "Remarks on Nominalization." In *Readings in English Transformational Grammar*, R. Jacobs and P. Rosenbaum, eds. Ginn.

—— 1973. "Conditions on Transformations." In *A Festschrift for Morris Halle*. S. Anderson and P. Kiparsky, eds. Holt, Reinhart and Winston.

—— 1975. "Questions of Form and Interpretation." *Linguistic Analysis* 1: 75–109.

Dougherty, R. C. 1970. "A Grammar of Coordinate Conjoined Structures: I." *Language* 46: 850–898.

—— 1971. "A Grammar of Coordinate Conjoined Structures: II." *Language* 47: 298–339.

Ervin-Tripp, S. 1973. "The Structure of Communicative Choice" in *Language Acquisition and Communicative Choice*, Anwar S. Dil, ed. Stanford University Press.

Fodor, J. A., T. Bever, and M. Garrett. 1974. *The Psychology of Language*. McGraw-Hill,

Fodor, J. A., and M. Garrett. 1966. "Some Reflections on Competence and Performance." In *Psycholinguistic Papers*, J. Lyons and R. Wales, eds. Edinburgh University Press.

—— 1967. "Some Syntactic Determinants of Sentential Complexity." *Perception and Psychophysics* 2: 289–296.

Fromkin, V. 1971. "The Non-Anomalous Nature of Anomalous Utterances." *Language* 47: 27–52.

Garrett, M., and S. Shattuck. 1974. "An Analysis of Speech Errors." *Quarterly Progress Report No. 113*, R.L.E.-M.I.T.

Grice, H. P. 1967. "Logic and Conversation." In *The Logic of Grammar*, D. Davidson and G. Harmon, eds. 1975, Dickenson.

Grosu, A. 1971. "On Perceptual and Grammatical Constraints." *Papers from the Seventh Regional Meeting, Chicago Linguistic Society*. University of Chicago Press.

—— 1972. "The Strategic Constant of the Island Constraints." *Ohio State Working Papers in Linguistics* 13.

Halle, M. 1962. "Phonology in Generative Grammar." *Word* 18: 54–72.

Hankamer, J. 1972. "Analogical Rules in Syntax." *Papers from the Eighth Regional Meeting, Chicago Linguistic Society*. University of Chicago Press.

Jackendoff, R. 1972. "Semantic Interpretation in a Generative Grammar." M.I.T. Press.

—— 1974. "Introduction to the $\overline{X}$ Convention." Indiana University Linguistics Club.

Katz, J. J. 1972. *Semantic Theory*. Harper and Row.

Kimball, J. 1973. "Seven Principles of Surface Structure Parsing in Natural Language." *Cognition* 2: 15–47.

Kiparsky, P. 1968. Linguistic Universals and Linguistic Change." In *Universals in Linguistic Theory*, E. Bach and R. Harms, eds. Holt, Rinehart and Winston.

Kiparsky, P., and C. Kiparsky. 1970. "Fact." In *Progress in Linguistics*, M. Bierwisch and K. Heidolph, eds. Mouton.

Labov, W. 1968. "Reflections of Social Processes in Linguistic Structures." In *Readings in the Sociology of Language*, J. Fishman, ed. Mouton.

—— 1970. "The Study of Language in its Social Context." *Studium Generale* 23: 30–87.

—— 1972a. "Negative Attraction and Negative Concord in English Grammar." *Language* 48: 773–818.

—— 1972b. "For an End to the Uncontrolled Use of Linguistic Intuitions." Unpublished paper.

Lakoff, G. 1969. "On Derivational Constraints." *Papers from the Fifth Regional Meeting, Chicago Linguistic Society*. University of Chicago Press.

—— 1971. "On Generative Semantics." In *Semantics*, D. Steinberg and L. Jakobovitz, eds. Cambridge University Press.

—— 1974. "On Transderivational Constraints. In *To Honor Henry and Rene Kahane*, Linguistic Research.

Lakoff, G., and J. R. Ross. 1972. "A Note on Anaphoric Islands and Causatives." *Linguistic Inquiry* 3: 121–125.

Langendoen, D. T. 1970. "The Accessibility of Deep Structures." In *Readings in English Transformational Grammar*, R. Jacobs and P. Rosenbaum, eds. Ginn.

Langendoen, D. T., and T. G. Bever. 1973. "Can a Not Unhappy Man be Called a Not Sad One? In *A Festschrift for Morris Halle*, S. Anderson and P. Kiparsky, eds. Holt, Rinehart and Winston. Reprinted, this volume.

MacKay, D. 1970. "Spoonerism: The Structure of Errors in the Serial Order of Speech." *Neuropsychologia* 8: 323–350.

Maclay, H., and C. Osgood. 1959. "Hesitation Phenomena in English Speech." *Word* 15: 19.

McCawley, J. 1973. A Review of Noam Chomsky's *Studies on Semantics in Generative Grammar*. Indiana University Linguistics Club.

——— 1970. "On the Application of Vice Versa." *Linguistic Inquiry* 1: 278–280.

——— 1974. *Grammar and Meaning*. T.E.C. Corp.

McNeil, D. 1969. *Developmental Psycholinguistics*. Harper and Row.

Miller, G., and N. Chomsky. 1963. "Finitary Models of Language Users. In *Handbook of Mathematical Psychology*, Vol. 2, R. D. Luce, R. Bush, and E. Galanter, eds. Wiley.

Perlmutter, D. 1972. *Deep and Surface Structure Constraints in Syntax*. Holt, Rinehart and Winston.

Ross, J. R. 1967. *Constraints on Variables in Syntax*. Indiana University Linguistics Club.

Ross, J. R. 1972. "Doubl-ing." *Linguistic Inquiry* 3: 61–86.

Schlesinger, I. M. 1971. "Production of Utterances and Language Acquisition." In *The Ontogenesis of Language*, D. Slobin and C. Ferguson, eds. Academic Press.

Schmerling, S. 1973. "Subjectless Sentences and the Notion of Surface Structures." *Papers from the Ninth Regional Meeting, Chicago Linguistic Society*. University of Chicago Press.

Slobin, D. 1966. "Grammatical Transformations and Sentence Comprehension in Childhood and Adulthood." *Journal of Verbal Learning and Verbal Behavior* 5: 219–227.

Slobin, D. 1971. "Developmental Psycholinguistics." In *A Survey of Linguistic Science*. W. I. Dingwall, ed. University of Maryland Press.

Tannenhaus, M. K., and J. M. Carroll. 1975. "The Clausal Processing Hierarchy . . . and Nouniness." In *Papers from the Parasession on Functionalism, Chicago Linguistic Society*. University of Chicago Press.

Valian, V. 1971. "Talking, Listening and Linguistic Structure." Unpublished Ph.D. dissertation.

Valian, V. and R. Wales. 1975. "What's What: Talkers Help Listeners Hear and Understand by Clarifying Sentential Relations." Unpublished paper.

Wells, R. 1947. "Immediate Constituents." *Language* 23: 81–117.

Yngve, V. 1960. "A Model and an Hypothesis for Language Structure." *Proceedings of the American Philosophical Society* 104: 444–466.

Zwicky, A. 1969. "Phonological Constraints in Syntactic Description." *Papers in Linguistics* 1: 411–463.

A Case of Apparent Ungrammaticality

D. TERENCE LANGENDOEN

Green (1971) claims that noun phrases like (1), which should be well-formed transformational variants of phrases like (2), are ungrammatical:

(1)   one of my friends' mother
(2)   the mother of one of my friends

Certainly, phrases such as (1) are unacceptable, as can be readily seen by considering sentences like (3) and (4), also given by Green:

(3)   *One of my friends' mother is coming.
(4)   *I had an argument with one of my friends' mother.

Green goes on the claim that when a plural head noun is substituted for the singular in (1), the resulting phrase is acceptable, as in (5):

(5)   One of my friends' parents are coming.

However, informants I have questioned on the matter also find (5) unacceptable, though perhaps not so bad as (3). To avoid the problem posed by the word *friends'* (is it pronounced [frénz] or [frénzɨz]?), I contrasted the following sentences and obtained the acceptability judgments as indicated:

(6)   *One of my children's friend is coming. (parallel to (3))
(7)   *One of my children's friends are coming. (parallel to (5))
(8)   One of my children's friends is coming.

Upon hearing (6) or (7), several informants in fact insisted that they contained grammatical lapses; that only (8) was correct English. But (8) contains a right-

---

Source: This article appears for the first time in this volume.

branching structure in which the head word is *one*, not *friends*, so, to repeat the question raised by Green at the end of her squib, "What is going on?"

To see what might be going on, let us examine other types of noun phrases of the surface form *NP of NP's N*, besides those in which the first NP is a quantifying word, such as *one*, *both*, and *all* (the only ones considered in Green's squib). When the first noun phrase is not a quantifying word, we find that left-branching interpretations are possible, though not preferred. There is, for example, the fairly well-known conundrum that is based on our spontaneous preference for right-branching over left-branching possessive structures.

(9)   The daughter of Pharaoh's son is the son of Pharaoh's daughter.

If one takes a consistently right-branching interpretation for the subject and predicate noun phrase in (9), one is left with contradiction: *the daughter. . .is the son . . .* (Similarly if one takes a consistently left-branching interpretation, but I have never heard of anyone ever doing this spontaneously.) To make sense of the conundrum, that is, find its tautological interpretation, one must associate a left-branching structure with either the subject or the predicate noun phrase (I get the impression that those who figure the conundrum out usually reinterpret the subject noun phrase in this way). This suggests that one arrives at a left-branching structure for noun phrases of the form *NP of NP's N* only if one is forced to on semantic or pragmatic grounds. Thus, consider a sentence like (10):

(10)   The commander of the army's belt-buckle needs polishing.

If *commander* is taken to be the head of the subject noun phrase in (10), one becomes aware of a number of anomalies: *the army has a belt-buckle*, *the belt-buckle has a commander*, and *the commander needs polishing*. However, if *belt-buckle* is taken to be the head of the subject noun phrase in (10), there are no anomalies and the sentence is ultimately understood in this way. The problem raised in Green's squib, then, is really the following. Surface strings of the form *NP of NP's N* may be parsed either as *NP [of NP's N]* (right branching) or *[NP of NP's] N* (left branching). If the first NP in the string is a quantifying word, the left-branching structure is always unacceptable; otherwise the left-branching structure is acceptable, but is only arrived at if the right-branching structure results in semantic or pragmatic anomaly.

This problem is an excellent test case for the theory of perceptual parsing of surface strings that has recently been proposed by Kimball (1974). If Kimball's theory can provide a reasonable and natural explanation for the phenomenon just described, there would then be considerable reason to consider that theory seriously as a part of an overall model of speech perception. Let us examine, then, what Kimball's principles predict about the parsing of strings of the form *NP of NP's N*.

First of all, let us provide the surface structures of the sentence (11), as they are given by English grammar:

(11)   The daughter of Pharaoh's son is handsome.

In (12), the surface phrase marker of (11) in which *daughter* is the head word of the subject noun phrase is represented; (13) represents the surface phrase marker of (11) in which *son* is the head word of the subject noun phrase:

(12)

(13)

Kimball's theory calls for top-bottom parsing as the sentence is being scanned, with as little look-ahead as possible (provided mainly to resolve local ambiguities, such as whether *that* is a complementizer, demonstrative determiner, or demonstrative pronoun), augmented with one specific bottom-top procedure that is called into play whenever a grammatical function word is encountered. The parsing principles he gives are basically language-independent schemata, which are fleshed out in accordance with structural properties of given languages (exactly in the way that grammatical theory provides rule schemata that are realized in different ways in the grammars of the various languages of the world). Therefore, from time to time, we will have to augment Kimball's principles somewhat for the English data under consideration.

In (14)–(21), we show how the surface phrase marker (12) for sentence (11) is built up in perception. First, the word *the* is encountered and recognized. In accordance with Kimball's top-bottom principle, and the facts of English grammar, the structure (14) is assigned:

(14)

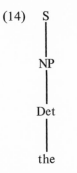

Next, the word *daughter* is recognized. Added to (14), the result, by Kimball's principle of Right Association, is (15):

(15)

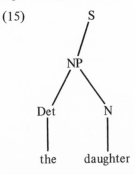

Next, the word *of* is recognized. As a preposition, it signals the beginning of a prepositional phrase. When a preposition phrase follows a subject noun phrase (such as *the daughter* in (14)), that phrase can be construed only as an adjunct to the subject noun phrase, and a new NP node must be inserted into the partial phrase marker (14) above the already existing NP node, in accordance with Kimball's one bottom-top principle "New Nodes."[1] This results in (16) in which, the "new node" is circled:

(16)

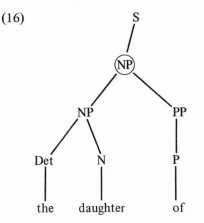

Next, the word *Pharaoh* is recognized.[2] This is categorized as a noun phrase consisting solely of a noun, and by Right Association it is subjoined to the preposition-phrase node, as shown in (17):

(17)

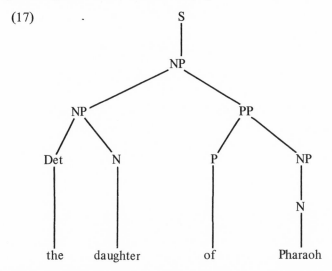

1. According to Kimball, "new nodes" are created exclusively by Chomsky-adjunction. I abandon that restriction in this paper, since I want to make use of the principle of New Nodes to create higher nodes that are not always copies of lower nodes. This constitutes my only departure from Kimball's theory, and it is not a major one.

2. More likely, the complex word *Pharaoh's* is recognized as a whole. For purposes of exposition, however, it is convenient to assume that the two morphemes in it are recognized sequentially.

Next, the possessive morpheme *'s* is recognized. As a function morpheme, it triggers the creation of the appropriate superordinate "new nodes," Det and NP. Grammatically, it may be associated with either the lower NP *Pharaoh* or the higher NP *the daughter of Pharaoh*. By the principle of Right Association, it must be associated with the lower NP. This results in the configuration shown in (18), in which the "new nodes" are circled:

(18)

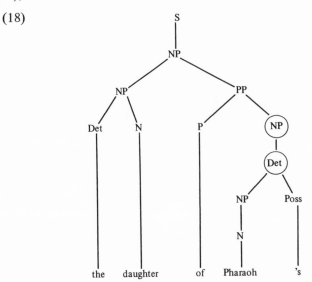

Next, the word *son* is recognized, and categorized as a noun. By Right Association, it is subjoined to the lower NP node (by Kimball's principle of Closure, also, it cannot be subjoined to the higher NP node):

(19)

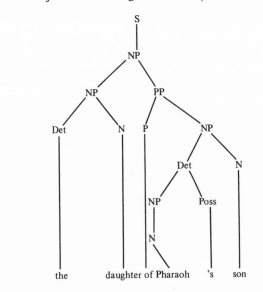

Next, the word *is* is recognized and categorized as a verb. By Closure, it cannot be subjoined to the subject noun phrase; by Right Association it must be subjoined to the S node, resulting in (20):

(20)

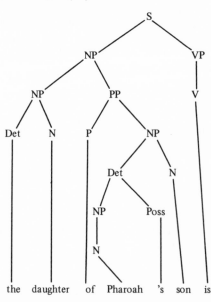

Finally, the word *handsome* is recognized, and categorized as an adjective, exhaustively dominated by the category adjective phrase. By Right Association, it is subjoined to the VP node, resulting in (21), which is identical to the surface phrase marker (12), as generated by the grammar of English:

(21)

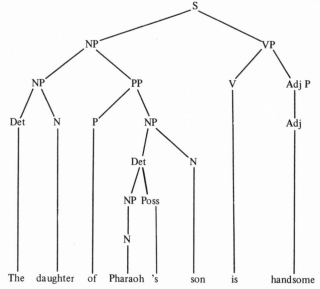

However, the interpretation of (21) is semantically anomalous; *handsome* is predicable of male subjects, and the subject of (21) is female. On the other hand, (11) has a nonanomalous interpretation, namely that provided by (13), in which the subject noun phrase designates a male. To arrive at (13), however, assuming that (12) = (21) has already been arrived at, one runs afoul of Kimball's principle of Fixed Structure. According to this principle, once a syntactic structure has been assigned to a string, it is difficult to reanalyze that string and assign it a new structure.

The principle does not say, however, that it is impossible to do so. What is needed is a specification of the conditions under which reanalysis of this sort can be carried out. Recall that the ambiguity of the subject noun phrase in (11) has to do with whether the possessive morpheme is associated with just the smaller noun phrase *Pharaoh* or with the larger noun phrase *the daughter of Pharaoh*. Suppose that in the course of listening to (11), at the point at which the possessive morpheme is encountered and by Right Association associated with the smaller noun phrase, an abstract mark "R" (interpretable as 'point of possible reanalysis') is made. When, at the end of the sentence, it is discovered that the structure that has been assigned receives an anomalous interpretation, the perceptual device remembers that it has entered "R", and undoes all of the structural analysis from point "R" on. That is, the device goes back to the point at which it has only the structure given in (17) left. It now recognizes the possessive morpheme *'s*, but this time associates it with the high NP *the daughter of Pharaoh*. This results in the configuration (22), in which, again, the "new nodes" are circled:

(22)

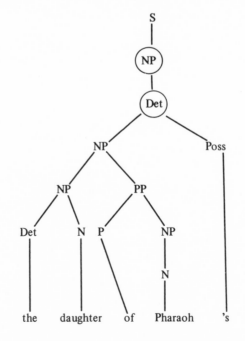

Next, the word *son* is rerecognized, assigned the category noun, and by Right Association, subjoined to the only available NP node, namely the one immediately below the S node. This results in (23):

(23)

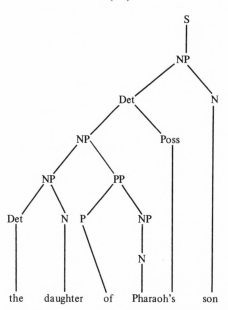

When *is* and *handsome* are encountered, the structure of the verb phrase is built up as before, and (24) results, which is identical to the surface phrase marker (13), as generated by the grammar of English:

(24)

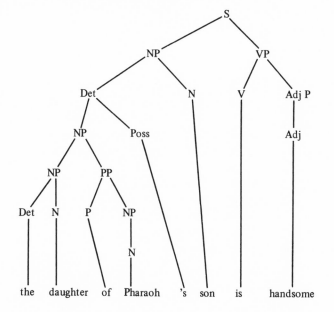

D. TERENCE LANGENDOEN

This model of how syntactic reanalysis is carried out makes a number of predictions, which strike me as correct, although I have not undertaken the experimental work necessary to show them correct. One is that constituent-structure ambiguities in which one interpretation is highly favored because of Right Association will go unnoticed, unless the favored interpretation is semantically or pragmatically anomalous. An even stronger prediction is that reanalysis is easier and much more likely to be carried out in sentences like (10) than in sentences like (11). The reason is that in (10), the point of possible reanalysis is exactly the point at which semantic and pragmatic anomaly is noticed (at that point, the anomalous phrases *the army's belt-buckle* and *the commander of the army's belt-buckle* will have been built up). In (11), on the other hand, the point at which the anomaly is first noticed comes considerably later than the point of possible reanalysis. It should be a relatively straightforward matter to design experimental materials in which one systematically varies the distance between the two points, and measures (for example) latencies to respond.

We return now to the problem that started us off: why are sentences like (6) and (7) unacceptable? Already, we can rephrase that question: why isn't reanalysis carried out when one hears these sentences? The answer, I believe, has to do with the fact that (6) and (7) are heard, not as semantically or pragmatically anomalous, but as syntactically anomalous. Consider first example (6). By Kimball's principles, at the point at which *friend* is encountered, the quantifying word *one* will have already been analyzed as the head of the subject noun phrase, and *friend* is then analyzed as the head of the noun-phrase object of the preposition-phrase adjunct to the word *one*. But, *one*, and similarly all quantifying words as heads of noun phrases with preposition-phrase adjuncts, requires that the head noun of the object of the preposition be *syntactically* plural, and *friend* is singular. To see that the requirement is a syntactic, and not a semantic one, consider examples (24)–(27):

(25) One of the boys is coming.
(26) *One of John and Bill is coming.
(27) *One of the team is coming. (i.e., where *team* means 'teammembers')

In general, as soon as an apparent syntactic anomaly is encountered, we assume that the listener either rejects the sentence in which it occurs as not part of his language, or that he mentally makes the simplest adjustment necessary to restore its grammaticality, on the assumption that the speaker made a simple syntactic error. In the case of (6), the simplest adjustment is to construe *friend* as *friends*, and in the absence of further anomaly, the sentence will be interpreted as such. In either case: rejection of the sentence as not part of the listener's language, or syntactic readjustment so as to make the sentence well formed syntactically, the reparsing routine will never be called into play, even though the result of reparsing would render the sentence grammatical.[3]

3. In other words, the adjustment of *friend* to *friends* is a simpler adjustment than reparsing; hence the latter will never be used.

In the case of (7), the head word of the object of the preposition-phrase adjunct to *one* is, as it should be, syntactically plural. However, the verb is also plural, which is syntactically wrong if the singular word *one* is the head word of the subject noun phrase. Therefore, again, the listener will either reject the sentence, or more likely, mentally adjust the verb from plural *are* to singular *is*.[4] Either way, reparsing of the subject noun phrase will not be undertaken.

What have we shown? First, Kimball's theory of surface-structure parsing receives strong independent support, in that, together with very reasonable assumption about what listeners do when they encounter syntatic anomaly as opposed to what they do when they encounter semantic or pragmatic anomaly, it explains the unacceptability of the sentences noted by Green. Second, since the distinction between syntactic and semantic or pragmatic anomaly is an integral part of what must be counted a very satisfying explanation for a puzzling phenomenon, that distinction must be maintained in an adequate theory of language. Finally, Green's unacceptable sentences are grammatical, not ungrammatical, as she claims. They are grammatical, because well-motivated rules of English grammar generate them; to constrain those rules so as not to generate them would badly complicate the grammar. What we have done is to provide an explanation for their unacceptability within the domain of perceptual parsing.

References

Green, G. M. 1971. "Unspeakable Sentences: Book 2." *Linguistic Inquiry* 2:601–602.

Kimball, J. 1974. "Seven Principles of Surface Structure Parsing in Natural Language." *Cognition* 2:15–47.

---

4. It is the fact that changing the verb to agree with the subject noun is an easier adjustment to make than the adjustment of a singular noun to a plural one (for whatever reasons) that accounts for the somewhat higher acceptability of (7) over (6).

Dative Questions: A Study in the Relation of Acceptability to Grammaticality of an English Sentence Type

D. TERENCE LANGENDOEN
NANCY KALISH-LANDON
JOHN DORE

1. GRAMMATICALITY AND ACCEPTABILITY

It is not always easy to determine the grammatical status of expressions in a given language, for at least three reasons. First, speakers' judgments that certain expressions are unacceptable do not guarantee that they are ungrammatical, since there may be language-independent[1] perceptual principles that make certain perfectly grammatical sentences seem ungrammatical (Chomsky, 1965; Bever, 1970; Kimball, 1974). Second, the converse is also true: Judgments that expressions are acceptable do not guarantee that they are grammatical (Otero, 1972; Langendoen and Bever, 1973). Finally, there are many expressions for which speakers do not give consistent acceptability judgments; such inconsistency has misled many linguists into postulating the existence of 'dialects' for which there is often no geographic, socioeconomic or other language-independent basis (Labov, 1972). In this paper, we consider a type of English sentence which has, until very recently, been considered ungrammatical because

---

1. We use the term 'language-independent' throughout this paper specifically to mean 'independent of the rules that generate the sentences of any given language'. The principles are certainly not to be considered 'independent of language itself', since they are intended to be rules according to which linguistic structures are perceived.

This work was supported in part by a faculty research award of The City University of New York.

Source: *Cognition* 2 (1974): 451–478. Reprinted, with minor additions, by permission of the publisher.

D. TERENCE LANGENDOEN, NANCY
KALISH-LANDON, AND JOHN DORE

the various linguists who have studied it have all found it unacceptable. We question the decision to label this type of sentence ungrammatical; first because it appears to lead to an *ad-hoc* complication of the rules of English syntax, second because there are many English speakers who find the sentence-type in question to be acceptable and third because there seems to be a language-independent perceptual principle that accounts for both the unacceptability of the sentence type and the variability found in those acceptability judgments.[2]

The decision to treat a given principle of language as part of the grammar of that language (competence); or alternatively as part of the system of perceptual rules, or of some other system of rules relating to language use (performance), is thus based on two considerations. First, we must evaluate the effect that incorporating the principle into the grammar may have on the expressive power of the theory of grammar. If incorporating the principle into the grammar requires greater theoretical expressive power than if the principle were not part of the grammar, that incorporation of the principle into the grammar is disfavored. However, if the principle does not relate to any system of language use—for example, if it cannot be shown to be a principle whereby listeners parse surface structures or assign relations among perceived constituents under the real-time constraints of the listening situation—then incorporating the principle into a system of language use is disfavored. Thus, four possibilities arise. First, the principle increases the expressive power of grammatical theory, and it can be interpreted as a principle of language use. Then we conclude that the principle is one of language use only. Second, the principle does not increase the expressive power of grammatical theory, and it cannot be interpreted as a principle of language use. Then the principle is one of grammar. Third, the principle increases the expressive power of grammatical theory, and it cannot be interpreted as a principle of language use. Then, despite the increase in the power of the theory, we must conclude that the principle is one of grammar. Fourth, the principle does not increase the expressive power of grammatical theory, and it can be interpreted as a principle of language use. Then we may conclude that the principle is one of grammar and that it is also one of language use; the decision for each component being made on the basis of whether the incorporation of the principle would or would not result in a simpler system. For example, the principle governing the appearance of the complementizer *that* in English finite subordinate clauses is a situation of this fourth type, and it is an open question whether those principles are to be construed as part of the grammar of English (Bever and Langendoen, 1971).

---

2. We say 'seems to be' rather than 'is' because we have not carried out empirical investigations on the principle in question. See below, Section 6.

2. THE INTERACTION OF THE DATIVE TRANSFORMATION WITH VARIOUS OTHER MOVEMENT TRANSFORMATIONS IN ENGLISH

There is a well-known syntactic transformation in English that puts the underlying indirect object into the position of the direct object; that is, immediately following the verb. The characteristic preposition of the indirect object (*to* or *for* in most cases) is then deleted (whether by the same rule that performs the movement of the indirect object or by a later rule of Preposition Deletion is of no concern to us here). We call this movement rule the Dative transformation (Fillmore, 1965; Ross, 1968; Kuroda, 1968; Klima, 1970; Fischer, 1971; Jackendoff and Culicover, 1971; Edmonds, 1972 all treat the Dative transformation in some detail). According to this transformation, we may derive the sentences in (2) from the structures that also underlie those in (1).

(1) (a) The traveler gave documents to the clerk.
    (b) My grandmother bought a radio for my sister.
(2) (a) The traveler gave the clerk documents.
    (b) My grandmother bought my sister a radio.

We now consider sentences in which the underlying indirect object is moved to a new position in the sentence; first those in which Dative has not applied, and second those in which Dative has applied (the asterisk '*' indicates those sentences which are unacceptable to the linguists that have studied sentences of this type):

(3) (a) i. *The clerk was given documents to by the traveler.
      ii. *My sister was bought a radio for by my grandmother.
    (b) i. The clerk was given documents by the traveler.
      ii. (*) My sister was bought a radio by my grandmother.[3]

---

3. Fillmore (1965) judges all sentences like (3bii) unacceptable. Jackendoff and Culicover (1971, p. 400) hold that such sentences vary in acceptability, depending on whether or not the indirect object comes to 'have' the direct object. Thus for them (3bii) would be acceptable, but not (i).

(i) *My sister was played a tune by my grandmother.

The issues raised by this difference of opinion on acceptability are interesting but not within the scope of this paper.

(Passive)

    (4) (a)   i. Harriet is tough to write letters to.
               ii. Harriet is tough to buy clothes for.
         (b)   i. *Harriet is tough to write letters.
               ii. *Harriet is tough to buy clothes.

(Tough Movement)

    (5) (a)   i. It's Harriet (that) I gave the watch to/ It's Harriet to whom I
                   gave the watch/ It's to Harriet (that) I gave the watch.
               ii. It's Harriet (that I bought the watch for/ It's Harriet for whom
                   I bought the watch.
         (b)   i. *It's Harriet (that) I gave the watch.
               ii. *It's Harriet (that) I bought the watch.

(Clefting)

    (6) (a)   i. These people, I wouldn't send a penny to.
               ii. Elsie, I wouldn't buy anything for.
         (b)   i. *These people, I wouldn't send a penny.
               ii. *Elsie, I wouldn't buy anything.

(Topicalization)

    (7) (a)   i. This is the person (that) Selma sold the car to/ This is the per-
                   son to whom Selma sold the car.
               ii. Do you know the person (that) I made this dress for?/ Do you
                   know the person for whom I made this dress?
         (b)   i. *This is the person (that) Selma sold the car.
               ii. *Do you know the person (that) I made this dress?

(Relativization)

    (8) (a)   i. Who(m) did you give this book to?/ To whom did you give this
                   book?
               ii. Who(m) did you make this dress for?/ For whom did you make
                   this dress?
         (b)   i. *Who(m) did you give this book?
               ii. *Who(m) did you make this dress?

(Question Formation)

According to the judgments just given, the interaction of Dative and Passive is opposite that of Dative and the other movement transformations considered. Dative must apply if the underlying indirect object is to undergo Passive; it must not apply if the indirect object is to undergo Tough Movement, Clefting, Topicalization, Relativization or Question Formation.[4] It is easy to see why failure

4. It is immaterial to us whether Relativization and Question Formation are two rules in English or two manifestations of the same rule (*Wh*-Fronting). Evidence that they are two rules is presented in Langendoen (1973).

to apply Dative leads to unacceptability when the indirect object is made subject by Passive: Such sentences are ungrammatical because Passive can move the noun phrase of a preposition phrase into subject position only if the preposition phrase immediately follows the verb (Jackendoff and Culicover, 1971, p. 398). What is not so easy to see is why the examples in (3b) are acceptable whereas the (b)-examples in (4)-(8) are not.

One possible explanation makes use of a fundamental formal difference between Passive and the other movement transformations under consideration. Passive is not an unbounded movement rule; the others are.[5] One could then claim that what makes the (b)-examples of (4)-(8) unacceptable is their ungrammaticality, and that they are ungrammatical because their derivations violate the principle that no indirect object that has undergone Dative may be moved by any unbounded movement transformation.

3. AN ATTEMPT TO EXPLAIN THE INTERACTION FROM UNIVERSAL GRAMMAR, WHICH FAILS

It would be highly desirable if we could formulate a principle of universal grammar from which the English-specific principle just formulated would follow as a direct result. The reason for this is that the most adequate formalization of the English-specific principle is in terms of a derivational constraint, the undesirability of which notion has, in our judgment, been amply demonstrated. (Chomsky, 1972; Baker and Brame, 1972; Langendoen and Bever, 1973).[6] A language-universal principle that has been suggested recently by Klima (1970) and Ruwet (1973) looks promising in this connection. In its crudest form, the principle states that syntactic transformations may not create structures that permit the existence of syntactic ambiguity that depends *solely* on the grammatical rela-

5. On this distinction, see Ross (1967). We say that a movement transformation is unbounded if it can move a constituent across an unlimited number of unmatched left brackets labeled S; otherwise a movement transformation is bounded. Thus, for example, Question Formation is unbounded because sentences like (i) are grammatical.

    (i)   Who(m) did you say that Georgette found out that Marian was known to have been seen with?

But Passive is bounded because sentences like (ii) are ungrammatical.

    (ii)   *Frieda was believed that they had heard from by Irene (i.e., as Passive of: Irene believed that they had heard from Frieda).

6. The derivational constraint would be formulated along the following lines. In a derivation, a noun phrase that has been moved by Dative may not be moved again by any unbounded movement rule. The best alternative to the derivational constraint within an *Aspects*-type theory would be to mark all noun phrases that undergo Dative with some arbitrary feature and add to the structural conditions on all unbounded movement transformations in English the stipulation that they are inapplicable to noun phrases carrying that feature.

D. TERENCE LANGENDOEN, NANCY
KALISH-LANDON, AND JOHN DORE

tions of two constituents in a sentence; we may call this the constraint on relational ambiguity principle (CRAP).[7] Among other things, CRAP can be used to explain the observation made by Chomsky (1965, p. 128) that although it is generally possible to topicalize direct objects in German, sentences in which the direct object cannot be distinguished inflectionally from the subject cannot undergo direct-object topicalization. That is, Chomsky claims that although there is a general process in German involving Topicalization and Subject Postposing that permits the derivation of sentences like (9) from structures like those underlying (10), (11) cannot be obtained from (12) because, if the derivation of (11) were allowed, (11) would have the same surface structure as (13), in which the two noun phrases bear the opposite grammatical relations:

(9) (a) Heute kommt die Frau. 'Today, the woman comes'.
    (b) Den Mann sieht die Frau. 'The man, the woman sees'.
(10) (a) Die Frau kommt heute. 'The woman comes today'.
    (b) Die Frau sieht den Mann. 'The woman sees the man'.
(11) *Das Mädchen sieht die Frau. 'The girl, the woman sees'.
(12) Die Frau sieht das Mädchen. 'The woman sees the girl'.
(13) Das Mädchen sieht die Frau. 'The girl sees the woman'.

As Chomsky observes, the ordinary mechanisms of transformational grammar would not be able to account for the cases in which the application of Topi-

---

7. For example, CRAP specifies that in English, one could not transformationally derive the sentence (i) from the same deep structure that underlies (ii):

    (i) Jill denounced Jack.
    (ii) Jack denounced Jill.

On the other hand, the principle does not disallow one or both of the derivations of (iii) and (iv), since the ambiguity involves more than just the grammatical relations of its elements:

    (iii) The ducks are ready to eat.
    (iv) The shooting of the hunters was a tragedy.

Klima's version of CRAP is somewhat different. It reads: 'When there are multiple occurrences of the same category in one construction, without lexical or morphological differentiation, then a simple algorithm exists for distinguishing their function and no transformation will have such an effect as to interfere with the effectiveness of the algorithm' (quoted in Ruwet, 1973, p. 426). This formulation, however, is defective in at least two critical respects. First, for 'transformation', Klima should have something like 'transformational derivation', since presumably he would want to allow the possibility of a derivation in which a transformation applies so as to interfere with the algorithm only to have a second transformation undo its effect. Second, his formulation is not couched in universal terms, since the algorithm Klima refers to will differ from language to language. In English, for example, the algorithm Klima posits for distinguishing the function of direct object from the function of indirect object is that the indirect object is the noun phrase that immediately follows the verb (in the absence of morphological evidence). Moreover, this algorithm, if true, is not a grammatical principle, but rather a principle of language perception (that is, a language-independent principle in the sense given in footnote 1). Hence it can have no bearing on the question of whether a given sentence is grammatical. For further discussion of Klima's version of CRAP, see section 5.1 and footnote 9.

calization and Subject-Postposing in German would result in an unacceptable sentence, since the cases involve 'accidents' of morphology to which the transformations in question could not possibly be sensitive. CRAP, however, provides what seems to be the most direct and intuitively satisfying account.[8]

Returning to the problem of the interaction of Dative with the various movement transformations in English, we see that CRAP also predicts that the (b)-examples in (4)-(8) are ungrammatical because there is nothing in the *structure* (including morphology) of those examples that permits us to determine which of the two object noun phrases in each is the direct object and which the indirect object. That is, if those examples were grammatical, they would be relationally ambiguous. This fact becomes clearer if we consider an example in which the direct object is animate:

> (14)　*Who(m) did Selma send the doctor?

If (14) were grammatical, there would be no dispute about its relational ambiguity. It would mean the same thing as either (15a) or (15b):[9]

> (15)　(a)　Who(m) did Selma send the doctor to?/ To whom did Selma send the doctor?
>
> 　　　(b)　Who(m) did Selma send to the doctor?

8. However, although the existence of CRAP as a linguistic universal would remove the need for a high-powered constraint (presumably a transderivational constraint) from the grammar of German, CRAP is itself a device as powerful as a transderivational constraint. In effect, it is an instruction to block a derivation given the existence of another derivation which results in the same surface structure as the first but with the constituents in different grammatical relations (or, both derivations may be blocked; see footnote 9). Thus the explanatory power of CRAP is strongly limited. It does not prevent the existence of grammars with rules that could create relational ambiguity but only prevents the derivation of relationally ambiguous sentences when those rules are used. It would be more interesting if there were a principle that really limited the class of grammars that could be acquired by stipulating that certain rules could not be a part of a grammar that had certain other rules because of the problem of relational ambiguity. But, apparently, there is no such principle.

9. As formulated in footnote 6, the English specific derivational constraint would actually block only the derivation of (14) from the structure that underlies (15a). The derivation of (14) from (15b) would be permitted, since Question Formation is moving the direct object, not the indirect object. From the version of CRAP given in the text, on the other hand, it would follow that both derivations would be blocked, since in both cases syntactic transformations that create an ambiguous structure are being applied. This contrasts with the German situation involving Topicalization and Subject Postposing, in which one derivation is not blocked because it does not involve the application of relational-ambiguity-creating transformations. Since none of the linguists we have cited who have investigated the problem under consideration took into account sentences like (14), we have no way of knowing whether they would judge (14) as unacceptable on both readings, or unacceptable only on the reading of (15a) and acceptable on the reading of (15b). We suspect that opinion would be divided on this matter, some finding that (14) is unacceptable on both readings, in conformity with our version of CRAP, and others that (14) is acceptable on the reading of (15b) only, in conformity with Klima's version of CRAP and the derivational constraint formulated in footnote 6. We take up this matter of varying acceptability judgments below in Section 6.

D. TERENCE LANGENDOEN, NANCY
KALISH-LANDON, AND JOHN DORE

Similarly, convincingly ambiguous examples could be constructed using any of the other unbounded movement rules together with Dative.

However, CRAP falsely predicts that the examples in (3b), which illustrate the interaction of Dative and Passive, are also ungrammatical, since structurally the surface-subject noun phrase could be taken to be either the underlying direct or indirect object. This fact, again, emerges most clearly when we consider an example that contains an underlying animate direct object:

(16) The rich client was offered the young lawyer by the senior partner.

That is, (16) is the passive version of either (17a) or (17b):

(17) (a) The senior partner offered the righ client the young lawyer (i.e., The senior partner offered the young lawyer to the rich client).

(b) The senior partner offered the young lawyer the rich client (i.e., The senior partner offered the rich client to the young lawyer).

To save CRAP, we must therefore specify that it blocks a derivation of a relationally ambiguous sentence only if at least one unbounded movement transformation is applied in it.[10]

10. Alternatively, one could eliminate reference to boundedness in the statement of CRAP if one could substantiate the claim that (16) cannot be derived from (17b) and that hence (16) is not relationally ambiguous. This could be done by strictly enforcing the requirement that the noun phrase made subject by Passive must either be immediately postverbal or contained in a preposition phrase that is immediately postverbal; in (17b), the noun phrase undergoing Passive is separated from the verb by another noun phrase.

By so restricting Passive, however, we would also be predicting that both sentences in (i) are ungrammatical:

(i) a. A book was given Mary by Nancy
     b. *A dress was bought Mary by Nancy

According to both Fillmore (1965) and Jackendoff and Culicover (1971, pp. 398, 400), only sentences in which a *for*-dative is made subject by Passive are unacceptable. Nevertheless, Jackendoff and Culicover accept the limitation on the structural description of Passive discussed above and derive sentences like (ia) from the structure that underlies (ii) by a later, optional rule they call, simply enough, *To* Deletion (1971, p. 404):

(ii) A book was given to Mary by Nancy.

But if Jackendoff and Culicover are right, then sentences like (16) remain relationally ambiguous, and CRAP continues to make the wrong prediction. To save CRAP without imposing the limitation on boundedness, one would have to insist that the proposed rule of *To* Deletion is not part of the grammar of English and that (ia), while acceptable, is nonetheless ungrammatical.

Now, as we observed in the opening paragraph of this paper, it is possible that a class of sentences can be considered acceptable but ungrammatical. But to show that such a class [for example, the class of sentences like (ia)] must be viewed in that way, one must be able to demonstrate a language-independent behavioral principle according to which those sentences are acceptable, despite their ungrammaticality. In particular, it will not suffice to say simply that such sentences are acceptable 'by analogy', for then the questions arise, by analogy to what, and why this analogy and not some other. In the case of (ia), we know of no language-independent principle that could be appealed to; indeed it is the very

But even this limitation is inadequate. Ruwet (1973) points out that the application of Question Formation (an unbounded rule) and a rule he calls Stylistic Inversion creates sentences with relational ambiguity in French; one example he cites is (18):[11]

(18) Quels soldats commandent ces officiers? 'Which soldiers command these officers?' or 'Which soldiers do these officers command?'

Exactly the same sort of ambiguity appears in German and English (in English it is limited to sentences containing the main verb *have* and no auxiliary verbs), as in the examples in (19):

(19) (a) Was hat diene Katze in den Pfoten?
      (b) What has your cat in its paws?

In light of such examples, it is clear that there can be no syntactic mechanism for ruling out relational ambiguity in all cases, whether language-universal or language-specific. This raises the possibility that there is some alternative explanation for the unacceptability of the (b)-examples in (4)-(8), which does not classify those examples as ungrammatical. One such explanation for the cases in (8b), in which Dative interacts with the application of Question Formation to the indirect object resulting in sentences which we henceforth shall call dative questions (DQs), has been proposed by Jackendoff and Culicover (1971). We consider now their proposal in detail.

4. CRITIQUE OF JACKENDOFF AND CULICOVER'S PERCEPTUAL-STRATEGY EXPLANATION FOR THE UNACCEPTABILITY OF DATIVE QUESTIONS

Although we limit our attention in this section and in what follows to DQs, what we have to say will largely carry over to sentences like the (b)-examples in (4)-(7).[12]

---

acceptability of (ia) that gives rise to the ambiguity of (16)! We conclude that (ia) is acceptable because it is grammatical, that (16) is relationally ambiguous, and therefore that CRAP, if it is to be saved from this particular objection, must make reference to the boundedness of the transformational rules involved.

11. Although Ruwet (1973) devotes the bulk of his article to a defense of CRAP from French syntax, he is prepared to abandon it if the two readings would not both be likely in a given context. But this amounts to an admission that the principle is not part of linguistic theory but at most a rhetorical principle: Relationally ambiguous sentences are avoided except in the case where only one interpretation is likely given the context.

12. We have some informally collected evidence that there is some variation in the acceptability of the (b)-examples in (4)–(7); in particular that the examples in (4b) are considerably less acceptable than the others. We are not prepared at the moment, however, to explain this variation.

D. TERENCE LANGENDOEN, NANCY
KALISH-LANDON, AND JOHN DORE

Jackendoff and Culicover's motivation for proposing a perceptually based account of the unacceptability of DQs, like ours, is based on the realization of the difficulty of accounting for the unacceptability of that sentence type in the grammar of English (see especially p. 411 of their article).[13] According to their account, DQs are unacceptable because a listener cannot determine from their perceived structure what grammatical relation to assign to the interrogative constituent. To show why this is so, Jackendoff and Culicover propose the following two-stage account of how listeners assign grammatical relations to noun phrases.

First, grammatical relations for noun phrases that occur in their underlying positions by undoing a bounded-movement rule (such as Passive, Dative or Subject-Verb Inversion) are established. Second, grammatical relations for noun phrases that have been moved by unbounded rules[14] are established by fitting them into any remaining perceived gaps. The crucial point is that although an unbounded-movement rule will always leave a gap (namely, the position formerly occupied by the moved constituent), the gap will not always be readily perceivable. Let us call this second stage of Jackendoff and Culicover's proposal for the perceptual determination of grammatical relations the Gap-Filling Principle (GFP). To see how GFP works, consider its application to DQs and their variants in which Dative is not applied:

(20) (a) What did John give to Mary?
 (b) What did John give Mary?
 (c) Who(m) did John give a book to?
 (d) *To whom did John give a book?

13. However, Jackendoff and Culicover, in another passage, express the view that the mechanisms that account for perceptual difficulty are to be accounted for in the grammatical description of a language. In connection with the transformation called Extraposition from NP, they say the following: "the constraint on Extraposition from NP, which is very awkward to state in terms of conditions on application of transformations, becomes much clearer in terms of the difficulty of correctly interpreting the resulting strings. By permitting problems of string interpretation as possible sources of *ungrammaticality* [emphasis ours], we can eliminate this otherwise unexplained constraint. However, we must leave open for the present the question of how to incorporate this innovation into the theory of grammar" (1971, pp. 406–407). Given what they say on p. 411, we charitably interpret this passage as containing a lapse; Jackendoff and Culicover, we believe, are not really proposing that a theory of grammar should contain within it a theory of how sentences are perceptually processed.

14. Jackendoff and Culicover's exact wording (1971, p. 410) is that "NPs which have been moved away from arbitrary positions (such as NPs fronted by *wh*-fronting) are then fitted into remaining gaps." As far as we can determine, rules which move constituents from arbitrary positions are coextensive with rules which are unbounded.

To explain the acceptability judgments in (20), Jackendoff and Culicover (1971) reason as follows (we change their example numbers to conform to ours):

> In each sentence, the presence of the *wh*-word signals that the interpreter of the sentence must look for a gap into which the *wh*-word can fit. In (20a), *to* follows *give*, which can never happen in a declarative sentence. One can thus conclude that *what* must have been fronted from between these two words. In (20b), *give Mary* is a permissible sequence in a declarative sentence, so *what* need not have come from between them. In fact, if it had, the impossible string **give something Mary* would have to be the corresponding declarative VP form. However, nothing follows *Mary*, and the verb *give* requires two objects. *Give Mary something* is a possible declarative VP form, so one can conclude that *what* has been fronted from the end of the sentence.
>
> In (20c), *give a book* is a possible string in a declarative VP, and the bare preposition at the end shows that *whom* must have come from the end of the sentence. In (20d) again *give a book* is a possible string, and so no gap is noticed at the stage where *Whom did John give a book* has been perceived. At this stage, the listener's hypothesis is that *whom* has been fronted from the end; hence the preposition *to* is expected to follow *book*, as in (20c). Imagine the hearer's consternation when the expected *to* does not arrive. The sentence is therefore judged unacceptable, since it is expected to be (20c) and then fails to conform to that expectation (p. 409).

To summarize, sentences like (20d) are said to be unacceptable because the gap left by the fronting of the questioned constituent is not noticeable; sentences like (20a-c) are acceptable because the gap is noticeable.

There are several respects in which this explanation for the judgments in (20) is faulty. First, consider the treatment of (20a). While it is certainly unlikely that the string *give to Mary* would appear in a declarative sentence,[15] it is certainly not impossible, since examples like (21) are certainly acceptable:

(21)   Whenever he is feeling charitable, John gives to Mary.

More seriously, consider a sentence like (22), which has exactly the same structure as (20a):

(22)   What did John write to Mary?

---

15. Jackendoff and Culicover do not intend for us to conclude that interrogative sentences are transformed back into declarative sentences in perception; it is just that in declarative sentences constituents generally appear where they also happen to appear in deep structure.

Since *to* can follow *write* in a declarative sentence, and probably does so quite frequently in ordinary usage, it would seem that listeners many times, if not invariably, would fail to notice a gap between *write* and *to* in (22); nevertheless, no one would find (22) unacceptable.[16]

Now consider (20d). According to GFP, this sentence is unacceptable because no gap can be perceived within its VP. Now consider (23), which is structurally parallel to (20d) except that where a nominal direct object appears in (20d) a sentential one appears in (23):

(23)   *Who(m) did John tell that Mary was staying?

Example (23) contains the surface VP *tell that Mary was staying*, which is impossible in a sentence not transformed by some movement rule. Moreover, the element that has been moved out of that VP must appear between the verb *tell* and the sentential object, and hence a gap must be noticeable in that position. According the GFP, therefore, (23) should be acceptable, but is not. Still another problem with GFP as it applies to (20d)-type sentences that it predicts that sentences like (14), repeated here for convenience, should be acceptable on the interpretation that the postverbal noun phrase is the indirect object:

(14)   *Who(m) did Selma send the doctor?

This is so because *who(m)* can be fitted into the gap following the postverbal noun phrase (but see footnote 9).

Thus, GFP, despite its intuitive plausibility, cannot as such provide a perceptually based explanation for the unacceptability of DQs. We must conclude either that there is some other language-independent account of their unacceptability or that, indeed, DQs are ungrammatical. One piece of evidence that would tip the scales against the latter conclusion would be the existence of a population of otherwise ordinary English speakers who find DQs acceptable. For such speakers it would be impossible to maintain the DQs are ungrammatical, since an acceptable sentence type can only be considered ungrammatical if there is a language-independent explanation for its acceptability (see Langendoen and Bever, 1973, for discussion). But for the sentence type under consideration, the problem up to now has been just the opposite: to find a language-independent basis for their unacceptability. Furthermore, there is no problem in accounting for the acceptability of DQs within the grammar of English, since

16. This is not due to any strict subcategorizational difference between *give* and *write*, but rather to the much greater likelihood of the direct object being left out of sentences with *write* than of sentences with *give*.

they arise upon application of generally accepted transformations to well-formed base structures.

Furthermore, the difference between the population that accepts DQs and the one that does not need not be viewed as a dialect difference in the strict sense that the two populations possess two slightly different internalized grammars. Rather, the difference could be just as plausibly explained on the basis of a difference between the perceptual mechanisms by which the two populations attempt to understand DQs. In the next section, we present the evidence that the relevant population exists; in the section following that, we provide an alternative to Jackendoff and Culicover's explanation of the unacceptability of DQs that accounts for the different acceptability judgments regarding DQs.

5. DEMONSTRATION THAT A POPULATION THAT ACCEPTS DQs EXISTS

5.1 Result of a Pilot Study on DQs

In a pilot study conducted with undergraduates at various campuses of the City University of New York and at Rutgers University in New Brunswick, New Jersey, we found that our subjects had no objections at all to DQs of any sort. In particular, we found that many of our subjects spontaneously interpreted genuinely ambiguous DQs like (14) exactly opposite to the way predicted by both GFP and Klima's version of CRAP (see footnote 9). That is, such a sentence would often be interpreted as (15a) rather than as (15b). On the basis of this pilot study, we conducted in the spring of 1971 more careful studies to substantiate the claim that many people from metropolitan New York City find DQs to be acceptable. We are particularly interested in subjects' responses to genuinely ambiguous sentences like (14) because rather than ask for acceptability judgments directly (a methodologically unsound technique, since one has no way of knowing whether the responses are bona fide acceptability judgments), we wanted to infer those judgments by indirect techniques. The fact that subjects can respond to DQs does not necessarily mean that they accept such sentences, but if they consistently respond to sentences like (14) in a way that indicates that they interpret them in the manner of (15a) (in which the postverbal noun phrase is taken to be the direct object), then for them DQs are acceptable because such interpretations are possible only if DQs are acceptable. The reason is that if a sentence like (14) is interpreted as (15b), Ss may be responding to it on the pattern of (i.e., on the analogy of) acceptable nonDQs, such as (20b), in which the inanimate direct object is questioned:

(20) (b) What did John give Mary?

If, however, Ss' responses indicate that they construe the postverbal noun phrase in a sentence like (14) as a direct object, there is no nonDQ model that they could possibly be using as a basis for those responses; hence the acceptability (in fact, grammaticality) of DQs for those Ss.

For Ss that do not accept DQs, the ability of interpreting (14) as (15a) need not be taken as evidence that GFP or Klima's version of CRAP (see footnote 9) is correct for those Ss, since again, those Ss may be using (20b)-type sentences as a basis for that interpretation in a task situation like those described below in section 5.2.

5.2 Two Experiments on DQs

In the first experiment, we constructed a questionnaire consisting of fifteen sentences, in which Ss were instructed to "add the word 'to' once to each of the . . . sentences so as not to change the meaning." This questionnaire is given in Appendix 1; for convenience we refer to it as the To-Insertion Form (TIF). The fifteen sentences were written in full capital letters with equal spacing between the words. They were of three types.

There were five sentences of the type (24):

(24) What did you show the landlord? [Example (1) on TIF].

These were control sentences, since they are undisputedly grammatical, and only the postverbal noun phrase can be reasonably construed as the indirect object.

Five sentences were DQs of the type (25):

(25) Whom did you give the ball? [Example (3) on TIF].

These were also control sentences, since, although they are of the type that we have seen have been considered ungrammatical, the postverbal noun phrase can be reasonably construed only as a direct object, and perhaps because of the coercive effect of the experimental situation it was almost always so judged.

Five sentences were ambiguous DQs of the type (26):

(26) Whom did you send the woman? [Example (12) on TIF].

These were the experimental sentences that we believed could be interpreted in two ways. Besides (26), we used the following sentences:

(27) Whom did you offer the man? [Example (2) on TIF].
(28) Whom did you lend the team? [Example (4) on TIF].
(29) Whom did you show the woman? [Example (9) on TIF].
(30) Whom did you refer the person? [Example (14) on TIF].

The fifteen sentences were arranged pseudo-randomly as to type. TIF was administered to 48 subjects consisting of undergraduates at Brooklyn College and Rutgers University, and of professionals at Bell Laboratories in Piscataway, New Jersey. The Ss were instructed that "there are no right or wrong answers: We are interested only in where you think the word [to] can be added."

The results of this experiment suggested several changes in the form. First, the task did not in any straightforward way require Ss to interpret sentences as they would if they were to encounter them spontaneously in speech or writing. The form was structured much like a typical Scholastic Aptitude Test question and so may have involved the Ss' conscious knowledge about English grammar. Second, we felt that the ordering of the first two sentences on TIF [examples (24) and (27) above] might be introducing perceptual-set bias, since the initial *what* of example (24) might start a pattern of response in which the postverbal noun phrase is the indirect object throughout. Third, we felt that examples (28) and (30) [examples (4) and (14) on TIF] were not entirely satisfactory. Example (28) seemed to cause may Ss trouble, and (30) was being uniformly interpreted in only one way (unlike the others), namely with the postverbal noun phrase as the direct object. Fourth, we felt that the use of *whom* rather than *who* throughout may have promoted the interpretation of that word as the indirect object (for many persons, *whom* is used spontaneously only when a preposition precedes).

Accordingly, a new form was devised, a form in which Ss were asked to "answer the . . . questions with a full sentence using the same verb." This form is shown in Appendix 2; we refer to it as the Answer Form (AF). In this form, we replaced *whom* by *who(m)* , with the instruction to "read 'Who(m)' as either 'Who' or 'Whom', depending on how you would say it in ordinary conversation." We interchanged the positions of examples (24) and (27), so that (27) became example (1) on AF and (24) became (2) on AF. We replaced examples (28) and (30) by the following sentences:

(31) Who(m) did you recommend the man? [Example (4) on AF] .
(32) Who(m) did you direct the person? [Example (14) on AF] .

We also instructed Ss that if they felt that more than one kind of answer was appropriate, to write additional answers, but not to cross out or erase their first answer, as we were particularly interested in their first response.

AF was administered to 79 Ss, who were undergraduates at Baruch and Hunter Colleges of C.U.N.Y. Shortly afterward, AF was administered to part of the same population that originally received TIF (30 in all), and TIF was administered to part of the same population that originally received AF (44 in all). This was done to insure against a confound of population difference with form differences.

Finally, we decided to try out TIF, with *who* replacing *whom* throughout, as shown in Appendix 3. This form was administered to 68 undergraduates at

D. TERENCE LANGENDOEN, NANCY
KALISH-LANDON, AND JOHN DORE

Brooklyn and Hunter Colleges and Rutgers University, none of whom had been previously used as Ss in this study, and to 44 undergraduates at S.U.N.Y. at Buffalo (we thank David Hays for his help in administering the form there). This was done specifically to test out hypothesis that *whom* is more likely to attract the word *to* than *who*, and to run the test on Ss from outside metropolitan New York City.

5.3 Results

In Table 1, the grammatical relations assigned to the postverbal noun phrases in the first TIF (using *whom*) and AF for the three experimental sentences that they have in common are tabulated. Comparing the same forms against the different populations on which they were administered, we find that there is no significant population difference, using the Chi-Square method. For example (27), $p < .5$; for example (29) $p < .5$; for example (26), $p < .5$.

If we now add the populations together by form we obtain the results given in Table 2 (the results of TIF using *who* on metropolitan New York City populations are also included in this table). The differences between AF and TIF using *whom* are significant, using the Chi-Square method. For example (27), $*p < .001$; for example (29), $*p < .001$; for example (26), $*p < .001$. The differences between AF and TIF using *who* are significant for two of the three sentences; for (27), $*p < .001$; for (29), $p < .3$; for (26), $*p < .001$.

TABLE 1

Forms vs Populations for the Three Sentences in Common to the To-Insertion (Whom) and Answer Forms

SENTENCE	POPULA- TION*	FORM**	INDIRECT OBJECT	DIRECT OBJECT	AMBIG- UOUS	NO INTERPRE- TATION	N
			POSTVERBAL NOUN-PHRASE IS:				
(27)							
Who(m) did you	A	AF	21	4	3	2	30
offer the man?	B	AF	73	6	0	0	79
[Ex. (1) on AF,	A	TIF	17	23	6	2	48
Ex. (2) on TIF]	B	TIF	14	23	1	6	44
(29)							
Who(m) did you show	A	AF	14	12	4	0	30
the woman?	B	AF	55	22	1	1	79
[Ex. (9) on AF and TIF]	A	TIF	12	28	8	0	48
	B	TIF	10	29	5	0	44
(26)							
Who(m) did you	A	AF	15	12	2	1	30
send the woman?	B	AF	45	30	3	1	79
[Ex. (12) on AF and TIF]	A	TIF	13	28	6	1	48
	B	TIF	13	30	1	0	44

*Population A: Brooklyn College, Rutgers University, Bell Laboratories
 Population B: Baruch College, Hunter College.
**AF: Answer Form; TIF: *To*-Insertion Form

TABLE 2

Answer Form vs To-Insertion Forms (both Whom and Who) for Metropolitan New York City Populations*

		POSTVERBAL NOUN-PHRASE IS:				
SENTENCE	FORM	INDIRECT OBJECT	DIRECT OBJECT	AMBIG-UOUS	NO INTERPRE-TATION	N
(27)						
Who(m) did	AF	94	10	3	2	109
you offer the	TIF (*Whom*)	31	46	7	8	92
man?	TIF (*Who*)	30	30	6	2	68
(29)						
Who(m) did	AF	69	34	5	1	109
you show the	TIF (*Whom*)	22	57	13	0	92
woman?	TIF (*Who*)	33	30	5	0	68
(26)						
Who(m) did	AF	60	42	5	2	109
you send the	TIF (*Whom*)	26	58	7	1	92
woman?	TIF (*Who*)	20	42	4	2	68

*For AF and TIF (*Whom*), the populations are Baruch, Brooklyn and Hunter Colleges, Rutgers University and Bell Laboratories.

For TIF (*Who*) the populations are Brooklyn and Hunter Colleges and Rutgers University.

In Table 3, the grammatical relations assigned to the postverbal noun phrases for the experimental sentences not in common to AF and the two TIFs are tabulated for the metroplitan New York City populations (again, since internal population differences are nonsignificant, the figures are added together). For the five experimental sentences, the differences between TIF using *whom* and TIF using *who* are nonsignificant, except for example (29). For (27), $p < .2$; for (29), $*p < .01$; for (26), $p < .7$; for (28), $p < .7$; for (30), $p < .3$.

In Table 4, we compare the results of TIF using *who* for the metropolitan New York City populations with those for the Buffalo population for all five experimental sentences. The differences for examples (27), (29), and (26) are significant; for (28) and (30) they are not. For (27), $*p < .001$; for (29), $*p < .05$; for (26), $*p < .001$; for (28), $p < .9$; for (30), $p < .5$. Finally, in Table 5, we give a detailed analysis of the AF responses to examples (29) and (26) [examples (9) and (12), respectively, on AF]. In this table, we correlate the responses to (29) and (26), which are the only minimal pair among our experimental sentences (they differ only in the verb). In addition, we distinguish between responses which are syntactically and semantically appropriate and those which are inappropriate. For example, (33) is an appropriate response to (29), whereas (34) is inappropriate:

D. TERENCE LANGENDOEN, NANCY
KALISH-LANDON, AND JOHN DORE

TABLE 3

Answer Form and To-Insertion Forms (Whom and Who) for the Sentences Not Common to Those Forms for Metropolitan New York City Populations*

		POSTVERBAL NOUN PHRASE IS:				
SENTENCE	FORM	INDIRECT OBJECT	DIRECT OBJECT	AMBIG-UOUS	NO INTERPRE-TATION	N
(31) Who(m) did you recom-mend the man? [Ex. (4) on AF]	AF	34	63	4	8	109
(32) Who(m) did you direct the person? [Ex. (14) on AF]	AF	2	94	2	11	109
(28) Who(m) did you lend the team? [Ex. (4) on TIF]	TIF (Whom) TIF (Who)	30 26	51 39	10 2	1 1	92 68
(30) Who(m) did you refer the person? [Ex. (14) on TIF]	TIF (Whom) TIF (Who)	7 8	77 56	5 1	3 3	92 68

*See Table 2 for the population breakdown by forms.

(33) I showed the woman a friend.

(34) I showed the woman a hat.

Both responses indicate that the postverbal noun phrase *the woman* in (29) was interpreted as indirect object; however the latter response is inappropriate be-cause the noun phrase that answers the question *who(m)*? is inanimate. A syntactically inappropriate answer would be (35):

(35) I showed the woman.

In (35), there is no second object; in fact the question is not really answered at all. For purposes of classification, *the woman* is assumed to be direct object, since that is how the sentence would be analyzed out of context.

TABLE 4

To-Insertion Form (Who) vs Population (Metropolitan New York City and Buffalo, New York)

		POSTVERBAL NOUN-PHRASE IS:				
SENTENCE	POPULATION*	INDIRECT OBJECT	DIRECT OBJECT	AMBIG-UOUS	NO INTERPRE-TATION	N
(27)						
Who did you	C	30	30	6	2	68
offer the	D	38	2	2	2	44
man?						
(29)						
Who did you	C	33	30	5	0	68
show the	D	27	9	6	2	44
woman?						
(26)						
Who did you	C	20	42	4	2	68
send the	D	27	11	4	2	44
woman?						
(28)						
Who did you	C	26	39	2	1	68
lend the	D	13	24	5	2	44
team?						
(30)						
Who did you	C	8	56	1	3	68
refer the	D	3	38	2	1	44
person?						

*Population C: Brooklyn and Hunter Colleges and Rutgers University
 Population D: SUNY at Buffalo

TABLE 5

Analysis of responses to Examples (29) and (26) in Answer Form

POSTVERBAL NOUN PHRASE IS:	BOTH RESPONSES APPROPRIATE	ONE OR BOTH RESPONSES INAPPROPRIATE	N
1. I.O. in both (29) and (26)	42	9	51
2. I.O. in either (29) or (26); D.O. in the other	12	12	24
3. I.O. in either (29) or (26); ambiguous in the other	2	0	2
4. D.O. in either (29) or (26); ambiguous in the other	2	0	2
5. Ambiguous in both (29) and (26).	3	0	3
6. D.O. in both (29) and (26)	19	6	25
7. No interpretation for one or both (29) and (26)	0	2	2
Total of 4, 5, 6	(24)	(6)	(30)
Grand total	80	29	109

5.4 Discussion

We consider here the following matters: (*a*) The differences in the responses to the two tasks, (*b*) the differences between TIF with *whom* and with *who* and the difference between the Buffalo and New York City populations, (*c*) the intrasentential differences, particularly on AF, and (*d*) the establishment of a New York City population that accepts DQs.

Concerning task differences, we find that in general AF favored the interpretation of the postverbal noun phrase as indirect object, whereas TIF favored its interpretation as direct object (but less so when the interrogative word was *who* rather than *whom*). Thus TIF provided a task that enhanced the appearance of the ability to interpret DQs in a way contrary to the predictions made by both GFP and CRAP. However, we are willing to discount that evidence on the basis of the relative artificiality of that task as compared to the question-answering task in AF and to rest our case for the existence of a population that accepts DQs on the AF responses.

Concerning the difference between TIF with *whom* and TIF with *who*, we note that although the difference is nonsignificant except for example (29), the difference is in the predicted direction: *Whom* is more likely to be taken as indirect object than *who*. The reason significance was achieved for (29) may be that there were relatively many ambiguous responses to it in TIF with *whom*. These responses were not included in the calculation for significance. However, we have no explanation why just this example deviated from the general pattern. On the other hand, the difference between the New York City and Buffalo populations on TIF with *who* convincingly shows that a population selected from outside New York City will treat DQs in conformity with the linguistic and psycholinguistic descriptions considered in Sections 2 through 4.

The most striking intrasentential variations are to be found between the three sentences in common to the two forms (26), (27) and (29) and two of the four sentences not in common to them, namely (30) and (32). For AF, the contrast is most striking between (27), in which 94 *S*s considered the postverbal noun phrase to be the indirect object and only 10 *S*s considered it the direct object, and (32), in which only 2 *S*s considered the postverbal noun phrase to be the indirect object and 94 *S*s considered it the direct object. For TIF (both *who* and *whom* varieties, New York City populations only), compare (27), in which 61 *S*s took the postverbal noun phrase to be an indirect object and 76 took it to be a direct object with (30), in which 15 *S*s considered the postverbal noun phase to be an indirect object and 133 *S*s considered it a direct object.

The reason for this set of differences has to do with a grammatical oddity inherent in examples (30) and (32). If we put them back into declarative form [replacing *who*(*m*) by *someone*], considering *who*(*m*) to be the indirect object, as most of our *S*s did, we obtain ungrammatical sentences:

    (36)   *You referred someone the person.

    (37)   *You directed someone the person.

The results are similarly ungrammatical if *who*(*m*) is considered the direct object. Thus we must assume that examples (30) and (32) are also ungrammatical, and that our *S*s were forced in the experimental situation to interpret them in terms of the closest salient grammatical sentences (Katz 1964). For (30) and (32), they are the following: [17]

(38) Who(m) did you refer the person to?
(39) Who(m) did you direct the person to?

This accords with the experimental facts, since in both (38) and (39), the postverbal noun phrase is the direct object.

We take up now the matter of most importance to us: The establishment of the existence of a population that accepts DQs, and for whom therefore DQs are grammatical. This, we claim, is shown in Table 5, in which we examine the responses to two non-problematic DQs in AF, examples (29) and (26). In section 5.1 above, we argued that if *S*s are consistently able to interpret the postverbal noun phrases of DQs as direct objects, then DQs for them must be acceptable, since there are no analogical grammatical sentences on the basis of which they could interpret DQs in that way. The number of *S*s that treated the postverbal noun phrases as direct objects in both (29) and (26) without error is 24, or 22 percent of the total number of *S*s that filled out AF. This means that at least one-fifth of our *S*s from metropolitan New York City find DQs acceptable. We suspect that the actual population, expressed as a percentage of fluent metropolitan New York City English speakers, is considerably larger than this figure would indicate, but we are content with having shown that it is at least this large.

6. AN EXPLANATION BASED ON THE PERCEPTUAL DETERMINATION OF GRAMMATICAL RELATIONS FOR THE VARIATION IN THE ACCEPTABILITY OF DQS

In this section, we show how the variation in the acceptability of DQs could be accounted for as a consequence of the different perceptual rules used by English-speaking listeners for assigning grammatical relations to noun phrases. We assume that such relations are assigned while the sentence itself is being actively processed, and that the end of each perceived constituent is a potential decision

17. This is so, since listeners would conclude from the fact that neither *refer* nor *direct* undergo Dative that the postverbal noun phrase must be the direct object. The minimum syntactic change, therefore, is to add the appropriate preposition (*to*) to the interrogative word. Our purpose in including these patently ungrammatical sentences in the questionnaires was to see whether they would be treated differently from DQs whose grammaticality status was the subject of investigation. And indeed they were.

D. TERENCE LANGENDOEN, NANCY
KALISH-LANDON, AND JOHN DORE

point for determining the grammatical relations that obtain within that sentence.[18] In (40), we give a schematization of a DQ, with the potential decision points (DPs) indicated underneath.

$$(40) \quad \frac{\text{Who(m)} \quad \text{did} \quad \text{you} \quad \text{V} \quad \text{NP}}{0 \qquad\quad 1 \qquad 2 \qquad 3 \qquad 4 \qquad 5}$$

In (41), we state the perceptual rules that are applicable in the processing of DQs and indicate for each rule the decision point in (40) at which it is applicable first.[19]

(41) a. Subject and object in inverted sentences (DP 3)

$$
\begin{bmatrix} \text{NP} \\ \text{Interr.} \end{bmatrix} \quad - \quad \begin{bmatrix} \text{V}_i \\ \text{Aux.} \end{bmatrix} \quad - \text{NP} - \text{X}
$$
$$
\qquad 1 \qquad\qquad\quad 2 \qquad\qquad\quad 3 \qquad\quad 4 \implies
$$
$$
\begin{bmatrix} 1 \\ \text{Obj. of V}_i \end{bmatrix} \qquad 2 \qquad \begin{bmatrix} 3 \\ \text{Subj. of V}_i \end{bmatrix} \qquad 4
$$

b. Interrogative indirect object (DP 4)

$$
\begin{bmatrix} \text{NP} \\ \text{Interr.} \\ \text{Animate} \\ \text{Obj. of V}_i \end{bmatrix} \quad - \text{X} \begin{bmatrix} \text{V}_i \\ +\text{Dative} \end{bmatrix} \text{Y}
$$
$$
\qquad\qquad 1 \qquad\qquad\qquad 2 \implies
$$
$$
\begin{bmatrix} 1 \\ \text{Ind. Obj. of V}_i \end{bmatrix} \qquad 2
$$

18. These assumptions can be strongly motivated simply from consideration of the rapidity and precision of speech comprehension. Although they have not received direct experimental support, the assumptions have also been used by other psycholinguists in the construction of more elaborate hypotheses that have received experimental support.

19. We assume that the system of perceptual rules is designed to recover essentially the surface structures of sentences (as in Kimball, 1974) and 'annotations' of those surface structures that indicate the deep grammatical relations and perhaps certain other aspects of deep structure, where those are different from surface structure. The rules in (41) are a subset of the annotating rules. We cast them in the form of transformational rules because that is a convenient and revealing framework. The subscript 'i' on the category symbol 'V' (for 'verb') is an abstract indicator of the clause in which that verb is the main verb; for simplicity, we assume that all the constituents mentioned in the rules of (41) are members of the same clause. The feature specification [+Dative] indicates that the verb permits application of Dative within its clause. The specifications [Dir. Obj. of V_i] and [Ind. Obj. of V_i] are assumed to substitute for the specification [Obj. of V_i]. Thus rule (41a) may mark certain noun phrases as objects of a particular verb; rules (42b, c, d) may then replace that specification with the more precise specifications as direct or indirect objects.

c. Interrogative direct object and postverbal indirect object (DP 5)

$$\begin{bmatrix} NP \\ Interr. \\ Obj.\ of\ V_i \end{bmatrix} - X \begin{bmatrix} V_i \\ +Dative \end{bmatrix} - (NP) - Y$$

$$\qquad 1 \qquad\qquad\qquad 2 \qquad\qquad\qquad 3 \qquad\qquad 4 \Rightarrow$$

$$\begin{bmatrix} 1 \\ Dir.\ Obj.\ of\ V_i \end{bmatrix} \qquad 2 \qquad \begin{bmatrix} 3 \\ Ind.\ Obj.\ of\ V_i \end{bmatrix} \qquad 4$$

d. Postverbal direct and indirect objects (DP 5)

$$X\ V_i \quad - \quad (NP) \quad - \quad NP \quad - \quad Y$$

$$\quad 1 \qquad\qquad 2 \qquad\qquad\quad 3 \qquad\quad 4$$

$$\quad 1 \qquad \begin{bmatrix} 2 \\ Ind.\ Obj.\ of\ V_i \end{bmatrix} \begin{bmatrix} 3 \\ Dir.\ Obj.\ of\ V_i \end{bmatrix} \quad 4 \Rightarrow$$

Rules (41a) and (41d) are independently needed for the perceptual processing of a wide variety of English sentence types and must be considered part of the set of listening strategies of everyone who is fluent in English. Rule (41c) embodies a specific case of Klima's 'simple algorithm' for picking out direct and indirect objects in the event an object has been moved out of postverbal position. It, too, may be presumed to be shared by everyone who is fluent in English.[20] Rule (41b), however, is limited to those speakers who accept DQs; it accounts in fact for their ability to interpret those sentences in the manner in which the grammar of English dictates that they must be interpreted. To see this, consider first how rules (41a, b, c, d) assign grammatical relations to sentences of the type (40), and second how rules (41a, c, d) do so. At DP 3, rule (41a) marks *who(m)* to be an object of the main verb and *you* the subject. At DP 4, rule (41b) specifies that *who(m)* is in fact the indirect object of the verb. At DP 5, rule (41c) is inapplicable (the interrogative noun phrase is already specified as the indirect object), but rule (41d) is applicable; it marks the postverbal noun phrase to be the direct object of the verb.

If rule (41b) is left out, the following perceptual derivation is obtained. At DP 3, as before, rule (41a) marks *who(m)* as an object of the main verb and *you* as subject. At DP 4, none of the rules of (41) are applicable. At DP 5, rule (41c) applies, marking the interrogative noun phrase to be the direct object and the postverbal noun phrase the indirect object. In case the postverbal noun

---

20. Hankamer (1973, p. 52) reports that he does not accept sentences such as (i) in which the direct object in a sentence that has undergone Dative is fronted:

(i) What did Harry sell Jerome?

We can explain his inability to accept sentences like (i), an inability which he alone among the numerous linguists that have investigated the dative construction has testified to, by saying that he lacks rule (41c). Accordingly, the interrogative noun phrase will be marked as an object, but not any particular kind of object, such as direct or indirect.

D. TERENCE LANGENDOEN, NANCY
KALISH-LANDON, AND JOHN DORE

phrase is animate, the result is not unacceptable, but if it is inanimate, the result is unacceptable, since it is not possible for an indirect object to be inanimate while the direct object is animate.[21] Thus DQs are acceptable in case listeners have internalized rule (41b) and unacceptable in case they have not.

At this point, we must emphasize that we have not demonstrated experimentally that English speakers who accept dative questions have internalized a perceptual rule like (41b), but only that the postulation of such a rule does provide an explanation for their ability to accept such sentences, without having to posit that they speak and understand a different dialect of English from everyone else. However, it should be possible to test experimentally whether a perceptual rule like (41b) exists. First, one must isolate two populations, one containing Ss that accept dative questions and the other Ss that do not. If Ss that accept dative questions do so on the basis of their having a rule that marks interrogative animate noun phrases as indirect objects as soon as they have heard a main verb that undergoes Dative, then such subjects should have demonstrably greater difficulty (as measured, for example, by latency to respond) in dealing with sentences like (42) than Ss that do not accept DQs:

(42) Who(m) did you send home?

The reason is that *who(m)* must be the direct object of *send* in (42), but Ss who employ (41b) upon hearing *send* will mark *who(m)* as indirect object and will have to correct that assignment once they discover that there is no other direct object, the correction being based on the principle that *send* cannot take an indirect object in the absence of a direct object. Since such corrections

21. Thus the rules in (41), like GFP and Klima's version of CRAP, do not account for the unacceptability of ambiguous DQs like (14), if indeed they are unacceptable (see footnote 9). We would account for their unacceptability within the framework of (41) by supposing that for those who find such sentences unacceptable the rules (41b) and (41c) apply simultaneously to mark the interrogative noun phrase as both direct and indirect object. The incoherence of such a marking is what makes such sentences unacceptable.

The perceptual rules in (41) have been formulated to handle acceptability judgments in simple DQs only. They may, however, be extended without difficulty to complex DQs and the other sentence types in (4)–(7). In the case of complex DQs, such as (i), one must suppose the existence of a perceptual rule that marks the clause that the interrogative noun phrase originates in (not necessarily unambiguously):

(i) Who(m) do you believe John sold the books?

Since this problem is independent of the problem of recognizing DQs, it will not be discussed further here. Second, there must be a way of recognizing subject noun phrases (like *John* in (i)) in case inversion of subject and auxiliary verb has not applied. This we assume is not a serious problem (it is accomplished, for example, by one of the perceptual strategies presented in Bever (1970)). To handle sentences in which Relative-Clause Formation, Topicalization, Cleft-Sentence Formation or Tough Movement, together with Dative Movement, have applied, one must generalize the specification of those noun phrases in (41) that receive interpretation as simple objects, direct objects, or indirect objects in appropriate ways.

must take time over and above the time required for straightforward comprehension, the prediction follows. On the other hand, the presence of a perceptual rule like (41b) should enhance *S*s' ability to understand sentences like
(43):

(43)   Who(m) did you write yesterday?

In (43), *who(m)* is the indirect object despite the fact that no direct object is
present in surface structure; *Write*, unlike *send*, does not require an indirect
object to cooccur with a direct object (this is so, even if the preposition *to* is
deleted), and this information may be assumed to be available to listeners.
Thus the claim that the acceptability of DQs depends on the presence of a
particular perceptual rule that not every English speaker possesses is empirically
testable in a straightforward way. Regardless of the outcome of experiments
testing the hypotheses advanced in this section, however, we believe that a solid
basis for considering that dative questions are grammatical in English has been
established.[22]

APPENDIX 1

To Insertion Form Using WHOM

Add the word 'to' once to each of the following sentences so as not to change
the meaning. There are no right or wrong answers: We are interested only in
where you think the word can be added.

1. What	did	you	show	the	landlord	?
2. Whom	did	you	offer	the	man	?
3. Whom	did	you	give	the	ball	?
4. Whom	did	you	lend	the	team	?
5. Whom	did	you	offer	the	candy	?
6. What	did	you	lend	the	captain	?
7. Whom	did	you	send	the	packages	?
8. What	did	you	give	the	teacher	?
9. Whom	did	you	show	the	woman	?

22. We regret that we read too late for inclusion in our theoretical discussion the interesting
and provocative paper by Hankamer (1973), in which he asserts, among other things, that
he can see no basis for distinguishing between rules of grammar and so-called perceptual
strategies. We hope that this paper will be viewed as providing at least one such basis.
Concerning Hankamer's proposed 'no-ambiguity condition', which bears considerable resem-
blance to the principles discussed and dismissed in Sections 3 and 4 and which appears
superior to them in a number of respects, we note simply that it is supported by remarkably
idiosyncratic and otherwise unjustified acceptability judgments, such as the one pointed
out in footnote 20. If those judgements cannot be supported, neither can the condition.
For further discussion of Hankamer's proposals, see Langendoen (1975).

D. TERENCE LANGENDOEN, NANCY
KALISH-LANDON, AND JOHN DORE

10. Whom	did	you	show	the	dress	?
11. What	did	you	offer	the	students	?
12. Whom	did	you	send	the	woman	?
13. Whom	did	you	lend	the	money	?
14. Whom	did	you	refer	the	person	?
15. What	did	you	send	the	boy	?

Name or social security number _____

Languages other than English you speak or have studied. If more than one,

list in order of decreasing fluency _____

_____

Have you taught English? ____ Yes ____ No

APPENDIX 2

Answer Form

Please answer the following questions with a full sentence using the same verb.
For example:
Q. Who(m) did you see?
A. I saw the man.

Read 'Who(m)' as either 'Who' or 'Whom', depending on how you would say it
in ordinary conversation.
If you feel that more than one kind of answer is appropriate, write additional
answers. Please do not change your first answer to each question. There are
no right or wrong answers. Your first answer is the best one.

1. Q. Who(m) did you offer the man?
    A.

2. Q. What did you show the landlord?
    A.

3. Q. Who(m) did you give the ball?
    A.

4. Q. Who(m) did you recommend the man?
    A.

5. Q. Who(m) did you offer the candy?
    A.

6. Q. What did you lend the captain?
    A.

7. Q. Who(m) did you send the packages?
    A.

8. Q. What did you give the teacher?
   A.

9. Q. Who(m) did you show the woman?
   A.

10. Q. Who(m) did you show the dress?
    A.

11. Q. What did you offer the students?
    A.

12. Q. Who(m) did you send the woman?
    A.

13. Q. Who(m) did you lend the money?
    A.

14. Q. Who(m) did you direct the person?
    A.

15. Q. What did you send the boy?
    A.

Name or Social Security Number _____

Are you a native speaker of English? ____ Yes ____ No

How long have you been a resident of Greater New York City _____

Have you ever taught English ____ Yes ____ No

APPENDIX 3

To-Insertion Form Using WHO

Add the word 'to' once to each of the following sentences so as not to change the meaning. There are no right or wrong answers: We are interested only in where you think the word can be added.

1. What	did	you	show	the	landlord	?
2. Who	did	you	offer	the	man	?
3. Who	did	you	give	the	ball	?
4. Who	did	you	lend	the	team	?
5. Who	did	you	offer	the	candy	?
6. What	did	you	lend	the	captain	?
7. Who	did	you	send	the	packages	?
8. What	did	you	give	the	teacher	?
9. Who	did	you	show	the	woman	?
10. Who	did	you	show	the	dress	?
11. What	did	you	offer	the	students	?
12. Who	did	you	send	the	woman	?

D. TERENCE LANGENDOEN, NANCY
KALISH-LANDON, AND JOHN DORE

13. Who   did   you   lend   the   money   ?
14. Who   did   you   refer   the   person   ?
15. What   did   you   send   the   boy   ?

Name or social security number _____

Languages other than English you speak or have studied. If more than one, list

in order of decreasing fluency _____

_____

Have you ever taught English? ____ Yes ____ No

REFERENCES

Baker, C. L., and M. Brame. 1972. Global Rules: A Rejoinder. *Language* 48: 51–75.

Bever, T. G. 1970. The Cognitive Basis for Linguistic Structures. In *Cognition and the Development of Language*, J. R. Hayes, ed. Wiley.

Bever, T. G., and D. T. Langendoen. 1971. "A Dynamic Model of the Evolution of Language." *Linguistic Inquiry* 2: 433–463. Reprinted in this volume.

Chomsky, N. 1965. *Aspects of the Theory of Syntax*. M.I.T. Press.

———. 1972. Some Empirical Issues in the Theory of Transformational Grammar. In *Goals of Linguistic Theory*, S. Peters, ed. Prentice-Hall.

Edmonds, J. 1972. Evidence that Indirect-Object Movement Is a Structure-Preserving Rule. *Foundations of Language* 8: 546–561.

Fillmore, C. J. 1965. *Indirect Object Constructions in English and the Ordering of Transformations*. Mouton.

Fischer, S. 1971. *The Acquisition of Verb-Particle and Dative Constructions*. Unpublished Ph.D. dissertation. M.I.T.

Hankamer, J. 1973. "Unacceptable Ambiguity." *Linguistic Inquiry* 4: 17–68.

Jackendoff, R., and P. Culicover. 1971. A Reconsideration of Dative Movements. *Foundations of Language* 7: 397–412.

Katz, J. J. 1964. "Semi-sentences." In *The Structure of Language*, J. A. Fodor and J. J. Katz, eds. Prentice-Hall.

Kimball, J. 1974. "Seven Principles of Surface Structure Parsing in Natural Language." *Cognition* 2: 15–47.

Klima, E. S. 1970. "Regulatory Devices against Functional Ambiguity." Unpublished paper.

Kuroda, S.-Y. 1968. "Review of Fillmore (1965)." *Language* 44: 374–378.

Labov, W. 1972. "For an End to the Uncontrolled Use of Linguistic Intuitions." Unpublished paper.

Langendoen, D. T. 1973. "The Problem of Grammatical Relations in Surface Structure." In *GURT: 1973*, K. Jankowsky, ed. Georgetown University Press.

———. 1975. "Acceptable Conclusions from Unacceptable Ambiguity." In *Testing Linguistic Hypotheses*, D. Cohen, ed. Hemisphere Press. Reprinted in this volume.

Langendoen, D. T., and T. G. Bever. 1973. "Can a Not Unhappy Person Be Called a Not Sad One?" In *A Festschrift for Morris Halle*, S. Anderson and P. Kiparsky, eds. Holt, Rinehart and Winston. Reprinted in this volume.

Otero, C. 1972. "Acceptable Ungrammatical Sentences in Spanish." *Linguistic Inquiry* 3: 233–242.

Ross, J. R. 1967. *Constraints on Variables in Syntax*. Indiana University Linguistics Club.

Ruwet, N. 1973. How to Deal with Syntactic Irregularities: Conditions on Transformations or Perceptual Strategies? In *Generative Grammar in Europe*, F. Kiefer and N. Ruwet, eds. Reidel.

Acceptable Conclusions from Unacceptable Ambiguity

D. TERENCE LANGENDOEN

Hankamer (1973) has proposed the following convention as a hypothesis of universal grammar:

(1) Structural Recoverability Condition (SRC): Rules involving variables are universally subject to a transderivational condition which prevents them from applying in such a way as to introduce structural ambiguity.

By subjecting only rules involving variables to the condition, Hankamer's proposal is a refinement of a principle originally proposed by Klima (1970), and discussed at length in Ruwet (1973), prohibiting the transformational introduction of structural ambiguity in general, a principle dubbed the Constraint against Relational Ambiguity Principle (CRAP) in Langendoen, Kalish-Landon, and Dore (1974). Hankamer's refinement is surely in the right direction, because many of our criticisms of CRAP do not go through against SRC, and Hankamer himself gives an effective argument against the cases covered by CRAP but not covered by SRC (pp. 60–63).[1] It is useful, therefore, to put Hankamer's hypothesis to the test, since its correctness bears crucially on the issue of whether transderivational constraints should be a part of the theory of grammar.

Hankamer considers two types of rules involving variables: deletion rules and movement ("chopping") rules (if other types of rules, such as "feature changing" rules, also involve variables, Hankamer speculates that they too would participate in SRC (p. 63)). He discusses one variable deletion rule at

1. Wherever page references alone are given, they refer to pages in Hankamer (1973).

I thank C. Kaniklidis and B. Lust for helpful discussions on many points of this paper.

Source: J. Wirth and D. Cohen, eds., *Testing Linguistic Hypotheses* (Washington-London: Hemisphere Publishing Corporation, 1975). Reprinted by permission of Halsted Press and Hemisphere Publishing Corporation.

length, Gapping, and derives the bulk of his motivation for SRC from consideration of that rule. Gapping, as Hankamer effectively argues, is not limited to
cases in which material is deleted from the middle of a conjunct, but is responsible for all deletions under identity in conjuncts, in which Regrouping has not
applied. Thus Gapping is allowed to delete nonmedial (peripheral) elements as
well as medial ones, and for this reason I shall refer to the rule in question
henceforth not as Gapping, but as Coordinate Deletion (CD, the term due to
Koutsoudas (1971)). Hankamer goes on to argue that in case a given structure
could be viewed as the output of CD applied to two or more different inputs, it
will in fact be the result of applying the rule to only one of those inputs, namely
the one in which the deleted material constitutes the beginning (the left periph-
ery) of the conjunct(s) to which it is applied (p. 29). The following illustration
(Hankamer's example (38)) is typical of the many different kinds of examples he
considers. (I indicate a permitted application of CD by enclosing the deleted
material in brackets, and a disallowed application of that rule by enclosing the
deleted material in brackets preceded by an asterisk; dashes indicate the first
conjunct):

(2) (a) Max gave Sally a nickel, and Harvey a dime.
     (b) _____, and [Max gave] Harvey a dime.
     (c) _____, and Harvey *[gave Sally] a dime.

Within a theory that does not permit transderivational constraints, in particular
within standard theory, it would appear that some sort of condition on CD is
required to prevent its application to (2c) to derive (2a). From a consideration
of various of the sentence types in which CD would have to be blocked,
Hankamer concludes that it may not even be possible to specify coherently all
of the different sorts of conditions that it would be necessary to impose on CD.
Moreover, even if they could be specified, there would be no explanation, within
such a theory, for the existence of such a large body of apparently unrelated
conditions. On the other hand, if transderivational constraints are permitted in
linguistic theory, one could eliminate this collection of conditions in favor of a
single, unified generalization, namely SRC.

This move, however, backfires. First, recall that SRC, by itself, merely
prohibits the introduction of structural ambiguity by rules involving variables;
it does not indicate how this prohibition is to be effected. One still needs, for
each rule, a condition governing which derivations involving its application are
to be allowed and which are to be blocked. As we have already seen, Hankamer
asserts that when CD would introduce structural ambiguity, just that derivation
in which CD deletes left-peripheral material is allowed. But sometimes more
than just left-peripheral material can be deleted by permitted applications of CD,
as is illustrated by Hankamer's own example (42) (repeated here as (3)):

(3) (a) Max wanted Ted to persuade Alex to get lost, and Walt, Ira.
     (b) _____, and Walt *[wanted] Ira [to persuade Alex to get lost] .

    (c) ———, and Walt *[wanted Ted to persuade] Ira [to get lost].

    (d) ———, and [Max wanted] Walt [to persuade] Ira [to get lost].

Suppose, however, there is more than one derivation in which left-peripheral material could be deleted by CD. In that case, the one in which CD deletes no non-left-peripheral string that contains NP is allowed, as is illustrated in examples like those in Hankamer's (64)–(67); consider (4):

  (4) (a) Max sent Sally the messenger last week, and Susan yesterday.

       (b) ——— and [Max sent Sally] Susan yesterday.

       (c) ——— and *[Max sent] Susan [the messenger] yesterday.

A more dramatic illustration of this point is provided in (5):

  (5) (a) Max wanted Ted to persuade Alex to see Mary, and Walt, Ira.

       (b) ——— and Walt *[wanted] Ira [to persuade Alex to see Mary].

       (c) ——— and Walt *[wanted Ted to persuade] Ira [to see Mary].

       (d) ——— and Walt *[wanted Ted to persuade Alex to see] Ira.

       (e) ——— and *[Max wanted] Walt [to persuade] Ira [to see Mary].

       (f) ——— and *[Max wanted] Walt [to persuade Alex to see] Ira.

       (g) ——— and [Max wanted Ted to persuade] Walt [to see] Ira.

In (5e, f, g), the deleted material includes left-peripheral material, yet only (5g) is grammatical. (For some reason, (5f) does not seem quite as unacceptable as (5e); I suspect this has to do with the complexity of the examples.) What distinguishes (5e, f) from (5g) is that the former contain NPs in the nonleft-peripheral material to be deleted, and the latter does not.

Thus, Hankamer is in the position of claiming that the applicability of CD is governed by SRC and the condition that CD cannot apply so as to delete nonleft-peripheral strings that contain NP. Let us call this latter condition the nonleft-peripheral NP condition (NLPNPC). But now, if we go back and examine all of Hankamer's examples, such as (2), that lead up to his positing SRC for CD, we observe that they all obey NLPNPC. For example, (2b) does not involve the deletion of a nonleft-peripheral string containing NP, while (2c) does. Thus NLPNPC, by itself (i.e., without SRC), handles all the cases considered by Hankamer, whereas the converse is not true: SRC (as we have already seen) alone cannot handle all of those cases. Therefore NLPNPC, not SRC, provides the more significant generalization concerning the applicability of CD. Moreover, since NLPNPC, unlike SRC, is a condition on a transformation, and as such is expressible in standard theory, it is also to be preferred on the grounds that its introduction does not increase the power of the theory of grammar. I return to this point later.

Since NLPNPC is more general than SRC in limiting the applicability of CD, we would expect it to be able to block applications of CD even in cases where structural ambiguity is not introduced. And, indeed, such is the case. Consider first examples (6)–(8), which illustrate the point that CD cannot delete just an object NP or PP:

(6) Jackendoff despises bassoonists and McCawley admires *[bassoonists].
(7) Show Rafael that you love him and tell *[Rafael] that he's wonderful.
(8) Leave the car in the garage and put the bus *[in the garage].

CD is blocked in these cases, not because there are other derivations of the reduced sentences involving CD, but because NLPNPC is violated. Second, NLPNPC predicts that CD may delete sentence-final adverbs not containing NP, but not those that do. As (9)–(10) show, this prediction is borne out:

(9) Laurie washed the car yesterday and [Laurie] mowed the lawn [yesterday].
(10) Laurie washed the car in the early afternoon and *[Laurie] mowed the lawn [in the early afternoon].

Thus NLPNPC receives very strong independent support.

Furthermore, in section 1.4 Hankamer in effect appeals to NLPNPC to account for what he takes to be apparent counterexamples to SRC. They are, however, real counterexamples to SRC, and apparent counterexamples only to NLPNPC. To see this, consider how Hankamer tries to explain away the counterexample in (11) (modeled on Hankamer's example (89)), in which CD *does* introduce structural ambiguity:

(11) (a) Marlene told me that Arnold left, and Dave that Ilse stayed.
     (b) _____ and Dave [told me] that Ilse stayed.
     (c) _____ and [Marlene told] Dave that Ilse stayed.

Concerning such counterexamples, Hankamer says (35): "This type of exception to [SRC] would disappear if there were a cliticization rule in English, whereby pronouns in immediate postverbal position become cliticized to the verb." By this, Hankamer apparently means that the object pronoun *me* in (11) is not to be analyzed as NP for purposes of limiting the applicability of CD. This, however, can only be interpreted as a way of preventing NLPNPC from blocking the derivation of (11a) from (11b), not of preventing SRC from doing so. As far as SRC is concerned, (11) is a counterexample, even if object pronouns in immediate postverbal position in English were to be transformed into carrots.

Moreover, if object pronouns in English are not NPs, how is NLPNPC to block the applicability of CD to (12)?

(12) Sam will sell me steaks and *[Sam] might buy [me] roasts.

To account properly for the fact that CD is applicable in (11b), but not in (12), NLPNPC must be modified so as to allow application of CD to delete non-left-peripheral strings that contain both a verb and its immediately following clitic pronoun, but no other NPs.

This completes our reanalysis of CD. Before we can give a formal statement of the rule, however, we must show how to handle another class of apparent counterexamples, namely those derivations in which the application of CD would result in the reduction of noninitial conjuncts to a single constituent other than VP. As (9) shows, reduction to VP alone is permitted. In all other cases, the remaining single constituents must be regrouped, as (13)–(15) show (labeled brackets indicate constituent structure, not deletion):

(13) (a) Buzhardt objected strenuously and St. Clair *[objected strenuously].
    (b) [NP Buzhardt and St. Clair]NP objected strenuously.

(14) (a) I admire Solzhenitsyn and *[I admire] Sakharov.
    (b) I admire [NP Solzhenitsyn and Sakharov]NP.

(15) (a) We went to the country last week and *[we went to the country] last month.
    (b) We went to the country [AdvP last week and last month]AdvP.

Assuming, with Hankamer and with Harries (1973), and against Ross (1967, 1970), Tai (1969, 1971) and Koutsoudas (1971), that CD (or Gapping) always operates on noninitial conjuncts and that it does so in one step at its point of application, and assuming a theory, such as standard theory, that disallows global rules, we must conclude that Regrouping either precedes or applies simultaneously with CD.[2] Since the structural analyses of the two rules can be collapsed and since there are no rules known to intervene between them, we present them together, formally, under the heading Conjunction Reduction:[3]

2. If CD precedes Regrouping and the former operates only on noninitial conjuncts then, in the case of (13) and (14), one would be unable to tell which NP (subject or object) in the first conjunction is the regrouping site. This may be obviated either by making Regrouping a global rule, so that it has access to the stage in the derivation immediately prior to CD, or by formulating CD so as to delete into left conjuncts when the nonidentical material is on a right branch and into right conjuncts when the nonidentical material is on a left branch, and by requiring CD to reapply to its own output. I reject the former as resulting in needless increased power in the theory of grammar, and the latter on simplicity grounds.

3. Circled "plus" signs indicate Chomsky-adjunction. The asterisk on the right conjunct indicates iteration. Option A in the structural change is CD, option B is Regrouping. The angled brackets are to be read so that *respectively* is added transformationally just in case Regrouping is applied and two categories are simultaneously regrouped. To complete this account of CR, we would have to add another operation, namely that of extracting a single identical rightmost constituent; what is sometimes called Node Raising (NR). NR operates independently of CD and Regrouping to derive (ib) from (ia):

(i) (a) [S[SJohn built [NPthe tower]NP]S and [SHarry destroyed [NPthe tower]NP]S]S
    (b) [S[SJohn built]S and [SHarry destroyed]S [NPthe tower]NP]S

It operates on the output of CD to derive (iib) from (iia):

(ii) (a) John built the tower and [John] then destroyed the tower.
    (b) John built and then destroyed the tower.

D. TERENCE LANGENDOEN

(16)　　　Conjunction Reduction (CR):

$$X_1 - Z_1 - X_2 - \langle Z_2 - X_3 \rangle - (and - X_1 - Z_1' - X_2 - \langle Z_2 - X_3 \rangle)*$$

1	2	3	4	5	6	7	8	9	10	11

$$\overset{opt}{\Longrightarrow}$$

(A)　1　2　3　4　5　6　ϕ　8　ϕ　10　ϕ

(B)　1 2$\oplus$6+8　3　4$\oplus$6+10　5　ϕ　ϕ　ϕ　ϕ　ϕ　ϕ

⟨*respectively*⟩

Conditions:　(1)　2 and 8; 4 and 10 are the same major category, and $2 \neq 8$; $4 \neq 10$.

(2)　A is precluded if:

(a)　$45 = \phi$ and 2 is not VP, or

(b)　3 or 5 contain NP other than a clitic pronoun adjoined to its V.

Condition (1) is familiar from all previous discussions of CR, for example Chomsky (1965, p. 212), Schane (1966), Ross (1967), and Hankamer (1971), to name a few. Condition (2a) specifies that only Regrouping (option B) is permitted if the reduction of conjunctions is to a single category other that VP. Condition (2b) is NLPNPC.

To summarize: close examination of Hankamer's argument for a trans-derivational constraint on CD to eliminate derivations that would result in structural ambiguity reveals that that argument fails, and that there is an alternative analysis within standard theory that not only accounts for the facts noted by Hankamer, but many others as well. Therefore his argument for SRC, based on CD, must be rejected. We turn now to his other arguments for SRC, based on other variable deletion rules, and on chopping rules. These arguments are derived from cases from a variety of languages, including, besides English, Japanese, Turkish, Navaho, French, and Slovenian. His discussion of the non-English cases, however, is inconclusive, and fails to provide real support for SRC.[4] I therefore restrict myself to consideration of his English cases.

Most of the English cases discussed, it turns out, involve the interaction of variable deletion and movement rules with the rule of Dative Movement. For

---

NR also operates on conjoined noun phrases (which may themselves result from Regrouping), as illustrated in (iii); note that the raised noun remains singular, with the verb showing plural agreement:

(iii)　(a)　[$_{NP}$[$_{NP}$A young [$_N$man]$_N$]$_{NP}$ and [$_{NP}$an old [$_N$man]$_N$]$_{NP}$]$_{NP}$ are here.

(b)　[$_{NP}$[$_{NP}$A young]$_{NP}$ and [$_{NP}$an old]$_{NP}$ [$_N$man]$_N$]$_{NP}$ are here.

It is beyond the scope of this paper to provide an adequate explicit statement of NR.

4. Hankamer never shows, for example, that the conditions on the rules discussed in these languages cannot straightforwardly be stated in terms of standard theory. His only objection to such statements is that they "would merely state the facts" (p. 51). I cannot take this objection very seriously.

example, Hankamer considers the interaction of this rule with the variable deletion rules of Comparative Deletion and "Ready Socks" (pp. 42-44),[5] and the
chopping rules of Relativization, Question Movement, and Topicalization
(pp. 51-53). Concerning the latter interaction, Hankamer argues that any
derivation involving the application of a chopping rule to an NP affected by
Dative Movement (that is, either the direct or the indirect object) must be
blocked. Hankamer's examples (128)-(129) and (133)-(134), given here as
(17)-(20), illustrate this restriction (I use "#" to indicate "unacceptable to
Hankamer"):

   (17) #Sally is a girl I would give my last dime.
   (18) #The bastard I lent my pipe tool never brought it back.
   (19) #The pipe tool I sold Jeremy was rusty.
   (20) #The book I was reading Susan is on the table.

These judgments confirm SRC, he argues, since application of any of the chopping rules in English to a direct or indirect object in a sentence in which Dative
Movement has applied would introduce structural ambiguity. Concerning
(19)-(20), Hankamer admits "the judgments are delicate" (p. 52), and points
out in footnote 18 (p. 53) that he has learned from B. Schapiro that some
people find sentences like (19)-(20) acceptable. He need not have had to con-
sult Schapiro on this point, however, if he had examined the transformational
literature on Dative Movement, such as Fillmore (1965), Kuroda (1968), and
Jakendoff and Culicover (1971), in which such sentences are uniformly considered acceptable. As Hankamer points out, the acceptability of (19) and (20)
is consistent with SRC, as long as (17) and (18) remain unacceptable, since one
need only add to the SRC that, for some English speakers, in the case of chopping rules applying to the configuration V NP NP, only the peripheral NP (the
direct object) can be chopped.

    Unfortunately, Hankamer has mistaken what Schapiro told him. What
Schapiro actually found was that some people (himself included) accept not
only sentences like (19) and (20), but also sentences like (17) and (18); it never
occurred to Schapiro that anyone would not accept the former type of sentence.
In a carefully controlled study of dative questions, Langendoen, Kalish-Landon,
and Dore (1974) found exactly the same thing as Schapiro; we go on to argue
that in fact all sentences like (17)-(20) are grammatical, and that the unacceptability of (19)-(20) for those that find them unacceptable is due to perceptual
principles. But regardless of the success of our arguments in support of this
contention, the existence of a dialect of English in which chopping rules introduce acceptable structural ambiguity is sufficient to refute SRC.

5. It is not clear to me why these rules are called variable deletion rules; they both seem to
involve the deletion of a constituent, namely NP. This is no consequence, however, since
one can reformulate the problem to be whether SRC is appropriate to constituent-deletion
rules.

Concerning Hankamer's treatment of the interaction of Dative Movement and the variable deletion rules of Comparative Deletion and "Ready Socks," much the same point can be made. Hankamer contends that the deletions indicated in (21) and (22) (his examples (97) and (99)), result in unacceptability:

(21) Jack persuaded more millionaires to go on diets than Harry sold #[millionaires] Cadillacs.

(22) Jack stole more Cadillacs than Harry sold millionaires #[Cadillacs].

In my judgment, whatever lack of acceptability these examples have is due to lack of parallelism between the two clauses, a performance matter, rather than to some degree of ungrammaticality due to the inapplicability of Comparative Deletion whenever structural ambiguity would be introduced (see also pp. 63–64, where Hankamer acknowledges the possibility effects of lack of parallelism on acceptability in similar cases). To see this, compare (21) and (22) with the following examples:

(23) (a) Jack sold more millionaires Cadillacs than Fred gave [millionaires] Continentals.

(b) Jack sold more millionaires Cadillacs than Fred gave Continentals to ?[millionaires].

(24) (a) Jack sold millionaires more Cadillacs than Fred gave the poor [Cadillacs].

(b) Jack sold millionaires more Cadillacs than Fred gave ?[Cadillacs] to the poor.

Thus I conclude that there is no blocking of Comparative Deletion affecting direct or indirect objects in sentences in which those NPs are affected by Dative Movement, again disconfirming SRC.

Hankamer illustrates the Dative Movement–"Ready Socks" Interaction with the following examples (his (104)–(105)):

(25) These socks are ready for you to take Harry #[these socks].

(26) Harry is ready for you to take #[Harry] these socks.

Whatever unacceptability these examples have, however, is due not to the inapplicability of Ready Socks, but to the choice of the main verb in the infinitive. By substituting for *take* a verb more prone to Dative Movement, such as *bring* or *give*, one improves the acceptability of examples like (24) and (25). Thus this case, too, rather than confirming SRC, disconfirms it.

Hankamer's remaining examples in English involve the application of the rightward chopping rule of Heavy NP Shift. He argues that SRC is needed to account for the contrast in acceptability between (27) and (28), which are analogous to his examples (151)–(155):

(27) *We expect to be executed everyone who was arrested in front of the palace.

(28) We sent to be executed everyone who was arrested in front of the palace.

Concerning this contrast, Hankamer says:

> Note that the inability of the immediate postverbal NP to undergo Heavy NP Shift correlates with the ability of the verb involved to have the subject of a sentence embedded as its object deleted by Equi. All Equi verbs have the restriction, all non-Equi verbs lack it.

> This is a correlation which can only be stated in transderivational terms. Heavy NP Shift is blocked just in case its output is a sentence which looks like a product of Equi with an extra NP tacked on at the end (p. 55).

This statement is extraordinary on two accounts. First, the "terms" of the proposed statement are hardly transderivational, since, as Hankamer admits (p. 56), there is no derivation in English in which one generates a sentence with an extra NP tacked on at the end. We have here an instance of a proposed constraint, call it transnonderivational, that blocks derivations on the basis of derivations of ungrammatical strings. Since the latter do not exist, neither can the constraint. Second, Hankamer states in the first part of the passage just quoted a condition on the applicability of Heavy NP Shift that is straightforwardly expressible in standard theory. Namely, Heavy NP Shift is inapplicable in case the verb preceding the NP to be shifted is marked as requiring Equi to apply when the subject of the object complement is identical to its own subject. Why Hankamer believes that the correlation can only be stated in terms that transcend standard theory escapes me.[6]

Even if one could somehow get around the objection just raised, there is a further problem raised by the fact that Heavy NP Shift is blocked even if the part preceding the shifted NP is not by itself a grammatical sentence, as (29) illustrates:

(29) *You can't expect to pay you everyone who borrows money and promises to pay you back.

A similar case arises in connection with CD, which Hankamer alleges may be blocked by SRC even though the nonblocked application of CD is in a "derivation" that results in an ungrammatical string. This is illustrated in (30) (Hankamer's (52)).

(30) (a) *Jack asked Mike to wash himself, and Sue to shave himself.
     (b) *_____ and [Jack asked] Sue to shave himself.
     (c) _____ and Sue *[asked Jack] to shave himself.

6. The possibility remains that (27) is grammatical, but unacceptable because it contains a perceptual "garden path." Such an explanation would be correct for a sentence like (i):

(i) ?We expect to be executed will be no fun.

Again, since there is no derivation of (30b), one can hardly call the principle that blocks (30c) transderivational. The existence of other derivations (even of ungrammatical strings) is simply irrelevant to the correct account of the ungrammaticality of sentences like (29) and (30).

This concludes my examination of Hankamer's empirically-based arguments for SRC. However, Hankamer, in section 2 of his paper, gives a number of purely theoretical arguments for SRC as well, based on such notions as recoverability of deletion, the power of linguistic theory, and the status of perceptual strategies. Suppose, then, for purposes of discussion, the empirically-based arguments did not weigh so heavily against SRC, so that if the theoretical arguments for it were strong, we might be led to consider it seriously as a hypothesis of universal grammar. Unfortunately, Hankamer's theoretically-based arguments backfire as badly as do his empirically-based ones.

Consider first Hankamer's argument concerning the notion of recoverability of deletion. He first points out that Chomsky's proposal (1965, pp. 144–145) concerning recoverability is inadequate, because it does not permit the existence of variable deletion rules. The question then becomes how best to extend Chomsky's proposal to deal with variable deletion rules. One way to do it in terms compatible with standard theory is to specify that the variable strings that act as deleter and deletee be nondistinct (as defined in Chomsky (1965, p. 182)), and be presented as terms in a fixed position in the structural analyses of such transformations, as is the case in my version of CD in (16). Hankamer's suggestion is that SRC is needed to capture the notion of recoverability for such deletions. First of all, he asks, what is the notion of recoverability? Hankamer defines it as follows:

[A] deletion is recoverable if, given only the statement of the rule effecting the deletion and the output of a particular application of the rule, the input to the rule can be uniquely determined. In order to meet this condition, a deletion rule would have to be so formulated or so constrained that it could never map two distinct inputs into the same output. Any rule which so neutralized the distinction between two different underlying structures would introduce ambiguity, and a deletion which introduces ambiguity is not recoverable (p. 30).

Hankamer goes on to argue that if deletions are recoverable in this sense, and if it is not possible to impose a set of restrictions on such rules so as to insure recoverability, then "it must be because there are independent constraints which block these rules when there is a possibility of nonrecoverable application" (40). This argument does not go though, however, because the first premise is false. I have already considered a case, example (11), in which Hankamer himself must admit that a variable deletion rule applies nonrecoverably in his sense. The fact that constituent-deletion rules can apply nonrecoverably (in Hankamer's sense) in cases where "sloppy identity" is sufficient is another instance in which the first premise of the argument is falsified. Thus Hankamer's notion of recoverability cannot be what is meant when we say that deletion rules must satisfy a condition on recoverability. A much weaker condition, such as the alternative suggested above, must be what is required, and SRC receives, accordingiy, no support from considerations of recoverability of deletion.

Hankamer also tries to show that the incorporation of a transderivational condition like SRC, rather than broadening the scope of the theory of transformational grammar, in fact narrows it. He says the following: "Note that the proposed condition [SRC] has the effect of *reducing* (original emphasis) the number of possible derivations; that is, it reduces the generative capacity of transformational grammars" (p. 37). Here, Hankamer reveals himself as totally confused about the meaning of reducing the generative capacity of a theory of grammar. That notion has nothing to do with the number of possible derivations in a grammar; generative capacity, rather, is defined as the class of languages that may be generated by all the grammars expressible in a given theory. The generative capacity of transformational grammars without SRC includes all those languages in which application of variable deletion rules introduces structural ambiguity, and includes no languages in which application of such rules fails to do so (except by accident). On the other hand, transformational grammars with SRC includes all those languages in which variable deletion rules fail to introduce structural ambiguity by virtue of the filtering effect of SRC, and no languages in which application of such rules does introduce structural ambiguity. Thus, the generative capacity of transformational grammars with SRC is distinct from, but not comparable with, the generative capacity of transformational grammars without SRC.[7] Hence, SRC receives no support from consideration of generative capacity.

Finally, there is the matter of the difference between rules of grammar, and rules of performance, such as perceptual strategies. Here again, I quote Hankamer:

[SRC], it should be noted, represents an explicit formulation of what has been called a "perceptual strategy." There has been some speculation about perceptual strategies and the role such devices might play in determining interpretations of ambiguous sentences and levels of acceptability . . .

One reason for the general neglect of this phenomenon is no doubt the widespread assumption that perceptual strategies belong in some as yet unexplored "performance model" and have nothing to do with "competence." Yet I know of no empirical test which could tell us whether a given sentence . . . is actually ungrammatical or only "unacceptable for performance reasons."

7. I thank G. Sanders for clarifying my thinking on this point.

Until such a test is suggested, it is vacuous to attribute some cases of ungrammaticality to violations of rules "in the grammar" and others to "performance constraints" (p. 36, note 12).

Concerning this passage, I observe first of all that SRC is not a formulation of a perceptual strategy. A perceptual strategy is a rule that listeners employ as they hear a sentence, in order to assign it a representation (e.g., of its meaning). SRC cannot possibly be such a rule, since it is not a principle for constructing linguistic representations in real time. Now it is certainly true that listeners generally do not notice structural ambiguities when presented with sentences that are structurally ambiguous, but that fact is certainly not due to their applying a rule that says in effect "don't notice structural ambiguity"; rather it is a by-product of the application of applying *bona fide* perceptual strategies. Take, for example, the set of strategies discussed in Langendoen (1976), by which the structurally ambiguous sentence (31a) is heard only as (31b), never as (31c):

(31) (a) Several of my children's friends are here.

(b) $[_{NP}$Several $[_{PP}$of $[_{NP}$ $[_{DET}$ $[_{NP}$my children$]_{NP}$'s$]_{DET}$friends$]_{NP}$ $]_{PP}$ $]_{NP}$ are here.

(c) $[_{NP}$ $[_{DET}$ $[_{NP}$Several $[_{PP}$of $[_{NP}$my children$]_{NP}$ $]_{PP}$ $]_{NP}$'s $]_{DET}$ friends$]_{NP}$ are here.

The apparent unambiguity of (31a) is due to the particular way that the perceptual parsing strategies in English work; it is not due to the application of a pseudostrategy that instructs listeners not to construct a left-branching parsing of a string of a certain sort when that string can also receive a right-branching parsing.

Second, concerning Hankamer's requirement of an "empirical test" for the difference between grammaticality and acceptability before any decision can be made about how to classify sentences along these dimensions, it should be pointed out that this amounts to the requirement of a discovery procedure. Short of lapsing into empiricism, there can be no discovery procedure for the distinction; what we have, rather, is a much weaker decision procedure for the distinction, having to do with whether it is possible to formulate independently motivated performance rules (to handle whatever cases we happen to be dealing with), and with the question of whether the incorporation of the rules that handle the phenomena in the grammar results in a weakening of the theory underlying it (see Langendoen, Kalish-Landon, and Dore, 1974, for further discussion). Hankamer's own suggestion of a possible discovery procedure, namely, that judgments that reflect acceptability are subject to semantic and morphological manipulation, whereas judgments that reflect grammaticality are absolute, certainly does not work as one can convince oneself by considering a grammatical, but unacceptable, sentence with degree 100 of center-embedding. Thus SRC receives no support from the consideration of perceptual strategies, either.[8]

To summarize the findings of our investigation of Hankamer's theoretically based arguments for SRC, we see that they fare no better than his empirically based arguments. There is no way that SRC can be justified as a principle of universal grammar, and therefore the hypothesis that it is such a principle is disconfirmed.

REFERENCES

Chomsky, N. 1965. *Aspects of the Theory of Syntax*, M.I.T. Press.

Fillmore, C. J. 1965. *Indirect Object Constructions in English and the Ordering of Transformations.* Mouton.

Hankamer, J. 1971. *Constraints on Deletion in Syntax.* Unpublished Ph.D. dissertation. Yale University.

———. 1973. "Unacceptable Ambiguity." *Linguistic Inquiry* 4: 17–68.

Harries, H. 1973. "Coordination Reduction." *Stanford University Working Papers on Language Universals* 11: 139–209.

8. In Langendoen (1972), I suggested that the unacceptability of sentences like (2c), (3a,b), (4c), (5b,c,d,e,f), etc., is due to the difficulty of interpreting such sentences using perceptual strategies for recovering deleted material, rather than to ungrammaticality as a result of violating condition (2b) on CR. I changed my mind on this matter, because I found I could express the restriction straightforwardly in terms of grammar (a restriction that also generalized to such cases as (6)–(8), which can only be out for grammatical reasons), but that I could not see any straightforward characterization in terms of perceptual strategies. This does not mean, of course, that some such characterization cannot be found that is superior to the formulation given in grammatical terms. In support of the contention that the phenomena are to be described outside the grammar, S. Greenbaum (personal communication) argues that the acceptability judgments in many of these cases are not as clearcut as Hankamer and I make them out to be, and that the variation may be explainable on extra-linguistic grounds. That may be so, but it does seem clear that the examples are not fully acceptable when contextual support is not provided. Greenbaum also correctly notes a difficulty with NLPNPC, which may cast some doubt on its general validity, namely that CD is also blocked if a non-left-peripheral string consisting of a manner adverbial (not containing NP, at least in surface structure) is deleted. This is illustrated in (i):

    (i) (a) Mary entered the room carefully and turned on the light.
        (b) _____ and [Mary] turned on the light [ϕ].
        (c) _____ and *[Mary] turned on the light [carefully].

One might want to argue that at the point at which CD applies, *carefully* is still represented as *in a careful manner* (i.e., as a string that contains NP; such a solution would of course be feasible only if *yesterday* does not receive the analysis *the day before today* and if CD is not the last rule in the syntax, contra Koutsoudas (1971)). Alternatively, one could add various types of adverb constructions to the list of constituents that, if non-left-peripheral, cannot be deleted by CD. Without much further detailed investigation, this question cannot be decided one way or the other. See also Kuno (1976).

Jackendoff, R., and P. Culicover. 1971. "A Reconsideration of Dative Movements." *Foundations of Language* 7: 397–412.

Klima, E. S. 1970. "Regulatory Devices against Functional Ambiguity." Unpublished paper.

Koutsoudas, A. 1971. "Gapping, Conjunction Reduction, and Coordinate Deletion." *Foundations of Language* 7: 337–386.

Kuno, S. 1976. "Gapping: A Functional Analysis." *Linguistic Inquiry* 7, no. 2.

Kuroda, S-Y. 1968. "Review of Fillmore, 1965." *Language* 44: 374–378.

Langendoen, D. T. 1972. "The Problem of Grammaticality." *Peabody Journal of Education* 50: 20–23.

———. 1976. "A Case of Apparent Ungrammaticality." In this volume.

Langendoen, D. T., N. Kalish-Landon, and J. Dore. 1974. "Dative Questions: A Study in the Relation of Acceptability to Grammaticality of an English Sentence Type." *Cognition* 2: 451–478. Reprinted in this volume.

Ross, J. R. 1967. *Constraints on Variables in Syntax.* Indiana University Linguistics Club.

———. 1970. "Gapping and the Order of Constituents." In *Progress in Linguistics*, M. Bierwisch, and K. Heidolph, eds. Mouton.

Ruwet, N. 1973. "How to Deal with Syntactic Irregularities: Conditions on Transformations or Perceptual Strategies?" In *Generative Grammar in Europe*, F. Kiefer, and N. Ruwet, eds. Reidel.

Schane, S. 1966. *A Schema for Sentence Coordination.* MITRE Corporation.

Tai, J. 1969. *Coordination Reduction.* Unpublished Ph.D. dissertation. Indiana University.

———. 1971. "Identity Deletion and Regrouping in Coordinate Structures." In *Papers from the Seventh Regional Meeting, Chicago Linguistic Society*, University of Chicago.

Can a Not Unhappy Person Be Called a Not Sad One?

D. TERENCE LANGENDOEN
THOMAS G. BEVER

Banal statements are given the appearance of profundity by means of the not un-*formation.... It should also be possible to laugh the* not un-*formation out of existence.... One can cure oneself of the* not un-*formation by memorizing this sentence:* A not unblack dog was chasing a not unsmall rabbit across a not ungreen field.

GEORGE ORWELL

1. ACCEPTABILITY AND GRAMMATICALITY

In this paper we present a current sample of the rationalist-structuralist approach to the study of language.[1] Specific results are discussed that may be of interest to researchers specializing in English syntax. But more important, the present investigation is an example of how to treat linguistic phenomena as the result of interactions among different systems of linguistic knowledge. We argue that certain acceptable sequences are in fact ungrammatical but they are deemed acceptable by virtue of their perceptual comprehensibility. This analysis reduces the generative potential of universal grammatical formalisms and thus strengthens the claims made about what the child must know to be able to learn language.

---

1. As pioneered by Jakobson and Halle (1956), Halle (1962), and Chomsky and Halle (1968). An earlier version of this paper was read by Langendoen at the 1972 Summer meeting of the Linguistic Society of America under the title "Prenominal Negation in English."

Source: S. Anderson and P. Kiparsky, eds., *A Festschrift for Morris Halle* (New York: Holt, Rinehart & Winston, 1973). Reprinted by permission of the publisher.

D. TERENCE LANGENDOEN
AND THOMAS C. BEVER

The goal of a linguistic grammar is to account directly for the grammatical status and structure of sentences. Many contemporary proposals in linguistics derive critically relevant facts using the assumption that sentence grammaticality is equivalent to string acceptability. Representative samples of acceptability judgments that have been interpreted as grammatical ones are given in (1)–(4):[2]

(1) (a) *A not happy person entered the room.
    (b) A not unhappy person entered the room.
(2) (a) *Who did you give this book?
    (b) Who did you give this book to?
(3) (a) *Did that the guests slept late inconvenience you?
    (b) Did it inconvenience you that the guests slept late?
(4) (a) *Tomorrow I expected him to be there.
    (b) Tomorrow I expect him to be there.

But, as Chomsky (1965) has pointed out, sentence acceptability is to be distinguished from grammaticality: acceptability can be characterized *within* grammar "only in terms of some 'global' property that is attributable, not to a particular rule, but rather to the way in which the rules interrelate in a derivation" (p. 12). Accordingly, the decision to interpret differences in acceptability in cases like (1)–(4) as differences in grammaticality has recently led to the development of formalisms that enable one to mark sentences as ungrammatical on the basis of properties of their derivations (derivational constraints) or even on the basis of properties of potential derivations of other sentences (transderivational constraints) (See in particular Lakoff, 1969, 1970, 1971).

The unnecessary use of such formalisms will lead to a trivialization of linguistic theory: the more descriptive potential a formal device has, the less revealing it is about the specific ability it respresents.[3] To accept these powerful formalisms as linguistic universals is to weaken the interest of the specific claims made about language acquisition and the antecedent properties of the child's mind. However, if there is no independently motivated theory of language

---

2. Examples (1) are adapted from Klima (1964), examples (2) from Fillmore (1965), examples (3) from Ross (1967), and examples (4) from Postal and Ross (1970).

3. There has been, so far, no formal proof that derivational and transderivational constraints of the kinds that have been proposed do actually increase the generative capacity of the class of grammars permitted by the theory. In fact, one can imagine derivational constraints which would restrict the generative capacity of linguistic grammars to that of finite-state grammars—for example a constraint that would limit the degree of self-embedding to some fixed finite amount (see the discussion of (5) in the text). However, it is intuitively clear that the ability to make reference at any stage of a derivation to any other stage or to make reference to other possible derivations increases the descriptive power that is available to the grammarian.

performance that accounts for differences in acceptability like those in (1)–(4) one must then accept the grammatical formalisms in question.

As a case in point, let us consider sentences which have center-embedding. If sentences such as (5a) were to be classified as ungrammatical and those such as (5b) as grammatical, then the grammar of English would require at least the power of derivational constraints:

(5) (a) *I watched the man the psychiatrist my mother recommended had worked with jump out the window.
    (b) I watched the man the psychiatrist had worked with jump out the window.

Although there is no fully agreed-upon behavioral theory that accounts completely for the difference in acceptability between (5a) and (5b), most researchers have been willing to recognize some behavioral theory as sufficiently plausible so that grammatical mechanisms are not required here (for example, Miller and Chomsky, 1963; Bever, 1970).

Similarly, were grammaticality the basis for the differential acceptability of English sentences such as (6) in which Relative Clause Reduction has applied, derivational constraints would be required within a grammar:

(6) (a) *The horse raced into the ring bolted.
    (b) The horse ridden into the ring bolted.

However, the behavioral explanation is sufficiently well documented in this case to show that (6a) and (6b) are both fully grammatical (see Bever, 1970; Bever and Langendoen, 1971). The unacceptability of (6a) is explained by appeal to otherwise motivated perceptual mechanisms.

In each of these cases, the grammar has been relieved of accounting for certain instances of differential acceptability by reference to other systems of linguistic knowledge. A considerable number of systems of language behavior have by now been isolated for study—among them, systems of rhetoric, conversational implicature, speech production, speech perception, and language acquisition. Any or all of these systems may provide a basis for acceptability differences independent of grammar. Paradigm examples have been like the case of center-embedding; that is, the unacceptability of a grammatical sentence, such as (5a), is described in terms of a behavioral process.

In this paper we shall be concerned with the problem posed by the contrast in acceptability between sentence (1a) and sentence (1b). We shall show that both (1a) and (1b) are ungrammatical but (1b) is acceptable and interpretable as a result of independently motivated processes of speech perception and conversational implicature. That is, the case of (1a) versus (1b) is one in which the acceptability of an ungrammatical string is accounted for in terms of its behavioral comprehensibility.

D. TERENCE LANGENDOEN
AND THOMAS C. BEVER

2. GRAMMAR OF NEGATED ATTRIBUTIVE ADJECTIVE PHRASES

Let us first examine the descriptive and theoretical problems that would be entailed by the decision to label (1a) ungrammatical and (1b) grammatical. To begin with, note that the two sentences (7a) and (7b), which correspond directly to structures underlying (1a) and (1b), do not differ in acceptability; both are fully acceptable and presumably also fully grammatical:

(7) (a) A person who was not happy entered the room.
    (b) A person who was not unhappy entered the room.

Therefore, there must be a restriction on either the Relative Clause Reduction Rule or the Adjective Phrase Preposing Rule to the effect that (1a) cannot be derived from (7a) but that (1b) can be derived from (7b). That the restriction must be on Relative Clause Reduction can be seen from the unacceptability of (8), the analog to (1a) in which the reduced relative clause follows the head of the noun phrase:

(8) *Someone not happy entered the room.

As Klima noted, however, Relative Clause Reduction is not restricted if the adjective, besides being preceded by *not*, is also modified either by an intensifier or by a following phrase or clause, as in (9):[4]

(9) (a) A not very happy/unhappy person entered the room.
    (b) Someone not very happy/unhappy entered the room.
    (c) A person/someone not happy/unhappy about the recent polls entered the room.

We therefore may state the restriction on Relative Clause Reduction as follows: a relative clause may not be reduced just in case it ends in the string *not* Adjective, unless the adjective is composed of a negative prefix followed by an independently occurring adjective. Formally, Relative Clause Reduction can be stated as in (10):

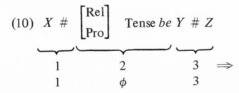

(10) $X \#$ $\begin{bmatrix} \text{Rel} \\ \text{Pro} \end{bmatrix}$ Tense *be* $Y \# Z$

$$\begin{matrix} 1 & 2 & 3 & \Rightarrow \\ 1 & \phi & 3 & \end{matrix}$$

4. Since the intensifier *enough* follows the adjective it modifies, there may be some disagreement as to the acceptability of sentences like (a):

(a) ?A not large enough box came with the coffeepot.

We shall treat such sentences as acceptable. If it should turn out that this is the wrong decision, the rules we propose can be adjusted accordingly.

Condition:[5] Inapplicable if
- (a) $Y = not$ Adj_1, and
- (b) $Adj_1 \neq$ [Neg] + Adj_2

Otherwise optional

The requirement that Adjective not be analyzable into [Neg] + Adjective$_2$ is necessitated by the fact that sentences like (11) are unacceptable (hence, by hypothesis, ungrammatical):

(11) (a) *Some not insolent students want to see the dean.
     (b) *Did he make a not untoward remark about me?
     (c) *His uncle left him a not dismantled clock.

The input of (11) to rule (10) satisfies the condition that makes the rule inapplicable: *insolent, untoward, dismantled* are not analyzable into [Neg] + Adjective since at most *-solent, -toward, -mantled* are categorized as adjective stems.

3. PROBLEMS FOR STANDARD THEORY

Upon closer examination the statement of the rule of Relative Clause Reduction in (10) turns out to be inadequate. First, note that there is an asymmetry in the acceptability judgments having to do with whether the modified element is a noun or an indefinite pronoun. We observed that (8), the analog to (1a) with an indefinite pronoun as head, was, like (1a), unacceptable. However, sentence, (12), the analog to (1b), is unacceptable, unlike (1b):

(12) *Someone not unhappy entered the room.

Thus the second part of the condition in (10) must be dropped in case the element immediately preceding the relative clause is an indefinite pronoun (*someone, something*).

However generic indefinite pronouns (*anyone, anything*) can be modified by reduced relative clauses of any sort whatever.[6] Consider in this regard the examples in (13), all of which are acceptable:

(13) (a) Anyone not interested may leave.
     (b) Anything not easy is worthwhile.
     (c) Melvin dislikes anything not fattening.

5. The subscripts on Adjective are for convenience only, to distinguish the full adjective (e.g., *unhappy*) from the adjective that follows the negative prefix (e.g., *-happy*). The symbol [Neg] should be read "negative prefix."

6. This was pointed out to us by J. R. Ross. See also Ross (1972, pp. 70–71).

D. TERENCE LANGENDOEN
AND THOMAS C. BEVER

This relaxation of the condition, however, does not extend to generically used nouns, as illustrated in (14):

(14) (a) *Any not interested person may leave.
      (b) *Any not easy project is worthwhile.
      (c) *Melvin dislikes any not fattening food.

Given the facts in (12)–(14), the condition on Relative Clause Reduction must be amended as in (15):

(15) Condition: Inapplicable if

(a) $X = X'$ N and $Y = not$ Adj_1 and $\text{Adj}_1 \neq$ [Neg] + Adj_2

(b) $X = X'$ $\begin{bmatrix} \text{Indef} \\ \text{Nongener} \\ \text{Pro} \end{bmatrix}$ and $Y = not$ Adj_1

The requirement that Adjective not be analyzable into [Neg] + Adjective_2 is not strong enough, however. Consider (16):

(16) *Sheila wants to meet a not unmarried man.

Clearly *unmarried* is analyzable into [Neg] + Adjective_2, yet (16) is unacceptable. The reason, apparently, is that *married* and *unmarried* denote two mutually exclusive states. It is sufficient for Relative Clause Reduction to be blocked if an explicitly negated negatively prefixed adjective and its unprefixed counterpart do not denote two ends of a continuous scale with respect to the noun being modified.[7] Thus we must alter the condition (15) to read as in (17):

(17) Condition: Inapplicable if

(a) $X = X'$ N and $Y = not$ Adj_1 and
     { $\text{Adj}_1 \neq$ [Neg] + Adj_2 or { Adj_1 or Adj_2 = [Noncontinuous]}}

(b) $X = X'$ $\begin{bmatrix} \text{Indef} \\ \text{Nongener} \\ \text{Pro} \end{bmatrix}$ and $Y = not$ Adj_1

Even with this modification the condition is still too weak. We must also specify that Adjective_1 and Adjective_2 have exactly the same meaning, save

---

7. Whether an adjective is marked as continuous or noncontinuous is not always clear and perhaps may vary from person to person in some cases. Thus one can imagine a person who categorized people into exactly two classes with respect to holiness—*holy* and *unholy*. Presumably such a person would refuse to accept the phrase *a not unholy man*, whereas another person who considers there to be a holiness continuum would accept it readily.

for the contribution of the negative prefix of Adjective$_1$. Examples are legion. Consider (18):[8]

(18) (a) *He emitted a not unearthly scream.
      (b) *Sam bought his wife some not unusual clothes.

We must therefore build into the restriction on Relative Clause Reduction the additional qualification that the rule is inapplicable if Adjective$_1$ and Adjective$_2$ differ in meaning beyond the difference supplied by [Neg]. Such a qualification, however, is not statable in the theory of Chomsky (1965) (the so-called standard theory), assuming that *-earthly* and *-usual* of *unearthly* and *unusual* are categorized as Adjective. To avoid this impasse, we would have to assign to all negatively prefixed adjectives like *unearthly* a special bracketing, analogous to the bracketing of *insolent*, in which *-earthly* is not given the label "Adjective" but rather some special label such as "Adjective-Stem." In this way standard theory could account for cases like those in (18).

Such a decision, however, leads to unacceptable consequences for lexical representation and hence cannot be generally applied.[9] Consider, for example, the lexical items *healthy* and *unhealthy*. Both items are polysemous, and in some of their senses, listed in (19), they differ only to the extent supplied by the prefix *un-*:[10]

(19) (a) *healthy*   i.   in a state of good health.
                        ii. conducive to good health.
                        iii. indicative of good health or of a rational or constructive frame of mind.

      (b) *unhealthy* i.   in a state of ill health.
                        ii. conducive to ill health.
                        iii. indicative of ill health or of an irrational or destructive frame of mind.

Accordingly, phrases of the type *a not unhealthy* N are acceptable when *unhealthy* is used in any of the senses of (19b). But both *healthy* and *unhealthy*

8. Our acceptability intuitions about cases like (18) have interesting properties. At first it appears that the sentences are acceptable; then, upon reflection as to their meaning, their unacceptability emerges. Our explanation for this in terms of the general solution proposed in Section 7 is the following: the sentences contain phrases that are superficially analyzable in terms of the perceptual schema (34c), but once they are so analyzed, their interpretation is seen to be anomalous (for example, "He emitted a slightly to moderately earthly scream" for (18a)).

9. The decision would be right only for those cases in which an adjective stem, by accident, is homophonous with a true adjective with an entirely different meaning. Neither of the cases in (18), however, strikes us as meeting this criterion.

10. The definitions in (19) and (20) are based on the entries that appear under *healthy* and *unhealthy* in *The American Heritage Dictionary*.

D. TERENCE LANGENDOEN
AND THOMAS C. BEVER

also have senses that are unmatched by corresponding senses in the other, as shown in (20):

(20) (a) *healthy*   iv. sizable
      (b) *unhealthy* iv. dangerous

The fact that *healthy* has the additional sense 'sizable' is not problematic.[11] However, the sense 'dangerous' for *unhealthy* does present a problem since phrases of the type *a not unhealthy* N, in which *unhealthy* is used in this sense, are unacceptable, as illustrated in (21):

(21) *Don't take any not unhealthy risks.

To adopt the solution that *unhealthy* with the sense 'dangerous' is not analyzable into the negative prefix *un-* and the adjective *healthy* would be incorrect since this sense of *unhealthy* clearly belongs with the others.[12] Therefore standard theory has no mechanism to account for the unacceptability of cases like (21).

These cases do not exhaust the list of difficulties for standard theory. Consider (22):

(22) (a) *The bishop favored the not impious regent.
      (b) *Maude wants to marry a not impotent man.

Semantically, the relation of *impious* to *pious* (similarly, *impotent* to *potent*) is that of *unhappy* to *happy:* They mean the same save for the contribution of the negative prefix. But phonologically they differ in the quality of the first vowel. Using Chomsky and Halle's (1968) informal spelling, *pious* is *pIous* and *-pious* is *-pEous*. The *E* of *-pEous* is derived from underlying *-pIous* by a laxing rule (and a subsequent rule which tenses vowels in prevocalic position). The laxing rule applies to a vowel which immediately follows a stressed syllable and which is not the final syllable in the word. Formally, the rule is (23):[13]

(23) $V \rightarrow [-\text{tense}] / [+\text{stress}] C_0 \underline{\quad\quad} C_0 V$

---

11. For some people, however, *not unhealthy* may acceptably be used to mean "slightly to moderately sizable," as in (a):

(a) The president fled to Venezuela with a not unhealthy share of the profits.

The significance of this fact is discussed in note 22.

12. Roughly, we may say that the sense 'dangerous' for *unhealthy* is derivable from the sense 'conducive to ill health' by generalizing the notion 'ill health' to 'harm'. Such a generalization, however, does not obscure the underlying relation of *unhealthy* to *healthy*.

13. Rule (23) is obviously related to Chomsky and Halle's rule (118d), the last line of their Auxiliary Reduction Rule I (1968, p. 125), which they develop to handle the reduction of the penult in words like *advisory* (from *advise* + *Ory*). What our discussion shows is that their rule (118d) has a more extensive application than they supposed.

The effect of rule (23) can also be seen in such examples as *infinite* (from *in + fInIt*—compare *finite*), *barometer* (from *baro + mEter*—compare *meter*), *relative* (from *relAt + ive*—compare *relation*), *bicycle* (from *bI + cIcle*), and *maturation* from *matUr + ation*—compare *mature*).

Consequently, *pious* and the *-pious* of *impious* do not differ in their systematic phonemic representation: both are represented *pIous*. But if *pious* and *-pious* have the same meaning and are represented alike phonologically, how can standard theory account for the unacceptability of (22)? The relevant factor, clearly, is that the two forms differ phonetically as a consequence of the application of the laxing rule in *impious*. However, standard theory cannot make reference to that difference in the formulation of a restriction on a syntactic transformation. And even if it could, there would be no way of referring to the pronunciation of the adjective *pious* in a derivation of a sentence that contains only the adjective *impious*. The constraint would have to refer to a quasi-phonetic form that does not appear in the derivation of the sentence in question, a possibility that does not exist within standard theory.[14]

One could argue that condition (17) handles most of the cases and that the remaining problems can be listed as idiomatic exceptions to the rule of Relative Clause Reduction. But such a list would provide no explanation of why just these cases are exceptional.

4. A SOLUTION WITHIN GENERATIVE SEMANTICS

Having shown that standard theory is incapable of providing a natural account of negated attributive adjective constructions, we will now demonstrate that generative semantics is more than adequate to the task. This should not be surprising, given the fact that the theory permits reference to all stages of a derivation at any given stage (derivational constraints) and even to other possible derivations (transderivational constraints).

Recall the problematic cases for standard theory, which are illustrated in (18), (21), and (22). In (18) we find examples like *unearthly* and *unusual*, in which the meaning of the full adjective is different from the compositional meaning of the negative prefix and the adjective that follows it (*-earthly* and *-usual*). One possible treatment for such cases within generative semantics is to specify a constraint that noun phrases of the type $X \, not \, \widehat{\text{Adjective}_1} \, \text{Noun}$, where $\text{Adjective}_1 = [\text{Neg}] + \text{Adjective}_2$, are ill-formed just in case the material that corresponds to Adjective_2 in a derivation of a noun phrase of the type $\widehat{X \, \text{Adjective}_2} \, \text{Noun}$ is different from the material that corresponds to Adjective_2 in the original derivation or in case there is no derivation that leads to a well-

---

14. See examples (d)–(g) in note 21 for other cases of this sort.

formed noun phrase of the latter type.[15]   The constraint is both derivational
(requiring simultaneous reference to a stage preceding lexical insertion and a
stage following relative clause reduction) and transderivational (requiring reference to other derivations or to the nonexistence of other derivations of a
certain type).

The case of (21) would receive a smaller treatment. Prior to lexical insertion,
the material corresponding to *healthy* in the derivation of (21) would be the
structure corresponding to the notion 'safe'. This semantic structure is not one
of the possible prelexical structures underlying *healthy* in the derivation of the
corresponding sentence (24):

(24)   *Don't take any healthy risks.

Thus (21) is ill-formed.

Finally, consider (22). To account for the unacceptability of this type of
sentence, we would simply add to the transderivational part of the constraint
that Adjective$_2$ in the phrase X Adjective$_2$ Noun is phonetically the same as
Adjective$_2$ in X *not* [Neg] + Adjective$_2$ Noun after the application of the
morphophonemic rules of vowel laxing.

5. A SOLUTION WITHIN
EXTENDED STANDARD
THEORY

Since the description of the cases under consideration appears to involve the
full panoply of power available to generative semantics, it is surprising that the
extended standard theory (Chomsky, 1971), with one modification, can also
account for these cases. It is not usually supposed that the extended standard
theory provides as much increased descriptive latitude over the standard theory
as does generative semantics. However, all that must be assumed is that reduced
relative clauses receive their semantic interpretation (including semantic amalga-
mation with the head noun) following the rule of Relative Clause Reduction
rather than in deep structure.

This assumption is not unreasonable in view of the possibility that there
are real, though subtle, differences in interpretation assigned to the object noun
phrases in (25a) and (25b):

(25)   (a)   I see an elephant that is small.
       (b)   I see a small elephant.

---

15. A generative semanticist could argue that his approach to this situation enables one to
avoid the ad hoc and arbitrary maneuver of considering *-earthly* and *-usual* to be adjective
stems rather than adjectives. For other arguments that claim that generative semantics offers an alternative to "arbitrary syntax," see Lakoff (1972) and Postal (1970).

To see these differences, suppose that (25a) and (25b) are the first premises of the two arguments whose second premises are given in (26):

(26) (a) An elephant is an animal.
      (b) An elephant is an animal.

Substituting *animal* for *elephant* whenever it appears in (25), we obtain (27):

(27) (a) I see an animal that is small.
      (b) I see a small animal.

For many people, (27a) would be considered a valid inference from (25a) and (26a), but (27b) would be considered an invalid inference from (25b) and (26b). Thus it would appear that (25b), which is derived from the structure that also underlies (25a) by Relative Clause Reduction and Adjective Preposing, differs semantically in an ever-so-slight way from (25a).[16]

Suppose, then, that we accept the view that there is a surface interpretation of Adjective-Noun combinations in English, and suppose that we are faced with the question of how to interpret the surface noun phrase configuration (28):

(28)   Adj₁

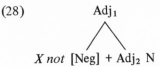

X *not* [Neg] + Adj₂ N

We proceed as follows. First we determine the senses of Adjective₁ that are compatible with the noun. We then construct the antonyms of these senses, assign the readings to Adjective₂, and declare that the interpretation is that of (29):

(29) X is slightly to moderately Adj₂ N

---

16. We believe, however, that the difference in interpretation between full and reduced relative clauses is rhetorical rather than semantic. That is, both (25a) and (25b) are ambiguous: the substitution of *animal* for *elephant* leads to a valid conclusion in one reading and to an invalid one in the other, and this is true for both examples. The reduced relative clause structure simply highlights the reading in which the substitution leads invalidly to the conclusion. This is so because the surface string Adjective Noun gives perceptual salience to the interpretation in which the adjective is to be judged in relation to the noun rather than in an absolute sense (that is, "small for an elephant"); the surface string in which the adjective is separated from the noun by the relative pronoun and the copula gives salience to the absolute interpretation of the adjective. This case is very much like that of sentences containing two quantifiers for which there is a preferred reading based on which quantifier comes first, as, for example, in *Many arrows hit few targets* and *Few targets were hit by many arrows*. Indeed it may turn out that all of the central cases motivating semantic sensitivity to surface structure can be explained by mechanisms outside the grammar (see Katz, 1972, Chap. 8).

D. TERENCE LANGENDOEN
AND THOMAS C. BEVER

The interpretation (29), however, is well-formed (grammatical) only if Adjective$_2$ is lexically represented as having at least one of the senses assigned to it by the interpretive rule. Given the surface noun phrases in (30), this rule would assign the interpretations in (31):

(30) (a) a not unhappy man.
     (b) a not unhealthy man.
     (c) a not unearthly scream.
     (d) a not unhealthy risk.

(31) (a) a slightly to moderately happy (in a state of emotional well-being) man.
     (b) a slightly to moderately healthy (in a state of good health) man.
     (c) a slightly to moderately earthly (not weird, ordinary) scream.
     (d) a slightly to moderately healthy (safe) risk.

Both (31a) and (31b) are well-formed interpretations since the independent lexical items *happy* and *healthy* within them have the interpretations assigned to them by the interpretive rule. But (31c) and (31d) are not well-formed since *earthly* does not mean 'not weird, ordinary' and *healthy* does not mean 'safe'.

To handle the unacceptability of phrases like *a not impious regent* in (22a), however, the Extended Standard Theory would have to have the power of examining the output of phonological rules such as (23), since the surface structure representations of such phrases would not distinguish them from acceptable phrases like *a not impossible situation*. Rule (23) is either a cyclic rule or a post-cyclic rule since it makes reference to stress placement. In either case the internal labeled bracketing would have been erased, destroying the information necessary for constructing a semantic representation. Therefore the theory would have to be modified further in one of two ways: either it would have to abandon the principle that labeled bracketing is erased after each cycle or it would have to permit the existence of derivational constraints that hold between surface structure and phonetic representation. Either choice would add descriptive power to the theory, thus reducing its explanatory capacity.[17]

17. Presumably, generative semantics and extended standard theory would treat cases of phrase-incorporated *not* with predicate adjectives in a similar manner. These cases appear to be governed by the same set of restrictions that applies to the prenominal cases, as exemplified in (a) and (b):

(a)   Harry was often not unfriendly

(b)   *Harry was often not $\begin{Bmatrix} \text{intrepid} \\ \text{impious} \end{Bmatrix}$

Generative semantics would mark cases like (b) as ungrammatical. Extended standard theory would include a generalized form of the interpretive rule (28)–(29) that could apply to predicate adjective structures as well. This, however, has some unfortunate consequences for the treatment of nonechoic, noncontrastive tag question formation, which has usually been taken as a paradigmatic example of a syntactic phenomenon. Consider (c)–(f):

6. A MOVE TO SAVE
STANDARD THEORY

To summarize, we have shown that if we are obliged to account within the grammar for the acceptability judgments concerning negated attributive adjective phrases in English, then standard theory must be abandoned in favor of either the much more powerful theory of generative semantics or a more powerful version of extended standard theory. It is clear that the problem with standard theory is the complexity involved in the theoretical extensions needed to make it sensitive to the internal morphology of adjectives with negative prefixes. Suppose we accept this limitation and add to standard theory the following universal constraint, which increases the restrictiveness of the theory: *no syntactic transformational rule is permitted to make use of the internal morphological structure of lexical items.*[18] The effect of this restriction on the statement of the rule of Relative Clause Reduction would be the elimination of that part of the condition on inapplicability that refers to the analysis of an adjective into a negative prefix and another adjective. Thus, the rule would now have the form (32):

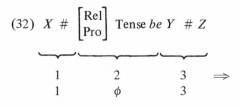

$$(32) \quad X \ \# \ \begin{bmatrix} \text{Rel} \\ \text{Pro} \end{bmatrix} \text{Tense } be \ Y \ \# \ Z$$

$$
\begin{array}{cccc}
1 & 2 & 3 & \Rightarrow \\
1 & \phi & 3 &
\end{array}
$$

(c) Harry [was not] unhappy, was he?
(d) Harry was [not unhappy], wasn't he?
(e) Harry [was not] happy, was he?
(f) Harry was [not happy], wasn't he?

Presumably, the surface interpretive rule would allow sentences like (d), (f) to be generated freely with the assumption that *not (un)happy* is a constituent. Sentence (f) would then be marked as semantically anomalous by virtue of the fact that no interpretive rule applies to simple constructions of the type *not* Adjective. That is, (f) would be marked as syntactically well-formed but semantically anomalous. This consequence, of course, is not further proof of the inadequacy of extended standard theory but is certainly at variance with the previously well-motivated assumption that tag formation is a syntactic process.

18. Note that feature-sensitive transformations such as Subject-Verb Agreement and polarity-adjustment rules (for example, the rule that specifies the conditions under which items like *any*, *ever*, and *at all* occur) are stated in terms of semantico-syntactic features, not word-internal morphemes. Thus the proposed universal restriction would have no adverse effect elsewhere in a standard theory account of English syntax. The restriction may have to be slightly modified, however, to allow for such phenomena as separable prefixes, as in German and Dutch.

D. TERENCE LANGENDOEN
AND THOMAS C. BEVER

Condition: Inapplicable if

$$X = X' \widehat{} \left\{ \begin{bmatrix} N \\ \text{Indef} \\ \text{Nongener} \\ \text{Pro} \end{bmatrix} \right\} \quad \text{and} \quad Y = not \, \widehat{} \text{Adj}$$

Otherwise optional

Rule (32) specifies that (1a) and (1b) are both ungrammatical, despite the acceptability of the latter. This simplifies the grammar but requires an explanation of the acceptability of (1b).

7. A BEHAVIORAL ACCOUNT OF THE MEANING AND ACCEPTABILITY OF A RELATED CONSTRUCTION

In order to understand the basis for the acceptability of (1b), it is necessary to consider the mechanism for the perception of speech. Recent research has isolated various systems of this component. The most pertinent to the present discussion is a set of perceptual strategies, operations which utilize information in surface strings to assign directly their deep structure relations. Recent experimental evidence supports the view that the words in a surface sequence are first assigned their possible lexical classification (see Garrett, 1970; and Conrad, 1972). Other experimental evidence supports the view that perceptual strategies are schemata which take the lexically labeled strings as input and mark them directly for deep structure relations, without processing intermediate levels of representation (see Fodor and Garrett, 1966; Bever, 1970; and Fodor, Bever, and Garrett, 1974). The best-studied example of such a strategy is one which assigns the "actor-action" relation to a clause-initial $\widehat{\text{NP V}}$ string (33):

(33) $\widehat{\text{NP V}} \rightarrow \text{NP}_{\text{actor}} \, \widehat{} \text{V}_{\text{action}}$

Of course, strategies such as (33) are not rules which define well-formedness since they allow exceptions. (For example, (33) is inappropriate to passive sentences or to object-first cleft sentences, as is reflected in their relative perceptual complexity.) Rather, such operations appear to be incorporated as an early stage of perceptual processing because of their general validity.

Such strategies also apply to assign relations within phrases. For example, rules like (34) would assign a particular relation correctly in almost every case in English:

(34) (a) $\text{Det} \, \widehat{} \text{Adj} \, \widehat{} \text{N} \rightarrow \text{Det} \, \widehat{} \text{Adj}_{\text{modifier of N}} \, \widehat{} \text{N}$

(b) $\text{Det} \, \widehat{} \text{Adv} \, \widehat{} \text{Adj} \, \widehat{} \text{N} \rightarrow \text{Det} \, \widehat{} \text{Adv}_{\text{modifier of Adj}} \, \widehat{} \text{Adj}_{\text{modifier of N}} \, \widehat{} \text{N}$

(c) $\text{Det} \overset{\frown}{} \text{Adv}_1 \overset{\frown}{} \text{Adv}_2 \overset{\frown}{} \text{Adj} \overset{\frown}{} \text{N} \rightarrow$

$\text{Det} \overset{\frown}{} \text{Adv}_{\text{modifier of Adv}_2} \overset{\frown}{} \text{Adv}_{\text{modifier of Adj}} \overset{\frown}{} \text{Adj}_{\text{modifier of N}} \overset{\frown}{} \text{N}$

The psychological interpretation for such labeled structures is a function of semantic analysis together with the analysis provided by such systems as rhetoric and conversational implicature. Consider, for example, (35):

(35) He has a not very expensive apartment.

Its literal interpretation is paraphrased in (36); note that *not* simply negates that part of the price dimension denoted by *very expensive*:

(36) He has an apartment which is expensive to a not very extreme degree.

However, the interpretation that is often given to sentences like (35) is something like (37):

(37) He has a slightly to moderately inexpensive apartment.

Thus the pure semantic interpretation of (35) does not correspond to the interpretation which is more likely to be associated with it. A possible conclusion is that the proposed semantic interpretation is wrong. However, that would incorrectly entail that the pure semantic interpretation of (35) is not a possible interpretation for it.

A more promising line of investigation is provided by Grice's theory of conversational implicatures (Grice, 1967), which assigns interpretation (37) to (35) as a function of the literal interpretation (36) together with inferences based on conversational "maxims." The maxim here would be that of "quantity": *make your (conversational) contribution as informative as required*.

Suppose (35) is given as an answer to the question (38):

(38) How expensive an apartment does Horace have?

In such a case the literal meaning of (35) is an apparent violation of the maxim of quantity: it answers a request for positive information about a continuum denoted by the unmarked adjective *expensive* with a denial of only one position on that continuum.[19] This leaves open all the other positions on the "expensive" side of the continuum—"rather expensive," "slightly expensive," and so on. Thus, the questioner is free to assume that the literal interpretation of the answer was not intended because it violates the maxim of quantity. The task then becomes to determine the intended interpretation. The questioner may reason as follows. If the answerer had intended to communicate any specific degree of expensiveness in conformity with the maxim of quantity, then he or she would have used one of the positive adverbs (e.g., *pretty*, *slightly*) with the adjective in

19. It is not necessarily a violation, however, since this may be all the information that is available to the answerer, in which case to say more would be in violation of the maxim of quality.

D. TERENCE LANGENDOEN
AND THOMAS C. BEVER

framing the answer. Thus, the questioner can assume that the answerer intended to indicate a range on the "inexpensive" side of the continuum. But that range cannot be the one denoted by *very inexpensive* since what was said was the explicit negation, namely, *not very expensive*. Hence, by exclusion, the questioner is left with the interpretation 'slightly to moderately inexpensive' as the intended meaning.

This line of reasoning and its conclusion are strengthened by an independent rhetorical principle, namely, that one should strive for parallelism: one should not answer a question using *expensive* with a construction using *inexpensive*. Accordingly, (39) as a response to (38) would be heard as slightly abrupt, almost disagreeable:

(39) He has a pretty inexpensive apartment.

Thus, if in fact Horace has a pretty (but not very) inexpensive apartment, the respondent to the question (38) has the choice of either the abrupt (39) or the polite but somewhat more prolix (35).

The analysis just given correctly predicts an asymmetry in the natural interpretations of answers to questions framed in terms of marked and unmarked adjectives. Consider the question-answer dialog (40), (41), as compared with the dialog (38), (35):

(40) How inexpensive an apartment does Horace have?
(41) He has a not very inexpensive apartment.

Example (41) does not contain the conversational meaning 'slightly to moderately expensive' but can be taken only literally as containing the meaning 'inexpensive to a not very extreme degree'. This is so because the use of the marked adjective *inexpensive* in the question in (40) conveys the presupposition that Horace's apartment is inexpensive to some degree. The respondent in this case cannot be interpreted as denying this presupposition. Thus the questioner here would conclude that the answer is vague because the answerer could not be more precise (that is, the answerer was actually obeying the maxim of quality).

In summary, then, we find that phrases of the type Determiner *not* Intensifying-Adverb Unmarked-Adjective Noun have possible nonliteral interpretations which would literally be rendered by Determiner *slightly to moderately* Marked-Adjective Noun. These interpretations are consequences of the application of rules that determine conversational implicatures. Moreover, it appears to be the case that these nonliteral interpretations can be supplied by speakers even in the absence of a conversational setting. To the extent that they can, the rules have become generalized (Grice, 1967, pp. 21–23); that is, they are part of a system of surface interpretive rules that are not part of the grammar of English.

8. WHY WE CAN SAY A NOT UNHAPPY PERSON EVEN THOUGH IT IS UNGRAMMATICAL

We can now explain the acceptability of sentences like (1b) in terms of the perceptual mechanisms. Consider the perceptual strategy in (34c). This operates correctly on sequences like (42) to assign the scope of the initial *not* as the following adverb:

$$(42) \quad \text{the not} \begin{Bmatrix} \text{very} \\ \text{clearly} \end{Bmatrix} \text{happy boy}$$

Since such strategies operate on a preliminary lexical-class analysis of the input as it is heard, they sometimes apply behaviorally in instances where their structural index is met only approximately. For example, consider the sentences in (43), each of which contains a negated attributive adjective, while the adjective contains an adverblike prefix:

(43) (a) Harry's not overdeveloped muscles were not up to the task.
(b) We worship a not all-powerful deity.
(c) A not supersaturated solution is what we need.
(d) They are certainly a not underdeveloped tribe.

Apparently, the *not* can combine a perception with the prefixes *over-*, *all-*, *super-*, *under-* by the application of (34c), provided that what remains after the prefix has been removed is an adjective that plausibly modifies the noun that follows it. In (43) this proviso is met; in (44) it is not, and the examples are accordingly unacceptable:

(44) (a) *Isidor has a not overweening personality.
(b) *The not overturned decision was the basis for his case.

The explanation for the acceptability of sentences like (1b) is of exactly the same form. The subject noun phrase is misanalyzed perceptually as in (34c), with *un-* being treated as a negative intensifying adverb that modifies the adjective *happy*.

Immediately most of the problematic acceptability judgments given in Section 3 receive their proper explanation. The most serious problem was that the adjective that remained after separating the negative prefix had to be perspicuous as an independent modifier of the following noun. But phrases containing negated adjectives cannot be misanalyzed in accordance with (34c) unless what follows the negative prefix is perspicuous as an adjective. If the mechanism that assigns lexical-class membership in perception cannot assign adjectival status to the element that immediately follows a negative prefix, then (34c) will not be activated.[20]

Now consider the interpretation that is given to the subject noun phrase of (1b), namely (45):

(45) a slightly to moderately happy person

Given that the negative prefix is classified in perception as an intensifying adverb (in the same class as *very*, but with negative sense), then (45) follows by virtue of the generalized conversational implicatures governing expressions of the type Determiner $\overset{\frown}{not}$ Intensifying-Adverb $\overset{\frown}{}$ Unmarked-Adjective Noun.   In fact (1b) does not have a literal interpretation, but of course that is just what we would expect, since on our analysis it is ungrammatical.

9. ACCEPTABILITY AND GRAMMATICALITY— REPRISE

Our analysis of the acceptability of sentences like (1b) represents a departure from the usual assumption that if a sentence is acceptable, it is grammatical.[21]

20. See note 8 for evidence that in cases like *a not unearthly scream* in (18a) a preliminary lexical-class assignment in conformity with the left-hand side of (34c) may be made, only to be rejected because it cannot be interpreted.

The fact that phrases like *someone not unhappy* in (12) are unacceptable follows from the fact that the schema (34c) operates on prenominal modifiers. The unacceptability of *a not unmarried man* in (16) results from the anomalous character of its interpretation, 'a slightly to moderately married man'.   Finally, the unacceptability of *the not impious regent* (22) results from the fact that *-pEous* is not a perspicuous representation of *pIous*.

21. One precedent for this departure is Chomsky's claim (1970, pp. 193–194) that phrases of type (a) are ungrammatical but acceptable:

(a) his criticism of the book before he read it

However, Chomsky does not cite any independent evidence from the theory of language use to support his contention; rather, his argument is simply that since his theory (the Lexicalist Hypothesis) predicts that (a) is ungrammatical, it must be so, even if it is acceptable.   More recently Otero (1972) has argued that certain Spanish sentences in which the verb agrees in number with the direct object rather than with the subject are acceptable but ungrammatical.   He, too, argues that since such factors cannot be handled within his grammatical framework, they must *ipso facto* be nongrammatical in nature.

Of course, in the absence of an independently motivated performance theory (or some other theory about a part of linguistic knowledge), the failure of a grammatical device to account for acceptability facts can be taken as evidence that more powerful devices are needed within the grammar.   For example, Lakoff and Ross (1972) assume the availability of a grammatical device that is sensitive to the phonological clarity of a morphological relationship.   Such a device is needed to account for the relative acceptability of sentences like (b) and (c):

(b) ?Max liquefied the metal faster than Sam could bring it about.
(c) *Max killed Boris faster than Sam could have brought it about.

It is commonly accepted that ordinary speech behavior is filled with ungrammatical utterances that are used simply because they are behaviorally simple and comprehensible in specific contexts. On our analysis (1b) is ungrammatical, but it is acceptable in most contexts due to the applicability of a general perceptual strategy, (34c). The methodological basis for this decision is straightforward. On the one hand, to treat such sentences as grammatical, while treating sentences like (1a) as ungrammatical, places extremely strong formal requirements on grammatical theory—in particular, a transderivational constraint that is sensitive to the output of the phonological component. On the other hand, the acceptability of such sentences may be accounted for in terms of an independently motivated perceptual theory. Thus we conclude that both sentences (1a) and (1b) are ungrammatical but that (1b) is acceptable because it is comprehensible.

This methodology is not only straightforward, it also offers a principled basis for the notion of "analogy" within the theory of language behavior. Our

---

Lakoff and Ross argue that (c) is unacceptable by virtue of a *grammatical* process that is sensitive to the clarity of the morphological relation between the causative form of the verb and the corresponding change-of-state form. Thus, *liquefy* in (b) is phonologically close to the corresponding intransitive, *liquefy*, while *kill* in (c) is phonologically distinct from the corresponding intransitive, *die*, thus rendering the sentence unacceptable. Lakoff and Ross simply assume that this unacceptability must be due to ungrammaticality and therefore that the grammar must include a device that can account for it. They use this device to explain the ungrammaticality of (c), in response to Fodor's point (1970) that (c) should be as grammatical as (b) if *kill* is actually derived from *cause to die*.

Independent of the arguments given by Fodor, there is a simpler explanation of the difference in acceptability between (b) and (c) than that offered by Lakoff and Ross. We can assume that both (b) and (c) are ungrammatical but that (b) is partially acceptable by virtue of the relative ease with which the listener can figure out what the *it* in the second clause might refer to. This interpretation would allow other aspects of performance to play a role in the relative acceptability of sequences raised but not explained by Lakoff and Ross. For example, (d) would be predicted as being more acceptable than (e) because of the relative clarity of *flute* in (d):

    (d) ?Flutists are strange: it doesn't sound shrill to them.
    (e) *Flautists are strange: it doesn't sound shrill to them.

Similarly, the relative productivity of the form which binds the pronominal referent should also correspond to the relative acceptability of such sentences, which is exactly the phenomenon asserted by Lakoff and Ross. Thus, sentences like (g) are more acceptable than those like (f) because "the productivity of the morphological process . . . also plays a role" (p. 122).

    (f) *Iroquoianists are strange: they think it should be a world language.
    (g) ?Australians are strange: they don't think it's too remote.

In sum, if the facts noted by Lakoff and Ross are interpreted as due to behavioral processes, then we can explain the different observations as all due to one fact, namely, *any* property of the morphologically bound form which makes it easier for the listener to isolate it facilitates the interpretation of a later pronoun as referring to it. Thus the interpretation that (b) and (c) are both ungrammatical not only simplifies the grammar, it also allows for the direct representation of a significant generalization about linguistic knowledge underlying the distribution of words and morphemes.

claim in section 8 was that certain adjective prefixes may be misanalyzed perceptually as intensifying adverbs which modify the adjectives to which they are prefixed. The process of perceptual misanalysis would appear to capture what is often meant by "analogy" in linguistic discussions. We now propose that appeal to "analogy" should be restricted to cases in which the analogy is generated within the behavioral systems of language use.[22] This means that analogy may be appealed to only in those cases in which there are independently verifiable mechanisms that could contribute to it, rather than leaving it open as an unconstrained grab bag to be used whenever needed (Chomsky, 1970). By restricting analogy in this way, it is at least possible that an explanation for it can be found.

We have shown that if certain strings can be analyzed as ungrammatical but acceptable, the empirical facts about negated attributive adjective phrases can be interpreted in a way that vindicates standard theory. This vindication is important primarily because standard theory imputes more limited and specific structures to linguistic knowledge. This in turn makes more precise claims about what is in the child's mind that allows the acquisition of language. Of course, it remains to be shown that standard theory can be vindicated in all the areas in which it is currently under attack. However, the clarification of the relation between acceptability and grammaticality can provide the basis for a revival of what we consider to be a prematurely rejected theory.[23]

REFERENCES

Bever, T. G. 1970. "The Cognitive Basis for Linguistic Structures." In *Cognition and the Development of Language*, J. R. Hayes, ed. Wiley.

Bever, T. G., and D. T. Langendoen. 1971. "A Dynamic Model of the Evolution of Language." *Linguistic Inquiry* 2: 433–463. Reprinted in this volume.

Chomsky, N. 1965. *Aspects of the Theory of Syntax*. M.I.T. Press.

22. Further evidence for the perceptual as opposed to the grammatical character of the analogy we propose is supplied by the observation in note 11. Since the lexical item *unhealthy* cannot mean 'unsizable', there is absolutely no way for a grammar constructed in accordance with standard theory to generate sentence (a) of note 11 with the interpretation it has. In perception, however, *healthy*, in the sense 'sizable', is perspicuous in that example.

23. For example, the contrast in acceptability between (2a) and (2b) would require a grammatical theory that allows for derivational constraints. But there is good reason to believe that (2a) and (2b) are both grammatical (see Jackendoff & Culicover, 1971, and Langendoen, Kalish-Landon, and Dore, 1974). For arguments that (3a) and (3b) are both grammatical, see Grosu (1972). Grosu, in fact, attempts the very ambitious task of showing that all of Ross's constraints are based on perceptual operations. Similarly (4a) and (4b) are interpretable as grammatical, with the unacceptability of (4a) being due to a perceptual operation that attaches an initial adverb to the nearest following verb, leading to an apparent temporal contradiction in the verb phrase (see Katz and Bever, 1976).

—— 1970. "Remarks on Nominalization." In *Readings in English Transformational Grammar*, R. A. Jacobs and P. S. Rosenbaum, eds. Ginn.

—— 1971. "Deep Structure, Surface Structure, and Semantic Interpretation." In *Semantics*, D. Steinberg and L. Jakobovits, eds. Cambridge University Press.

Chomsky, N., and M. Halle. 1968. *The Sound Pattern of English*. Harper and Row.

Conrad, C. 1972. *Studies of the Subjective Lexicon*. Unpublished Ph.D. dissertation, University of Oregon.

Fillmore, C. J. 1965. *Indirect Object Constructions in English and the Ordering of Transformations*. Mouton.

Fodor, J. A. 1970. "Three Reasons for Not Deriving 'Kill' from 'Cause to Die'." *Linguistic Inquiry* 1: 429–438.

Fodor, J. A., and M. Garrett. 1966. "Some Reflections on Competence and Performance." In *Psycholinguistics Papers*, J. Lyons and R. Wales, eds. Aldine.

Fodor, J. A., T. G. Bever, and M. Garrett. 1974. *The Psychology of Language*. McGraw-Hill.

Garrett, M. 1970. "Does Ambiguity Complicate the Perception of Sentences?" In *Advances in Psycholinguistics*, F. D'Arcais and W. Levelt, eds. North Holland.

Grice, H. P. 1967. "Logic and Conversation II." Unpublished paper.

Grosu, A. 1972. *The Strategic Content of Island Constraints*. Unpublished Ph.D. dissertation., Ohio State University.

Halle, M. 1962. "On the Bases of Phonology." *Word* 18: 54–72.

Jackendoff, R., and P. Culicover. 1971. "A Reconsideration of Dative Movements." *Foundations of Language* 7: 397–412.

Jakobson, R., and M. Halle. 1956. *Fundamentals of Language*. Mouton.

Katz, J. J. 1972. *Semantic Theory*. Harper and Row.

Katz, J. J., and T. G. Bever. 1976. "The Fall and Rise of Empiricism." In this volume.

Klima, E. S. 1964. "Negation in English." In *The Structure of Language*, J. A. Fodor and J. J. Katz, eds. Prentice-Hall.

Lakoff, G. 1969. "On Derivational Constraints." In *Papers from the Fifth Regional Meeting, Chicago Linguistic Society*, University of Chicago.

—— 1970. "Thoughts on Transderivational Constraints." Unpublished paper.

—— 1971. "On Generative Semantics." In *Semantics*, D. Steinberg and L. Jakobovits, eds. Cambridge University Press.

—— 1972. "The Arbitrary Basis of Transformational Grammar." *Language* 48: 76–87.

Lakoff, G., and J. R. Ross. 1972. "A Note on Anaphoric Islands and Causatives." *Linguistic Inquiry* 3: 121–125.

Langendoen, D. T., N. Kalish-Landon, and J. Dore. 1974. "Dative Questions: A Study of the Relation of Acceptability to Grammaticality of an English Sentence Type." *Cognition* 2: 451–478. Reprinted in this volume.

Miller, G. A., and N. Chomsky. 1963. "Finitary Models of Language Users." In *Handbook of Mathematical Psychology*, Vol. II, R. Luce, R. Bush, and E. Galanter, eds. Wiley.

Otero, C. 1972. "Acceptable Ungrammatical Sentences in Spanish." *Linguistic Inquiry* 3: 233–242.

Postal, P. 1972. "A Global Constraint on Pronominalization." *Linguistic Inquiry* 3: 35–60.

Postal, P., and J. R. Ross. 1970. "A Problem of Adverb Preposing." *Linguistic Inquiry* 1: 145–146.

Ross, J. R. 1967. *Constraints on Variables in Syntax*. Indiana University Linguistics Club.

—— 1972. "Doubl-ing." *Linguistic Inquiry* 3: 61–86.

The Argument from Lurk

ROBERT M. HARNISH

1. INTRODUCTION

In his interesting and influential article "On Declarative Sentences," Ross presents a number of arguments for the position that all declarative sentences contain a higher performative clause in underlying structure, a clause that would have roughly the following lexical representation:[1]

(1) I state to you [$_S$ $_S$].

One of these arguments (which Ross attributes to Perlmutter) is the argument from *lurk*.

Although this argument for the higher performative analysis of declaratives has not played a particularly important role in subsequent discussions, it seems to me to have methodological import independent of its syntactic success or failure. It is important because the data Ross describes (and data like them) can be viewed as a particularly revealing challenge for two opposing ideologies implicit in current linguistic theory. On the one hand, there are those who view a total theory of language as a homogeneous system utilizing as few, but as powerful, rules as possible, rules that apply uniformly throughout the system (see Postal, 1972, or Lakoff, 1970). On the other hand, there are those who view a total theory of language as a system of intricately connected, but conceptually distinct, subtheories (see Katz, 1972, or Langendoen and Bever, 1973). It is of course the conviction of both camps that their approach will result in the simplest and most revealing overall theory.

---

1. Nothing in the discussion that follows turns on this being exactly the right lexical representation for Ross's feature bundles.

Source: *Linguistic Inquiry* 5(1975): 145–154.
Reprinted by permission of the publisher.

In what follows I want to treat Ross's proposal (not unfairly I think, and hope) as a part of the first trend in current linguistic theory, and I wish to advance a proposal of the second sort.

2. ROSS'S ARGUMENT AND ITS CRITICS

Ross notes that sentences like (2a, b) are "awkward," while sentences like (3a, b) are not:

(2) (a) ?*Max$_i$ believes that he$_i$'s lurking in a culvert—actually, of course, he$_i$'s here with you.

   (b) ?*[Pat and Mike]$_{NP_i}$ testified that they$_i$ lurked near your house last night.

(3) (a) Max believes that I am lurking in a culvert—actually, of course, I'm here with you.

   (b) Pat and Mike testified that I lurked near your house last night.

These sentences, Ross claims (1970, p. 234), fall under the following generalization:[2]

(I) The subject of *lurk* and the subject of the next highest verb cannot be identical.

Ross also notes that (4a, b) are "awkward" and would clearly agree that (5a, b) are not.

(4) (a) ?*I am lurking in a culvert.

   (b) ?*I lurked near your house last night.

(5) (a) Max is lurking in a culvert.

   (b) Max lurked near your house last night.

In the theory of higher performatives, both (4a, b) and (5a, b) are given underlying representations like (1); the theory thus predicts that (4a, b) will conform to generalization (I) and thus be ungrammatical, but that (5a, b) will not so conform and so will not be for *this* reason ungrammatical. Since this is what is observed to be the case, the higher performative analysis gains support.

In their replies to Ross, however, both Anderson (1971) and Fraser (1971) have claimed that generalization (I) is spurious. They point out that sentences like (6a, b) are quite grammatical.

(6) (a) He admits that he was lurking around.

   (b) I deny that I was lurking around.

2. I will deal with Ross's qualification with respect to factives in section 3.3.

Moreover, there appear to be grammatical "simple" sentences of the forbidden sort:

(7) (a) I was lurking near city hall. (Fraser)
      (b) I wasn't lurking anywhere. (Anderson)

How then are we to account for the awkwardness of Ross's awkward examples without predicting that the nonawkward examples will be awkward too? I shall make a proposal that has the consequence that the above awkwardness is not purely grammatical—which is to say, *contra* Ross, that it is not purely syntactic and (perhaps *contra* Anderson) that is not purely semantic.[3]

3. A PRAGMATIC PROPOSAL

The proposal I wish to outline here has three characteristics:

(a) *Syntax:* There are no special restrictions on the subject of *lurk* of the sort suggested by Ross.

(b) *Semantics:* In the reading of *lurk* there is a clause to the effect that (i) the referent of the subject (of *lurk*) supposes his or her whereabouts to be relevantly secret at the time indicated by the temporal specifier of the sentence, and (ii) he or she has no legitimate business being there.[4]

(c) *Pragmatics:* Assume for the time being something like Searle's (1969) analysis of stating, questioning, requesting, etc. Also assume his generalizations that (i) when a psychological state is mentioned in the sincerity rule, the performance of the act counts as the expression of that state (ii) in the performance of a speech act, one implies the satisfaction of the preparatory

---

3. I think Anderson realizes this when he says that lurking is something one may predicate of oneself if joking, or if forced to, or if denying it. The first two conditions I consider pragmatic, not semantic. I will account for these observations.

4. This needs a lot of work, as Anderson has pointed out in discussion. To see that the secretive aspect of lurking must be relativized, just imagine the preceding examples uttered by a secret agent over the phone to his director, or consider the plurals like *We were lurking around* where the inclusive *we* collects those among whom secrecy is not relevant.

Also, since *hide* can be intransitive too (*I am hiding* as well as *I am hiding the gold*), these clauses help to distinguish them semantically. *Hide* involves concealment from observation (not necessarily intentional), whereas *lurk* involves secrecy and the absence of good intent (perhaps also the presence of some ill intent). No wonder children play "Hide and Seek" but not "Lurk and Seek." Since hiding involves only concealment from observation, we can say *I am hiding from* . . ." However, lurking involves more, and we do not say *I am lurking from* . . . Finally, notice that sentences with *hide* can be awkward in the way (4a) is. Imagine the serious utterance of *I am hiding from everyone*. I do not have (and probably never will have) a complete theory of lurking. However, my purpose here is to make an alternate viewpoint plausible.

conditions (Searle, 1969, p. 65). Finally, assume that a *serious* utterance is one uttered with the intention to communicate – to effect understanding.[5]

If (*a*)-(*c*) are even roughly right, I think that it is possible to account for the examples cited and some new data as well. I shall deal mainly with declaratives, since that is the context in which the discussion originated and I want this case to be fairly plausible.

3.1. Simple Declaratives

Suppose that declarative sentences are generally used to perform speech acts of stating, asserting, informing, etc., and that Searle is right in claiming that the sincerity rule for this informative class of speech acts is that the speaker must believe the proposition expressed to be true. Then, insofar as a speaker utters a declarative sentence seriously and means what he says—intends that he should be understood—we would expect this utterance to be awkward or odd when the time of utterance is the same as the tense on *lurk* and the subject of *lurk* is first person. The reason is simple. When the tense of *lurk* is the same as the time of utterance (present tense), the subject must suppose himself unobserved at the time of utterance. But if the subject of *lurk* is first person, then the speaker must suppose himself unobserved at the time of utterance. If it is a serious speech act of the informing class, the speaker expresses to the hearer the belief that he or she is, at the time of utterance, unobserved. But now we have the "awkward" situation of the speaker attempting to inform someone and in the very attempt compromising a belief that the performance counts as expressing. Since these are the only (relevant) conditions for the speech act to defeat itself, we should expect that any other combination of person and time would not be awkward or at least not quite so awkward. The examples seem to bear this out.[6] Consider the paradigms in Table 1.[7]

The only case that is (for me) really awkward is the first person present progressive.[8] With this case the awkwardness arises because the content of the

---

5. I do not want to suggest that there are no other ways to state the pragmatic facts. Indeed, I think there might be a better way, and I shall try to spell it out on another occasion (Bach and Harnish, forthcoming). Again, it is the interplay among the three types of phenomena that I am trying to investigate here.

6. There is also a pejorative connotation to *lurk*. It is not something one is supposed to do, so not something one freely *admits* doing. But this fact in itself does not explain the *lurk* data. First, it is not awkward to admit *having* lurked (though it may be disreputable). Second, other pejorative expressions can be predicated of oneself freely, e.g., *torturing this child*, and so the explanation is not sufficient.

7. In the chart "*" and "?" indicate levels of awkwardness, not degrees of grammaticality.

8. I will deal here with only the singular cases. Similar remarks will, I think, carry over to the plural.

TABLE 1

| PERSON | TIME | | |
	PAST	PRESENT	FUTURE
Affirmative	I lurked	?I lurk . . . (habitual)	?I will lurk . . .
1st	I was lurking	?I am lurking	?I will be lurking
2nd	You lurked . . .	?You lurk . . . (habitual)	?You will lurk . . .
	You were lurking	?You are lurking	?You will be lurking
3rd	He lurked . . .	He lurks . . .	He will lurk . . .
	He was lurking	He is lurking	He will be lurking
Negative	(All OK)	I do not lurk . . . (habitual) I am not lurking (All OK)	(All OK)

belief expressed has the "component" (B), yet the information is being revealed to the hearer at t_0 (as indicated in (S)):

(B) Speaker is unobserved during
$t_{-n} \cdots t_0 \cdots t_{+n}$.[9]

(S) Speaker informs hearer of (B) at t_0.

Thus, the interval of secrecy that I am committed to believing, by what I say, includes the point in time at which I compromise that secret by seriously uttering that sentence. In this way the speech act defeats itself in the present progressive.[10]

The nonawkwardness of the rest of the clear cases is easily explained, because there is no conflict between the belief expressed and the supposition that the speech act is being seriously performed. When the referent of the subject of *lurk* is someone other than the speaker, then his or her secrecy is not in conflict with the conditions for serious performance of the relevant speech act. When *lurk* is not in the present tense, then the information conveyed (at t_0) concerns secrecy at some other time and there is again no conflict. Finally, when the sentence is negative, we find no awkwardness because the speaker is *not* committed by the assertion of expressing the belief that he or she is unobserved or secretive. Thus again there is no conflict, which explains another observation of Anderson's.

9. Here I adopt Katz's notation for temporal specification (see Katz, 1972, Chap. 7). This represents an unspecified interval around the time of utterance t_0.

10. Notice that this would, if true, account for Anderson's observation that one can predicate *lurk* of oneself if joking, for after all when one is joking one is not being serious, so there is no bind.

Let us turn now to the questionable or borderline examples. I think their fuzziness can be explained by this sort of account. Consider the first person cases. These will be awkward to the extent that the speaker believes that his or her *future* secrecy will be compromised by the present assertion.[11] To the extent that this secrecy will *not* be compromised, the utterance will not seem awkward. There are a variety of ways this can happen: the hearer can be exempted from the secrecy requirement, the speaker can suppose that other factors will cause the hearer not to compromise his or her secrecy, etc.

With second person present and future sentences, the reason is almost exactly the same, but the speaker and hearer are reversed. In the present progressive, the assertion will be true only if the hearer is relatively secret at some interval around the time of utterance. But serious utterance of this conflicts with such secrecy, and so the act is defective and the sentence seems odd. Notice that the perfective *You have been lurking* is not nearly so odd. I suspect this is because completion of the activity is suggested; thus, there is no present relevance and hence no compromise.

In the case of the habitual present, the assertion will be odd to the extent that it is supposed that the repeated action extends to the present; hence, this statement is compromised to some extent by the utterance for the same reason as reports of present lurkings would be. As evidence, notice that when the present is explicitly precluded, as with *You only* used to *lurk around her window*, the sentence is not odd in at all the same way, just unusual.

With second person future cases, it is clear that by informing the hearer of what he or she will be doing, one is revealing knowledge that compromises that very activity on the part of the hearer; thus, it is natural that these cases will be awkward.

This sort of account will also explain some facts not clarified by Ross's proposal. Ross notes (1970, p. 235) that the following is awkward, though not as awkward as those given earlier:

(8) ?Susan told Max$_i$ that he$_i$ should not lurk near her house any longer.

Notice that it is the occurrence of *any longer* that is creating the oddity:

(9) Susan told Max$_i$ that he$_i$ should not lurk near city hall under any circumstances.

The reason here is exactly the same as we found with the second person present above, but in this case the telling is being *reported*, not just imagined being done. For me, prefixing *It is not true that* to (8) relieves it of all awkwardness, and this indicates that it is the interplay of the telling and what is told that causes the oddity.

---

11. Notice that this possibility is foreclosed in the past tense, so nonawkwardness is virtually guaranteed. Of course, if there were time machines (assuming the notion is coherent), the past would behave in this respect like the future.

3.2. Simple Imperatives and Interrogatives

Nothing I have said so far suggests that this account must be restricted to declaratives and assertions. Indeed, being basically semantic and pragmatic, it is easily extended.

With imperatives we would expect that unless the speaker is supposed to be in on the secret, the utterance will be awkward for the obvious reason that in issuing the request he thereby reveals his awareness of the act.

With interrogatives the story is more complex. On the one hand, there will be an awkwardness of the sort so far discussed. This is suggested by the fact that the chart for simple interrogatives looks exactly like the one for simple declaratives. In the case of the second person present progressive *Are you lurking* ... ?, the oddity could be accounted for by the fact that the interval of secrecy being "questioned" includes the time at which the speaker (potentially) compromises it. This is revealed by the felicity of a *no* answer, but not of an affirmative one.

With first person cases like (10), the oddity is compounded by another pragmatic conflict:

(10)   *Am I lurking ... ?

One of the preparatory conditions for a serious (nonexamination) question is that the speaker not already possess the information requested. So, by the pragmatic principle (cii) given in section 3, the utterance of (10) should count as implying that the preparatory conditions are fulfilled, i.e. that the speaker does not know if he is lurking or not. But people usually do know their present mental states as well as what they are doing (or trying to do), especially when what is done is not described causally. Thus it is quite odd to ask seriously (nonrhetorically) the (nonexamination) questions (11a-e):

(11)   (a)   *Do I have a headache?
       (b)   *Do I like beans?
       (c)   *Am I seeing an after image?
       (d)   *Am I brushing my teeth?
       (e)   *Am I typing this paper?

But it is not odd at all to ask the following questions:

(12)   (a)   Did I (will I) have a headache?
       (b)   Do I *really* like beans?

Nor is it odd to ask of oneself whether one is doing something under a causal description, since one may not know if the effect has been or is being achieved:

(13)   (a)   Am I cleaning my teeth?
       (b)   Am I bothering you with my typing?
       (c)   Am I convincing you with my argument?

ROBERT M. HARNISH

Following this chain of implications, speakers who utter (10) seriously are implying that they do not know something that it is very odd to suppose that they do not know. This, then, is another dimension of awkwardness that supplements the first.[12]

3.3. Complex Sentences

So far nothing I have said affects sentences like (2) and (3). However, I think that the above account can be generalized in a natural way, using the following principle:

(C) Any sentence that commits the speaker to expressing, at the time of serious utterance, belief in (B) will have an element of this sort of (*lurk*) oddity. The converse is also the case.

Since neither (2) nor (3) so commits the speaker, neither is predicted to have this sort of oddity. I think this is correct for both cases. But this is not to say that they cannot be odd for some other reason. Indeed, in the previous section I noted just such a source. For instance, in normal circumstances (2a) leaves one wondering why Max believes such a thing. The origin of this judgment is different depending on whether we take (2a) with or without the appended clause. With the appended clause present, we have ascribed to Max a belief that we know not to be true, because of the (assumed) truth of the appended clause. Without the appended clause, and in normal circumstances, the utterance of (2a) suggests that Max's belief is false. This probably arises because the speaker has made a weaker than normal remark (*Max_i believes he_i is lurking*) and so has some reason for not making the stronger remark (*Max is lurking*); we infer that Max is not lurking, though he thinks he is, and we wonder why he should think such a thing. In appropriate circumstances this oddity does not arise. Just imagine a conversation concerning the properties of some new belief-inducing drug or posthypnotic suggestion, in which the doctor announces to his colleagues that because of the injection, Max (now) believes that he is lurking in a culvert. Also, it should be clear that none of this has anything special to do with *lurk*. All of the previous remarks carry over mutatis mutandis to cases like (14).

(14) Max_i believes that he_i is brushing his_i teeth—actually, of course, he_i is here with you.

---

12. Notice that if we factor out the first kind of pragmatic oddness in the utterance of sentences like (10), and if *lurk* has a clause in its semantic representation of the sort suggested, then it ought to be conceptually possible to take (10) in such a way as to be "questioning" the *secrecy* of the act—since this is not something obviously known to the speaker. I think it is, but I doubt that this is *linguistically* possible with (10) without special prompting. I am not sure why this is.

Finally, Ross remarks (1970, fn. 28) that sentences with *lurk* and first person subject cannot be embedded as complements of factive verbs without oddity. I do not think that this is a peculiarity of factive verbs—at least as they are characterized by the Kiparskys. The correct generalization is something like (C). Thus, (15a-c) are all odd, but (15a) is not factive. Since (15a) conforms to (C), it is predicted to be odd.

(15) (a) *It is true that I am lurking here.
     (b) *I know that I am lurking here.
     (c) *I realize that I am lurking here.

Notice that this holds for interrogatives as well, and that the distribution of oddities is the same for these complex sentences as for the simple complements, further supporting the explanation above:

(16) (a) *Do you realize that I *am lurking* here?
     (b) ?Do you realize that I *lurk* here?
     (c) ?Do you realize that I *will lurk* here?
     (d) ?Do you realize that I *will be lurking* here?
     (e) Do you realize that I *lurked* here?
     (f) Do you realize that I *was lurking* here?

4. CONCLUSION

In this paper I have suggested that oddities of the sort mentioned by Ross be accounted for by a fairly special sort of interplay among syntax, semantics, and pragmatics. Of course, I have not shown that *no* single-level, homogenous theory of language can account for these facts. Nor do I suggest that all of the details are right. I mainly want to suggest another way of looking at some linguistic phenomena, in the hope that others might look at linguistic phenomena in this way too.[13]

REFERENCES

Anderson, S. 1971. "On the Linguistic Status of the Performative—Constative Distinction." Indiana University Linguistics Club.

Bach, K., and R. Harnish. *A Theory of Speech Acts* (forthcoming).

Fraser, B. 1971. "An Examination of the Performative Analysis." Indiana University Linguistics Club.

Katz, J. 1972. *Semantic Theory*. Harper and Row.

13. I want to thank Haj Ross for comments on this paper and Bruce Fraser and Jerrold Katz for helpful discussions on both the details and the implications of this approach.

Lakoff, G. 1970. "Linguistics and Natural Logic." *Synthese 22:* 1/2.

Langendoen, D. T., and T. G. Bever. 1973. "Can a Not Unhappy Person Be Called a Not Sad One?" In *A Festschrift for Morris Halle*, S. Anderson and P. Kiparsky, eds. Holt, Rinehart and Winston. Reprinted in this volume.

Postal, P. 1972. "The Best Theory." In *Goals of Linguistic Theory*, S. Peters, ed., Prentice-Hall.

Ross, J. 1970. "On Declarative Sentences." In *Readings in English Transformational Grammar*, R. A. Jacobs and P. S. Rosenbaum, eds. Ginn.

Searle, J. 1969. *Speech Acts*. Cambridge University Press.

Social Differentiation
of Language Structure

MANFRED BIERWISCH

1. INTRODUCTION

It is an empirical fact that generally in a speech community several varieties of language, or even different languages, are used. Furthermore, native speakers are very well aware of the differences between such varieties and of the effects these differences may have in communication. It is not at all obvious, however, how such varieties are to be delimited, how they function in producing the effects in question, and what the nature of these effects is. There are several branches of linguistic research dealing with one or another aspect of the indicated problems: dialectology, stylistics, and sociolinguistics are the more obvious ones.

In the present paper I will sketch a conceptual framework which allows for a systematic exposition of some of these problems, thus integrating them into a general theory of language, and connecting them at the same time to the pertinent extralinguistic conditions, mainly of the social structure of speech communities. The problems I have in mind, although intimately related to the form and meaning of linguistic expressions, do not belong to semantic, syntactic, or phonological structures as such. In a certain sense the phenomena in question presuppose, rather, the grammatically determined form and meaning of linguistic expressions; they consist in the grammatical (including lexical) differences between concuring language varieties and their evaluation according to certain socially determined conditions obtaining in the speech community. Again, what we are concerned with here is not a speech community's socioeconomic, political, or cultural structure as such, but only the way in which this structure determines the differentiation and evaluation of properties of linguistic expres-

Source: György Szépe, ed., *Acta Linguistica Academiae Scientiarum Hungaricae* (Hungary).
Reprinted by permission of György Szépe.

sions. In other words, the question underlying the following considerations is: how are certain aspects of linguistic structure related to the social structure in a linguistically nonhomogeneous speech community? To be more specific, let us assume that $L_1, \ldots, L_n$ are the language varieties concurrently used in a certain speech community C.[1] The first problem then is to identify the different L_i (with $i \leqslant i \leqslant n$) or, what amounts to the same thing, to distinguish the different L_i from each other. This in turn means determining the membership of arbitrary well-formed expressions e in the various L_i. An interesting solution to this problem must of course explain, how the members of C, i.e., the native speakers, differentiate the L_i in question and how they succeed in assigning expressions they use to different language varieties. I will argue below that two varieties L_i and L_j can be distinguished if and only if there are structural differences between expressions of L_i and expressions of L_j that are somehow related to certain extralinguistic factors in the social structure of C determining the verbal communication.

The nature of this relation can basically be described as a convention among the members of C to use expressions of a certain variety L_i if the communication proceeds under certain conditions c_i, "convention" being understood here in the sense specified more precisely by Lewis (1969). That is, there is common knowledge among members of C that, given the condition c_i, they are supposed to use, and generally will use, expressions with properties characteristic of L_i rather than expressions with properties characteristic of some L_j different from L_i. Once a convention of this type is established in C, the fact that a speaker uses expressions with the characteristics of L_i allows his audience to infer something about his assessment of the conditions according to which the communication is to take place. What an expression, by virtue of such conventions, conveys by its formal properties as a member of a certain L_i, can most naturally be called its connotation. This concept, if made precise, and delimited from certain other senses in which the term is sometimes used, provides a basis sufficiently general to characterize the effects of different language varieties that native speakers are aware of. In other words, what a speaker-hearer realizes as stylistic, social, regional, and other values of linguistic expressions is precisely the conno-

1. This assumption already presupposes the notion of a speech community. It is not at all clear how this notion is to be made precise. Obviously, it cannot be defined as a (or the) population using the same language, since this would wrongly exclude multilingual speech communities and presuppose the very notion of "same language," which is warranted only as long as we consider the idealized case of a linguistically homogeneous speech community. In fact, a useful notion of speech community cannot be specified in purely linguistic terms; it must rather rely on a theory of social communication and it must have access to concepts of socioeconomic structures and processes. This does not necessarily mean that it is independent of linguistic concepts, but only that it cannot be established on the basis of the theory of linguistic structure alone. (Notice that it is difficult, though possible, to avoid circularity here; see below). There might be, moreover, several different but related notions of speech community with varying degrees of narrowness. For the time being I will simply take the specification of C for granted.

tation these expressions convey, in addition to their regular denotative meaning or conceptual content. It is only to be expected that an account of heterogeneity along these lines will differ from traditional accounts, both in the limits it sets and in the relations it recognizes between the phenomena in question.

After this preliminary exposition, I will turn to a more careful discussion of the problems concerned. Before going into detail, it seems to be worthwhile, however, to consider briefly some more general, methodological questions concerning the phenomena of linguistic heterogeneity.

2. LINGUISTIC STRUCTURE AND LINGUISTIC HETEROGENEITY

The foregoing considerations point more or less clearly to the two-sided nature of the phenomena observed in a linguistically nonhomogeneous speech community. From the point of view of linguistic structure as such, we are dealing with conditions of language use, that is, with extralinguistic factors determining linguistic performance. Presupposing the speaker-hearer's knowledge of the linguistic structure of different classes of expressions available to the individual members of C, we are concerned with how this knowledge is exploited according to varying conditions of verbal communication.[2] From another point of view, however, these conditions must be taken as constituting a system of knowledge per se, according to which linguistic performance is organized. Insofar as the members of C are aware of concurring language varieties and the effects associated with them, they (tacitly) know the pertinent conventions determining the use of these varieties and the resulting connotations. Otherwise, they would not be able to organize their speech behavior accordingly.[3] Let us call a theoretical account of this knowledge a theory of linguistic heterogeneity, with social connotation as one of its key concepts. It seems to be clear then that this theory and the theory of linguistic structure, i.e., the linguistic theory in the usual sense, jointly account for linguistic performance of speaker-hearers in a

2. This does not necessarily mean that every member of C has at his disposal, both as speaker and hearer, the full range of all expressions of all concurring language varieties. I will briefly return to this point below. At this point it is sufficient to note that if elements of one rather than another variety are used, this is a question of the usage of these varieties, not of their structure.

3. If we try to associate this latter point of view with an existing theoretical trend, the domain of pragmatics comes to one's mind next. And it may well be, in fact, that a systematically developed theory of language varieties and their connotations will absorb an essential part of the phenomena envisaged under the heading of pragmatics. For the time being, however, such speculations are premature, and it seems to me to be more worthwhile at the present stage to concentrate on developing the necessary theoretical tools according to the pertinent empirical issues rather than relying on readymade classificatory schemes.

nonhomogeneous speech community.[4] In other words, accepting the scope of linguistic theory in a way motivated by Chomsky (1965), we must complement this theory by a theory of linguistic heterogeneity, thus extending it to the more general case of nonhomogeneous speech communities.[5]

It remains to be shown how the theories envisaged are related to each other. It is already clear that an account of the relation between different language varieties in a heterogeneous speech community must be able to refer to the structural properties of linguistic expressions. Hence, a theory of heterogeneity logically presupposes a linguistic description based on a proper linguistic theory. It will be seen below that in fact intrinsic grammatical details are relevant here.

So far the picture is fairly clear. One kind of knowledge is added to—or rather imposed on—another kind of knowledge, and the corresponding theories can be related accordingly, i.e., heterogeneity is analyzed in terms of linguistic structure, with specific concepts added where necessary. The situation becomes somewhat more complicated, however, if we are to consider the relations among coexisting language varieties not as an accidental phenomenon occurring in concrete speech communities, but rather as an inherent possibility of natural language.

What is at issue here is not the fact that actual speech communities in general are not linguistically homogeneous and thus do not meet the relevant idealization made explicit by Chomsky (1965, p. 3-4). The question is rather whether the conditions of linguistic heterogeneity must be traced to the underlying principles of linguistic structure if such an idealization is dropped. What this question in fact means can be made precise in the following way. Let L_i be an arbitrary homogeneous language (or language variety). Linguistic theory must then determine a particular grammar G_i which explicitly accounts for all the structural properties of the expressions of L_i. As Chomsky has argued repeatedly, this means that linguistic theory fully determines the linguistic knowledge acquired by an ideal speaker-listener who is exposed to L_i. Our question can now be formulated as follows: Can L_i have different grammars G_i and G_i' depending on whether it is taken in isolation or within a system of more or less

4. Of course they do this only partially, since neither of these theories includes, for example, an account of the concrete psychological processes of speech production and perception. As pointed out, though, we are concerned here only with different systems of knowledge underlying the actual processes of speech behavior.

5. With drastic oversimplification the situation might be represented diagramatically as an extension of the competence-performance distinction to the following diagram:

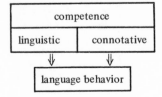

closely related varieties? Or in terms of language acquisition: If two speakers S and S' acquire L_i under different conditions, as a first (and perhaps only) language and as a second or third variety, must their respective linguistic knowledge perhaps be described by different grammars G_i and G'_i? If so, in which way can the grammars differ? Are these differences to be accounted for by linguistic theory?[6] The answer to this question is not at all clear in advance. Chomsky has left it open by restricting himself to the primary concern of characterizing the structure of linguistic competence resulting from a homogeneous speech community. It is now clear, however, exactly where problems of heterogeneity can enter into the principles of linguistic theory: if we assume—as I think we plausibly should—that neither the grammars G_i and G'_i envisaged above can be outside the class of possible grammars that linguistic theory has to specify in any case, their difference can only be a question of choosing between two (or more) descriptively equivalent grammars within that class. This selection is jointly determined by universal constraints on possible grammars compatible with a given set of linguistic expressions, and general criteria of evaluation. Hence, if phenomena of linguistic heterogeneity are anchored in the principles of linguistic theory, they must be traced either to certain aspects of constraints to be imposed on descriptively adequate grammars, or to ingredients of the evaluation criteria.[7] As far as I can see this is the only way phenomena of linguistic heterogeneity may be relevant for the theory of linguistic structure (but see footnote 8). In section 8 this contingency will be given a somewhat more concrete content.

To conclude the methodological considerations, we have arrived at the following picture. Besides the fact that the theory of linguistic heterogeneity obviously presupposes linguistic theory, the latter might also depend in a certain respect on the former. This mutual dependence need not result in circularity, however, since different aspects of linguistic theory are involved. What an account of heterogeneity presupposes is the class of possible structural descriptions

6. This question must be relativized, of course, to certain idealized conditions in order to avoid accidental differences in the resulting grammars. i.e., differences due to idiosyncratic incidents and hence definitely outside the scope of linguistic theory. In other words, we must be concerned with something like an ideal speaker-listener in a systematically heterogeneous speech community. That is, we modify the assumptions on which Chomsky proposes to base linguistic theory only by discounting the condition of a completely homogeneous speech community and retaining all other considerations.

7. It is worth noting that these considerations have already been illustrated quite clearly by Klima (1964). He studied the different principles for case marking of pronouns in four coexisting styles of English and formulates their respective grammars, on the one hand taking each style in isolation, and on the other one taking one style as a modification of another. The resulting pairs of grammars are clearly distinguished in terms of the evaluation measure, namely by the shortness of rules. By the same token Klima establishes certain structural relations between the four dialects. Although he does not discuss the question raised here, his exposition would lead to the same conclusion. See section 8 below for further discussion.

of linguistic expressions as well as the class of possible grammars from which they can be derived. What on the other hand an account of heterogeneity might affect are the general conditions to be imposed on descriptively adequate grammars and the criteria for selecting among descriptively equivalent grammars. In terms of the penetrating discussion in Chapter 1 of Chomsky (1965) the first kind of dependence concerns those parts that guarantee the descriptive adequacy of linguistic theory; the second kind of dependence concerns the part which eventually leads to explanatory adequacy.

3. SOME EXAMPLES AND SOME FACTS

The examples to start the discussion are ever present, almost to the point of being trivial, and can easily be extended in several directions. Their only purpose is to bring into focus crucial properties of well-known phenomena:

(1) (a) He couldn't provide any money.
  (b) [i: kudnə kɔf ʌp no loli]
      'e couldn't cough up no lolly.
(2) (a) The policeman didn't do anything.
  (b) [də kɔpə nɛvə dʌn nʌfiŋk]
      The copper never done nuffink.

Let us assume that the (a)-sentences in (1) and (2) are synonymous with the respective (b)-sentences, i.e., that they are true under the same conditions. This assumption is in reasonable agreement with the intuitions of native speakers whose language contains sentences like (1) and (2). In spite of this synonymy, the (b)-sentences convey something different than the (a)-sentences for those speakers who are able to interpret correctly the formal differences. What the sentences in (1) as opposed to those in (2) have in common will be called their cognitive or denotative meaning, or for short their meaning. What the (a)-sentences have in common as opposed to the (b)-sentences will be called their connotative meaning, or for short their connotation. In general, a speech community has the verbal means to designate these connotations more or less precisely. The connotation of the (a) cases would be called "Standard English" or "normal style" or something similar, as opposed to the substandard style of the (b) cases. In other words, there are linguistic expressions whose denotative meaning is the connotation conveyed by classes of expressions. One of the aims of a theory of linguistic heterogeneity must therefore be to provide a principled basis for the explication of the meaning of these expressions.[8]

8. There is a very general problem here. If one were to include a principled account of the meaning of all linguistic expressions in the scope of semantic theory and therefore in the theory of linguistic structure, the theory of linguistic heterogeneity would become a part of linguistic theory, which is moreover presupposed in yet a different sense than that discussed

I have used synonymous pairs of sentences to illustrate the distinction be-tween meaning and connotation. It is obvious, however, that (denotative) synonymy is by no means a condition for connotative differences. Thus (1b) has the same connotation with respect to (1a) and (2a). Conversely, formal dif-ferences between synonymous expressions do not necessarily carry different connotations. Thus, (3) is not only synonymous with (1a), but has also the same connotation:

(3) He wasn't able to provide any money.
(4) (a) I think that the length of John's skis is greater than that of Mary's.
    (b) I think that John's skis are longer than Mary's.

The sentences in (4) are another obvious example for the same fact. The impor-tant conclusion to be drawn from these trivial observations is this: formal differ-ences between classes of expressions that do not correspond to parallel differ-ences in meaning constitute different varieties if and only if there is a pertinent difference in connotation. Otherwise the formal differences are possible variants within the same variety. In other words, connotation and language variety as used here are interdependent concepts.

If we compare more than just pairs of sentences (or varieties to which they belong), we can easily detect further structure within the connotations:

(5) (a) He has cut himself.
    (b) [iːz kʌʔ izsɛwf]
        'es cut 'isself.
    (c) [iːz kʊt ɪsɛn]
        'es cut 'issen.

These three synonymous sentences do not only exhibit a difference between Standard English (5a) versus nonstandard varieties, but also a regionally deter-mined difference among the latter. (5b), like (1b) and (2b), belongs to the Cockney (London) variety of Southern English, (5c) belongs to the Western variety of Yorkshire. Thus we get a further split of the connotation "non-standard" along a spatial dimension. The examples in (5) then provide a rudi-mentary structure of connotations which might be represented in the following way:

---

in section 2. Notice, however, that such a view would turn the explication of every part of general factual knowledge into a linguistic task. Thus, by this token physics, sociology, and every other science would become a part of linguistic theory. A provisional and fairly vague answer would be that semantics as a part of linguistic theory has to specify the general principles according to which the meaning of linguistic expressions is made up, whereas the specification of the concrete details in particular domains of denotation may be a joint task of semantics and other theories. But I do not want to deal here with this problem any further, since it is by no means specific to the domain of linguistic heterogeneity. For a more detailed discussion of the general problem see, e.g., Schnelle (1973, p. 78 ff.).

(6)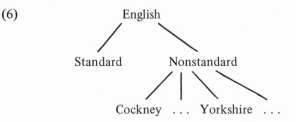

I do not wish to suggest that branching diagrams must be the adequate formal way of representing the interrelation of connotations, but merely that there is a certain kind of structure the general principles of which are subject to empirical motivation. In fact the different connotations and the dimensions on which they are organized might form a more complicated structure than a single branching hierarchy. To mention just one problem, within the spatially undifferentiated standard variety there might be several strata (or ranks) such as formal, neutral, colloquial, or vulgar varieties differing mainly (but not only) by characteristic lexical rules. The same dimension might also be found for subvarieties of the different regional dialects (though not all of its values may be relevant). In short, connotations—and the language varieties to which they are attached—are not merely an unstructured set but are related by general principles, organization according to separate dimensions being one of them. This fact has to be reflected in the internal structure of the individual connotations themselves.

The next point to be noted concerns another obvious property of connotation: expressions with different connotations might cause a specific kind of deviancy. The combination of (2a) and (1b), for example, within one coherent utterance would make the whole inconsistent as to its connotation; the same would be true in a different way for a combination of (2b) and (5c) if judged by a native speaker of Cockney and/or Yorkshire. This kind of inconsistency can be illustrated not only between but also within sentences. On the other hand, there can be expressions with indefinite connotation which can be combined with expressions of different connotation. For example, (5a), which is neutral as to its stylistic rank, can become part of an utterance with colloquial or vulgar connotation if preceded by "Good Lord" or "Oh shit." Hence, connotations do not only show the previously mentioned differentiation and the pertinent internal structure, they also exhibit possibilities and restrictions of combination. Someone who favors Saussurean terms might think of a paradigmatic and a syntagmatic aspect of connotation.

So far I have considered and I will continue to consider examples of different varieties that in an intuitive sense belong to one language, in order to simplify the discussion. There is no a priori reason for excluding the relationship between varieties existing within separate languages. Thus French expressions can be contrasted to our examples if one considers a Canadian speech community, in which both French and English are spoken, or German examples like (7)–

Standard German and the Berlin regional variety—might convey the pertinent connotations if opposed to (1) for British people living temporarily in a German-speaking community:

(7) (a) Er konnte kein Geld hergeben.
     (b) [dea kɔntə keːn jɛlt aɔsspukŋ]
          Der konnte keen Geld ausspucken.

The connotational dimension relevant in these cases is that of different nationalities, a concept that must be defined and sharpened within the framework of a theory of society. The point at issue here is the distinction between different languages and different varieties within one language. Although this distinction is closely related to formal linguistic properties, plenty of problems show that it cannot be clarified on this basis alone.[9] What I would like to point out is merely that a principled answer to the question "what is one language?" requires in part a theory of linguistic heterogeneity explaining the connection between linguistic structure and those social factors establishing the dimension of nationality as opposed to social structures giving rise to other kinds of connotation.

4. ON THE NATURE OF CONNOTATION

Given the preliminary characterization of connotation and some of its properties, we can explore its character somewhat more closely.

As a first step, we may notice that all aspects of linguistic structure can be relevant to connotation. The examples above easily illustrate the point. Phonological properties, which so far have attracted the most systematic investigation in this respect, contrast Standard English [nʌθiŋ, kʌt] versus Cockney [nʌfiŋk, kʌʔ]. Morphological differences show up in Standard English *himself* versus Cockney *hisself* versus Yorkshire *hisson*. A syntactic difference is illustrated by Standard English simple negation versus Cockney double negation, or more precisely the negative concord in Cockney; lexical differences are exhibited by Standard English *policeman, money* versus Cockney *copper, lolly*.[10] To be sure, there are interesting differences in the role these aspects may play concerning the various dimensions of connotation. Phonological factors, for example, contribute

---

9. To give just one example, in many respects Dutch dialects are more similar to low German varieties than the latter are to southern German dialects. But the latter two are nevertheless taken as varieties of one language, while the former two belong to different languages—for sound but clearly extralinguistic reasons. The problem here is parallel to that mentioned in footnote 1 concerning the notion of speech community.

10. The special question whether semantic differences can have connotative effects will be taken up at the end of section 5, where it will be seen that it is a problem of a fairly different character.

primarily, but not only, to the regionally determined varieties, while lexical distinctions are prominent in the stylistic levels, professional and other group jargons, etc. But in spite of such differences these aspects may jointly determine the specific connotation of linguistic expressions. More precisely, structural properties can be connotatively relevant because they contribute to the fact that a specific phonetic structure is related to a particular meaning. What I have in mind can perhaps best be seen by the following example. The verb *cough up* in (1b) contributes to the connotation not because of its phonological form as such, since this word also occurs in standard English, though with a different meaning, nor because of the concept 'provide, bring out,' which it expresses, since this concept of course can also be expressed in a connotatively different way. Its substandard character rather depends on the fact that this concept is related to that phonological form. Similarly, the negative concord in (1b) and (2b) contributes to connotation because it determines a form that does not express double negation, as it would in standard English, but just simple negation.

More generally, we may say then that the connotation k of an expression e depends on the fact that e relates a certain phonetic structure p to a certain denotative meaning m.[11] Every property of e involved in its relating a specific phonetic structure p to its meaning m may thus be a point of contact for the connotation k associated with, or manifested by, e.

The next point to be clarified has two facets. First, although we have separated connotation explicitly from (denotative) meaning, it is still something that the utterance of a linguistic form means; in other words, a connotative expression really conveys something in addition to its meaning. And second, this connotative information is conveyed in a completely different way than denotative meaning.

Let us start with the first aspect. It was in fact one of our initial assumptions that the speaker-hearers in a nonhomogeneous speech community are aware of what connotations express. But this is not a vague allusion, however, it has to be taken quite seriously. In order to see this, let us think for example of a telephone call to a London police station, the speaker consistently using sentences of the variety to which (1b) and (2b) belong. The policeman called will understand, first, that the speaker is an inhabitant of London, and, second, that he does not have a very respectful attitude toward his present audience. As a second thought the policeman might wonder whether he is perhaps being

---

11. As far as I can see, this explication of the concept of connotation was first proposed, albeit in a different framework, by Hjelmslev (1953, p. 114–25). Having defined a semiotic system as the interdependent connection of a content plane and an expression plane, Hjelmslev introduces a connotative semiotic as a system whose expressions plane is itself a semiotic system. In other words, content and expression of a denotative sign as an interdependent whole are correlated with an additional content functioning as its expression. The inverse case, incidentally, i.e., a semiotic system whose content plane is itself a semiotic system, is called by Hjelmslev a metasemiotic system.

deceived intentionally, just as he might with respect to the proper content of information. And he might further conclude that this is more likely so with respect to the first than to the second, since he knows that almost everybody has at his disposal the expressions of different stylistic levels, using them according to varying situations, whereas mastery of a regional dialect is characteristic of the pertinent people and hence a well-directed means of deception, if occasion arises.[12] Examples like this are apt to show that connotation is a specific kind of information, which can have a clear and definite character, that the means to freely convey it are available to the speaker-hearer in varying degrees and may therefore be used as a means of deception.[13]

The second aspect, the difference in manner of conveying denotative meaning and connotation, can best be foregrounded by contrasting what might be considered as two ways of transmitting the same information. Compare, for example, (2b) with something like (8):

(8) I'm a native of working-class London (and I'm telling you that) the policeman didn't do anything.

Roughly speaking, what in (2b) is distinctly divided into meaning on the one hand and connotation on the other is transformed into pure denotative, propositional meaning in (8). As far as this is essentially correct, the difference between (2b) and (8) immediately brings out the way connotation functions, as opposed to denotative meaning: (8) specifies truth conditions, it describes a fact, where (2b) exhibits a characteristic component of the fact itself.[14]

12. The last point is brought up by Searle (1969, p. 44–45) in a different context by means of the somewhat more drastic example of an American soldier captured by Italian troops. In order to make the Italians believe he is a German, the soldier pronounces a line from a German poem he remembers. What Searle has in mind is the fact that in uttering *Kennst du das Land wo die Zitronen blühn* the American does not mean what the words say. I would add that far from caring about the denotative meaning of the sentence he relies on the connotation "German," because this is precisely the information he—deceptively—intends to convey. This case differs crucially from the police station example in that the audience is supposed not to understand the meaning, but still somehow to realize the connotation of the sentence, which in this case belongs to the dimension of nationality—also a highly invariant characteristic of a person.

13. Free choice of the means of conveying and recognizing particular connotations is restricted by a variety of factors, ranging from knowledge of the relevant linguistic structures to the strategies and skills brought to bear in actually applying the knowledge. An important role is, of course, played by the kind of linguistic means predominant in distinguishing the concurring language varieties. The conditions for building up the pertinent knowledge, and the skills and mechanisms for applying it, depend in turn on the social structure and the speaker's position in it.

14. There are several other more or less appropriate ways in which to paraphrase the distinction. One way would be to use Bühler's (1934, p. 28) notion of a Symptom as opposed to a Symbol to characterize connotation vs. meaning. Although this might be suggestive in some respects, it nevertheless would require crucial qualifications. I will therefore refrain from pursuing such possibilities.

It might be noted that this observation can be generalized to certain forms of complex behavior where no denotative meaning is involved. Clothing is an obvious example showing farreaching parallels with the principles of connotation. Characteristic formal properties of clothes convey information about the conditions of those who wear them. Just like language varieties, different types or styles of clothing are related to various dimensions of social conditions. A more intricate case is the different varieties of music, whose formal characteristics may mean something in precisely the way discussed above.[15] What all these phenomena have in common is the fact that there are traditionally or conventionally fixed structural properties that mean something precisely because their existence is part of the conditions they are pointing out.

The comparison of (2b) with (9a) and (9b) turned on a (partial) description of the conditions to which the connotation of (2b) pertains. We can narrow such description to the linguistic expressions as such directly, since natural languages, as already mentioned, contain expressions denoting the connotative aspect of language varieties. Using such expressions one can get sentences that fulfill or contradict by way of connotation their own descriptive content:

(9) (a) [ʔaːm tɔːwkɪn kɔkniː]
          I'm talking Cockney.
     (b) [ʔaː nɛvə sæi nʌfɪŋʔɪŋ kɔkniː]
          I never say nuffink in Cockney.

What is going on here is similar to what Katz (1972, p. 192–220) has defined as metalinguistic truth and falsehood. (9a) is true because of its connotation, whereas the connotation of (9b) contradicts its meaning. These properties have to be accounted for in a theory of linguistic heterogeneity. At present I have mentioned them to show from a slightly different angle what connotations say and how this relates to meaning.

The last point I would comment on is the distinction between the structure of connotations and the affective, emotional, and other ingredients they very often carry. There are at least two reasons why connotations easily acquire such ingredients. The first is that they are bound to conditions determining the general and occasional social relations among communicating people. Such relations are typically bound up with the vital interests of the members of a speech community. They provide the basis for cooperation or conflict, for solidarity or antagonism. Hence the emotionally colored impact of connotations is likely to vary with the intensity or abatement of social conflicts and agreements, the underlying interests, and the position of the speaker-hearer within them. The second reason is the specific way that connotations express something: as they do not describe a property or condition, but show it directly by one of its pertinent features, they are apt to elicit a more direct attitude from both the speaker and the hearer than a mere denotative representation would do.

15. An interesting concrete example is the so-called Janizary music, certain features of which were used by European composers of the eighteenth century to convey the connotation "exotic." I am indebted to Professor Georg Knepler for this remark.

In spite of these tendencies, there is a structural relation among the different connotations, and it is only this underlying structure that makes emotional values possible. It is easy to see that this structure must be neutral as to affective evaluation, and that it is open to different emotional interpretations, so to speak. Thus, ingroup and outgroup people may have fairly different attitudes toward the jargon of the group, although both may identify the same linguistic properties as well as the same social conditions to which they belong. Similarly a worker and a bourgeois may evaluate the distinction between standard and nonstandard varieties rather differently, but still they are both aware of the same conditions which they are related to. This emotionally neutral structure of connotation is what I am concerned with in the present paper.

One final remark. It is well known that the term "connotation" is used in various ways. Many uses have little or nothing in common with the concept discussed here. Vagueness and emotional character are features very often attributed to connotation. Sometimes the term is simply used to cover elusive and accidental aspects of meaning which seem to escape any systematic account of semantic structure. A slightly more precise view considers as connotation typical or occasional associations cooccurring with a given concept. The idea of power and majesty associated with the concept 'lion', or the idea of peace and repose as well as death associated with 'night' are typical examples. A fairly different, theoretically oriented conception is the approach of Osgood, Suci, Tannenbaum (1957), which is widely interpreted as an account of affective or connotative meaning. Whatever stand one might take with respect to Osgood's notion of "semantic differential," it has no bearing on the present approach. Probably the most widely held conception of connotation is that expressed by Bloomfield (1933, p. 151-157). Although it has much in common with the present view, it is broader, kept largely vague, primarily because Bloomfield does not regard it as subject to theoretical explication. He gives a lot of examples of much the same type as those considered here, commenting that "The most important connotations arise from the social standing of the speakers who use a form." But he also writes that "the number *thirteen*, for instance, has for many people a strong connotation."

This is by no means a complete list of what has been understood as connotation. But the difference between these and similar notions from the one proposed here—as well as possible similarities—are, it is hoped, sufficiently clear by now.

5. SOCIAL CONDITIONS OF
LINGUISTIC HETEROGENEITY

Before turning to a more detailed account of how connotations are related to properties of linguistic structure, I will briefly consider the social correlates that have been claimed to be a constitutive condition for them. For obvious reasons this can be done only in a highly provisional and intuitive way.

As already mentioned, connotations associated with language varieties must be referred to different dimensions. As far as I am aware, they can be related to two types of factors in social structure: relations between classes and groups of varying size and conditions of constitution, and relations between individual partners in typical situations. These are certainly not strictly separable types of relations, but there are sufficiently clear distinctions that can be taken as starting points.

The function of language varieties reflecting the first type of social relations is supposed to contribute to the identity of the group; the speakers affirm their membership within the group by adhering to the specific linguistic means established as a characteristic convention obtaining in the group. The function varies with the size, the stability, and the constitution of the group. It plays a different role for macrogroups and small groups, for long-term historical formations and short-term configurations, etc. In particular, there is no simple and obvious correspondence between the strength of social and economic conditions on the one hand and the linguistic pecularities on the other hand. Thus the fundamental distinction between the economically determined social classes need not have a direct reflection in the system of language varieties in a speech community. It is rather mediated by regional divisions and social ranks in various ways.

Provisionally the following dimensions may be distinguished in the present domain:

(Ia) *Geographic or regional divisions*, as studied mainly in dialectology. Although this dimension is generally treated as the regional aspect of language, it is surely obvious that it is essentially the spatial reflection of social and economic conditions.

(Ib) *Social stratification* of the speech community, correlating, but not identical, with social ranks and class structure. Although this differentiation seems fairly clear on the surface, a theoretical account encounters serious problems. The content of this dimension is certainly determined to a high degree by the historical type of society realized in a speech community. The dimensions (Ia) and (Ib) tend to show a close interrelation in the following well-known sense: a regionally less restricted variety is generally regarded as higher social rank than a regionally more restricted one, if both concur in the same region. In particular, if there is a standard variety whose local range comprises the range of a class of varieties differentiated on dimension (Ia), it usually occupies the highest rank on dimension (Ib).[16]

(Ic) *Special groups, professional branches, cliques*, and other more or less stable associations exhibiting linguistic characteristics. This dimension

16. This is no explanation of the notion "standard variety." At best, it is a necessary condition. I also do not want to exclude the possibility of more than one variety occupying the top in (Ib). In such a case we would have a multilingual speech community.

too is interrelated, though differently, with (Ib). I need not comment on this in detail.[17] Linguistically, distinctions on this dimension are manifested primarily by lexical and idiomatic peculiarities.

The function of connotations bound to the second type of social relations is to identify mutual status and attitudes of partners in communication. The distinctions that can be made in this domain seem to fall into two dimensions:

(IIa) *Relatively constant relations between speaker and audience*, based on conventions of intercourse. Different forms of address and honorifics are typical examples conveying this type of connotation. Although at a first glance phenomena like these seem to belong to the realm of linguistic structure proper, and are generally so treated, they have all the properties of connotations discussed above. The difference between *Du* and *Sie* in German for instance has no bearing on denotative meaning but indicates the degree of familiarity between speaker and hearer according to strictly fixed conventions.

(IIb) *More or less stable types of situation*, differing with respect to certain kinds of regimentation of social behavior. Most characteristic of this dimension are phenomena usually treated as value styles, i.e., vulgar, colloquial, neutral, formal style, etc.[18] A deeper understanding of the principles at work in this area might easily show that actually more than one dimension must be distinguished. What seems to be relevant, however, is the fact that the characteristic effect of, say, formal or vulgar style is based on the existence of social conditions. Only the adherence to or the deviation from the conventions attached to them make formal, casual, vulgar, or other levels a matter of taste.

In other words, given the conditions of type (I), speakers coordinate their communication according to dimensions of type (II), where partners are relevant for (IIa) and types of situations for (IIb). Again, (IIa) and (IIb) are not fully independent, and both can be related to (I).[19]

17. It might be remarked, however, that from the present point of view scientific language has a connotation on this dimension, as science is a social endeavor carried out by a specific social group.

18. It should be remarked that "style" is a notoriously hybrid notion. Only one of its various facets is relevant in the present context, and the term is used here only as a rough indication.

19. A somewhat different classification of varieties according to their conditions of use has been proposed by Gregory (1967). He distinguishes 'dialectal' varieties and 'diatypic' varieties. The former are described as reflecting reasonably permanent characteristics of the *user*, the latter as reflecting recurrent characteristics of user's *use* of language in situations. There are some similarities between this distinction and that between type (I) and (II) proposed here, although Gregory's classification relies on different criteria. It remains to be seen whether these criteria (characteristics of the user, characteristics of use) can eventually be reduced to social conditions of the type proposed here, as I would strongly suggest.

It is furthermore reasonable to assume that the dimensions sketched so far must be open to further subdivision in several ways. This is most obvious for the regional differentiation, but it holds for other dimensions as well. Such subdivisions are particularly relevant in the case of interrelations between different dimensions.

Clearly, (Ia) through (IIb) are only a highly tentative characterization of main coordinates in the social structure of a speech community according to which its language varieties receive their connotations. They must not be taken as a substitute for a serious theoretical account relating phenomena of linguistic differentiation to the structure of society, its economic basis, and its social superstructure. Otherwise, one would be restricted to empiristic observations instead of trying to explain how mediating social structures function in determining different language varieties. These remarks enable us, nevertheless, to make the following points. What linguistic expressions convey by way of connotation, and the internal structure of connotations, is based on discernible aspects of the social structure of the speech community. It is this structure that provides the purport of connotations and imposes conditions on their mutual relationship and possible combination. The formal means I will use in the following to represent connotations must therefore be taken not as arbitrary entities, but as theoretical terms receiving an interpretation somehow along the lines suggested above. The categories of this interpretation must be taken from the theory of social structure, i.e., this interpretation will be given in such terms as social class, group, institution, etc. I am not in a position to make any specific claims in this direction, but it seems obvious that this presupposes a principled analysis of the conditions of communication in close connection with the analysis of the conditions of production initiated by Marx.

Quite a number of the problems involved in these considerations have been treated fairly extensively by Soviet linguistics under the heading "forms of existence" (*formi suščestvovanija*) of a given language.[20] In terms of the foregoing discussion we can say that the language varieties of a speech community, related to each other on dimensions such as (Ia) through (IIb), make up a system of forms of existence of a language, if there is a standard variety in the sense suggested above to which all varieties are structurally related.[21] This notion brings into relief the systematic, socially determined character of linguistic heterogeneity in a speech community; it stresses in particular the key role of the standard variety and the specific historic character that its function imposes on the whole system of forms of existence of a language.

There is one additional point in connection with the foregoing considerations. It is immediately obvious that the different social dimensions to which

20. See Serebrennikov et. al. (1970, Chaps. 6–8) for a comprehensive survey and detailed illustration.

21. Although intuitively plausible, the concept of structural relatedness of two language varieties is still in need of explanation. This problem will be taken up in section 7.

cooccurring varieties are related may have a strong impact on the potential subject matter that a given variety is used to communicate about. Formally this problem is related to the range of denotative meanings available in a given variety. Even if we make no specific claims as to the expressive power of different varieties, it is obvious that certain varieties are more suitably adapted to certain topics than others. In fact, the specific formal properties of varieties with connotation along (Ic), i.e., professional jargons or special group varieties, derive to a large extent from precisely this type of adaptation. As a result, certain facts are expressed more naturally in one variety than in another, however this notion is to be made precise.[22] Given this indirect correlation between range of subject matter and connotation, we can explain a secondary phenomenon of heterogeneity. For example, to talk in Cockney about Hegelian ideology or astrophysics would convey not only the general connotation of Cockney because it is Cockney that is being spoken; it would have an additional effect produced by the very fact that Cockney is being used to deal with this topic. More generally, whereas connotation was described as the effect of how a certain meaning is formally related to a phonetic representation in some L_i, the present effect is based on the fact that it is so related at all.[23] The most drastic phenomenon of this type might be called verbal taboo, the restriction of not talking about certain things under conditions appropriate to a given language variety.

6. TOWARD AN EXPLICATION OF CONNOTATION

I will turn now to a more precise formulation of the framework to be proposed. Let C be a speech community and E_C the full set of linguistic expressions underlying possible, nondeviant utterances available to members of C. More precisely, we will assume that $E_C = \{e_1, e_2, e_3, \ldots\}$ is a (potentially infinite) set of expressions, where $e_i = (m_i, p_i)$ for any i is an ordered pair of a semantic represen-

22. There is a highly intricate problem here. Are we entitled to assume that everything that can be expressed in one variety—i.e., can be the denotative meaning m of an expression e in L_i—can also be expressed in every other variety? In other words, can we extend the effability hypothesis of Katz (1972) or the principle of expressibility of Searle (1969) from language (whatever "language" means in this case) to language variety? Such an extension seems to be problematic even as a (somewhat artificial) theoretical postulate. It might turn out that it can be maintained only if we allow the eventual introduction of new lexical rules. But although this is possible in every language for principled reasons, as discussed in Bierwisch and Kiefer (1969), it might crucially change the affected variety by introducing expressions with different connotations. In any case, it is not necessary at this point to take a stand on this question, since both answers are compatible with what follows.

23. A rough parallel from a nonlinguistic area would be the distinction between different types of headwear on the one hand and using or not using any headwear in certain situations on the other.

tation m_i and a phonetic (or graphic) representation p_i and m_i is the (denotative) meaning conveyed by an utterance of p_i under appropriate conditions.[24] Thus using M to designate the set of possible meanings m_i available to members of C, and P to designate the set of possible p_i, E_C as well as every subset of it can be characterized a proper subset of the cartesian product $M \times P$. The specification of such subsets of $M \times P$ is, of course, a matter of systems of grammatical rules. We will turn to this aspect in the next section.

Let us next assume that there is for every speech community C a finite set $K_C = \{k_1, k_2, \ldots, k_n\}$ of connotations, where the k_j represent (configurations of) conditions in the social structure of C relevant for distinguishing different language varieties used in C. According to the discussion in the previous section, we have to recognize a certain structure imposed on K_C. Its formal character will be considered below. The elements of K_C must be related in a characteristic way to the expressions used in C. We will express this by postulating a mapping f, which assigns to each $e_i \in E_C$ at least one connotation k_j. An expression is said to manifest the connotation k_j related to it, and the resulting pair (e_i, k_j) will be called a connotative expression. The relation of manifestation thus introduced is a formal reconstruction of how an expression conveys the information about the social conditions of communication represented by its connotation. The question of how f determines the connotation k_j on the basis of the formal properties of an e_i manifesting it will be taken up in the next section.

Given the mapping f, we immediately get for every k_j a subset E_j of E_C consisting of all elements e_i manifesting k_j. The corresponding set of connotative expressions (e_i, k_j) may be called a connotative set and represented by the ordered pair (E_j, k_j). With certain qualifications to be discussed below the sets of expression E_j entering a connotative set will be used to explicate the concept of language varieties assumed at the outset. Finally it is obvious that K_C together with the function f splits E_C up into a family of subsets $\mathcal{F} = \{E_1, \ldots, E_n\}$. I will call this family of sets of expressions together with the connotations determining it a connotative system. The structure of this system clearly depends on the conditions imposed on K_C and f. Before I discuss these conditions and their consequences for the system of connotative sets, I will illustrate the assumptions introduced so far by a highly idealized example.

Although constrained by very restrictive conditions, the example will serve to clarify in part the ideas underlying the explication of connotation and hetero-

24. Thus the p_i should be thought of as phonetic transcriptions in the sense of, e.g., Chomsky and Halle (1968, p. 293ff). The crucial dependence of phonetic representations on the linguistic knowledge as described by systems of grammatical rules will be taken care of later on. For the time being I take the p_i simply for granted. I also do not worry here about the details of the semantic representations m_i, assuming that a reasonable semantic theory will provide the general form of the m_i which includes besides the conceptual structure (or propositional content) a specification of presuppositions, conditions on possible reference, and illocutionary force regularly associated with an utterance of the p_i associated with m_i. Katz (1972) and Lewis (1972) can be taken as different programs in this direction.

geneity to be proposed. Let us consider a connotative system meeting the following restrictions:

(10) (a) E_c is divided by $K_C = \{k_1, \ldots, k_n\}$ into n disjoint subsets $E_1, \ldots, E_n$, i.e., each $e_i \in E_C$ belongs to one and only one E_j.

 (b) The different E_j all have the same range of meanings, i.e., the set M_j of meanings occurring in the $e_{i_j} \in E_j$ is the same for all E_j such that $M_j = M$ for $1 \leqslant j \leqslant n$.

 (c) There is no ambiguity within the different E_j, i.e., each $m_i \in M$ occurs precisely once in an expression $e_{i_j} \in E_j$.

 (d) There is no synonymy within the different E_j, i.e., each $P_{i_j} \in P_j$ occurs exactly once in an expression $e_{i_j} \in E_j$.

Notice that no claim is made with respect to the various P_j. They may be disjoint or not. All that is required by (10) is that in no E_j the same phonetic representation is paired with the same meaning. If the P_j are assumed to be disjoint, then it follows from (10d) that the total set E_C does not contain any ambiguities. On the other hand, every expression of E_C has at least $n - 1$ synonyms, each belonging to a different E_j and hence manifesting a different connotation. A connotative system meeting (10) can obviously be represented by a matrix as represented in (11).

(11)

M	m_1	m_2	m_3	$\cdots$	m_i	$\cdots$	K_C
P_1	p_{1_1}	p_{2_1}	p_{3_1}	$\cdots$	p_{i_1}	$\cdots$	k_1
P_2	p_{1_2}	p_{2_2}	p_{3_2}	$\cdots$	p_{i_2}	$\cdots$	k_2
$\cdot$	$\cdot$	$\cdot$	$\cdot$		$\cdot$		$\cdot$
$\cdot\cdot$	$\cdot$	$\cdot$	$\cdot$		$\cdot$		$\cdot$
$\cdot$	$\cdot$	$\cdot$	$\cdot$		$\cdot$		$\cdot$
P_n	p_{1_n}	p_{2_n}	p_{3_n}	$\cdots$	p_{i_n}	$\cdots$	k_n

Clearly, each pair of lines (M, P_j) represents the set of expressions of one E_j manifesting the connotation k_j. In the framework of this matrix, the column to which a phonetic representation belongs determines its meaning, whereas the line in which it occurs determines the connotation of the expression to which it belongs. We can describe these two types of determination as constituted by two types of convention. The first type of convention concerns the pairing of phonetic and semantic representation, that is, it establishes the columns for any given E_j, as far as that pairing is conventional at all and not subject to universal conditions restricting the class of possible languages. As Lewis (1969) has argued, this convention can best be understood as coordinating verbal communication according to the sound-meaning relation represented by the expressions of a given E_j. The (tacit) knowledge involved in this relation constitutes a speaker-hearer's linguistic competence in the proper or narrower sense, represented by systems of grammatical rules. The second type of convention concerns the conditions under which a certain convention of the first type applies. In other words, it determines which system of rules is followed under which conditions. The implicit knowledge involved here typically governs linguistic behavior in a heterogeneous speech community. For the sake of reference we will call it the connotative competence of a speaker-hearer.

I do not mean, of course, that in a speech community C whose possible expressions could be displayed in a matrix like (11), every speaker-hearer can freely select between the lines in (11). For reasons inherent in the very structure of C he may lack the necessary linguistic knowledge. I mean only that if a choice is made (which may be completely unconscious), it is determined by the convention relating a given E_j to certain conditions in the social structure of C represented in the corresponding k_j.

If we give up or several of the conditions in (10) we can no longer represent E_C in a simple, complete matrix like (11). As long as we retain condition (10a), that of disjoint connotative sets, it is only the complete and unique correspondence within the columns that gets lost: A more realistic view of heterogeneity, however, requires us to recognize also possible conflation of lines. Remember the neutral status of sentences like (5a) "He has cut himself" as opposed to those obtained by prefixing it with "Good Lord" versus "Oh shit." Dialectology and sociolinguistics provide plenty of more intricate cases. Instead of relaxing step-by-step the conditions imposed by (10) and showing that the basic considerations still hold in the resulting generalizations, I will turn directly to the general structure of possible connotative systems.

Let us first consider the conditions to be imposed on K_C reflecting the linguistically relevant aspects of the social structure of C. As we have seen above, this structure shows several possible dimensions, which may in turn be divided into subdomains, thus leading to hierarchies like that provisionally indicated in (6). Different dimensions may furthermore be interrelated in various ways with one (complex) condition being subordinated to or composed of more than one more general condition. This means that a partial ordering, that is an asymmetric, transitive, two-place relation R, must be imposed on K_C such that the pair (K_C, R_C) represents the connotations and their interrelation pertaining to a given speech community C.

Notice next that the ordering imposed on K_C must be reflected directly in the system of subsets E_j created by the members of K_C in the manner assumed above. In other words, if k_1 is dominated both by k_2 and k_3, i.e., if $R_C(k_2, k_1)$ and $R_C(k_3, k_1)$, then E_1 is (part of) the intersection of E_2 and E_3. Similarly, if k_1 dominates both k_2 and k_3, then E_1 must be the union of E_2 and E_3. To illustrate this requirement by a concrete example, let us assume that the sentence "Oh shit, he has cut himself" manifests the connotation Vulgar Standard English, which is dominated in K_C both by Vulgar (style) and Standard English. The set of expressions to which it belongs should be the intersection of Standard English expressions and those manifesting the connotation Vulgar. Intuitively, the higher a connotation ranks with respect to R_C, the less specific are the conditions of communication it represents, and hence the larger is the set of expressions normally admitted.

Let us finally consider the mapping f, which has been left fairly vague so far. It seems to be a natural requirement that an expression e_i has only one connotation, in spite of the fact that it can be a member of various interrelated sets, as just discussed. Thus, "Oh shit, he has cut himself" does not manifest the three connotations Standard English, Vulgar, and Vulgar Standard English, but just one, Vulgar Standard English. This then means that $f(e_i) = k_j$ is a function whose value is uniquely determined for every $e_i \in E_C$.

In order to reconcile these requirements, the internal structure of the connotations must reflect the structure of the hierarchy of connotative sets induced by K_C. This can be achieved in an obvious way by reconstructing K_C and the partial ordering R_C imposed on it in the following manner.

Let $\mathcal{A} = (A, \wedge, \vee, K_C)$ be an algebraic structure with $A = \{a_1, a_2, \ldots, a_m\}$ being a finite set of elementary connotations, and $\wedge$ and $\vee$ algebraic operations satisfying the usual axioms of Boolean operations.[25] The elements of K_C are now represented as primary Boolean combinations over A meeting the following conditions:

(12)   (a)   If $k_i = x$ and $k_j = x \wedge y$, then $R_C(k_i, k_j)$.
      (b)   If $k_i = x$ and $k_j = x \vee y$, then $R_C(k_j, k_i)$ for x, y arbitrary primary Boolean combinations over A.

It is easily verified that $\mathcal{A}$ represents the structure of (K_C, R_C) just by the internal composition of the elements of K_C, since a Boolean algebra is a particular type of partial ordering.

The connotative sets (E_j, k_j) are now determined on the basis of the function f in the following way. Obviously, any $k_j \in K_C$ has the form $k_r \wedge x$ for an arbitrary (including empty) Boolean combination x and some $k_r \in K_C$. (Thus $k_j = k_r$ for empty x.) We want now the set E_j corresponding to (E_j, k_j) to consist of all expressions manifesting the connotation $k_j \wedge x$. That is, the connotative expression $(e_i, a_1 \wedge a_2)$ should be a member of (E_1, a_1) of (E_2, a_2), and of

---

25. That is, $\wedge$ and $\vee$ are specified by the following axioms:

    (i) $x \wedge y = y \wedge x$ (commutativity)
    (ii) $x \wedge (y \wedge z) = (x \wedge y) \wedge z$ (associativity)
    (iii) $x \wedge (x \vee y) = x$ (absorption)
    (iv) $(x \wedge y) \vee (x \wedge z) = x \wedge (y \vee z)$ (distributivity)
         and the parallels with $\wedge$ and $\vee$ interchanged. x, y, z are arbitrary Boolean combinations over A.

The axioms (iii) and (iv) can be considered as rules reducing Boolean combinations in an obvious way. Boolean combinations over A that cannot be further reduced by means of these rules will be called primary Boolean combinations.

MANFRED BIERWISCH

$(E_1 \cap E_2, a_1 \wedge a_2)$. We thus postulate a mapping F from K_C on E_C meeting the following condition:

(13) $F(k_j) = E_j$ iff $E_j = \{e_i | f(e_i) = k_j x\}$ for $k_j \in K_C, e_i \in E_C$ and all (possibly empty) Boolean combinations x over A.

On the other hand, if the k_j of a connotative set has the form $k_r \vee k_s$ with k_r, $k_s \in K_C$, we want the corresponding E_j to contain not only the e_i with $f(e_i) = k_r \vee k_s$ but also those manifesting one of the connotations k_r or k_s. Hence we add the following condition:

(14) $F(k_j \vee x) \supseteq E_j$ if $E_j = \{e_i | f(e_i) = k_j\}$

or, what amounts to the same:

(15) $F(k_j) = E_j$ iff $E_j = \{e_i | f(e_i) = k_r\}$ for $k_j = k_r \vee x$ for arbitrary (including empty) x and $k_j, k_r \in K_C$.

As (13) and (15) can easily be collapsed, we get the following complete specification of F:

(16) $F(k_j) = E_j$ iff $E_j = \{e_i | f(e_i) = k_r\}$ where either $k_r = k_j \wedge x$ or $k_j = k_r \vee x$ for arbitrary x, and $k_j, k_r \in K_C$, and $e_i \in E_C$.

On the basis of F we can now generally specify the connotative sets used in C and the corresponding family of sets:

(17) (E_j, k_j) is a connotative set in E_C with respect to K_C iff $F(k_j) = E_j$ with $k_j \in K_C$.

(18) $\mathcal{F} = \{E_j | F(k_j) = E_j$ for $k_j \in K_C\}$ is a family of sets representing the connotational structure of E_C with respect to K_C.

It can easily be verified that F is a homomorphism from the algebraic structure $(A, \wedge, \vee, K_C)$ into the set system $(\mathcal{F}, \cap, \cup)$ with respect to the relation R in K_C and set inclusion in $\mathcal{F}$.[26]

Notice that we have changed somewhat the notion of a connotative set suggested at the beginning of this section. A set E_j now contains not only the expressions manifesting k_j but also all those expressions manifesting a k_r subordinated to k_j in terms of R. This is because we required the relation of set inclusion in $\mathcal{F}$ to reflect the partial ordering in K_C and simultaneously f to be a unique function. The latter is of particular interest, since this was the crucial assumption underlying the comments on conventions in the case of the simplified example (11) above. They carry now over to the general case with overlapping sets of expressions. More specifically, a connotative expression $(e_i,$

26. In fact, what we have specified is just the projection of a set of interfering properties on a set of objects characterized by combinations of these properties. E_C is the set of classified objects, A is the set of properties, and K_C contains the combinations of properties actually occurring with elements of E_C.

$a_j \wedge a_k$) belongs to the set of expressions by means of which two conventions are followed simultaneously, one imposed on the other, so to speak, while $(e_i, a_j \vee a_k)$ is valid for two conventions followed alternatively. Both belong, though in different ways, also to the conventions holding under conditions a_j and a_k.

Summarizing the foregoing discussion we can now specify a connotative system of a speech community C in the following way:

(19) $K = (E_C, \mathfrak{C}, f, \mathfrak{F})$ is a connotative system, iff
- (a) E_C is the set of well-formed expressions e_i underlying possible utterances in C with $e_i = (m_i, p_i)$ being a pair of a semantic and a phonetic representation.
- (b) $\mathfrak{C} = (A, \wedge, \vee, K_C)$ is an algebraic structure with $A = \{a_1, a_2, \ldots, a_m\}$ being a set of elementary connotations, $\wedge$ and $\vee$ Boolean operations, and $K_C = \{k_1, k_2, \ldots, k_n\}$ a specified set of primary Boolean combinations over A.
- (c) f is a function mapping E_C on K_C such that $f(e_i) = k_j$ iff (e_i, k_j) is a connotative expression with e_i manifesting k_j in C.
- (d) $\mathfrak{F}$ is a family of sets over E_C as defined in (18).

Having clarified to a certain extent the formal structure of a connotative system[27], I will add some remarks concerning its substantive content.

27. A connotative system as specified in (19) could probably be viewed as a particular type of what Lieb (1968, 1970) has called a communication complex. Although Lieb proposes, as far as I can see, the most elaborated formal theory of phenomena related to those discussed here, I do not specifically rely on it for the following reasons.

(i) Language varieties (*Sprachausprägungen*) are discussed by Lieb only informally; in fact, they show up only in Lieb, 1970, where they are not given a special theoretical status. Therefore, nothing particular can be gained from Lieb's theory for the problem at hand, even if the proposals made here could be construed as a reasonable extension of it.

(ii) In particular, Lieb is not concerned with the problem of how varieties are to be marked off and how the relations among them are to be theoretically reconstructed; he does not consider the notion of connotation or whatever might replace it. (In fact, he is primarily interested in reconstructing the notion of "stage" and the succession of stages in time.)

(iii) Lieb claims that there is a principled distinction between a system and a grammar of a language, where, roughly speaking, the latter is a description of a language, while the former is something different from both the language and its description, distinguished from a grammar mainly by the fact that it does not depend on any claims of a general theory of grammar. Whatever a system of a language in Lieb's sense might turn out to be, and he is fairly vague in this respect, the fact that he refuses to explain the relation between subsets of a communication complex in terms of grammatical rules underlying them deprives his theory of much of the interest it might otherwise deserve. In my view, it is precisely the explanation of language varieties in terms of alternating (systems of) grammatical rules that must be searched for. The next section is concerned with this problem.

These remarks are not meant, of course, as an evaluation of Lieb's theory in general, which would require a much more careful discussion.

Notice first of all that for $n = 1$ the connotative system accounts for the particular case of a completely homogeneous speech community with $E_C = E_1$ being the only language variety used in C, distinguished only from languages outside C by the unique connotation k_1.[28]

Second, there is still a wide range of possibilities in choosing a set of elementary connotations A compatible with the conditions imposed on the representation of (K_C, R_C) by means of $\mathfrak{A}$. In order to avoid arbitrariness, the specification of $\mathfrak{A}$ should therefore be supplemented by substantive restrictions on the choice of A, that is, by statements about possible elementary connotations. Such statements are mainly motivated by the general possibilities of social structure and their interaction with linguistic differentiation. They will concern not only the inventory A as such but also the possibilities of forming elementary Boolean combinations over A. Thus it seems to be, for example, a reasonable hypothesis that there are general limitations to form conjunctions of elementary connotations referring to regional restrictions with those related to certain levels of social stratification. Statements of this type, which can formally be expressed by conditions on the elements of A as well as on the primary Boolean combinations admitted in K_C, express general substantive properties of connotational structure and are in a sense parallel to claims concerning the system of phonological features as formulated in Jakobson and Halle (1956) and further developed in Halle and Chomsky (1968).

The most important condition to be imposed in this sense on A directly is its subdivision into a set of domains, each domain being a separate set of elementary connotations. We therefore add to (19b) the following clause:

(20) A is the union of mutually disjoint sets $A^1, A^2, \ldots, A^k$ with $A^i = \{a_1^i, a_2^i, \ldots, a_{n_k}^i\}$ for $1 \leqslant i \leqslant k$. A^i is a domain of A.

One immediate consequence of (20) should be that two elements of the same domain cannot be conjoined, as no connotatively consistent expression can manifest a connotation referring simultaneously to two concurring conditions of the same domain. Thus, no expression can consistently be formal and vulgar style at the same time. We can express this as a condition on K_C, which we take to be the set of consistent connotations, in the following way:

(21) Let x and y be disjoint subsets of the same dimension of A combined by $\wedge$, and z an arbitrary (including empty) primary Boolean combination over A. Then $x \wedge y \wedge z$ is an inconsistent connotation. No inconsistent connotation can be an element of K_C.

Thus K_C does not contain in particular elements like $a_j^i \wedge a_k^i \wedge z$. For the sake of later reference we will designate inconsistent connotations by ϕ with the con-

28. Although in most cases this situation would be merely a methodological idealization, it need not be so in principle. It might in fact be an adequate account of real speech communities in an early stage of social and economic development. (Notice in this connection that often a tribe designates itself and its language by (a derivation of) its equivalent for *man*, thus identifying the only connotation realized in C with the condition of being human.)

dition $k_j \wedge \phi = \phi$ and $k_j \vee \phi = k_j$. The union $K_C \cup \{\phi\}$ thus becomes a Boolean algebra with zero elements. Obviously, $F(\phi) = \Phi$, if we assume that E_C contains only connotatively consistent expressions. There is, by the way, a certainly not incidental similarity between domains of A and antonymous sets of semantic markers as defined in Katz (1972, p. 159).

Notice that one can reasonably look for a general characterization of the dimensions that elementary connotations can enter—as we provisionally did in the previous section—while the identification of individual elementary connotations is to a large extent dependent on the concrete historical facts of a speech community. This does not include the possibility of giving universal characterizations also for some particular elementary connotations, if the necessary prerequisites stemming from the theory of structure of society are available, just as phonological features are universally characterized on the basis of acoustic and articulatory prerequisites.

Third, several concepts can be introduced on the basis of (19) that are of interest for a theory of heterogeneity.

Let us first distinguish tentatively between language and language variety in the following way:

(22) E_j is a language of C if the following holds:
    (a) the k_j of the pertinent connotative set (E_j, k_j) is an upper boundary in K_C, that is, there is no k_i with $R_C(k_i, k_j)$:
    (b) all E_i included in E_j, that is, all connotative sets (E_i, k_i) with $R_C(k_j, k_i)$, are structurally related to E_j.

This is not, of course, a full specification of the notion of a language. It merely separates languages from other connotative sets by the condition that, one, it is not properly included in another subset in E_C, and, two, all its connotative subsets are structurally related. How the crucial notion of structural relatedness can be specified at least partially will be discussed below. According to (22), a speech community is multilingual if there is more than one upper boundary in K_C meeting the condition (b). (22) does not say anything about the intricate problem of identifying the same language spoken in different speech communities, say French in France and Canada. Obviously, structural relatedness is crucial in this respect too. There are now various ways in which the concept of variety can be construed. One possibility is to make it a relational concept:

(23) E_j is a variety of E_i in C, iff $R_C(k_i, k_j)$ for the pertinent connotative sets (E_j, k_j) and (E_i, k_i).

By this definition, a language is not a variety of any other set of expressions. One might also try to specify an absolute notion of variety. One trivial, and certainly not very interesting way would be to take all sets of $\mathcal{F}$ as varieties. More in agreement with current usage of the term would be a definition along the following lines:

(24) E_j is a variety (in C), iff $k_j \in A$ (and $k_j \in K_C$) for the pertinent connotative set (E_j, k_j).

One might furthermore add the condition of structural relatedness of the subsets
of E_j. By this definition only connotative sets bound to elementary connotations would be (proper) varieties.

Taking into account the substantive aspect of A mentioned before, one
might furthermore split up the notion of variety into dialects, styles, jargons,
etc., according to the particular substantive domain to which k_j belongs.

It goes without saying that definitions of this type are provisional suggestions to make precise the more or less vague terms currently used. They are
clearly in need of more extensive justification than I can provide here.

Finally, I will take up the problem of sequential combination of connotative
expressions. It seems to be a reasonable consequence of what has been said so
far to adopt the following convention:

(25) Let (e_1, k_i) and (e_2, k_j) be connotative expressions. The concatenation $e_1 \frown e_2$ then manifests the connotation $k_i \wedge k_j$ of the complex
connotative expression $(e_1 \; e_2, \; k_i \wedge k_j)$, if $e_1 \frown e_2$ underlies a single
utterance.

Thus for the concatenation of $(e_1, a_1 \vee a_2)$ and $(e_2, a_2 \wedge a_3)$ we get by (25) the
new connotation $(a_1 \vee a_2) \wedge (a_2 \wedge a_3)$, which reduces by the rules mentioned in
footnote 25 to $a_2 \wedge a_3$. Whether two expressions are to be considered as underlying one coherent utterance or not depends on conditions outside the scope of
the present discussion.[29] The convention (25) permits us, however, to restrict
essentially the range of E_C. Since we can derive the connotation of complex
utterances (with certain exceptions to be mentioned at the end of the paper)
from those based on sentences (or parts of sentences like "Good Lord!", etc.),
we can restrict E_C to the domain of sentences, thus limiting the range of f to the
usual scope of grammars. This greatly simplifies the task of specifying f. On the
other hand, (25) permits us to determine formally the connotative consistency
of arbitrary complex utterances, or larger texts for that matter, which is an
interesting problem in stylistics. Obviously a (complex) expression is said to be
connotatively inconsistent, if it manifests an inconsistent connotation in the
sense of (21).

7. GRAMMAR AND CONNOTATION

So far the assignment of connotations to expressions has been taken for granted.
A specification of the function f providing this assignment is of course a crucial

---

29. One condition of particular interest is this: e_1 must not be a clause introducing reported
speech, having e_2 as its complement, since "And then John asked him: Parlez-vous
Français?" certainly does not manifest the connotation "English $\wedge$ French."

task for any account of what we have called connotative competence. As I have argued above, f cannot depend on simple surface properties of expressions, but must have access to the full range of their structural properties, and it furthermore cannot be specified by indicating fixed lists of expressions. Hence f must be determined by means of the systems of grammatical rules generating the expressions in question. This leads to the following obvious procedure. First we introduce a function f' assigning connotations to the rules of grammars. Then we say that an expression e_i manifests the conjunction of just those connotations assigned by f' to the rules generating it. The assignment of connotations to rules must and can be learned, since it has a finite domain and a finite range. This knowledge controls in a sense the application of grammatical rules with respect to the conditions encoded in the connotations. We thus get a plausible picture of connotative competence, which shows that it is simultaneously a kind of knowledge, and a condition on the use of linguistic knowledge, as discussed in section 2. I will now develop this basis idea in a sequence of steps, with necessary oversimplification in many respects.

First we make available some general concepts. Presupposing that a theory of linguistic structure will provide a general scheme of a grammar G, we can define with respect to it the concepts of derivation and rule base of e_i making precise the notion of full structural characterization of e_i:

(26) For every expression $e_i \in L(G)$, where $L(G)$ is the set of expressions generated by G, there is a unique sequence of structural representations $D_i = (x_{i_1}, x_{i_2}, \ldots, x_{i_n})$ with the following properties:

(a) $x_{i_{j+1}}$ is determined by the application of a rule r_{i_j} of G to a subset of the preceding $x_{i_1}, \ldots, x_{i_j}$ in accordance with the conditions of rule application imposed on G for $1 \leqslant j < n$;

(b) D_i contains two designated elements $x_{i_s} = m_i$ and $x_{i_t} = p_i$ with $e_i = (m_i, p_i)$.

D_i is the derivation of e_i with respect to G.

(27) The sequence of rules $RB_i = (r_{i_1}, r_{i_1}, \ldots, r_{i_{n-1}})$ uniquely associated with D_i is the rule base of e_i with respect to G.

Although one might think of G as specified somehow along the lines of Chomsky (1965), supplemented by an appropriate semantic component, I have been fairly general in defining the concepts of derivation and rule base.[30] Clearly, lexical rules must be included in G and hence in the pertinent RB_i.

We will furthermore stipulate that the function $f'(r_i) = k_j$ assigns to r_i the connotation k_j, giving us the connotationally conditioned rule r_i/k_j. For reasons that will become obvious later, r_i might be an elementary rule notationally included in a rule schema with collapsed environments. In other words, in a rule

---

30. What I do not consider here is the inclusion of admissibility conditions in G. While it can easily be defined what it means to say that a rule has been applied, it is more difficult for conditions. If one were to recognize language-specific conditions within a grammar, as has been proposed several times, certain amendments would be required here and later on.

schema different environments may have different connotational conditions assigned to them. We are now ready to define the notion of connotative expression in terms of connotationally conditioned rules:

(28) (e_i, k_I) is a connotative expression with e_i manifesting k_I with respect to G and f' iff;
   (a) RB_i is the rule base of e_i with respect to G;
   (b) $f'(r_{i_j}) = k_j$ for $1 \leqslant j \leqslant n - 1$;
   (c) k_I is the primary Boolean combination obtained from $k_1 \wedge k_2 \wedge \ldots \wedge k_{n-1}$.

As the next step we have to face the problem of how to relate connotatively conditioned grammars to sets of connotative expressions and to connotative systems in general. Basically, there seem to be three possible approaches. We can account for a connotative system by an aggregate of homogeneous grammars, or by one heterogeneous grammar, or by combining somehow the first and the second approach. I will briefly discuss them one after the other.

Let us first define a homogeneous grammar in the following way:

(29) G_j is a (connotatively conditioned) homogeneous grammar iff every $e_i \in L(G_j)$ manifests the same connotation k_j with respect to G_j and f'. We will say in this case that G_j is homogeneously bound to k_j.

The most natural way to specify f' in this case is to assume that $f'(r_i) = k_j$ for all rules of G_j. Notice that $L(G_j)$ in the sense of (19) constitutes a connotative set (E_j, k_j) with the special restriction that the connotation is $k_j \wedge x$ with empty x for each $e_i \in L(G_j)$. An aggregation of two homogeneous grammars is now formed by assigning the conjunction of their respective connotations to the sentences belonging to the intersection of the generated languages. More formally:

(30) Let G_i and G_j be homogenously bound to k_i and k_j respectively. The connotatively conditioned aggregate of G_i and G_j is formed by assigning the connotation $k_i \wedge k_j$ to every $e_i \in L(G_i) \cap L(G_j)$.

The language generated by G_i may be a proper subset of that generated by G_j (or inversely). Notice in particular that if the elements of $L(G_i)$ and $L(G_j)$ manifest the connotation k_i and k_j respectively, with $k_j = k_i \vee k_m$, then the elements of their intersection manifest the connotation k_i, as $k_i \wedge (k_i \vee k_j)$ reduces to k_i. The aggregate-formation for grammars without intersecting languages trivially changes nothing in the assignment of connotations to $L(G_i)$ and $L(G_j)$. Since no claim has been made to the contrary in (30), it is possible that an expression generated by G_i as well as by G_j may have different derivations with respect to the different grammars. We will therefore say that two grammars form a strong aggregate if they provide the same D_i for every e_i generated by both of them. Obviously, aggregate formation as introduced in (30) can be extended to any finite set of grammars in a straightforward way. This then allows for an explicit formulation of the first approach mentioned above:

(31) Let $\mathcal{G}$ be a connotatively conditioned (strong) aggregate of the grammars $G_1, G_2, \ldots, G_k$.
$\mathcal{G}$ is a (strong) aggregate of homogeneous grammars for the connotative system K with (E_j, k_j) being a connotative set of K for every $k_j \in K_C$ of K iff
(a) for every G_i of $\mathcal{G}$ there is a connotative set (E_j, k_j) of K such that $L(G_i) = E_j$ and G_i is homogeneously bound to k_j;
(b) for every (E_j, k_j) of K for which there is no G_i with $L(G_i) = E_j$ by (a), there are grammars G_i and G_m in $\mathcal{G}$ such that G_i and G_m are homogeneously bound to k_i and k_m, respectively, $k_j = k_i \wedge k_m$, and $E_j = L(G_i) \cap L(G_m)$.

The idea expressed in this definition is fairly simple. Every connotative set of the connotative system is either generated directly by a (homogeneous) grammar, or else it is the intersection of two (or more) such sets. It can be proven on the basis of rather general assumptions about grammars that for every system of sets $\mathcal{F}$ that can be generated by a finite set of grammars at all there is always an aggregate of grammars which assigns to them the connotations required in K on the basis of the conventions adopted above.

The idea underlying (31) corresponds quite nicely to some of our earlier considerations. Clearly, any G_i now corresponds to a connotative set as defined in (16) and (17), the connotation to which it is bound determining the social conditions under which it is appropriately used. Subsets with more restricted connotations are specified by two (or more) grammars simultaneously. The grammars thus express directly the conventions which are applied under the conditions represented by the connotations to which they are homogenously bound. Conventions followed simultaneously are described now by grammars with overlapping output.

In spite of its plausibility, there are several objections to be leveled against this approach. By positing separate grammars for all connotative sets not formed by intersection, an aggregate of grammars cannot account explicitly for different kinds and degrees of structural similarity among the various sets generated by the different grammars. Closely related varieties of the same language must be treated in the same way as those of completely different languages. As one consequence of this, there can be a large amount of descriptive redundancy, so to speak, particularly if we consider strong aggregates, where the grammar of a subset must simply repeat in part the grammar of the pertinent superset. An aggregate of grammars hence does not give in general a plausible account of the linguistic knowledge of a member of a heterogeneous speech community. Instead of patching up these deficiencies, I will turn to the more interesting second approach.

The crucial notion here is that of a connotatively heterogeneous grammar. Let me illustrate this by means of the simplest possible case, that of a grammar which generates just two disjoint connotative sets. In other words, if G is the grammar in question, we assume that $L(G) = E_1 \cup E_2$, furthermore that $E_1 \cap E_2$ is empty, and finally that there is an f' such that every e_i of E_1 manifests k_1, while every e_i of E_2 manifests k_2, with respect to G and f'. Obviously, there must be at least one rule in the derivation D_i of every e_i of E_1 with k_1 assigned to this rule by f'. Let us call the set of these rules the k_1 part of G. Similarly there must be a k_2 part of G. Furthermore, if G is not just a composition of two completely disjoint grammars, there must be a third part of it, consisting of all those rules applicable in derivations of elements of E_1 as well as E_2. Let us assume that f' assigns the connotation $k_1 \vee k_2$ to these rules, and call them the $k_1 k_2$ part of G. It is this part which makes a heterogeneous grammar particularly interesting, since it allows us to save in part the unnecessary redundancy of aggregates of grammars mentioned above, expressing now at the same time explicitly the structural relatedness of the generated subsets. This becomes still more obvious if we define the subgrammar G_1 of G as the k_1 part plus the $k_1 k_2$ part, and similarly G_2 as the k_2 part plus the $k_1 k_2$ part. It is easily verified that $L(G_1) = E_1$ and $L(G_2) = E_2$ with E_1 and E_2 as defined above. Let me illustrate the notions discussed so far by a very simple example, which however shows at the same time that G (and hence G_1 and G_2) may have rule ordering imposed on it, and furthermore that G_1 and G_2 may differ with respect to the ordering of identical rules:

(32) Let (G, f') designate the (ordered) set of connotatively conditioned rules
$(r_1/k_1 \vee k_2, r_2/k_1, r_3/k_2, r_4/k_1 \vee k_2, r_3/k_1, r_5/k_1 \vee k_2)$
then $G_1 = (r_1, r_2, r_4, r_3, r_5)$
and $G_2 = (r_1, r_3, r_4, r_5)$

In order to make the example work in the intended sense, we must of course assume that there is no derivation of G whose rule base consists only of r_1 and/or r_4 and/or r_5. Otherwise, G would generate a third subset E_3 with expressions manifesting the connotation $k_1 \vee k_2$, and hence contain a third subgrammar G_3 consisting of the $k_1 k_2$ part only. Whether G of (32) contains this third subgrammar depends on the conditions of rule application associated with G and/or on the content of the rules, which I cannot specify here in detail.

On the background of these informal considerations we will define the notion of a heterogeneous grammar more generally in the following way:

(33) G is a connotatively conditioned heterogeneous grammar with respect to f' and a consistent set of connotations K iff for the triple (G, f', K) the following holds:
(a) for every $e_i \in L(G)$ there is a unique $k_j \in K$ such that (e_i, k_j) is a connotative expression with respect to G and f', that is, $f(e_i) = k_j$ with respect to G and f';

(b) the function f thus determined induces a homomorphism from K into the set of subsets of $L(G)$ according to the definition of F given in (16) above.

The idea underlying this definition is intuitively this. Given an assignment of connotations to the rules of G and the definition of manifestation of connotations based on it as in (28), we get a set of connotations K manifested by the various expressions of $L(G)$. If we apply the function F defined in (16) above, the output of G automatically subdivides into subsets (E_j, k_j) on the basis of the internal structure of the elements of K. The resulting family of sets over $L(G)$ is the connotational structure of $L(G)$ with respect to f' and K. The crucial point now is that the connotative sets generated in this way are determined by pertinent subgrammars of G in the way illustrated fragmentarily in (32). In other words, there is a subgrammar G_i of G with $L(G_i) = E_j$ for every connotative set (E_j, k_j), and G_i is determined by general conditions on the connotations assigned the rules of G. The details of these conditions are somewhat complicated, and they depend, as shown already by means of (32), on the content of the rules and the conditions on rule application. With a certain oversimplification, however, the general principle is this: A rule conditioned by the connotation k_j is valid under the (social) condition represented by k_j; it is valid for the conditions represented by k_i and k_j with these conditions obtaining simultaneously, if its connotation is $k_i \wedge k_j$; and it is valid for either the conditions represented by k_i or those represented by k_j if its connotation is $k_i \vee k_j$. In other words, every (complex) condition represented by a k_j selects a special subgrammar G_i out of G representing the convention appropriately followed under that condition. To speak metaphorically, the heterogeneous grammar G resembles an organ with the subgrammars G_i selected by the k_j being the organ stops, the registers set by the k_j (whereas, to stretch the analogy even further, an aggregate of grammars resembles a set of overlapping separate instruments). The resulting subgrammars are formed mainly by a partition of the lexicon of G if the subsets are primarily distinguished by their respective vocabulary, as in the case of professional jargons; they consist of sometimes very intricate sequences of selected phonological, morphological, or syntactic rules in the case of social and regional dialects. What is most important, however, is that G and f' together completely control the resulting connotative sets. Hence every change either in G or in the assignment function f' of a heterogeneous grammar G leads to a change in the resulting family of connotative sets.

We can now complete the exposition of the second approach by the following definition:

(34) G_C is a connotatively conditioned heterogeneous grammar of the connotative system K iff there is a triple (G, f', K) as defined in (32) with the following condition:
(a) $G = G_C$ and $L(G_C) = E_C$ of K;
(b) $K = K_C$ of K.

MANFRED BIERWISCH

The overall grammar G_C thus defined retains the advantage of the corresponding aggregate of grammars, while overcoming some of its inadequacies. In particular it is possible to express in G_C the structural relationship between the various connotative sets in E_C by means of greater economy of the resulting grammar. Roughly speaking, two varieties are the more related, the more rules of G_C are valid for both, these rules being marked by the appropriate disjunctive connotation. Nevertheless, G_C is by no means a simple conflation of the corresponding aggregate of grammars into one overall grammar, arrived at just by erasing repeated rules. Rather a farreaching reorganization may be required, as already shown by trivial examples like (32). It is easy to see furthermore that fairly different grammars G_C (all constructed according to the same general scheme of possible grammars) can meet the conditions of (34) with respect to a given connotative system. This remark leads to an important general point.

As is well known from the study of homogeneous grammars, a grammar G uniquely determines its language $L(G)$, while a language L may have different grammars, even those accounting for the same range of structural properties of L. Thus, as Chomsky (1965) has shown with great clarity, an explanatory theory of linguistic structure must provide not only a general scheme of possible grammars, but also a way to select the correct or optimal grammar with respect to a given set of linguistic data. This goal can be approached in two ways: first, by enriching the substantive conditions imposed on descriptively adequate grammars, thereby restricting the class of possible grammars in general; and second, by specifying an evaluation criterion that selects the highest valued grammar from a set of otherwise equivalent candidates. The two approaches are not mutually exclusive alternatives, and both are intimately connected to empirical insights into the basic principles of natural language.

These considerations carry over directly to the problem of specifying possible heterogeneous grammars. Notice that we have construed G_C as a grammar in the strict sense of linguistic theory. The only difference in constructing and evaluating a heterogeneous rather than a homogeneous grammar is that the former is based on additional data concerning the connotative aspect of language and the heterogeneity induced by it. Here we are facing the question raised in section 2, whether problems of heterogeneity can affect the theory of linguistic structure. It is possible, though by no means clear in advance, that the conditions selecting an optimal homogeneous grammar remain unchanged if an optimal heterogeneous grammar is at issue.[31] It would be more than premature to make any serious claims in this respect at the present stage of development.

---

31. Consider the principle of rule ordering as an example. As provisionally indicated in (32), reconstructing different external rule ordering in a heterogeneous grammar forces one to repeat the same rule at two different places with different connotations assigned to it. It remains to be seen whether the significant generalizations achieved by means of explicit as opposed to only implicit rule ordering justify a repetition of rules in a heterogeneous grammar.

The problem of determining the optimal heterogeneous grammar is connected to a major flaw in the second approach discussed so far. According to the underlying assumptions, G_C must generate all kinds of varieties, even completely unrelated sets of expressions of E_C, particularly if C is a multilingual speech community. Thus we would have, e.g., English and French generated by one unified grammar for bilingual areas of Canada. Although such an account might provide interesting insights in certain cases of linguistic interference, creolization, and so on, it would be unjustified as a general principle. This then leads to the third approach.

The ingredients of this variant have already been developed. It differs from the foregoing approach only by admitting the possibility of accounting for a connotative system by a set of heterogeneous grammars instead of only one overall grammar. Intuitively, we will assume that E_C is divided on the basis of purely structural conditions into two or more disjoint subsets, which in themselves may be connotationally heterogeneous. Each of these subsets will then be accounted for by one heterogeneous grammar in the sense of (33), these grammers together forming a (trivial) aggregate of heterogeneous grammars specifying the total connotative system. Let the triple $(\mathcal{G}, f', K_C)$ represent such as aggregate of heterogeneous grammars for the connotative system K. Its explicit definition is straightforward, given the above definition of $\mathcal{G}$ and (G, f', K). Hence I will omit it here. The crucial problem now is that of determining the conditions for splitting up the overall grammar G_C posited by (33) into well-motivated separate grammars forming the aggregate $\mathcal{G}$. This problem is obviously connected to that of specifying the notion of structural relatedness relied upon in the definition (22) of language as opposed to variety. I strongly submit that its solution finally depends on the specification of conditions selecting optimal (heterogeneous) grammars, as discussed above. Hence the separation of grammars for languages, dialects, and other varieties can be motivated only insofar as we are able to incorporate substantive insights into the pertinent theoretical framework.

It should be mentioned in this respect that empirical research on which the necessary generalizations concerning the principles of linguistic heterogeneity can be based has already begun. Becker (1967), presenting an extensive fragment of the phonological component of a heterogeneous grammar for three German dialects, and Labov (1972) and Klima (1964), presenting small but revealing fragments of the syntactic component of heterogeneous grammars for different dialects of English, give important examples. The general assumptions implicit in such work are precisely those leading to the notion of a heterogeneous grammar as defined above.[32]

Let us assume now for the sake of argument that there is a set of conditions selecting a certain $(\mathcal{G}, f', K_C)$ as the optimal account for the data of a given

32. Another aspect of the penetrating study of Klima (1964) will be taken up in the next section.

speech community C. According to all previous assumptions, this system would represent the heterogeneous competence, i.e., the linguistic plus the connotative competence, of an idealized speaker-hearer of the linguistically heterogeneous speech community C. Notice, however, that this involves an idealization of a particular sort. It would be the competence of a kind of superego of C, that is, of a speaker who knows completely all the varieties used in C. As pointed out repeatedly, this knowledge need not exist in any one of the members of C, and we may wonder whether it is more of an artifact than an idealization. In any case, it is worthwhile to consider also another, weaker idealization characterizing the objective of a theory of heterogeneity, the competence of particular though still idealized (in the sense of footnote 6) speaker-hearers in a heterogeneous speech community. It might turn out that the competence of particular speakers in this sense is always a well-defined, proper substructure of the overall aggregate $(\mathcal{G}, f', K_C)$. This, if true, would be an important empirical finding. In this case no additional theoretical apparatus would be required. There are, however, reasonable alternatives to be explored, one of which I will take up in the next section.

8. EXTENSION RULES

So far we have reduced the function f assigning connotations to expressions to f' assigning connotations to rules. We have furthermore stated certain general conditions that f' must meet with respect to aggregates and heterogeneous grammars. In this section I consider one way to specify more detailed properties of f'. More specifically, I will indicate how f' can be constructed, at least in part, for a given heterogeneous grammar. This will be done in connection with what might be called a local viewpoint of heterogeneity as opposed to the global view followed above.

What I have in mind is the following. In the previous section we ended up with the notion of an optimal (aggregate of) heterogeneous grammar(s) for a given connotative system. Let us call the orientation toward this system the global view. It already implies the possibility that the subgrammar generating a certain variety within the heterogeneous grammar may differ from an optimal grammar of the same variety taken in isolation. We may go now one step further and consider the possibility that there are different optimal heterogeneous grammars for the same (part of a) heterogeneous system, depending on what is taken as the basic, or initial, variety. This orientation is what is meant by the term 'local viewpoint'. To give a concrete example, consider two speakers with full mastery of both Standard English and Cockney, but one starting with Cockney incorporating Standard English later on, the other starting with Standard English incorporating Cockney. Do both speakers end up with the same (relative or local) optimal grammar? The example may be artificial, the problem certainly not.

In fact, Klima (1964) studied a very similar problem by means of a fairly detailed and realistic example. He compares four varieties of English differing with respect to surface case marking of pronouns. Starting with Standard English he describes each of the other varieties once by an optimal adaptation of the standard grammar, once by an independent optimal grammar which would result if the variety were not acquired as an extension of previous knowledge.[33] The difference between the optimal adaption and the optimal isolated grammar, according to Klima's analysis, concerns the content of certain rules as well as their relative ordering.

In order to clarify our local view of heterogeneity we need a more precise concept of an extended grammar G' specified with respect to a certain grammar G. An extended grammar in turn will be constructed by means of extension rules, to which connotations are assigned in a well defined way.

The term 'extension rule' was introduced, to the best of my knowledge, by Klima (1964). However, a large variety of facts discussed mainly in connection with language change is more or less directly related to it, even if the term is not applied. Informally, an extension rule in a certain obvious sense is an ordinary grammatical rule inserted in a given grammar G such that the resulting grammar G' specifies a language L' different from $L(G)$. Given this fairly simple idea of extending a grammar G to a modified grammar G', many derived notions can be considered. Thus, assuming that G is the optimal grammar of L (in the sense discussed above), G' may or may not be the optimal grammar of L'. If it is not, it may still be the optimal extended grammar with respect to G, given certain conditions evaluating possible extensions. Considering furthermore repeated extensions, we get an extended grammar G'' specifying another related language L''. G'' can now be an optimal extended grammar with respect to G or G' or even with respect to the optimal grammar of L', if that is different from G'. These and other related concepts, if made precise and motivated by pertinent empirical considerations, will essentially contribute to a more detailed account of the notion of structural relatedness mentioned above.[34]

---

33. Actually, what Klima does is a little bit different. He construes the four varieties as a sequence of extensions from L_1 to L_2 to L_3 to L_4, not as extensions of the same initial variety L_1. He shows in particular that there is an optimal ordering of the stepwise extension determined by internal structural properties of the varieties in question. I am not concerned here with this additional problem, although it has some bearing on the question of what the resulting adaptation would be in the various possible combinations of an original dialect and the extensions.

34. It might be noted in passing that problems of extending and adapting a grammar must finally be placed in a much wider context, including not only problems of coexistent language varieties and language change, but also crucial topics of language acquisition. These wider perspectives are, of course, outside the scope of the present paper.

Extension rules and extended grammars as considered so far involve the transition from one set of expressions L to another set L' sharing a larger or smaller subset of identical expressions.[35] We are interested however in a kind of extension, where G' generates both L and L', assigning different connotations to the expressions according to their membership in L and/or L'. Klima's concept of extension rule has been reconstructued in precisely this sense by Butters (1971). He contrasts extension rules relating sentences of one dialect to the grammar of another to the mechanism accounting for deviant utterances.

In terms of connotative sets we can characterize the problem as follows. If (E_1, k_1) and (E_2, k_2) are two connotative sets, we have considered so far the situation $L(G) = E_1$ and $L(G') = E_2$ and G' is an (optimal) extended grammar of E_2 with respect to G. We now want a heterogeneous grammar that generates E_1 as well as E_2 and assigns to them moreover the appropriate connotations. Before stating this more generally, let us first clarify what the appropriate connotations should be.

For the sake of argument, we will assume that E_1 and E_2 are both connotatively homogeneous.[36] We will furthermore assume that G' is formed from G by adding only one extension rule, say r_e. The relation between the grammars and their respective languages can then be represented by the following diagram:

(35)

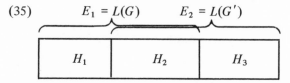

$$E_1 = L(G) \qquad E_2 = L(G')$$

| H_1 | H_2 | H_3 |

Clearly, H_3 must consist of all those expressions whose rule base contains at least one occurrence of r_e. The subsets H_1 and H_2 on the other hand, consist of all expressions whose rule base does not contain r_e, the crucial difference being that the expressions of H_1 would be in the scope of r_e, while those of H_2 are not. The latter distinction can be made precise in the following way. Every grammatical rule r can be represented as an ordered pair (SD, SC) of a structural description and a structural change. An expression e_i is in the scope of r if and only if its dervation D_1 contains an x_j that meets the structural description of r. In other words, both H_1 and H_2 contain expressions that do not undergo in their derivation the SC of r_e: however, only the expressions of H_1 somewhere in their derivation meet the structural description of r_e. Notice that the inter-

35. Notice that at least theoretically L and L' can be completely disjoint, even if G' is formed from G by only one extension rule. Suppose, for instance, that this rule would be an unconditioned nasalization of vowels. If we assume that every $e_i \in L(G)$ has at least one vowel, then L and L' would have no element in common.

36. This can be done without loss of generality. By definition, a connotative set (E_j, k_j) consists of all and only the expressions with the connotation $k_j \wedge x$ with arbitrary x. Hence we need only require that x is left unchanged for any expression of the sets we are considering. We will see that this requirement can easily be met.

section H_2 of E_1 and E_2 may be empty. In this case every expression of E_1 and E_2 is in the range of r_e.

Consider now the connotation that must be assigned to the elements of H_1, H_2, and H_3, respectively. Clearly, the elements of H_2 cannot have any formal property according to which they manifest either k_1 or k_2 distinctively. In other words, they manifest the connotation $k_1 \vee k_2$. The elements of H_3, characterized by the application of r_e, manifest the connotation k_2, whereas the elements of H_1, characterized by the relevant nonapplication of r_e, manifest k_1.

According to these considerations, the appropriate assignment of connotations in $E_1 \cup E_2$ is as follows: e_i manifests k_1 iff it is an element of $E_1 = E_2$; it manifests k_2 iff it is an element of $E_2 = E_1$; it manifests $k_1 \vee k_2$ otherwise. It is easily verified that this assignment is in accordance with the definition of connotative sets given above.

What has been said with respect to an extension rule added to G in order to form G' applies *mutatis mutandis* also to a G' formed from G by eliminating a rule of G. Since moreover one way to represent reordered rules of G in a derived grammar G' is repetition of the same rule on a different place in G', as mentioned above, all relevant types of rule change can be accounted for at least in principle in the way outlined so far. Admitting finally more than one change in G in order to yield G' we now arrive at the following general characterization:

(36) G_{ij} is an (optimal) heterogeneous extended grammar of $E_i \cup E_j$ with respect to G_i iff
(a) $L(G_i) = E_i$ and $L(G_{ij}) = E_i \cup E_j$;
(b) $f(e_i) = k_i$ iff $e_i \in E_i = E_j$;
(c) $f(e_i) = k_j$ iff $e_i \in E_j = E_i$;
(d) $f(e_i) = k_i \vee k_j$ otherwise;
(e) $P = (r_{e_1} \cdots \cdots r_{e_n})$ is a sequence of rules in G_{ij} which, if added to or deleted from G_i, yield a grammar G_j with $L(G_j) = E_j$.
(P is the optimal sequence meeting condition (e).)

Notice that G_{ij} is not necessarily identical to G_{ji} taken as a heterogeneous extension from an optimal grammar of E_j to an optimal extended grammar of $E_i \cup E_j$. As an illustration, think of optimal grammars of E_i and E_j having different underlying phonological representations for the same lexical entries. The necessary phonological extension rules would then be different in G_{ij} and G_{ji}.

In order to complete the rough account of heterogeneous extended grammars, we must specify the function f' assigning connotations to the rules of G_{ij}. By assumption, we already know f' for G_i, the grammar to be extended. On this basis, we can specify the assignments as follows:

(37) Let P be the sequence of rules in G_{ij} extending G_i to G_j. Then for $r_e \in P$
(a) $f'(r_e) = k_j$ for every r_e added to G_i to yield G_j;

MANFRED BIERWISCH

(b) $f'(r_e) = k_j$ for every r_e dropped from G_i to yield G_j;

(c) $f'(r_e) = k_i \vee k_j$ otherwise.

If E_i is already connotatively heterogeneous, we retain this heterogeneity if k_i is replaced in (b) and (c) by the value of $f'(r_e)$ in G_i. Every heterogeneity already present in G_i then carries over to G_{ij}. This assignment as well as the definition (36) can be extended from pairs to arbitrary sets of grammars and may finally be relativized to the connotative system, to which the sets of expressions belong. I will not go into these details.

We still have another gap to fill, however. We have not yet determined how expressions of H_1 in the example above receive their connotation, or more generally, what it means for an expression to be in the range of a rule which does not apply. As can be seen from (37a), the rule responsible for the delimitation of H_1 receives the connotation k_2, which is manifested as desired by the expressions of H_3. Expressions in H_1, however, must manifest k_1, as argued above. The consequence to be drawn from this situation is obvious. The increment of a rule whose structural description is met, but whose structural change does not apply, should be the complement of the connotation assigned to that rule. In our example the complement is simply k_1. A more general solution requires a formal specification of the complement c/k_i of a connotation k_i. This will be done on the basis of the elementary connotations and the domains to which they belong in the following way:

(38) Let $A^i = \{a_1^i, a_2^i \cdots a_n^i\}$ be a domain in the set A of elementary connotations, then $c/a_j^i = (a_1^i \vee \cdots \vee a_{j-1}^i \vee a_{j+1}^i \vee \cdots \vee a_n^i)$ for $1 \leqslant j \leqslant n$.

The operator $c/$ thus defined corresponds closely to logical negation. More precisely, it extends the Boolean algebra $\mathfrak{A}$ to an algebra with (domain restricted) complementation.[37] Since every k_j is by definition a primary Boolean combination of elementary connotations, the definition of $c/$ extends immediately to the full set of possible connotations.[38] Having thus explained the complement

37. The operator $c/$ is the direct analogue of the antonymy operator defined in Katz (1972, p. 160) for antonymous n-tuples of semantic markers. Given the analogy between antonymous n-tuples and domains of connotators mentioned earlier, this is a natural consequence.

38. Actually, we must define the interaction of $c/$ with the operations already introduced. This is done in the usual way by de Morgan's laws: we add the following to the axioms in footnote 25:

$(\vee)$ $c/(x \wedge y) = c/x \vee c/y$

This (and its analogue with $\wedge$ and $\vee$ exchanged) together with (38) allows one to eliminate $c/$ from every Boolean combination, and we will therefore require that primary Boolean combinations do not contain $c/$.

Notice in this connection that by condition (21) for a_j^i and a_k^i from the same domain $a_j^i \wedge a_k^i = \phi$. Thus if, e.g. $A^1 = \{a_1, a_2, a_3\}$ we get the following reduction for $c/(a_1 \vee a_2)$:
$c/a_1 \wedge c/a_2 = (a_2 \vee a_3) \vee (a_1 \vee a_3) = (a_2 \wedge a_1) \vee a_3 = \phi \vee a_3 = a_3$.

of k_j for arbitrary connotations, we can complete our account of the effect produced by connotatively conditioned rules. The connotative effect of an applied rule has been defined in (28). We must now add the effect of a rule which does not apply although its structural description is met. Given (28), we adopt the following extension of it:

(39) Let $D_i = (x_1, x_2 \cdots\cdots x_n)$ be the derivation of e_i with respect to G. For every connotationally conditioned rule r_j/k_e such that x_i meets the structural description of r_j and r_j is not the ith element of the rule base RB_i of e_i, the connotative expression (e_i, k_i) defined in (28) is changed to (e_i, k_p) with k_p being the primary Boolean combination obtained from $k_1 \wedge c/k_e$.

Instead of running through further technical details showing that the adopted conventions produce in fact the desired result, I will briefly comment on their intuitive meaning.

Notice first that if G were a homogeneous grammar then the situation described in (39), i.e., nonapplication of a pertinent rule, would result in a violation. In a heterogeneous grammar the result is different. The expression in question is not marked as ungrammatical, but excluded from the appropriate connotative set, i.e., from that variety for which the rule in question is responsible.[39] For a concrete example, consider Klima's L_3, that variety of English which has case marking for pronouns like "That is her," "It was him," etc. If we take it in isolation, that is as output of a homogeneous grammar, then an expression like "It was he" would simply be a violation. In the context of a heterogeneous grammar, the same expression is marked as non-L_3 and ends up as Standard English.

These considerations also show that (39) must be restricted to obligatory rules. If a rule r_i/k_i of a heterogeneous grammar is optional, its nonapplication to an expression e_i within its range does not say anything with respect to the connotation manifested by e_i. Thus, negative concord, for example, is an optional rule with varying contexts for certain English dialects (see Labov (1972) for details). If it applies, the connotation of the resulting expression is accordingly specified. If it does not apply, the connotation is left open, at least with respect to this particular property.

More generally we may note that a given variety is not only characterized by those rules which specifically apply to its expressions, but also by rules of other varieties which are typically avoided. In other words, if placed in a heterogeneous context, the rules constituting a specific convention may have a two-sided function. Their application affirms that the convention is followed; their (relevant) nonapplication demonstrates that the convention is avoided.

39. In fact, the result of not applying a relevant rule as defined in (39) for a connotatively conditioned grammar is the analogue of rule violation as treated in Lakoff (1970). Notice that in a connotatively homogeneous grammar the nonapplication of only one rule is sufficient to get $k_i \wedge c/k_i = \phi$, i.e., a (connotatively) inconsistent expression.

As an interesting consequence of these considerations, notice that a connotative set of expressions may change if the heterogeneous grammar by which it is generated (together with other sets, of course) is modified with respect to the connotations of its rules. In other words, a language variety may change if only the connotation, but not necessarily the content, of the rules in a heterogeneous grammar is modified. This seems to me a fairly interesting explication of one part of the mechanism of language change. In fact, one possible step in language change is the exclusion of a rule from the conditions of communication to which it originally pertained, and its eventual relegation to different communicative conditions.

Let us finally return to the distinction of the local and global view of heterogeneity. We have outlined the notion of a heterogeneous extended grammar. It is based on a stepwise incorporation of related varieties into one heterogeneous grammar. For each step of this kind the resulting change in the connotations assigned to grammatical rules is defined. It remains to be seen whether an optimal extended heterogeneous grammar can finally differ from an optimal heterogeneous grammar in general, i.e., whether different speakers may come up with different grammars for the same set of varieties.

9. CONCLUDING REMARKS

I have tried to show that the widespread problems of linguistic heterogeneity can be dealt with in a sufficiently precise framework that can be construed as a natural complement to, or extension of, the theory of linguistic structure developed on the basis of homogeneous languages. The concept of connotation or some equivalent of it seems to be an indispensable factor of such a framework. The formal apparatus I have proposed to make that concept precise, and to relate it to social conditions of communication on the one hand and to properties of heterogeneous linguistic systems on the other, is not an achievement in itself. Its relevance completely depends on the degree to which it can be related to existing empirical insights, providing them with a wider perspective, and on further empirical results to which it eventually may contribute. The formal aspect of the proposed framework nevertheless deserves some interest. It is certainly not an accident that Boolean conditions on the use of expression and on grammatical rules underlying them are a natural way to represent the relevant features of a wide variety of problems.

I should finally point out certain serious limits of the approach developed here. The concept of connotation has been introduced to explicate the type of knowledge that determines the use of expressions on the basis of their grammatical form with respect to the social conditions of communication. The knowledge involved has been related to grammatical rules in terms of connotational conditions. It is obvious, however, that conditions on the use of expressions in the sense developed here should include phenomena like frequency distribution of specific vocabulary, characteristic limits in syntactic complexity, inclination toward applying (or avoiding) certain optional rules, say, of phonetic reduction, etc. Colloquial English, for example, is characterized not only by certain syntactic and phonological rules underlying its utterances, but also by restrictions on syntactic complexity, frequency of certain idioms and stereotypes, etc. The common denominator of all the phenomena just mentioned is that of frequency distribution, or probability of rule application, for that matter. These phenomena cannot be explained in terms of grammatical rules alone. They cannot even be restricted to the domain of sentences. Syntactic complexity or use of characteristic vocabulary is not a property of sentences but of sets of sentences, or texts. Whether the account of connotation proposed here can finally be extended to include frequency phenomena insofar as they are a consequence of conditions on communication is unclear to me. But even if another approach would be necessary to deal with that aspect, heterogeneity in the sense discussed here remains an interesting topic on its own.

REFERENCES

Becker, D. A. 1967. *Generative Phonology and Dialect Study: An Investigation of Three Modern German Dialects.* Unpublished Ph.D. dissertation, University of Texas.

Bierwisch, M., and F. Kiefer. 1970. "Remarks on Definition in Natural Language." In *Studies in Syntax and Semantics*, F. Kiefer, ed. Reidel.

Bloomfield, L. 1933. *Language.* Holt.

Bühler, K. 1934. *Sprachtheorie.* Gustav Fischer.

Butters, R. R. 1971. Dialect Variants and Linguistic Deviance, *Foundations of Language* 7: 239–254.

Chomsky, N. 1965. *Aspects of the Theory of Syntax.* M.I.T. Press.

Chomsky, N., and M. Halle. 1968. *The Sound Pattern of English.* Harper and Row.

Gregory, M. 1967. "Aspects of Varieties Differentiation." *Journal of Linguistics* 3: 177–198.

Hjelmslev, L. 1953. *Prolegomena to a Theory of Language.* Indiana University Publications in Anthropology and Linguistics.

Jakobson, R., and M. Halle. 1956. *Fundamentals of Language.* Mouton.

Katz, J. J. 1972. *Semantic Theory.* Harper and Row.

Klima, E. S. 1964. Relatedness between Grammatical Systems. *Language* 40: 1–20.

Labov, W. 1972. Negative Attraction and Negative Concord in English Grammar. *Language* 48: 773–818.

Lakoff, G. 1970. *Irregularity in Syntax.* Holt, Rinehart and Winston.

Lewis, D. K. 1969. *Convention: A Philosophical Study.* Harvard University Press.

—— 1972. "General Semantics." In *Semantics of Natural Language*, D. Davidson and G. Harman, eds. Reidel.

Lieb, H. H. 1968. *Communication Complexes and Their Stages*. Mouton.

—— 1970. *Sprachstadium und Sprachsystem*. W. Kohlhammer.

Osgood, C. E., G. J. Suci, and P. H. Tannenbaum. 1957. *The Measurement of Meaning*. University of Illinois Press.

Schnelle, H. 1973. *Sprachphilosophie und Linguistik*. Rowohlt.

Searle, J. R. 1969. *Speech Acts*. Cambridge University Press.

Serebrennikov, B. A. 1970. *Obščee Jazikoznanie*. Izdatel'stvo 'Nauka'.

Logical Form
and Implicature

ROBERT M. HARNISH

In another work (1972, Chap. I), I presented the doctrine of logical form as a program committing one, at least in part, to representing those features of a sentence that play an essential role in entailments. Of course the notion of entailment, as well as its analysis, is not uncontroversial. However, it seems fairly central to the notion of entailment that if a sentence S entails a sentence S', then S' would, in virtue of its meaning,[1] have to be true if S were true (Massey, 1970, p. 3). If this is even in part the province of a theory of logical form, then such a theory will, in the long run, be affected by the correctness of proposals as to the presence or absence of entailments between sentences in the language to which that theory of logical form applies.

In this paper I investigate some proposals that bear directly on the issue of the logical form of certain kinds of sentences in English by way of their claim (or assumption) that a relation of entailment does or does not hold between certain kinds of sentences. In one case I want to argue that a relation of implication, not entailment, holds. In another group of cases I want to argue that entailment, not presupposition, holds.

---

1. This clause cannot be dropped on pain of allowing statements true by 'physical necessity' to be sufficient for entailment.

Source: This article appears for the first time in this volume. The main parts of this essay were written in 1969 and slightly revised and expanded as Chapter III of my thesis. This version is essentially that of my thesis, with minor revision. I have held off publishing these thoughts on Grice until he released at least some of his own material. I want to thank Kent Bach, Sylvain Bromberger, Noam Chomsky, Jerry Fodor, Bruce Fraser, Paul Grice, Jerrold J. Katz, and Judith Jarvis Thomson for the many helpful discussions I have had on the topics of this paper. Needless to say, not everyone agrees with everything I say.

CONJUNCTION REDUCTION: THE PROBLEM

'Tom and William arrived' does not mean the same as 'Tom arrived and William arrived'; for the first suggests 'together' and the second an order of arrival.

Strawson (1952, p. 80)

If I can call the same object red and green with equal right, it is a sure sign that the object named is not what really has the green colour, for that we must get a surface which is green only.

Frege (1884, § 22)

It has been known for a long time that there are certain verbs for which the derivation of a sentence with conjoined subjects from conjoined sentences is implausible (Strawson, 1952, p. 79; Lakoff and Peters, 1969). Sentence (1) is not derived from (2):

(1) John and Bill met.[2]
(2) John met and Bill met.

because the conjoined simple sentences 'John met' and 'Bill met' are not well formed. However, along with such examples are those of another sort that require a slightly different argument, and it is on these examples that I want to focus my attention. The cases divide into at least two classes, verbs and adjectives, but I think it will be obvious that the same phenomena is illustrated by both classes.

Verbs

It is sometimes claimed that (3) has problems in its derivation analogous to the proposed derivation of (1) from (2):

(3) Russell and Whitehead wrote *Principia*.

On the standard account, (3) would come from (4i) and (4ii):

(4) (i) Russell wrote *Principia*.
(ii) Whitehead wrote *Principia*.

The argument against deriving (3) from (4) goes as follows:

(5) (i) Sentence (4i) is false.
(ii) Sentence (4ii) is false.
(iii) Therefore, sentence (4) is false.
(iv) Two sentences with the same meaning cannot have different truth values at the same time with the same referents.

2. Displayed sentences are to be interpreted in the usual manner. Where necessary I will use corners.

(v) Since (3) is true and (4) is false they cannot have the same meaning.

(vi) Transformations do not change meaning.

(vii) Therefore (3) cannot be derived from (4).

Clearly, there are a number of places at which one could challenge this argument, but I want to challenge steps (5i) and (5ii). That is, I want to deny that (4i) and (4ii) are false.

The first thing to ask is why one might think that (4i) and (4ii) are false. Although I have no proof, I think the reason is as follows. If someone else asks

(6) Who wrote *Principia*?

and someone answers,

(7) Russell and Whitehead wrote *Principia*.

it is claimed that (7) *entails*

(8) Russell and Whitehead wrote *Principia* together.

If someone asks (6) and someone answers,

(9) Russell wrote *Principia*.

then (9) is also taken to *entail* that

(10) Russell wrote *Principia* alone.

However, this reading of (9) is inconsistent with the favored reading of (7), and since the favored reading of (7) is deemed true, (9) must be false.

The argument as stated turns on (7) entailing (8) and (9) entailing (10). Since I want to challenge the claim that the correct relation both between (7) and (8) and between (9) and (10) is entailment, we need some term for the whole family of relations that hold between sentences of these types—as well as perhaps between other things. For this I (hesitantly) settle on 'implies' and its cognates ('implication') mainly because it has in the philosophical literature the proper ambiguity. It has been used (by Russell) to mean 'entail' and it has been used by others to mean 'suggest,' 'indicate', etc. I will use IMPLICATION for this generic relation, reserving 'Implication' for a more specific class of IMPLICATIONS which exclude entailments. I call a person who maintains that the relation of IMPLICATION in question is entailment a 'strong theorist'.[3] To break the strong theorist's argument we need only establish (11):

(11) Either (7) does not entail (8), or (9) does not entail (10).

In the end, I will try to establish (11).

---

3. I borrow the term from Grice (1967), though I am not sure he would agree with its application here.

As a first step in this direction, we should attempt to isolate what part of sentences (7) and (9) support the purported entailments. Clearly, the subject expressions here play no favored role. It must then be all or part of the predicate expressions that support the purported entailments. We call IMPLICATIONS of the sort alleged between (7) and (8) 'together-IMPLICATIONS' and those between (9) and (10) 'alone-IMPLICATIONS'. How are we to understand (A) and (B)?

(A) A ϕ-ed C alone.

(B) A and B ϕ-ed C together.

As it stands, (A) is multiply ambiguous[4] for most substitution instances of ' ϕ '. Consider the instance: ' A moved that table alone'. We do not want to take it that *that* table was the only thing he moved (ever) or even on some occasion. Nor do we want to take it that A was the only person ever to move that table. Rather we take it as

(A') A alone ϕ-ed C.

on the occasion in question. This reading is similar to

(A'') A ϕ-ed C by himself.

But this is still ambiguous. Here we do not mean 'by himself' in the sense in which one may want to 'be by himself' for a while. We want to read (A'') as either

(A''') (i) A ϕ-ed C by himself.   (not jointly with anyone)
       (ii) A ϕ-ed C by himself.   (without anyone else's help)

I will not distinguish between (A'''i) and (A'''ii) here, as either of these will do as the sense I want for (A). It is very hard to distinguish a joint enterprise from one person's enterprise aided by another.[5] As for (B), most instances of this also are ambiguous. However, I do not want to consider the reading of (B) as in: A and B added the numbers together—that is, A and B added together the numbers. Rather, I want it in the sense of

(B') A and B together ϕ-ed C.

But here again I do not want it to be understood as simple concurrence. It is not that they each ϕ-ed *at the same time*. If that was so, there would be two ϕ-ings at some time. But in the sense I want, there was only one ϕ-ing—and A and B

4. These remarks are the result of a very helpful discussion of these cases with Judith Jarvis Thomson.

5. By far the most interesting and compelling discussion of these matters I have seen is in Ware. As far as I can tell, Ware's study reinforces my belief in the necessity of drawing the distinctions mentioned.

were both doing it.[6] Unfortunately, this is not too helpful since I do not know the principle for counting most acts. I want to say that for *A* and *B* to travel together (to *C*), it is not sufficient that they both be traveling to *C* at the same time. Nor even on the same vehicle. In some sense they must be intending to spend most of their time together *while* traveling to *C*. At the moment I cannot make this more precise.

Even though it is the predicate that supports the IMPLICATION there are a number of differences among predicates, as can be illustrated with some examples. In testing one's intuition here it is important to keep a number of things in mind. First, it must be remembered that we are trying to discover the contribution of the predicate expressions as abstracted from all *particular* contexts of utterance. Second, that it takes place in a communication situation. Imagine, then, what I shall call the 'minimal context': where someone asks 'who ϕ-ed?' with no stage setting and the answer is an instance of one of the schemata that follows. If this is not observed, it is easy to construct situations when the IMPLICATIONS of all of these forms vary wildly. Where the schematic letter '*C*' appears in a predicate, it is to stand in for some noun phrase that identifies a particular token of the type appropriate to the verb. For example, $\ulcorner A$ and *B* read $C\urcorner$ could be $\ulcorner A$ and *B* read *War and Peace*.$\urcorner$ Third, the cases often break down into two groups that I have not distinguished. For instance, with $\ulcorner A$ and *B* remembered $C\urcorner$ as opposed to $\ulcorner A$ and *B* read $C\urcorner$ it is not possible for logical reasons that *A* and *B* remembered *C* in any stronger sense than temporal concurrence. Thus, the absence of a together-IMPLICATION is a degenerate or limiting case. This is not so with the second example. It is logically possible for two people to read the same book (token). I would think that this knowledge about 'remember' on the part of language users is what keeps this kind of utterance from having the IMPLICATION in question. Nevertheless, it is still *true* that there is no such IMPLICATION. Consider the following examples:[7]

(12) No Alone-IMPLICATIONS:
      (i) *A* sidled up to *C*.
     (ii) *A* remembers *C*.
    (iii) *A* ignored *C*.
    (iv) *A* raved about *C*.
     (v) *A* promised to *C*.
    (vi) *A* belongs to *C*.
   (vii) *A* scratched the *C*.
  (viii) *A* went to *C*.
    (ix) *A* left for *C*.

6. This locution must be watched, because I think that 'Jones and Smith both moved the table' itself implies that they did *not* move it together.

7. Carole Taylor is to be thanked for her assistance with these, and with (27).

(13) No Together-IMPLICATIONS:

    (i)   *A* and *B* remembered *C*.

    (ii) *A* and *B* ignored *C*.

    (iii) *A* and *B* raved about *C*.

    (iv) *A* and *B* promised *C*.

    (v) *A* and *B* read *C*.

    (vi) *A* and *B* ran the mile.

    (vii) *A* and *B* drew circles.

(14) Weak Together-IMPLICATIONS:

    (i)   *A* and *B* left for C.

    (ii) *A* and *B* sidled up to *C*.

    (iii) *A* and *B* invited *C* over.

    (iv) *A* and *B* scratched *C*.

    (v) *A* and *B* went to *C*.

    (vi) *A* and *B* shot the *C*s.

    (vii) *A* and *B* replied to *C*.

    (viii) *A* and *B* discovered *C*.

    (ix) *A* and *B* crossed C.

(15) Weak Alone-IMPLICATIONS:

    (i)   *A* replied to *C*.

    (ii) *A* shot the *C*s.

    (iii) *A* invited *C* over.

    (iv) *A* sang to *C*.

    (v) *A* sold *C* to *B*.

    (vi) *A* accepted *C*.

    (vii) *A* argued with *C*.

    (viii) *A* called *C*.

    (ix) *A* caught *C*.

(16) Strong Together-IMPLICATIONS:

    (i)   *A* and *B* moved *C*.

    (ii) *A* and *B* washed *C*.

    (iii) *A* and *B* cleaned *C*.

    (iv) *A* and *B* painted *C*.[8]

    (v) *A* and *B* drew *C*.

    (vi) *A* and *B* wrote *C*.

    (vii) *A* and *B* pushed *C*.

    (viii) *A* and *B* bought *C*.

(17) Strong Alone-IMPLICATIONS:

    (i)   *A* moved *C*.

    (ii) *A* washed *C*.

    (iii) *A* cleaned *C*.

    (iv) *A* painted *C*.

8. As in 'painting a wall' vs. 'painting a portrait'.

   (v)   *A* drew *C*.
   (vi) *A* wrote *C*.
   (vii) *A* pushed *C*.
   (viii) *A* threw *C* to *B*.
   (ix) *A* answered *C*.
   (x)   *A* confessed to *C*.
   (xi) *A* ate the *C*.[9]

Notice that most cases use the schematic letter '*C*' for the object phrase. This suggests that in many cases the internal structure of the object plays no role in the IMPLICATION. Consider (16i) again. It seems to me that the following C-variants of (16i) have the same strong together-IMPLICATION:

$$
(18) \quad \text{A and B moved} \begin{cases}
\text{(i)} & \text{this table.} \\
\text{(ii)} & \text{a table (specific).} \\
\text{(iii)} & \text{the tables.} \\
\text{(iv)} & \text{some of the tables.} \\
\text{(v)} & \text{all of the tables.} \\
\text{(vi)} & \text{a few of the tables, etc.}
\end{cases}
$$

However, in some cases the object plays a crucial role via its interactions with the contribution to the truth conditions of the verb:

(18) (a)   (i)   Who drew a circle? (must be nonspecific)
           (ii) *A* and *B* drew a circle. (implies specific?)
(18) (b)   (i)   Who drew that circle? (token)
           (ii) *A* and *B* drew that circle. (token)
(18) (c)   (i)   Who wrote *The Butterfly*?
           (ii) *A* and *B* wrote *The Butterfly*.
(18) (d)   (i)   Who discovered the calculus?
           (ii) Newton and Leibniz discovered the calculus.

In (18a, ii), both *A* and *B* *could* have drawn different circles, but this is not so in (18b, ii).[10] Likewise, it is *possible*, but highly *improbable*, that in (18c, ii), both *A* and *B* happened to write the same book, in the same way that Newton and Leibniz made the same discovery. Indeed, it is probably this very improbability that helps give rise to the IMPLICATION that *A* and *B* wrote *The Butterfly* together. This is legitimate because some IMPLICATIONS can be a function of (shared) background knowledge. There are many more complications here that I am not going to go into.

---

9. Contrast this with 'John tasted the cake'. Sentence (17 xi) implies that John ate the whole cake. But 'John tasted the cake' does not imply he was the only one to have tasted the cake or that he tasted the whole cake. This might be related to what have been called 'unit concepts' like 'see', 'touch', etc. One can be said to have seen the car even if one saw only (strictly?) the left side. See Clark (1965) for an extended discussion of this.

10. What if *A* and *B* both held the pencil?

At the moment it seems to me that the verbs listed as having strong IMPLI-
CATIONS form a natural class. I call these 'chore' verbs for obvious reasons. It
would be interesting to see how this class of verbs (when filled out with more
examples) relates to the taxonomies of Ryle, Vendler, and Kenny. Unfortunately, these taxonomies are in no better shape than mine—some are worse,
since they are contradictory.[11] Most of the strong IMPLICATIONS look as if they
are what Kenny calls performances, but this needs further work.

Adjectives

A perfectly analogous argument to (5) can be constructed using certain adjectives. It could be claimed that

> (19) The flag is red and white.

cannot be derived from (20i) and (20ii):

> (20) (i) The flag is red.
> (ii) The flag is white.

because

> (21) (i) Sentence (20i) is false.
> (ii) Sentence (20ii) is false.
> (iii) Therefore (20) is false.
> (iv) Two sentences with the same meaning cannot have different
> truth values at the same time with the same referents.
> (v) Since (19) is true and (20) is false they cannot have the same
> meaning.
> (vi) Transformations do not change meaning.
> (vii) Therefore (19) cannot be derived from (20).

A version of this argument has been put forward recently in a discussion of the
assignment of logical form. Ackermann writes: "Consider this argument: 'The
flag is black and white. Therefore, the flag is black.' An appropriate flag would
provide a counterexample, since we assert 'The flag is black' only where the flag
is plain black or nearly so" (1970, p.64). While I would agree that this is the
normal implication when making the assertion, I do not agree that this has to be
a part of the meaning of the statement, nor does it have to affect its logical
form.

Returning to the grammatical version of the point, there are many places
where one could challenge argument (21), but I will focus only on (21i) and
(21ii). Again we must ask why one might think (20i) and (20ii) false. The
strong theorist might reason as follows. Suppose someone asks,

> (22) What color is the flag?

---

11. See Harnish (1975a) for additional discussion.

and I answer

(23) (The flag is) red and white.

But if someone asks (22) and I answer,

(24) (The flag is) red.

then (24) entails that

(25) (The flag is) all (only?) red.

Since (25) is inconsistent with (23) and (23) is (supposedly) true, (24) which entails (25) must be false. The reasoning again turns on (24) entailing (25). To block the strong theorist we need only establish (26):

(26) Sentence (24) does not entail (25).

In the end I will try to establish (26).

The question of what elements in the sentence support the purported entailment is, in the case of adjectives, easy—it is the adjective. To see this we need only exhibit adjectives which fail to support this IMPLICATION. I call the IMPLICATION between (24) and (25) a case of 'all-IMPLICATION.' Now consider the following:

(27) No All-IMPLICATION:
     (i) X is spotted.
     (ii) X is dirty.
     (iii) X is stained.
     (iv) X is torn.
     (v) X is patched.
     (vi) X is dented.
     (vii) X is wet.
     (viii) X is on fire.
(28) Weak All-IMPLICATION:[12]
     (i) X is twisted.
     (ii) X is curved.
     (iii) X is steep.

It will be a condition of adequacy on a complete account of this phenomena in verbs and adjectives that one be able to explain why the expressions fit into the category they do vis-a-vis these IMPLICATIONS. With IMPLICATIONS we cannot *assume* that differences between verbs and so on turn (solely) on differences in their logical (semantic) representation, because IMPLICATIONS turn also on contextual knowledge and *shared background information*. This means that it is possible that nonessential properties of the referents can contribute to IMPLI-

---

12. Sylvain Bromberger is thanked for suggesting the first of these for me.

CATIONS. With verbs this distinction is harder to make clear because it is not clear in what sense verbs refer. Nevertheless, it could be the case that the reason, for example, that

(29) *A* and *B* imagined *C*.

does not have a together-IMPLICATION is simply our shared belief that the event token specified by the verb in uttering (29) is not the type of token which ever is a shared "activity." Although it may be a logical truth that two people cannot perform the same act token of *imagining C*, it may not be—and this is all that I want to illustrate.

In the rest of this section I want to argue for two things. First, that the strong theorist is wrong in thinking that the IMPLICATIONS mentioned are *entailments*, and second, that the relationship really is one of *implication* in a specific sense (to be specified shortly). I want to argue, moreover, that the theory that the relationship is one of implication can explain phenomena that the strong theorist cannot explain. I will now present some evidence for thinking the strong theorist wrong.

PRIMA FACIE EVIDENCE FOR A MISTAKE

I want to claim that in supposing there to be an entailment between (7) and (8), (9) and (10), and (24) and (25), the strong theorist has mistaken entailment for implication. I have two kinds of arguments to suggest that it is not entailment.

First Kind of Argument

For verbs:

(30)   (i)   Suppose that Russell and Whitehead wrote *Principia*.
       (ii)   Suppose that 'Russell wrote *Principia*' is false.
       (iii)   Suppose that 'Whitehead wrote *Principia*' is false.
       (iv)   Then 'Russell did not write *Principia*' is true.
       (v)   And 'Whitehead did not write *Principia*' is true.
       (vi)   By conjunction, 'Russell did not write *Principia* and Whitehead did not write *Principia*' is true.
       (vii)   Therefore neither Russell nor Whitehead wrote *Principia*.[13]
       (viii)   But this conflicts with (i), so suppositions (ii) and (iii) must be false.

13. This should strike one as at least suspicious. Unfortunately, I do not at the moment see how to decide if it is valid *in English* or not. The standard treatments of translation in logic texts which allow us to render ⌜neither Fx nor Fy⌝ as ⌜not Fx and not Fy⌝ and to tender ⌜Fx and Fy⌝ for ⌜F x and y⌝ are of no help. This is because rejecting (30) amounts to rejecting at least one of these translations—and pretty clearly the last one, since it looks equivalent to what I want to conclude.

For adjectives:

(31) (i)   Suppose that the flag is red and white.
      (ii) Suppose 'the flag is red' is false.
      (iii) Suppose 'the flag is white' is false.
      (iv) Then 'the flag is not red' is true.
      (v)   And 'the flag is not white' is true.
      (vi) Then 'the flag is not red and the flag is not white' is true.
      (vii) So the flag is neither red nor white (see footnote 13).
      (viii) But this conflicts with (i), so assumptions (ii) and (iii) must be false.

Second Kind of Argument   If P entails Q, then it cannot be the case that $\ulcorner$P and not Q$\urcorner$ is true; $\ulcorner$P and not Q$\urcorner$ is a contradiction.

For verbs, suppose that

(32) (i)   'Russell wrote *Principia*' entails 'Russell wrote *Principia* alone'.

then it should be the case that

      (ii) 'Russell wrote *Principia*, and he did not write it alone'.[14]

is a contradiction. But it doesn't seem to be, so (32) is false and not a case of entailment.

For adjectives, suppose that

(33) (i)   'the flag is red' entails 'the flag is all red'.

then it should be the case that

      (ii) 'the flag is red, but it is not all red'.

is a contradiction. But it does not seem to be, so (33i) is false and not a case of entailment.

A Potential Objection

One way the previous arguments could be stopped is by claiming that the crucial expression 'write' is *ambiguous* as between, say, 'write collectively' and 'write singly'. Thus, in (32i) if true, 'wrote' means 'wrote singly' whereas (32ii) is false if the first occurrence of 'wrote' means 'wrote collectively' and contradictory if not. Argument (30) would then just be invalid by equivocation on 'wrote'.

No philosopher has made this move that I know of. However, McCawley (1968) has taken this line with an example sufficiently close to mine that I think the points on both sides will carry over.

14. Sylvain Bromberger suggests: "Russell wrote *Principia* and Whitehead wrote *Principia* and they wrote it together."

McCawley says, (I have renumbered the examples),

"Consider now another class of sentences which has been proposed as an argument for deriving some conjoined noun phrases from conjoined sentences, namely sentences such as

(34) John and Harry went to Cleveland
This sentence is ambiguous, allowing the two paraphrases
(35) John and Harry each went to Cleveland
(36) John and Harry went to Cleveland together" (1968, pp. 152ff.).

It is not clear from the text how we are to think McCawley takes (35) and (36). They are not themselves perfectly precise. How then do we answer such (nonindependent) questions as

(Q1) Does (36) entail (35)?
(Q2) Are (35) and (36) compatible?
(Q3) Are (35) and (36) contradictories?

Although McCawley does not go on to discuss (34), he does discuss the sentence

(37) Those men went to Cleveland.

which he claims has "exactly the same ambiguity as" (34), and so we can assume that whatever is required to represent the ambiguity of (39) will be required for (34). Thus McCawley's analysis of (37) can serve as the basis for answering our questions about (34). McCawley's proposal is to

(38) "subcategorize noun phrases which have set indices into two types, which I will call joint and nonjoint. Joint noun phrases allow adjuncts such as *together*; nonjoint noun phrases allow adjuncts such as *each*. Attached to each set index in deep structure will be a specification of [+ joint] or [- joint]. Some verbs allow only a nonjoint subject, for example, *erudite*; some allow either a joint or a nonjoint subject, for example *go* . . . Semantically, the distinction between joint and nonjoint relates to the order of quantifiers. In the one reading (joint) of [37], the meaning is that there was an event of 'going to Cleveland' in which each of the men participated; in the other reading (nonjoint), the meaning is that for each man there was an event of 'going to Cleveland' in which he participated; symbolized very roughly,

(39) (a) Joint: $\exists_{y} \forall_{x \in M}$ 'go to Cleveland' (x, y)

(b) Nonjoint: $\forall_{x \in M} \exists_{y_x}$ 'go to Cleveland' (x, y_x)" (1968, pp. 152–153).

I do not see that we will get much help from (39).[15]   Rather, we must turn to the informal remarks for help in answering questions (Q1)-(Q3). On the one hand, the choice of 'nonjoint' instead of 'disjoint' as the label for (35) suggests that (35) and (36) could both be true (of the same occasion). On the other hand, toward the end of (38) we are told that the joint reading of (34), that is, (36), would read something like

(40)   There is an event of going to Cleveland in which John and Harry participated.

For the nonjoint reading of (34), that is, (35), we get something like

(41)   For each of John and Harry there is an event of going to Cleveland in which he participated.

I take it that if (41) is true (and John $\neq$ Harry) then it follows that there are at least two events of the type: going to Cleveland. However, (40) entails only that there is one event of this type. So (40) could be true and (41) false. But since (40) and (41) were supposed to be translations of (36) and (35) respectively, we have an answer to (Q1): (36) does not entail (35) on McCawley's way of taking them. It is also clear that both (40) and (41) could be true, so the answer to (Q2) is "yes" and to Q3 is "no"—for John and Harry might have gone to Cleveland twice, once satisfying (40) and once satisfying (41). But suppose that they have been to Cleveland only once. Then if (40) is true, (41) is false. How about the converse? (41) entails that there were two events of going to Cleveland, and (40) that there was one such event. It seems plausible to argue that if there are *two* such events, then there is not *one* such event. But this would be to move too fast, for all we can conclude so far is that there is not *just one* such event.

15. It is not clear how "rough" (39) is supposed to be—which is unfortunate because of the fanfare which usually accompanies the introduction of logic into syntax (usually only logical *notation* at that). Now, it is clear that there is nothing magical about the explanatory power of expressions like 'x', '∃', 'x ∈ M' in themselves. Either they must be explained upon introduction or we must be allowed to assume that they are being used with the force conventional in the relevant literature. Since we are told almost nothing about the expressions in (39) we must assess it as standard. But then it is just jibberish. Among its defects are:

It is not well-formed. (a) says literally: there is a y such that for all x's in the set M the expression 'go to Cleveland'. (b) is just as bad.

(39) is supposed to say something about events, but nothing indicates that this is so.

Even if we add event predicates, the use of quotes precludes a going-to-Cleveland event. And what exactly *is* a going-to-Cleveland event? Is it a type or a particular? How is John's going-to-Cleveland related to it? The serious use of logical notation should at least indicate what direction our translation would take us, but we get precious little from (39).

Even if we get the quotes out and solve the previous problems, do we want to say that 'go to Cleveland' is two-place predicate—as seems to be required by the notation '(x, y)'? Why not say it is a one-place predicate or a three-place predicate?

I leave deciphering '$x \in M$', 'x_y' and '(x, y_x)' as an exercise to the reader.

If we can establish (42),

> (42) 'There are two events of going to Cleveland' entails 'It is not the case that there is one event of going to Cleveland',

we could establish that if (41) is true, then (40) is false. Is (42) true? Consider the following:

> (43) (i) There are two people here.
> (ii) Therefore, there is one person here.
> (44) (i) The number of people here is two.
> (ii) Therefore, the number of people here is one.
> (45) (i) Two people are in the room.
> (ii) Therefore, one person is in the room.

Are these valid? First, suppose you bet me that there will be 20 people at the talk tonight. We arrive and there are 25 people there. Who wins? There may be some temptation in both directions, but that seems to be because the question is underdetermined. It seems that the sentence

> (46) There will be 20 people there.

can be used to make the following claims:

> (47) (i) There will be at most 20 people there.
> (ii) There will be exactly 20 people there.
> (iii) There will be at least 20 people there.

Of course I do *not* want to claim that (46) is ambiguous and has (47) as its senses. Suppose that in the situation imagined, I had been complaining about the poor attendance at talks and you reply with (46)—against the mutual understanding that 20 people is a good turnout. In this context, what you said could have been paraphrased as (47iii), and so you would win the bet. Another context could have changed the force of my utterance to either of the other two.[16] So questions and examples like the previous one will not decide the validity of (43)–(45).

16. But it is at least very odd to say,

> (a) There wasn't one person there.

when there were two people there, because (a) at least suggests or implies that nobody was there. Also notice that

> (b) There weren't 10 people there.

suggests, implies, etc., that there were less than 10 people there. It would again be odd at least, to say (b) if there were 15 people there. Since $0 < 1$, the generalization to be captured from (a) and (b) is that sentences of the form

> (c) There weren't n G's there.

imply sentences of the form

> (d) There were less than n G's there.

I expect that this can be explained along the Gricean lines explored in this paper.

Second, notice that the standard logicist translations of sentences like (44) render the arguments invalid. For instance, Hempel writes:[17]

(48)   "Let us now express precisely the meaning of the assertion that a certain class C [e.g., of people in the room] has the number 2, or briefly, that $n(C) = 2$. Brief reflection will show that the following definition is adequate in the sense of the customary meaning of the concept 2: there is some object x and some object y such that (1) $x \in C \ldots$ and $y \in C$, (2) $x \neq y$ and (3) if z is any object such that $z \in C$, then either $z = x$ or $z = y$." (1945, p. 375)

Applying this to (45) we get

(49)   (i) $(\exists x)(\exists y)$ (x is in the room & y is in the room & $x \neq y$ & (z) (z is in the room $\supset$ $(z = x \lor z = y)$))
       (ii) $(\exists x)$ (x is in the room & (y) (y is in the room $\supset$ $y = x$)).

and (i) is true iff (ii) is false. Of course the fact that various philosophers have chosen to translate sentences this way does not show that this is the *correct* translation. However, I will accept these translations provisionally,[18] and so will accept (42). This in turn shows that if (41) is true, (40) is false. And this, in conjunction with its converse established earlier, yields the conclusion

(50)   If John and Harry have only been to Cleveland once, then (40) is true iff (41) is false.

Recall that (40) was McCawley's explication of what he meant by (36) and (41) was his explication of what he meant by (35). Consequently, we can substitute into (50), yielding

(51)   If John and Harry have only been to Cleveland once, then (36) is true iff (35) is false.

If we could discharge the antecedent in (51) we could answer (Q2) as "no" and (Q3) as "yes," which in turn will give us some grip on the logical force of the purported senses of (51). Can the antecedent of (51) be discharged? I do not see any natural way to do it.[19] So in all that follows I will make the assumption

17. See also Quine (1959, § 39) for a similar analysis of 'the Apostles are twelve'.

18. It does have some merits, as Hempel points out. For the defects of logicism see *inter alia* Benacerraf (1965). Notice that even if the critics of logicism can make their claim that numbers are not sets stick, this in itself does not show that the translations offered for numerical statements are wrong, since they do not entail that view nor are they entailed by it.

19. For instance, it might be thought that we can just build the uniqueness condition into the sentences themselves and thereby dispense with the troublesome antecedent. But how would this go? Consider.

   (a)   John and Harry went to Cleveland once in their lives.

This may, on the proposal above, be said to have the readings of (b) and (c):

   (b)   John and Harry each went to Cleveland once in their lives.

(which could be true) that the antecedent is true and thus

(52)   (36) is true iff (35) is false.

The questionable antecedent could be carried along as a premise and my arguments would not be affected. However, (52) is more convenient to work with.

Given (52), we can now answer (Q2), as "no" and (Q3) as "yes." But this raises serious doubts as to the adequacy of (35) for saying what (41) says. That is, if McCawley wants (34) to be ambiguous, and to have one of its senses be such as to require that if true, then (41) is the case, then, (35) is a poor way of stating it. On most people's understanding of (35), it need only be the case that both Harry and John traverse some distance and arrive in Cleveland. Nothing more is claimed, although of course more may in fact be true. So (35) does not seem to have the right logical properties to make (41) a translation of it. A more accurate rendition of the sense that (41) is supposed to capture would be

(53)   John and Harry went to Cleveland separately.

One advantage that (53) has over (35) is that it fairly clearly has the properties we determined (41) to have (and which it was not clear that (35) had):

(54)   (i)   (53) entails that there were (at least) two events of going to Cleveland.
        (ii) On the assumption that John and Harry have been to Cleveland only once, our questions (Q1)-(Q3) get answered as before.

I call this an advantage of (53) over (35) because although (40) explicates (36) and we have concluded that (40) entails the falsity of (41), it is not at all clear that (36) entails the falsity of (35). In fact I think that (36) entails (35).

In summary, McCawley claims that (34) is ambiguous. It has a joint and a nonjoint reading. As explications of what he takes the ambiguity to be, McCawley has offered (40) and (41), which he seems to think are captured by (36) and (35) respectively. I have argued that the nonjoint reading, i.e. (41), is better captured by (53) than (35). I conclude that McCawley's claim is that (34) can mean either (36) or (53).

Replies

I do not think that McCawley is correct in claiming that (34) is *ambiguous* as between (36) and (53)—or between (36) and (35), if (35) ≠ (53). I want to con-

---

(c)   John and Harry went to Cleveland together once in their lives.

Unfortunately, (b) and (c) can both be true, because the scope of the adverb is 'went . . . together' and 'went . . . ' and they may have done each of these once in their lives. Another proposal might be to add on the phrase 'and John and Harry only visited Cleveland once in their lives' to (34), (35) and (36). It looks like this would support the requisite entailments and allow us to drop the antecedent, but I have not thought it out. Again, it is very unnatural.

tend that what McCawley gives as two readings for (34) are simply two of the most common kinds of circumstances that do *in fact* satisfy (34). That is, (34) is certainly *vague* or *indeterminate*,[20] but that it is *ambiguous* requires some argument. That it is *not* ambiguous also requires some arguments. Here are a few.

Suppose, as McCawley suggests, that (34) is ambiguous as between (36) ($\equiv$(40)) and (53) ($\equiv$(41)). Assume the following two sets of circumstances:

> $C\,1$: the circumstances such that John and Harry meet halfway to Cleveland and continue there together.
>
> $C\,2$: the circumstance such that John and Harry meet a quarter of the way to Cleveland and continue there together.

I. *First Argument*

1. Since $C\,1$ obtains, (34) is true. Certainly it can be said of both of them that they went to Cleveland.
2. $C\,1$ makes (34) true iff either it makes (36) or (53) true, because these are the possible readings of (34).
3. If $C\,1$ makes (36) true it is because they went at least part of the way together.
4. But, then, by parity of reason, $C\,1$ will make (53) true also, for they traveled at least part of the way separately
5. But we established earlier that (36) and (53) were contradictories, so no circumstance can make them both true at the same time.
6. So, if $C\,1$ cannot make (36) true without making (53) true, it cannot make (36) true, and the same for (53).
7. But, then by 2, $C\,1$ cannot make (34) true.
8. But this contradicts our assumptions $C\,1$ and 1.
9. But since $C\,1$ could be true and 1 is true, our assumption that (34) is ambiguous must be rejected.

II. *Second Argument*

1. Same as I.1.
2. A sentence is true only if one of its senses 'represents' circumstances that obtain.
3. So one of the senses of (34) must represent $C\,1$ (from 1, 2, assumption). Call this sense 'S_3'.
4. Either S_3 = the sense of (36) or (53), or it does not.
5. But $S_3 \neq$ the sense of (36) nor the sense of (53) because $C\,1$ makes S_3 true, but not the sense of (36) nor (53) (from 3-6, argument I.)
6. So S_3 is a new sense of (34).

---

20. I do not think that these are the same: 'father' is *ambiguous* as between (at least) 'biological father' and 'member of a religious organization who . . . ', 'grandfather' is *indeterminate* as between 'maternal grandfather' and 'paternal grandfather', and 'paternal grandfather' is *vague* (do hermaphrodites count? etc.). However, for my purposes I need not distinguish this last pair of properties.

7. But now consider $C\,2$.
8. *Mutatis mutandis*, reapply steps 1–6.
9. So there is a new sense S_4 of (34).
10. Reapply steps 1–9 for as many times as there are rational numbers.
11. Therefore, on McCawley's assumptions, (34) has at least as many senses as there are rational numbers.

III. *Third Argument*[21]

If (34) is ambiguous, it should have two senses each of which can have semantic properties and relations such as analyticity, redundancy, contradictoriness, etc. For instance, the sentence

(55) He fed her dog biscuits.

is ambiguous between

(56) He fed her (dog biscuits).
(57) He fed (her dog) biscuits.

Consequently, if we add information to (56) or (57) that is contained in the sentence already, we will produce a redundancy. Moreover, it should be possible to construct a sentence that is redundant on one sense but not on the other—given the knowledge we might have of those senses.[22] Thus the sentence

(58) He fed her dog biscuits for dogs.

will be redundant on the sense of (56), that is,

(59) He fed her (dog biscuits) for dogs.

but not on the sense of (57):

(60) He fed (her dog) biscuits for dogs.

Now consider McCawley's proposed ambiguity again. Since one of the senses of (34) is supposed to be (36), it should be *redundant* on one sense to say,

(61) John and Harry went to Cleveland and they went together.

That is, given that (34) is supposed to be able to mean (36), then (61) should be able to mean,

(62) John and Harry went to Cleveland together and they went together.

Native informants have unanimously rejected (62) as a reading for (61). More-

21. The first of these is due to Jerrold J. Katz (in conversation)—who also suggested Bever's ambiguity example, "He fed her dog biscuits." This conversation prompted me to make (and aided me in making) my arguments more explicit.
22. This is because to be two senses they must differ in some way. One then picks one's predicate to reflect this semantic difference.

over, on McCawley's analysis, we ought to be able to get (61) as contradictory[23] that is, as

(63) John and Harry went to Cleveland separately and they went together.

Again, native informants unanimously reject (63) as a possible sense of (61).

By now it should be getting clearer that the addition of 'separately' or 'together' to (34) does not constitute a more adequate formulation of one of its *senses*, but is rather a more *specific* statement. The relation of (34) to (36) and (53) is more like genus to species than a sentence to its paraphrases.

In summary, I take it that the original arguments against the strong theorist stand, so far, and we turn now to an alternate account of the relationship.

GRICE'S THEORY OF IMPLICATION

In this section I present what is the main point of the first parts of this paper: reasons for believing that the relationship in question is one of implication. Since this is an empirical hypothesis and one of the best ways of challenging a theory is to provide a more adequate alternative, I shall try to make this part as persuasive as possible.

In an important series of papers, published and unpublished, H. P. Grice has been developing a theory of the relationship among an expression, its meaning, the speaker's meaning, the implications, and so on, of the utterance. Some of this structure is indicated in (64):[24]

(64)   total content (signification) of an utterance (remark)

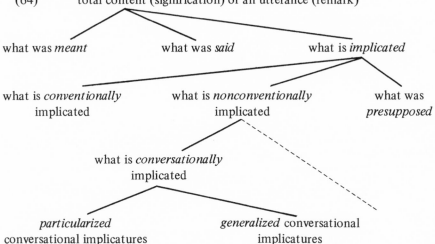

23. Again assuming that they went just once.

24. This diagram is meant to be only suggestive. There is no readily apparent interpretation of the domination lines that is coherent. It is an interesting and important question how these notions are related. The dotted line will be filled in.

One convenient way of investigating Grice's theory is by tracking down various branches of this tree.[25]

In a number of places (1961, p. 444; 1967; 1968, p. 225), Grice has attempted to draw, both pretheoretically and theoretically, a distinction between what someone stated or said on an occasion, and what was implied or implicated.[26] To focus our attention on saying and implicating, Grice invites us to consider the following dialogue (1967, II, p. 4):

> (65) (i) S (to H): How is C getting on in his job at the bank?
>   (ii) H (to S): Quite well, he likes his colleagues and he hasn't been sent to prison yet.

Grice wants to claim that H did not *say* that C is the sort of person who might yield to monetary temptations, but S's saying (65ii) suggested, indicated, implied it—that is, his saying what he did *implicated* it.

This raises two related problems. One, how does one tell whether something is said or (just?) implied on a given occasion? Two, what is it to say or imply something? If we had necessary or sufficient conditions for saying or for implying, then we might be able to answer the first question, and if we had a way of assigning cases, we might be able to construct necessary or sufficient conditions. So anybody's discussion of one question is likely to include probes into the other, and Grice is no exception. What is true in Grice's case, I think, is that the different problems get different emphasis in these various discussions. The first question gets more emphasis in the earlier works, the second in the latter. We can take them up in this order.

In an early paper Grice (1961) discusses four cases "in which . . . something might be said to be implied as distinct from being stated." Although his main purpose seems to be to decide cn the "vehicle" of the implication in each case, in the course of this Grice suggests some useful diagnostic tests:

1. *Nondetachability* (of the implication from what is asserted): "*Any* way of asserting what is asserted . . . involves the implication in question" (1961, p. 446).

25. I will not be concerned here with Grice's theory of meaning. But it is important to know how utterer's meaning and utterance type meaning are related to saying and implying. Especially vexing is the relationship between utterer's meaning and implicature. One strong supposition worth looking at is that what one implicates (as well as what one says) is always a species of what was meant, differences being traceable to different ways in which various intentions are to function and different reasons the audience is intended to have. It would be important for this strong view that one not be able to imply that p and not mean that p, and to get at this one might need to know if one could imply unintentionally (as might a Republican who said that Nixon was the best president that money could buy).

26. The reason for the disjunction is that Grice's terminology has shifted from the first pair to the second. The shift to 'implicature' frees him from the unwanted 'logical' use of 'implies', and the shift to 'said' is a generalization from 'state'. I can report what someone said in cases besides what they stated, for instance, when I report that he said that you are to leave the room.

2. *Noncancelability* (of the implication without canceling the assertion): "One cannot take . . . [another] form of words for which both what is asserted and what is implied is the same as [the first] . . . and *then* add a further clause withholding commitment from what would otherwise be implied, with the idea of annulling the implication without annulling the assertion" (1961, p. 446).

3. "If accepting that the implication holds involves one in accepting a hypothetical 'if p then q' where 'p' represents the original statement and 'q' represents what is implied, then what the speaker said (or asserted) is a vehicle of implication, otherwise not" (1961, p. 445–6).

These tests will be of assistance only to the extent we are able to tell when the conditions mentioned in them are met. However, the first two conditions appeal to the notion of two statements being the same, while the third appeals to the notion of 'involving one in accepting,' and one may protest that these notions are less clear than the notions we were testing for. Still, if we do not press too hard I think they can be of some utility. This does perhaps indicate that progress is more likely to be made by turning to the second set of problems mentioned earlier. We can conveniently reformulate that set as the following triple question:

(Q1) What is it for someone to *say that p*?

(Q2) What is it for someone (or something) to *implicate that q*?

(Q3) What are the main kinds of implicature?

We take these up in turn.

Saying that *p*

Without further remarks, (Q1) as stated blurs an important distinction—or rather, can be taken as asking two nonequivalent questions—depending on whether we view 'p' as a variable or as a schematic letter. Taking it as a variable is to take (Q1) to be equivalent to

(Q1a) What is it to *say* something?

Taking it as a schematic letter or place holder shifts the emphasis to the place held: What is it to say p? This is better put: Given that something was said,

(Q1b) *What* was said? (How do we identify (or specify) what goes into the place held?)

We can put these questions as requests that the theorist fill out the following two schemas correctly:

(Q1a') *Saying Attribution*: (x) (x said something if and only if x . . .).

(Q1b') *Saying Specification*: (x) (If x said that p, then one identifies p if and only if one specifies . . .).

What does Grice have to say that bears on (Q1a) and (Q1b)?

SAYING SPECIFICATION

Grice does not say too much about this question. At one point (1967, II, p. 5) he does remark that, "for a full identification of what the speaker had said one would need to know (a) the identity of x [the referent(s)], (b) the time of utterance, (c) the meaning, on the particular occasion of utterance, of the phrase ... [uttered]". Although Grice is here talking about a particular example, there is no indication that any of (a)–(c) are peculiar to it. So we can perhaps generalize this remark to the following Gricean instantiation of (Q1b'):

(66) To identify what x said [within the total signification of the utterance] (on some occasion) one must identify (specify)
   (a) The identity of the referents (if there was reference).
   (b) The time of utterance (if there was temporal specification).
   (c) The meaning of the expression uttered on that occasion of utterance.

Clause (c) has the effect of insuring that

(67) "In the sense in which I am using the word 'say', I intend what someone has said to be closely related to the conventional meaning of the words (the sentence) which he has uttered."

Thus, a person who understood English and supposed the speaker to be speaking literally, but knew nothing of the context, could only know that in uttering "He's in the grip of a vice" the speaker had *said* of some male that at the time of utterance (whenever that was) either he was unable to rid himself of some bad character trait, or he was caught in a particular kind of tool. Clause (a) is left vague on purpose, since Grice wants to leave it open "whether a man who says (today) 'Harold Wilson is a great man' and another who says (also today) 'The British Prime Minister is a great man' would, if each knew that the two singular terms had the same reference, have said the same thing" (1967, II, p. 5). However, there is *some* tension now with (c), for the two sentences certainly do not mean the same thing (in English), on any reading. But then it is not clear what the status of (c) is in the identification of what is said. Since that is the most natural way of reading the quotation, some additional elucidation is called for.

SAYING ATTRIBUTION

The saying specification (66) does not, of course, tell us under what circumstances it will be true that someone has said something. In his later works Grice has taken a number of steps toward an analysis of 'U said that p'. One of the first things Grice wants to say (1967, V, p. 13) is that

(68) 'U *said that p*' entails 'U did something x':
   (1) by which U *meant that p*

(2) which is an occurrence of an utterance type (sentence) S such that
   (i) S *means* '*p*'
   (ii) S consists of a sequence of elements (e.g., words) ordered in a way licensed by a system of rules (syntactic rules)
   (iii) S means '*p*' in virtue of the particular meaning of the elements of S, their order, and their syntactic character.

Grice abbreviates (68, 2) to read

(2′) which is an occurrence of a type S which means '*p*' in some linguistic system (1967, V, p. 14).

From this it *looks* like we will get a definition of 'saying' like the following:

(69) *U* said that *p* iff
   (1) By uttering *X*, *U* meant that *p*
   (2) When uttered by *U*, *X* meant '*p*'.

But Grice does *not* want to subscribe to (69). Grice considers (69, 1,2) to be the definiens for '*U conventionally meant* that *p*' which is introduced as a technical term (1968, p. 228). Why does Grice think that '*U* said that *p*' is not equivalent to the coincidence of utterer's occasion-meaning and applied timeless meaning? Apparently because

(70) "There are, I think, at least some sentences whose timeless meaning is not adequately specificable by a statement of the exemplary form" (1968, p. 227).

If this were not the case, Grice seems to think that it would be possible to defend (69). Grice gives as an example of such a sentence:

(S1) Bill is a philosopher and he is, therefore, brave.

A specification of timeless meaning for (S1) might go,

(71) "One meaning of (S1) includes 'Bill is occupationally engaged in philosophical studies' and 'Bill is courageous' and 'That Bill is courageous follows from his being occupationally engaged in philosophical studies' and that is all that is included" (1968, p. 228).

But rather than argue that (71) does *not* exemplify the schema for (applied) timeless meaning specification, and so is not exemplary, Grice *seems* to accept it as a good specification of timeless meaning and then he *goes on* to argue that even though

(i) By uttering (S1), *U* meant that Bill is . . .

and

    (ii) When uttered by U, (S1) meant "Bill is . . ." . . .

it may *not* be the case that

    (iii) U *said* that Bill is . . . and that his being courageous *follows from* his being a philosopher . . .

This is because Grice wants to claim that U *indicated*, but did not *say* (in his favored sense) that Bill's being courageous follows from his being a philosopher:

    (72) "I wish to maintain that the semantic function of the word 'therefore' is to enable the speaker to *indicate*, though not to *say*, that a certain consequence holds" (1968, p. 228).

Thus, Grice contends that concordance of (applied) timeless meaning and occasion-meaning is not *sufficient* for 'saying that'. Quite simply, if metaphorically, a person (and a sentence) can mean more than they *say*. But I think it is misleading to pin *this* disparity on the nonexemplariness of a certain meaning specification—or at least we need to be told how/why the said specification is not exemplary. What (72) indicates is that the utterance-meaning/speaker-meaning distinction cuts across the saying/implying distinction. That is, if (69) were correct, then in diagram (64), what the speaker meant by uttering x, and what x has meant, would determine what was said. But this may not be correct, since it seems that what is *implicated* can be a part of what is meant (by U, or X, or both). Since what is said may be only a *part* of what is meant, Grice needs some way of factoring out a central core of meaning that will help determine what is said. Grice wants to

    (73) "be able to explain or talk about what (within what U meant) U *centrally* meant: to give sense to 'in meaning that p, U *centrally* meant that q' " (1967, V, p. 14).

As far as I know, Grice has not yet produced an analysis of 'centrally meant,' but he does suggest one role that it will play in the *definition* of *said that*:

    (74) " 'U said that p' is true iff U did something x:
        (1) by which U *centrally* meant that p.
        (2) which is an occurrence of a type S, part of the meaning of which is 'p' " (1967, V, p. 14).

In (1968, p. 228), Grice expands on his program for getting an analysis of 'saying that'. It includes

    (75) (i) specifying conditions for a limited range of central or fundamental speech acts: Y-ing;
        (ii) Defining each Y-ing that *p in terms of occasion-meaning, or important elements in the analysis thereof;

(iii) Stipulating that
In uttering X, U will have *said that* *p if
(1) U has Y-ed that *p;
(2) X embodies some conventional device the meaning of which is such that its presence in X indicates that its utterer is Y-ing that *p.

It would seem that one defect of all these preliminary analyses, ((68), (74), (75))—insofar as they are *necessary* conditions—is that the clause requiring that the speaker mean that p (or *p) is too strong.[27] Suppose that someone thought that 'hoi polloi' meant 'the upper classes'. Then, by uttering 'he likes to associate with (the) hoi polloi' he would have meant that he likes to associate with the upper classes. But of course this is not what he *said*. When his mistake is pointed out to him, he agrees that he hadn't said what he meant—he had said that p, but meant that q, when q was in fact incompatible with p. Grice could, of course, say that his 'favored' sense of 'say' is not the sense above, but without more in the way of independent characterization of this sense (or use) of 'say' the move is not helpful. It is interesting to note that in his earlier paper (1961, p. 444) Grice drew the contrast not between *saying* and implicating, but between *stating* and implicating (he then used 'implying'). This may have been better since I find it more plausible to deny that I *stated* (or *asserted*) that p when I meant that q. However, this move would rule out all 'nonindicative' central speech acts.

Implicating that q

I think that the same distinction made for 'saying' carry over to 'implicating'. We get

(Q2a) *Implicature Attribution*: (x) (x *implicated* something iff . . . x . . .)
(Q2b) *Implicature Specification*: (x) (if x implicated that q, then one specifies q iff one specifies . . .)

To my knowledge, Grice has not attempted either to formulate necessary and jointly sufficient conditions for implicating nor to give a general procedure for identifying, on an occasion, what has been implicated—although at one point ("Conditionals," p. 4) he does offer the following partial characterization:

(76) S *implicates* that q (to H) if:
(i) S says that p (to H)
(ii) S does not say that q (to H)
(iii) By saying that p (to H) S meant, conveyed, implied, suggested, indicated that q (to H).

---

27. I owe this version of the complaint to a conversation with Anthony Woozley. An earlier version of this complaint (mine) was met by Jerrold Katz in conversation.

Rather, Grice has turned his attention mainly to sorting out different kinds of implicature and analyzing their modes of operation.

Some Kinds of Implicature

In his work so far, Grice distinguishes three major species of implicature: conventional implicature, conversational implicature, and presupposition. Since Grice has very little to say about the last category, we can look at it first.

PRESUPPOSITION

Grice's main example of presupposition is (77):

> (77) (a) 'Smith has left off beating his wife' presupposes that
> (b) Smith has been beating his wife.

Moreover, Grice is working with the 'semantic' notion of presupposition in the sense that "the truth of what is implied is a necessary condition of the original statement's being either true or false" (1961, p. 445). However, he also is willing to allow that in this case the *speaker* can be said to have presupposed (implied) that (77b). Presumably this is either a derived use of 'presupposition', or the speaker is said to have implied it in some way *because* what he said presupposed it. Grice does not spell this out, but he does say one curious thing about this case. He says that we should have "at least some inclination to say that the presence of the implication was a matter of the meaning of some of the words in the sentence, but we should be in some difficulty when it came to specifying precisely which this word or words are, of which this is true" (1961, p. 447). What is curious is that it seems clear that the guilty words are "left off." Synonyms preserve the presupposition (e.g., "quit"), and nonsynonyms do not (e.g., "started" or "begun thinking about").

CONVENTIONAL IMPLICATURES

In conventional implicatures:

> (78) "The conventional meaning of the words used will determine what is implicated, besides helping to determine what is said" (1967, II, p. 6). "What is conventionally implicated is part of the meaning/force of the utterance" (1967, III, p. 1).

One of our earlier examples falls under this category. Consider:

> (79) He is a philosopher; he is, therefore, brave.

Grice comments,

> (80) "I would wish to maintain that the semantic function of the word 'therefore' is to enable the speaker to *indicate* though not to *say*,

that a certain consequence holds . . . I would adopt the same position with regards to words like 'but' and 'moreover' " (1968, p. 228).

(81) "The presence of this implicative is clearly a matter of the meaning of the word 'therefore' " ("Conditionals," p. 4).

Later (1967, III, p. 8) Grice entertains the idea that

(82) "a model case for a word which carries a conventional implicature is 'but'."

In his early paper (1961), Grice considers the example "[2] She was poor but she was honest" which is said to imply some contrast between *poverty* and *honesty*. Grice wants to claim the following:

(83) (i) "It would be . . . incorrect to say in the case of [2] that what he said (or asserted) implied that there was a contrast between, e.g., honesty and poverty.

(ii) I should be inclined to say . . . that the speaker could be said to have implied whatever it is that is implied; that in the case of [2] it seems fairly clear that the speaker's words could be said to imply a contrast . . .

(iii) The implication is *detachable*: had I said 'she is poor and she is honest' I would assert just what I would have asserted if I had used the original sentence; but there would now be no implication of a contrast between, e.g., poverty and honesty.

(iv) as regards [2], the fact that the implication obtains is a matter of the meaning of the word 'but' . . ." (pp. 445-447).

We have, then, the following cases of conventional implicature:

(a) p therefore q : q follows from p (perhaps: p provides good reasons for believing q).

(b) p but q : p contrasts with q.

One might question the correctness of witholding some of this from what is said. Suppose someone says, "Sartre is a philosopher; he is, therefore, brave." Now, it might very well be true that Sartre is a philosopher and that he is brave, but that the *reason* we are willing to say he is brave has nothing at all to do with his being a philosopher, but rather with his work in the Resistance. Thus I would reject the statement above as false, but to do this it would have to be the case that what was said comprises the notion of his being a philosopher providing grounds for thinking him to be brave, because the other two clauses are true.

This is not the case with 'but'. If one says that Jackie is wealthy, but a brunet, one implies a contrast between wealth and hair color. However, in this case one is inclined to say that the statement is true even though the implicate is (probably) false, indicating that it is not a part of what was said.

I do not want to deny there is a class of conventional implicatures, but I will continue to be suspicious until more examples are adduced, and their conventionality is explicated.

CONVERSATIONAL
IMPLICATURE

In contrast with conventional implicatures (which turn on the meaning of the words used) there is a class of implicatures that turn not only on what a person says but also on principles governing discourse. As such, Grice's theory is the latest, and most sophisticated, in a line of attempts to account for what has variously been called *contextual* or *pragmatic* implication.[28] These implications turn on saying what is said in a discourse of a certain kind. The kind of discourse at issue is one governed by the *Cooperative Principle*:[29]

> (84) "Make your conversational contribution such as is required, at the stage at which it occurs, by the accepted purpose or direction of the talk-exchange in which you are engaged" (1967, II, p. 7).

Under this principle come the following *maxims*.[30] The first are those relating to *what is said*:

28. For a survey discussion up to 1960, see Hungerland (1960) and the references there.

29. Some have been misled by Grice's remarks. For instance, Elinor Keenan's interesting paper (1974) is somewhat marred by the supposition that her data from Madagascar are counterexamples to Grice's theory of conversation. Keenan's mistake is to assume that for maxims to be universal, they must be *categorically* observed. But this need not be so. Grice's theory of implicature requires just that the speaker and hearer(s) be observing the cooperative maxims. This assumption is necessary for Grice's theory of implicature to work, but it is also sufficient. Grice nowhere says, nor would want to say, that all conversations are governed by the cooperative maxims. There are too many garden-variety counter-examples: social talk between enemies, diplomatic encounters, police interrogation of a reluctant suspect, most political speeches, and many presidential news conferences. These are just some of the cases in which the maxims of cooperation are not in effect and are known not to be in effect by the participants.

Since Grice's theory is basically conditional (if any conversation is governed by the cooperative maxims, then we can explain such and such implicatures in such and such a way), it will not do for falsifying it just to show that the antecedent is false. What must be done to falsify this theory, and what Keenan does not report doing, is to find examples of cooperative exchanges where the maxims are violated in the requisite way and none of the predicted implicatures are present.

However, Keenan does ask the important question: why don't the Malagasy cooperate with information? And to this question she has an interesting suggestion. Apparently the Malagasy are so closely knit that possessing information another lacks gives one status over them. Thus, reluctance to cooperate on information could be viewed as a natural consequence of the general reluctance to relinquish advantages in status.

30. This raises the general question of how to discover new maxims and how to justify the claim that some maxim 'governs' discourse. A rough and ready principle I have used is the following: the supposition that maxim M governs conversations affords the best available explanation for the (pretheoretically identifiable) implication that p, in such and such contexts.

(85) *Quantity*
 (1) Make your contribution as informative as necessary.
 (2) Do not make it too informative.
(86) *Quality* (supermaxim: "try to make your contribution one that is true") (1967, II, p. 8)
 (1) Do not say what you believe to be false.[31]
 (2) Do not say what you lack adequate evidence for.[32]
(87) *Relation*: Be relevant.[33]

Relating to *how* what is said to be *said*:

(88) *Manner* (supermaxim: "Be perspicuous")
 (1) Avoid obscurity of expression.
 (2) Avoid ambiguity.
 (3) Be brief.
 (4) Be orderly.

And Grice observes (1967, II, p. 9) that there will need to be other kinds of maxims, e.g., esthetic, social (politeness), moral.[34]

31. It is interesting to note that Sir David Ross considers this a *prima facie* duty arising from: "The implicit understanding not to tell lies, which seems to be implied in the act of entering into conversation" (Ross, 1930, p. 21). A slightly stronger version of this can be found in Urmson (1952, p. 224): "Whenever anyone utters a sentence which could be used to convey truth or falsehood there is an implied claim to truth by that person, unless the situation shows that this is not so (he is acting or reciting or incredulously echoing the remarks of another) . . . it is understood that no one will utter a sentence of a kind which can be used to make a statement unless he is willing to claim that the statement is true . . . The word 'implies' is being used in such a way that if there is a convention that X will be done in circumstances Y, a man implies that Y holds if he does X." I say that this account is slightly stronger because stated as a maxim it enjoins one to speak (what one believes to be) the truth (and not just to *refrain* from speaking what one believes to be falsehoods), and because it appeals to the existence of a *convention* to explain the implication. However, if I understand Grice correctly, the maxims are not conventions at all. They are a "part" of what it is to be verbally cooperative and so lose the feature of arbitrariness so dear to most accounts of conventions (See e.g., Lewis, 1969, for a more adequate statement. For a critique and reformulation, see Schiffer, 1972, Chap. V.).

32. Urmson (1952, pp. 229–230) again notes that "Whenever we make a statement in a standard context there is an implied claim to reasonableness . . . it is, I think, a presupposition of communication that people will not make statements, thereby implying their truth, unless they have some ground, however tenuous, for those statements . . . There is a convention that we will not make statements unless we are prepared to claim and defend their reasonableness."

33. This maxim turns out to be so central and important in conversational implicature that it is not clear that it belongs on equal footing with the rest. I suspect that maxims are (at least partially) ordered with respect to weight, etc. and that relevance is at the top, controlling most of the others.

34. I find this a bit misleading. It is easy to see how the maxims given might fall under the cooperative principle, but it is not at all obvious that esthetic, social, or moral maxims need contribute to rational cooperation. Indeed, moral maxims may well preclude obedience to other maxims. (Presumably, one was not obliged to give all necessary information when the

From these maxims it is obvious that the purpose mentioned in the Co-operative Principle is *here* taken to be the exchange of information. But there are, as Grice acknowledges (1969, II, p. 9), many other purposes of a talk exchange such as to influence the actions of others. Thus these maxims must be generalized and supplemented for a complete theory.[35]

According to Grice, participants in a talk exchange may fail to fulfill a maxim in many ways. Since Grice is not always completely consistent in the use of his terminology, we adopt the neutral term 'infringement' for any failure to fulfill a maxim (or the CP). Saying that *A* infringed a certain maxim simply means he failed to fulfill it. This use commits us to nothing regarding the *way* the maxim was not fulfilled or the *consequences* of not fulfilling it. Of the four ways discussed, only three of them give rise to implicatures: (90), (91), and (92).[36]

(89) seems to be the only infringement that does not give rise to implicature:

> (89) One may *opt out* by indicating plainly that he is unwilling to cooper-
> ate. ("I cannot say anything more.")

In violating a maxim one is likely to mislead. Grice does not say very much about this as a way of infringing a maxim distinct from the others to follows. In fact, sometimes he uses 'violate' where I have picked 'infringe'.

Gestapo came calling.) Part of the problem here is that we have no suggestions as to what any of these new maxims might look like. Grice's only example of a social maxim is: be polite! Moreover, it is not clear what Grice has in mind as an "esthetic" maxim. Perhaps the best research strategy to adopt is first to imagine ideally cooperative conversations, ideally esthetic (?) conversations, etc. Then turn to the project of seeing how these maxims interact in actual contexts.

35. The project of supplementing and generalizing *these* maxims to nonconstative cases is distinct from the project mentioned earlier of finding other sorts of maxims. Generalizing these maxims, or finding special cases for other (classes of) speech acts, presumably yields maxims falling under the cooperative principle. The only maxims mentioned so far that are specifically constative are the maxims of Quantity and Quality, so these are likely candidates for supplementation or generalization. Analogues for requesting (as a type of speech act, asking a question might fall under this) could be:

Quantity′ (a) Do not request too little. ("Breathe.")
          (b) Do not request too much. ("Bring me the moon.")
Quality′ (a) Do not request what you do not want. ("Leave the room, but I don't want you to.")
          (b) Do not request what you do not have a reason for requesting. ("Leave the room." "Why?" "I don't know.")

Furthermore, the original maxims of Quantity and Quality should probably be generalized from just *saying*. This is because implicatures can work off of what is presupposed but not said, as well as what is said.

36. I want to emphasize that these are not exclusive ways of infringing a maxim. As far as I can tell, clashes are just a special subclass of violations—where the violation is forced, or seen as forced, by having in the circumstances competing maxims.

(90) One may quietly and unostentatiously *violate* a maxim.

These two infringements, (89) and (90), seem to be logically distinct. That is, if *A* opts out of a maxim, he does not infringe it "quietly and unostentatiously" and thus violate it. Conversely, if *A* violates a maxim, he has not indicated plainly that he is "unwilling to cooperate" and thus opted out. In (91), a maxim may be infringed, but its infringement is explained by supposing it to conflict with another maxim.

(91) One may be faced with a *clash* between one maxim and another.

Consider Grice's example. Suppose *A* is planning with *B* an itinerary for a holiday in France. Both know that *A* wants to visit his friend *C*. *A*: "Where does *C* live?" *B*: "Somewhere in the south of France."

GLOSS: (1) *B* is not opting out. (2) *B* has infringed the first maxim, Quantity (say as much as necessary). (3) (2) can be explained only by supposing that *B* is aware that to be more informative would be to infringe the second maxim, Quality (have evidence for what you say). (4) So *B* implicates that he does not know which town *C* lives in.

Notice first that it seems to be in the nature of the clash that in the particular circumstances the speaker cannot fulfill both of the maxims in question at once. However, it is not in the nature of the clash that any *particular* maxim must override the other. In this case, the second maxim of Quality overrides the first maxim of Quantity. Notice also in (3) Grice claims that this is the only supposition that would explain (2), but he gives no reason to believe this to be true— although it may be.

There are two ways of viewing this clash. From the speaker's point of view he must, in the circumstances, either infringe the first maxim of Quantity or the second maxim of Quality, and he must make a choice—between giving not enough information and giving groundless information. If the speaker does not opt out of the second maxim of quality (by saying "I do not know exactly") then the hearer is faced with an infringement he can explain (or explain away) by positing that there was a clash and that the speaker opted for fulfilling the second maxim of Quality.

On the speaker's side, this suggests an ordering or weighting of the maxims and it is not too hard to find a plausible explanation. If it can be assumed that the speaker *S* is observing at least the CP, then *S* will pick quality over quantity if only because truly groundless information has at least as good a chance of being wrong as right, and as such would probably not be helpful—thereby violating the CP.

On the hearer's side, this suggests that there is a metaprinciple at work, which I will call the Principle of Charity:

> (*PC*) Other things being equal, construe the speaker's remark so as to violate as few maxims as possible.

Since, however, some maxims may be more highly weighted than others we need the Weighted Principle of Charity (for pairs of maxims):

> (*WPC*) Other things being equal, construe the speaker's remark so that it is consistent with the maxim of higher weight.
>
> or If the speaker has infringed one or other of a pair of maxims, other things being equal, assume that he has chosen to infringe the lowest valued maxim.

Now we can reconstruct Grice's Gloss in more detail and perhaps eliminate the appeal to "explanations" in favor of an appeal to a sufficient condition. We will assume that B knows that A is observing the maxims, CP and the metaprinciples:

> GLOSS: (0) B said that p. (1) B has not opted out. (2) B's saying that p in this context infringes Quantity-1. (3) So some p' (more informative than p) would not have infringed Quantity-1. (4) So B could have said that p', but if he had said that p' then under the (ex hypothesi) assumption that B is obeying Quality-2, he would had to have had evidence for p'. (5) If B had no evidence for p' and said that p', he would have violated Quality-2. (6) Assume that B has no evidence for p'. (7) Then: (i) If B says that p, he infringes Quantity-1. (ii) If B says that p', he infringes Quality-2. (8) Apply the WPC to (7): Do not infringe Quality over Quantity, so do not say that p'. (9) B said that p (and not p') thereby satisfying (8). (10) So (6) (plus general principles) is sufficient for (9), so B has no evidence for p'. (11) So B has implicated that he does not know which town C lives in.

The final infringement of a maxim that Grice discusses is flouting:

> (92) The speaker may *flout* a maxim—he may blatantly fail to fulfill it.

It is this class of infringements that gives rise to conversational implicatures. The speaker S *exploits* a maxim when S flouts a maxim, with the consequence that the hearer H knows that S's utterance does not fall under (89)–(91) and so H must reconcile S's saying what he said with the supposition that S is obeying the conversational maxims and/or the cooperative principle.

Here (as indicated by '□') are some examples of Grice's (1967, II) that involve exploitation, the procedure by which a maxim is flouted for the purpose of getting in a conversational implicature. Though a maxim is infringed at the level of *what is said*, the hearer is entitled to assume that the maxims (or the CP) is being observed at the level of *what is implicated*.

Quantity-1 Make your contribution as informative as necessary
□ *A* is writing a recommendation for his philosophy pupil *C* to *B*. It reads: "Mr. *C*'s command of English is excellent and his attendance at tutorials has been regular. Yours, etc."

> GLOSS: (of *B*'s reasoning): (1) *A* cannot be opting out, for he need not have written at all. (2) *A* cannot be unable, through ignorance, to say more since *C* was *A*'s pupil. (3) Therefore, *A* must be wishing to impart some information that he is unwilling to write down. (4) This supposition is tenable only on the assumption that *A* thinks that *C* is no good at *X*-ing. (5) Therefore, this is what he is implicating.

The end of a review of a sleazy American novel is an analogous case: "The print is tolerably readable and all the pages in the last two chapters are correctly numbered" (*Punch*, 1969, p. 354). Although this carries a definite implication of worthlessness, it would have been quite strong had this been the total review. The mechanism behind this implication may well underlie the force of the slogan 'damn with faint praise'.
□ Tautologies like: "war is war" and "boys will be boys" flout the first maxim of Quantity.

> GLOSS: These are totally uninformative at the level of what is said, but they are informative at the level of what is implicated. The hearer's identification of their information content at this level depends on his ability to explain the speaker's selection of this *particular* patent tautology.

I do not find this completely satisfactory. We still need some argument to show that these are not idiomatic, for instance. Notice that if this was *purely* conversational, it ought to work appropriately for almost any tautology of the relevant type. But consider: "Tables are tables"; "Pencils will be pencils." These simply do not have the requisite implicature *except* as being read (by the hearer) as conscious plays by the speaker on the standard tautologies. As such, the principles that yield the requisite implicatures in the standard cases yield the requisite implicatures in these cases (e.g. pencils usually break or have some characteristic defect). Notice how hard it is to figure out what the first of the tautologies above would implicate even in the appropriate contexts. This application of Quantity-1 still needs more work, since the mechanism generating the specific implications is still obscure.[37]

---

37. Consider a remark like "Church's discussion may or may not be helpful here." Clearly this can (would) be taken as a certain suggestion, not as just the utterance of a tautology. Or, "There are movies and there are movies" is used to stress that there are certain (contextually determined) differences between movies.

Although Grice does not mention contradictions, since they also carry no information it might be supposed that they can function the same way as tautologies in generating implicatures. Cases are hard to find, however, the following might be considered: "Contemporary philosophers are not (really?) philosophers." "It is raining and it isn't." "Fairest Cordelia, that art most rich being poor" (*King Lear*, 1, i).

Quantity-2 Do not give more information than is required.
□ *A* asks "Is it the case that p? and *B* answers: "It is certain that p" or "*p*, and I am certain of it, everybody knows it."

> GLOSS: (of *A*'s reasoning): (1) If *B*'s volubility is undesigned it may raise doubt whether *B* is as certain as he says ("The lady doth protest too much"). (2) If it is thought of as designed, it would be an oblique way of conveying that it is to some degree controversial whether or not p.

I find these very suspicious. The gloss does not exhibit any of the structural complexity of the working-out schema.

Quality-1 Do not say what you believe to be false.
□ Irony: *A* and *B* both know that *A*'s friend *X* has just sold *A*'s business secrets. A: "X is a fine friend."(*P*).

> GLOSS: (by *B*) (1) *A* has flouted the first maxim of quality. (2) *A* knows that I know this. (3) *A* has not opted out, nor is there any obvious clash. (4) Therefore, *A* must be trying to get across some other proposition *Q*. (5) For me to be successful it must be some obviously related proposition. (6) The most obviously related proposition is the contradictory of the purported one. (7) Therefore, this is the proposition that *A* is trying to get across.

I find this suspicious for two reasons. First, why should we suppose that the contradictory is the most obviously related proposition and not, say, the Existential Generalization of *P*, or the result of substituting the name of *B*'s mother for the subject expression in *P*, etc? Second, the contradictory of *P* is "*X* is not a fine friend" and it at least has to be argued that this *entails* that *X* is not a friend at all. It is at least possible that without stress on "fine" I might still only be denying him a certain *rank* as a friend. But suppose it does entail that *X* is not a friend, this does not, certainly, entail that he is an enemy, rival, villain. Presumably many people are not *A*'s friends who also are not *A*'s enemies. Notice, I am *not* denying that in the context, there is the implication that *X* is a cad; rather I am complaining that this fact has not been captured by the description Grice gives of both the upshot and the way it is achieved.
□ Metaphor: A: "You are the cream in my coffee."(P).

GLOSS: (1) P is categorically false. (2) Therefore the contradictory of what *A* has made as if to say will strictly speaking be a truism. (3) Therefore, it cannot be *that*, that *A* is trying to get across. (4) The most likely supposition is that *A* is attributing to his audience some feature in respect of which the audience resembles (more or less fancifully) the mentioned substance. (5) Therefore, this is what is implicated.

Again, why is (4) supposed to be true? Why is *this* the "most likely" supposition? I take it that Grice would like to *explain* metaphor along these lines rather than appeal to some sort of loose 'metaphor-conventions' to sanction the move to (4)—that is, the move to (4), and others like it, is to *explain* metaphorical use of language. But then we need some principles to guide our search for the correct supposition. I do not see why the proposition Grice gives is the "most likely."

Quality-2 Do not say what you lack adequate evidence for.
☐ Grice's only example of this is where someone says, in suitable circumstances, "She is probably deceiving him this evening," thereby implicating that she is (the sort of person who is) given to deceiving her husband. The implicature is supposed to be off of the contextually determined fact that the speaker has no evidence for what he said, so the hearer must find a proposition that the speaker might have sufficient evidence for, such as the above.[38]

Relation Be relevant.
☐ At a genteel tea-party, *A*: "Mrs. X is an old bag." (Appalled silence). B: "The weather has been quite delightful this summer, hasn't it?"

GLOSS: (1) *B* has flouted the maxim of relation—it is not relevant to *A*'s remark. (2) He thereby implicates that *A*'s remark should not be discussed or that *A* has committed a social gaffe.

I find this case suspect because it is not at all obvious how to fill in the reasoning between flouting the maxim and the implication, which must be possible if it is to be a conversational implicature.

---

38. This example is complicated by the fact that we do not know from the description of the case whether 'deceiving him' is meant literally or is a general euphemism for (the more specific euphemism) 'sleeping with someone'. (For the record, note that within the context of a discussion about said wife, a person remarking "She probably is sleeping with someone tonight" would normally be taken to mean that she is probably sleeping with someone *else* (other than her husband) tonight. Presumably this is because otherwise the remark would have added no new relevant information to the talk exchange.) I find the example more plausible but more complicated on the euphemistic reading. The complication is that the hearer must first recover what the speaker more specifically meant, then, given that, determine what was implicated. Much of the same machinery and pattern of inference are involved in both steps.

We can now try to characterize conversational implicatures as follows (1967, II, p. 13):[39]

(93) *S conversationally implicates* that *q* to *H* iff:

    (1) *S* implicates that *q* to *H*;

    (2) *H* presumes that *S* is observing the conversational maxims (or CP) when *S* says that *p* to *H*;

    (3) If *S*'s saying that *p* is *S*'s total contribution to the conversation at that point, then *S*'s saying that *p* is not consistent with the presumption that *S* is observing the conversational maxims (or CP);

    (4) The supposition that *S thinks, is aware*, that *q* is required to make *S*'s saying (or making as if to say) that *p* consistent with the presumption that *S* is observing the conversational maxims (or CP);

    (5) *S* thinks (and would expect *H* to think that *S* thinks) that it is within the competence of *H* to work it out or grasp intuitively that (4).

WORKING-OUT SCHEMA

Since it is a necessary condition on something being a conversational implicature that it at least be capable of being worked out, we should be able to schematize this working out as follows (1967, II, p. 14):[40]

(94) (1) *S* said that *p*.

    (2) If *S*'s saying that *p* is his total contribution to the conversation at this point, it is not consistent with the presumption that *S* is observing the conversational maxims (or CP).

    (3) There is no reason to suppose that *S* is not observing the conversational maxims (or CP).

    (4) The supposition that *S* thinks that *q* is required to make *S*'s saying that *p* consistent with the presumption that *S* is observing the conversational maxims (or CP).

    (5) *S* knows that I can see that (4).

    (6) *S* has done nothing to block (5).

    (7) Therefore *S* intends me to think that *q*.

    (8) So, *S* has implicated that *q*.

In this reasoning *H* makes use of at least the following information:

(95) (1) The conventional meaning of the words;

    (2) The identity of the referents;

    (3) The conversational maxims (or CP);

    (4) The context of utterance;

---

39. Grice mentions all but (3).
40. Grice mentions all but (2).

(5) Background knowledge;

(6) The mutual belief that S and H share knowledge of (1)–(5).

At this point we must notice that the implicature that q has been carried by S's saying that p on a particular occasion in virtue of special features of the context. These kinds of conversational implicatures Grice calls *particularized* conversational implicatures. As he says: "There is no room for the idea that an implicature of this sort is *normally* carried by saying that P" (1967, II, p. 21).

GENERALIZED CONVERSATIONAL IMPLICATURE

Grice coins the category of *generalized* conversational implicatures for cases where saying that p would *normally* carry such and such an implicature. The fact that a generalized conversational implicature carries a normal implicature is liable to make it appear similar to a conventional implicature. As examples of generalized conversational implicatures, Grice gives the following:

(96) 'x is meeting a woman this evening'[41] implicates 'the woman is not his sister, mother, wife, or close platonic friend'.

(97) 'x went into a house yesterday and found a tortoise inside the front door' implicates 'the house was not his own'. The same could be said of 'a car,' 'a garden,' 'a college'.

Grice claims that sometimes there is no such implicature. For example,

(98) I've been sitting in a car all morning.

41. But does 'x is meeting an adult human female this evening' carry the *same* implication? It seems not, and this creates the following difficulty (emphasized by Chomsky, in conversation); Grice wants to say that any *way* or *manner* of saying the same thing is likely to have the same generalized implicature. So if the above does not (in all likelihood) have the requisite implicature it should not count as another way or manner of saying (the same thing as) the original. And this would be the case if either (i) these two expressions did not count as 'saying the same thing' when uttered in the appropriate context, or (ii) these were not different 'ways' or 'manners' of saying the same thing. There is reason to deny both (i) and (ii). First, recall that 'what is said' was in part a function of (or at least 'closely related to') the conventional meaning of the words uttered (1967, II, p. 5) and presumably the two expressions in question are paraphrases. So, other things being equal, one would expect the same thing to have been said. Second, under the maxim of Manner (relating *how* what is said is to be said) we find: "be brief." And clearly we could generate an implicature off of the expanded paraphrase. (For instance, A says, "I'm going to meet Bobby," B says, "Is Bobby a man or a woman?" A says, "(Well) Bobby's an adult human female." I would think that A implied something like the opinion that he did not view Bobby as particularly attractive or desirable in a feminine way, and he did this by conspicuously picking this verbose equivalent thereby (conspicuously) avoiding the word 'woman' and so disavowing some of its usual suggestions in these contexts. That it has these suggestions cannot be doubted in view of pairs like: 'She is a real (good, etc.) woman' vs. 'She is a real (good, etc.) adult human female'.)

If this is correct it is an interesting question why there is no implicature in (98), but there is in the following:

(99) x climbed into a car yesterday and found a tortoise behind the seat.

Notice that the explanation cannot turn on a difference in the verbs in (99) and (98), because the same verb in different VP's can have or fail to have the requisite implicature. Consider the following:

(100) (i) 'I slept in a chair last night' does not imply 'the chair is not mine'.

(ii) 'I slept under a table last night' does not imply 'the table is not mine'.

(iii) 'I slept $\begin{Bmatrix} \text{in a house last night} \\ \text{on a boat last night} \end{Bmatrix}$' does not imply 'the house/boat is not mine'.

(iv)? 'I slept in a car last night' does imply 'the car is not mine'.

(v) 'I slept in a small room last night' does not imply 'the small room is not mine'.

(101) (i) 'I found a ring yesterday' does imply 'the ring is not mine'.

(ii) 'I found an error yesterday' does not imply 'the error was not mine'.

(102) (i) 'I read a book yesterday' does not imply 'the book is mine'.

(ii)? 'I lost a book yesterday' does imply 'the book is mine'.

I have as yet no explanation for these differences.

Grice concludes that a conversational implicature possesses certain features:

(103) (1) Since observance of the conversational maxims is a necessary condition for calculating a conversational implicature, a generalized conversational implicature can be *canceled* by either *explicitly or contextually opting out*.

(2) Since calculation of a conversational implicature requires only:
(i) Contextual information
(ii) Background information
(iii) What is said
and not the *manner* in which it is said, then any way of saying what is said is likely to have the same conversational implicature. Since a generalized conversational implicature is fairly insensitive to context and background information, it should have a high degree of nondetachability.

(3) Since calculation of the conversational implicature requires prior knowledge of what is said, the conversational implicature is not a part of the meaning-force of what is said.

(4) Since what is said may be true and what is conversationally implicated is false, the implicature is not carried by what is said, but only by, "The saying of what is said or by 'putting it that way' " (1967, II, p. 25).

Clause (4) is not at all clearly true and seems to conflict with the claim in (103, 2). In (4) Grice seems to be invoking his old criteria of cancelability as the test for whether *what is said* is the vehicle of the implication. But since implicature is not entailment and can always be canceled, it is not clear what truth or falsity has to do with it at all.

(103) (5) In many cases the conversational implicature will be a disjunction.

A Problem with This Account

The possibility of (103, 5) raises some questions about the completeness or adequacy of Grice's characterization of the generalized conversational implicature. Reconsider Grice's examples:

(104) I found a tortoise in a house yesterday.

is said to conversationally implicate

(105) The house was not mine.

How would we get this implicature on Grice's scheme? Presumably, the first maxim of quantity is being exploited. 'A house' conveys less information than might be desired. In normal circumstances the speaker might legitimately suppose that the hearer would like him to be more specific. But there are many ways of being more specific here:

(106) I found a tortoise in $\begin{Bmatrix} \text{my} \\ \text{Nixon's} \\ \text{Aunt Martha's} \end{Bmatrix}$ house yesterday.

Again, feature (103, 5) predicts that my saying that I found a tortoise in a house yesterday should implicate an open disjunction of the form

(107) The house was mine or the house was Nixon's, or the house was Aunt Martha's . . .

However, none of these are implicated. All that *is* implicated is that it is *not* my house. Fortunately for Grice's theory, the description above does not satisfy all of his conditions for a conversational implicature. In particular, it doesn't satisfy condition (1): that S implicates that q to H, because it does not satisfy condition (iii) on Implicature: that by saying that p to H, S implied, suggested, indicated, etc., that q (to H).
Since it is false that I implicated that

(108) The house was $\begin{cases} \text{mine.} \\ \text{Nixon's.} \\ \text{not Nixon's.} \\ \text{Aunt Martha's.} \\ \text{not Aunt Martha's.} \end{cases}$

ROBERT M. HARNISH

it is false that I *conversationally* implicated that (108). For this reason we must assume that the *range* of the possible disjunction in (5) is determined by what is implicated. However, the theory now cannot explain why the implicature is there in the first place.[42] One way to get the requisite implicature might be as follows. We distinguish between a *primary* and a *secondary* implicature. A secondary implicature is whatever can be reasonably inferred by the hearer (given shared background knowledge and beliefs) from the primary implicature in the context. In the case above the hearer reasons as follows:

(109) (1) X said he found a tortoise in a house yesterday.
(2) We both know (and know that we both know) that the conversational maxims are being observed.

42. The point can be put more precisely as follows:

(1) Feature (5) allows for the possibility of many implicata Q, R, etc.
(2) (i) Either (2)–(5) define conversational implicata Q, R, etc. or,
(ii) (1)–(5) define conversational implicata Q, R, etc.
(3) Suppose (2i): then by definition, the set of implicata (on a particular occasion) is determined by the predicate (roughly):

(a) X is required to make S's-saying-that-P, consistent with the supposition that S is observing the conversational maxims.

(4) Thus, (3a) can explain (via the working-out schema) how P, etc., get implicated. But,
(5) (3a) predicts that

(b) The house was Aunt Martha's.

is an implication of "I found it in a house."
(6) But (5b) is not such an implication, so (3a) cannot be sufficient.
(7) Suppose (2ii): Then by definition the set of implicata (on a particular occasion) is determined by the predicate:

(c) (i) x is implicated (i.e., suggested, implied, but not said) and (ii) x is required to make S's-saying-that-P, consistent with the supposition that S is observing the conversational maxims.

(8) Then (7c) does not predict that (5b) is an implicata of "I found it in a house," because (5b) does not satisfy condition (i) on the predicate (c).
(9) However, now condition (ii) on the predicate (c) does not provide us with an explanation of why

(d) The house was not mine.

gets conversationally implicated, because it does not provide us with an explanation of why (d) gets implicated at all.
(10) This result seems counter to the whole point of Grice's discussion of conversational implicature.

Although it is true that conversational implication is a species of implication, its relationship to the genus is not the usual one of having the properties of the genus *plus* some new property essential to the species. Rather a conversational implication is an implication *generated in a certain way*: by exploiting a maxim on the assumption that the hearer will be able to apply the working out schema. For our part, we want to see if we can find an explanation for the implicature on the basis of exploitation and working out.

(3) Therefore, the first maxim of Quantity is being observed.

(4) The speaker should assume that I am interested in knowing what house it was found in.

(5) Therefore, he is flouting the first maxim of Quantity.

(6) Since the speaker is obeying the conversational maxims, he is observing the maxim of Relation: be relevant. Thus the most charitable assumption consistent with the exploitation of the first maxim of Quantity is that he doesn't know anytning more about the house (that he thinks is relevant).

(7) Therefore, he *primarily implicates* that he doesn't have any more pertinent information about the house.

(8) Since one usually knows what houses one possesses, we may reasonably infer that this was not one of them.

(9) Therefore, he *secondarily implicates* that the house was not his.

Notice that this way of handling the case has the advantage that it explains why, in a conversation about, say, Aunt Martha's house, the speaker would be taken to implicate that the tortoise was not in Aunt Martha's house. This is because the gap between the primary and secondary implicature is bridged by background knowledge and beliefs—and in the course of a conversation various pieces of information that influence the inference can be conveyed. It seems to me that there is liable to be a complex interaction here (and other places, of course) among various pieces of information and the different maxims—although I have no clear data to support this hunch. This also suggests that the terminology 'generalized' implicature is misleading. What appears to happen is that such implicatures stand unless they are explicitly or contextually cancelled. Such 'standing' conversational implicatures are presumably sustained by a variety of mutual beliefs among participants in the talk-exchange.

FIRST SOLUTION TO THE PROBLEM PROPOSED

We now return to our problem cases. We have decided that the IMPLICATION is not entailment, is not a *part* of what is said. The question then becomes, what kind of implicature they are: conventional, particularized conversational, or generalized conversational. Here we must be careful, for although we have been given five features of conversational implicatures, we do not have and may never have a decision procedure to settle the question of whether q—which is a part of the total signification of the utterance of a sentence—is a conversational implicate or an element in the conventional meaning of the sentence (1967, III, p. 3). To make any case for the existence of a conversational implication, it is necessary (and perhaps not sufficient) to exhibit the reasoning that generates it. As Grice says:

(110) "Any such case [for the existence of a conversational implicature] would at least have to be supported by a demonstration of the way in which what is putatively implicated could have come to be implicated (by a derivation of it from conversational principles and other data); and even this may not be sufficient to provide a decisive distinction between a conversational implicature and a case in which what was originally a conversational implicature has become conventionalized" (1967, III, p. 4).

Thus, to make even a plausible case for our favored relation being a nonconventional implicature, the exact steps for its generation must be specified. This is a requirement I will try to strictly observe.

Our earlier results showed that the implications were cancelable, but not (easily) detachable. Since these are two of the properties of the generalized conversational implicature, it is plausible that this is the correct category. However, if we try to apply the paradigm it is not clear how it is supposed to work. The main problem is to find an adequate sense in which one *exploits* a conversational maxim in uttering our sentences. This should make us suspicious. Nevertheless, we will try to construct an explanation along these lines.

Adjectives

The only plausible maxim to be exploited is Quantity-1: be as informative as is necessary. Suppose Jones asks: "what color is the flag?" and Smith replies: "(the flag is) red." Thus

(111) (1) (i)   Smith said that the flag was red.
            (ii) Smith did not say that the flag was red all over.
            (iii) Smith's saying that the flag was red suggested or implied that it was red all over.
            (iv) Therefore, Smith implicated that the flag was red all over.
      (2) Smith supposes that Jones is aware that Smith is observing the general maxims.
      (3) The supposition that the flag is red all over is required to make Smith's saying that the flag is red consistent with the first maxim of quantity.
      (4) Jones is aware that Smith knows it is within Jones' competence to work it out that (3).
      (5) Smith has done nothing to block (3).
      (6) Therefore Smith thinks that the flag is red all over.

The exploitation of the first maxim of Quantity comes about by having the choice of sentences:

(112) The flag is $\left\{\begin{array}{ll}\text{(i)} & \phi \\ \text{(ii)} & \text{partly} \\ \text{(iii)} & \text{all}\end{array}\right\}$ red.[43]

But if we read 'the flag is red' as I want to—'the flag is at least partly red', then *both* 'the flag is partly red' and 'the flag is all red' are *more* informative than 'the flag is red'. The problem is why it implies 'all' rather than 'partly' since they are both compatible with the first maxim of Quantity. This is a case like the one we mentioned earlier as raising questions about the completeness of Grice's characterization of the generalized conversational implicature. According to feature (103, 5), in many cases the conversational implicature will be a disjunction and that is just what we have here. However, only the 'all' statement is really implicated—whereas the theory predicts that both will be.

Our difficulty here is analogous to our difficulty with 'a house'. With the house example we saw that saying 'I found a tortoise in a house yesterday' did not conversationally implicate (via exploitation of the first maxim of quantity) that the house was Aunt Martha's or Nixons's—even though these were assumptions that would make what I said compatible with the maxims—because I didn't implicate these at all. Likewise with 'the flag'; I do not implicate at all that the flag is partly red, so I don't conversationally implicate it. But analogous to the house example, we still need to explain how the implicature arises in the first place. With the house example, we got the implicature through the distinction between primary and secondary implication. How can we get it with the flag

43. Notice that 'the flag is red' does not *mean* 'the flag is partly red' because this entails that it is not all red. As evidence for this entailment consider

  (a) The flag is partly red and it is all red.

Since this is a contradiction, 'the flag is partly red' entails 'the flag is not all red'. As further evidence notice that contraposition seems to hold: if the flag is all red it follows that that flag is not partly red. Furthermore, Chomsky has pointed out (in conversation) the following curiosity. Suppose that I am right about the meaning of 'the flag is red'. Consider

  (b) The red flag (is on the table).

Here, in prenominal position, we feel disinclined to say that a flag so picked out need only have *some* red in it. Rather it should be distinctively or predominantly red. But if prenominal adjectives are gotten in a grammar by Rel-Clause Reduction and Adjective-Preposing, then transformations seem to change meaning. Alternately, if they do not change meaning, then either 'The flag is red' does not mean 'The flag is at least partly red', or 'The red flag is . . .' does not mean 'The flag which is predominantly red is . . .', but only implies it. I am more inclined toward the latter way out. But then one needs to explain why 'The flag that is red . . .' seems not to carry the same implication. One proposal might be along the lines that the attributive use is in some way more characteristically referential and so would carry more of an implication because of maximum identificatory power. Unfortunately, there are many nonreferential occurences of prenominal adjectives where the difference still seems to show up: 'I am looking for a red flag' versus 'I am looking for a flag that is red'.

example? It might go the same way as follows. Recall that we introduced our sentence in response to the question, 'What color is the flag?' (what I earlier called the 'minimal context'). It can reasonably be supposed that when a person asks a question of the form

(113)   What ϕ is the X?

he wants enough information about the ϕ of the X so that if he wanted to pick out X with respect to ϕ, he could. To say that the flag is at least red is to provide less identificatory information than that it is all red.[44]

44. Fodor observed (in conversation) that questions of the form (a) 'Who ϕ-ed?' do not always ask for a complete specification of X with respect to ϕ. For example, (b): 'Who has a key?' can be used to ask for a specification of *someone* with a key, not *everyone* with a key. Now, on the Katz-Postal (1964) theory of interrogatives, (b) has the deep structure shown in (c):

(c)

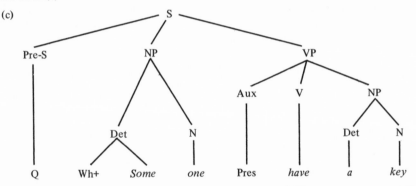

The reading of 'Q' expresses the fact that the utterance of (b) counts as a request that a hearer provide a sentence synonymous with what is dominated by S, except that more semantic information should be included in the constituent which in the interrogative is in the scope of Wh, and which the answerer believes to be true. (Unfortunately, unless Frege is right, the answer 'John' will not count as an answer to the question since proper names have no sense and so do not contribute markers to the reading of the answer.) Ignoring this, it is clear that something like the proper interpretation is assigned to (b) by this theory since it in effect asks for substitution instances on 'someone'. The problem is, rather, that it is not clear how we get the other interpretation of (b), i.e., give me identifying expressions for all the people with keys. This is the common reading one finds in exam questions: 'who holds that all *a priori* statements are analytic?' Here I am asking for *everyone* (within the scope of the discussion) who held that all *a priori* statements are analytic. Now, do we want to say that (most) questions of form (a) are *ambiguous* as between a 'someone' and an 'everyone' reading? If one takes this line, it is difficult to specify the underlying structure for the 'everyone' reading. I do not think that we can simply substitute 'every' for 'some' in (c). I do not know how to interpret 'Wh+ everyone' in a way that guarantees what we want. Notice that if 'who' can come from 'Wh+ everyone', then we could not define a rejected question as before. If I ask 'who has a ϕ?' I can answer (and not reject) the question by replying 'everyone has a ϕ'. Rather, I think that the most plausible line for a person to take (who thinks that questions like (a) are *ambiguous*) is to offer two interpretations of 'Q'; one asks for at least *some* additional semantic information, the other asks for *all* additional semantic information. This approach, however, has its own obvious drawbacks.

Given this, we can account for the implicature stated as a blunt fact in (111, 1) (iii) and shortcircuit the unwanted implicatures of (107). The hearer's (questioner's) reasoning is as follows:

(114)   (1) Jones said that the flag is (at least) red.

          (2) Jones did not say that the flag is all red.

          (3) We both are observing the conversational maxims, etc.

          (4) Therefore, Jones is observing the first maxim of Quantity.

          (5) Under the circumstances, Jones can reasonably assume (and assume that I assume him to assume) that I would like ϕ-identifying information about x.

          (6) Given assumption (5), Jones has flouted the first maxim of Quantity.

          (7) The most charitable assumption consistent with (4) and (5) is that no further information is needed (for ϕ-identification).

          (8) Therefore, Jones *primarily implicates* that no further information is needed (for ϕ-identification).

          (9) But if the flag were other colors besides red, other information would be needed, but since (7), then there are no other colors.

        (10) Therefore, Jones *secondarily implicates* that the flag is *all* red.

Notice that one advantage of treating 'the flag is all red' as a conversational implicature and not as an entailment is that in a conversation requiring the identification of a certain color, one can point to an American flag and say 'that flag is magenta' without implicating that it is all red. In this case, the implicature is *contextually* canceled. This is analogous to the first feature Grice gives of a general conversational implicature—that its implication can be canceled by either explicitly or contextually *opting out*.

Verbs

We turn now to sentences like

(115) Russell wrote *Principia*.

(116) Smith and Jones moved the table.

Again there is a certain difficulty in seeing how to apply the theory. Rather than assume that the explanation for the IMPLICATIONS will be the same for both (115) and (116), I will attack them one at a time.

I would prefer to assume that questions of form (a) have only the one sense, but that the context determines when the scope of the question is stronger than (or is intended to be taken as stronger than) the minimal as determined by the meaning of the sentence. Unfortunately, I have no theory of how the context can determine the force of the utterance in the appropriate way.

Consider the following dialogue again:

(117) (i) *H*: Who wrote *Principia*?
       (ii) *S*: Russell wrote *Principia*.

The most obvious way of handling the implication in our theory is to appeal again to the first maxim of Quantity. Again, we can suppose that the hearer-*cum*-questioner is requesting ϕ-identifying information about *Principia*. The hearer-*cum*-questioner (*H*) upon hearing the answer reasons as follows:

(118) (1) *S* said that (at least) Russel wrote *Principia*.
       (2) *S* did not say that Russel alone wrote *Principia*.
       (3) We are both obeying (and know that we both know we are obeying) the conversational maxims.
       (4) *H* supposes that *S* knows that *H* is requesting authorship-identifying information, and that all information *necessary* for this is relevant.
       (5) Since *H* supposes *S* to fulfill (3), *H* supposes *S* to be obeying the maxim of Relation: be relevant.
       (6) Since *H* supposes *S* to fulfill (3), *H* supposes *S* to be obeying the first maxim of Quantity.
       (7) But on supposition (5), *S* is flouting the first maxim of Quantity by uttering (117 ii) (in this context).
       (8) To make *S*'s saying that (117 ii) consistent with supposition (6), the most charitable assumption is that no further information is needed for ϕ-identification.
       (9) Therefore, *S primarily implicates* that no further information is necessary for ϕ-identification.
     (10) But if Russell wrote *Principia* with someone else, (8) would be false.
     (11) Since *H* is supposing (8) is true, Russell did not write *Principia* with someone else.
     (12) Therefore *S secondarily implicated* that Russell alone wrote *Principia*.

Consider the following dialogue:

(118) (i) *H*: Who moved the table?
       (ii) *S*: Smith and Jones moved the table.

Besides the implication that no one else helped them move the table, there is the implication that they moved it together. It is this latter implication that I want to investigate

Unfortunately, here there seems to be no obvious way of appealing to the first maxim of Quantity. As a clue to what is going on, notice what kinds of cases would make the implication false. For example,

(119) First Smith moved the table, then Jones moved the table.

This suggests to me that it is possible that the single temporal specification in (118ii) could be playing a role in the implication. Notice that the conjoined sentence

(120) (i) Smith moved the table and (ii) Jones moved the table.

tends, if anything, to imply that they did *not* move it together. Again it is possible that picking twin temporal specification contributes to carrying the implication of two separate act-tokens. This phenomenon is similar to Strawson's examples (1952, p. 80):

(121) (i) They got married and had a child.
       (ii) They had a child and got married.

Some logicians have claimed that these two sentences are equivalent (that 'and' is the English analogue of the standard connective '&') while other logicians (among them Strawson) have claimed that (121) is a counterexample to such a view. Grice, subscribing to the former view, has tried to explain the *prima facie* difference between (121i) and (121ii) as due to an implicature, not to the meaning of 'and'. Grice handles this case by appealing to a submaxim of Manner, to the effect that one should make the order of telling reflect the order of the events.

In an analogous fashion, choosing the conjoined-subject sentence (118, ii) over the conjoined-sentence sentence (120), or vice versa, implies something about the nature of the event. The problem is finding the necessary feature of the sentence and finding a suitable submaxim. In Grice's account of Strawson's example there was an appeal to similarity of temporal order. What can I appeal to? As a start consider the following:

Super Submaxim: Be representational; in so far as possible, make your sayings "mirror" the world.

With this *Tractatus*-like maxim available, we can see Grice's submaxim as fitting one "dimension" of mirroring, *time:*

Submaxim of Time: In so far as possible, make the order of saying reflect the order of events.

Another dimension of mirroring might be *space:*

Submaxim of Space: In so far as possible, if objects a, b, c, ... ϕ together, put their names together when reporting this ϕ-ing.

These may not be as farfetched as they seem. At times we seem to utilize in our sayings the paralellism between our sayings and the world. Consider: "Sam read Plato, Aristotle and Descartes in that order." What order is *that* order? Clearly it is not the left-to-right order of the words 'Plato', 'Aristotle,' and 'Descartes', but rather the temporal order in speech which the left-to-right order represents in English. The use of 'that' in this way here requires that the temporal order of saying mirror that of the reading.

Does the submaxim of space contain a pun on 'together'? Consider the difference in implication between the following:

(122) (i) Sam was in New York last week, and John was in New York last week, and Fred was in New York last week.

(ii) Sam and John and Fred were in New York last week.

For me, (122ii) implies that they were in New York together, while (122i) does not. In fact (122, i) weakly implies that they were not together in New York last week. The question is what (122ii) shares with (118ii) such that an implication is generated, but which (122i) and (120i) lack. At the moment, only the condition specified by the applied submaxim seems to sort these cases. Using this submaxim we can, perhaps, account for the implicature in (118ii) that they moved the table together in a way that resembles (114) and (118).

PROBLEMS WITH THE FIRST PROPOSAL

Besides the obvious deficiencies of vagueness, overhasty generalization, one-sided diet of examples, and so on, the explanation sketched in the previous section has at least the following limitations. One, the theory so far does not explain why some adjectives and verbs contribute to an implicature and others do not. Two, previously I said that we ought to be suspicious of our difficulty in identifying the appropriate maxim for exploitation and utilization in the working-out schema. I think those suspicions were justified. In fact, not all of the working-out schema was utilized, as a glance back at (94) will show. In particular, clause (94, 4) requires that the output of the schema have the form

(123) S thinks (is aware) that q.

whereas our implicata had the form

(124) q (e.g., 'The flag is all red.')

But clause (94, 4) is a reflex of a condition on conversational implicature— it is the supposition (123) that is required for maxim consistency. Thus technically our cases were not cases of conversational implicature. In a way this is good, for certainly when I say 'The flag is red' I am not trying to get you to work it out that I think that the flag is all red. I may be being coy or noncommittal, but I need neither think that the flag is all red nor need I be trying to get you to think that I think that the flag is all red. Nevertheless, I want to claim that something like this implication *is* generated by saying that *p*. In this respect our cases from some of the paradigmatic examples with which Grice introduces and illustrates the notion of conversational implicature. In cases like (65ii) and (96), the probable context is one where the speaker wants to *communicate* a certain belief or piece of information without *saying* it —as if he might want to leave the 'I didn't *say* that' bridge unburned. But notice that I did not cite Grice's example (97) in the list above. All along I have been working off of the parallelisms between the house example (97) and my examples, and it strikes me that the house example falls under criticisms above, too. In saying 'I found it in a house', I am not trying to get you to work it out that (I think that) the house was not mine. The implication is carried regardless of this. It is not something I might care to avoid *saying* but nevertheless want to *communicate*. The conclusion that the working-out schema does not (completely) apply has serious consequences. As Grice says;

(125) "The presence of a conversational implicature must be capable of being worked out; for even if it can in fact be intuitively grasped, unless the intuition is replaceable by an argument, this implicature will not count as a *conversational* implicature; it will be a *conventional* implicature" (1967, II, p. 13).

This might lead us to believe that the phenomena I am trying to explain is conventional, but it cannot be—first, since the implications are cancelable, and, second, because there is no obvious way to tie the implication to the words in question without creating difficulties. Thus, even if conventional implication is distinguished from entailment, it cannot be *attached directly* to the adjective because conjoined predicates like 'red and white' would then have incompatible conventional implications. But if the implication is not conventional and not conversational, what is it? There are at least two alternatives. First, we could either modify the definition of conversational implicature and the working-out schema by (*a*) making the appropriate condition *disjunctive*, i.e., $\ulcorner S$ thinks that q, or $q\urcorner$; or (*b*) we could simply replace $\ulcorner S$ thinks that $q\urcorner$ by q in the definition, and let $\ulcorner S$ thinks that $q\urcorner$ be inferred by the hearer via the first maxim of Quality: do not say what you believe to be false. But since q is not a part of what is *said*, the maxim does not literally apply. The second alternative is to attempt to isolate another kind of implicature that does not necessitate the use of exploitation and the fullblown working-out schema. This kind of implication would lie 'between' conventional implication and generalized conversational implication.

Second Solution Proposed: Direct and Indirect Implicature

Recall that we earlier noted that Grice distinguished four ways in which a maxim could be infringed: by opting out, by violation, by clash, and by flouting. Grice *seems* to reserve the title 'conversational implicature' for those aroused by flouting a maxim. What then of the others? Since they also turn on supposing the maxims to be in effect thay can be said to be broadly 'conversational' too. If all nonconventional implicatures should turn out to be conversational (in the sense of turning on maxims of conversation), then we could adopt some other term like 'pragmatic' for the genus, and reserve 'conversational' for those gotten by flouting. However, this generalization is by no means clearly true. So I will adopt the terminology of *direct* and *indirect* (conversational) implicatures. *Indirect* implicatures require that a maxim be flouted, whereas *direct* implicatures require that the highest-valued maxims are intended to be observed, at the level of what is said. Nonconventional, but nonconversational implicatures might be called 'contextual'.

These two kinds of implicature seem to have at least one important difference. With indirect conversational implicature, the hearer is intended to reason from the speaker's saying that p to his implicating that q, that it would be reasonable (on Grice's theory of utterer's occasion-meaning[45]) to say that the speaker meant that q. This will not be the case with direct implicature since the speaker need not be aware that the hearer is making the inference generating the implicature. Consider again

(126) The flag is red.

On the assumption that the speaker is obeying the conversational maxims, the speaker is obeying the following maxims:

(127) (i) Be as informative as necessary.
       (ii) Be relevant.
       (iii) Have evidence for what you say.

These obviously can interact in various ways and for this reason it is useful to state them separately. However, I want to suggest[46] another maxim that combines them in a specific way:

(128) *Maxim of Quantity-Quality:* Make the strongest relevant claim justifiable by your evidence.

This maxim is ordered with respect to the other three—it applies unless one of the others overrides it (either explicitly or contextually).

45. See for instance Grice (1969), redefinition IV (B).

46. In his earlier paper, Grice makes use of a similar principle: "One should not make a weaker statement rather than a stronger one unless there is a good reason for so doing" (1961, p. 451). In his interesting study of this principle, O'Hair ends up with the following version: "Unless there are outweighing good reasons to the contrary, one should not make a weaker statement rather than a stronger one if the audience is interested in the extra information that could be conveyed by the latter" (1969a, p. 45). This can be viewed as spelling out what "strongest relevant" might come to in my maxim.

We have been assuming that if p entails q, and q does *not* entail p, then p is stronger than, more informative than, q. This was supposed to be a sufficient condition on relative strength of information. One problem is that, on this account, if p is contradictory or logically false, then it will (trivially) entail any contingent statement q, but q will not entail it. So by this criterion contradictions will be stronger than, more informative than, any contingent statement, and this does not seem right. One way out might be to analyze entailment along the lines of recent work in 'relevance' logic (see Anderson and Belnap, 1968).

Nor can the suggested criterion be turned into a necessary condition. This would preclude the possibility of independent statements bearing relations of strength. Yet we feel that a statement to the effect that Jones' phone number is 1213 is more informative than that someone has been happy. So we want an account that meets the following conditions (if possible):

(1) Logical truths and falsehoods are least informative and get rank 0. (If logicism is correct, then mathematical statements would be uninformative. Perhaps we could say

On hearing (126), the Hearer reasons as follows:

(129) (1) S is obeying all the maxims, so he is obeying Quantity-Quality.
      (2) The claim that the flag is red and some other color would be stronger than the claim that it is red, because $\ulcorner p$ and $q \urcorner$ entails p, but not conversely.
      (3) Therefore S is directly implying that the flag is not red *and* some other color, and therefore that the flag is only red.

The same reasoning will work for "Russell wrote *Principia*." And the nonconventional implicature branch of (64) should look something like (130):

(130)

| | Nonconventional Implicature | | |
| | Conversational | | Contextual |
	Direct	Indirect	?
Particular			
Standing (Generalized)			

---

that what is informative is not the statement that p, but the realization that p *is* a mathematical truth.)

(2) If p, q are not of rank 0, then if p entails q, but q does not entail p, then p is stronger than q.

(3) Logically independent statements can bear relations of strength.

I have no analysis that meets these, but see Smokler (1966) and O'Hair (1969b) for some relevant discussion.

Another line of attack might be to postpone the search for a general criterion of information strength, and turn instead to more specific submaxims of information. Steps in this direction have been taken by Fogelin (1967, I.6). There he considers statements related by the traditional square of opposition and offers us two principles that range over them:

(P 1) Do not employ an I or an O proposition in a context where you can legitimately employ an A or an E proposition (p. 21).

And its 'corollary':

(P 2) Do not affirm one subcontrary if you are willing to deny the other (p. 21).

It is convenient to restate (and perhaps generalize) (P2) as (P2'):

(P 2') Affirm one subcontrary iff you are willing to affirm the other.

Given (P 2') it is clear that the use of one subcontrary will suggest that one would affirm the other as well, and that "subcontraries tend to collapse together" (p. 22). To say that some As are B is conversationally taken to mean that some are and some are not; likewise, with saying that some As are not B. It is important to note that this implication is contextually dependent. Consider Fogelin's case of a prison guard who announces that some of his prisoners have escaped, when they all have. The implication is dependent on the presumption that if more were missing, he would know. Contrast this with another case (due to Merrilee Salmon): I am driving past Jones' house, the light is on, and I say: 'Somebody must be home.' I certainly do not imply that somebody is not; and this is because (I contend) I am not supposed by the hearer to be in any position to know.

CONCLUSIONS

I want to emphasize exactly how weak my conclusions are even on the assumption that all of my arguments are sound. I am *not* claiming that I have shown that sentences like the ones I have been interested in are correctly gotten by conjunction reduction. Indeed, I think that evidence will eventually turn up that will show that they are *not* gotten by conjunction reduction—but this is presently just a hunch. Nor am I claiming that there are not other arguments besides (5) and (21) that would show that the sentences at issue could not come from conjunction reduction. Finally, I am not claiming that there is nothing wrong with these arguments except the steps that I have isolated for discussion. All I claim to have shown is that one argument in support of two of the premises of (5) and (21) is not sound because it has a false premise—that (7) entails (8) and (9) entails (10). I have given two sets of considerations against that view: direct counterargument and a theory of why one might have thought the relation was entailment. Now, it might turn out that my use of Grice's theory here is incorrect, and it might be that some more obviously adequate explanation can be found. Still, this paper will have the value of having demonstrated that in that case Grice's theory is simply too strong, that it can be applied very naturally to a domain that should be explained some other way. This would tell us that (and perhaps to some extent how) we must constrain the theory. This is one of the reasons that I have been at special pains to keep my examples and explanations as close to Grice's examples and explanations as possible.

FURTHER APPLICATIONS

If, contrary to my suspicions, the general mode of explanation investigated in this paper holds up and even is confirmed by independent arguments, then I think it would be profitable to take seriously the possibility of extending this kind of explanation to other data uncovered by linguists and philosophers and to their proposals.

Presupposition

Consider the following observation of Chomsky's:

> (131) "Two of my five children are in elementary school.

> The statement of [131] presupposes that I have five children; if I have six children, the statement is without truth value. In quite another sense, [131] presupposes that three of my five children are not in elementary school. That is, it would be natural for the hearer to assume this, on the basis of the statement [131]. On the other hand, if, in fact, three are in elementary school, [131] is not devoid of truth value; in fact it is true. Hearing [131], one is entitled to assume that three of my children are not in elementary school,

perhaps by virtue of general conditions on discourse of a sort that have been discussed by Paul Grice in his work on 'conversation implicature' " (1972, p. 112).

I agree with the substance of these remarks and I think that I can apply Grice's theory to the example. However, I will not subscribe to the current practice of distinguishing various 'senses' of presupposition. I will always use 'presuppose' as a relation between two statements such that if p presupposes q, then q is a necessary condition for the truth or falsity of p.[47] Now I want to reconstruct Chomsky's remarks in an explicitly Gricean framework. But first notice that the claim that (131) presupposes that I have five children, together with the usual account of presupposition, entails that a certain plausible account of its logical form is incorrect. That is, one might think that (131) has, on one level of analysis, the form

(132) I have five children and two of them are in elementary school.

But whereas (131) was said to lack a truth value if

(133) I have five children.

is false, (132) would be false if (133) were false. So if Chomsky and the usual accounts were right about (131), it could not have the form of (132).[48]

I am not at all confident about the correct ascription of logical form to (131), but for our purposes it is sufficient to assume that it is not (132) and that "two of my five children" is, on some level of analysis, a complex referring expression. Next we assume that the grammar can assign some representation of conceptual as well as logical (in the narrow sense) structure to (131). We can provisionally identify this as what a sentence literally and standardly/conventionally means. Further, let's assume that an expression means, on the occasion of its utterance, what it standardly means (this need not always be the case, see Grice (1969), Schiffer (1972)). Now, given a time of utterance, we can follow (66) and identify *what is said*. We suppose the hearer to be able to do this. If the hearer believes that the conversational maxims are being observed, then in particular the hearer believes that the maxim of Quantity-Quality is being observed. Thus, the hearer reasons:

(134) (1) S is obeying all the maxims so he is obeying Quantity-Quality.
       (2) The claim that three (or more) of S's five children are in elementary school would be stronger than the claim that two are—because the first entails the second but not vice versa.

47. This is slightly inaccurate, since I am tempted to follow Katz and others in 'extending' logical relations to sentences not conventionally used to make statements, but used to ask questions, issue commands, and so on.

48. Unless some way can be found for 'bracketing' off certain clauses in a conjunction and marking them for this logical property (see Grice, 1967, later lectures, and the last sections of this work).

(3) Therefore, given (1), S is directly implying that it is not the case that three or more of S's five children are in elementary school.

(4) Therefore, S is directly implying that three of S's five children are not in elementary school.

It strikes me as plausible that much of what has been said in the recent literature on presupposition can be reinterpreted in terms of implicature. Whether it all can, and whether this would result in the best overall theory of language, is a matter for future research and present faith.

Indirect Speech Acts

Consider again the sentence given earlier:

(135) Who has a (the) key?

Notice that in uttering (135), one could be performing the act of questioning, but one could also be performing the act of requesting a key. No doubt some philosophers (and linguists) would be inclined by this to the view that (135) is ambiguous.[49] I have referred to this kind of case as 'speech-act' indeterminacy or 'force' indeterminacy, to distinguish it from the usual kind of ambiguity. It is very common. For instance, the sentence

(136) I will be at your party tonight.

can be used to make a promise, make a threat, vow prediction, express intention, and so on. When one considers these kinds of cases, one is no longer quite so tempted to say that (135) is ambiguous, because by parity of reasoning, (136) would be five ways ambiguous. The mistake is to attach the force of the utterance too tightly to the meaning of the sentence uttered. These considerations lead me to think that (135) is not in fact ambiguous, but rather that the difference in the force of its utterance is to be accounted for contextually.

The conversion of question into requests is quite widespread in English speech. One of the most powerful classes of these is simple yes/no questions. Consider the following examples:

(137) (i) Will you pass the salt?

(ii) Won't you pass the salt?

(iii) Would you pass the salt?

(iv) ?Wouldn't you pass the salt?

(v) Can you pass the salt?

---

49. W. Alston (1963, IV) says, for instance, "'Can you reach the salt?' sometimes means *please pass the salt*, sometimes *Are you able to pass the salt?* and perhaps sometimes *I challenge you to try to reach as far as the salt.*"

(vi)   ?Can't you pass the salt?
(vii)   Could you pass the salt?
(viii)   ?Couldn't you pass the salt?
(ix)   *Should you pass the salt?
(x)   ?Shouldn't you pass the salt?

Notice two things. First, all of the sentences without initial question marks or star will take 'please' appended to them, while none of those with question marks or star prefixed will take 'please' appended to them. It is sometimes suggested that the possibility of so placing 'please' is a necessary (and perhaps sufficient) condition for a sentence being imperative. This may or may not be correct for the sentence type 'imperative', but if it is meant to suggest that if a sentence will not take 'please' it cannot be used to make a request or give an order then it must be mistaken: (137x) will not take 'please' but can be used to make a request. So also can "Should you be pulling the kitty's tail, Johnny?", which clearly can have the force of a request to stop. I think that this can be explained. Second, there is a natural hierarchy of 'strength' or politeness in the examples. The ordering for me and others of (137) from weakest (most polite) to strongest (most rude) is: (vii), (iii), (v), (i), (ii). Since conversations will also be governed by maxims of politeness, this data will have to be explained. One would like to find some (semantic?) property that correlates with this ordering. I have no indisputable candidate.

Returning to our original concern, we want to explain the conversion of interrogatives like 'who has a key?' and 'Will you pass the salt?' into requests like 'Somebody, give me a key' and 'Pass the salt'. Or, to put it another way, how do we get to what the speaker meant (to communicate) on that occasion from what the sentence means? The general form of the conversion (for these examples) is from (138) to (139):

(138)   He requested information about $\begin{Bmatrix} \text{the key.} \\ \text{the salt.} \end{Bmatrix}$

(139)   He requested $\begin{Bmatrix} \text{the key.} \\ \text{the salt.} \end{Bmatrix}$

What precisely is the question asked on these occasions? We have already spelled out the key example. For the salt example, the question is harder, for some people claim that 'will' is ambiguous. This is analogous to the sentence: 'I will be at your party tonight'. The basic senses seem to be: 'intend to' and 'predict that'. It should not be too hard to get the force of a promise, threat, and vow contextually off of the intend-reading. For the moment I am content to work with the assumption that 'will you pass the salt' is two ways ambiguous: (roughly) 'Do you intend to pass the salt?' and 'Do you think your passing the salt will come about?' I will work off of the intention reading because its connection with the request is more direct.[50] In effect what the hearer does is ignore part of the object of the request—the request *for information*. Instead, it is taken as a request for what the information is *about*. What would warrant this on Grice's account? Most plausibly it is the maxim of Relevance. The hearer must suppose that it is not *really* information that the speaker wants. It is of course easy to construct cases where it is *prima facie* obvious that the person does not want information and so must want something else (presumably). Consider Katz's case (personal communication) where the speaker says:

"Can you lift the log that is crushing my leg?" One might then argue, on the assumption that 'can' here means 'ability':

> Surely the addressee must ask himself how it could be relevant to the speaker's immediate needs to have the addressee provide information about his physical prowess. Surely, too, the addressee must conclude that the speaker's utterance is only an apparent violation of the maxim, not a real one, since he knows that the speaker is in no position to indulge in irrelavancies. Given this, it can be shown that the speaker's utterance conversationally implicates a proposition expressing a request for aid.

But of course if we are to get this implication conversationally, then the maxim of Relevance must be flouted, but to be flouted, it must be flagrantly violated— or as Grice puts it, X flouts a maxim if he "*blatantly* fails to fulfill it." So it is not the case that the speaker can just 'apparently' violate the maxim—he must really do so, and for a reason.

Now, although it can be the case in certain circumstances that it is obvious that the maxim of Relevance is being exploited, this is not so with my two examples. In Katz's example, the context is loaded so heavily toward a request for aid that the working-out schema seems almost otiose. If the speaker had simply mumbled something unintelligible we would have taken it to be a plea for help. The problem with my examples, on the other hand, is that the context does not have this kind of weight and so we still need an explanation of how the content of the question is related to the content of the request. To put it another way, the speaker asks a question (about x), the hearer understands this question (about x) and for some reason supposes it to flout the maxim of Rele-

---

50. It is not fair asking now for a principle by which the hearer selects that reading (over the prediction reading) before performing the requisite reasoning. It might be the case that the reasoning at issue will contribute to the determination of which the hearer selects. It is not implausible, for instance, that selection is made in accordance with the maxim of Relevance, so if Relevance is used in working out the implication, the possibility of such a working-out can confirm the original selection. The picture I am suggesting, then, is that in the communication situation the hearer forms hypotheses as to what the speaker meant on the basis of what 'what he uttered' means, and tests each hypothesis contextually in some vaguely understood way, being guided by the maxims. In this procedure the maxim of Relevance seems to play a uniquely central role. This is reflected by its similarity to the Cooperative Principle.

vance, and he then (somehow) concludes that it is a request (about x). Why does he assume it is a request about x and not about y? It may be obvious that it is, but so far all the hearer need supply is some z that would make requesting z conversationally relevant. Why should he suppose $z = x$?[51] The best reason I can think of is that what the questioner says is *more* relevant if the content of his utterance is considered relevant and only its *force* irrelevant. The hearer's job is then lightened in that he need only find the relevant speech-act type. However, we should not be overly impressed by the fact that a question is a request for information about x. This seems to suggest that a request *tout court* is the simplest hypothesis consistent with the supposition that the speaker is obeying the maxims. But this might only be an accident. Nevertheless, one can wonder why questions have been favored as forms of polite request—although there certainly are other kinds:

(140) I sure would like some salt.
       I wish I had some salt.

Either of these could count (on occasion) as a request for salt. These are expressions of desire (notice that they will not take 'please'), but the way they could generate a request is fairly straightforward on Gricean lines. It would be interesting to know what the limits to this kind of speech-act conversion are, if there are any.[52]

51. Recently, I understand, this problem has gone under the title of the problem of 'Whimperatives'. This is of course just one case of a very general phenomenon (see Searle, forthcoming, for an interesting discussion and a speech-act solution to this problem).

52. It is interesting to note that an opinion close to mine was reached by Robert Heinlein, who probably can be said not to have any philosophical/linguistic axes to grind. In his book *Stranger in a Strange Land*, a Martian (Mike Smith) is brought to Earth. His instruction in English is underdescribed, but apparently it consists mainly of memorizing a dictionary (he has total recall of course) and an oldfashioned grammar. He uses his (memorized) dictionary to translate English into Martian when possible. E.g., "Smith used English as one might use a code book, with tedious and imperfect translation" (p. 14). Because of the way he understands English, Smith understands sentences quite *literally*, and many humorous situations develop because "He knows a number of words, but . . . he doesn't have any cultural context to hang them on" (p. 37). Under this description of Smith's linguistic competence, it is intructive to consider the following episode. Smith is suspected of having the ability to levitate objects. He is being put to the test by Jubal and Jill. The dialogue (with slight alterations) is as follows:

Jubal: "Mike, sit at my desk. Now, can you pick up that ash tray? Show me."
Mike: "Yes, Jubal." Smith reached out and took it in his hand.
Jubal: "No, no!"
Mike: "I did it wrong?"
Jubal: "No, it was my mistake. I want to know if you can lift it *without* touching it?"
Mike: "Yes, Jubal."
Jubal: "Well, are you tired?"
Mike: "No, Jubal."
Jill: "Jubal, you haven't *told* him to—you just asked if he could."

Moore's Paradox

Given the second maxim of quality it would be natural to try to account for the oddity of such sentences as

(141)   Snow is white, but I don't believe it.

by appealing in some way to conflict between what is said and what should be implicated, etc. And *if* this were to be the sort of account offered, it would have to be direct implicature that is appealed to, not indirect, since the maxim is not flouted.

Interestingly enough, Grice does not want to explain Moore's paradox conversationally: "On my account, it will not be true that when I say that p, I conversationally implicate that I believe that p . . . the natural thing to say is that he has *expressed* (or at least purported to express) the belief that p . . . the nature of the connection will, I hope, become apparent when I say something about the function of the indicative mood" (1967, III, p. 2).

This strikes me as a better line to take. The oddity of sentences like (141) do not seem to turn on the accidents of conversation. It seems like a much tighter relationship. Moreover, given Grice's early remarks on implication it would seem that it should not be implicature at work. If the relation between p and ⌐I believe that p⌐ were one of implication, then one should be able to cancel it. But Moore-type sentences just *are* such an attempt. This suggests the implication is not cancelable and so not conversational at all. What then of Grice's proposal? According to his later theory of meaning, indicative mood indicators are correlated (by 'procedures') to speakers' beliefs. For example, Grice imagines the following procedure:

(P)   "To utter the indicative version of σ [an indicative sentence] if (for some A) U wants/intends A to think U thinks . . . (the blank being filled in by the infinitive version of σ)" (1968, p. 65).

Jubal: (looking sheepish) "Mike, will you please, without touching it, lift that ash tray a foot above the desk?"

Mike: "Yes, Jubal." (The ash tray raised, floated above the desk) (p. 112).

I think that Heinlein is right here. A person who learns English from a dictionary and a grammar would need some "cultural context" to justifiably take the *prima facie* question as a request.

Or consider the (unconsciously) interesting example from Frederic Brown:

Carmody grinned. "You want me to get graphic, but I'll fool you. I'll just ask you this—should I see her again?" "No," said Junior mechanically, but implacably. Carmody's eyebrows went up. "The devil you say. And may I ask why, since you haven't met the lady, you say that?" "Yes. You may ask why." That was one trouble with Junior; he always answered the question you actually asked, not the one you implied (p. 8).

Furthermore, according to definition D.2, this would specify the meaning of the mood indicator for U (and for those who shared the procedure).

Turning again to sentences like (141), we can see that it is in the indicative mood and so applying (P) to it yields the result that it is to be U's policy:

(142) To utter (141) if U intends A to think U thinks that snow is white, but that U does not believe that snow is white.

Now, one might suggest that the oddity of (141) be accounted for on the basis of the oddity of the belief expressed in (142). After all, A is to think the following schema to be truly instantiated by U:

(143) UBp & $UB(\sim UBp)$

The problem with this line is that it may be *unusual,* but it does not seem odd in the *way* that the Moore sentences are. For a person could believe that p and not believe that he believes it: a person might believe that such and such a race is inferior, but not believe that he believes it. Not to allow this would force all racism to be explicit, and that seems very implausible. So we really do not yet have an account of the oddity of Moore's sentences. If this is correct, then we must turn to either a speech-act explanation (one like Searle's, 1969), or try to make the conversational hypothesis work. Perhaps when (or if) Grice develops a theory of speech acts we can look there for an account of Moore's Paradox.

Factives

The Kiparskys, in their interesting paper "Fact," claim that there is a set of 'predicates' such that sentences containing them have the property that speakers presuppose that the complement sentence is true. Thus, for the Kiparskys, presupposition is a relation between a person, a sentence, and a truth value (truth). But what is this relation? The Kiparskys do not say very much about it. They do distinguish it from both assertion and belief, and they note its traditional property (due to Frege) of being invariant under negation. However, this is not an analysis. We want a definiens for (144).

(144) In uttering $S(S')$, x *presupposes* that S' is true iff . . .

I do not know how to complete (144), but I think there are some wrong ways of putting the Kiparskys' point.

1. Someone first encountering the Kiparskys' relation of presupposition might be tempted to fashion it into something more familiar—say, a relation between a sentence and a belief. They might propose that

(145) $S(S')$ presupposes that x believes that S'.

But there are serious problems with (145) if we mean by 'presuppose' what it has been taken to mean since Frege and Strawson (1952):

>(146) X's belief that S′ is a necessary condition for the truth-or-falsity of S(S′).

The problems arise as follows. First, it makes the truth value of what one says depend on one's beliefs, even when what is said is not about those beliefs. For suppose that x utters S(S′) and does not believe that S′. Since the presupposition is false, S(S′) has no truth value (by (146)). Second, the analysis in (145) makes it almost impossible to lie with factives. To lie is at least to (intentionally) assert that p, while believing that p is false. But on the account above, if I believe that S′ is false, this is sufficient to guarantee that S(S′) has no truth value, and so cannot be asserted to be true, except from ignorance or by mistake. These cases are bound to be rare, however, since people usually know what sentences they believe to be false.

2. Suppose that someone were to say that factive sentences presuppose their complements in the Strawsonian sense that

>(147) S(S′) *presupposes* S′ iff the truth of S′ is a necessary condition for the truth-or-falsity of S(S′).[53]

Now, one of the interesting things about (147) is that it conflicts with the standard philosophical analysis of many factives, so if this is what the Kiparskys were to mean, the standard accounts would be wrong if the Kiparskys were right. The standard analysis of 'know', for instance, is

>(148) x knows that p if and only if
>   (i) x believes that p.
>   (ii) p is true.
>   (iii) x is justified in believing that p.

On this analysis, if any of (i)–(iii) are false, then ⌜x knows that p⌝ is false. But if the relationship where one of presupposition, then if any of (i)–(iii) were false, then ⌜x knows that p⌝ would lack a truth value. How do we decide which is correct? Here are some considerations in favor of the standard analysis, as against the presuppositional view.

First Argument

1. Assume: 'I know that the earth is flat' presupposes 'The earth is flat'.
2. 'The earth is flat' is false.
3. So, 'I know that the earth is flat' has no truth value.

---

53. It is not to be thought that this definition is unproblematic. In fact, it can be shown that 'necessary condition' cannot mean 'logically necessary condition' in the sense of standard logic, for all presuppositions would then be logical truths, by a familiar argument.

4. So, 'I do not know that the earth is flat' has no truth value.
5. So 'I know that the earth is flat' and 'I do not know that the earth is flat' each have no truth value.
6. So 'I know and I do not know that the earth is flat' has no truth value.
7. But 6 seems just false, so we must reject assumption 1.

Second Argument[54]

1. If my car has not been stolen, then I cannot know that it has been stolen.
2. Assume: my car has not been stolen.
3. Then I cannot know that my car has been stolen.
4. Then it is not possible that I know that my car has been stolen.
5. Then it is necessary that I do not know that my car has been stolen.
6. Then I do not know that my car has been stolen.

But now, from the assumption that 'My car has been stolen' is false we derived the result that I do not know that my car has been stolen. But then it must be true, not neither true nor false, as the presuppositionalist would have it.

One weakness of the standard analysis is that it fails to account for the fact that embedded sentence in both positive and negative factives are held to be true by the speaker, or at least this is implied. Consider the following;

(*Affirmative Factives*) John knows that his car has been stolen.
　　　　　　　　　　　　 "　remembers　　　　　　　　"
　　　　　　　　　　　　 "　realizes　　　　　　　　　"
　　　　　　　　　　　　 "　regrets (it)　　　　　　　"
(*Negative Factives*)　　John doesn't know that his car has been stolen.
　　　　　　　　　　　　　 "　　remember　　　　　　　"
　　　　　　　　　　　　　 "　　realize　　　　　　　　"
　　　　　　　　　　　　　 "　　regret　　　　　　　　"

The presuppositional theory can, at one level at least, handle this, since presupposition has traditionally been taken to be invariant under negation. But how can the standard 'entailment' theorist account for this? Is it perhaps some form of implication? In the case of positive factives, the answer is straightforward entailment. It is the class of negative factives that gives the entailment view trouble.

A BRACKETING PROPOSAL

In the middle lectures, Grice introduces what he calls a 'bracketing device' used to "indicate the assignation of common ground status" to some of the clauses in the analysis of indicative conditionals (1967 IV, p. 10). He then illustrates its utility in a variety of cases. I would like to try to bend this device to our present

54. A variant of this argument appears in Wilson (1972). As far as I know, these were arrived at independently.

concerns.[55] As a first step we could claim that what has been considered 'presupposition' is really 'common ground' on Grice's story. If we suppose (148) to have the standard analysis as in (149a), then the bracketed analysis would be as indicated in (149b), thus representing that the truth of p is to be common ground:

(149) (a) xKp iff xBp & xJBp & p
   (b) xBp & xJBp [&p]

The denial of (149b) would then be as in (150):

(150) $\sim$(xBp & xJBp [&p])

Being common ground, p will not be affected by operators like negation, and so the negated version of (149b) would be (151):

(151) $\sim$$xBp$ $\vee$ $\sim$$xJBp$ [&p]

On this view, negative factives would have the force of an assertion of the disjunction above. But this does not seem correct. Negative factives are not normally taken that way. They normally have the force of a denial of the belief condition. We can get this result by imposing more structure on (149) as follows:

(152) xKp iff xBp [& xJBp [&p]]

Using the principle (0),

(0) Operators go to the least deeply embedded condition first

we get the result that the denial of (152) would be required (153):

(153) $\sim$$xBp$ [& xJBp [& p]]

The principle (0) suggests that the brackets are penetrable, and that an operator can attach itself to one of these embedded conditions. To say how this can happen, what makes it happen, and what all this machinery means is to give the beginnings of a genuine theory.

If the bracketing does not reflect the truth-conditional semantics of the expression, then what does it reflect? So far, I have hedged on this by talking of indicating common ground in the utterance of the expression. What I want to suggest about the bracketing is that it is somehow a part of a system that relates what an expression means in the dialect to what the speaker means in uttering it. Where exactly it goes, and what its exact interpretation is, remains a bit of a mystery to me. We can start with the idea that the least deeply embedded condition specifies what the speaker primarily meant in uttering the expression, while the rest of the conditions are proposed as shared suppositions, in order to get to the point of the remark. That is, the speaker is indicating that he assumes

55. Although Wilson (1970) does not mention this device in her discussion of negative factives and offers a slightly different account, she may have had some of this material in mind also.

that he and the hearer will both assume that such-and-such is true for the purposes of discussion.

But now that justification clause is in the way. It is not proposed as common ground that x is justified (in believing that p) when one utters a negative factive. We are in a dilemma. The standard analysis requires this clause to be there in the positive cases, but by the bracketing device it will be there in the negative cases as well where we do not want it. But to eliminate it from the negative cases it seems necessary to eliminate it from the positive cases as well or be *ad hoc*.

There are at least a couple of ways out. We could, one, argue that the justification clause is *not* in the positive cases either, or, two, argue that there is a reason for excluding it from the negative cases.

1. If we were to take the first way out we then need to see how we can distinguish 'knows that' from 'be aware that' and 'realize that', for the previously present justification clause seemed to do just that. Also, we need to explain how evidence and justification *can* be the topic of discussion without much stage setting when ascribing knowledge or ignorance (especially if we stress 'know' in these ascriptions), but not, for example, awareness that p.

One way of supplying this information might be to say that there is a generalized conversational implicature of justification when one ascribes knowledge that p. On this view the 'analysis' of knowledge would be

(154) (a) Truth conditions: $x\mathrm{B}p \ \& \ p$.
       (b) Generalized implicature: $x\mathrm{JB}p$.

The *saying* that $x\mathrm{K}p$ would *implicate* that x was justified in believing that p.

To make this line plausible one would have to give some sort of reason why the implicature is there with 'know' and not with 'aware' (maybe it is conventional implicature and not generalized conversational), and also one would have to explain how we can (or seem to) deny the justification clause in making the negative ascriptions. How can denial go to the implicature?

2. If we take the second way out and let the justification clause remain in the positive cases, then we need to find some way of 'removing' it from the total content of the remark in the negative cases. One way to do this would be to read the justification clause as something like

(155) $x\mathrm{JB}p$ iff x is justified in believing that p

Then we could say that if denial goes to the belief clause (by bracketing), then that entails that it is not the case that $x\mathrm{JB}p$. Of course this does not entail that x has no evidence for p, just that if x does not believe that p, then x is not justified in believing that p. We would then get the result we want if we required common ground to be consistent with what was meant (as well as shared beliefs about the context; we will make this more explicit shortly).

In sum, I do not know exactly what is the best way of handling these facts, and I have sketched a pair of proposals that might be pursued. Assuming some reasonable account can be given, what more can be said about the basis and justification of the bracketing?

Let us first agree that many conversations are governed by maxims that enjoin us from being overly ambiguous and nonspecific. On the standard analysis of negative factives, they have the form of disjoined negations. Thus, if this is what the speaker meant to communicate, he might well be cited for violating a maxim; if the bracketing of the positive case were left as in (149b), the denial would still be unspecific or ambiguous:

(156) $\sim x\mathrm{B}p \lor \sim x\mathrm{JB}p \; [\& \, p]$

The bracketing convention (in the negative cases) comes in to reduce ambiguity and increase specificity. The negative operator goes to just one condition. So with negation, (149a) is interpreted as (152); the ordering of constituent conditions is *completed* so that ambiguity or equivocation is avoided.

What is the status of this bracketing device? Is it a part of the language, a conventional device that serves a purpose like the one sketched above? Or is it just a principle of interpretation based on conversation or discourse? I don't know, but the latter seems more plausible to me. On this account we could say the bracketing reflects our expectations about what a speaker will mean based mainly on our previous experience with the point or topic of such remarks in the past. If these experiences were to change, our expectations would change and so the bracketing would change. This account has the virtue of meshing in an obvious way with our earlier justification for the device, but it also meshes with a fact we alluded to earlier—the fact that in certain circumstances, context can force a change in bracketing. In a context in which it is obvious that $x\mathrm{B}p$, the negative factive will not be interpreted as the denial of $x\mathrm{B}p$. The general principle seems to be.

(0′) If C is a condition in the analysis of an expression E, and C is contextually satisfied, then the operator is taken as going to the next most deeply embedded condition consistent with what is meant and context.

Thus, if the context is such that it is clear that $x\mathrm{B}p$, then (0′) predicts that the negative factive will be taken as a denial that $x\mathrm{JB}p$. And if the context is such that it is clear that both $x\mathrm{B}p$ and $x\mathrm{JB}p$, then the negative factive would be taken as the denial of p. This would explain why negative factives seem to be arranged on a scale of difficulty with regard to what they will be taken to mean, as well as why the scale of Table 1 is the way it is.[56]

56. It is not too difficult to find a context in which 2 and 3 are true. Many a situation from epistemology will do. It is harder to construct one for 4, but consider the following dialogue:

S: I didn't know that you were married.
H: You still don't.

Here I think it plausible to say that the force of H's remark was that of a denial that he was married; a denial that p. It is a very instructive exercise to try to figure out exactly how this comes about.

TABLE 1.

CONTEXT	OPERATOR	FACTIVE	FORCE OF NEGATIVE FACTIVE
1. ϕ(None of the conditions clearly antecedently true)	'not'	'know'	$\sim x\mathrm{B}p\ [\&\ \phi\ [\&\ p]\,]$
2. $x\mathrm{B}p$	"	"	$[x\mathrm{B}p\ \&]\ \sim x\mathrm{J}\mathrm{B}p\ [\&\ p]$
3. $x\mathrm{B}p\ \&\ p$	"	"	same
4. $x\mathrm{B}p\ \&\ x\mathrm{J}\mathrm{B}p$	"	"	$[x\mathrm{B}p\ \&\ x\mathrm{J}\mathrm{B}p\ \&]\ \sim p$

There remain a host of questions concerning this proposal, and two are of some immediate concern. First, what are the rules or principles besides (0) and (0') that give us Table 1 as output from the initial bracketings as input, plus context? Second, what accounts for the fact (assuming it to be one) that negative factives of this sort are taken as denial of the *belief* condition? If this is explained on the basis of expectation on the basis of experience, then why did it develop this way in the beginning? Of course it could be that it just happened that way. But as we will see shortly, it does not seem to be a fact just about 'know', but other factives as well, and this requires some explanation, if only an account in terms of what the speaker is more likely to have evidence for (in accordance with the maxims of Quality) and will therefore be supposed to mean.

EXTENDING THE PROPOSAL

With some reservations it looks like the proposal above can be extended in two directions: to other operators besides negation, and to other factives besides 'know'.

TABLE 2.

CONTEXT	OPERATOR	FACTIVE	FORCE
ϕ	possibly	know	possibly $x\mathrm{B}p$ . . .
ϕ	unlikely	know	unlikely that $x\mathrm{B}p$ . . .
ϕ	uncertain	know	uncertain that $x\mathrm{B}p$ . . .
ϕ	must	know	x must $\mathrm{B}p$ . . .
ϕ	hopefully	know	hopefully $x\mathrm{B}p$ . . .
ϕ	finally	know	finally $x\mathrm{B}p$ . . .

Other Operators It seems to me that, at least in an unbiased context, the sentences reflected in Table 2 would be taken primarily as remarks about belief.

Other Factives The same sort of analysis and bracketing seems to work with other factives like

(157) realize; recognize; remember; be aware; admit

For instance, if we suppose the following to be roughly right:

(158) x is aware that p iff $x\mathrm{B}p\ [\&\ p]$

then the denial of (158) has just the force we take it to have—as the denial that x believes that p. The same seems to hold for 'realize', and for one common propositional use of 'recognize'. Also, if we suppose 'admit' to have an analysis something like (159):

(159) x admits that p iff x says that p [& p]

then the negative factive: x didn't admit that p, comes out right, as primarily a denial that x said (or would say) that p. Perhaps other cases could be handled as these.

Illocutionary Generalizations

At the end of Chapter 3 of *Speech Acts*, Searle gives a number of "generalizations" over speech acts (1969, p. 65). We can summarize two of them as follows:

(EXP) "Whenever there is a psychological state specified in the sincerity condition, the performance of the act counts as an *expression* of that psychological state."

(IMP) "In the performance of any illocutionary act, the speaker *implies* that the preparatory conditions of the act are satisfied."

Given a tentative analysis of various illocutionary acts, these principles can be used to do some work. For instance, fairly plausible accounts can be given for Moore's Paradox and various cases of contextual implication. However, Searle does note something he may not appreciate the importance of: "If it really is the case that the other rules are functions of the essential rule, and if some of the others tend to recur in consistent patterns, then these recurring ones ought to be eliminable" (1969, p. 69). Searle suggests that these regularities may go into the general theory of illocutionary acts, but it would be worthwhile to explore the possibility that these generalizations might be special cases of a theory superordinate even to the general theory of illocutionary acts; say, the general theory of conversations.

Before we can do this, we must be clearer about the force of these principles. I am not sure how Searle intends us to take these remarks: as (contextual) *definitions* of the notions of expressing and implying, in performing a speech act, or as *empirical* generalizations over expressings and implyings. By using such phrases as 'counts as' he suggests the former, but by calling these 'tentative generalizations' he suggests the latter. I think the latter is what he wants, or should want. This is because the notions of 'expressing' and 'implying' are pulling some weight in these generalizations. This can be seen by substituting 'exponentiation' for 'expression' and 'diagonalizes' for 'implies' in these generalizations. If these really were contextual definitions, it should make no difference what word we decided to define, but clearly we have lost a great deal of explanatory utility in these substitutions. But if these are really generalizations then the antecedent meaning of the words 'expresses' and 'implies' will be important. To test these generalizations we need to know what it is to express a psychological state or to imply that a certain condition is satisfied. As far as I can tell Searle never does this.

With both expressing[57] and implying[58] there is a range of characteristic circumstances in which we would say that something has been expressed and implied. I think that ones that come the closest to what Searle may have in mind are the following:

(E)   (S's) doing ϕ (timelessly-) *expresses* (the psychological state) ψ if:
    (i)   If S were to ϕ, then if
    (ii) H were aware that S had ϕ-ed, then
    (iii) Probably H would conclude that S was in ψ, at least partly on the basis of the awareness in (ii).

(I)   (S's) doing ϕ (timelessly-) *implies* that p if:
    (i)   If S were to ϕ, then if
    (ii) H were aware that S had ϕ-ed, then
    (iii) Probably H would conclude that p, at least partly on the basis of the awareness in (ii).

57. Among the variety of circumstances that would make it true to say that someone expresses a psychological state would be

(A) S expresses ψ if
    (i)   (optional for achievement sense) S is in state ψ.
    (ii) S does something ϕ such that:
        (a) if H were aware that S had ϕ-ed, then
        (b) H probably would conclude that S was in ψ, at least partly on the basis of the awareness in (a).
(B) S (intentionally) expresses ψ if
    (i)   (optional for success sense) S is in state ψ.
    (ii) S does something ϕ with the intention that:
        (a) if H were aware that S had ϕ-ed, then
        (b) H probably would conclude that S was in ψ, at least partly on the basis of the awareness in (a).

58. Among the variety of circumstances that would make it true to say that someone implies something would be

(A) S's doing ϕ implied that p if
    (i) S ϕ-ed.
    (ii) H is aware that S has ϕ-ed.
    (iii) H concluded that p, at least partly on the basis of the awareness in (ii).
(B)   In doing ϕ, S implied that p (to H) if
    (i) S does ϕ.
    (ii) S does ϕ with the intention that:
        (a) H be aware that S has ϕ-ed.
        (b) H conclude that p, at least partly on the basis of the awareness in (a).

Notice that in these definitions, expressing a psychological state is just implying that you are in that state. This is not implausible.

We can now give at least sufficient conditions for (EXP) and (IMP), and I will call these analyses (EXP') and (IMP'):

(EXP')   If there is a psychological state ψ mentioned in the sincerity condition of ϕ-ing, then ϕ-ing *expresses* that state ψ if: S ϕ-es and
(i)   If H were aware that S had ϕ-ed, then
(ii)   Probably H would conclude that S was in ψ, at least partly on the basis of the awareness in (i).

(IMP')   In the performance of an illocutionary act of ϕ-ing the speaker S *implies* that the preparatory conditions p of the act are satisfied if: S ϕ-es and
(i)   If H were aware that S had ϕ-ed, then
(ii)   Probably H would conclude that p, at least partly on the basis of the awareness in (i).

We now turn to the task of deriving (EXP) and (IMP) via deriving (EXP') and (IMP') from facts and principles not specifically illocutionary and constitutive. We will start with (IMP') since (EXP') may require material that Grice has not yet developed.

1. (IMP)

We can get (IMP') without using any special illocutionary constitutive rules given a fact and two plausible principles:

Fact: On Searle's account, preparatory conditions are necessary for the performance of the illocutionary act they are conditions for.

P1.   If ψ is a necessary condition for having ϕ-ed, then being aware that S has ϕ-ed is a basis for concluding that ψ.

P2.   If ψ is an immediate consequence of ϕ and one is aware that ϕ, then one will probably conclude that ψ.[59]

We can now argue thus:

1.   Suppose that S has ϕ-ed.
2.   Suppose H were aware that S had ϕ-ed.
3.   Then H probably will conclude that p (from *Fact*, 2, and *P 2*)
4.   Then H could conclude that p at least partly on the basis of 2 (from *Fact*, 2, and *P 1*)
5.   Then probably H would conclude that p, at least partly on the basis of 2 (from 3 and 4)

59. For the purposes of the argument it is sufficient that q is an immediate consequence of p if q is a logical consequence of p and q may be inferred from p by a single intuitively correct principle of inference (like simplification or *modus ponens*).

6. So given *Fact*, *P 1* and *P 2*, then if 1 then if 2 then 5 (conditional proof from above)
7. But 'If 1 then if 2, then 5' is the sufficient condition for (IMP')
8. So given *Fact*, *P 1* and *P 2* we can conclude that

In the performance of an illocutionary act of ϕ-ing, the speaker implies that the preparatory conditions of the act are satisfied.

2. (EXP)

Before turning to this argument it should be noted that the 'counts as' phrase has dropped out of (EXP'). This is in keeping with its empirical character as well as reflecting my belief that the relationship between the psychological state and the act is *not* conventional.

We cannot derive (EXP') on the model of the derivation of (IMP') because the sincerity condition is not a necessary condition for the performance of the act. The obvious question is: what might support the hearer's inference from the fact that the speaker performed the act to his being in a certain psychological state? There are at least three ways it could go. First, we might try to get (EXP') just using some other generalization about action and reasoning. Second, we might try to get it by concocting a 'Gricean' theory of illocutionary acts that would not appeal to the notion of special illocutionary constitutive rules, and then try to state the generalizations over *this* theory. Of course, some combination of these might be necessary. I want to take a quick look at the prospects and problems associated with these suggestions.

Generalization about Action and Reasoning We might suppose that most speakers count among their everyday beliefs something like (G):

(G) People usually believe (want, intend to do, ... ψ ...) what they state (request, promise, ... ϕ ...)

(We postpone the question of why and on what basis might people hold such a general belief.) Then given (G) we could argue roughly:

1. Suppose that S has ϕ-ed.
2. Suppose H were aware that S had ϕ-ed.
3. Suppose S believed (G).
4. Then H would probably conclude that S was in ψ, at least partly on the basis of 2. (from above, *P 2* and (G))
5. So we have it that given *P 2* and (G), if 1, then if 2, then 4.
6. But this is sufficient for (EXP').

To this there are a number of immediate objections.

One could object that this is no advance on Searle because we have *lost* a generalization, since (EXP) was of the form

For any illocutionary act, if ... then ——.

and (G) is just a list, pairing certain acts with certain states. But I think that the contrast is illusory. This is because Searle has no *general* procedure for determining the necessity for, or content of, the sincerity condition for each act. Thus the universal quantifier is just a summary for a conjunction of particular facts about a particular analysis. For the purposes of the theory it would have been no different had the 'generalization' been formulated as

If S performs an act n, then S expresses the psychological state n.

Given that we had some pairing between acts and states the only difference between this (and (G)) and Searle is that it refers to the pairing via a number rather than some rubric like 'sincerity condition'. The work this rubric does could equally be done on the scheme above by saying simply,

If S performs act n, then if n is paired with a psychological state n, then S performs n *sincerely* iff S is then in state n.

In the absence of a deduction of the sincerity condition from the essential condition or illocutionary purpose of the act, both 'generalizations' are essentially lists.

One may also object that we have given no account of how or why people might come to hold a belief like (G). I suspect that such a belief could arise from at least two sources: projections from one's own case, and observations of and inferences concerning others. Both of these could interact and support each other and become more refined over time, giving rise to the often highly specific expectations we have of others and expect others to have of us.

Finally, it may be objected that we have given no reason to suppose that (G) might be the *basis* of the inference to the psychological state. Here is one slight consideration on its behalf. Suppose that a study was indicating that (G) was wildly wrong, that people most often lied, requested what they didn't want, and soon, and it also gave an account of why we thought the opposite. Suppose it was very convincing. Under these circumstances, any H who had been persuaded of this would surely be reluctant to infer from S's having ϕ-ed that S was in state ψ.

A Special Consequence of Conversational Maxims One may find the first proposal implausible, and it may be false. It could be that the basis of the inference to ψ is not anything like (G), but rather the belief that S is obeying some general conversational principles. One problem here is that Grice's theory of conversation is geared to the accepted purpose of the talk exchange (at that point). So to make the connection between Grice and Searle we must connect the illocutionary act with the accepted purpose of the talk exchange. But there may be no *accepted* purpose to the talk exchange at that point, though the *speaker* may have a purpose at that point. Indeed, the conversation may be *given* purpose at a point *by* the speaker's purpose(s) in making the utterance he makes. If we view (most sorts of) conversations as a sequence of illocutionary acts, governed by certain principles of cohesion, relevance, and the like, then the move to conversations will *not* bypass illocutionary acts in providing an account of (EXP).

A "Gricean" Theory of Illocutionary Acts I think the most promising thing to do here is to first find a natural and general way of categorizing the purposes of a talk exchange (both at a point and over time), and then try to correlate these with illocutionary acts that might be performed in fulfilling those purposes. Since maxims of Quality seem to be a function of the purpose of the talk exchange, it should be possible to get the sincerity conditions on illocutionary acts via the maxim of Quality for the correlated sort of conversation. Such a project is clearly beyond the scope of this study.

GLIMPSES BEYOND

There are a number of (kinds of) cases not so far discussed that might yield to a Gricean analysis of one sort or another. Certainly this possibility should be pursued. I shall just mention and gloss a few of them briefly.

Intentional Verbs

If I say that John kicked the dog this morning I imply that he kicked the dog intentionally (and voluntarily). Certainly this does not *entail* that John kicked the dog intentionally (or voluntarily) because one can say without contradiction that John kicked the dog, but he did it accidentally or unintentionally. With some other verbs this is not the case. If I say that John stumbled on the dog this morning I do not imply that he did it intentionally or voluntarily. The generalization seems to be

If it is possible to ϕ intentionally (or voluntarily) then in saying that x ϕ-ed, one will imply that x ϕ-ed intentionally (or voluntarily).

What is the basis of this generalization? Is it a generalized conversational implicature? Perhaps it is no more than the general belief that acts that can be so performed usually are so performed.

Opaque Simplification

It is sometimes said that if Jones wants (hopes that, etc.) p and q, it does not follow that Jones wants p, nor does it follow that Jones wants q. For instance, if Jones wants ham and eggs for breakfast, it is claimed that it does not follow that Jones wants ham for breakfast nor that he wants eggs for breakfast.

However, I think that this case should be handled just as we handled the earlier cases of conjunction reduction. We could well contend that the *reason* one thinks that it does not follow is that the conclusion commits one to the view that Jones wants *only* ham for breakfast, etc. However, by the maxim of Quantity-Quality and the inference outlined earlier, we could contend that the commitment is via implicature, not entailment.

Completion Verbs

It is often claimed that remarks like (160a) presuppose (160b, c):

(160) (a) x has not stopped ϕ-ing.
      (b) x was ϕ-ing.
      (c) x (had) started ϕ-ing.

There are other cases as well:

(161) (a) x (has) finished ϕ-ing.
      (b) x was ϕ-ing.
      (c) x (had) started ϕ-ing.

The reason for supposing this to be presupposition is mainly invariance under negation:

(162) (a) x has not stopped ϕ-ing.
      (b) x was ϕ-ing.
      (c) x (had) started ϕ-ing.

There are at least two possible nonpresuppositional treatments available in Gricean terms: a bracketing theory and a conversational theory.

Bracketing

Suppose that at some level of representation the analysis of (160a) was something like (163):[60]

(163) [x started (or was) ϕ-ing &] x is not now ϕ-ing.

Then (160a) would *entail* (160b, c,). But the denial of (163), i.e. (162a), would be (164):

(164) $\sim x$ started ϕ-ing $\lor$ x is now ϕ-ing

although by bracketing it would have the force of (165):

(165) x started ϕ-ing & x is now ϕ-ing.

Conversational

Suppose the analysis of (161a) is, at some level of representation,

(166) x started ϕ-ing & x terminated ϕ-ing.

60. For instance see Ayer, 1936, p. 76.

Then we have it that saying that x finished is a stronger remark than saying that x started, since finishing entails starting, but not vice versa. Consequently, the denial of finishing should be a weaker remark than the denial of starting.[61] The denial of (166) would be (167):

(167) $\sim x$ started ϕ-ing $\lor \sim x$ terminated ϕ-ing.

But if the first disjunct is taken as sufficient for the truth of (167), then the speaker will have produced a weaker remark than is relevant and suitable. So he will have implicated that the first disjunct of (167) is not true, i.e. that x (has) started ϕ-ing.

Subject-oriented Adverbs

It has been noticed (Lehrer, 1975) that there are adverbs that have the property that combined with certain nonfactive verbs like 'believe' they *imply* that the complement of the verb is true, or is false (or perhaps just that the speaker believes it):

(168) (a) Wisely, cleverly John believes that p.
   (b) p (or perhaps, xBp).

(169) (a) Foolishly, John believes that p.
   (b) not p (or perhaps, xB $\sim p$).

However, these adverbs combined with factives like 'know' produce oddity:

(170) ?Wisely, cleverly John knows that p.

(171) ?Foolishly John knows that p.

These adverbs are to be distinguished from another group like 'correctly', 'erroneously', and 'falsely', which have the property that combined with certain nonfactive verbs like 'believes' *entail* that the complement is true, or that it is false:

(172) a. Correctly John believes that p.
   b. p.

(173) a. Falsely, erroneously John believes that p.
   b. not p.

When these are combined with certain factives like 'know', they produce oddity:

(174) ?John correctly knows that p.

(175) ?John falsely, erroneously knows that p.

---

61. This does not follow truth functionally from our working definition of strength, but it is a reasonable requirement.

Suppose that semantically these groups of adverbs are operators that have an effect on logical syntax, and that the effect of 'foolishly' and 'cleverly' as opposed to 'falsely' and 'correctly' is the following:

(176) Foolishly $(xBp) \Rightarrow xBp$ & $(\sim xJBp \lor \sim p)$

(177) Falsely $(xBp) \Rightarrow xBp$ & $\sim p$

(178) Cleverly $(sBp) \Rightarrow xBp$ & $(xJBp \lor p)$

(179) Correctly $(xBp) \Rightarrow xBp$ & p

Next, suppose part of the communicative force of an operator is to emphasize what is contributed by the operator, and to subordinate what is inherited from the operand to something like common ground. Then the bracketed result for the above would be:

(176') $[xBp$ &$]$ $(- xJBp \lor \sim p)$

(177') $[xBp$ &$]$ $\sim p$

(178') $[xBp$ &$]$ $(xJBp \lor p)$

(179') $[xBp$ &$]$ p

We can get the entailments recorded in (172) and (173) from (177) and (179) by elementary logic. How can we get the implications recorded in (168) and (169), and the remaining oddities? Suppose that (169a) has the bracketed semantic representation of (176') (repeated):

(176') Foolishly xBp: $[xBp$ &$]$ $(\sim xJBp \lor \sim p)$.

Now, given the conversational maxims to avoid equivocation we might suppose that the primary content of the remark will be taken to be one of the disjuncts left unbracketed. Given the maxim of Quality-2, the speaker is to say (mean) only what he has adequate evidence for. But other things being equal, it is much more likely that the speaker has evidence that $\sim p$ than that he has evidence that x has insufficient evidence that p—what do most speakers know about the epistemic biographies of others? So, by charity, the speaker will be taken to primarily mean that $\sim p$, and also to imply, that xBp.

Suppose that (168a) has the semantic representation of (178') (repeated):

(178') Cleverly xBp: xBp & $(xJBp \lor p)$

By the same reasoning as above we have it the speaker will be taken to mean that p, and also to imply, that xBp.

Notice that this explanation leans heavily on there being or not being certain shared beliefs between speaker and hearer. For instance, if it is common knowledge that nobody is in any position to be able to claim that p, then the speaker will (be taken to) primarily mean that x is not justified in believing that p in saying that foolishly xBp, as for example in (180b) as opposed to (180a):

(180) (a) Foolishly xB that the earth is flat.
      (b) Foolishly xB that there were exactly five trillion mosquitoes in Panama in 1903.

We can account for the oddities recorded in (174), (175) and (170), (171) along the same lines.

The oddity of (174) arises from the redundancy of the operation, since the knowledge claim already commits one to the truth of p. The oddity of (175) arises from the conflict between the commitment to the truth of p via 'knows' and the falsity of p via the operator.

The oddity of (171) arises from the implication by the operator that $\sim p$, and the commitment to p via 'knows'. The oddity of (170) can be accounted for by the redundancy of the implication of the operator, given the commitment to the truth of p via 'knows'. Notice finally that (182) is not odd;

(181) Foolishly x does not know that p

since on this account by bracketing (182) becomes $\sim xBp$, and 'foolishly' will go with 'believe'.

Repeaters

It is sometimes said that among sentences like those of (182)–(184), the (a) sentences presuppose the (b) sentences:

(182) (a) John kicks it again.
      (b) John kicked it previously.
(183) (a) John kicks it too, also.
      (b) Somebody (else?) kicked it.
(184) (a) John kicks it a second (nth) time.
      (b) Somebody (John?) kicked it a first ($n - 1$) time.

The reason for calling this presupposition is again the invariance under negation:

(185) (a) John did not kick it again.
      (b) John kicked it previously.

Suppose that (182a) is represented something like (186):

(186) [x kicked it before t_0 &] x kicks it at t_0

Then the denial of (186), i.e. (185a), would be (187), though the conversational force of (185a) would be (188):

(187) $\sim x$ kicked it before t_0 $\lor$ $\sim x$ kicks it at t_0.
(188) x kicked it before t_0 & $\sim x$ kicks it at t_0.

Depending on larger issues, one could view 'again' as the surface remnant of the second conjunct, or as an operator on the main clause forming a second conjunct semantically.

However, we still need an account of why the bracketing favors the conjunct indexed (by t) earliest in time. Perhaps this is just a part of the meaning of expressions like 'again' as opposed to 'before'.

It might be objected to this proposal that it cannot be a general account of repeater words. The reason sometimes given is that we have sentences like (189) which cannot, it is claimed, be given a conjunctive analysis as in (190):

(189) I promise not to do it again.
(190) I did it before t_0 and I promise not to do it after t_0.

It is not clear why (190) cannot be the analysis of (189), but apparently it is thought that conjunction can connect only constatives. But this is false as can be seen by the felicity of (191):

(191) I did it before, but I promise never to do it again.

An adequate semantics must reflect the fact that connectives can connect non-constatives, but that is not my obligation here.

Miscellaneous

Finally, I should just mention some additional cases that pose an interesting range of challenges to this sort of explanation.

☐ "Not all the tables are round" seem to imply that (the speaker believes that) most of the tables are round.

☐ Many euphemisms may have their origin in uses of language governed by conversational principles similar to Grice's discussion of metaphor. Consider the likely origins of such phrases as:[62] 'go to the bathroom'; 'sleep(ing) with'; 'going to be sick'.

☐ "I used to like spinach" seems to imply that I do not now like spinach. In fact, to a lesser extent, the use of the past tense often carries the implication that the activity or state indicated by the verb no longer is present: "I wanted to live in Rome"; "I lived in Rome"; I believed that p.

☐ "He walked halfway to New York" seems to imply that he did not walk all the way to New York. "He lifted his arm halfway to his head" seems to

62. Some more common euphemisms clustering around the usual taboo subjects of sex, excrement, death, and related interests are: make love to (with?), lost her virtue/honor, loose woman, ?do it, streetwalker (Boston: working girl), ?gay, birthday suit/clothes, house of ill repute, little girls' room, senior citizen, passed on, etc. It is important to distinguish euphemisms ('passed on') from clinical or technical terminology ('expired', 'deceased') and both of these from the common terms ('die'), slang ('croaked'), and idioms ('kicked the bucket'). I am not sure how to do this in general, but for various particular semantic fields it seems moderately clear how it should go.

imply that he did not lift his arm to his head. These implications can be canceled, as when one prefixes the above with "In the course of walking all the way to New York . . . ".

☐ "I haven't played tennis for ten years"[63] seems to imply that I had played tennis before that.

☐ "Have you mastered the topspin lob yet?" seems to imply that I expect you to (try to) master the topspin lob. "I haven't mastered the topspin lob yet" seems to imply that I expect (or will try) to. Perhaps this is simply a case of conventional implicature off of 'yet'—though notice that it is cancelable: "I haven't ϕ-ed yet, and I don't ever expect to."[64]

In this essay I have tried to make plausible the application of major portions of Grice's framework for the analysis of the total content of an utterance. I have also used this as an opportunity to raise certain questions about, and suggest various extension of, that theory. No doubt my execution has been defective in detail, even in major detail. Nevertheless, I do remain fairly convinced that the Gricean vision is basically correct, and it is just a matter of more work and further elaboration to make that conviction stick.

REFERENCES

Ackermann, R. 1970. *Modern Deductive Logic*. Doubleday and Company.

Alston, W. 1963. "Meaning and Use." *Philosophical Quarterly* 13, no. 51: 107–124.

Anderson, S. 1971. "On the Linguistic Status of the Performative-Constative Distinction." Indiana Linguistics Club.

Anderson, A., and N. Belnap. 1968. "Entailment." In *Logic and Philosophy*, G. Iseminger, ed. Appleton-Century-Crofts.

Ayer, A. 1946. *Language, Truth and Logic*, 2d ed. Dover Books.

Benacerraf, P. 1965. "What Numbers Could Not Be." *Philosophical Review* 74, no. 1: 47–73.

Bennett, J. 1969. "Entailment." *Philosophical Review* 78, no. 2: 197–236.

Brown, F. *Honeymoon in Hell*. Bantam Books.

Caton, C. 1963. *Philosophy and Ordinary Language*. University of Illinois Press.

63. Perhaps this sentence is just ambiguous as between: "It has been ten years since I last played tennis." and "It is not true that I have been playing tennis (as an activity) for ten years." However, I think that the former is not a sense of the sentence; rather the sense is "I have not played tennis during the last ten years" and the first sense can be seen as being implied in a way that should now be clear.

64. Glenn Ross brought these last two examples to my attention. See Wilson (1975) and Harnish (1975b) for further remarks.

Chomsky, N. 1972. "Some Empirical Issues in the Theory of Transformational Grammar." In *Goals of Linguistic Theory*, S. Peters, ed. Prentice-Hall.

Clark, T. 1965. "Seeing Surfaces and Seeing Objects." In *Philosophy in America*, M. Black, ed. Cornell University Press.

Davidson, D., and G. Harman, eds. 1975. *The Logic of Grammar*. Dickenson Publishing Co.

Fogelin, R. 1967. *Evidence and Meaning*. Humanities Press.

Frege, G. 1884. *Grundlagen der Arithmetic*. Translated by J. Austin as *The Foundations of Arithmetic*. 1953. Harper and Row.

Grice, H. P. 1961. "The Causal Theory of Perception." In *Perceiving, Sensing, and Knowing*, R. Shwartz, ed. 1965. Doubleday and Company.

——. 1967. *William James Lectures*. Unpublished Xerox. Lecture II, "Logic and Conversation," has been published in Davidson and Harman. 1975.

——. 1968. "Utterer's Meaning, Sentence-Meaning and Word-Meaning." Reprinted in *The Philosophy of Language*, J. Searle, ed. 1971. Oxford University Press.

——. 1969. "Utterer's Meaning and Intentions." *Philosophical Review* 78, no. 2: 147–177.

——. "Conditionals." Unpublished undated Xerox.

Harnish, R. 1969. "Conjunction Reduction and Implication." M.I.T. Press. Unpublished Xerox.

——. 1972. *Studies in Logic and Language*. Ph.D. dissertation, M.I.T.

——. 1975a. "Verb Toxonomies and Entailment." University of Arizona. Unpublished Xerox.

——. 1975b. "Review of Wilson (1975)." *Times Linguistic Supplements*, Sept. 1975.

Hempel, C. 1945. "The Nature of Mathematical Truth." Reprinted in *Philosophy of Mathematics*, P. Benacerraf and H. Putnam, eds. 1964. Prentice-Hall.

Hungerland, I. 1960. "Contextual Implication." *Inquiry* 3, no. 4: 211–258.

Katz, J. 1972. *Semantic Theory*. Harper and Row.

Katz, J., and P. Postal. 1964. *An Integrated Theory of Linguistic Descriptions*. M.I.T. Press.

Keenan, Elinor. 1974. "The Universality of Conversational Implicatures." Unpublished Xerox.

Kiparsky, P., and C. Kiparsky. 1971. "Fact." In *Semantics*, D. Steinberg and L. Jakobovits, eds. Cambridge University Press.

Lehrer, A. 1975. "Interpreting Certain Adverbs: Semantics or Pragmatics?" *Journal of Linguistics* 11: 239–248.

Lewis, D. 1969. *Convention: A Philosophical Study*. Harvard University Press.

Massey, G. 1970. *Understanding Symbolic Logic*. Harper and Row.

McCawley, J. 1968. "The Role of Semantics in a Grammar." In *Universals in Linguistic Theory*, E. Bach and R. Harms, eds. Holt, Rinehart and Winston.

O'Hair, S. G. 1969a. "Meaning and Implication." *Theoria* 35: 38–54.

O'Hair, S. G. 1969b. "A Definition of Information Content." *Journal of Philosophy* 66, no. 5: 132–133.

Quine, W. V. O. 1959. *Methods of Logic.* Holt, Rinehart and Winston.

Reibel, D., and S. Schane, eds. 1969. *Modern Studies in English.* Prentice-Hall.

Ross, Sir David. 1930. *The Right and the Good.* Oxford University Press.

Searle, J. 1969. *Speech Acts.* Cambridge University Press.

———. 1975. "Indirect Speech Acts." In *Syntax and Semantics*, vol. 3, P. Cole and J. Morgan, eds. Academic Press.

Smokler, H. 1966. "Information Content: A Problem of Definition." *Journal of Philosophy* 63: 201–211.

Strawson, P. 1952. *Introduction to Logical Theory.* Methuen.

Schiffer, S. 1972. *Meaning.* Oxford University Press.

Urmson, J. 1952. "Parenthetical Verbs. Reprinted in C. Caton, ed. 1963.

Von Writht, G. 1957. *Logical Studies.* Routledge and Kegan Paul.

Ware, R. n.d. "Two Models of the Mental Life of Groups." University of Calgary, Xerox.

Wilson, D. 1970. "Presupposition II." M.I.T., Xerox.

———. 1972. "Presuppositions on Factives." *Linguistic Inquiry* 3: 405–410.

———. 1975. *Presuppositions and Non-Truth-Conditional Semantics.* Academic Press.

Pragmatics and Presupposition

JERROLD J. KATZ
D. TERENCE LANGENDOEN

The idea that there are *contextual presuppositions* over and above *semantic presuppositions* has been gaining in popularity in both linguistics and philosophy.[1] Some linguists and philosophers even argue that the semantic notion of presupposition should be abandoned in favor of the contextual one. The aim of this paper is to show that, on the contrary, there is no need at all for a contextual notion of presupposition, and moreover, that the claims on behalf of this notion are based on a conceptual confusion about the relation between grammar and pragmatics. We will examine the most influential argument for contextual presupposition, namely, that of Karttunen (1973),[2] which summarizes and builds on earlier work. Besides showing that this argument is invalid, we will show why an adequate conception of the relation of grammar and pragmatics makes any such notion as contextual presupposition entirely unnecessary.

SEMANTIC PRESUPPOSITION.

The notion of semantic presupposition enters contemporary philosophy of language and linguistics from the work of the nineteenth-century logician and philosopher Frege (1892). Frege was primarily interested in developing an account of the logical form of sentences in which meaningfulness was not a sufficient condition for statementhood. For Frege, the condition under which declarative sentences make a statement (bear a truth value) is that each of their

1. See, for example, Green (1968); Lakoff (1971); Horn (1972); Morgan (1973); Stalnaker (1974).
2. Also see Karttunen (1974; to appear).

Source: *Language* 52, no. 1 (1976). Reprinted by permission of the publisher.

referring expressions succeed in referring to an appropriate object or objects. The content of such presuppositions on Frege's view is a function of the grammatical structure of sentences.

A contextual presupposition differs from a semantic presupposition in that the content of the latter condition is determined by the grammatical structure of a sentence type, whereas the content of the former condition is determined also by features of the context in which a sentence token occurs. Contextual presupposition naturally applies to utterances, while semantic presupposition naturally applies to sentences of a language. Moreover, the fact that both kinds of presupposition are conditions whose satisfaction normally requires a relation between something linguistic and the world ought not obscure this difference.

Those who first developed a semantic theory within the theory of transformational-generative grammar characterized the level of semantic representation as consisting of formal structures from which the semantic properties and relations of sentences can be determined. Thus the optimal semantic representation of a sentence in a grammar is whatever formal structure provides the simplest basis for predicting whether it is meaningful, ambiguous, analytic, synonymous with such-and-such other sentences, etc. (Katz, 1972, Chap. 1). The specification of such semantic properties and relations was left open-ended, in order to accommodate further cases that might turn out to be predictable from the semantic representations developed to predict meaningfulness, ambiguity, analyticity, etc. Presupposition was incorporated into semantic theory on the hypothesis that it is one of these further cases (Katz, 1965, pp. 597-98; 1966, pp. 211-20).

Introducing presuppositions as one of the semantic properties and relations that must be predicted from an optimal semantic representation raises questions both about the interpretation of this notion, for example, whether it should be interpreted logically, situationally, or in some other manner, and about the proper formal devices to use in constructing semantic representations. Both these questions came in for discussion (Katz, 1972, pp. 127-50). A noteworthy contribution to these discussions came in a paper by Langendoen and Savin (1971). They saw clearly that the formal devices required for constructing semantic representations from which presuppositions could be predicted would have to be part of the same machinery that provides a compositional analysis of the meaning of a sentence. Their empirical survey of the facts about how the presuppositions of the components of a complex sentence are related to the presupposition of the complex sentence as a whole led them to formulate the hypothesis (1):

(1) Each of the presuppositions of a component sentence in a complex sentence is a presupposition of the entire complex sentence.

But counterexamples were soon pointed out. Morgan (1969) observes that (1) fails for sentences like (2):

(2) If Jack has children, then all of Jack's children are bald.

As Austin (1963) points out, sentence (3), the consequent clause of (2), by itself presupposes the existence of people who are children of Jack's.

(3) All of Jack's children are bald.

He writes: "Not only (3) but equally '[Jack's] children are not bald', presupposes that [Jack] has children. To talk about those children, or to refer to them, presupposes that they exist" (p. 17). Yet as Morgan observes, (2) presupposes nothing beyond the existence of Jack, so that here the presupposition of a component sentence of a complex sentence is not a presupposition of the entire sentence. Further, as Katz (1972) and Karttunen (1973) observe, the presuppositions associated with an expression in a sentence are not in general presuppositions associated with the complex sentences in which such a sentence appears as a verbal complement because referentially opaque verbs remove such presuppositions. Thus, in a sentence like (4), there is no presupposition that Santa Claus exists:

(4) Bob believes that Santa Claus came last night.

As Karttunen (1973, p. 173) puts it, one must distinguish between "holes," "plugs," and "filters"; that is, positions that let the presuppositions associated with the expressions appearing in them become presuppositions of the entire sentence, positions that do not let them become presuppostions of the entire sentence, and positions that sometimes do and sometimes do not let them become presuppositions of the entire sentence.[3]

Thus we might restrict the formulation of the Langendoen-Savin hypothesis so that it avoids such counterexamples by restating it as (5):

(5) Each of the presuppositions of a component sentence in a complex sentence is a presupposition of the entire complex sentence just in case it is associated with an expression that appears in a hole.

But (5) amounts to no more than a triviality, since holes have been so far characterized as positions that let the presupposition of the expression occupying them become presuppositions of the entire sentence. Therefore, the problem is twofold. An adequate semantic theory must set up machinery to explicate formally these metaphorical notions of holes, plugs, and filters; then, it must provide in terms of such machinery, the projection mechanism that explains (5) and (6) and tells us when the filters are open and closed:

---

3. Karttunen actually speaks of the predicates, not the positions of their arguments, as constituting the holes, plugs, and filters. This difference, however, is immaterial to the discussion.

(6) None of the presuppositions of a component sentence in a complex
sentence is a presupposition of the entire complex sentence if they are
associated with expressions that appear in a plug.

This is done in Katz (1972; in press) as part of the formal theory of compositional semantic interpretation. In the next section, we briefly sketch how that
machinery works.

FORMALIZATION OF
SEMANTIC PRESUPPOSITION

Katz (1972, pp. 167) proposes that the referential positions in propositions
(senses of sentences) be formally represented by the notation of enclosure within
heavy parentheses, to distinguish them from nonreferential positions. Besides
nonreferential positions created by verbs of propositional attitude, such as
believes in (4), the subject of "exists" is nonreferential in our sense. The position occupied by 'poisonous mushrooms' in (7) is nonreferential, but the position this expression occupies in (8) is referential:

(7) Poisonous mushrooms exist.

(8) Poisonous mushrooms killed the elephant.

Since (7) asserts that there are poisonous mushrooms, it cannot be represented
as presupposing the existence of poisonous mushrooms. If it were so represented, it would be described as having its truth condition included in its condition of statementhood, and it would be mistakenly marked as analytic (Katz,
1972, pp. 172–78).

The sense of 'referential' represented by a pair of heavy parentheses is different from the standard one in terms of substitutivity of identicals (Katz, 1972,
p. 141), since, supposing that *toadstools* is coreferential with *poisonous mushrooms,* we can substitute the former for the latter in (7) as well as (8) preserving
truth, yet as we have just seen we cannot regard the term position of (7) as
referential in the sense of presuppositional reference. Thus the interpretation of
an occurence of heavy parentheses in a reading is simply that it is a necessary
condition on the (assertive) proposition represented by the reading being a statement (that is, either true or false) that the reading enclosed within these heavy
parentheses refer appropriately. The interpretation of a component reading not
enclosed within heavy parentheses is, correspondingly, that the statementhood
condition of the proposition in question is independent of whether the reading
refers. The assertion of (4) makes no claim about anyone in the world about

whom Bob has a belief whereas the assertion of (9) does make a claim about someone in the world about whom Bob has a belief:[4]

(9) Bob knows that the burglar came last night.

We are now in a position to explicate the notions of "hole" and "plug" and to explain (5) and (6), leaving the question of filters until after this explication and explanation are finished. At the lexical level, some verbs, such as *believe*, *exist*, *want*, etc., will have to be represented by readings in which categorized variables marking term positions are unenclosed by heavy parentheses; while others, such as *kill*, *know*, etc., will have to be represented by readings in which such categorized variables are enclosed with heavy parentheses. Thus, some parts of lexical readings have the form displayed in (10) and other parts of lexical readings have the form displayed in (11):

$$(10) \quad (\ldots \overset{[\ ]}{\underset{\langle\ \rangle}{X}} \ldots)$$

$$(11) \quad (\ldots (\overset{[\ ]}{\underset{\langle\ \rangle}{X}}) \ldots)$$

4. It is also possible for an entire complement to be in referential position; thus, the contrast between referential and nonreferential positions in (4) and (9) is matched in (i) and (ii):

(i) Alice believes (thinks, etc.) that it is raining.
(ii) Alice regrets (realizes, etc.) that it is raining.

The predicates in sentences like (ii), in which the reading of the object complement is in referential position, have been called 'factives' by Kiparsky & Kiparsky (1971). We retain their terminology, but not their construal of factive presupposition as a condition on the speaker's beliefs; that is, one that makes the utterance of the entire sentence anomalous in case the speaker's beliefs do not include the proposition expressed by the complement of the factive predicate. We do this because the adoption of this notion of "speaker presupposition" leads to absurd consequences (Katz, 1973). Rather, we consider the truth of the complement sentence to be a necessary condition for the entire (declarative) sentence in which it occurs to be true or false. The condition, in other words, is a semantic presupposition of the same sort that obtains in the case of ordinary referring expressions.

We can interpret this requirement that the complement of a factive predicate must be true in order for the sentence as a whole to be true or false as equivalent to a requirement that its reading succeed in corresponding to an actual state of affairs. The formal treatment of the presuppositions associated with the complements of factive predicates follows directly. We categorize the variables whose values represent objects of predicates like *regret*, *believe*, etc., and subjects of predicates like *be amazing*, *be certain*, etc., for readings of the complement sentences; such variables will be enclosed in heavy parentheses just in case they are associated with factive predicates. Thus, in (ii), the reading for *it is raining* is substituted for a variable enclosed in heavy parentheses, while in (i), the reading for *it is raining* is substituted for a variable not enclosed in heavy parentheses.

JERROLD J. KATZ
AND D. TERENCE LANGENDOEN

We can formally explicate the notion of a hole as a term position in a proposition represented in the form (11) and the notion of a plug as a term position in a proposition represented in the form (10). In the semantic representation of (8), the variable in the reading for *kill* that is categorized for a reading of the subject of the sentence is enclosed in heavy parentheses, and therefore the reading of the subject is placed in referential position by virtue of the projection rule substituting the reading of *poisonous mushrooms* for this categorized variable. Essentially the same thing happens in the semantic representation of (9). The variable in the reading of "know" that marks the position (or one of the positions) for terms that stand for the things about which something is asserted to be known is enclosed in heavy parentheses. Moreover, it is categorized for a reading of the subject of the embedded sentence, that is, the reading of *the burglar* in (9). This reading thus is placed in a referential position when the projection rule substitutes it for the aforementioned categorized variable. Hence, on the interpretation of heavy parentheses—that readings enclosed in them must succeed in referring to an appropriate object or objects if the entire sentence is to make a statement—we explain (5) with respect to these examples.

The explanation of (6) can be given in terms of the examples (4) and (7). The latter is straightforward. In (7), the variable categorized for the reading of the subject of the sentence is not enclosed in heavy parentheses, so that when the reading of *poisonous mushrooms* is substituted for it by the projection rule, the reading is placed in a nonreferential position. In (4), the interpretive process works as follows. The lexical reading for *believe* will contain a categorized variable or categorized variables for readings that appear as the terms of the proposition functioning as the object of belief, that is, the proposition that a sentence like (4) says that someone thinks is true. One such variable will be categorized for the reading of the subject of the sentential complement of *believe*. Now, the sentence that appears as the complement of *believe* in (4) would, outside this context, presuppose the existence of something answering to the description in its subject noun phrase, since *come* will have a lexical reading in which the term of the predicate is enclosed in heavy parentheses. But as the reading of a subject of a sentence appearing as the complement of *believe*, this reading will be substituted for the variable in the reading of *believe* categorized for such readings. Hence, it will be taken out of a position enclosed by heavy parentheses and put into one not so enclosed. Thus on the interpretation of heavy parentheses, this projection process explains (6) with respect to these examples.[5]

Before we turn to filters, let us summarize this discussion. The semantic property of presupposition can be formally defined in terms of the occurrence of readings enclosed by heavy parentheses. The definition, which is spelled out in greater detail in Katz (in press), is (12):

---

5. For further discussion, see Katz (in press).

(12) The presupposition of a proposition P (sense of a sentence) is the requirement that all and only the readings $R_1, \ldots, R_n$ enclosed in heavy parentheses in the reading R of P succeed in referring to their appropriate object(s).

This expresses the condition for the statementhood of sentences like (4), (7), (8), and (9). Moreover, the normal operation of the projection rule, together with independently motivated representations of the semantic structure of particular lexical items, automatically provides a formalization of the metaphorical notion of plugs and holes.

We now take up filters. The notion of a filter is actually a misleading metaphor. Unlike the notions of holes and plugs, which though metaphorical do correspond to a formalism in readings (i.e., holes and plugs have a structural realization in the difference between referential and nonreferential positions), the notion of a filter cannot be cashed in terms of a comparable formal device. The cases covered by this notion are just the ones in which semantic interpretation rules change holes into plugs or plugs into holes.

How did the notion of a filter arise? Compare (13) with (2):

(13) If Jack has sisters, then all of Jack's children are bald.

As Morgan (1969) and Kartuunen (1973) both observe, sentences like (13) presuppose that the person referred to by the subject in the antecedent has children. Now, this observation, together with the observation that sentences like (2) do not presuppose that there are such children, shows that the term position occupied by the subject in the consequent of such conditionals behaves like a hole on some occasions and like a plug on others. Karttunen jumps to the conclusion that he had found a new type of semantic entity with the properties of both holes and plugs. But there is another explanation possible on which there is no such new kind of entity. We can say, instead, that in cases like (13) the position in question is a hole, and in cases like (2) it is a plug. If we say this, we must provide a rule of semantic interpretation that converts holes into plugs, that is, changes referential positions into nonreferential positions, under the conditions that obtain in examples like (2).

Such a rule is proposed in Katz (in press). The rule would appear as a reading of a syntactic element in the same manner that antonymy rules appear as the reading of the "Neg" element (Katz 1972, pp. 157-71), and it would operate on a reading in its scope by deleting occurrences of heavy parentheses in the reading. We may refer to this rule as the 'heavy-parentheses wipe-out rule' (HPWR). We shall first provide independent motivation for HPWR and then show how it can be used to handle cases like (2).

Katz (in press) uses HPWR to explain the semantic fact that generic sentences like (14), in contrast to nongeneric ones like (15), do not have referential presuppositions:

(14)   The owl is nocturnal.

(15)   The owl is awake.

That is, the statementhood of a sentence like (14) does not depend on there being some actual owl or any owls, past, present, or future, referred to by its subject. This fact would be explained if the syntactic feature [Generic] (or whatever syntactic element is used instead of such a feature) has HPWR as its lexical reading and at the syntactic level the genericness of (14) is accounted for by marking the subject noun phrases (or the whole sentence) [Generic]. Then the application of HPWR to the reading of the subject in (14) removes the heavy parentheses around the term position of the predicate *is nocturnal*. In contrast, neither the subject noun phrase nor the entire sentence (15) is marked as [Generic], so that the heavy parentheses around the term position of the predicate *is awake* are not removed and thus appear in the reading of the sentence. We note further that HPWR must operate on the heavy parentheses around every term position of a predicate in its scope, so that the presuppositional requirement for every term of a relation is canceled if any one is. This further clause is needed to handle the fact that sentences like (16) have no presupposition:

(16)   The owl interbreeds with the cat.

Given that we have the rule HPWR, we can employ it to explain why a sentence like (2) does not presuppose the existence of children of Jack's, even though the existence of such children would be presupposed by the consequent sentence in isolation. The meaning of a conditional sentence in natural language normally involves the notion of what would be the case were some possibility to become an actuality. Let us call this aspect of their meaning their "hypotheticality." It is just this aspect that is lost when conditional sentences of natural language are translated by the material conditional of logic. For example, if we translate (17) as (18), then any denial of the claim made by (17) must assert that Saul will convert to Islam:

(17)   If Saul will convert to Islam, he will get into Egypt.

(18)   Saul will convert to Islam $(=P) \supset$ Saul will get into Egypt $(=Q)$.

That is, on the translation (18), I cannot deny the claim (17) without committing myself to the claim that Saul will convert to Islam, which it is absurd to think I commit myself to in denying (17). For the denial of (17) is, ex hypothesi, $\sim(P \supset Q)$, and this is equivalent to $\sim(\sim P \vee Q)$, which is $P \& \sim Q$, which implies P.

Now, however we choose to represent hypotheticality, it must follow from the representation that the predicate(s) of the antecedent clause(s) of a conditional fall in the scope of hypotheticality, and as a consequence the truth conditions associated with the proposition(s) expressed by these antecedent clause(s) —when they appear as isolated sentences—are nullified. That is, hypotheticality is a plug for truth conditions. The truth conditions of (17), for example, do not include the truth conditions of (19):

(19)   Saul will convert to Islam.

The details of how we represent this plugging do not concern us here (cf. Katz, in press). What is of concern here is that the case of conditional sentences is, as it were, the inverse of the case of generic sentences. Whereas in generic sentences the presupposition is wiped out but the truth conditions remain, in the antecedent of a conditional, the truth condition is wiped out but the presupposition remains.

This fact raises the question of what happens to constituents in other clauses of a sentence that are anaphoric to a constituent in a clause that has had its presupposition or truth-condition contribution wiped out. The anomaly of (20) shows that anaphora relations extend the scope of HPWR:[6]

(20)   The owl is nocturnal and it is awake.

That HPWR also applies to impose a nonpresuppositional characterization on constituents that are anaphoric to ones that have been hypotheticalized is clear from the fact that (21) does not presuppose that the pronoun subject of its second clause refers to some actual state of affairs:

(21)   If Saul converts to Islam, it will kill his mother.

HPWR is triggered by an anaphoric relation to a constituent whose presupposition or truth-condition contribution has been eliminated. It removes the heavy parentheses around the reading of the anaphoric constituent. Therefore, this operation of HPWR explains why in (2), but not in (13), the sentence does not presuppose that the subject of its consequent clause refers—no appropriate anaphora relation obtains in (13) to cause the subject of the consequent clause to become nonreferential:

(2)   If Jack has children, then all of Jack's children are bald.

(13)   If Jack has sisters, then all of Jack's children are bald.

The situation is somewhat more complex, however. From examples like (22), we see that the application of HPWR does not depend on anaphora as it is understood is syntax, but rather on meaning inclusion:

(22)   If Jack has children, then all of Jack's sons are bald.

6. The anomaly of (20) results from the adjective *awake* being inherently nongeneric, as can be seen from the fact that (14) is ambiguous between a generic and nongeneric sense, but (15) has only a nongeneric sense.

JERROLD J. KATZ
AND D. TERENCE LANGENDOEN

In (22), as in (2), the subject of the consequent clause is not presupposed to refer; thus the reading of the terms whose heavy parentheses are removed by such applications of HPWR must contain the reading of the corresponding constituent in the antecedent clause whose presupposition or truth-condition contribution has been eliminated.[7,8]

7. It turns out that even Karttunen's definition of "semantic" filtering for conditional sentences (1973, p. 178) cannot be accommodated within a formal grammatical theory, since it is stated in terms of deductive entailment. Thus, according to his account, sentences like (i) and (ii) also do not presuppose that Jack has children:

(i) If it is true that Jack has children, then all of Jack's children are bald.
(ii) If Jack has grandchildren, then all of Jack's children are bald.

However, what is made hypothetical in (i) and (ii) is not the predicate *have children* (applied to *Jack*), but rather *be true* (applied to the proposition *Jack has children*) and *have grandchildren* (applied to *Jack*). In neither case is there any expression in the consequent clause whose reading is included in the reading of the predicate of the antecedent clause. Hence by the formal semantic theory sketched in the third section, the heavy parentheses around the categorized variable for which *Jack's children* is substituted are not removed, and the presupposition of the existence of children of Jack's remains. The carrying out of the deductions that would lead users of sentences like (i) and (ii) to conclude that that presupposition does not obtain must be viewed as being performed outside of the grammar itself, along the lines proposed below.

8. Karttunen (1973) claims that presupposition filtering takes place not only in conditional sentences, but also in compound sentences in which the connectives *and* or *or* are used. Thus, he argues, the presupposition that Jack has children appears in sentences (i) and (iii), but not in (ii) and (iv):

(i) Jack has sisters, and all of Jack's children are bald.
(ii) Jack has children, and all of Jack's children are bald.
(iii) Jack has no sisters, or all of Jack's children are bald.
(iv) Jack has no children, or all of Jack's children are bald.

This claim, we contend, is false. For simplicity, let us just consider cases with *and*, like (ii). Concerning this sentence (=Karttunen's (16a)), he says the following: "The interesting case is (16a). As far as I can see, it does not presuppose that Jack has children. If it should turn out that the first conjunct is false, then the whole conjunction surely ought to be false, not indeterminate or truthvalueless" (p. 176). Furthermore, this is all that Karttunen says by way of justifying his claim that sentences like (ii), in which the first clause asserts what the second clause presupposes, do not contain a presupposition associated with the second clause; unlike the stiuation with conditional sentences, there is no independent semantic property of the sentence type which can be thought of as providing the basis for the presupposition filtering (such sentences are not hypothetical). Thus, the claim that *and* and *or* result in filtering rests ultimately only on the intuitions of the investigator.

Suppose, then, we assert that in (ii), the presupposition that Jack has children remains, and in general that *and* and *or* are never by themselves associated with filtering of presuppositions. We now show that the two claims make different predictions about the relation between conjoined sentences and their counterparts with conjoined noun phrases, and that only the latter claim is consistent with the hypothesis that the two sentence types have the same logical form (assuming, as we do, that presupposition is part of logical form). Consider the following sentences:

THE ARGUMENT FOR CONTEXTUAL PRESUPPOSITION

We have sketched above a treatment that accounts for hole and plug phenomena in terms of rules that convert holes into plugs in the process of deriving the semantic interpretation of a sentence compositionally. Thus, even though we have only given a sketch, we can begin to see how the initially heterogeneous behavior of semantic structures classified under the heading of filters will assume regular form and be describable by rules of the semantic component in a straightforward way. Thus far, then, nothing prevents the full treatment of presuppositional phenomena from being handled entirely within the semantic component of a generative grammar.

However, Karttunen (1973) claims that there is a further filtering phenomenon that cannot be handled within the strict confines of formal grammar. Karttunen argues that in sentences like (23), which are parallel in structure to sentences like (13), rather than (2), the presupposition arising from the factive verb *regret* in the consequent may still be filtered out:

(23) If Nixon appoints J. Edgar Hoover to the cabinet, he will regret having appointed a homosexual.

According to Karttunen, in contexts in which it is believed that Hoover is a homosexual, (23) does not presuppose that Nixon will have appointed a homosexual (just as (2) does not presuppose that Jack has children) even though, by virtue of the fact that *regret* is a factive, like *know* in (24), Nixon's appointing a homosexual is a presupposition of (25):

(24) Bob knows that Nixon was behind Watergate.
(25) Nixon will regret having appointed a homosexual.

Moreover, Karttunen argues that the simplest form of the presupposition filtering mechanism for conditional sentences would treat the filtering of presuppositions under purely semantic conditions as a special case of filtering in context, namely, as the case where the context is null. As he puts it:

(v) Jack has children, and all of Jack's children have children.
(vi) Jack and all of Jack's children have children.

Suppose Jack does not have children. On Karttunen's analysis, (v) is false and (vi) is truth-valueless (fails to make a statement). On our analysis, both (v) and (vi) are truth-valueless (fail to make statements). Thus (v) and (vi), on Karttunen's analysis, cannot have the same logical form, thus forcing him to give up the generalization that conjoined sentences and their counterparts with conjoined noun phrases always have the same logical form, a generalization which holds outside of cases of this sort (cf. Harnish, in this volume). On our analysis, on the other hand, the generalization is secure. A parallel argument goes through for cases with *or*. Hence, our analysis, in which *and* and *or* are not associated with presupposition filtering, is to be preferred to Karttunen's.

JERROLD J. KATZ
AND D. TERENCE LANGENDOEN

The effect of these revised filtering conditions is to make the notion of pre-supposition relative with respect to linguistic contexts, that is, to sets of sentences whose truth is taken for granted. We can no longer talk about the presuppositions of a compound [i.e., complex] sentence in an absolute sense, only with regard to a given set of background assumptions (1973, p. 185).

It may be observed, prior to considering the validity of this argument, that it fits nicely into the general tendency within generative semantics, as noted by Katz and Bever (in this volume), to attack the notion of a formal grammar in the sense of a system of rules that mechanically assigns structural descriptions to sentences. Karttunen's treatment of presupposition makes the assignment of structural descriptions that include a specification of presupposition relative to knowledge of whether the context under consideration is null or one in which some particular set of background assumptions are true. In Karttunen's treatment, although we can formally state various conditionals about a sentence like (23) specifying the belief conditions under which the sentence presupposes the same things that its clauses presuppose, we cannot detach the consequents of such conditionals without destroying the formal character of the system in which the conditionals are expressed. This is because detachment of the consequents would require supplementing these systems with statements expressing truths about the world. Thus, Karttunen's argument, that grammars treating presupposition as an absolute property (computable from the grammatical structure of a sentence) should be replaced by grammars treating presupposition as relative to context, implies that either grammars can make no predictions about what the presupposition of a sentence is or generative grammars must be abandoned in favor of grammars that determine the assignment of properties like presupposition nonformally. Since making no predictions about a property that obviously should be predicted is hardly an attractive alternative, Karttunen's argument coincides with the arguments that Lakoff and other generative semanticists have been making on behalf of the claim that the absolute notion of grammaticality must be abandoned in favor of a notion of relative grammaticality.[9] Therefore, the issue here between a contextual and semantic theory of presupposition is part of the larger issue of whether an adequate grammar of a natural language is a formal system.

PRAGMATICS AND PRESUPPOSITION

To see what is wrong with Karttunen's argument, we need to begin with the theory of linguistic communication that developed out of the work of transformational-generative grammar over the past two decades. This theory bases its account of how speakers of a language L communicate in their language on a model of online processing mechanisms for speech production and

9. See, for example, Lakoff (1971a, b).

recognition that embodies a grammar of L. The nature of the relation between a grammar (a theory of linguistic competence) and a model of production and recognition (a theory of linguistic performance) has so far been studied most extensively in connection with syntactic and phonological phenomena.[10] It is clear, however, that a complete account of this relation will also require a study of the role of semantic competence in a performance model.

A beginning was made in the study of the role of the competence/ performance distinction in semantics during the early 1960s in the first attempts to characterize a semantic component of a transformational grammar. Katz and Fodor (1963, p. 174) suggested that the semantic competence of speakers consists in whatever nonsyntactic and nonphonological information about the structure of the sentences speakers have when there is no information at all about their contexts, or alternatively, when they occur in zero contexts such as in an anonymous letter. Katz and Fodor drew a sharp distinction between what may be called "grammatical meaning," the meaning of a sentence type in the language, and "utterance meaning," the meaning of a particular token or use of a sentence type on some specific occasion. Within their framework, Chomsky's distinction between "well-formedness" and "acceptability" is paralleled by the distinction between "meaningfulness," which is a property of sentence types, and "significance," which is a property of tokens, or utterances. For example, (26) is meaningful; that is, it has a grammatical meaning in English, but a token of (26) rotely and uncomprehendingly spoken by nursery school children would not be significant:

(26) I pledge allegiance to the flag of the United States of America.

On the other hand, (27) is not meaningful in the language, but a token of this semantically deviant sentence used by John's golfing partners to describe his poor performance might be fully significant in the context:

(27) Golf plays John.

This leads to the following difference between a grammar and a performance theory at the semantic level. A grammar is a system of formal rules that provides a sound–meaning correlation in the language: it associates a grammatical meaning with each sentence type. A semantic performance theory is a system of rules that specifies how contextual factors interact with grammatical structure to determine an utterance meaning for each token of a sentence type: it concerns itself not with sentence types but with their spatiotemporal tokens, and not with grammatical meaning but with utterance meaning. Thus, we may regard a semantic performance theory as a *theory of pragmatics* (Katz, in press).

The problem to which a theory of pragmatics addresses itself is how to account for the divergence of utterance meaning from grammatical meaning.

10. See, for example, Chomsky (1965); Chomsky & Halle (1968).

JERROLD J. KATZ
AND D. TERENCE LANGENDOEN

For example, the grammatical meaning of (28)

(28) We have a genius in the White House now

is, roughly speaking, that the U.S. president at this time is endowed with extraordinary intellectual ability, whereas the utterance meaning of current tokens of (28) is very likely exactly the opposite. We may conceive of a theory of pragmatics as a function of the form $PRAG$ $(x, y) = z$. The arguments x and y are, respectively, a sentence S together with its structural description in an optimal grammar and a full specification of the relevant contextual information about a particular token of S. The value z is a representation of the utterance meaning of this token in the specified context. Properly constructed, such a function will account for the divergence of utterance meaning from grammatical meaning by providing an utterance meaning that is appropriately different from the grammatical meaning of the sentence in all and only those contexts that themselves determine aspects of the semantic content of the utterance.

The question of how the utterance meaning of a token is represented can be reduced to the question of how grammatical meaning is represented by taking the representation of the utterance meaning of a sentence token to be the grammatical meaning of some sentence different from the sentence type for this token. Thus a theory of pragmatics, like a grammar, can be regarded as a sound–meaning correlation, only not one for the language, but one for particular context–utterance pairs. Thus, in certain contexts at the present time, (28) is used to communicate the opposite of its grammatical meaning, and so the value of PRAG should be the semantic representation of (29) in the grammar of English:

(29) We have a moron in the White House now.

It is not important here to specify the nature of the rules that comprise PRAG, since what we have said so far is enough to bring out the fallacy in Karttunen's argument.

This conception of pragmatics and its relation to formal grammar is that knowledge of the grammar of a language provides the speaker with knowledge of all the sentences of the language and of all their correlated meanings, while knowledge of the principles in PRAG provides the speaker with knowledge of how to exploit information about an utterance context to express a meaning using some sentence of the language with which that meaning is not correlated in the language. Thus, knowledge of both grammar and pragmatics provides speakers with their ability to speak ironically or sarcastically (as in our example), their ability to speak concisely, and so on.

There is one feature of this ability that speakers gain by having knowledge of pragmatic principles in addition to their knowledge of the grammar that calls for special attention. We normally employ this ability to speak *very* concisely.

We say such things as (30),

(30) John is here

but by so doing express the statement that some specific person with the name
'John' is at some particular, definite location. Therefore, the sentence whose
reading is the output of PRAG should be as fully spelled out as is necessary to
uniquely specify the actual statement made on the occasion. On some occasion where a token of (30) occurs, the output of PRAG might be the reading
of the sentence (31):

(31) The person named "John Jacob Jingleheimer Smith," who is employed
      by the Smith and Wesson Company, who is seven feet tall, etc., etc.,
      etc., is at 11:59, December 31, 1974, at the very center of Times
      Square in New York City.

The extra information, such as John's middle and last names, his job, his height,
and so on would be the information that the participants in the speech situation
themselves use to pin down the referent of the subject, the time of utterance,
and the intended location.

In the context that Karttunen imagines, the participants in the speech
situation all believe that J. Edgar Hoover is a homosexual and each knows that
the others share this belief. Thus it is reasonable to suppose that (23) is another
instance of concise speech, in that it does not contain some constituent expressing the belief that J. Edgar Hoover is a homosexual, but nonetheless makes the
statement that Nixon will regret the appointment of Hoover because it is the
appointment of a homosexual. That is, we can take the token of (23) in the
situation Karttunen constructs to make this statement even though the sentence used to make it lacks the information that Hoover is a homosexual because we can assume that the information is shared by the participants, that
they know it to be shared, and that they can employ PRAG in addition to their
knowledge of the grammar. Thus it is reasonable that the output of PRAG for
the case of the use of (23) in Karttunen's context is the reading of (32), which
represents the utterance meaning of this token of (23):

(32) If Nixon appoints J. Edgar Hoover, who, as we all know, is a homo-
      sexual, to the cabinet, he will regret having appointed a homosexual.

Therefore, contrary to Karttunen's claim, there is no need for a notion of
contextual presupposition to handle the facts about filtering in connection with
the critical case. The semantic interpretation of (32) provides exactly the right
presuppositions for (23) in the context assumed. HPWR will apply to remove
the heavy parentheses around the reading of the complement of *regret* that come
in by virtue of this verb's factivity. HPWR performs this operation because, as
in the case of (22), the reading whose heavy parentheses are removed bears the
relation of meaning inclusion to the corresponding constituent in the antecedent

clause whose truth-condition contribution has been eliminated. Clearly, we must construe *a homosexual* in the consequent of (32) not only to be a specific homosexual but, in fact, the same one identified by the name *J. Edgar Hoover* in the antecedent. This construal will be required to obtain the right contextual presupposition on Karttunen's analysis. Hence, (32) will not presuppose that Nixon will have appointed a homosexual, accounting for the fact that the utterance meaning of (23) in the context that Karttunen supplies does not presuppose it either, even though (23) itself does have the presupposition.

This reply to Karttunen is quite general. Whenever a Karttunen-type argument for a contextual presupposition *C* is made (that is, one along the lines he set out for the presupposition about the belief that J. Edgar Hoover is a homosexual) we may recast *C* in terms of a constituent of the sentence that expresses the statement made on the occasion, the sentence whose reading is the output of PRAG for the appropriate arguments. Moreover, when such "presuppositions" do not hold, it will not be possible to justify a correspondingly richer statement. For example, if the participants of the situation do not believe J. Edgar Hoover to be a homosexual, then the use of (23) would be *too* concise to be understood in the intended way. Under these conditions, the utterance of (23) could be understood to mean that if Nixon appoints Hoover to the cabinet, he will regret having appointed a homosexual, someone other than Hoover, because Hoover's new cabinet post will put him in the position to expose the homosexual Secretary of Agriculture and Nixon will regret that.

Karttunen obtains his conclusion about the desirability of contextualizing presupposition by holding constant the sound–meaning correlation in the grammar with respect to context. That is, he uses the meaning correlated with a sentence type as the meaning of any of its tokens. This requires him to contextualize presupposition, since he now must make features of the meaning of utterances vary with the context, such as whether it is Hoover or some Secretary of Agriculture that Nixon is said to regret having appointed. We, on the other hand, contextualize the assignment of meanings to tokens, allowing the meaning of a sentence token to diverge from the meaning of its type. This is the role of PRAG. We thereby require no contextualization of presupposition. We keep as competence what is competence by taking as performance what is performance.

GENERALIZING THE ARGUMENT

Although the argument developed in the previous section was used exclusively in connection with the notion of contextual presupposition, its application is far broader. It can be applied generally to show that any contextualized property or relation (as opposed to pragmatic rules that comprise PRAG) is eliminable on the basis of a purely grammatical property or relation in the way that we eliminated Karttunen's notion of contextual presupposition on the basis of the notion of semantic presupposition. Let us consider one further contextual notion to illustrate the generality of our argument.

Grice (1975) distinguishes *conventional implicatures*, which rest on the meanings of the words in a sentence, from what he calls *conversational implicatures*, which rest also on various principles governing discourses. Conventional implicatures are simply semantic entailments. The example Grice often uses to illustrate this notion is (33):

(33) He is an Englishman; he is, therefore, brave.

Someone who asserts (33) conventionally implicates that his being brave is a consequence of his being English. This consequence relation rests on the meaning of *therefore*. Sarcasm is one of Grice's examples of conversational implicature, as when someone says (34) to mean that someone else is a poor friend:

(34) He's a fine friend.

The speaker can conversationally implicate this, according to Grice, because the discourse governing maxim not to say what you believe to be false is flouted so excessively. Noticing that the use of (28) to mean (29) discussed above is a case of the same sort raises the question of whether a special notion of conversational implicature is necessary. Might it too be definable on the basis of grammatical notions within the framework of the conception of pragmatics outlined above?

We can define the notion of a conversational implicature as follows. Someone conversationally implicates P in saying S in the context C just in case (*a*) PRAG assigns the reading R as its output for a structural description of S and appropriate information about C, and (*b*) the proposition that R represents semantically entails P. Consider the example of a use of (28) to mean (29). The speaker succeeds in denigrating the president's intelligence because the hearers know enough about the speaker's political beliefs to know that he or she cannot be using (28) literally and that he or she could not hope or want to deceive them with so flagrant a lie. Therefore, they construe the speaker to conversationally implicate that the president is stupid. Now the discourse-governing principles (here taken to be among the rules comprising PRAG) that enable us to account for the hearers construing the speaker to have sarcastically implicated that the president is stupid would also permit us to assign (29) as the utterance meaning of this use of (28). Hence this case of a conversational implicature can be handled by the notions of utterance meaning and of semantic entailment. An extension of this procedure to other cases would say that the notion of a conversational implicature, like that of a contextual presupposition, is unnecessary as a basic construct of pragmatics.

An elimination of conversational implicature as a basic notion of pragmatics does not, of course, deny the usefulness of Grice's hypotheses about discourse-governing principles. These may well be a major part of the PRAG mechanism

JERROLD J. KATZ
AND D. TERENCE LANGENDOEN

for assigning utterance meanings to sentence tokens. However, the possibility of an elimination raises a serious question about the homogeneity of the phenomena in the domain that Grice covers under the notion of conversational implicature. Such an elimination must ignore such things as Searle's (1969: 57) 'normal input and output conditions', for example, that the speaker believes that the hearer speaks the language the speaker is talking in, that the hearer is not deaf, and so on. These are not part of the utterance meaning of the sentence token but simply things that the hearer can infer from the speaker's behavior. Let us introduce the notion 'speaker implicature' to cover the various things that the speaker gives the hearer the right to infer about his beliefs, knowledge, and so on, which are not matters of utterance meaning and hence not conversational implicature in our reconstructed sense. Now, the question arises about Gricean cases like uses of (35) in which the hearer infers that the speaker does not know which of the two rooms the woman is in.

(35) My wife is either in the kitchen or in the bedroom.

Grice treats such an inference as turning on a clash between maxims. The speaker infringes on the maxim of quantity by not saying which room. If the speaker is not opting out, he must be presumed to be avoiding a conflict with the maxim of quality and thus he implicates that he does not know which room she is in. Consider the proposition P that the speaker does not know (have adequate evidence for saying) which room his wife is in. Is P a conversational implicature in our sense, that is, part of the utterance meaning, or a speaker implicature, that is, something inferable about the speaker like the fact that the speaker believes the hearer knows English? We do not wish to take a strong stand for either answer. We are aware of various considerations that might establish one or the other. For example, we think one is inclined to say in the case of a clearly sarcastic use of (34) that the speaker *asserted* that John is a poor friend, but we think that one is not similarly inclined to say in the case of a normal use of (35) that the speaker *asserted* that he did not know which of the two rooms his wife was in. This suggests that P is a speaker implicature. If this is right, then the phenomena covered under Grice's term 'conversational implicature' are not homogeneous as Grice's theory supposes. This would show that there are really two distinct phenomena and that there need to be new principles to explain the distinction between them.

WHAT PRAGMATIC NOTIONS
REALLY ARE

We have shown that the interpretation of sentences in context does not require the abandonment of the semantic notion of presupposition or the relegation of semantic presupposition to the status of a special case of contextual presupposition. We have argued further that consideration of the manner in which grammars and pragmatic theories interact shows that it is rather the contextual notion of presupposition that is unnecessary. For this interaction between competence and performance theories is exactly what one finds elsewhere in the theory of communication; competence theories define grammatical properties and relations (e.g., grammaticality, ambiguity, rhyme, etc.) while a performance theory assigns tokens to types. For example, the part of the performance model that accounts for sentence recognition is a system for assigning tokens of sentences (utterances) to their proper sentence-types in the grammar. Looked at in this way, it becomes clear that Karttunen's pragmatic notion of presupposition is not even the same kind of notion as that of semantic presupposition. Semantic presupposition is a condition of statementhood. If the *semantic* presupposition P of a sentence S holds in a context C where S is used, then the assertion is either true or false, while if P does not hold in a context C where S is used, then the assertion is neither true nor false. On the other hand, if the *contextual* presupposition P of a sentence S holds in a context C where S is used, then S carries some particular meaning M in C rather than some other meaning; for example, that it is Hoover Nixon regrets appointing rather than the Secretary of Agriculture. But if P does not hold in a context C where S is used, then S does not carry the meaning M in C. Therefore, the two notions are completely different. Contextual presupposition differs in being a condition for determining the proper utterance meaning of a sentence. It is not a condition of statementhood. It is, rather, part of a theory of how sentence tokens are assigned to semantic types in an account of their utterance meaning.

Finally, this difference between a grammar and a performance theory that accounts for utterance meaning shows why grammars and the notions defined in them (like semantic presupposition) are formal, but performance theories and the notions defined in them (like contextual presupposition) are not formal. The function of a grammar is to describe the structure of sentence types and to explain grammatical properties (like semantic presupposition) in terms of sentence structure. Since there is nothing that prevents us from representing the structure of a sentence type formally, a grammar is a formal theory. On the other hand, the function of such a performance theory is, as we have just seen, to assign sentence tokens to semantic types, and therefore, such a theory makes use of contingent truths both to specify the spatiotemporal events that are assigned to semantic types and to determine to which semantic types these events are assigned e.g., contingent truths about the speakers' intentions and beliefs that play a role in every current pragmatic theory. But making use of such contingent truths immediately renders the theory nonformal, since something other than the form and arrangement of symbols in strings determines the theory's treatment of its subject.

REFERENCES

Austin, J. L. 1963. "Performative-Constative." In *Philosophy and Ordinary Language*, C. E. Caton, ed. University of Illinois Press.

Chomsky, N. 1965. *Aspects of the Theory of Syntax*. M.I.T. Press.

Chomsky, N., and M. Halle. 1968. *The Sound Pattern of English*. Harper and Row.

Fillmore, C. J., and D. T. Langendoen, eds. 1971. *Studies in Linguistic Semantics*. Holt, Rinehart and Winston.

Frege, G. 1892. "On Sense and Reference." *Translations from the Philosophical Writings of Gottlob Frege*, P. T. Geach and M. Black, eds. 1952. Blackwell.

Green, G. 1968. "On *Too* and *Either*, and Not Just on *Too* and *Either*, Either." *Papers from the Fourth Regional Meeting, Chicago Linguistic Society*. University of Chicago.

Grice, H. P. 1975. "Logic and Conversation." In *The Logic of Grammar*, D. Davidson and G. Harmon, eds. Dickenson.

Harnish, M. 1976. "Logical Form and Implicature." In this volume.

Horn, L. 1972. *On the Semantic Properties of Logical Operators in English*. Unpublished Ph.D. dissertation. University of California, Los Angeles.

Karttunen, L. 1973. "Presuppositions of Compound Sentences." *Linguistic Inquiry* 4:169–193.

———. 1974. "Presupposition and Linguistic Context." *Theoretical Linguistics* 1:181–194.

———. To appear. "Remarks on Presupposition." In Murphy, Rogers and Wall, eds.

Katz, J. J. 1965. "The Relevance of Linguistics to Philosophy." *Journal of Philosophy* 62:590–601.

———. 1966. *The Philosophy of Language*. Harper and Row.

———. 1972. *Semantic Theory*. Harper and Row.

———. 1973. "Interpretive Semantics Meets the Zombies." *Foundations of Language* 9:549–596.

———. In press. *Propositional Structure: A Study of the Contribution of Sentence Meeting to Speech Acts*. Thomas Y. Crowell.

Katz, J. J., and T. G. Bever. 1976. "The Fall and Rise of Empiricism." In this volume.

Katz, J. J., and J. A. Fodor. 1963. "The Structure of a Semantic Theory." *Language* 39: 170–210.

Kiparsky, P., and C. Kiparsky. 1971. "Fact." In Steinberg and Jakobovits, eds. 1971.

Lakoff, G. 1971a. "Presupposition and Relative Grammaticality." In Steinberg and Jakobovits, eds. 1971.

———. 1971b. "The Role of Deduction in Grammar." In Fillmore and Langendoen, eds. 1971.

Langendoen, D. T., and H. B. Savin. 1971. "The Projection Problem for Presuppositions." In Fillmore and Langendoen, eds. 1971.

Morgan, J. L. 1969. "On the Treatment of Presuppositions in Transformational Grammar." *Papers from the Fifth Regional Meeting, Chicago Linguistic Society*. University of Chicago.

——. 1973. *Presupposition and the Representation of Meaning.* Unpublished Ph.D. dissertation. University of Chicago.

Murphy, J., A. Rogers, and R. Wall, eds. To appear. *Proceedings of the Texas Conference on Performatives, Presuppositions and Conversational Implicatures.*

Searle, J. R. 1969. *Speech Acts.* Cambridge University Press.

Stalnaker, R. 1974. "Pragmatic Presuppositions." In *Semantics and Philosophy*, M. K. Munitz and P. K. Unger, eds. New York University Press.

Steinberg, D., and L. Jakobovits, eds. 1971. *Semantics.* Cambridge University Press.

Global Rules and Surface Structure Interpretation

JERROLD J. KATZ

It has apparently gone unnoticed that the principles of surface structure interpretation introduced in developing the extended standard theory (EST) are as much global rules as any of the global rules of generative semantics (GS).[1] It is clear that this been generally overlooked in linguistics, for on the one hand Chomsky and his followers decry GS for employing global rules, and on the other Lakoff, McCawley, and their followers rejoice at the discovery of new evidence supporting global rules. The present paper explores some of the consequences of the fact that EST also contains global rules.

Surface interpretation rules (SIR) are global because they relate noncontiguous tree structures in the same derivation.[2] That SIR relate noncontiguous structures follows directly from both of the following: (a) they are an essential mechanism in EST for providing syntactic information required in the semantic interpretation of certain kinds of sentences; and (b) they obtain such information from tree structures representing surface syntactic form and apply it in the semantic interpretation of tree structures representing deep syntactic structure (or in the semantic interpretation of pairs of a surface phrase marker and an underlying phrase marker). This is evident from remarks of Chomsky's like the following:

> the theory of grammar should be reconstructed along the lines . . . base:
> $(P_1, \ldots, P_i)$ (P_1 the K-initial, P_i the post-lexical (deep) structure of the

---

1. Manfred Bierwisch has also observed this (I owe him thanks for fruitful and enjoyable discussions on this point).

2. This is true of SIR that pick up information about focus and presupposition (in Chomsky's sense), SIR that pick up information about the scope of quantifiers and negative elements, and of every other SIR so far proposed (Chomsky, 1972, pp. 62–119).

Source: This article appears for the first time in this volume.

syntactic structure which is a member of K); transformations: $(P_i, \ldots,$ $P_n)$ $(P_n$ the surface structure, $(P_1, \ldots, P_n) \in K)$; phonology: $P_n \rightarrow$ phonetic representation; semantics: $(P_i, P_n) \rightarrow$ semantic representation (the grammatical relations involved being those of P_i, that is, those represented in P_1) (1972, pp. 113-114).

The same point emerges when we examine the arguments offered for SIR. Grounds are adduced to show that the underlying phrase marker P_i does not contain certain syntactic relations needed to assign derived readings to a sentence as a representation of its meaning. Then, it is observed that these syntactic relations are found in the surface structure representation P_n. Thus, SIR are motivated on the grounds that the semantic component needs rules that can refer to phrase markers at both the deep and surface levels of syntactic structure in order to provide information about such syntactic relations in the interpretive process.

As a consequence of the fact that EST contains global rules, a number of disputes between GS and EST become pointless. But, more interestingly, some of the arguments employed against GS in these disputes can be turned against EST. One such argument is Chomsky's argument against GS that its introduction of global rules constitutes a dangerous liberalization of transformational theory (1972, pp. 123-129). He pointed out that broadening linguistic theory to allow such rules enormously increases the range of possible grammars and thus makes the task of explaining how the child is able to select among the members of the set of possible grammars a much larger problem than it is in the narrower theory on which grammatical rules relate contiguous structures. Chomsky claims that the selection problem on such a broadened linguistic theory is so great as to rule out language acquisition within the empirical conditions under which it is known to occur.

Another argument, which does not depend on psycholinguistic applications of linguistic theory, is that, on straightforward grounds of inductive simplicity, global solutions to grammatical problems should rank well below transformational solutions (Reichenbach, 1938). Framing hypotheses about the grammatical rules of a language (or the universals of language) is like a "goodness of fit" task such as finding a curve for a set of data points. In trying to find the relation between two variables, simplicity dictates that we choose the curve with the least average cruvature—that is, the curve whose shape most closely approximates the overall form of the set of observed points. Curves could be fit that oscillate between the observed points in any one of an indefinitely large number of unusual ways. The simplicity considerations that prevent us from making such interpolations are not just a matter of elegance but reflect the weight of evidence from past experience. Previous successes with the practice of choosing curves with the least average curvature warrants a second-level induction to the effect that future use of this practice ought to be successful, since the evidence is that unobserved functional relations ought to be like the observed ones. Now, the indefinitely wide range of additional options allowed by systems permitting global rules in relating structures in a derivation corresponds to the different kinds of oscillations found in perverse interpolations. Here, too, simplicity requires a choice of the hypothesis that represents a minimization of such options (with respect to the class of hypotheses that are consistent with the available data). Thus, the total evidence of past experience warrants a second-level induction to the effect that continuing the practice of choosing transformational solutions ought to continue to produce successful solutions. Because of this extensive second-level evidence that unknown relations between structures in derivations ought to be like the known ones in also holding between contiguous structures, acceptance of global solutions would require exceedingly strong evidence. For such evidence would have to be stronger than all this second-level evidence in order for it to be rational to decide in favor of a global solution. Thus, nonglobal solutions to grammatical problems ought to be exhausted before any global solution is tried, not for the sake of elegance, but because the evidence to date makes it far more likely that their solution *is* nonglobal.

Since the notion "transformational rule" has not yet been constrained sufficiently to prevent an indefinitely wide range of imaginable grammatical principles from being expressed in the form of transformational rules (Chomsky, 1972, p. 125), it might seem an insignificant matter whether we take the further step and allow global rules as well. But this is not so. It is important to restrict the kinds of principles that can be used in constructing grammars because only when such restrictions are strong does linguistic theory make revealing claims about the nature of language and provide explanations for the acquisition of languages. Chomsky's argument, then, is a sound one. It, together with my supplement, shows that theories allowing global rules are *a priori* less desirable than theories that do not allow them, other things equal. This means that we have methodological grounds for requiring strong empirical evidence in their favor before permitting them into descriptions of grammatical phenomena.[3] Therefore, it seems reasonable to agree with Chomsky that stronger empirical evidence for global rules than anything that generative semanticists have yet come up with is required to justify the introduction of global rules.[4]

3. It is, of course, not completely clear how strong such empirical evidence would have to be. Interestingly, it is the absence of suitably strong restrictions on the rules of standard transformational theory that prevents us from being able to say exactly how heavy this burden of proof is.

4. Various arguments are now beginning to appear that show that this evidence is vulnerable to direct criticism, e.g., there are transformational solutions to problems for which global solutions have been urged. Both Quicoli (1973) and Emonds (1973) provide refutations of the global derivational approach to classical Greek case agreement phenomena proposed in Andrews (1971) and in Lakoff (1970). Quicoli and Emonds demonstrate more viable transformational solutions without any recourse to global power or arbitrary indexing devices. In the same paper, Emonds demonstrates that two other arguments for global

Agreeing with Chomsky on this, however, translates directly into disagreement with him over EST, since EST poses the same danger for the progress of linguistics and psycholinguistics as GS in this respect. We seem, then, to be caught in a quandary. On the one hand Chomsky has given convincing *a priori* arguments to make us wary of global rules, and on the other he has offered apparently strong empirical arguments to make us think we should adopt them (in the case of SIR). Interestingly, Chomsky has also provided a form of argument that indicates at least the beginning of a way out of this quandary.

The idea of a global rule, as far as I know, was first thought of by Chomsky (1965). He considered it a possible alternative to distinguishing between syntactic well-formedness and acceptability. He wrote:

> Note that it would be quite impossible to characterize the unacceptable sentence [multiply center-embedded sentences] in grammatical terms. For example, we cannot formulate particular rules of the grammar in such a way as to exclude them. Nor, obviously, can we exclude them by limiting the number of reapplications of grammatical rules in the generation of a sentence, since unacceptability can just as well arise from application of distinct rules, each being applied only once. In fact, it is clear that we can characterize unacceptable sentences only in terms of some "global" property of derivations and the structures they define (pp. 11–12).

This consequence leads Chomsky immediately to reject the assimilation of acceptability to well-formedness and the corresponding necessity to prevent the grammar from generating unacceptable sentences. He does not explain why he regards the possibility he is rejecting to be the worst of the choices. But presumably he had in mind something like his argument concerning the implications for a theory of language acquisition. Whatever the reason, once the consequence that the sentences in question can be handled only with global rules is exhibited, Chomsky categorizes these sentences as well formed but to some degree unacceptable, and thus takes them to constitute problems for a theory of performance. Chomsky then supports this claim explaining the loss of full intelligibility of multiply center-embedded sentences in the following terms: the complexity of the syntax of such sentences overloads the information-storage capacity of immediate memory and the processing of their syntactic structure blocks.

A parallel strategy for the present quandary is to take features that arise

---

rules, the argument in Ross (1972) and the argument in Postal (1972), are invalid and that the phenomena in question can be accounted for within ST. Three further papers, Perry (1973), Barone (1972), and Soames (1974), provide arguments to show that the theory of global rules may very well be either internally inconsistent or incoherent. I wish to thank Constantine Kaniklidis for a number of enjoyable discussions of the literature on global rules. His work on this subject will be highly important when it appears.

from focus in surface structure, like natural-answer relations, as belonging to a domain of language use outside semantic competence, just as Chomsky saw comprehension difficulties with center-embedded sentences as belonging to a perceptual domain outside syntactic competence. One suggestion along these lines is to use the criterion implicit in Chomsky's decision to treat the unacceptability of multiply center-embedded sentences as extragrammatical in order to argue that such properties be taken as rhetorical (and stylistic) (Katz, 1972, pp. 417–434). Given this criterion, which we may state as (C),

> (C) A phenomenon is counted as extragrammatical just in case we can avoid complicating grammatical rules or weakening the constraints on grammatical rules by treating it outside the grammar and we can construct an explanation of it in terms of principles of some independent psychological or cognitive system.

we would have to show that properties such as natural-answer relations can be accounted for as people's expectations about the structure of the sentence they are about to read or hear which are based on (*a*) psychological factors concerning ease of transition from sentence to sentence in a discourse and (*b*) stylistic factors relating form and content. Chomsky argued that the only natural answers to (a), (b), and (c):

$$
\text{(b) \quad Was it} \left\{ \begin{array}{l} \text{an ex-convict with a red SHIRT} \\ \text{a red-shirted EX-CONVICT} \\ \text{an ex-convict with a shirt that is red} \end{array} \right\} \text{he was warned about?}
$$

(a) … an ex-convict with a red SHIRT
(b) Was it … a red-shirted EX-CONVICT … he was warned about?
(c) … an ex-convict with a shirt that is red

among (d), (e), and (f) are (d), (e), and (f) respectively. (Chomsky, 1972, pp. 91–93).[13]

> (d) No, he was warned about an ex-convict with a red TIE
> (e) No, he was warned about a red-shirted AUTOMOBILE salesman
> (f) No, he was warned about an ex-convict with a shirt that is GREEN

Pairings such as (a) with (e) or (f) do not represent the natural answer to the question. These facts are not in doubt. Nor is Chomsky's explanation of such facts:

> The focus is a phrase containing the intonation center; the presupposition, an expression derived by replacing the focus by a variable. Each sentence, then, is associated with a class of pairs (F, P) where F is a focus and P a presupposition, each such pair corresponding to one possible interpretation. In terms of these notions we can begin to explicate such notions as natural (presupposition sharing) response. Thus for a sentence S interpreted as (F, P) to be a natural response to a sentence S' interpreted as (F', P'), it must be the case that P = P'. Furthermore, F and F' must be paired in some natural way (1972, p. 100).

Nor even is Chomsky's claim that the intonation center of S cannot in general be given on the basis of the underlying phrase marker(s) of S. The controversial claim is that the class of pairs (F, P) for a sentence "must be determinable from the semantic interpretation of sentences if we are to be able to explain how discourse is constructed and, in general, how language is used" and therefore these facts about natural-answer pairs, and other aspects of focus, "provide strong counter-evidence to the standard theory, ... that semantic interpretation must be entirely determined by deep structure" (p. 100–101). Why must (F, P) pairs be determinable from the semantic interpretation of sentences? Whatever light they shed on the ways we go about answering questions should be obtained without bringing the semantic component into the picture. The reason is that the relations dealt with in the semantic component are logical relations, and natural answer relations are no more purely logical than the relations underlying loss of intelligibility in multiply center-embedded sentences are purely syntactic. The basic fact in the latter case is that, from the viewpoint of constituent structure, multiply center-embedded sentences are syntactically equivalent to singly or doubly center-embedded sentences, which *ex hypothesi* are well-formed. Chomsky's point about the need to bring in a global property of derivations to characterize the unacceptable multiply center-embedded sentences is simply a consequence of the fact that such center-embedded sentences are equivalent in syntactic structure to acceptable multiply center-embedded sentences. This equivalence makes it necessary to resort to a global property of derivations. The basic fact in the case of natural answer relations is quite parallel. It is that, from the viewpoint of semantic structure, nonnatural answers are semantically equivalent to natural answers: they are synonymous (on a sense). Consider the nonnatural answers (g), (h), and (i) to the questions (a), (b), and (c) respectively.

(g)   No, he was warned about an ex-convict with a TIE that is red
(h)   No, he was warned about an automobile salesman with a red shirt
(i)   No, he was warned about a green-shirted EX-CONVICT

The sentences (d) and (g) are synonymous, (e) and (h) are synonymous, and (f) and (i) are synonymous; that is, each member of these pairs has exactly the same entailments as its co-member. Hence, one would have to go beyond semantics in the logical sense in which this notion appears in ST in order to characterize the nonnatural question/answer relations here. Hence, just as one had to resort to a global property of grammatical derivations to characterize the unacceptable multiply center-embedded sentences, one would have to resort to a global property of grammatical derivations to characterize the nonnatural answers to a question. This could not be done on the basis of semantic representations because synonymous sentences receive the same semantic representation. One would have to find appropriate differences between the grammatical structure of natural and nonnatural answers at some other level in the grammar. Chomsky's introduction of SIR, which locate such differences at the level of surface structure representation, is just such an appeal to a global property. Therefore, the examples of natural answer and other focus determined relations that Chomsky brings up as evidence against ST is no stronger evidence than are the examples of multiply center-embedded sentences.

The appearance that such examples give of being strong counter-evidence to ST is due to little more than the widely held supposition that these features of language use must be determinable from the semantic representation of sentences. But this is surely no less question begging than the supposition of those against whom Chomsky argued for a grammaticality/acceptability distinction that comprehension and production difficulties with multiply center-embedded sentences must be determinable from the syntactic representation of sentences. There is a competence/performance distinction to be drawn at the semantic level just as there is a competence/performance distinction to be drawn at the syntactic level. In the latter case, it is between the constituent structure of sentences and their production and perception. In the former, it is between the logical structure of sentences and the pragmatics of their use. Broadening the notion of semantics from the logical notion, which was what Postal and I employed in the formulation of the thesis that transformations are semantically neutral, to include various extralogical features of sentences that relate to their use, though perhaps likely to go unnoticed because of prevailing skeptical attitudes toward meaning, is nonetheless, illegitimate in a framework that defines the concern of linguistic theory in terms of an ideal speaker-hearer's knowledge of a language.

Moreover, it is not as if there is no alternative explanation of natural answer and other focus-determined relations that is at least as suggestive as the explanation of comprehension failure in terms of the processing breakdown resulting from an overload of immediate memory. Such an alternative explanation, in rhetorical terms, is that what makes an answer natural is that it does not depart (any more than it has to by virtue of being an answer) from the form of the question in ways that are arbitrary from a stylistic viewpoint.[5] The rationale here is that arbitrary departures make the transition from sentence to sentence in a discourse more difficult than it need be by making the reader or hearer check to see if the change has some stylistic significance. Since such checking will not be repaid in stylistic coin, it will be a waste of time and computation and thus decrease the ease of transition (Katz, 1972, pp. 417–434). Given this explanation, the semantic component need not be asked to take on the burden of treating natural-answer relations in addition to the logical relations it was designed to handle. The situation is exactly parallel to Chomsky's treatment of center-embedded sentence. Just as he distinguished acceptability from well-

5. Examples of nonarbitrary departures can be found in Katz, 1972, pp. 422–423.

formedness, so we distinguish rhetorical relations like natural answer from logical relations like answer.[6]

If the same kind of account can be systematically developed for the other phenomena that arise from focus in surface structure, then all such phenomena can be taken to constitute problems for the theory of performance too, since there is no question but that SIR weaken the constraints on gramatical rules, that Chomsky's explanation and ours both distinguish between the grammatical and the extragrammatical on the basis of the same criterion, and that the principles that would express how people form their expectations about the intentions of those with whom they are communicating are as much a part of an independent psychological or cognitive system as the principles that would express how people process the syntactic structure of sentences in speech perception.

This strategy does not get us all the way out of the quandary. The pattern of argument we have modeled on Chomsky's does not apply in cases of actual logical relations, like those involved in scope relations of quantifiers and negative constituents (Chomsky, 1972, pp. 103-111). In these cases, it is necessary to show that deep syntactic structure contains all the information required to determine these logical relations. To show this two sorts of considerations are relevant: first, considerations showing that the arguments for the insufficiency of deep syntactic structure are flawed logically, for example, because they do not show that the cases in question are transformationally related or because the deep syntactic structures from which they argue have not been shown to be the correct deep structures for the sentences; second, considerations—of a more general nature—showing that it is implausible to think that surface (or any other transformationally derived) structure contains information relevant to determining the logical relations of sentences. Considerations of the first kind are found in Binnick (1973, pp. 162-176), Katz (1972, pp. 435-440), Hall-Partee (1971), Katz and Martin (1967).

Considerations of the second kind are rare. One example, however, is the fact that there is no general principle to explain why deep syntactic structure, which is sufficient to express all sorts of logical relations in the semantic structure of sentences, should be insufficient to express such scope relations in connection with a certain restricted class of sentences (Katz, 1972, pp. 439-441). Without such a principle, the existence of some empirical evidence ought not, in and of itself, make us anxious to abandon so strong a limitation on the power of transformations as the requirement that these rules be meaning preserving. Now, admittedly, this latter consideration, by itself, is not strong enough to make SIR seem implausible, given the accumulation of arguments for them. But with the exposure of SIR as global rules, we can strengthen our position by including both Chomsky's argument concerning the danger of global rules for

---

6. This distinction can be made very sharp by the argument in Katz, 1972, p. 424, showing that features like natural answer cannot be semantic because the natural answer is often synonymous with a number of unnatural answers.

the theory of acquisition and our argument concerning their second-level disconfirmation.

As I indicated at the beginning of this paper, if SIR are global rules, then their existence does not constitute an issue between GS and EST. Thus, the revelation about the status of SIR allows us to complete the argument developed in several earlier papers that there is *no* general theoretical question at issue in the dispute between GS and EST (Katz, 1973). This argument claimed that the models of grammar proposed by both GS and EST are essentially the same, being, in a technical sense, notational variants.[7] Since an equivalence claim even as strong as this allows room for genuine disagreement about how statements on language ought to be formally expressed, the controversy between GS and EST can still seem be substantial. But since the question of whether or not global rules have a place in grammar can no longer appear to be a point at issue this controversy can no longer seem so substantial.

The real issue in linguistics is, therefore, whether we can maintain the tightest restrictions on grammatical rules—in particular, the restriction of rules outside the base to transformational rules and the restriction of these to transformations that are meaning preserving—or whether these restrictions should be relaxed to include provision for global rules in grammars. GS and EST are together on the side of relaxing restrictions, while ST is on the side of keeping them tight. However, it is not exactly the old standard theory that faces the combined forces of GS and EST. As the result of the convergence of a number of lines of criticism of global rules in GS and EST, a new standard theory is emerging. We have considered one line of such criticism already in our discussion of Chomsky's claim that natural-answer relations provide evidence for SIR. Examples of various similar lines of criticism of GS include some recent discussions by Bever, Langendoen, Katz, and others. Each case uses an argument like the one Chomsky first used in connection with the distinction between syntactic well-formedness and acceptability. Each tries to show that some phenomenon originally used to motivate a global rule is better explained outside the grammar on the basis of some cognitive or psychological system that utilizes information from the grammar, e.g., the psychological system of perceptual strategies for the recognition of syntactic structure, and the pragmatic system for determining aspects of the meaning of sentence tokens (utterances) not determined by the meaning of their type (in the language). Unification of the explanatory paradigms underlying these lines of criticism would form a general theory of linguistic ability that interrelates the grammar to other psychological and cognitive systems. By offering a systematic way of dealing extragrammatically with the phenomena cited by GS and EST grammarians as evidence for widening the notion of grammar to include global rules, such a theory offers a

---

7. Roughly, two models are notational variants just in case, for any grammar in the enumeration of one, there is a strongly equivalent grammar in the enumeration of the other.

chance of maintaining the most restricted of the three contending theories of grammar.

APPENDIX

This paper was written in 1973. It thus makes no mention of the very recent development of the revised extended standard theory (REST) proposed in Fiengo (1974) and Chomsky (1975) and (To appear). The principal revision is that semantic interpretation rules operate only on phrase markers representing surface structure. The elimination of semantic interpretation rules operating on underlying phrase markers is accomplished by the introduction of a theory of transformational rules, called "trace theory," on which the movement of an element or the deletion of one leaves a "trace" of the syntactic structure prior to the movement or deletion operation. This theory of transformational operations makes the claim that there is a "trace record" in the case of each such transformational operation where the syntactic information from deep structure is necessary for semantic interpretation and that no subsequent transformational operations erase such traces. This claim permits semantic interpretation rules to operate exclusively on surface phrase markers.

The significance of the revision of EST in REST (aside from its interest as a theory of movement transformations) is that it provides a theory of the organization of grammar that is consistent with the rest of the methodology of Chomskyan linguistic theory. As we have shown in the body of this paper, SIR conflict with Chomsky's long-standing methodological principle precluding increases in the range of possible grammars which would render linguistic theory inadequate as a model of acquisition. Thus, the principal advantage is the restoration of consistency obtained by the elimination of global rules in favor of semantic rules that interpret only one level of syntactic structure.

It is important to note in this connection that no new evidence is brought into the debate between EST and ST. The evidence for REST is just the original evidence for EST. Any evidence for trace theory is independent of this debate. This is logically the case insofar as there is no reason why trace theory could not be incorporated into ST. There is no inconsistency in a version of ST with a trace theory conception of movement transformations. The issue between EST and ST is not whether surface structure is sufficiently rich but whether deep syntactic structure is too poor to provide all the syntactic information necessary to restrict semantic interpretation rules to underlying phrase markers.

On the other hand, the addition of trace theory increases the amount of evidential support that is required for such an alternative to ST. Since, as we have seen, without a theory of transformational operations like the trace theory Chomsky's extension of ST is inconsistent with his methodology, it is necessary to adopt trace theory and with it the burden of providing further empirical support for the overall theory. Logically speaking, if trace theory is false, then things are bad for EST, while if trace theory is true, things are in no way different from what they were in the controversy between ST and EST.

REFERENCES

Andrews, A. 1971. "Case Agreement of Predicate Modifiers in Greek." *Linguistic Inquiry* 2: 127–151.

Barone, J. 1972. "On Lakoff's Characterization of Derivational Constraints. Unpublished paper.

Binnick, R. I. 1973. Review of *Studies in Linguistic Semantics*. *General Linguistics* 13 : 162–176.

Chomsky, N. 1965. *Aspects of the Theory of Syntax*. Mouton.

—— 1972. *Studies on Semantics in Generative Grammar*. Mouton.

—— 1975. "Questions of Form and Interpretation." *Linguistic Analysis* 1: 75–109.

—— To appear. "Conditions on Rules of Grammars." *Public Lectures, 1975 Linguistic Institute*, University of South Florida.

Emonds, J. 1973. "Alternatives to Global Rules." Glossa 7: 000

Fiengo, R. 1974. *Semantic Conditions on Surface Structure*. Unpublished Ph.D. Dissertation. M.I.T.

Hall-Partee, B. 1971. "On the Requirement that Transformations Preserve Meaning." In *Studies in Linguistic Semantics*, C. J. Fillmore and D. T. Langendoen, eds. Holt, Rinehart, & Winston, pp. 1–22.

Katz, J. J. 1972. *Semantic Theory*. Harper & Row.

—— 1973. "Interpretive Semantics Meets the Zombies." *Foundations of Language* 9 : 549–596.

Katz, J. J. and E. Martin. 1967. "The Synonymy of Actives and Passives." *The Philosophical Review* 76: 476–491.

Lakoff, G. 1970. "Global Rules." *Language* 46: 627–639.

Perry, T. 1973. "On Arguing for Global Rules." Indiana University Linguistics Club.

Postal, P. 1972. "A Global Constraint on Pronominalization." *Linguistic Inquiry* 3 : 35–60.

Quicoli, C. 1973. "Remarks on Case Agreement in Greek." Unpublished paper, M.I.T.

Reichenbach, H. 1938. *Experience and Prediction*. University of Chicago Press.

Ross, J. R. 1972. "Doubl-ing." *Linguistic Inquiry* 3 : 61–86.

Soames, S. 1974. "Rule Orderings, Obligatory Transformations, and Derivational Constraints." *Theoretical Linguistics* 1, 116–138.

Index